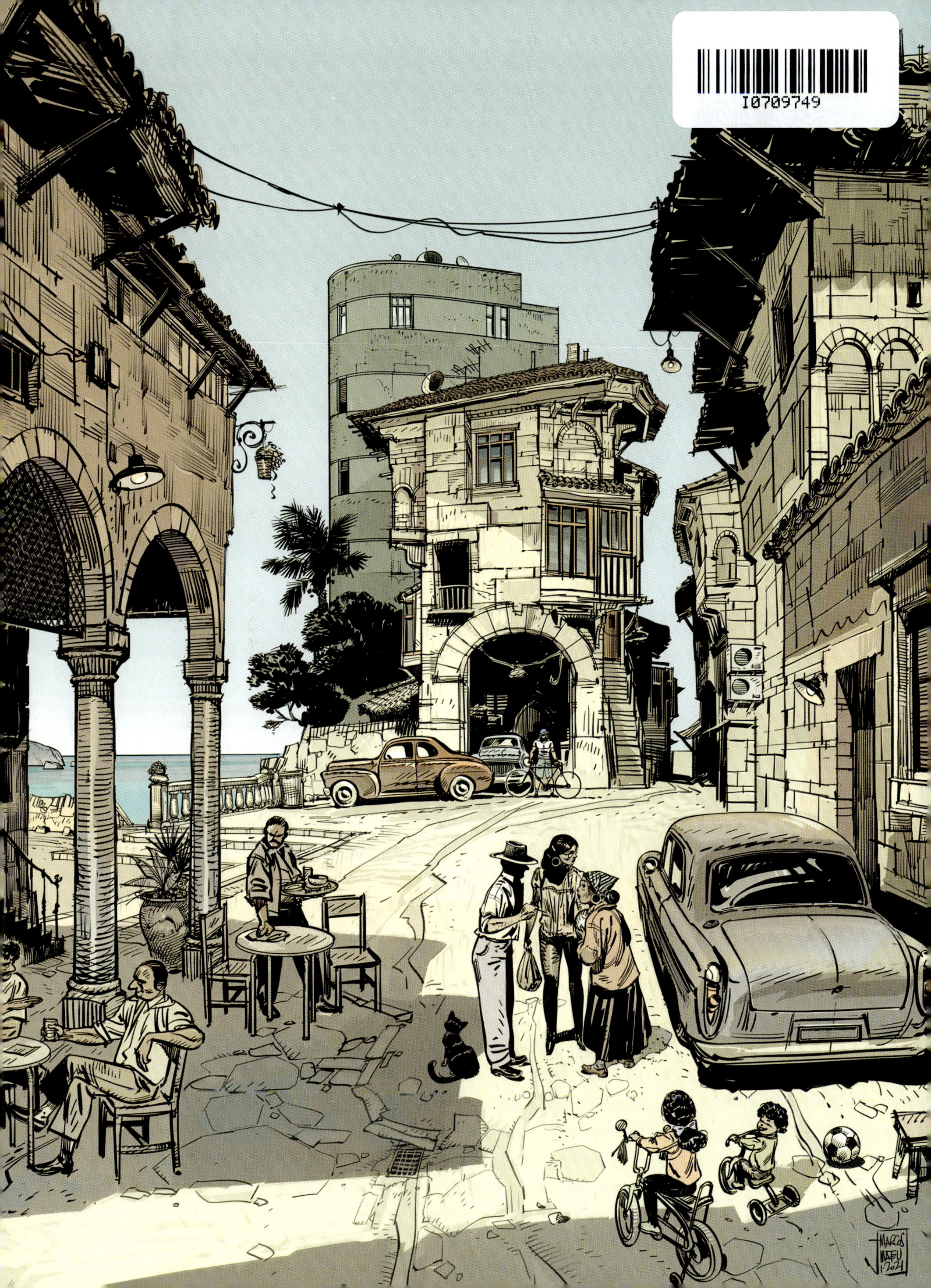

I0709749

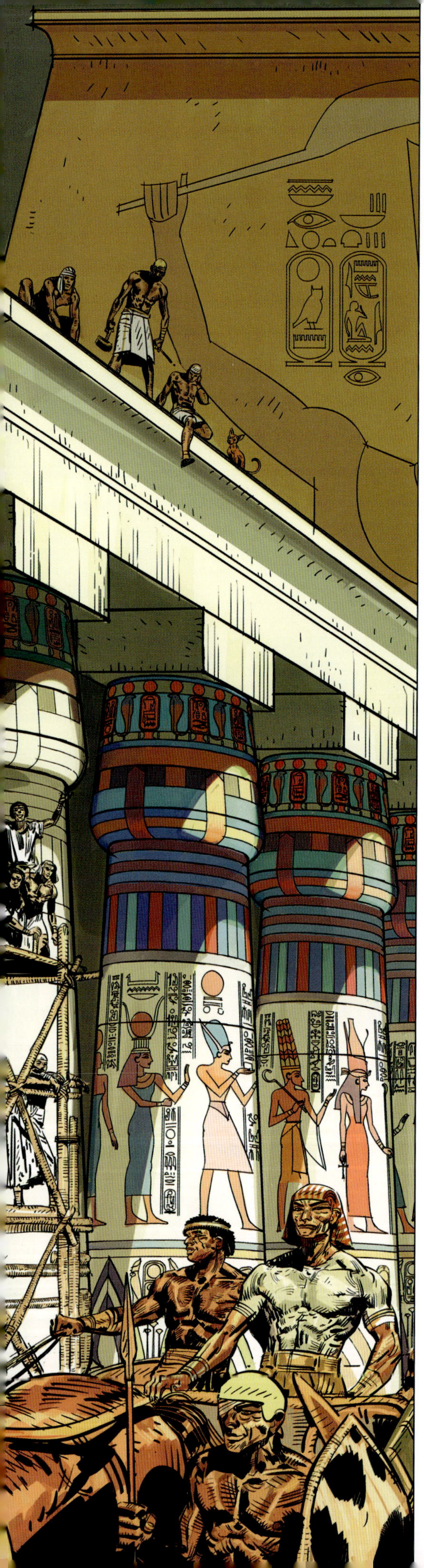

—TO ALFIE AND ARIANNA

· SPECIAL THANKS TO:
JOAN MATEU
MARGALIDA MESTRE
CARME MATEU-MESTRE

· THANKS TO ANTONI BALLESTER,
AND TO EVERYONE WHO SUPPORTED
THE MAKING OF THIS BOOK.

Copyright © 2024 Design Studio Press. All Rights Reserved.

All text and artwork in this book are copyright © 2024 Marcos Mateu-Mestre.
No parts of this book may be reproduced or transmitted in any form or by any means,
electronic or mechanical, including photocopying, xerography, and videography
recording without written permission from the publisher, Design Studio Press.

While inspired by real events, places, and personalities, the portrayal of these
elements in this book is often exaggerated or altered for artistic and dramatic effect.
Characters and scenarios are products of the author's creative mind, and any
resemblance to actual individuals or events is purely coincidental.

Copy Editor: Melissa Kent
Proofreader: Sara DeGonia
Graphic Designer: Marcos Mateu-Mestre

Published by Design Studio Press
Website: www.designstudiopress.com
Email: info@designstudiopress.com

Printed in China | First Edition, October 2024

10 9 8 7 6 5 4 3 2 1

ISBN: 978-1-624650-81-9

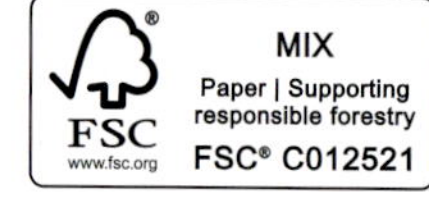

FRAMED ENVIRONMENT DESIGN

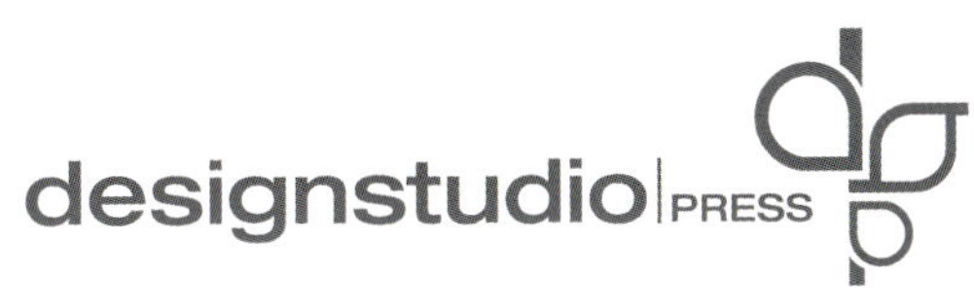

TABLE OF CONTENTS

Introduction...**007**

Chapter 1:

General Introduction **009**
The Purpose of a Design 010
    Reading the Script...010
        Geography..010
        Establishing Geography on Paper 011
    Visual Research, A Journey of "Archaeological" Discovery 013
        Doing the Actual Research 014
        A Research Philosophy / What to Look for, and How..014
        Talking to the Experts 015
        The Internet 016
        On Physical, Hard-Copy Books 017
        Visiting the Actual Locations 018
    General Shape Language 019
        Straight vs. Curved 019
    Big vs. Small—Organizing Shapes and Distributing the Visual Weight 022
        Silhouette Language 022
    Centers of Attention. A Shot-Composition Philosophy That Also Applies to Location Design.......................023
        One-Two Punch vs. Many Punches 022
    How a "Big vs. Small Shapes" Philosophy Works for Environmental Design 024
    Period and Geography / Identifying Shapes 025
        Shape Identity 025
        Practical Cases 025
    Creating Mood and Tone through Location 029

Chapter 2:

Developing Two Versions of the Same Location (and Why)..**033**
Setting up the Story Point That We Want to Tell through Visuals.......................................034
Johnny's Automotive Shop: East-Coast Location 034
        American Northeast, Red-Brick Buildings 035
    Getting into Specifics / The Alleyway's Buildings 038
    Sidney Walks into the Shop 044
    Establishing the Final Design 046
    The Second-Floor Office 048
    Elevation, Plan, and Profile Views 050
    Designing the Props 052
Arianna's Automotive Shop: Mediterranean Location 054
        Original Idea and Preliminary Sketches 054
    The Interior 060
    References and Research 061

Chapter 3:

Building Up to a Historical Epic..**065**
    An Ancient Egyptian Settlement / Preliminary Research 066
A "Working-Class" Area..069
An Upper-Class Environment 079
    Using Line Quality to Help Define Character 079
    Setting up a Location with an Establishing Shot 080
Understanding a Location as a Cinematic Environment 082

Chapter 4:

Pushing the Shape Language...**091**

    A Basic Checklist of Some Available Shapes to Play With....................................092

    Straight and Extended vs. Jagged and Compressed...093

Exploring the Language Possibilities of Geometrical Shapes..096

    Angular, Cubic Shapes..096

        Quick, Distinctive Shape Studies...100

Very Basic Geometry Applied to an Interior..102

    A Cinematic Use of This Stylized Location...106

Pushing the Complexity...108

    Curved, Round Shapes..112

        Thought Process...113

    Curved, Round Interiors...116

Chapter 5:

Weather, Lights, Camera, Action!..**123**

    Visualizing an Environment at Every Stage of the Story......................................124

        A Home's Living Room..124

    Weather Comes into Play (A Village Exterior)...128

        Preliminary Sketches..128

        Exploring a Few Story Moments...132

Pushed and Stylized Lighting...136

Chapter 6:

Nature Tells Its Tale...**141**

    Elements of Nature..142

        Trees...142

    Visual Progression...146

    Mountain Country. Shape Harmony vs. Shape Contrast.......................................148

        Changing the Shape Language...150

Different Environment Sections for Different Story Moments.......................................152

        Scattered Rocks Valley..157

        Narrow Canyon..158

        Canyon Walls Shape Analysis..159

        Scorpion Desert: The Final Stretch...160

Chapter 7:

A Path to Fantasy: The Creative Thought Process—Part 1...................................**163**

    Fantasy Loosely Inspired by Reality..164

    1: Starting the Process..164

    2: Looking Past the Big Shapes / Architectural Details...167

    3: Testing Ideas / Starting the Design Process...168

    4: First Solid Step...171

    5: Shape and Dynamics Language: Further Research...171

    6: Integrating Abstract Concepts So Everything Gels...172

    Further Pushing the Look...176

A Path to Fantasy: Living in that World—Part 2..**178**

    Getting into the Actual Fabric..178

    Developing Interiors..183

    Adding Complexity..186

    In and Around the Village..190

    A Villager's Family Hut..192

    Preparing to Design a Throne Room...194

    Characters—Stylized Version...196

    Throne Chamber's Exterior..198

    Camera and Lighting: Cinematic Possibilities...206

    A Big, Final Celebration..208

Epilogue..**212**

Index...**214**

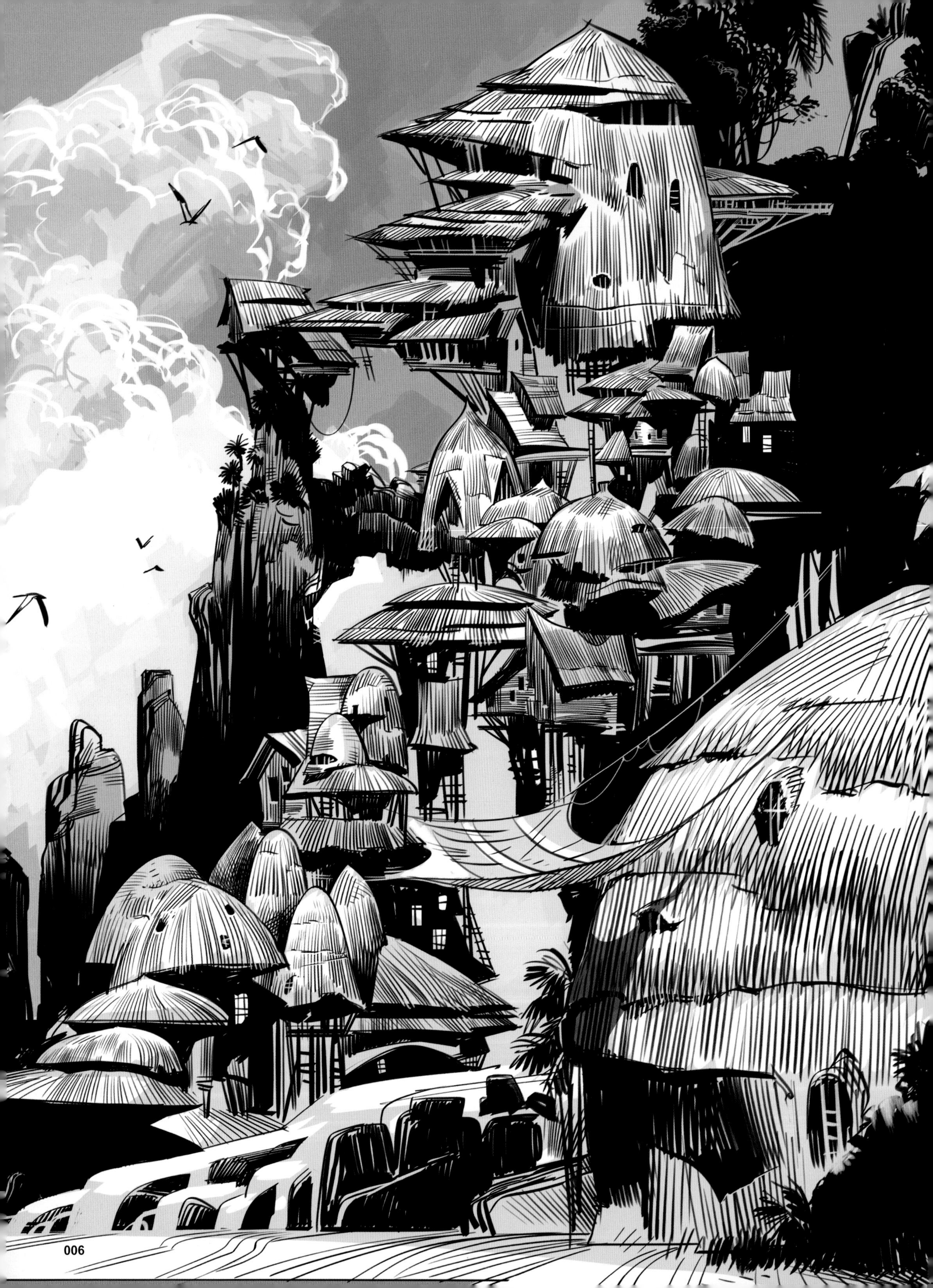

INTRODUCTION

The environment in which a scene develops serves as yet another player in the story. It interacts with the characters while communicating not just the historical period and geography but also informing what is happening and the emotional tones in which it is happening. And like the main characters, its appearance can be altered through the use of lenses, lighting, and camera framing in order to evolve as the story unfolds.

Each environment exists in context to all the other locations, in different degrees of contrast or similarity, to cater to the emotional impact the story needs at that time. It is essential then that before we start designing we have a clear understanding of the script and the characters who inhabit it.

The examples provided in this book illustrate numerous case scenarios while developing a number of tools that help us visualize how things might be worked out. A wide variety of options will be presented, but the exact approach will always depend on the particular case and challenge, and even more so on the unique vision and personality of each one of us.

So, without further ado, let's get this ball rolling.

— MARCOS MATEU

Los Angeles
6·2023

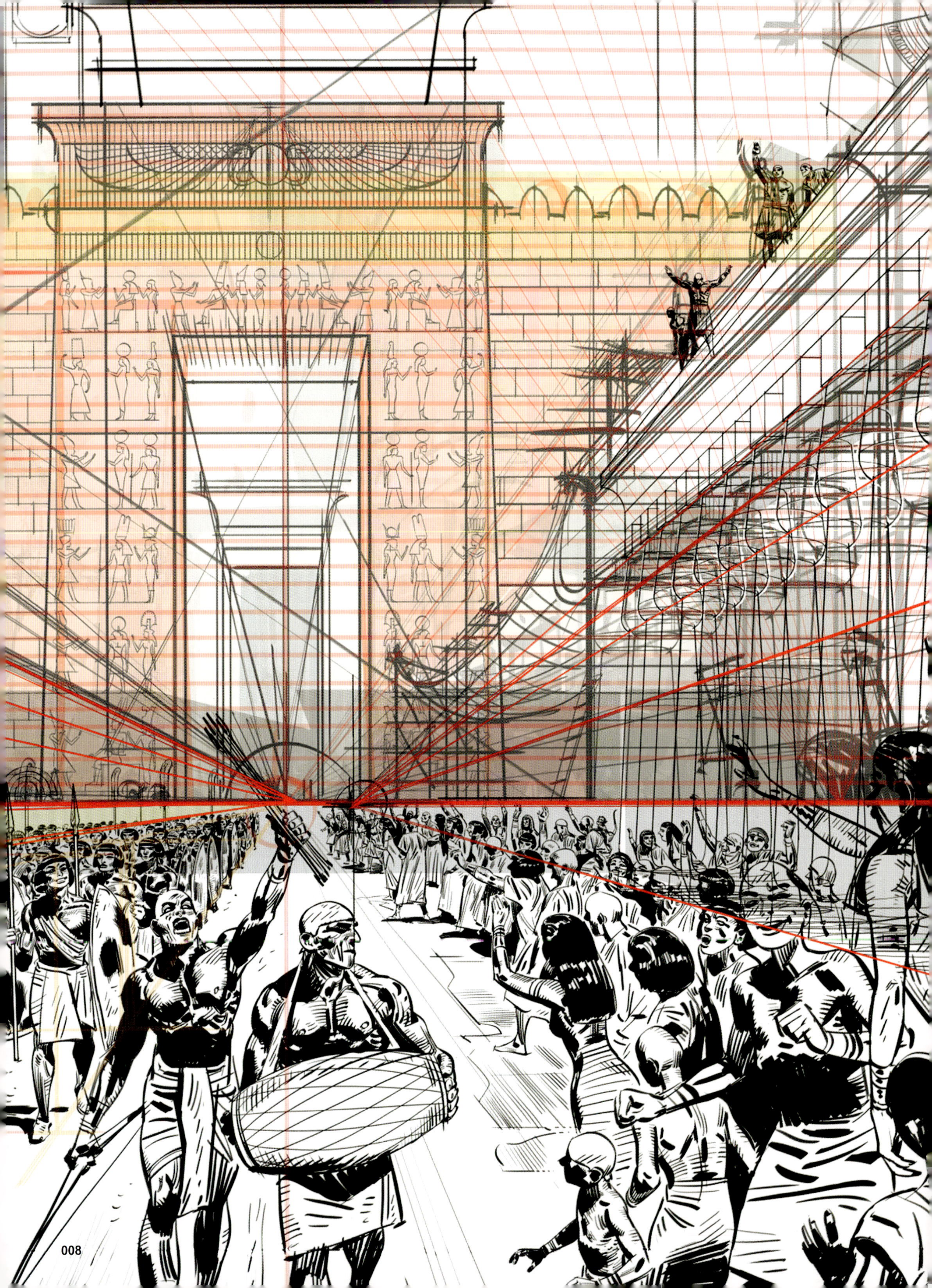

1

GENERAL INTRODUCTION

Each environment or location is an important element of the story and can play a big part in the introduction and representation of who the characters are and what their emotional moment is within the narrative.

Because of that, coming up with an environment involves not only a good sense of design but also a full understanding of the characters and the story it is meant to serve, as well as the emotional flow of each and every sequence within the general context. A good design combined with an appropriate camera position and choice of lighting is an important tool that allows us to convincingly tell our story.

There are a number of visual devices that help to give a design the overall flavor that is appropriate for the world and the characters. For example, an enclosed, dark environment generally does better representing mystery, danger, or stress toward the unexpected, whereas an open and well-lit environment mostly does well expressing calm, joy, hope. Softer, rounder shapes often indicate a kinder environment, while an angular and more jagged design is usually more appropriate for harsher, not-so-friendly moments or characters.

Using these simple ideas, we can imagine that an environment designed as a narrow space, shielded from light, with maybe just a few small openings to let in enough light for a dramatic contrast, with harsh shadows projected by surrounding angular shapes, would normally lead us to fear more for our safety than open, softer, and more balanced spaces. However, if an open and bright space happens to be a deadly desert with overwhelming light and harsh, punctual shadows, it could play out as the kind of environment the characters might want to avoid. **Although there are some general rules, these are definitely not "one size fits all."** It is the goal of this book to explore the many elements one must take into account and put into play when developing environmental concepts and ideas.

THINGS TO PAY ATTENTION TO FROM THE GET-GO:

1) Read the script. **Understand the story, characters, and the general tone** (dark, comedic, epic, etc.).

2) Do **visual research** focusing on the **time period, geography, and tone.**

3) Explore **visual rhythms with shape and volume language** (angular vs. curved, big vs. small, wide vs. narrow, complex vs. simple, etc.) and how all of these affect the emotional perception of the location.

4) Analyze what makes something look and feel the way it does. Explore the details that represent the fundamental points of an environment and how they express its style, time period, geographical location, and character.

5) Try out possible solutions and look at them in context. **Sketch** while visualizing the story and its mood and tone.

READING THE SCRIPT

If you wrote the script yourself, then obviously you have a natural knowledge and understanding of the storyline and characters. But usually a script is provided to us. It is recommended to have a pen and notepad handy to write down a short description of the characters and action on each page in order to build an overall understanding of the main events, in chronological order.

GEOGRAPHY

It is important to start clarifying an overall sense of each individual location that appears in the story and how all of these locations relate to one another geographically. What is their relative position and distance to each other? Thinking about scale, is one location bigger than the other? What is their overall look? Is this one in a flat valley, a narrow gorge, or a high mountain range?

In a dense forest or a desert? Is it a populated city or a small village? How we can use these facts to best depict each moment in the story?

This **sense of geography** will evolve by rereading the script, discovering new facts, and continuing to develop ideas along the way.

In addition to making notes about visually recognizable facts, it is important to annotate the story's **emotional flows** (intense vs. down moments, buildups, twists and turns, conflicts and resolutions) as well as the **time of day,** lighting, or any special **weather conditions.** Start thinking of ways to use the environments to represent and emphasize all of these nuances.

*(And always remember to write down **the script's page number** right next to the corresponding note to be able to find the scene whenever needed. Also prepare **any questions** for the department heads or supervisor.)*

Reading the script this way provides a first solid look at what the story needs in terms of set design, **how many locations** there are, and **which of these are the most relevant,** setting the tone for the rest of the look and feel of the narrative.

ESTABLISHING GEOGRAPHY ON PAPER

Now, with this new annotated version of the script in hand, it is time to start sketching a **general map of the locations** where the story takes place. These could be scattered around the whole planet, located in a specific area within a country, or simply contained within a very small apartment. The map makes it easier to get a visual sense of **where all the settings are relative to one another,** like the position of one village toward another, the orientation of a barn near a forest, or the position of a house's living room with regard to the balcony. This makes it easier to figure out what we see from any one specific point, depending on the direction the camera is looking.

It is also important to have an idea of the **distances between locations.** How long and in which direction would a character need to travel to get from point A to point B? Does it takes days to get from one place to the other, or merely seconds? Where are the **main landmarks in the story,** like a mountain range, a lake, or the corner of a particular city block? This will determine where the cameras need to point in order to capture the landmarks in the shot, and they can serve not only as backdrops for a number of scenes but also to establish a sense of geographical orientation for the audience. This can be as basic as making sure that the view at the end of a specific street or out of a featured apartment's window remains consistent throughout.

Other things to figure out are **the direction of any main roads or streets** to be featured in the story. This will be essential when it comes to planning a chase sequence, for example. Are certain streets parallel or perpendicular to each other? This helps establish a meaningful interaction between the movement and direction of all vehicles involved.

Having a map of the whole location will also be necessary when trying to figure out the **sunlight direction,** especially sunrise and sunset, and which locations are front lit or backlit at any particular **time of day.** A location's direction must remain consistent, unless there is a reason for it to change in the script.

There is the same need for proper geography **inside every structure** that is featured in, and relevant to, the story. Connections must be established between, for instance, a **house** and its front yard or backyard. How does the living room connect to the kitchen, or how do any of the rooms connect to a hypothetical swimming pool? Or in the case of, say, a **military stronghold,** where should the watch post be located? How about the ammunition depot, the commander's meeting area—where do the soldiers eat?

All of this planning will pay off when setting up any action that takes place there, such as the arrival of a new general and their interaction with everyone at the stronghold, or a fierce battle during an assault on the compound with troops moving around as they position and reposition themselves.

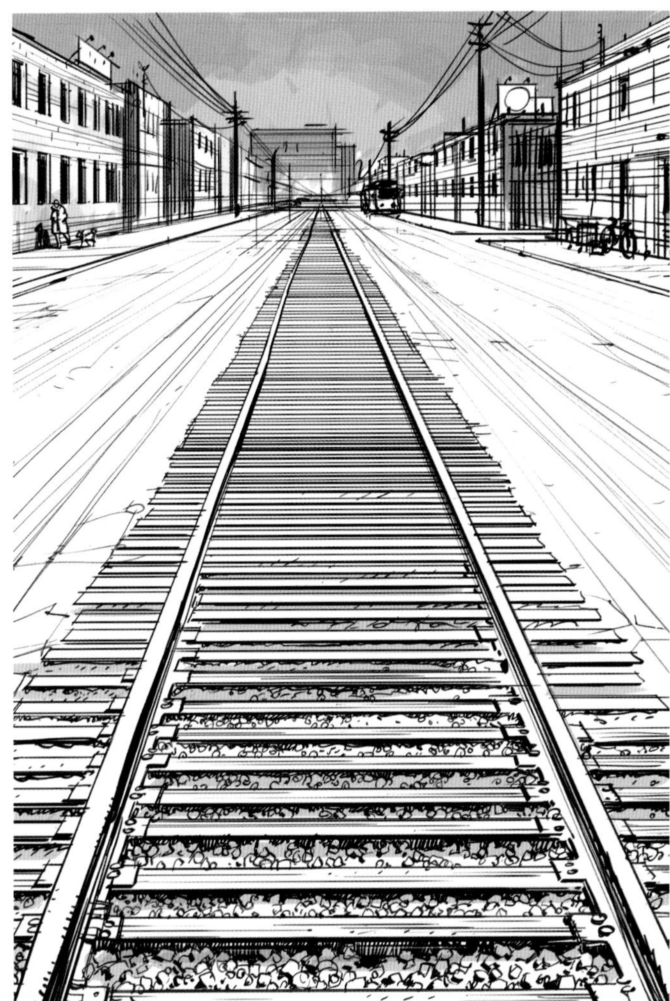

A rough but functional map will need to be created for the purpose of establishing a consistent and coherent geography throughout every shot of the story. **Start with very sketchy drafts** to quickly play with different ideas, and eventually make decisions based upon those. Also, use these sketches to open a discussion with other members of the team if this is part of a bigger production.

The camera will follow her car along Main Street (a wide street with train tracks right smack in the middle), past an incidental couple having an argument (this couple will later be deemed witnesses at a legal trial regarding whatever action Sidney ends up being involved in on this day). From Main Street she will take a right turn onto 2nd Street, proceed to the dead end, and park. Then she will head for the staircase that leads to Johnny's office on the second floor of Warehouse #2. An argument will ensue inside the office.

On the next page is a geography map based on a hypothetical script in which Sidney drives her car up to the building where Johnny's office is, in a back alley somewhere in a rather rundown industrial area.

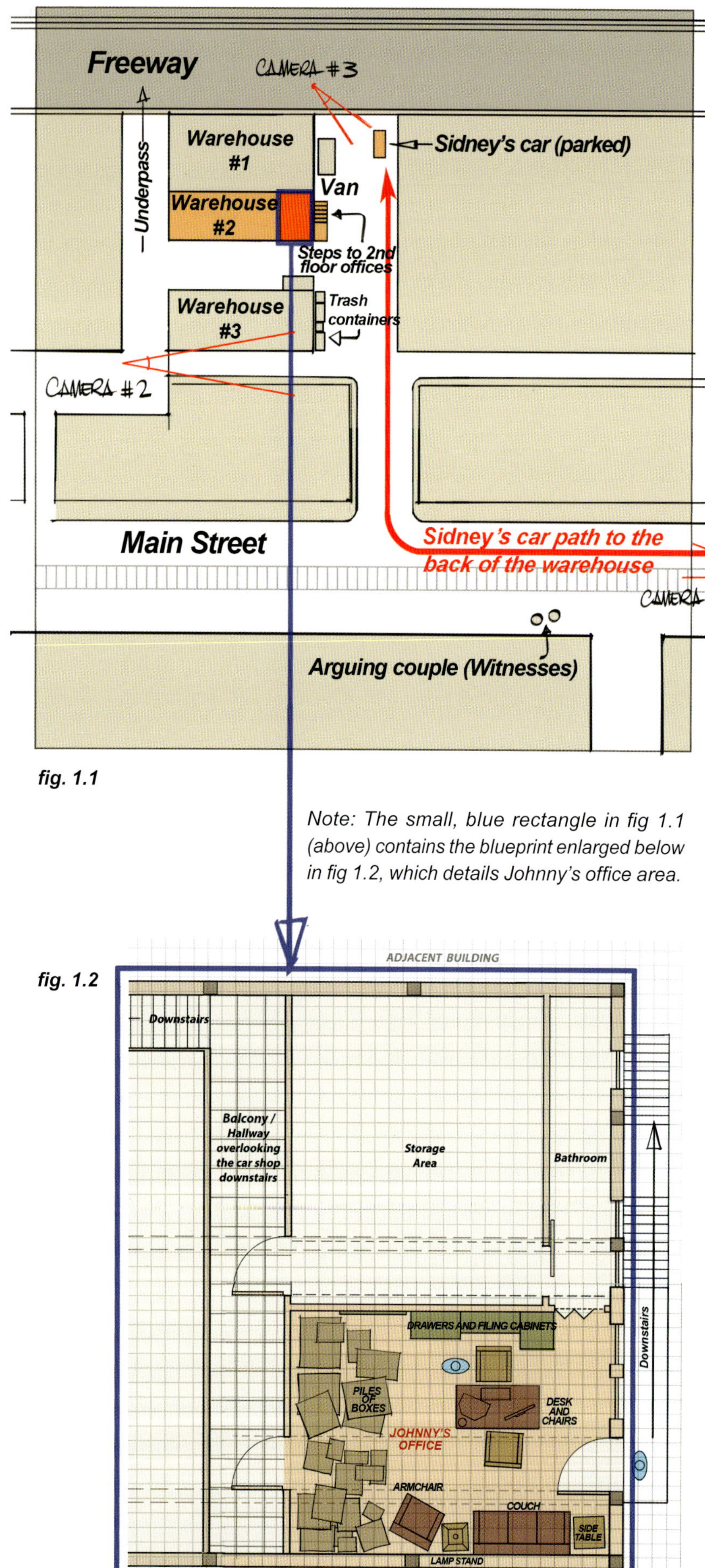

fig. 1.1

Note: The small, blue rectangle in fig 1.1 (above) contains the blueprint enlarged below in fig 1.2, which details Johnny's office area.

fig. 1.2

These are examples of **location maps,** as described in the previous paragraph. They include all the specific details needed for the development of the action the script describes, meaning the streets and alleys featured in the action as well as ones that will serve as specific backdrops or geographical landmarks, giving the audience a proper sense of orientation.

Other than that, details will subsequently be added in the design and visual development of that particular location.

Normally, drawing these maps involves a process of thinking and rethinking, adjusting and readjusting, making all the pieces of the puzzle work with one another. It must make sense for the action of the story, as well as the distances and the size relationships and proportions between the different parts of the location, all while making sure everything results in a visually interesting location. (Further examples of all these will be developed in detail in Chapter 2.)

Regarding geography maps that clearly tackle the basic facts and needs of a story, always remember that they will be read and accessed by many artists and production people during the filmmaking process.

And even when they are created by and for a single person's use, as in the case of a graphic novel with a single author, remember that given the amount of locations and production time involved in any one of these projects (normally many months), you will need to— at a glance— be able to easily understand the spacial relationship from one set to the next and know where you are at all times and how all the elements relate to each other, without much guesswork.

Fig. 1.1: This detailed view of the overall area includes not only the building where Johnny has his office and the warehouses immediately adjacent to it but also the full network of streets, alleys, and the freeway that make up the full geography of the area and give a complete context of the place.

Fig. 1.2: The enlarged plan shows the details of Johnny's office that is part of Warehouse #2, as contained in the blue rectangle above.

This is another biggy. Visual research is a really fascinating process that I feel is equivalent to one of archaeological discovery, a process during which things tend to take shape almost in a natural way as we combine the needs of the script with our personal style and vision for the project. And when, at some point, after all this researching, we find a design and style path that feels just right, on a personal project it might become difficult to steer our instincts away from this overall direction or to envision the project in any other way. Conversely, when working on a larger project as part of a bigger team, this will become a discussion that involves many thoughts and opinions.

I find this whole process similar to having a mound of shapeless clay on a table that we want to sculpt into a torso. It is not a torso yet, it doesn't even remotely resemble one, but it is definitely a material we know can potentially be made into a great sculpture.

So, let's start at the beginning. For many historical or geographical themes and subjects, it is natural to have preconceived ideas based upon movies, graphic novels, or literature we have seen or read. But how accurate or distorted are these media portrayals compared to a true, researched, and historical reality? For example, how did an actual Viking invasion look?

It should come as no surprise that all the clichés regarding this and many other subjects are not rooted in fact. Knowing how things looked in reality is the best base upon which to build. Then begin the process of visual stylization by departing from this informed research to come up with your own version, be it more or less realistic, stylized, or straightforward, pushed or fantastical. It is like studying proper grammar and classic literature to then eventually push our means and imagination and, finally, compose a piece of surreal poetry.

Now, do we want the visuals of our story to be historically and geographically accurate, or do we want to create our own fantastic or mythological versions? And in the latter case, how far do we push our designs? Are we talking about visuals that will be a slightly cooler and designed version of the real, historically accurate thing? Or is the intention to go way past that point?

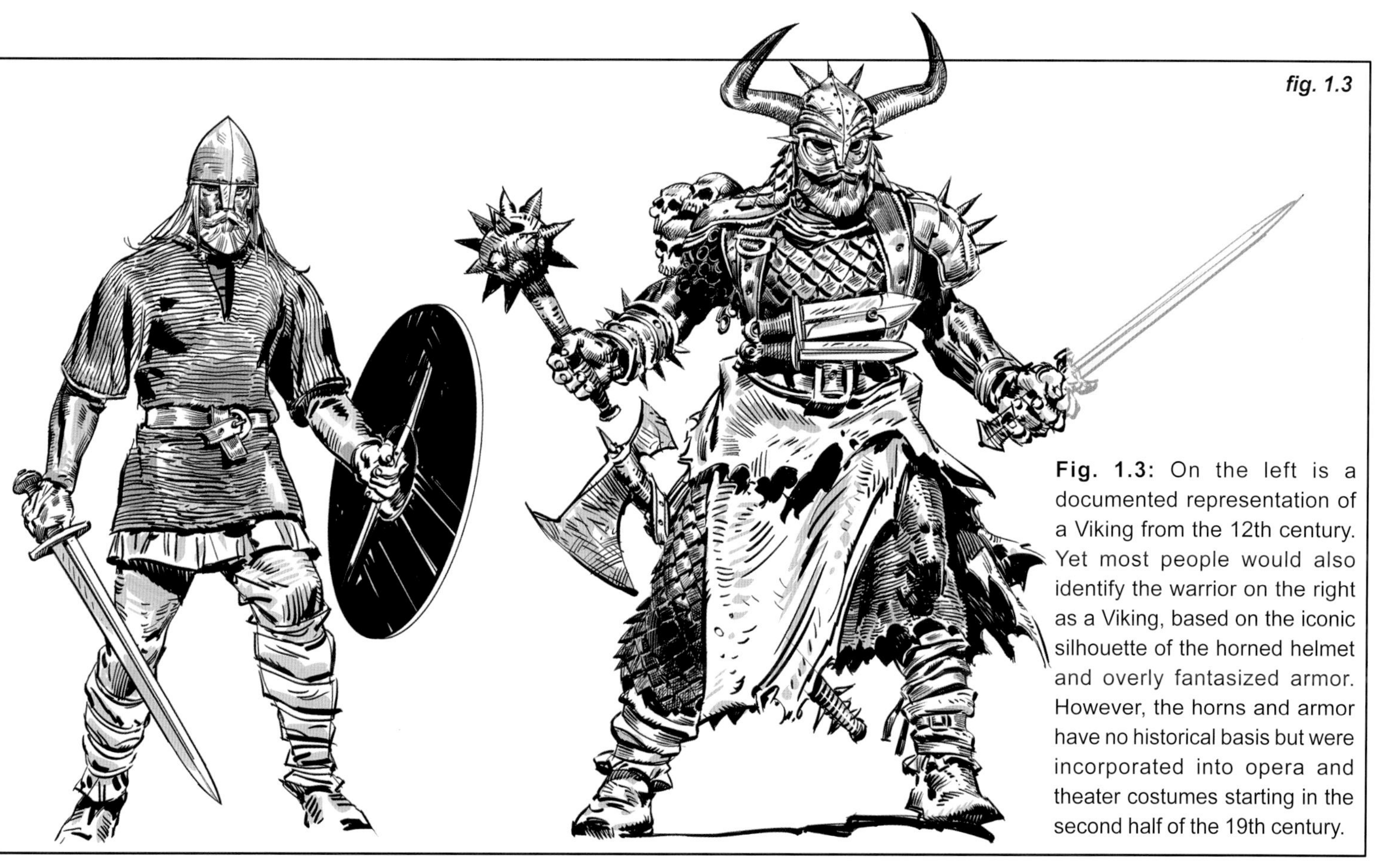

fig. 1.3

Fig. 1.3: On the left is a documented representation of a Viking from the 12th century. Yet most people would also identify the warrior on the right as a Viking, based on the iconic silhouette of the horned helmet and overly fantasized armor. However, the horns and armor have no historical basis but were incorporated into opera and theater costumes starting in the second half of the 19th century.

It is wise to explore all these options before making a final decision, even when you think you have a very clear idea of the level of stylization or general design direction from the very beginning. Sometimes we get to make these decisions with total freedom while developing our own personal project, and other times we are tasked with creating something for a studio's art department under more or less detailed ideas and visions for the project.

Either way, it is always interesting to broaden your vision by **doing further research on environments, characters, and costume designs. This will always provide an enhanced understanding of the world we are aiming to portray,** in one way or another, and offer a **much broader range of choices** that will help improve the creative process and make it more enjoyable. And then we can dial things up or down after that, depending.

So **let's get to know the "grammar" well,** let's go through the thought processes, and then let's decide whether we want to do straight prose or maybe complex poetry.

This **solid foundation,** whether we want to stick to reality or create our own pushed stylization, always makes for a **solid visual construction,** which is the kind of work that (independent from the choice of style) will ultimately and hopefully stand the test of time.

DOING THE ACTUAL RESEARCH

How do we find reliable information? Mostly through books, online sites, taking a research trip—camera and sketchpad in hand—or talking directly to experts on the subject.

Traditionally, designers would accumulate a **personal visual reference library** that might be comprised of hundreds or even thousands of books.

As one purchases and gathers these valuable tools, it can be very tempting to buy books that include references that are unusually hard to find, even when they are not needed for a current project. What if you visit a secondhand bookstore and discover a book with hundreds of photographs of Italian submarine interiors from World War II? That would be hard to pass up, even if that information is not useful at that very moment, simply because it is not that common of a subject, and if you ever did need it, it would be hard to find.

At this point, things like budget, or even having a studio roomy enough to house such a collection, can be a challenge. That is where other sources, like **public libraries,** become valuable.

And obviously, there is **the internet,** although in my opinion, nothing compares to the feeling of having physical books in hand. I remember many years ago buying a book, *London, In Color.* It was a secondhand copy and it showed the British capital in the 1950s. Added bonus, the book was published in the '50s, so it really was a little time capsule in itself—not just because the photographs and the visual information they provided were great but because of the quality of the paper from the '50s, the smell of that old book itself, the printing system used, and the quality of the color, clearly from that specific period. **That book was not just about the 1950s, it was from the '50s.**

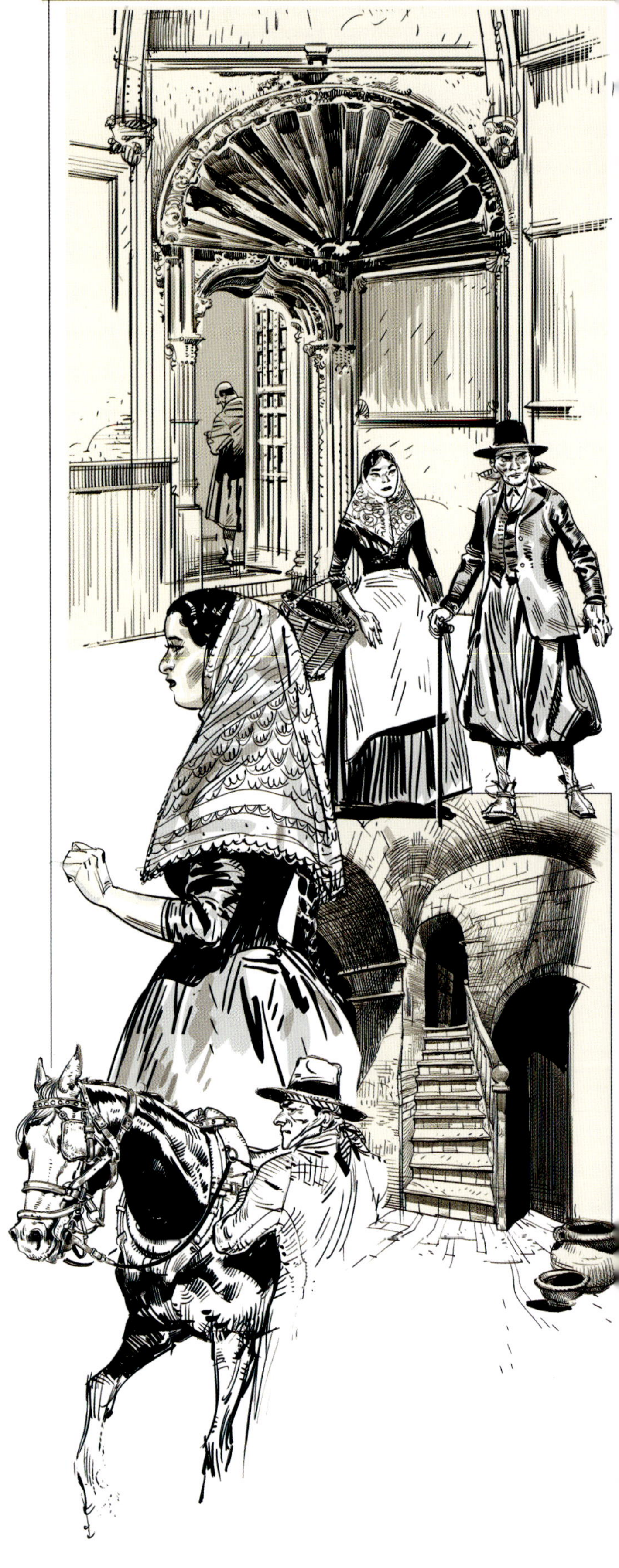

This type of feeling can really improve the research experience, which, in my opinion, always reflects in the final work. Circling back to the beginning, that's why I call it "archaeological" research, because we find one answer here, another one there, and then another bit of information somewhere else.

Next thing you know, the reality of that time period or culture *materializes in front of you.* That time, that place **becomes real.** You can see how everything worked back then or how things look and feel in a specific location in the world now, and suddenly, **you are there.** It really is a wonderful feeling, and it is the motivation for things to come, whatever direction we want to take it, realistic or extremely stylized.

So, let's start our research and make decisions based on it. Wherever it leads, let's **use the visual information to create the right designs and environments that enhance our characters, their tone, and their moment within the story,** for that is the ultimate goal of successful location design and cinematography.

A RESEARCH PHILOSOPHY / WHAT TO LOOK FOR, AND HOW

It is normal to begin by **diving into a sea of unorganized information.** Just soak in the overall look and atmosphere that a certain location exudes, in order to start gaining a superficial idea of flavor and possibilities. This is **the time to get excited about the location,** to feel lucky about getting to do a story that takes place in that specific environment. We live on a planet that, from both the natural and the historical sides, is exceptionally rich and often astonishing, no matter what the specific target of our research might be.

Eventually, after a while of "swimming" in this information of potential ideas, it starts to become more clear **what might actually be useful** while simultaneously revealing what is **not needed,** the elements that can be discarded and do not fit with the vision.

Be aware of giving in to preconceived ideas. If the particular geographical locale, be it a city, valley, country, castle, or anywhere else, is someplace you have been fortunate enough to have visited in the past, it may be tempting to feel, "I got this," and to cling to whatever visual aspects of it spoke the loudest, what was special and distinctive about it.

Or maybe you have seen documentaries or artwork reflecting life in this particular part of the world or period in history, and these were so impressive and inspiring that it feels like the perfect jumping-off point for the general vibe and direction of the project, even though this information has been filtered through the eyes of other artists, be they painters or documentarians.

Despite those interesting preconceived notions, it is always recommendable to remain **open to what you might keep finding during this research process.** Locations and historical periods are very complex, and as we continue to investigate the available information through books, documentaries, websites, and more, one might discover crucial information that was not considered in the first place.

So, let's consider a few more excellent ways to acquire information.

TALKING TO THE EXPERTS

In developing a project a few decades ago, part of which depicted the **Balearic Islands during the Middle Ages,** a few panels were especially challenging in terms of visual research. These scenes portrayed Catalan-Aragonese and North African **warriors** from the 13th and 14th centuries, plus a single small panel with a view from the sea of **Palma, the capital of Mallorca, the largest of the islands.** Not finding enough information about the armor, weapons, caparisons (the large decorative cloths covering the horses), and the troops' heraldic colors, I decided to contact a PhD in the history of the Islands who agreed to meet in his studio and spent a good amount of time discussing the specifics I was looking for.

He was such an enthusiast of the general topic that the discussion went long and included much more than the immediate information I was seeking. He provided a ton of historical **context.** This is an important point because, although one normally focuses on the details that demand first attention, **knowing more than what is strictly required for the matter at hand is always extremely helpful.**

Say there is a battle that is the subject of a scene, and in the process of looking for a **first layer of information** (armors, flags, weapons) we learn a lot of **collateral information** about the way those armies campaigned, their strategic formations, and how the war machines in that particular battle worked. Beyond the battlefield, we might find out how they cooked and what they ate, how they sheltered from the weather, when they wore armor, and when they did not. The warriors would certainly wear chain mail, swords, and helmets for battle, but not when "going to the bakery for bread." All of this additional information will enrich our knowledge of the period and make our job easier and better when finally putting pencil to paper, so that throughout the story we can properly represent not only this or that battle, this or that castle, this or that banquet, but the idea of that historical period overall, which will show up in every frame either by the confidence we have in our knowledge or through the casual depiction of background characters' everyday activities behind the main foreground action.

And one more thing. Regarding that **small panel view of the city of Palma,** I was very lucky to come across a history book (no internet at that time) that explained the evolution of the city throughout the centuries with its different and growing defensive walls and perimeters, as well as the different skylines as seen from the Mediterranean Sea. I bought the book just for that one image, which gave me the foundation to get that (really small, by the way) panel as accurate as possible. It was not only worth it but necessary. These details are what makes a project to come to life!

THE INTERNET

The internet puts so much of the world within reach from the comfort of your home.

The upside: An incredible amount of information to pick and choose from without having to walk from bookstore to bookstore. Not having to engage in lengthy explanations to the store's owner of what you are searching for. Not having to wait long for a book to arrive in the mail.

And yet, **on the downside,** no more walks from bookstore to bookstore. No conversations with the shop owner about a subject you might both be passionate about. Not having the tactile experience of physically browsing through thoughtfully created and printed books one after the other. No more walking amongst shelves and shelves of reverently and patiently stored knowledge.

Neither way is perfect, but let's consider for a moment that an essential part of what we are doing is illuminating the human experience, and no matter how practical, convenient, and sometimes plain necessary it is to get things done at a fast clip, what we gain in practicality we might lose in human touch and personal communication. Nowadays, I like to take the internet as a jumping-off point and then, whenever possible, combine it with other, more traditional, means as described in the pages of this chapter.

Also, not everything to be found in books is available online. Physical books still have a lot to offer, and the amount of knowledge stored within them, dating from centuries back, is a powerhouse not to be dismissed.

Now focusing on the **virtual world,** the research process is similar to what is normally recommended for other means. Start with broad thoughts, ideas, and searches about an overall time period, location, and culture. Then narrow it down to be more in tune with the vision for the project.

Returning for a moment to that word "caparison" from the previous page really comes in handy here as an example. When I was mentioning the elements that were of common use in a medieval battle, I had difficulty finding the right English word to describe the large cloths that covered the horses during combat. The way I managed to find it is representative of the general approach to looking for visual information. For that specific word, I **started with a broad search** on jousting, as I knew these cloths were heavily used on those occasions too. So, the first step was a general internet search for images using the keywords "jousting medieval horse armor," as I intended to find images with the written names of the armor and harness parts. This search led to a sketch that did that, although in Italian. So, next I tried online translations of the Italian words that described that cloth, yet when translated into English it still was not the word I was looking for.

So, I restarted, this time with a **more specific** search for "*armor cloth cover medieval horse,*" which finally led to a page that contained the line "*templar armour explained—***horse coverings.**"

In that good and brief article I found the word **"caparison"** referring to that specific piece. After that, a Wikipedia search **specifically** on "caparison" and then a search for the **images** associated with this word finally confirmed that that was the word I was seeking.

So, back to the point in question, always **start searches with very broad concepts and then slowly narrow the scope.** Remember to consult **various sources** along the way to see if they **confirm one another** so that the information you are gathering is as truthful and reliable as possible.

Another very important source of online information is **video.**

Besides seeking out photos or illustrations, videos can be a huge source of knowledge and inspiration. Seeing things play out in motion, in front of us, can have great impact on the visualization of our narrative worlds and it is yet another invaluable layer of information. However, be sure to keep both eyes wide open and confirm all this data through different sources, because the level of accuracy of video materials will range anywhere from totally authentic to completely false.

An additional benefit of researching online is access to a huge amount of **music and sound.** Have you ever tried drawing a high school scene out of the 1950s in total silence? Then worked on the same while scene listening to "golden oldies" from that era one after the other? Not the same. At all. The second way will most likely turn out to be a very memorable experience with all that added context, which in turn, may inform the drawings and be felt by the audience.

As I have mentioned in my previous books, **we cannot give anything we do not have.** If you give someone a football, it is because you have a football. If you make someone happy, chances are it is because you are happy, and the same with miserable, and so many other things. When listening to the right kind of music for the story (and the same goes for sound effects— try drawing a WW2 bomber scene while playing the sound of B-25 engines in the background), chances are this sound experience will end up embedded in the spirit of the scene. In a way, "all" we need to manage to do then is grab that sound, that music, that passion for the situation, time, circumstance, that rhythm, that beat, and translate it into **images,** narrative panels, and full scenes. This process will help your work become exponentially more authentic, more real. And let's keep in mind that indeed we are drawing, but ultimately what we are really doing is telling stories and expressing mood. So get the audience into your world and don't let them out.

ON PHYSICAL, HARD-COPY BOOKS

In my experience growing up in a beautiful but small town on the Mediterranean island of Mallorca in the 1970s–80s with somewhat limited resources, searching for the right reference books required a lot of walking from store to store, browsing around, or directly explaining to the bookseller what I was looking for. I would eventually find the needed visual references scattered among a number of books and bookstores, one bit of information at a time, often having to trek back home with quite a heavy load under each arm. It usually took several trips before I could feel happy with the resources I had gathered and was ready to go into the studio to finally put pencil to paper.

Sometimes all the bookstore owner could do was to recommend a book that they didn't have in stock at the time and order it from the mainland (Spain), a process that might take a few weeks, or they would just simply give me directions to another store in town where I might be able to find that targeted material, which meant more mileage on my sneakers.

The point is, back then information was more scarce and took much longer to acquire, making the process more inconvenient and uncertain than today, yet at the same time really **exciting and immersive.** There was a sense of physicality involved, having to get up and out of the studio for an actual "hunting" experience so that every time I found that one particular piece of information I was looking for, it really felt like a victory and a big achievement. In time, I ended up building **my own reference library,** book by book, experience by experience, which became a great personal resource and an asset to have in one's studio.

The origin of my personal library is linked to my days in London, when I was working at Amblimation Studios between 1991 and 1994. Prior to that I had always worked on a freelance basis, so my contact with other artists was quite limited. Then, all of a sudden, I was at a big studio with hundreds of other professionals.

My first position was that of a background artist (painting the environments behind and around the characters with good ol' brush, pigments, and paper). Being part of that department I saw for the first time other team members who had their own reference materials available right there on their shelves. Some of them really excelled at it, with shelves and shelves full of books on so many different topics. These collections included not only works by other renowned artists but also landscape and urban photography of different parts of the world, the evolution and design of historical tools and artifacts, costume design, you name it.

I realized that having that wealth of knowledge nearby was not only very informative for visual information while working on a project but, even in the case none was needed at the time, the amount of excitement, inspiration and curiosity they contained was really strong and certainly helped create a very solid sense of purpose and involvement that helped build a unique view and connection to our work.

That motivated me to start putting together my own resources, and soon I realized London was one of the best places to be for this. Entire areas of town were populated with extraordinary bookstores, from very general to very specialized, readily available for fascinating shopping trips or simply general exploration. Not to mention the massive amount of reference materials one could find in the dedicated bookstores at any of the fantastic museums, and on so many fascinating subjects. That meant I could visit the exhibits to learn about past cultures and the art and architecture they created, their tools used in everyday life, see tons of authentic

armors, uniforms and pieces of weaponry used in conflicts, from ancient to modern, and then be able to take home masterfully put together books as a visual and written record of what I had just seen and experienced. After that, trips to bookstores became a part of my regular routine, especially on weekends, and certainly well into my move to Los Angeles a few years later.

However it is approached, going through the research process toward the desired goals acts like a passage, a quest of sorts that takes us from the first original idea all the way through the final visual experience as part of a meaningful journey. And as the creative, hectic, and stimulating experience unfolds, any project will require a lot of our energy to be put in motion and transferred toward the final objective, a path to be enjoyed because all along our mind is focused on a wonderful goal that only we can put together and eventually make into a reality, which is the purpose of our work and the study of this book: to create worlds that were not there before.

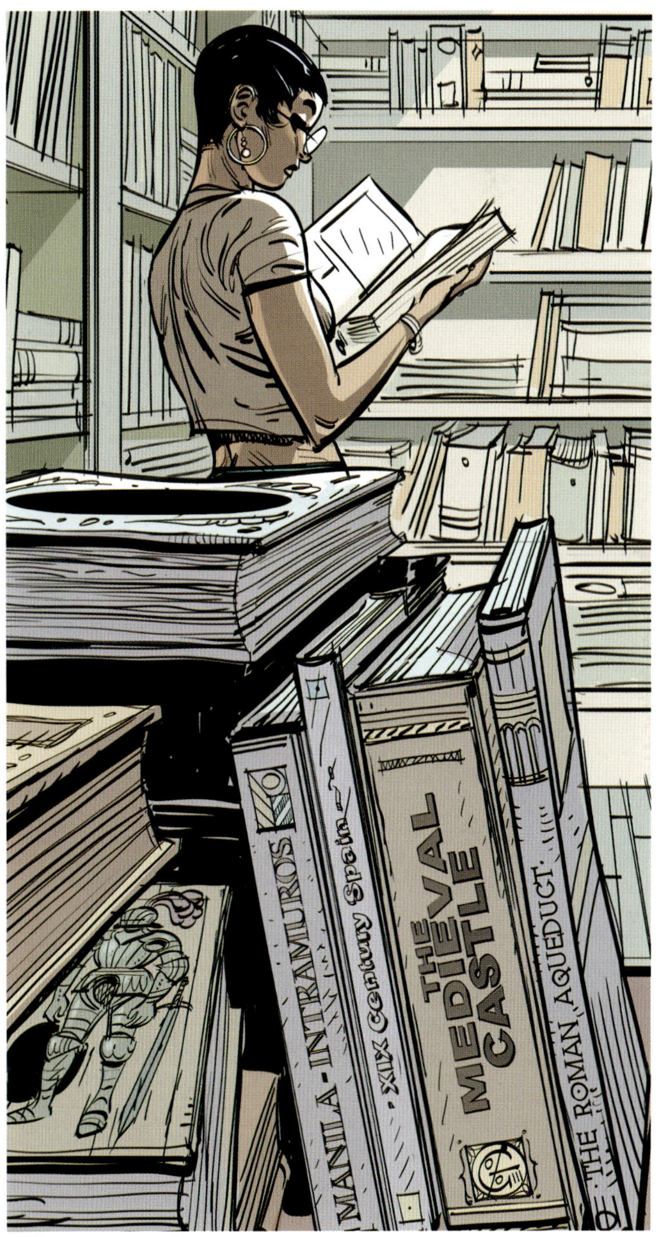

Another way to accrue a good amount of visual information is to travel to where the story is set. Grab your sketchpad, pencil, and camera and explore the physical places, feel them, see them, understand them, draw and photograph them. It is great when we have the opportunity to experience locations firsthand, because places are not just buildings but also full environments with a sense of light and atmosphere, sounds, people, food, language, accent, culture, a sense of pace, and an overall, incredible sense of context. All of these things are more impactful when seen and experienced on the spot, if possible.

Having the chance to be there also allows us to understand how light behaves at that location. (Chapter 5 will address how lighting and weather can dramatically influence the experience and perception of a place, especially when telling a story and augmenting the emotions the characters are going through.) This on-site knowledge will always allow better access to a good number of visual narrative options that would otherwise be more limited by just seeing the place in photographs. This is something I had the opportunity to put into practice a number of times, including some works that involved views of my own hometown (figs. 1.4, 1.5).

When you are out and about making your sketches, especially in the case of architecture, always pay attention first to scale and proportions. These are an essential part of what a place feels like and are the skeleton upon which everything else sits.

I will quickly refer now to an approach I explain in my book, *Framed Perspective, Vol. 1,* that applies in this case (*Chapter 11, Notes on Freehand Drawing and Sketching*). It is a practice I used when teaching drawing from a model, a simple yet very helpful exercise: I would place an object on the desk, or even a photograph of a landscape or a city neighborhood (simple views, nothing too complicated), and ask the student to look at it, pay attention to the broad shapes first and then the secondary details, and make sure they kept as much information as possible in mind, starting with the basics and **at least** enough to execute a general depiction.

I would then conceal the reference away from their view, and they would put pen to paper and start sketching.

When drawing the subject purely from memory, it is interesting to realize just how many of the essential facts we remember, and how many important details we have either forgotten or simply failed to pay any attention to in the first place.

Now that the students understood the elements they needed to be aware of to execute a decent rendering, I would bring out the model again so they could take a second look and make a more informed analysis of it, **aware now of the details they really needed** to pay special attention to. This is an exercise that, if repeated consistently, turns out to be of great help.

Once on location for the real work, it will be easier to glance up and down between the model and the sketchpad, on and on in cycles, and to know exactly what to look for and what to get out of every quick glimpse at the model so that our sketches are really informational and accurate and we can get more accomplished in a shorter amount of time. Regardless, especially now with smartphones, always complement your on-site reference gathering work with photographic images that can provide a level of accuracy that a sketch could hardly offer.

I would recommend, if you ever travel away from home to places that feel very different, try to do good research **before** you get on that plane. Read about the location, and watch documentaries and movies that were shot there. If you have any friends or acquaintances who live there, ask their advice. And once you arrive, interact with the locals as much as possible. Try to avoid returning home with only the "postcard" experience. Always aim to go beyond the surface, beyond simple appearances, and try to give an extra layer of meaning to whatever subject you have in your hands through the many contextual details you have, consciously or unconsciously, observed.

fig. 1.4

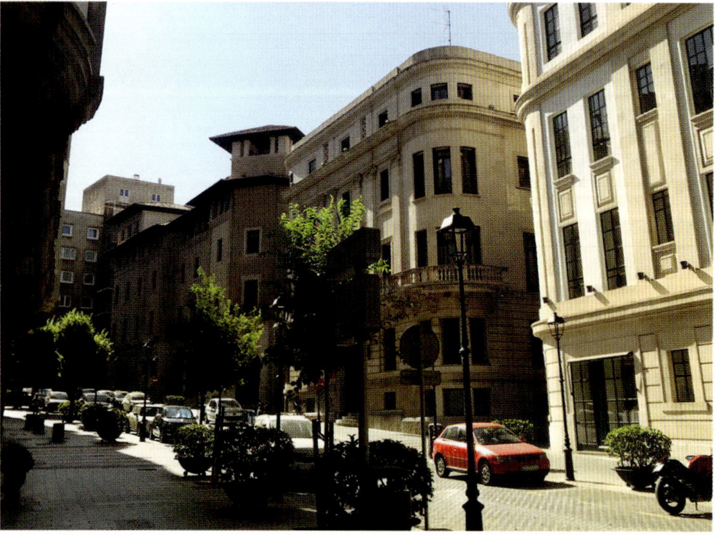

fig. 1.5

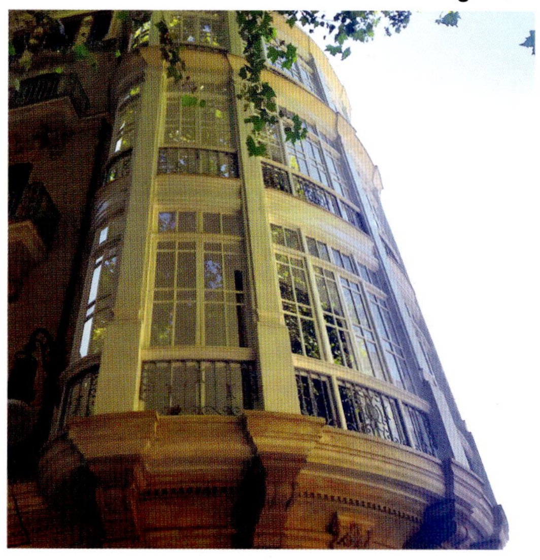

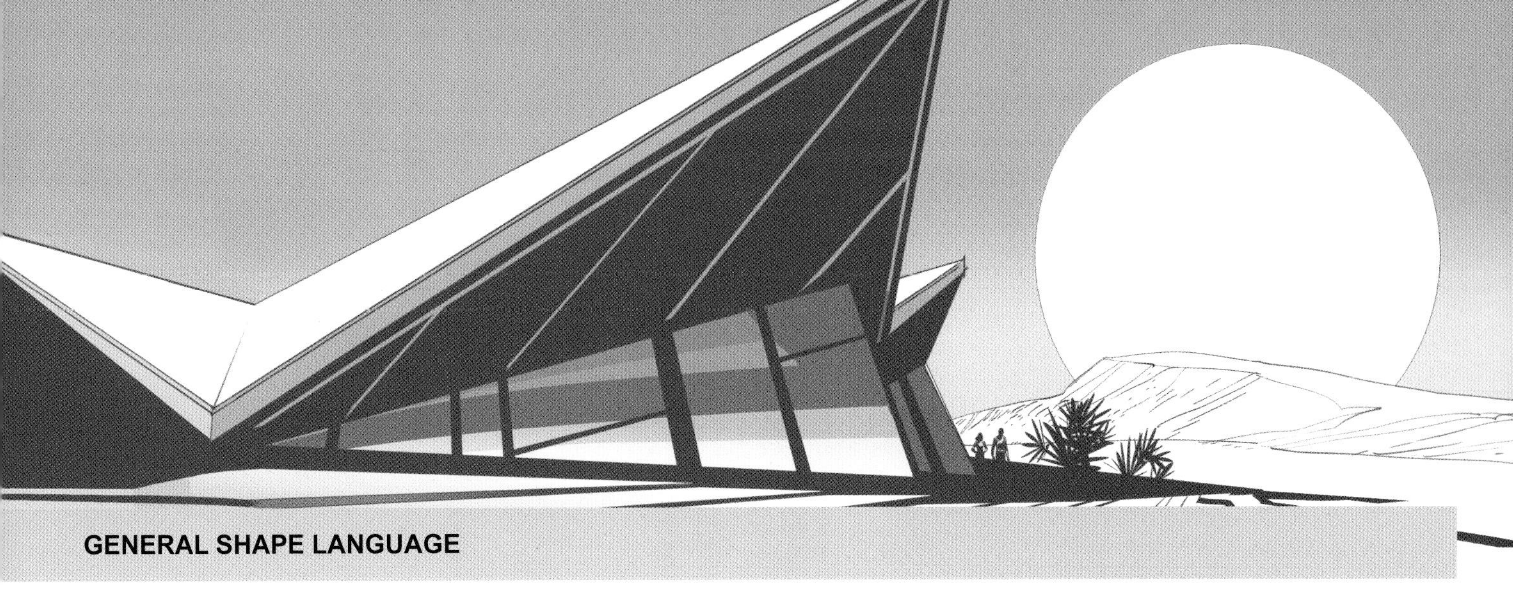

STRAIGHT VS. CURVED

fig. 1.6

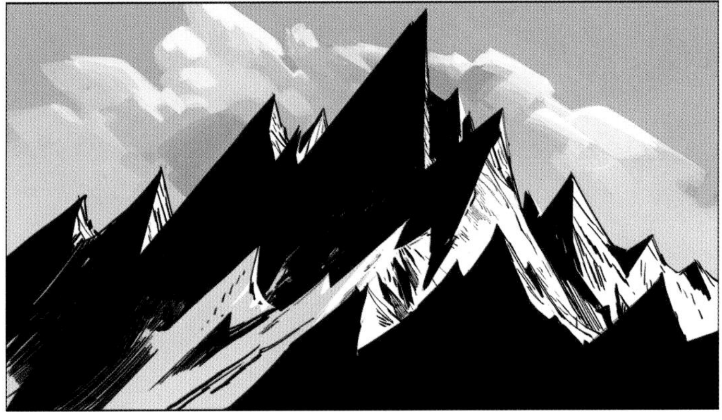

fig. 1.7

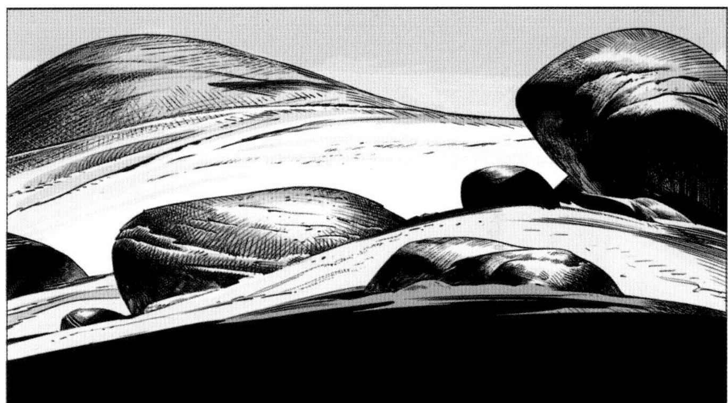

The first impression of a location (meaning whether it is dark and somber vs. bright and inviting, easy-flowing vs. abrupt, overwhelming vs. friendly) will likely stay with the viewer for most if not the entire duration of the story and will nail down their perception and emotional response to that particular place. This type of reaction is connected to the design itself (and the lighting), **including its shape language through the favoring of angular vs. round elements, continuous vs. interrupted flow,** and more.

Figs. 1.6, 1.7: The two images above could both be described simply as "rock formations." Yet the emotional impression on the audience will be like seeing two opposite worlds that make for two very different story experiences.

fig. 1.8

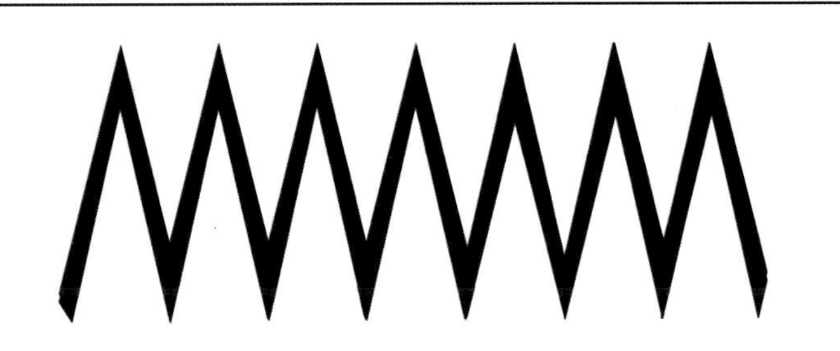

fig. 1.9

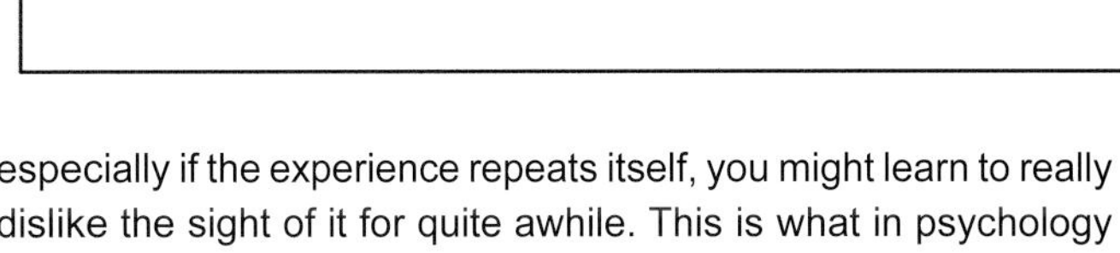

Figs. 1.8, 1.9: Overall, angular designs usually come across as harsher, more uncomfortable, and less welcoming than a rounder, softer-edged design would. Still, if the story manages to equate positive actions with angular shapes or negative actions with softer shapes, it could still work as a visual language for the project. Don't forget, as much as you might love a sun-dried tomato omelette, if you happen to be eating one when something really bad happens, especially if the experience repeats itself, you might learn to really dislike the sight of it for quite awhile. This is what in psychology they call a **conditioned reflex.**

The next page shows a few more quick shape sketches based on these principles.

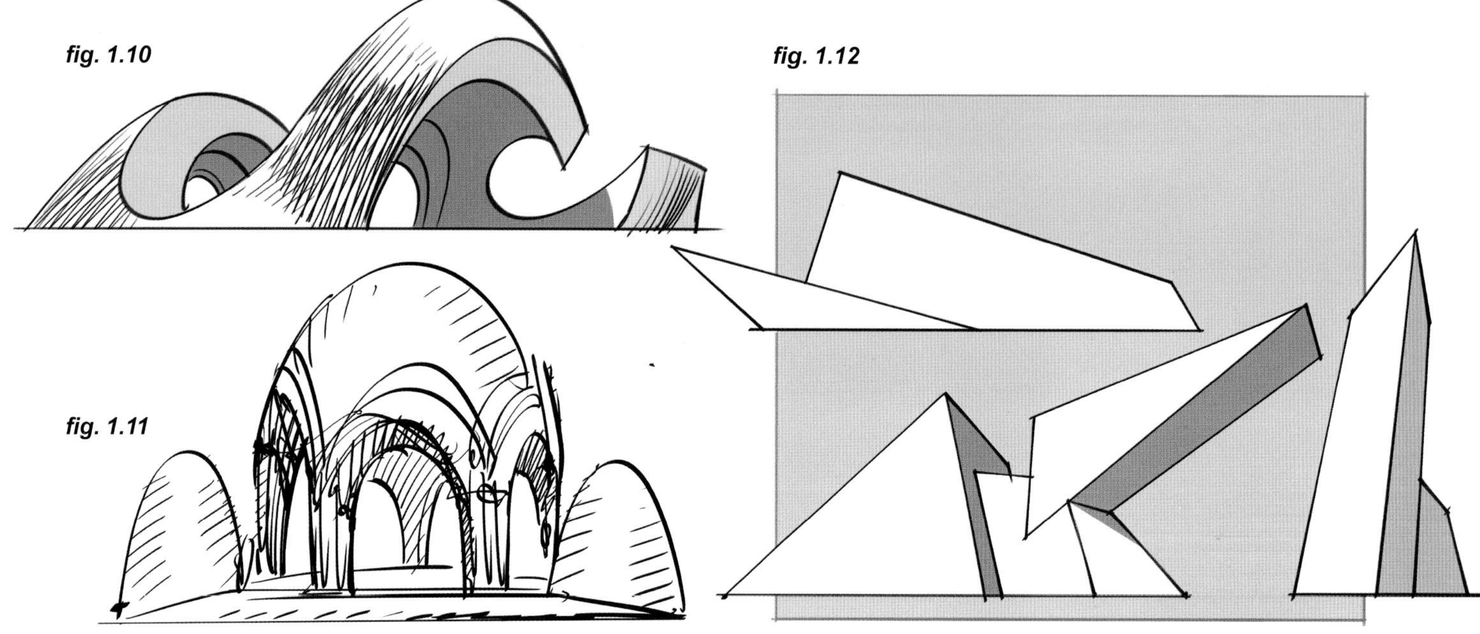

fig. 1.10

fig. 1.11

fig. 1.12

Figs. 1.10–1.12: These simplified and very stylized "round" vs. "angular" sketches show ways to emphasize and commit to a very clear visual shape language. The design philosophy we eventually decide to apply to our locations can be based on these elements, plus others such as the contrast between tall vs. short, top-heavy vs. bottom-heavy, and more.

It is important to decide what type of shape language to use for every location, character, and tone of the moment, and how to keep it consistent during the full narrative so that the audience can emotionally identify, link, and relate certain types of shapes with associated facts, experiences, feelings, and characters in the story.

Figs. 1.13, 1.14: The more rendered sketches show how lighting is also a determining factor in the emotional perception of the subject by emphasizing the volume, actual shape, and the flow of lines.

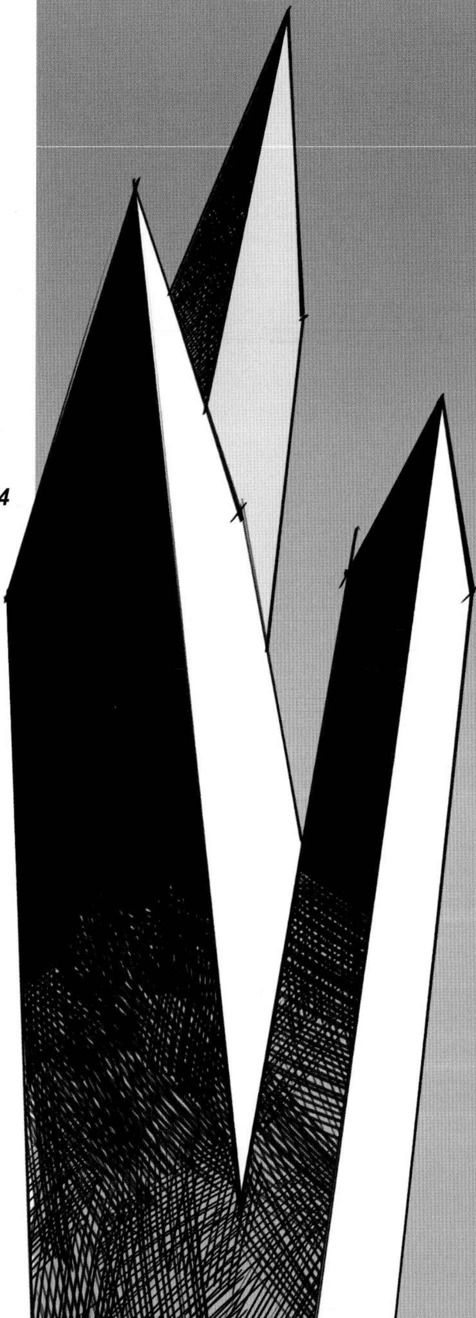

fig. 1.14

fig. 1.13

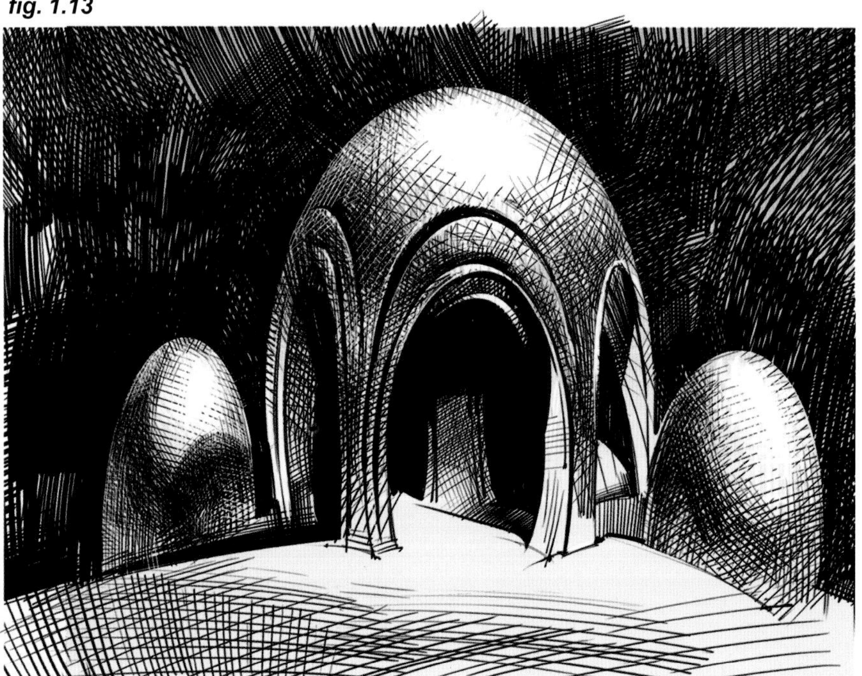

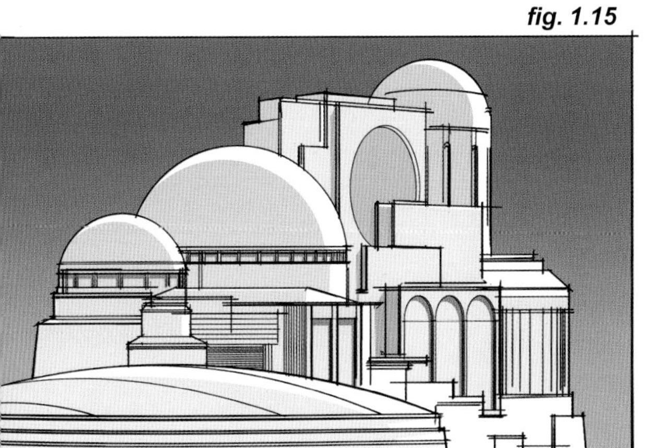

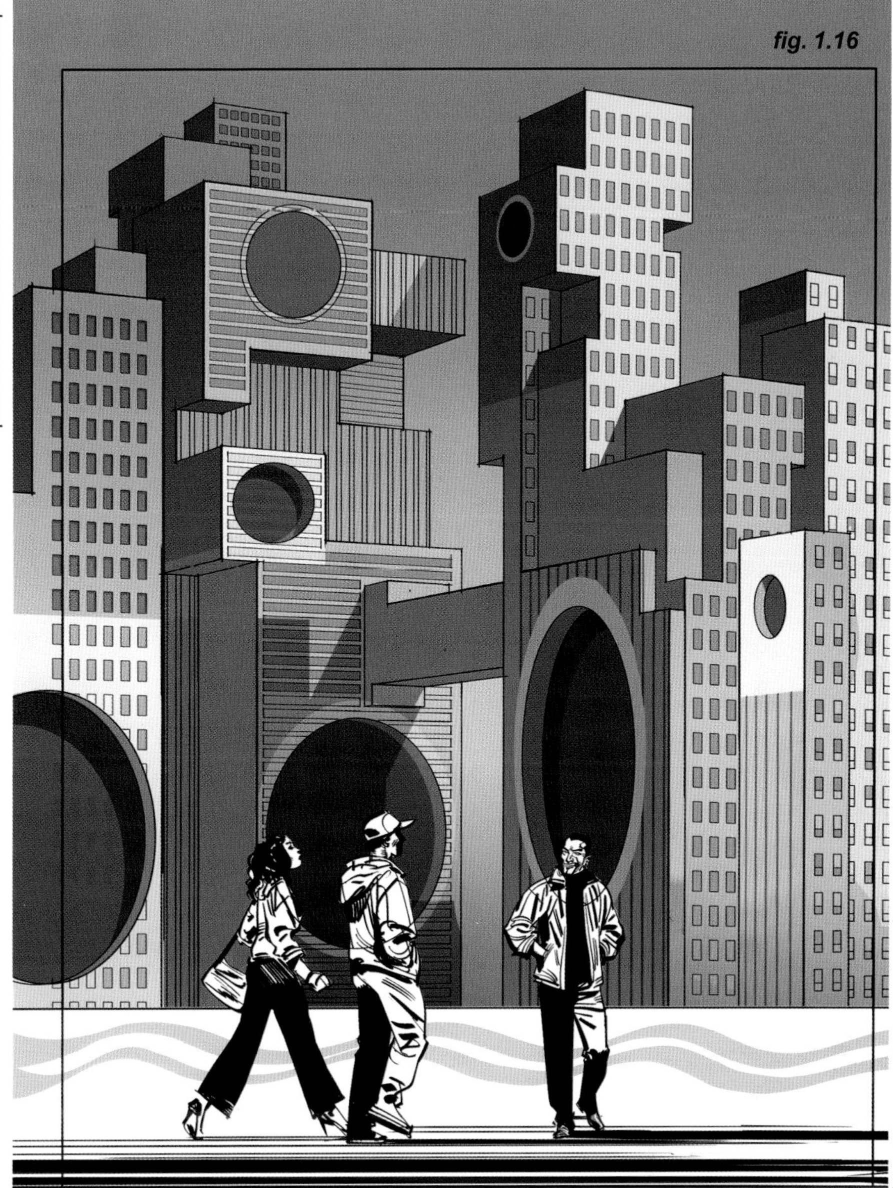

The examples on this page are the results of combining and juxtaposing both line languages (curved and straight/angular) in a stylized fashion. The mixing of these contrasts can create interesting patterns and rhythms for the visuals of a specific location or environment in which contrast or juxtaposition can be a story point.

Fig. 1.15: Preliminary sketch for a fantasy-style palace, using domes and angles.

Fig. 1.16: A street scene on the outskirts of an industrialized city. Vertical, cubic buildings have circular elements within their architectural design as strong, graphic statements.

Fig. 1.17: Combining a nomadic style of life with an ancient palace's ruins. The overwhelming straight, tall gate contrasts with the softer, wavy shapes of the nomads' tents, as well as the sand dunes.

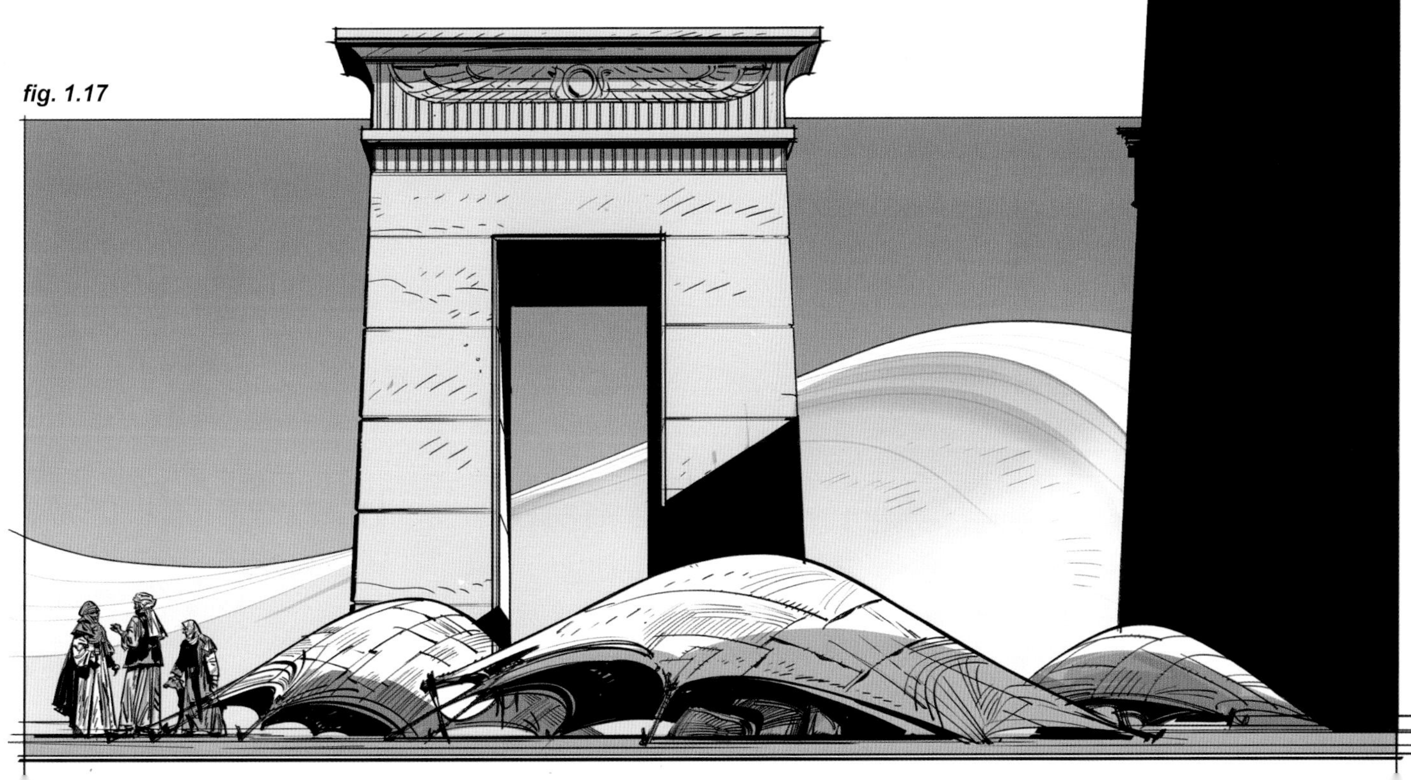

SILHOUETTE LANGUAGE

As seen in other books of this *Framed* series, the **quick readability** of a composition or a design is of the essence, especially when it is part of a visual narrative. Once the **main areas of attention** have been established in the **proper order of visual importance,** (yellow being the number one in figs. 1.18, 1.20)*,* the details can be added (figs. 1.19, 1.21).

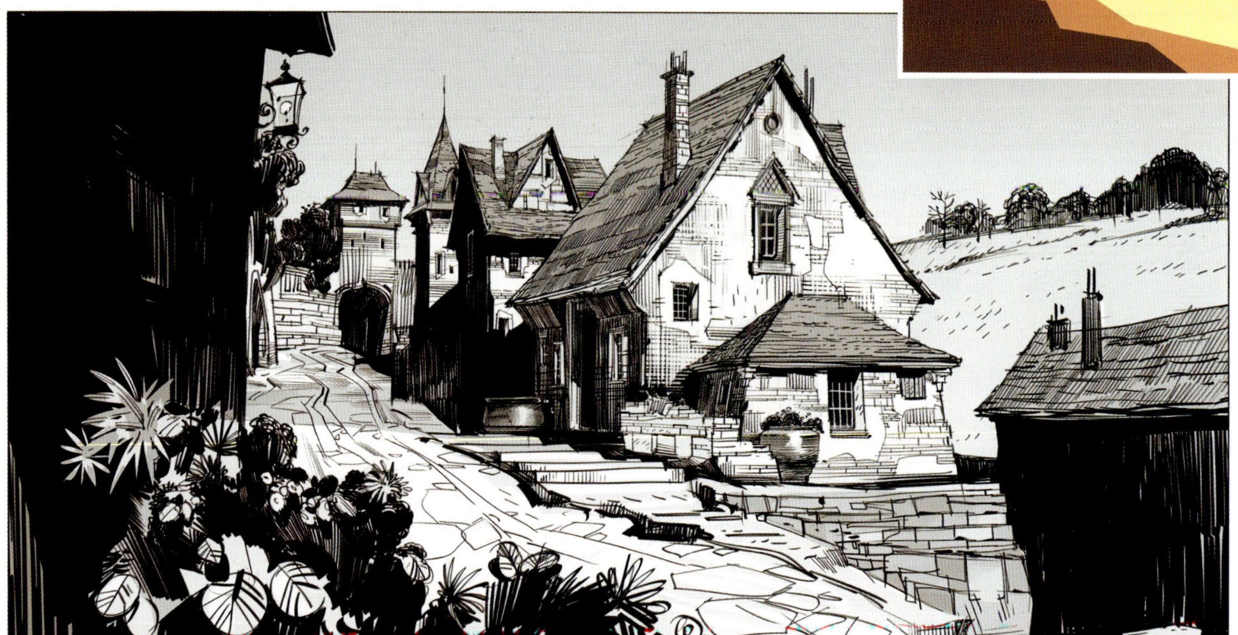

fig. 1.18

fig. 1.19

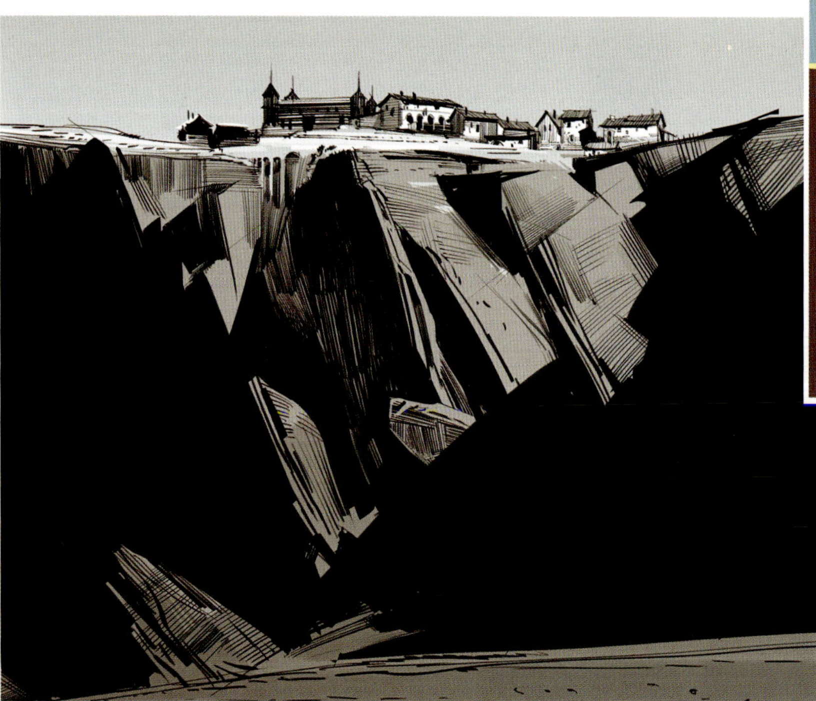

fig. 1.20

fig. 1.21

Unless there is a reason to make things look flat and equally relevant within a shot as part of a visual strategy (like when trying to make a location look boring by comparison to others), having a scene in which there is no depth and no visual priorities will always be a problem. It is important to focus the audience's attention, not spread it everywhere equally. This same philosophy also applies to designing the shapes within a specific environment.

A ONE-TWO PUNCH VS. MANY PUNCHES

A scene can have one or more centers of narrative attention, and therefore the level of complexity among them will vary. This can range from essentially two elements to many more that will need to be organized in order of importance.

Fig. 1.22: This aerial view of a European medieval village has a central defensive tower as the main statement, with the surrounding village as its visual background.

Fig. 1.23: The **"one punch" (1)** of the fortification is emphasized by being surrounded by a—comparatively speaking—visual counterpunch. The **counterpunch (2)** is the group of much smaller, equal-size buildings in the surrounding area, which comes as a second read.

fig. 1.22

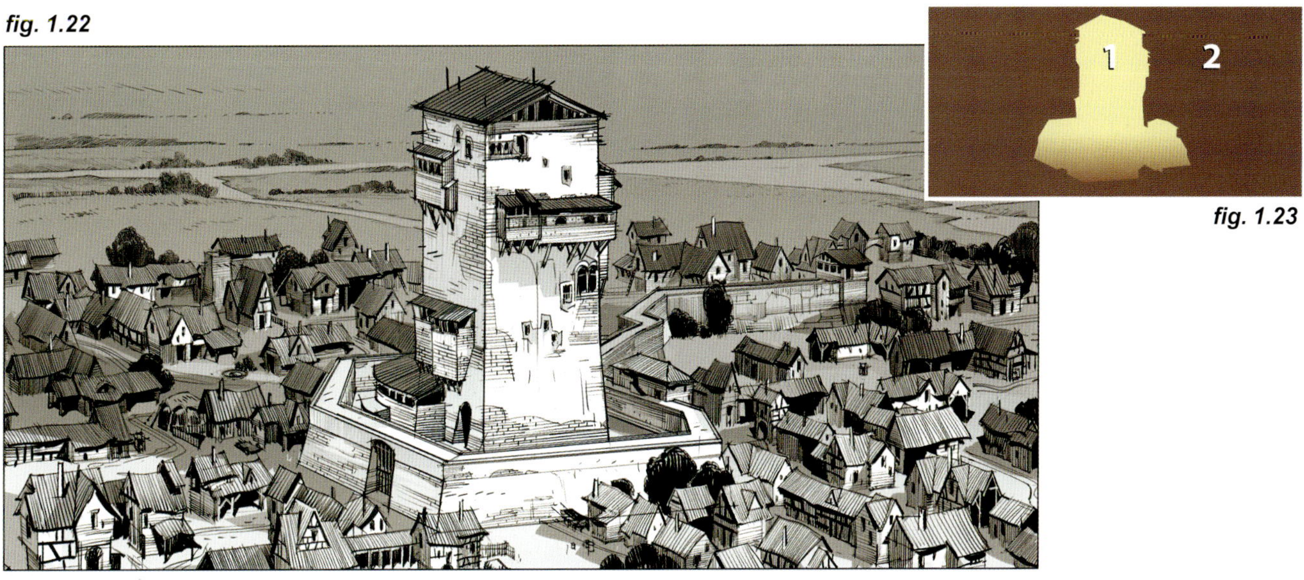

fig. 1.23

Figs. 1.24, 1.25: This next composition shows a more complex case where the relevant elements are more numerous and therefore need a bit more thought and strategizing when establishing a visual order. See how elements 1, 2, and 3 work in a way that—although combined into a single composition—each one has its own place of relevance within the scene:

(1) The first and most important read are the two characters, made prominent by being placed in the foreground, plus their size and strong lighting contrast with their immediate surroundings.
(2) The second read is the temple, a dominant piece of architecture in the far background that rises up above the rest.
(3) The third and final read is the lower, backlit houses that provide a dark background against which the characters stand out.

fig. 1.24

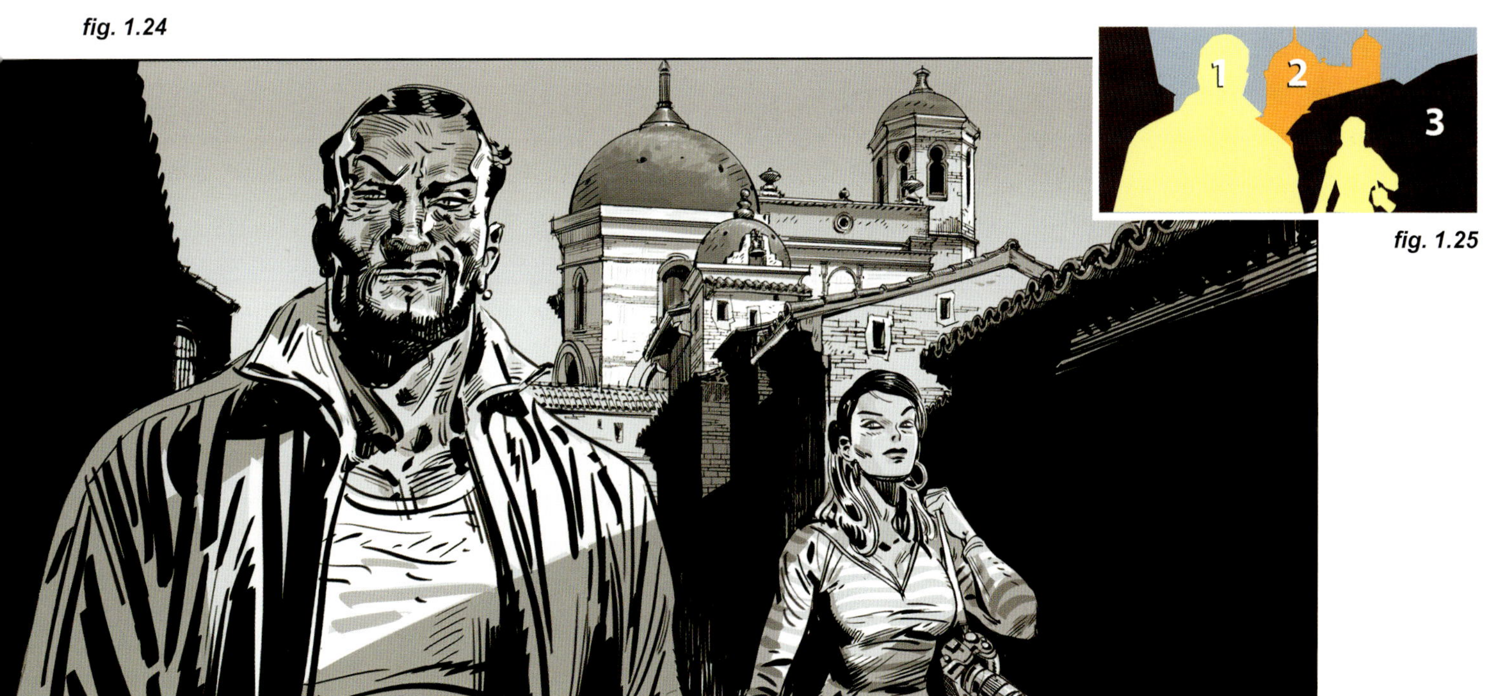

fig. 1.25

Fig. 1.26: Combine big and small shapes to form rhythms within a location that break up a potential monotony, create interesting weight distribution, focus attention, and overall give it a more vibrant feeling. And unless the story requires said monotony or repetition, this approach pushes the work in a more vibrant, interesting, and appealing direction.

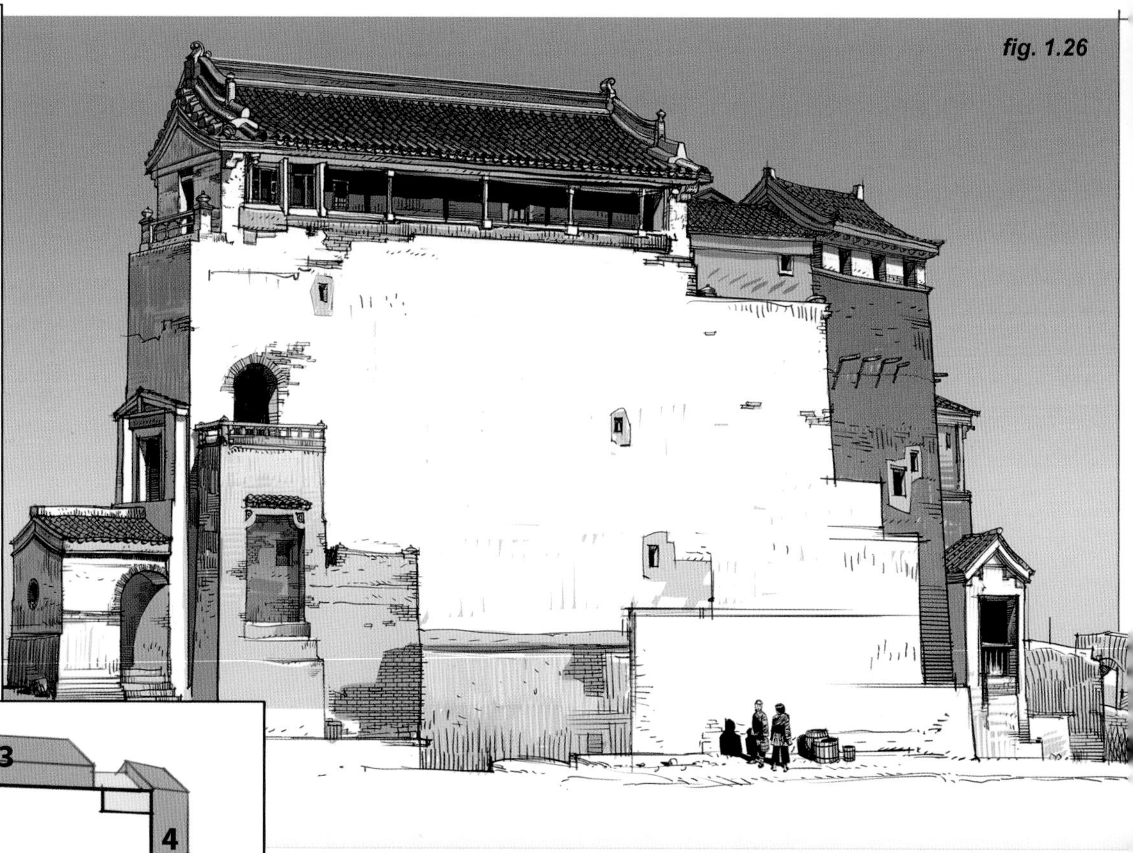

fig. 1.26

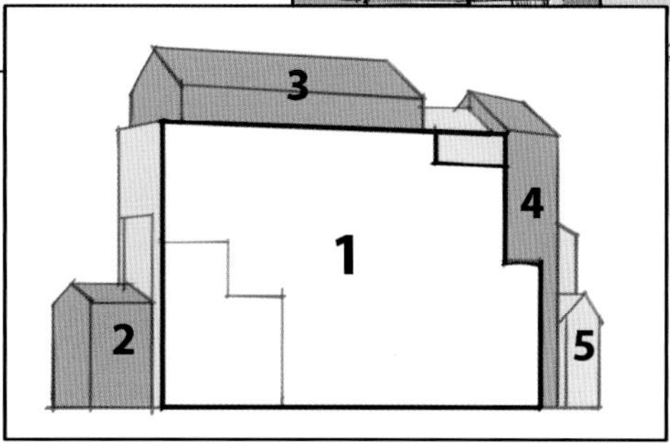

fig. 1.27

Fig. 1.27: These same shapes and volumes simplified.

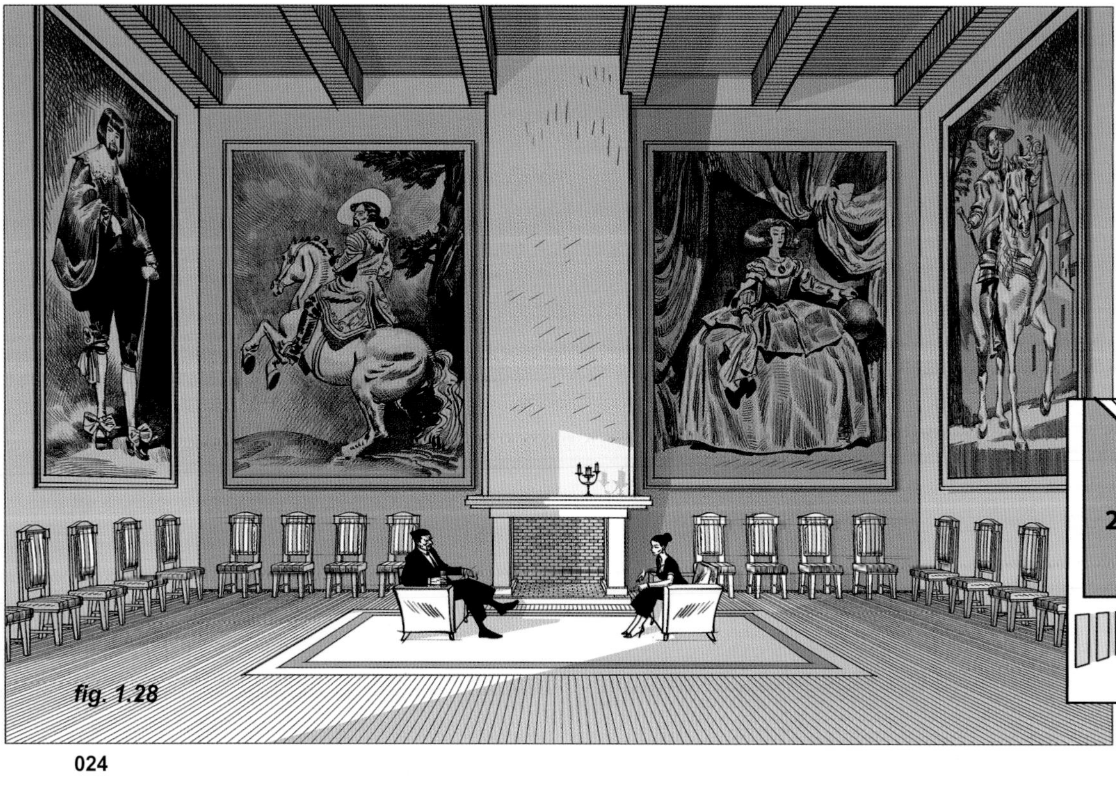

Fig. 1.28: The size imbalance and contrast between the characters, seats, fireplace, and paintings helps create an interesting sense of drama in the world where these two characters exist.

Fig. 1.29: These same shapes and volumes simplified.

fig. 1.

fig. 1.28

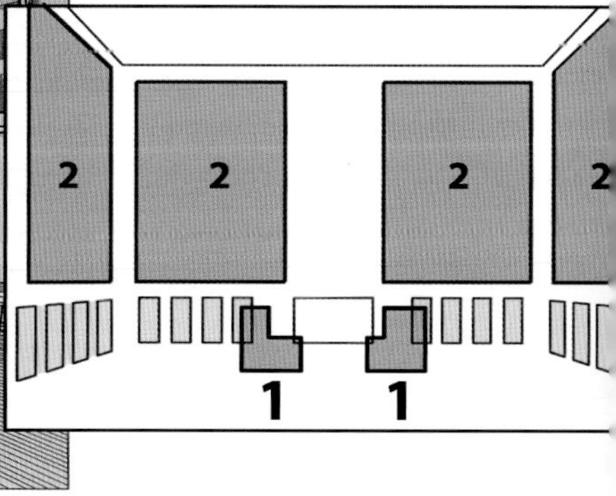

SHAPE IDENTITY

What gives something its distinctive look? What makes a Gothic building look Gothic? What essential elements make a Renaissance costume look like it belongs to the Renaissance and not to a different period? Ideally, even an audience that knows nothing about the story should be able to determine its basic parameters (location, time period, tone) just by glancing at our designs. Is the story a period piece? If so, what period is it? What about geographical location? Where does it take place? Is the tone of the story somber? Comedic? Realistic? Stylized?

How do we visualize these characteristics? What process do we follow to clearly state and represent what gives all these elements their clear **personality and sense of singularity?**

Whenever we travel out of our own cultural and linguistic environment, we are usually most intrigued by what other people do differently than us. For the most part, new details in the customs, traditions, art, language, architecture, light, accents, and life organization stand out to us and grab our immediate attention. No matter how many similarities there may be between our way of life and theirs, these can easily become secondary in our perceptions because we are already familiar with them. Generally, we are there to be exposed to the differences and to be fascinated by them.

When it comes to visually representing a variety of **architectural styles,** it is natural to go through a similar process, first noticing and underlining their differences and uniqueness in order to represent them in a distinctive manner. After we understand these differences, they can be emphasized more or less depending on the narrative needs.

PRACTICAL CASES

Here are a few examples of what we were just talking about. There are two basic cases.

When styles are completely different, the visualization of each one's particularities is easy to pinpoint and depict.

fig. 1.30

fig. 1.31

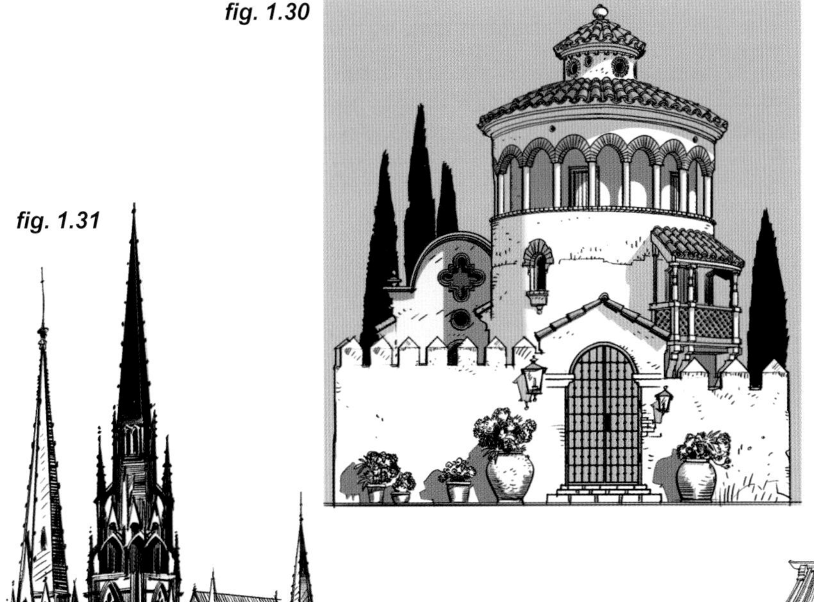

Fig. 1.30: Inspired by Southern Spain

Fig. 1.31: Inspired by European Gothic style

Fig. 1.32: Inspired by Japanese Edo period

When juxtaposing such different styles within the context of the same story, there is a bit more freedom in the process of stylization, because the basic shapes of these buildings already communicate radically different time periods and geography very easily identifiable in the blink of an eye.

But what happens when the differences between the identifying, distinctive shapes of a location are a lot more subtle?

fig. 1.32

When styles are very similar, it is important to focus on the few things that most clearly represent the differences between them.

When trying to figure out the specific singularities of an architectural style, it is good not only to study and analyze its characteristics in isolation but also to compare it with other similar styles. This comparison helps to emphasize the details and aspects that make the former really distinctive from everything else.

To visualize this **let's consider two similar architectural styles: Baroque and Rococo.** They have a lot in common. Once we understand their basic characteristics, how can we make them both quickly identifiable and unique?

First, consider the two styles in context. Previous to them, there was the **Renaissance** (approximately **1400–1600),** which applied many of the classic Greek and Roman principles with perfectly designed, balanced, symmetrical, and geometrical lines. By the early **1500s,** new views on the Christian religion were developing in Northern Europe, and as a result, **Protestantism** was born. Given its new understanding and approach to religion, temples became more austere and simple in their designs and atmosphere than the ones in Southern Europe. So, around **1600,** as a reaction to this and in order to make them more enticing, energizing, and appealing to people, Catholic temples became even more ornate, grandiose, and dramatic, enhancing a sense of dynamics, curves, diagonals, oval shapes, movement, contrasting light, and emotions far beyond what the Renaissance, its predecessor, ever achieved. Thus, the **Baroque** style was born.

Now fast-forward to the first half of the **1700s.**

Private life started gaining more value than big, ostentatious, public displays. While the extreme ornamentation and theatrics of the Baroque style lived on, it now became more intimate, less emotionally overwhelming, and more naturalistic. The twisted, curved, and extremely decorative forms that ruled until then went through a process of adaptation in order to better serve the new philosophy and approach to life. They became less heavy and more delicate, with more asymmetric components than its very geometrical ancestor, the Baroque style. There is more of a human scale to it, a more mundane tone if you will, less related to religion. More light was let in, and brighter colors were used. This was the **Rococo** period, also called "late Baroque," since it really was a natural evolution that adapted to a new perception of life.

So again, on spotting the identifying shape language that gives personality to an architectural style, here is a case where both differences and similarities do somehow share a common space. It is time to zero in on the differences and make a big fuss out of them, so let's investigate the elements and details that are available in order to achieve this goal.

Fig. 1.33: Some of the **similarities** are elaborate ornamentation, an opulent sense of exuberance, and motifs inspired by nature, as visualized in these two side-by-side examples. So having noticed these similarities, how do we make distinctive visual statements between these two styles to establish clear **differences?**

The **Baroque** style is **bolder,** with **more depth** and **three-dimensionality.** It is intricate and elaborate, yet more **imposing, dramatic, serious,** and mostly of a **religious** character or nature.

When it comes to color, its tones are **stronger,** more **saturated,** and combined with a dramatic **use of darks.**

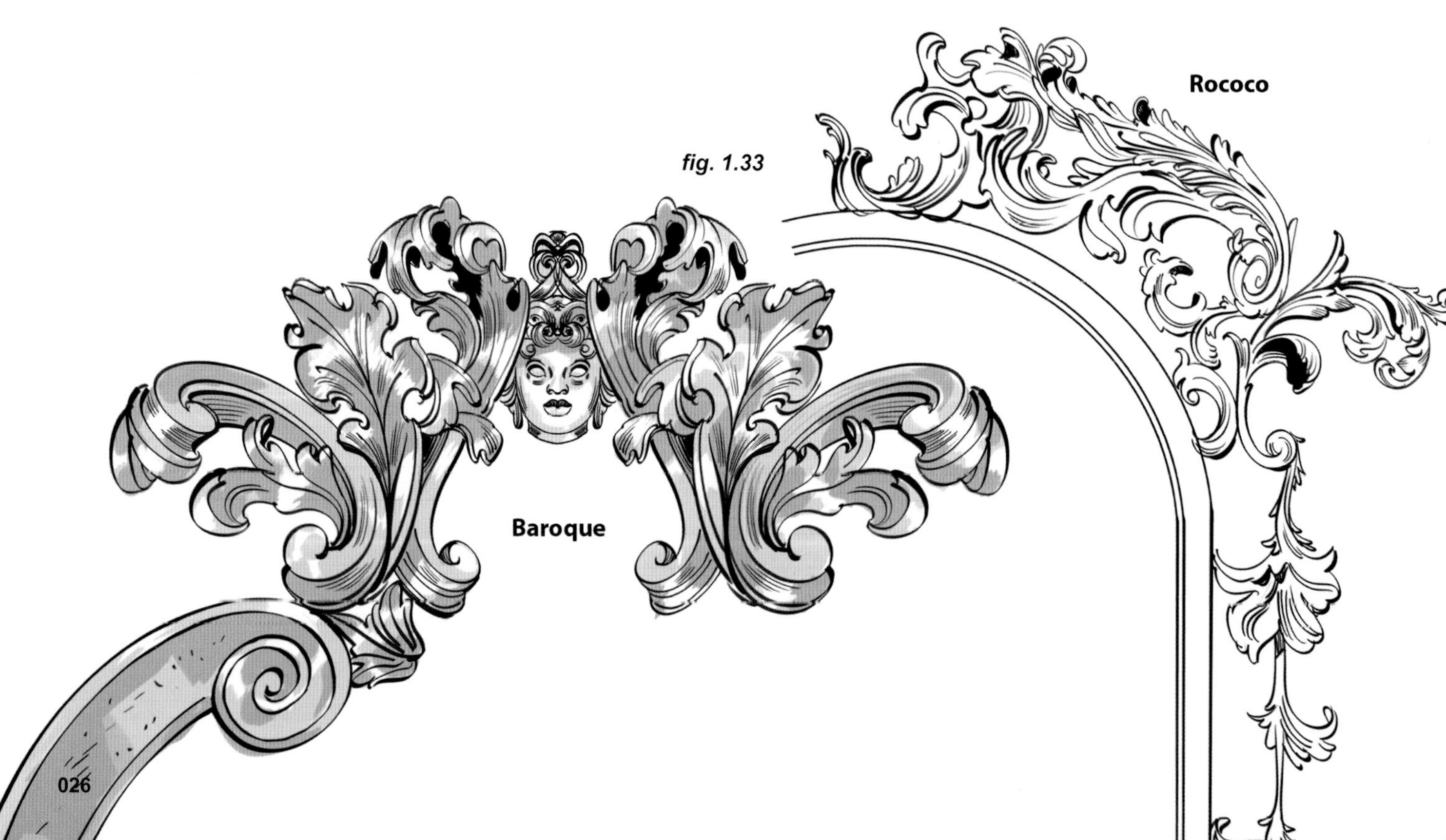

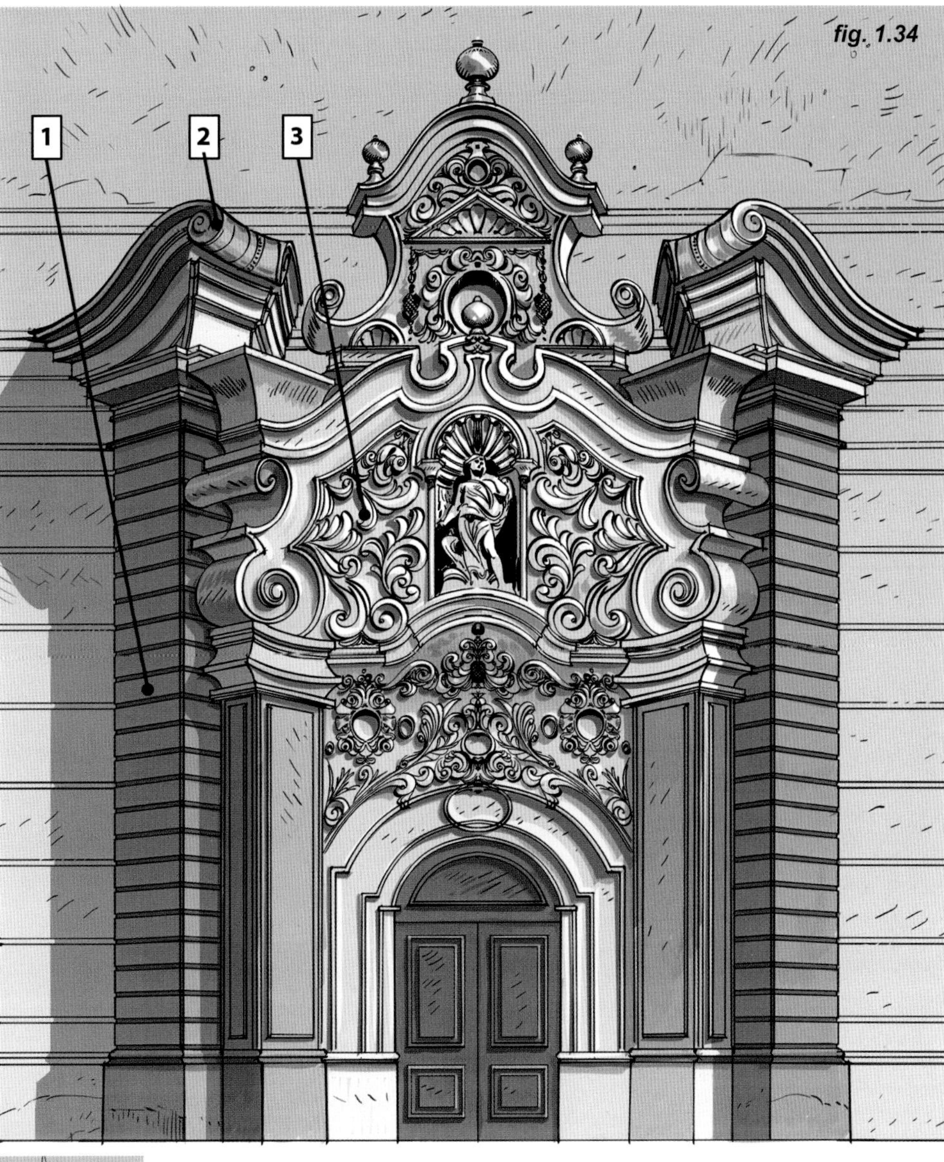

Fig. 1.34: As a result of observing these characteristics, this image emphasizes elements such as **(1) strong pilasters, (2) volutes,** and **(3) scrolls,** showing them as thick and bold elements that create the essential structure, while other smaller, more intricate elements just play around them.

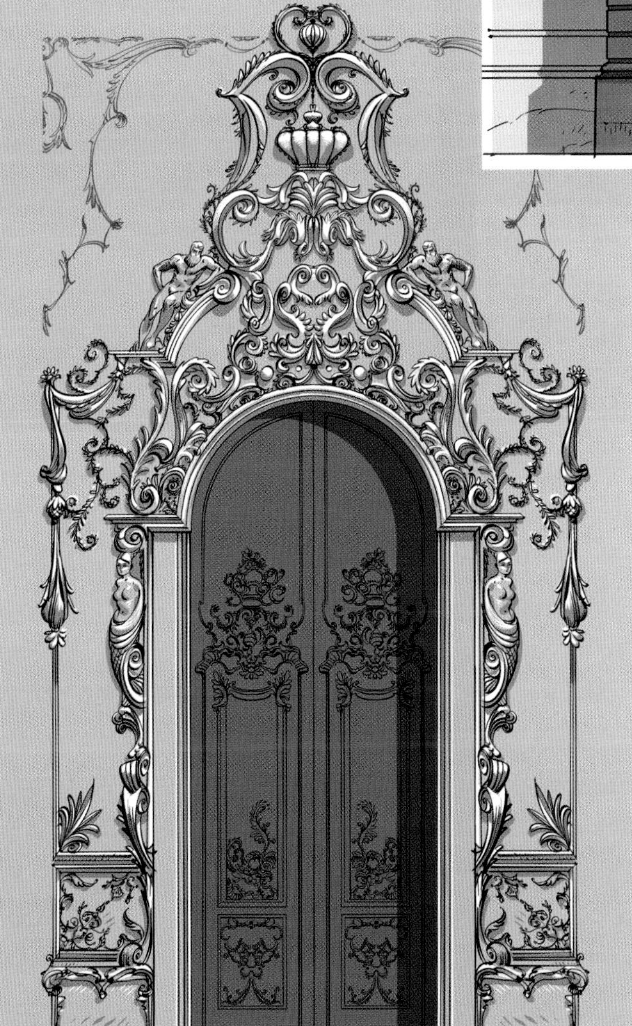

Fig. 1.35: The **Rococo** style incorporates **flatter** elements rather than volumetric ones and has a **lighter, more decorative tone** that comes across as **airy and more carefree.** The shapes are **thinner** overall, more **delicate** and **stylized.** With regard to color, it favored lighter **ivory and pastel tones.**

In essence, this general working philosophy applies to all aspects of design, whether **locations or characters,** when it comes to making them truly distinctive.

It is ultimately based on a very simple principle. Imagine designing a character, both its physical attributes and costume. Then ask, if you were to go to a comic convention disguised as it, would people around you immediately know who it was? Would it be **distinctive and easily identifiable?**

Being aware of the core characteristics of an architectural style facilitates our ability to establish a proper look in our designs, whether juxtaposed against each other in the same shot or even when shown individually, so that we can clearly establish the visual spirit of any given time period and place.

Spotting similarities and differences in locations' styles is an important part of our visual language, and everything just mentioned can be especially applicable to a number of cases.

Let's say we are telling the story of two characters who are constantly **at odds,** yet at the end they find a way to get together in **good harmony.** As always, we will try to find visual ways to support this. This is when differences and similarities between two architectural styles can come into play. During the introduction and development of their story, both characters could live in houses or apartments that are very different in style, symbolizing their different views and personalities, yet we could design both locations so that certain areas within them are closer in style or layout color. That way, we can shoot, draw, frame, or visualize the last, most harmonious scenes in these areas, as they peacefully come together in that **"common space."**

Another case in which the juxtaposition of different styles could come into play would be if we want to portray the **passage of time** within a location—a city, for example. In this case we will need to show the different historical styles that might be part of the growth of that city, neighborhood, or building in a visual way. At this point, I can't help but recall something that happened to me the first time I ever visited the United States—a good example of how **distinctive** the visual personality of one place versus another can be. It was during a short visit to the capital, Washington, DC. The first night, as I was waiting in line to check in to the hotel, I had a casual conversation with the gentleman ahead of me. I guess I mentioned it was my first time in the country because he asked me where I was from. When I said, "Europe," he said, "Oh great, you are going to love DC. This whole part of the country feels very European."

I thought that was an interesting comment. I was excited to start taking in the sights the following morning, and when I did, I have to say, I loved it. I found it fresh, exciting, and with a clear connection to the "Old World." After visiting and walking around for a few days, I realized what that man meant. There were definitely plenty of Georgian, Federal, and Neoclassical-style buildings, and then some. I was seeing everything around me and thinking, "He was right. All these buildings were clearly inspired by European architecture." And yet, there was something that felt *very* American and *very* non-European to me. I thought about it for days, analyzed it—what was it? It was clearly right in front of my eyes, but I couldn't put my finger on it—until it hit me.

When you walk around pretty much any European city, small town, or village, you will see buildings from those periods I just mentioned (in that particular country's style, obviously). Especially in certain parts of the old continent, like the UK and France, two countries that had outsized influence on the nascent United States, the architecture might look extremely similar to what one can see in Washington, DC, including more recent, modern buildings as well. But in Europe, there remains a lot of evidence of what came before that. Georgian buildings, Neoclassical buildings, and the like are the direct historical product of everything else

that preceded that time, and many of these older buildings are still standing to this day.

In a nutshell, Europe reminds me of the growth rings of a tree. It starts with a little core at the center and then grows, evolves, and expands from there (just like the Muir Woods cut-out tree scene in *Vertigo).* What I found incredibly distinctive about DC is that all those old, European-style buildings from the 1790s–1800s look like they appeared there out of nowhere, with no "Old World" architectural precedents anywhere to be seen, like a tree that was born already 100 years old. Visually, to me this was at the core of my experience in Washington, DC. For sure, if I had to design a story happening in that district, this idea would be in the back of my mind the whole time, affecting the totality of my work.

Given the nature of our business, it is very important that the characters, locations, props, etc. that are projected on-screen or drawn on paper are consistently recognizable in form, shape, and character throughout the narrative. The visual statements must be clear and deliver our message properly. For example, if we depict medieval Europe, it is important to portray the flavor and atmosphere of that time and place in a convincing manner. So, what makes any potential design look medieval? Or central European? Or elegant? Cheerful? Dangerous? Neoclassical? Gothic? Welcoming? Ominous? Modern? What makes an Indian jungle look Indian and not Central American? **What makes *any* element look, feel, or come across the way we need it to in order to support the message of the story?**

After detailed analysis of our visual references, we will have to make a number of choices that will inform our visual language. The quality of these decisions about how to show the visual elements will determine our level of success. **Consistent, recognizable shapes and tone are elements that will constantly come into play** and will affect the locations as much as they will affect the characters within, creating a level of **contrast between environments that can have different—and purposeful— degrees of strength,** from relatively similar to extremely different.

An audience that does not know anything about the story should be able to understand its basic parameters just by glancing at our designs.

In this example, let's consider a random geographical location, say, modern-day Paris.

The first step is to get visually and atmospherically acquainted with the city through visual research. Absorb the general flavor, possibilities, options . . . This is going to take awhile. It has to. We need peace of mind. **Enjoy the process of discovery,** and give yourself time to absorb this journey of getting to know the subject.

And then dive into content that has come before. Other artists, filmmakers, and journalists have been feeding us visual references and ideas about this location for ages. Many movies, graphic novels, and documentaries take place in Paris. Should these be taken into account as sources of visual inspiration, even though we are in the process of creating **our idea, our vision, and our version of Paris?** Normally, **we want our story, our narrative, to be unique.** Yet this is a location that has been explored a thousand times already, and some of these visions, although very personal to their creators, have sometimes **become generally accepted as cultural icons.** So, we might want to consider whether to include them—or to contradict them—in order to make our personal statement even stronger and with a more dramatic impact.

Can you imagine a story taking place in the French capital without ever showing the Eiffel Tower or the Seine River, and the very emblematic period buildings on both shores? Well, yes, of course, but that in itself might be a story point. From the moment we show a distant skyline that includes the iconic metal tower from 1889, we immediately know where we are.

But maybe the goal for this story, although set in Paris, is to make it feel universal, a drama that could happen anywhere. If we show too many Parisian icons or focus too much on them, the point of making this a human drama without specific geographical borders or boundaries could be lost.

Let's push this a bit further. So the story takes place in current-day Paris, fine, but current-day Paris also includes buildings and areas from the 1200s, the 1700s, right beside modern-day structures and skyscrapers. Such an opportunity for contrast makes for great storytelling and drama. Now let's add to that; let's say it's a spy story.

As usual, playing up contrast emphasizes the value and significance of each and every element (remember, a shadow means nothing without a light to compare it to). So, maybe the plot takes the main character from a very modern area to the narrow streets of a more historical one, or vice versa, the character could move from a centuries-old neighborhood to a more modern one.

What if the main character needs to start in a place that feels warm and closer to us, so that we feel the same way about them? But the director wants them coming from either the modern part of town to eventually travel to the older part of town as part of the adventure, **or possibly the other way around,** originating in the historical part of town and ending up in the modern area later on. How do we represent each one of these areas as likable and warm, or unwelcoming and cold, as needed? It depends on what elements of each of the areas (old and modern) are featured. So, in order to know which visual elements to focus on, do the **research** and, after that, start **sketching** and developing ideas.

The following **design philosophy options** could be applied to this case.

A: They *come from* **OLD TOWN—*LIKABLE***: Would look organic, quaint, human-scale, more in touch with nature, made of wood and stone, picturesque rooftops, small shops, maybe flowers on balconies, social, people standing around talking to each other.
B: They *go to* **MODERN DISTRICT—*UNLIKABLE***: Focus on cold, dark, more metallic and impersonal elements.

And now, let's reverse the tone.

AA: They *come from* **MODERN DISTRICT—*LIKABLE***: Focus on the comfortable, sophisticated, elegant aspects of it, with cool, modern, and convenient devices around.
BB: They *go to* **OLD TOWN—*UNLIKABLE***: Illustrate how claustrophobic it can feel; stonework will look heavy and dark, dirty, rundown, not taken care of, woodwork in serious need of repair, same with the rooftops.

Now we know what to look for because **it is a matter of nailing the right tone** (welcoming or unwelcoming) **independently from the part of town that represents it** (old or modern).

So, based on this principle, these two environments could look something like the examples on the next pages.

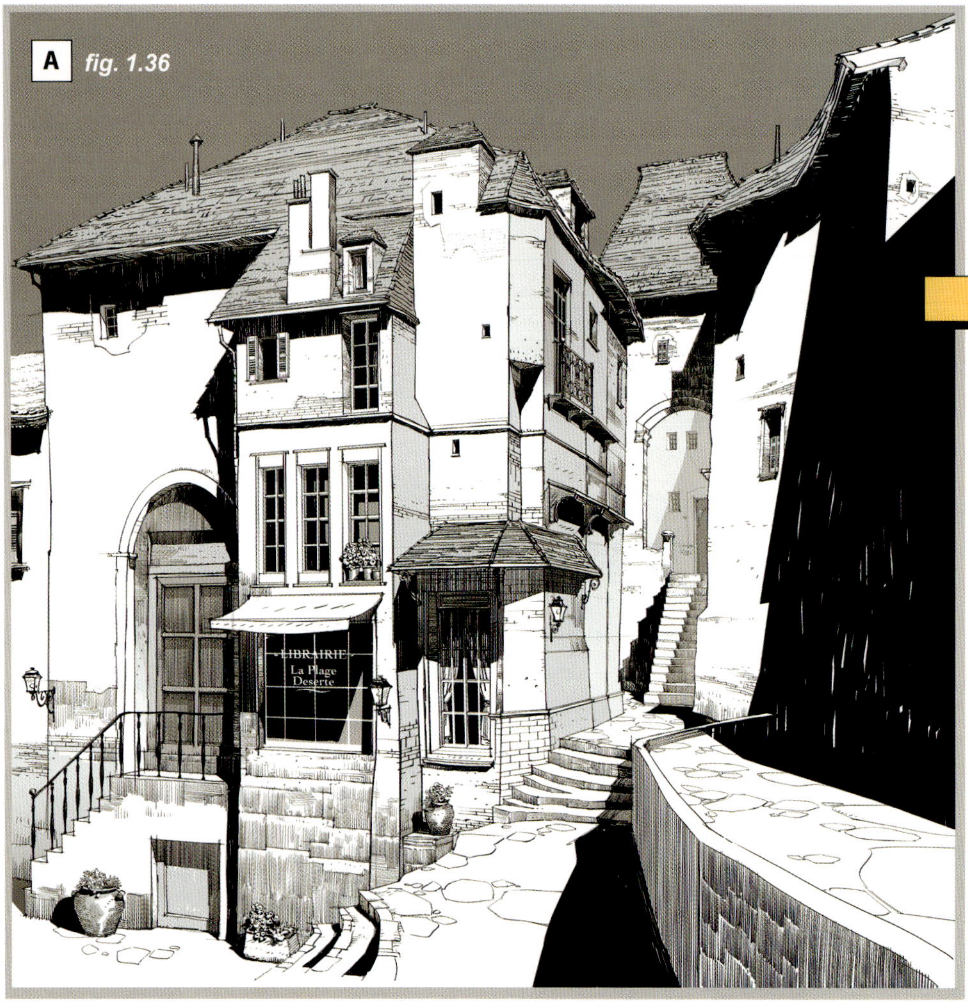

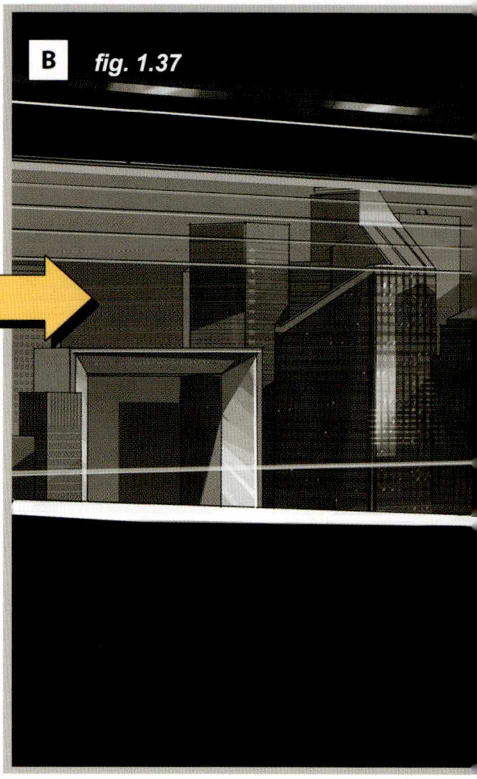

Let's look at these concept design options: **A** to and **AA** to **BB**.

Fig. 1.36: (A) The narrow streets of the old town are seen as bright, appreciated, and taken care of. The rugged textures are limited to specific areas in order to keep the old, human-scaled, quaint, and historical flavor going. Details such as flower pots and gentle curtains on the windows express the pride the inhabitants of this neighborhood take in their surroundings.

Fig. 1.39: (BB) On the contrary, **the same neighborhood** shows a more troubled place by playing with deeper, darker, more rundown textures. Areas of shadow have been enlarged to dim the mood of the area. This adds up to not just a sense of history but also of potential danger. Essentially the same area just turned into a way more **uninviting** place.

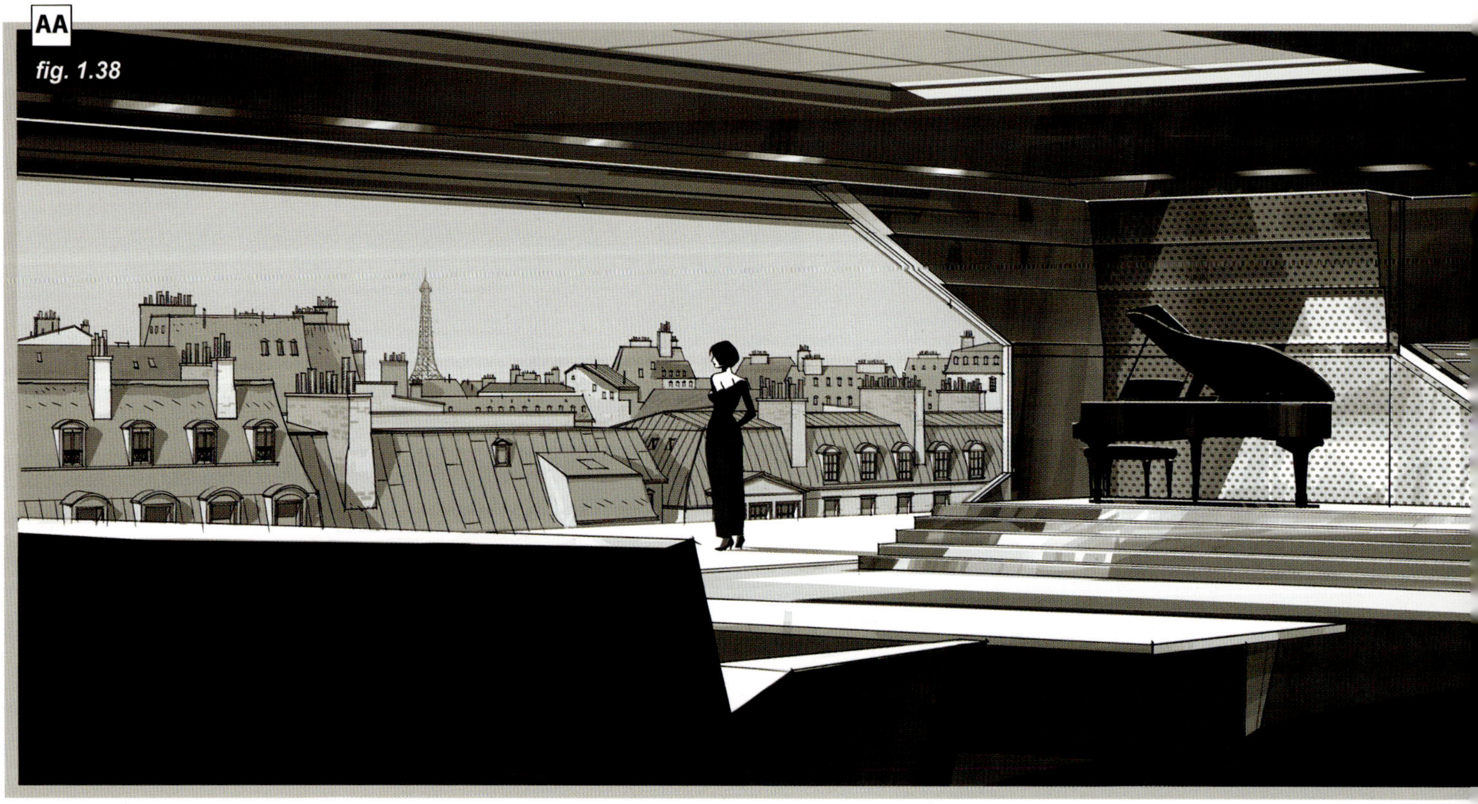

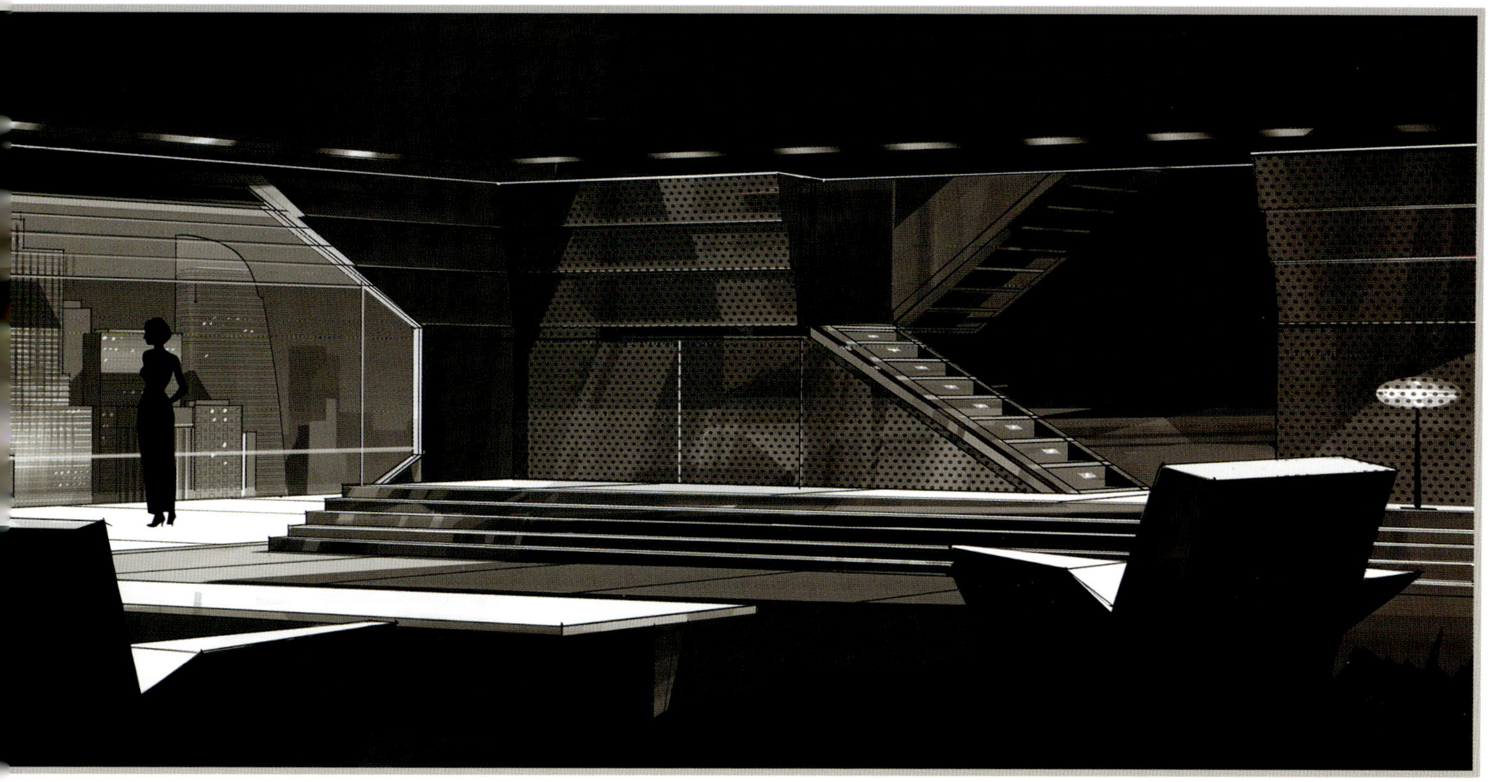

Fig. 1.37: (B) Meanwhile, **the cool and high-tech loft** on the other side of town shows a location not only modern but also dark, bare and cold, mostly lacking the human touch. The view is of a harsh, massive business district.

Fig. 1.38: (AA) This same cool and modern location now looks much brighter, with a view of a softer, more inviting, and organic-looking older part of town. Including elements such as the grand piano further reduces the tension of the place. In essence, this is a location we might want our hero to come from originally.

So, our hero's journey is not simply from modern to old, or vice versa, but from warm and inviting to dark, unwelcoming, and dangerous, independent of the physical location itself.

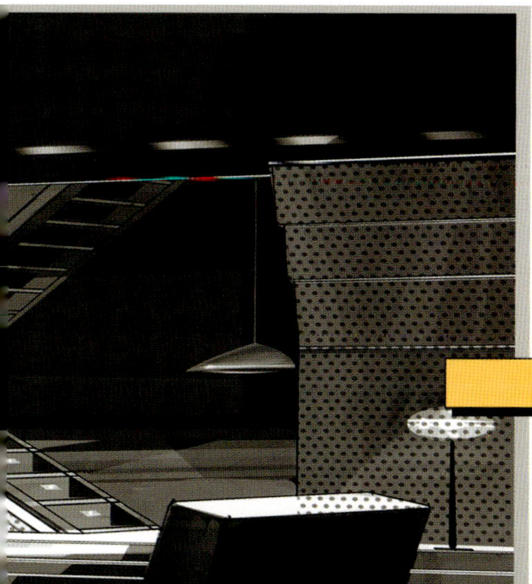

fig. 1.39

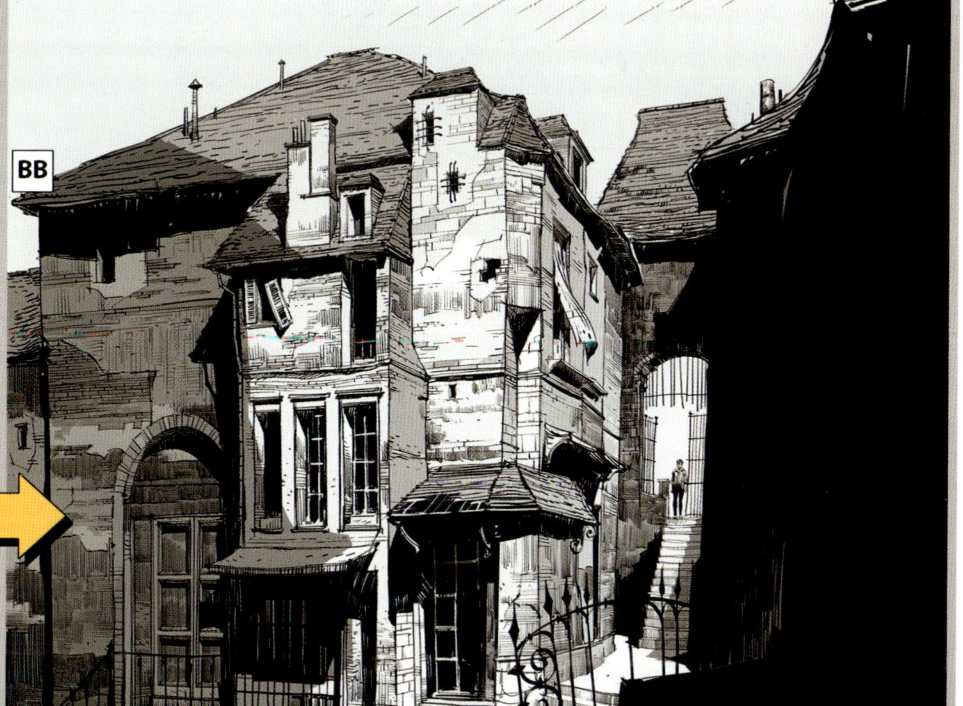

BB

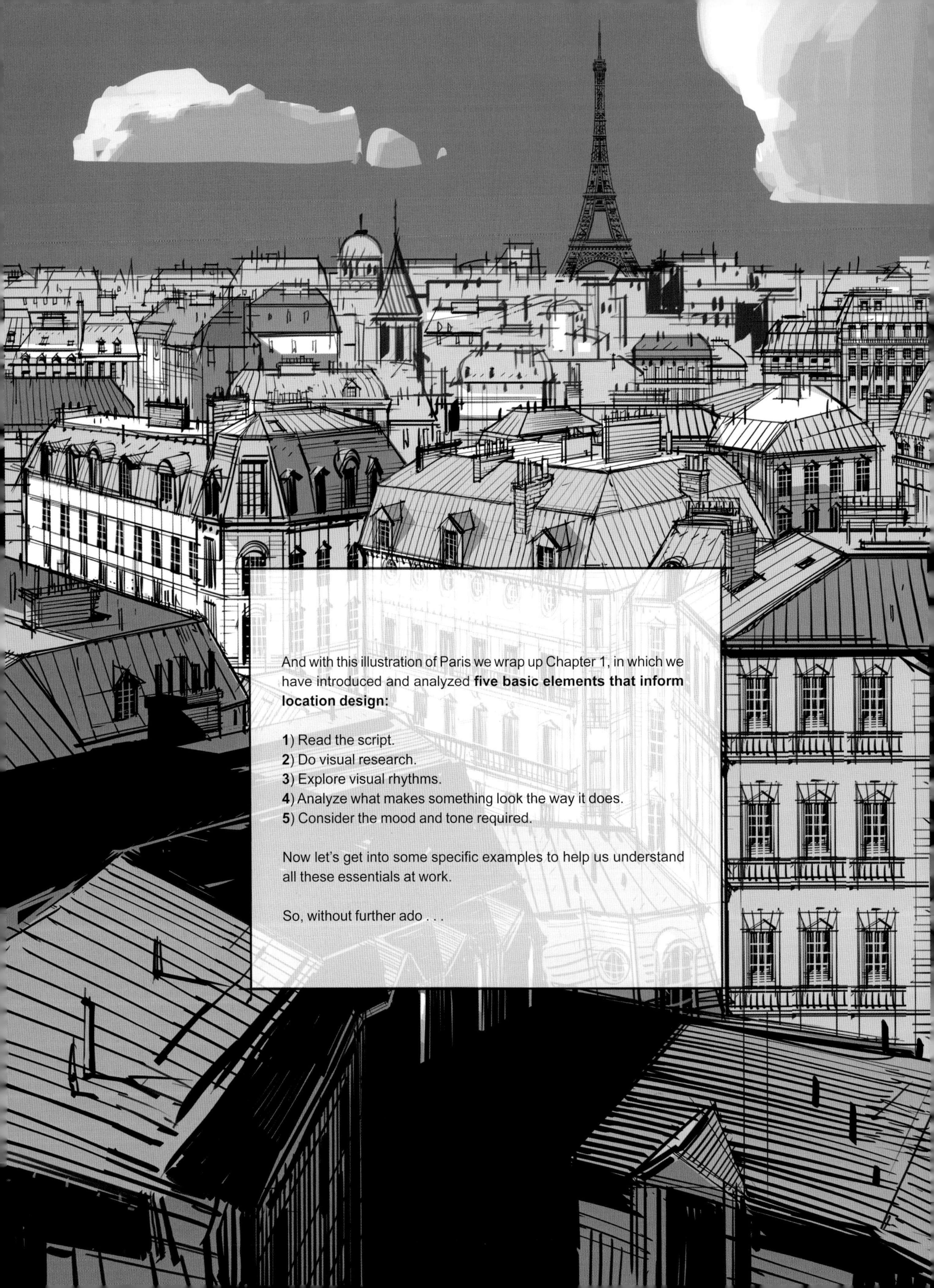

And with this illustration of Paris we wrap up Chapter 1, in which we have introduced and analyzed **five basic elements that inform location design:**

1) Read the script.
2) Do visual research.
3) Explore visual rhythms.
4) Analyze what makes something look the way it does.
5) Consider the mood and tone required.

Now let's get into some specific examples to help us understand all these essentials at work.

So, without further ado . . .

DEVELOPING TWO VERSIONS OF THE SAME LOCATION

(AND WHY)

Using the tools from Chapter 1, let's create **two distinctive locations based on the same idea, an automotive shop.** By setting them in two very distinct geographical locations and cultures, this exercise will show how two different auto shops can indicate two contrasting worlds and experiences.

This can play really well from a narrative point of view. Let's imagine the following story idea: two business partners **(Johnny and Arianna)** had decided to part ways, and **we want to show how their lives played out very differently after that** (remember, contrast is an excellent way to create drama, comedy, excitement, sense of adventure, etc.).

One way to communicate this visually is by establishing specific parallels between the two ensuing lives after their split-up, like having them both run the exact same kind of business (auto shop) but clearly differentiated by the particular characteristics of the two distinct cultural and geographical locations they moved to. For example, a generic, cold-weather city somewhere on the East Coast of North America for Johnny, and a small town in a warm-climate area in the Mediterranean for Arianna.

Before putting ideas down on paper, let's first start a visual research process through reference books, online images, and personal archive photographs as we search for a basic visual structure for our locations.

Here is a description of the location based on a hypothetical script in which **Johnny** receives a visit from a third character named **Sidney:**

After the phone call, Sidney gets in her old (1970s) car and drives along Main Street, where the beat-up train tracks run beside it. The whole area feels like the industrial outskirts of a city somewhere on the East Coast of North America, with its typical red-brick buildings all around. Incidentally, she goes past a young couple having an argument on the sidewalk. Although Sidney does not pay much attention to them, they will later become important witnesses to the action that ensues. Eventually she turns right on 2nd Street that leads to an alleyway where Johnny's Automotive Shop is located.

She parks in this relatively narrow and definitely industrial-looking alley, gets out of the car, and walks toward the auto shop, passing by the old fire escape at the back, which leads to the second floor of this two-story, red-brick building.

Once in the shop she asks one of the mechanics if Johnny is in, to which he replies, "Yeah, he's up in the second-floor office." As Sidney walks toward the interior staircase, the mechanic advises her that, "You'll need to take the emergency stairs outside. Johnny keeps the inside door locked at all times." Sidney looks at him, pauses, and then says a brief, "Thank you."

Keeping in mind that later we will design the "parallel setup" in the Mediterranean region, **let's first design the following American sets:**

1. **Main Street** with the train tracks
2. The **alley** where the car shop is (with a few parked cars, trash containers, etc.).
3. The auto repair **shop interior**
4. The **business office** on the second floor

As established earlier, after reading the script and making notes, go ahead and start looking for photographic reference materials in order to get acquainted with the overall look and feel of that geographical area. Then get into the specific details, which include buildings, roads, vehicles, furniture, and all the rest.

Here is a selection of the reference material that was put together for this location.

Note: For legal reasons, of all the references originally gathered to design this location (from books, the internet, etc.), the only ones reproduced here are photographs from the author's personal archive. These particular ones were not taken in the American Northeast but were also used as reference because they very closely resemble that part of the country.

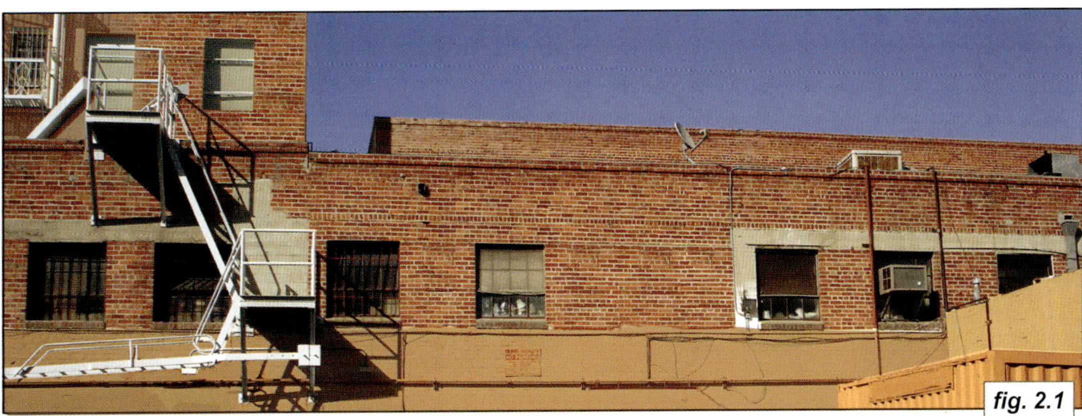

fig. 2.1

fig. 2.2

fig. 2.3

Figs. 2.1–2.6: Normally, photo references are not used in a literal way, meaning don't directly copy the setup unless tasked with realistically portraying a known landmark building or area. For the most part, references inspire the general look first and then the more precise, particular details of the place next.

These will be redesigned, re-stylized, and recomposed as per the needs of the story. The reference will inform relevant elements such as overall atmosphere, architectural style, its distinctive culture, even the weather conditions. These details and elements all add to the authenticity of the location.

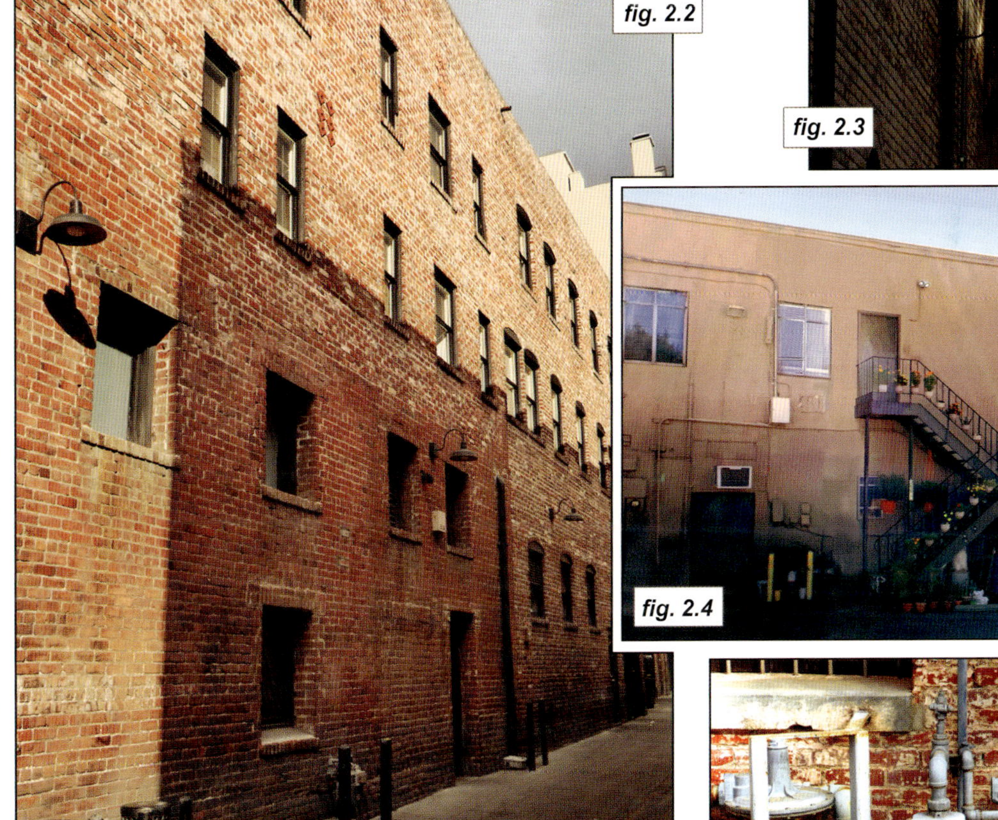

fig. 2.4

fig. 2.5

These references are perfect to inspire not just the specific architectural style but rather a general sense of staging and overall layout of the location.

Fig. 2.4: This picture provides a very interesting and suggestive depiction of what a back alley with two-story buildings and an escape staircase to the top floor can look like.

So, all these compositional elements will help portray the red-brick building style necessary as the backdrop for our story.

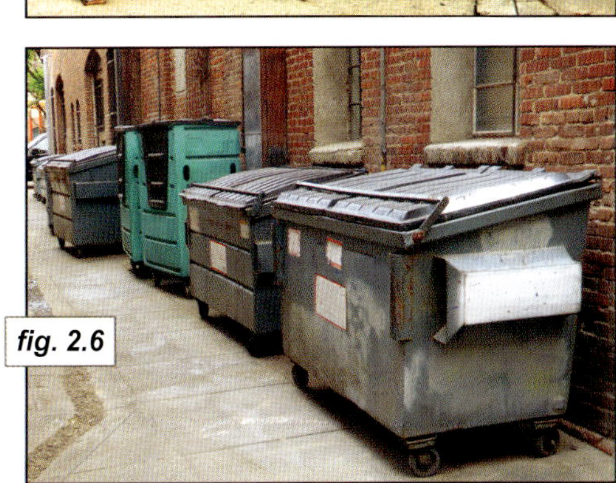

fig. 2.6

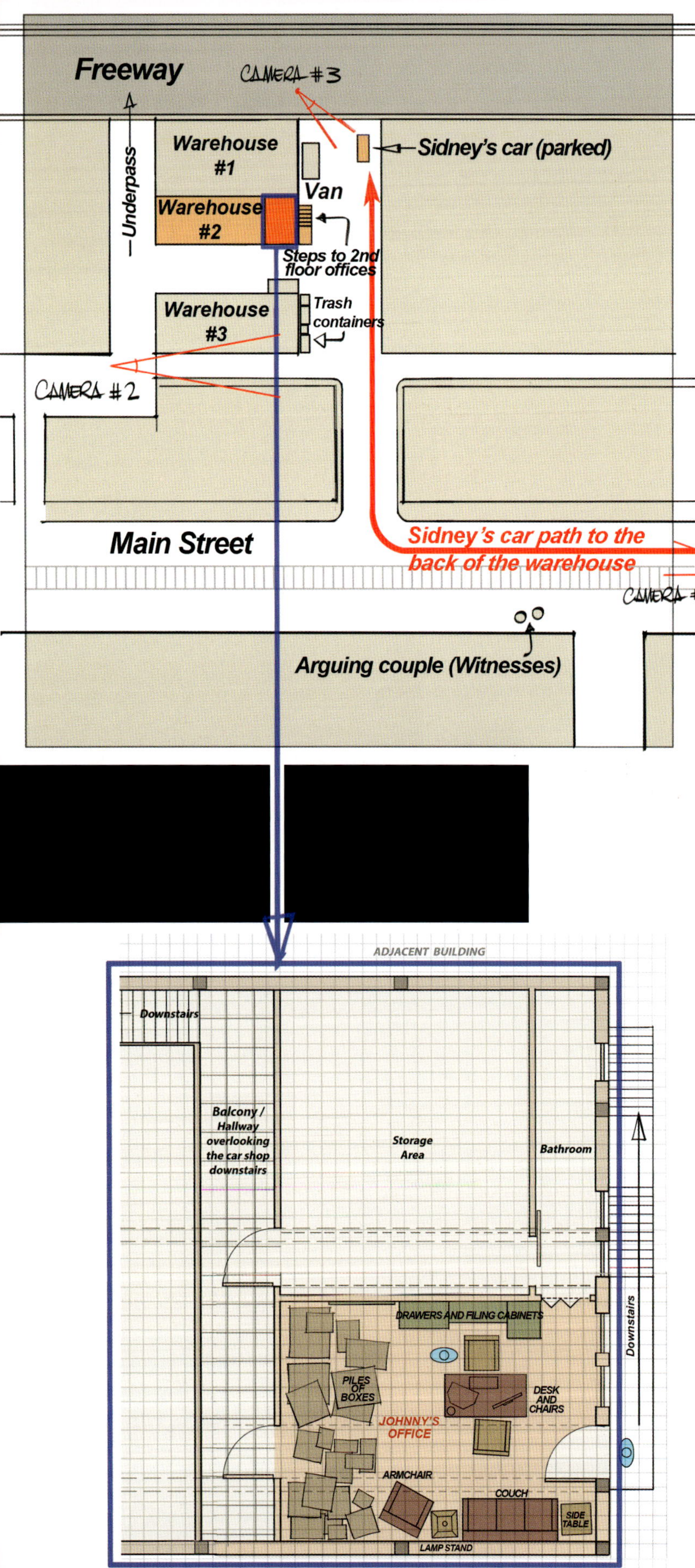

The location maps from page 012 actually refer to the very same location we are developing now, so let's consider them in more detail.

Based on this map and all of the references previously put together (see pages 034–035), we now have enough materials to start thinking about the excerpt from the script on page 034. What does the scene need, and **how can the location design help reflect that?**

As beautiful as this imaginary city may be, it is established that we have not chosen the most appealing area for this set but specifically a rather worn-out, secluded one. So, the **overall elements** this environment needs are:

A degree of isolation, a sense of the industrial outskirts away from crowds and away from witnesses (besides the arguing couple). Snowy and cold weather conditions could establish a major visual difference to Arianna's Mediterranean location.

These are the basic elements, but now, how do we stage them? **How do we build a general sense of structure that brings all of this together in a visually compelling way?**

Here is an idea: let's emphasize **a sense of progressive claustrophobia** so that there is a sense of increasing intensity to the scene. Start with the wide avenue. Looks barren. It is not quite taken care of, the buildings feel aged and used. Old, washed-out advertisements that were glued to those walls at some point in the past are still visible. There are abandoned shopping carts and train tracks that scream "rusty and industrial." The streets are nearly deserted.

And that's the widest, most open, and spacious part of the location.

Then, the **funnel effect.** The streets get narrower, the buildings smaller, and cul-de-sac alleyways end abruptly at an elevated freeway.

That is where the auto shop and Johnny's second-floor office are located. This claustrophobic feeling shows that if something happens there, it stays there. (Specifics about the actual office will be discussed later, on page 046.)

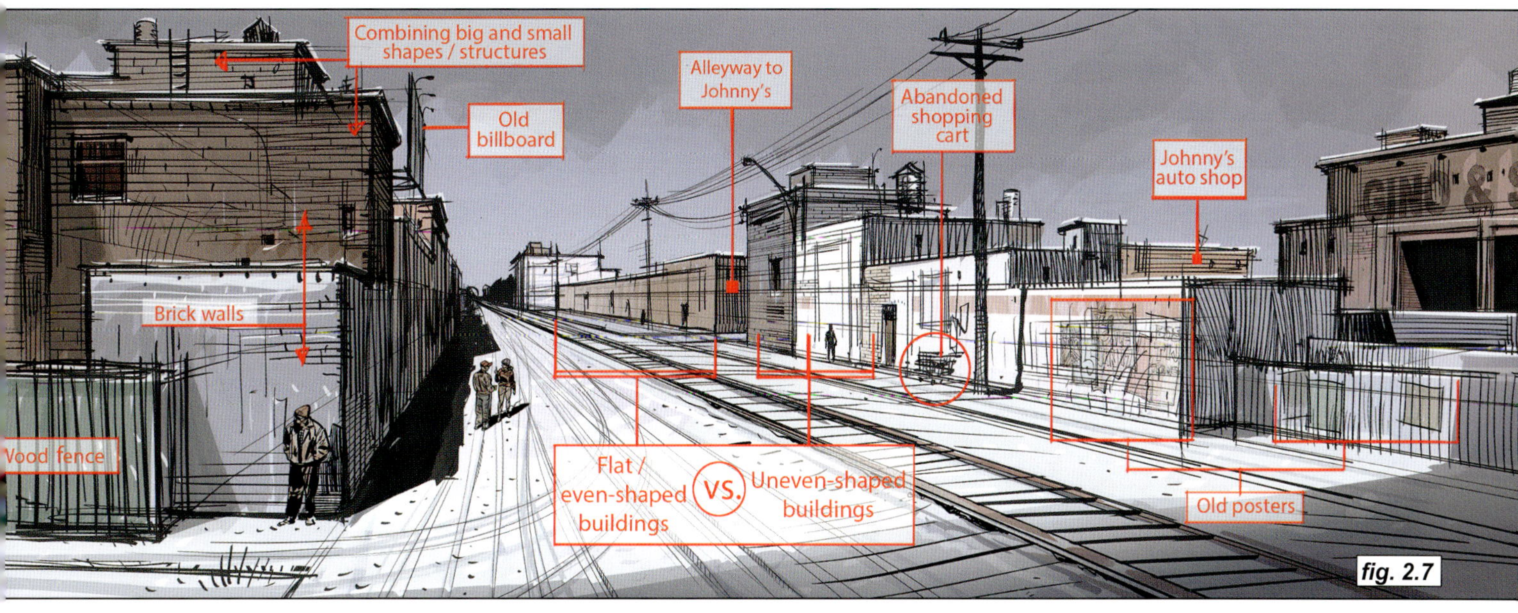

Fig. 2.7: Preliminary sketch of Main Street. Wide, cold, impersonal and industrial-looking. The little notes in red are pointing at key design elements, including Johnny's auto shop, the alley that leads to it, and some key atmospheric elements such as the abandoned shopping cart, the old posters on walls, etc.

Sketch a few different versions at first until hitting upon the overall feel and atmosphere. **After that, do the cleaner, final drawings (which we will get to soon).**

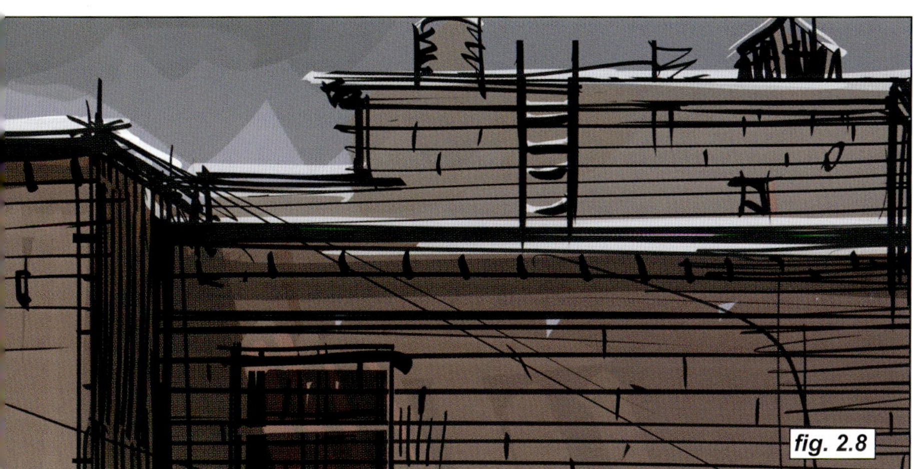

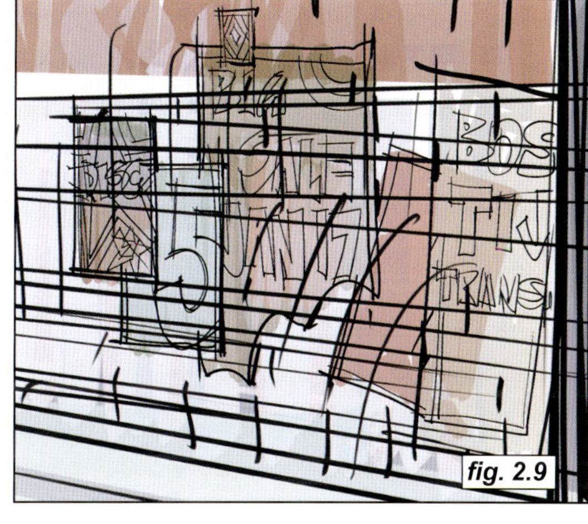

Figs. 2.8–2.10: Details like streetlights, utility poles, the abandoned shopping cart, and the old, weathered posters on the wall are to be **included in the fabric of our design work from our earliest sketches.** (The steps from sketch to final line work are on pages 040–043.)

Fig. 2.11: Always **include characters,** whether specific to the story or generic, in order to keep the overall scale correct. Also, make sure they are accurate to perspective.

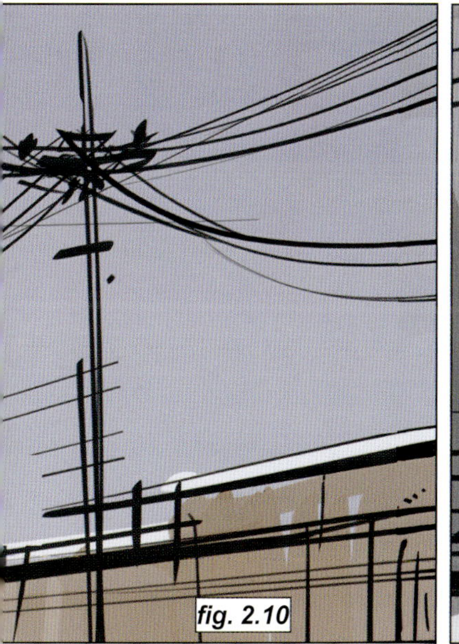

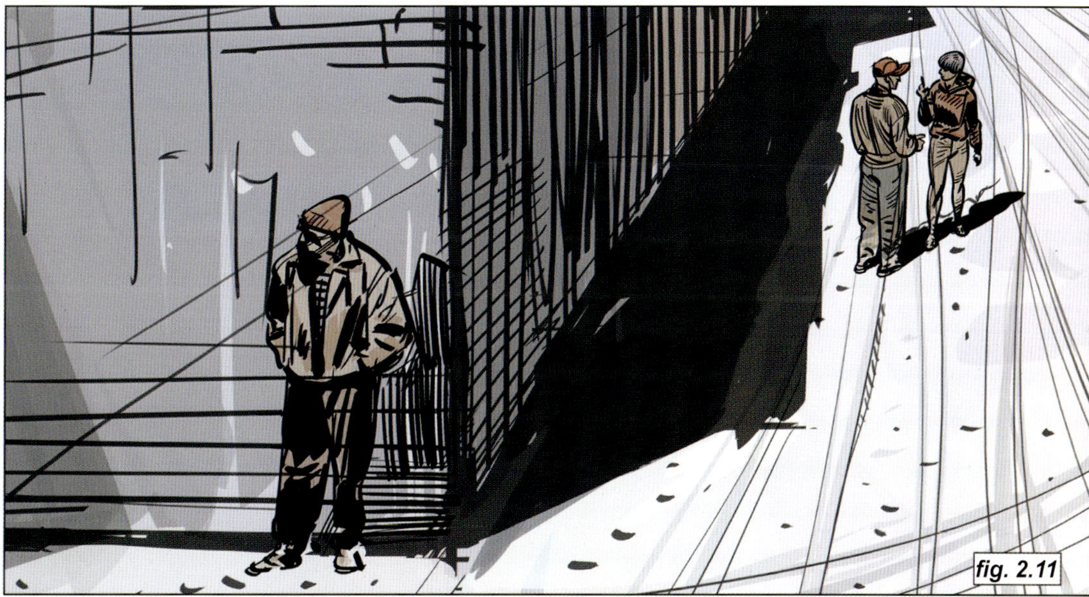

Figs. 2.12, 2.13: After this "broad strokes" approach, it is time to start down a more detailed path, studying and practicing the materials, textures, and qualities of the architectural elements at play.

Here are two examples of red-brick buildings which show how to use a more precise drawing style to explore options for the location's architecture.

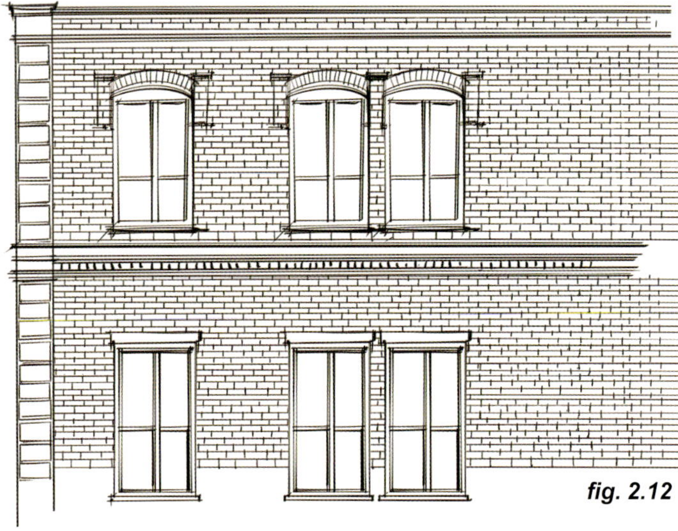

fig. 2.12

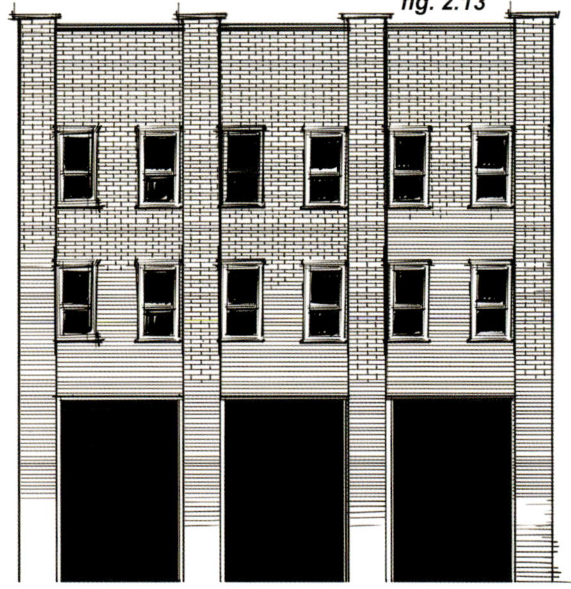

fig. 2.13

Getting familiar with these is very helpful as a first step, as we get more and more into the particulars and the personality of each building to be featured in the area.

Now for the **look of Johnny's automotive shop and the surrounding buildings** in the alley. All this previous research and practice will make it easier to better imagine design options for each building.

Here is an exploration of the thought process about the front of Johnny's auto shop building that faces the alleyway where Sidney parks her car:

Fig. 2.14: In this version the bigger entrance for the cars is on the other side, as this side shows only a regular door (yellow) and a number of trash cans to the left.

Fig. 2.15: This look is inspired by the photo reference (fig. 2.4, page 035). The problem here is that given the double flight of steps, the staircase protrudes too far for an alley that narrow.

Fig. 2.16: Looks good, but an issue is that most of the time the camera will be positioned on the left **(1)** looking right **(2),** and therefore the staircase would potentially obstruct the view of the garage's car entrance where Sidney will stop and ask for directions to the office.

Fig. 2.17: This version addresses and resolves all the issues of the previous sketches, **so let's go with it.**

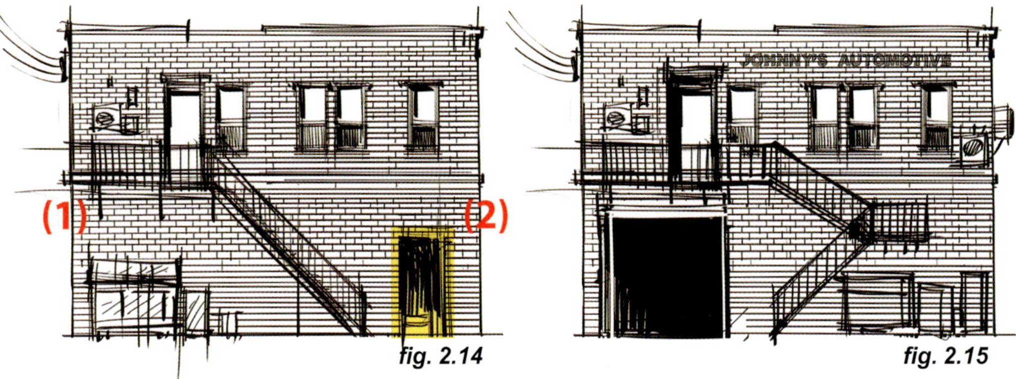

fig. 2.14   fig. 2.15

Note: In all four versions, (1) indicates the side of the building facing toward Main Street, and (2) indicates the side facing toward the end of the alleyway, cut off by the elevated freeway.

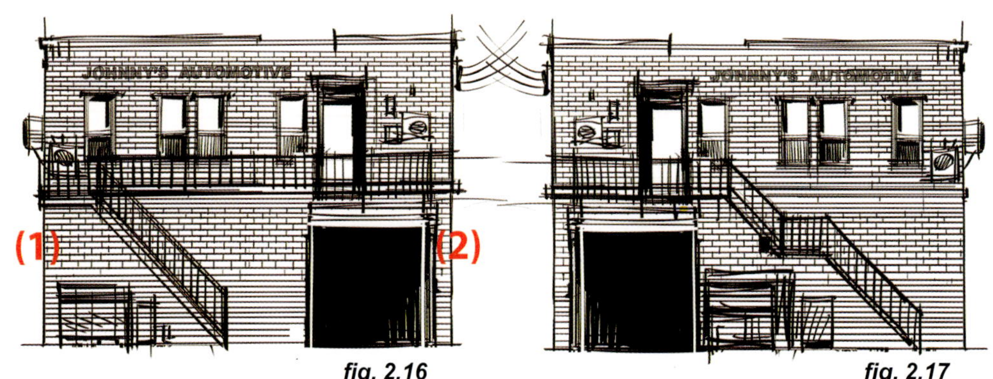

fig. 2.16   fig. 2.17

Once the auto shop has a solid start as the focal point in the sequence, it is time to move on to designing the surrounding buildings. How will they compare to Johnny's? One option is to make Johnny's look less important, more unassuming than the others, not the type of structure that would garner too much attention, while keeping in mind the overall cold and monotonous feel of the area. Yet, it should not be completely overshadowed by them either, because that kind of contrast would again put too much attention on it. All that being said, it needs to have a personality that makes it slightly more interesting than the others, which the staircase helps with.

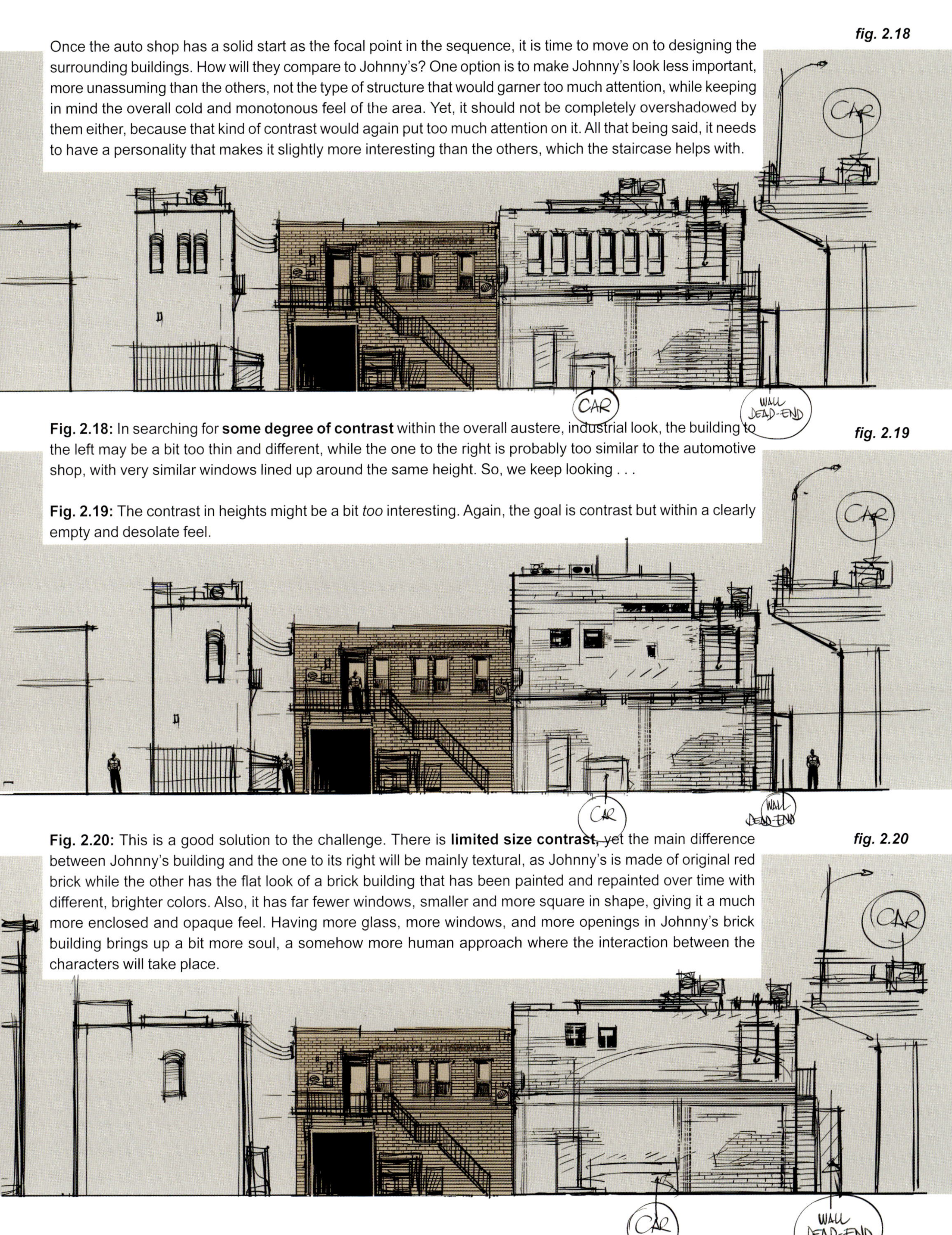

Fig. 2.18: In searching for **some degree of contrast** within the overall austere, industrial look, the building to the left may be a bit too thin and different, while the one to the right is probably too similar to the automotive shop, with very similar windows lined up around the same height. So, we keep looking . . .

Fig. 2.19: The contrast in heights might be a bit *too* interesting. Again, the goal is contrast but within a clearly empty and desolate feel.

Fig. 2.20: This is a good solution to the challenge. There is **limited size contrast**, yet the main difference between Johnny's building and the one to its right will be mainly textural, as Johnny's is made of original red brick while the other has the flat look of a brick building that has been painted and repainted over time with different, brighter colors. Also, it has far fewer windows, smaller and more square in shape, giving it a much more enclosed and opaque feel. Having more glass, more windows, and more openings in Johnny's brick building brings up a bit more soul, a somehow more human approach where the interaction between the characters will take place.

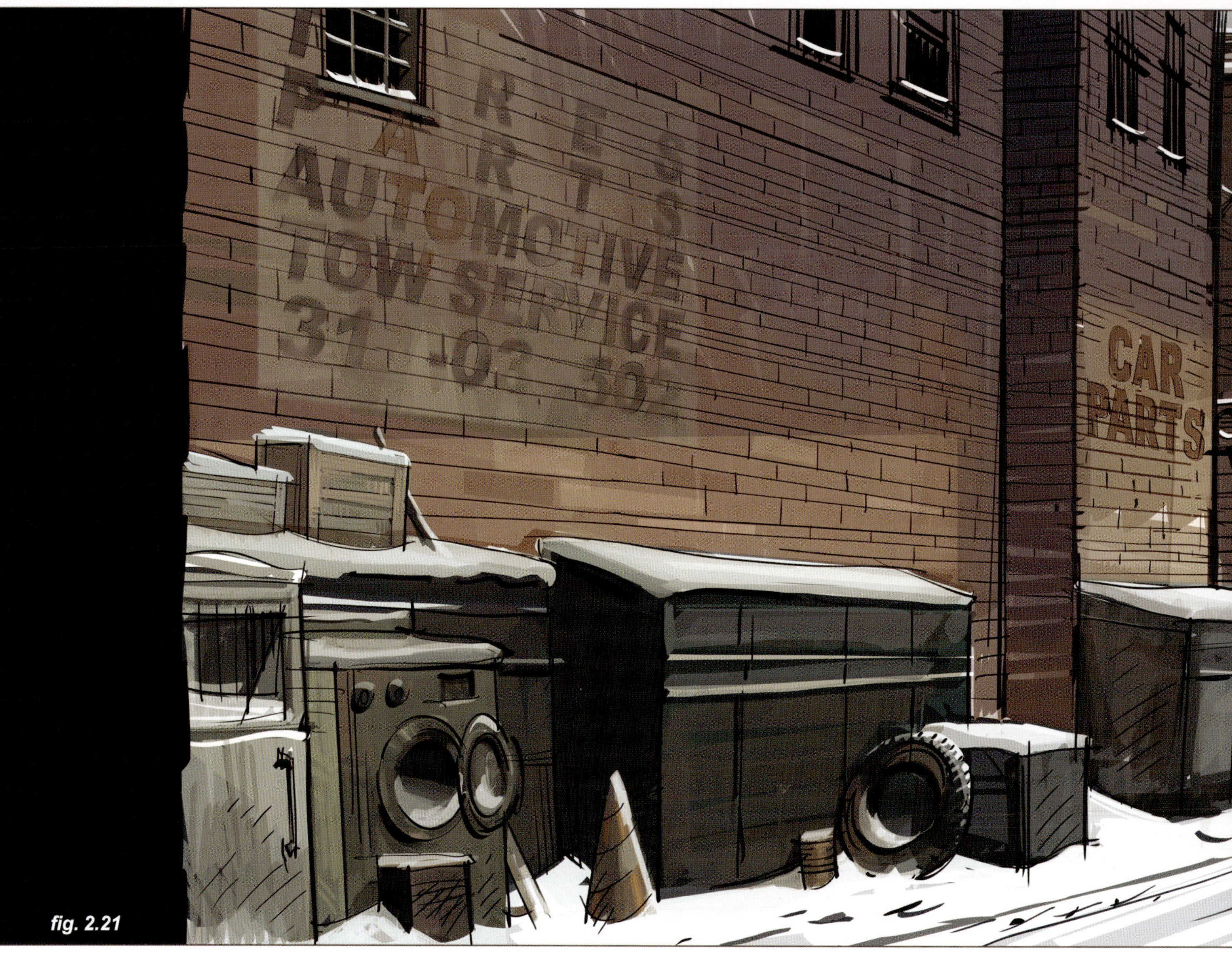

fig. 2.21

Fig. 2.21: And here is a first, rough perspective of the dead-end alleyway based on all the previous work.

To recap, we started with the design of the flat facades of the buildings (pages 038–039) and then moved onto a proper (preliminary) perspective view of the whole alley, choosing a camera position that could work for a movie, graphic novel, or storyboard. It is a good way to make sure all the previous ideas feel right as one full environment or location.

The previously mentioned "end of the funnel" sense of claustrophobia for this alley is enhanced by the piling up of waste containers, disheveled industrial rubble, tire tracks in the snow, and the tall wall at the end, doubled down by the view of the elevated concrete freeway towering above it and ultimately terminating this "no way out" cul-de-sac. All of these certainly seal the deal.

This place has become its own geographical capsule, and every action that takes place here will feel remote and disconnected from the rest of the world.

Another tool for our presentation—the quick wash of color—helps establish the tone and nails that sense of a certain dreariness that identifies this location with a desaturated look.

This environment is one more example of the fact that **a location should be designed with the purpose of visually supporting the story** and narrate it in a way that, if dialogue were missing, it would still communicate the moment, tone, and meaning of what is happening. Even in our everyday interactions and conversations with people, studies show that only a relatively small percentage of the information we receive out of the exchange comes from the verbal aspect of it, from what someone literally tells us. Everything else is about body language, tone of voice, and context. The same exists with our line of work. Environmental designs succeed when they are created **with a purpose.** In essence, first **understand what the story is about,** moment to moment, and then decide **what must be done to express this visually** through shapes, atmosphere, and designs.

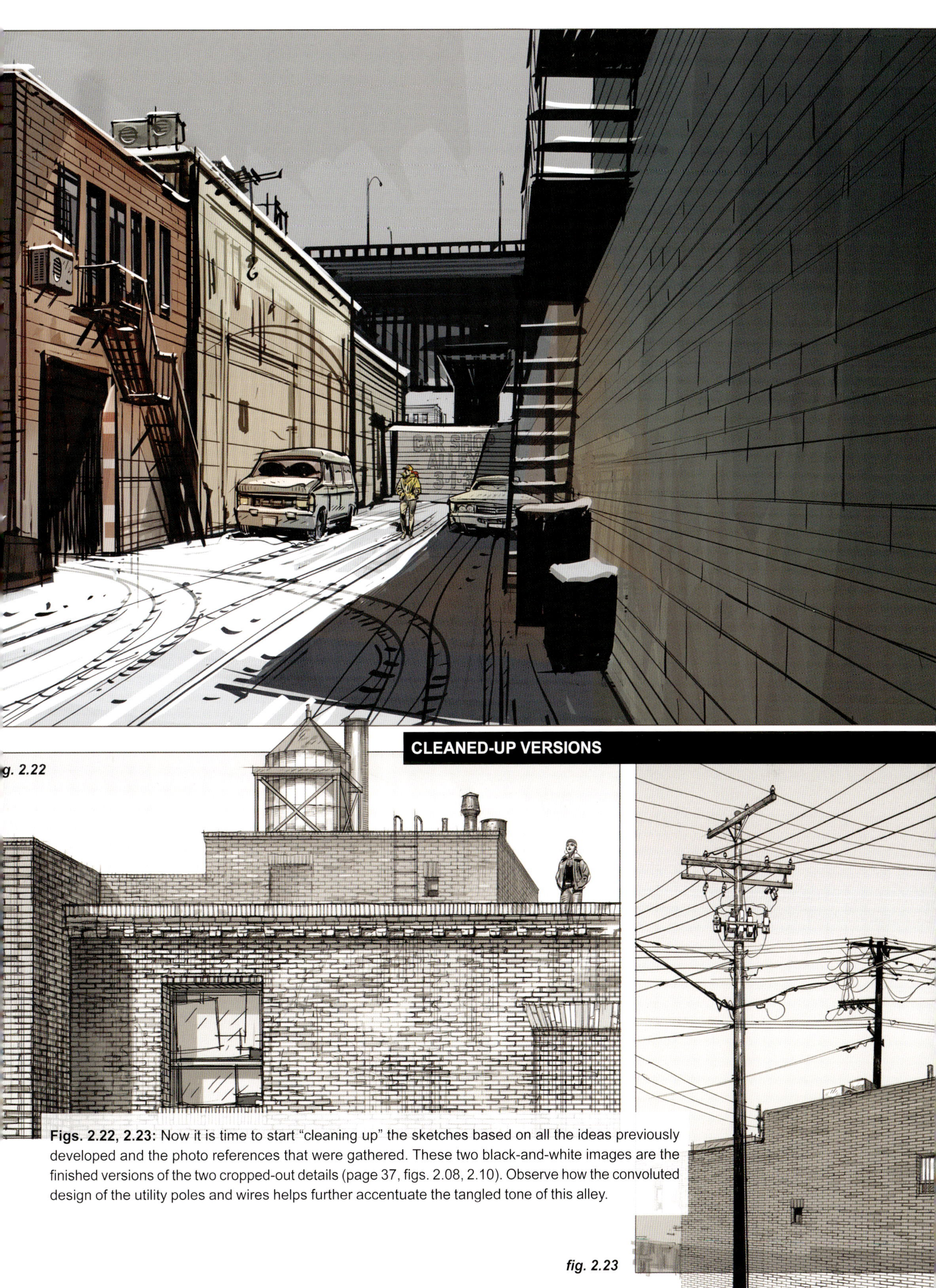

Figs. 2.22, 2.23: Now it is time to start "cleaning up" the sketches based on all the ideas previously developed and the photo references that were gathered. These two black-and-white images are the finished versions of the two cropped-out details (page 37, figs. 2.08, 2.10). Observe how the convoluted design of the utility poles and wires helps further accentuate the tangled tone of this alley.

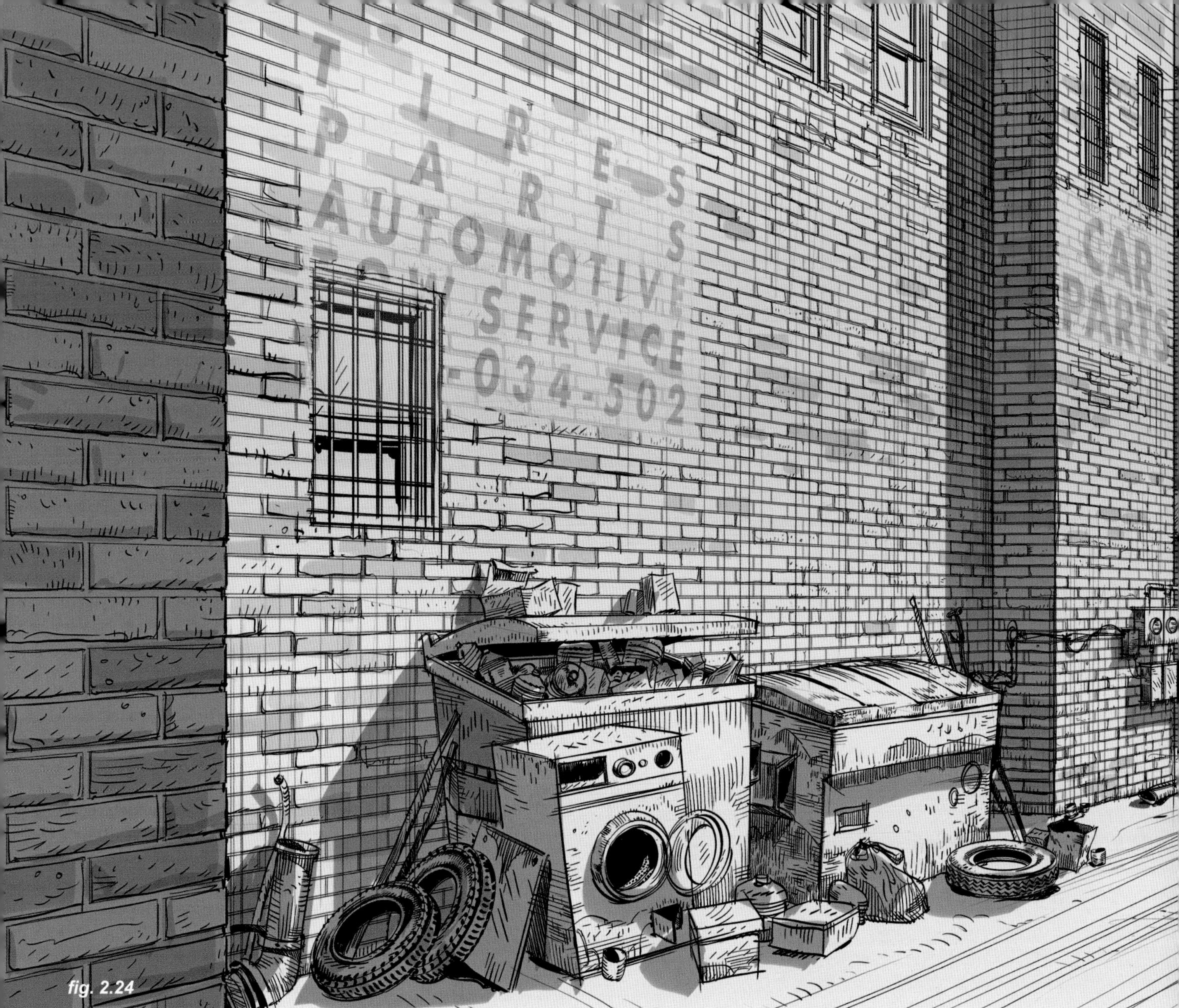

fig. 2.24

Fig. 2.24: This cleanup pass shows a more precisely detailed view.

This is a more accurate use of the photo references beyond the first sense of shape and proportions. It is important at this point to indicate a level of detail and texture in the components of the environment. How rundown or pristine do the items look? Are the surfaces rough or more polished, regular or irregular? Some general characters were added for a better sense of scale and proportion, and it is crucial that the perspective feels right so that there are no issues regarding the image's credibility.

Even though this environment will eventually be depicted under a thick layer of snow, for now the snow has been removed in order to reveal details that otherwise would remain concealed. Remember, these types of drawings need to be inspirational but also informational, so that the next artist who receives them can make proper sense of them for the purposes of painting them or creating 3D models based on them. For that it is also very helpful to provide different views and angles of the same area through additional drawings and photo references.

Another important thing to pay attention to is that the size and scale of the bricks on the various walls of all the buildings make sense when compared to each other.

A good knowledge of perspective is always essential. Here a simple trick was used to make the perspective of these brick walls realistic and accurate in a short amount of time.

Fig. 2.25: First, draw the flat wall.

Fig. 2.26: Then, having accurately blocked the shape and perspective of the buildings (red outline), all it takes is to adapt the flat drawing of the brick wall to the existing area in perspective so that it fits perfectly.

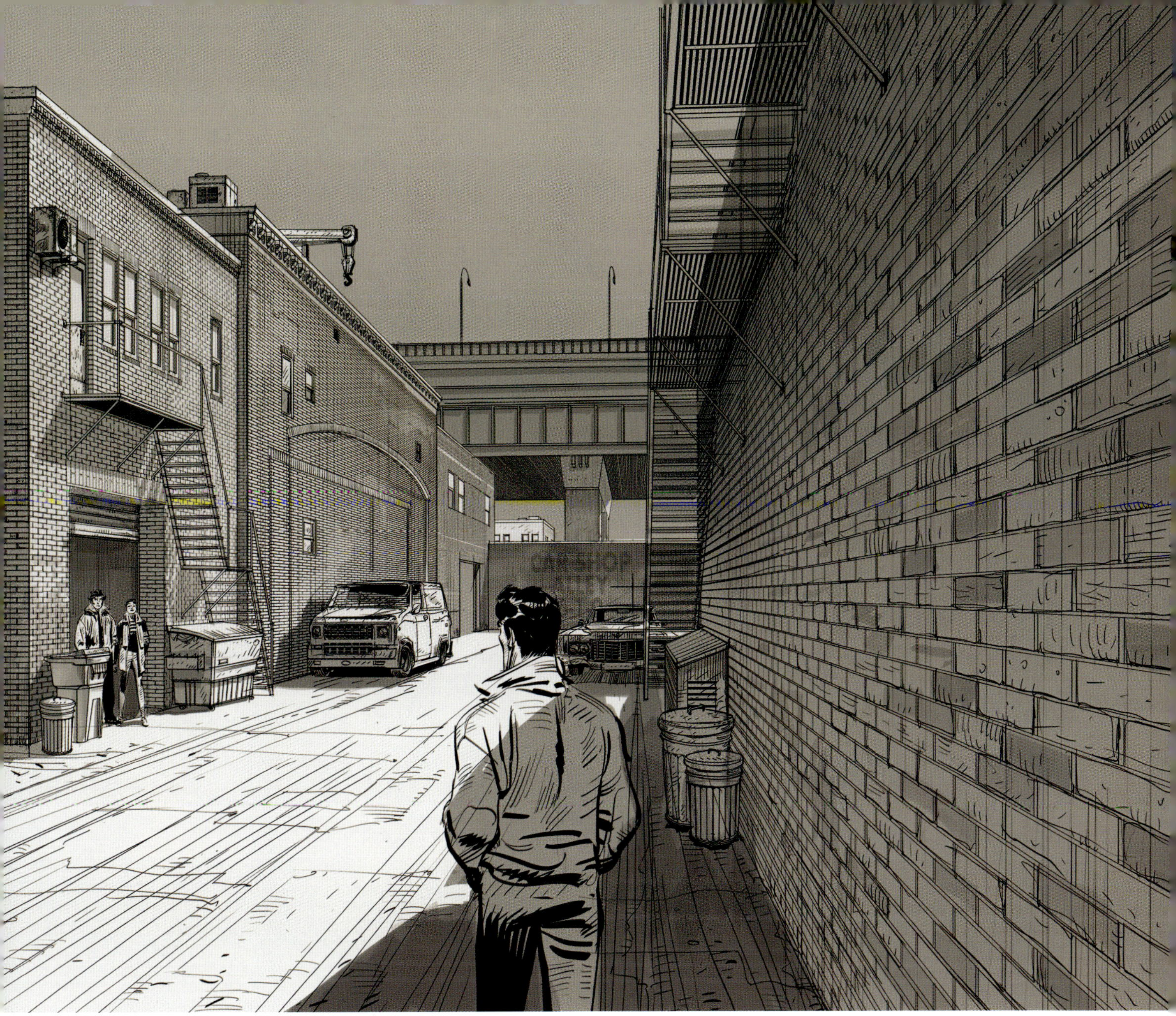

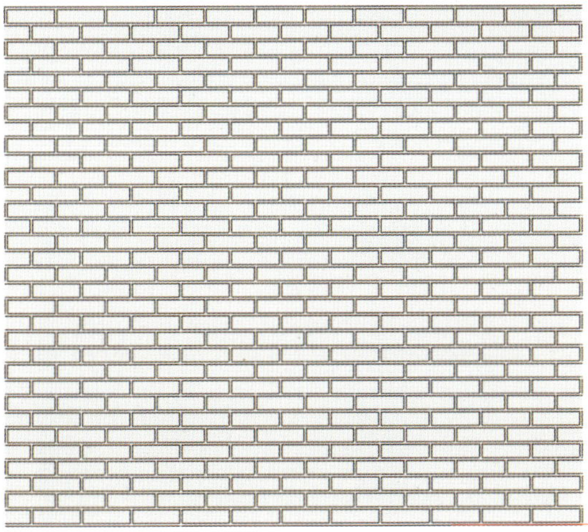

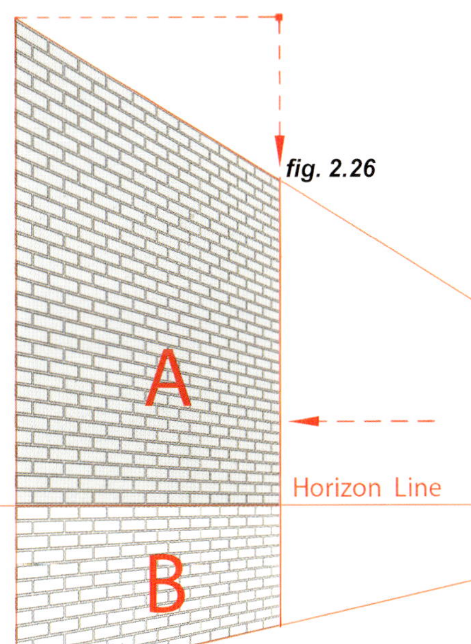

fig. 2.25

To adjust the flat view into perspective inside the area, use two Photoshop tools from the Edit menu: Free Transform and then Transform/Skew.

First place the wall **(A)** above the horizon line. The flat wall was squeezed sideways and the top-right corner brought down to adjust it to the red outline, making sure the bricks do not look distorted, too wide or too narrow, within the perspective. Once the proportion of the foreshortened bricks looks good, select and erase any remainder of the wall outside the red lines, if needed.

After that, flip the bricks vertically **(B)** so that the perspective is consistent **above and below the horizon.**

Sidney enters the automotive shop, looking for Johnny in order to discuss her business with him.

We decided earlier that the whole design philosophy would be based on playing up the visual contrast between this location and the automotive shop that Arianna (Johnny's former business partner) has set up somewhere in the sunny Mediterranean, after they parted ways.

We also decided as part of this visual language to make everything in Johnny's location feel consistently colder, dimmer, with a more grave or serious tone to it, and to have the interior of the shop favor more straight, angular lines, in contrast with the more organic feel of curved lines in the architecture of Arianna's Mediterranean location.

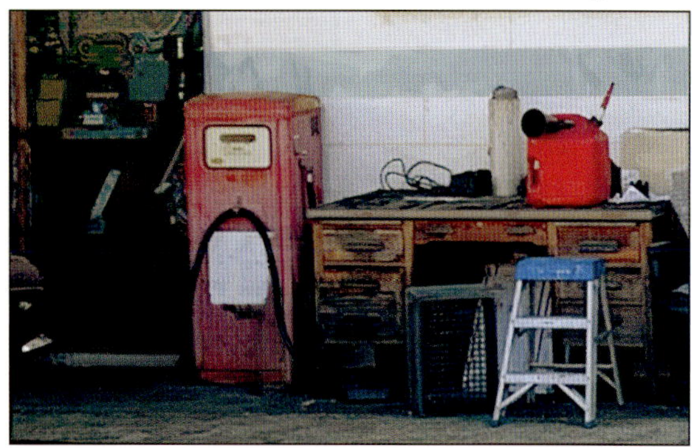

fig. 2.27

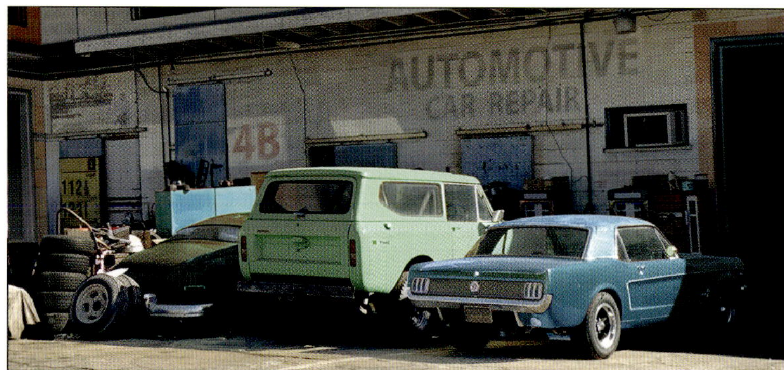

fig. 2.28

fig. 2.29

Figs. 2.27, 2.28: As usual, a process of gathering references takes place before proceeding with the early designs and sketches. These images provide not only specific ideas and descriptions of the items that fill the location but also inspire the general type of atmosphere, tone, and lighting.

Figs. 2.29, 2.31: These personal photo-based sketches of auto shops are a **first exploration of these ideas.** Here is a chance to study the sense of space, details, and compositional options. The graphic language of these reflect the **angular shapes** we were just talking about. Also reflected is an overall level of **organization and order,** obviously within the expected natural dynamics of a place like this.

Fig. 2.30: Additional tools reference and details.

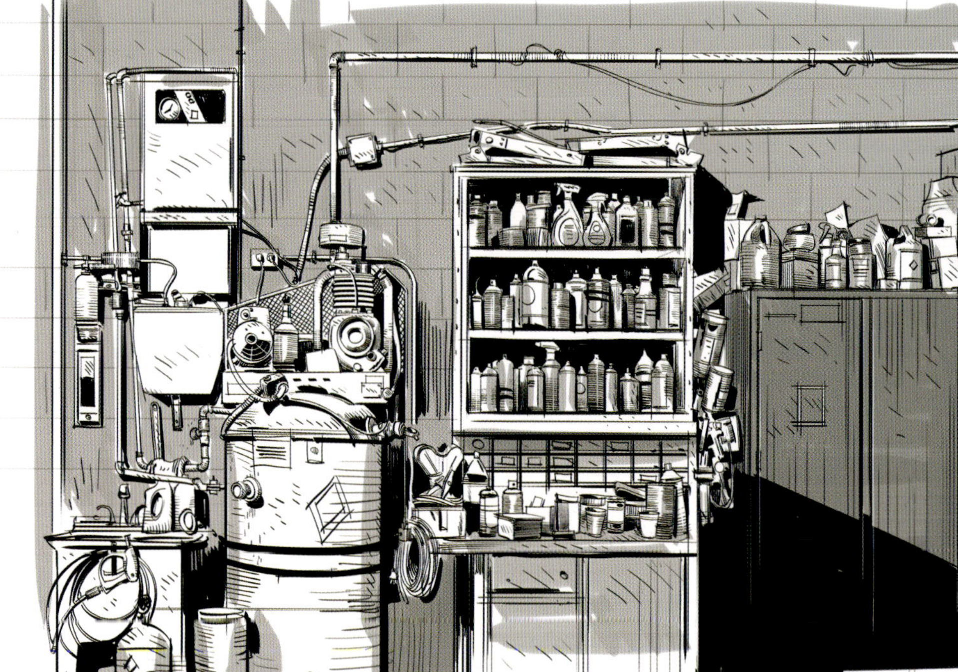

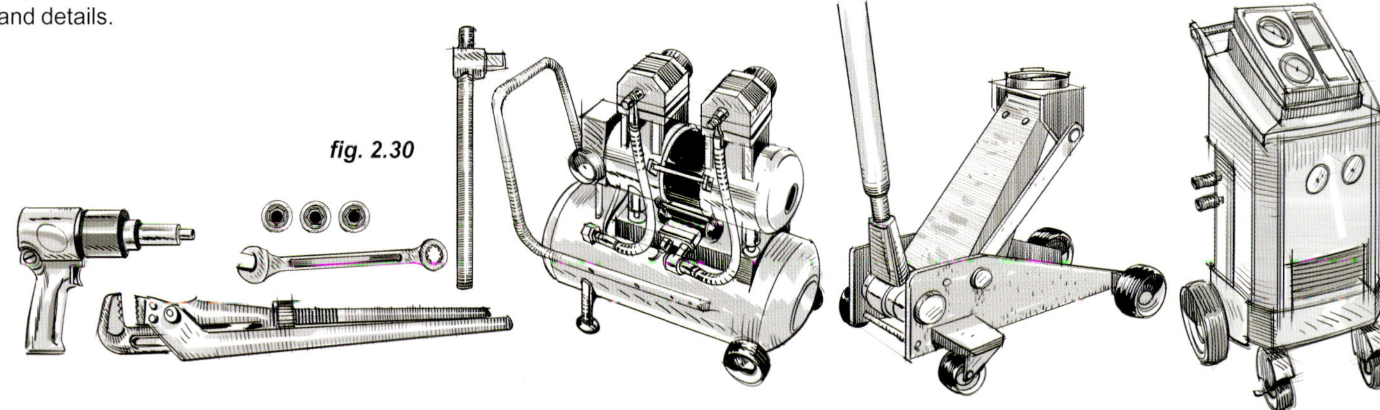

fig. 2.30

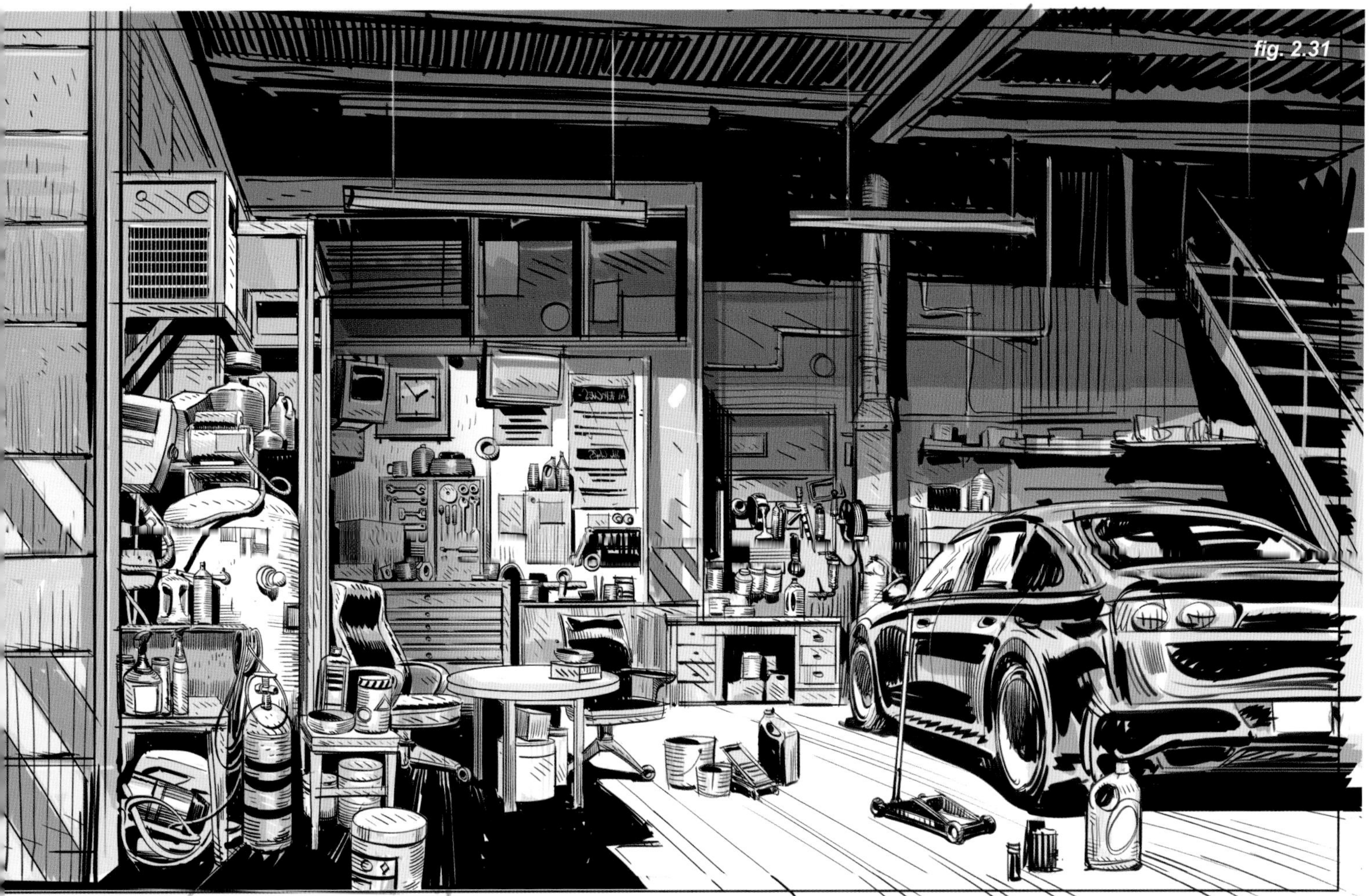

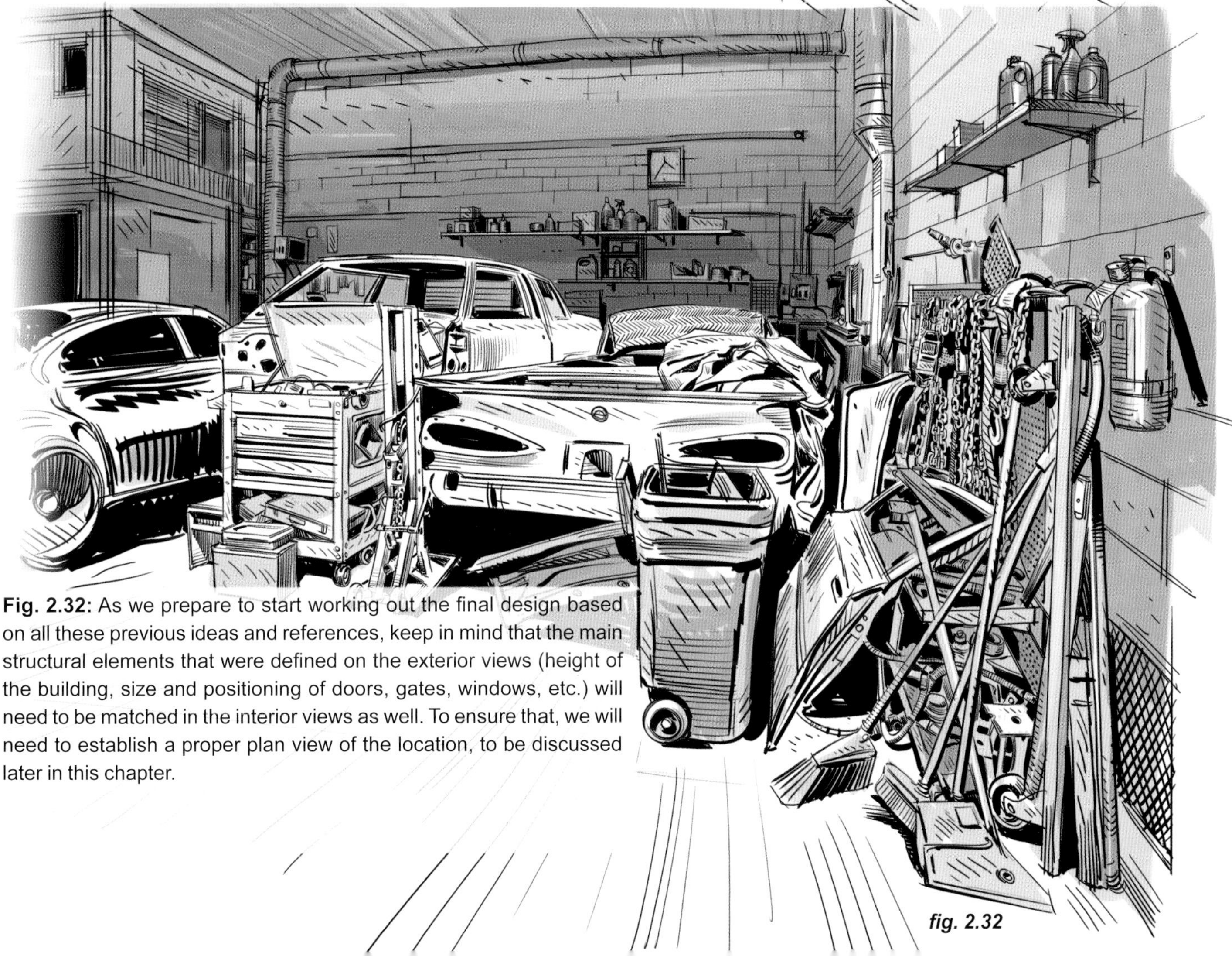

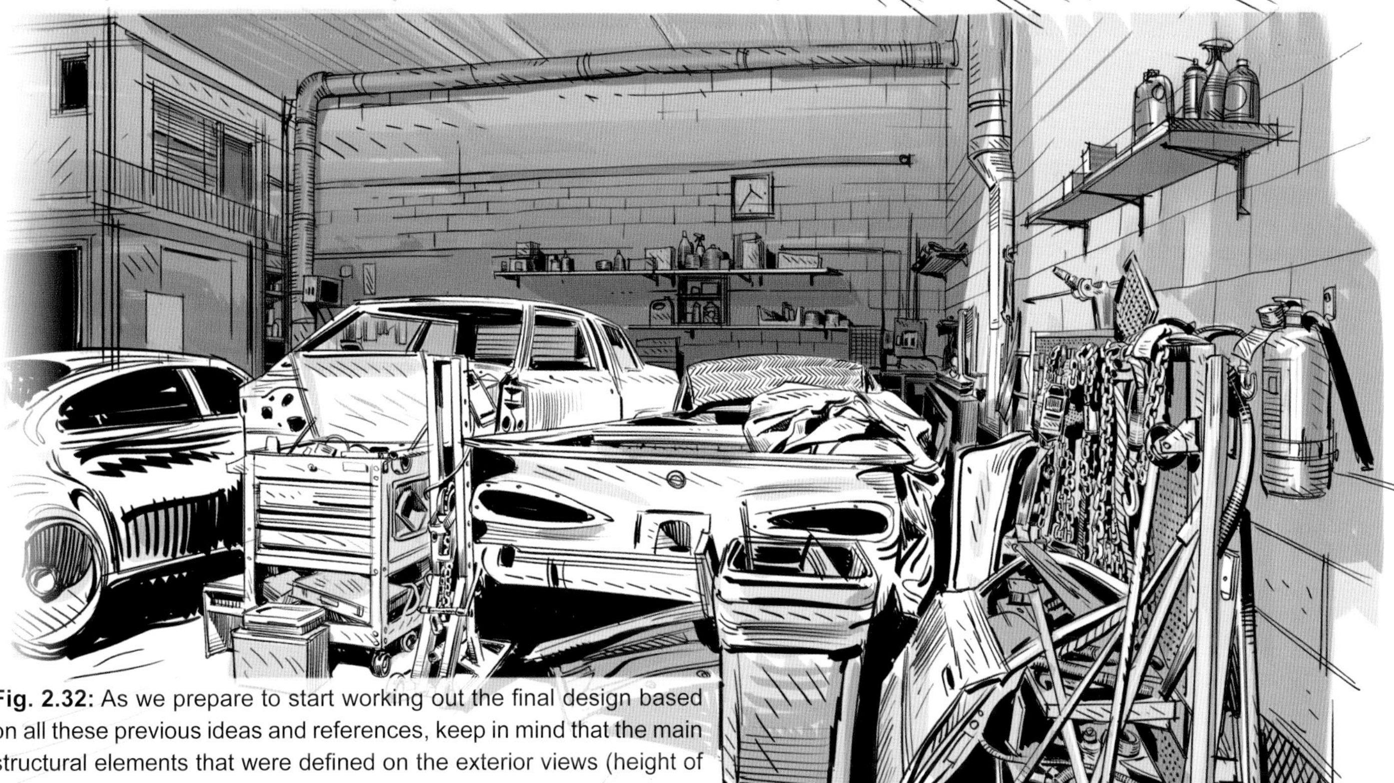

Fig. 2.32: As we prepare to start working out the final design based on all these previous ideas and references, keep in mind that the main structural elements that were defined on the exterior views (height of the building, size and positioning of doors, gates, windows, etc.) will need to be matched in the interior views as well. To ensure that, we will need to establish a proper plan view of the location, to be discussed later in this chapter.

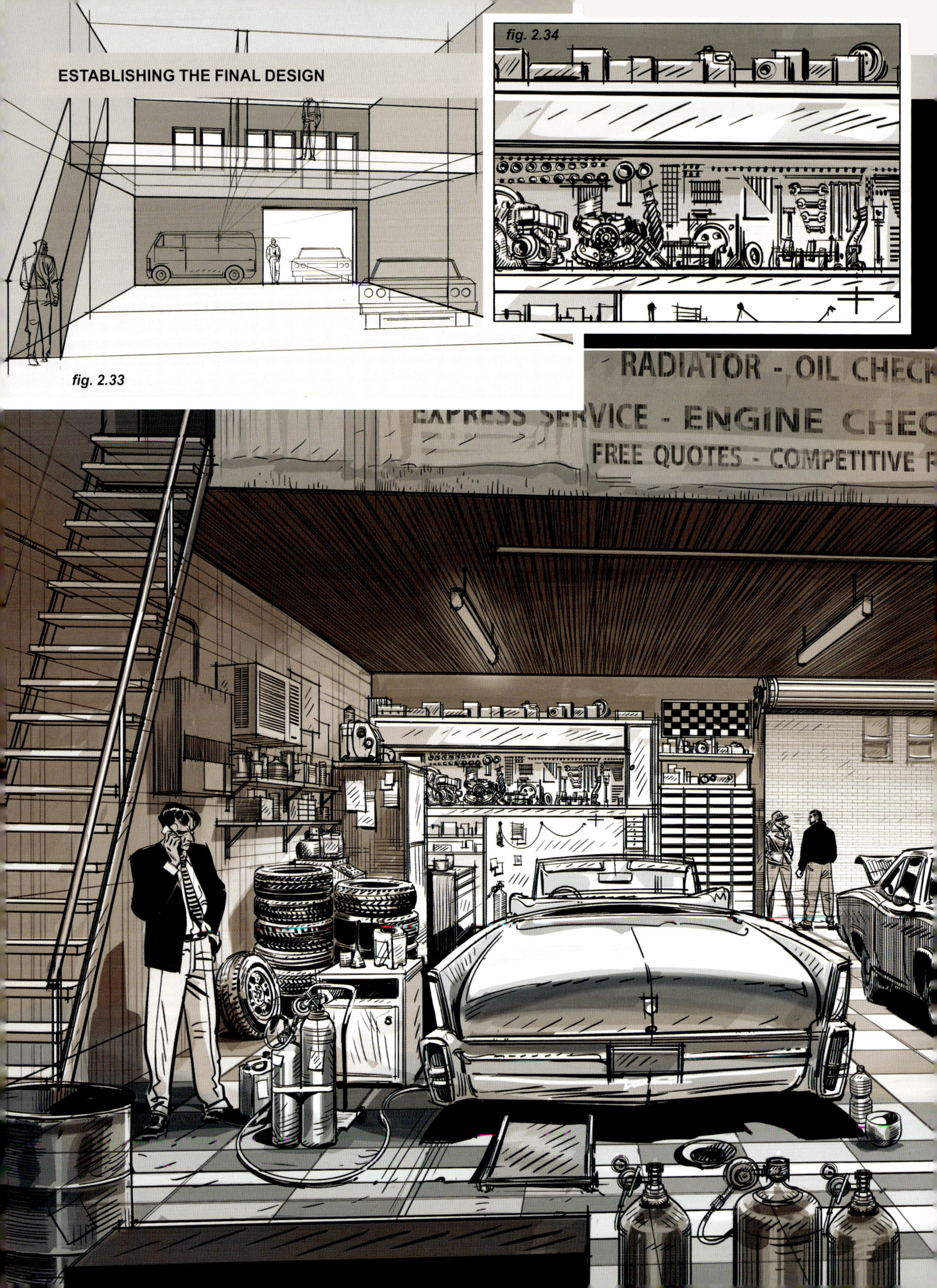

ESTABLISHING THE FINAL DESIGN
fig. 2.33
fig. 2.34
RADIATOR - OIL CHECK
EXPRESS SERVICE - ENGINE CHEC
FREE QUOTES - COMPETITIVE P

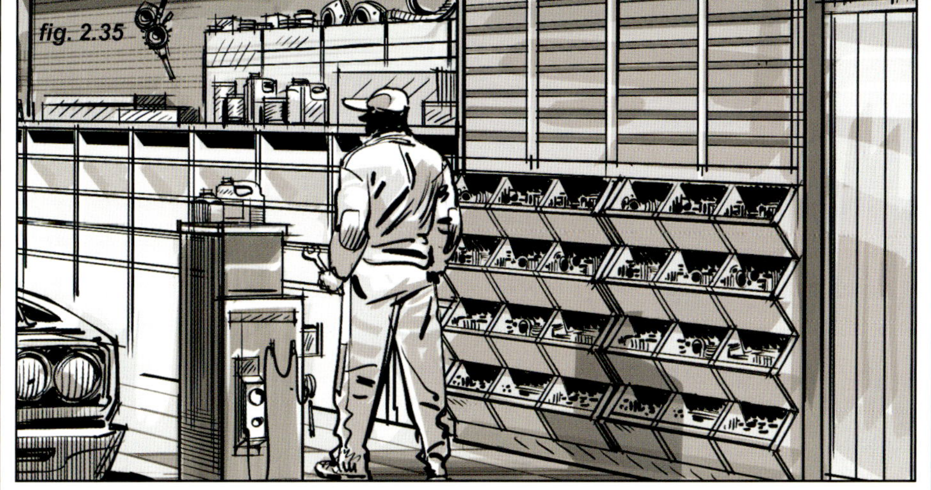

fig. 2.35

fig. 2.37

Fig. 2.33: Overall **perspective sketch.**

It is essential at some point to create all the structural work for the building (top views, front views, perspective drawings, etc.) and have them available to be referred to at any given time. It is the only way to ensure that all the parts of the structure match and correlate with each other, both within the location as well as between its interior and exterior.

Depending on the case, the exterior may need to be designed first if that is the most important location, and then the interior is made to match it, or vice versa if the interior is the one that dictates the action.

In either case, these locations might need to be built physically as live-action sets, or in 3D for animation, and will need to make complete sense.

Fig. 2.36: As usual there are some exceptions to this rule. For example, the sketch below shows a building's exterior in which there is a big step down from the upper structure to the lower one. That would imply that once the camera is inside that space, there would be a staircase of about 40 steps to descend from one level to the next. Although this large drop looks great and dramatic from the outside, on the inside it would become excessive and impractical. So, it is okay to keep the "40 steps look" for the exterior, but reduce it to about 20 steps when building the interior, as long as the discrepancy is credible and not too obvious.

Figs. 2.34, 2.35: These particular details are conceived to make this garage feel linear and angular overall, in contrast to Arianna's auto shop.

Fig. 2.37: Finished design.

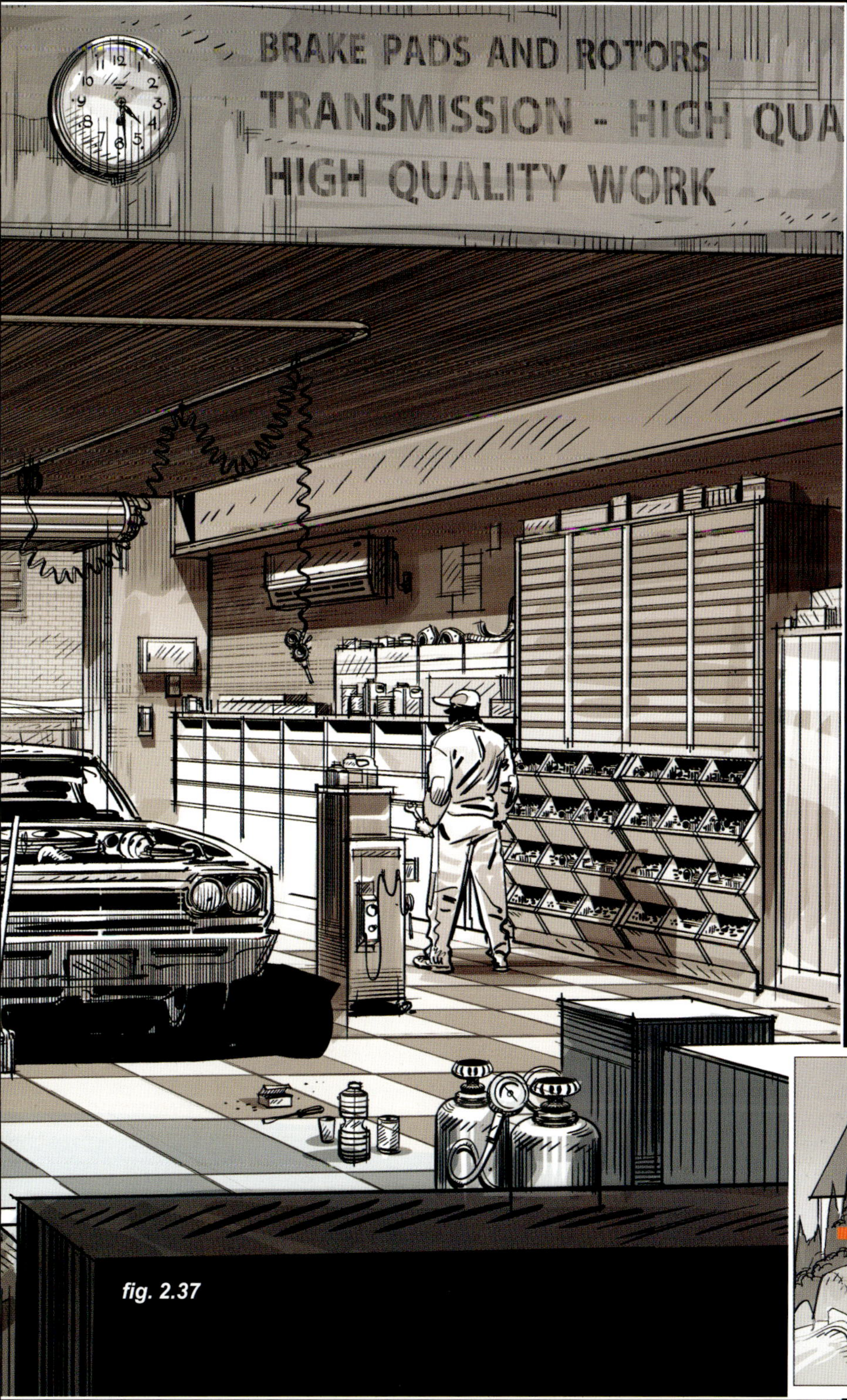

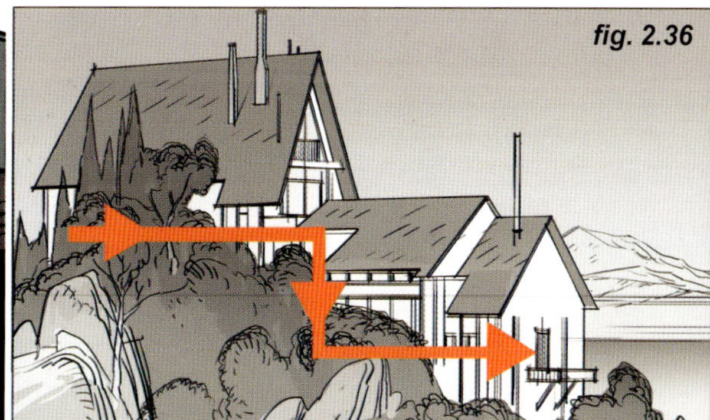

fig. 2.36

Sidney was told to take the exterior emergency staircase to the second floor to meet Johnny in his **office,** so this is the next location assignment.

In most cases, this will remain **consistent** with the previously established idea of the overall **"angular shapes"** design for this general location (as discussed in pages 019–021). Within these parameters, this area can include **Johnny's workspace and a bit of a storage,** with his desk, filing cabinets, chairs, boxes full of spare parts, and an old A/C unit displaying a certain level of "organized chaos."

Our imaginary script points out that the red-brick buildings in this area have easily been there for about a century and, as focused as Johnny is on running his business, it is fair to say he doesn't upgrade his surroundings much. Therefore, most of the lighting fixtures, filing cabinets, and furnishings will have been there for many decades, most likely passed down from previous owners, so it would make sense that the general vibe of his office is a bit **outdated and retro.**

Fig. 2.38: As usual, the search for visual reference information comes early in the creation of the set. Then it is analyzed to create a proper line and shape language. Remember the discussion in chapter 1, page 025, "Identifying Shapes." What are the lines and the volumes of the elements in the location that will give them the appropriate visual flavor?

It is essentially the **calligraphy of the environment,** and as such we will need to understand what makes them look the way they do.

Figs. 2.39, 2.40: These rough sketches show two steps of the process by temporarily positioning the main elements and giving an initial idea of how everything can fit in the space, servicing the story action and the chosen visual style.

Usually the script will mention a **description** of the office, especially if any items play a relevant role within the story or if the characters interact with them specifically. For example, "He points at the calendar on the wall," "Sidney sits on the couch next to the door as she starts talking," "Johnny left his jacket hanging on the coat rack," etc.

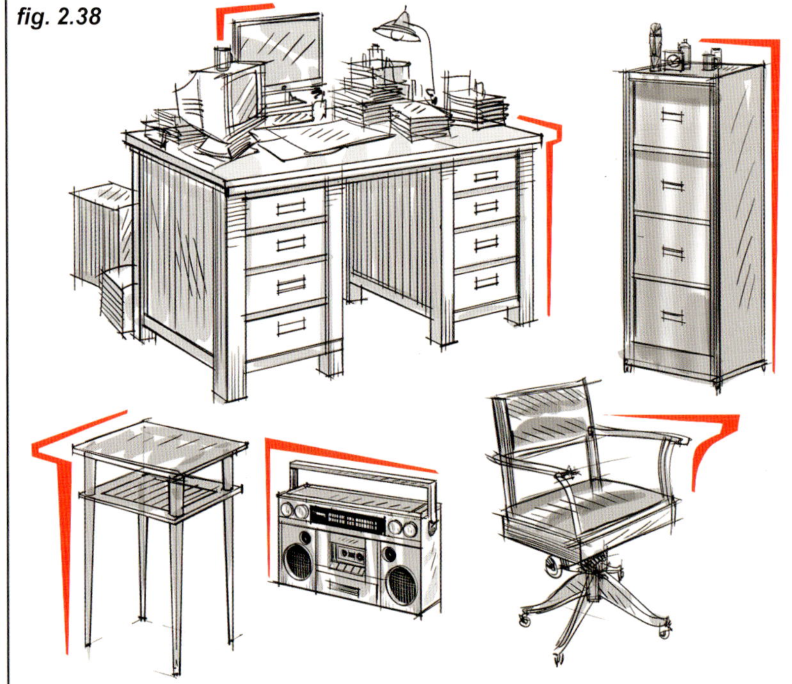

fig. 2.38

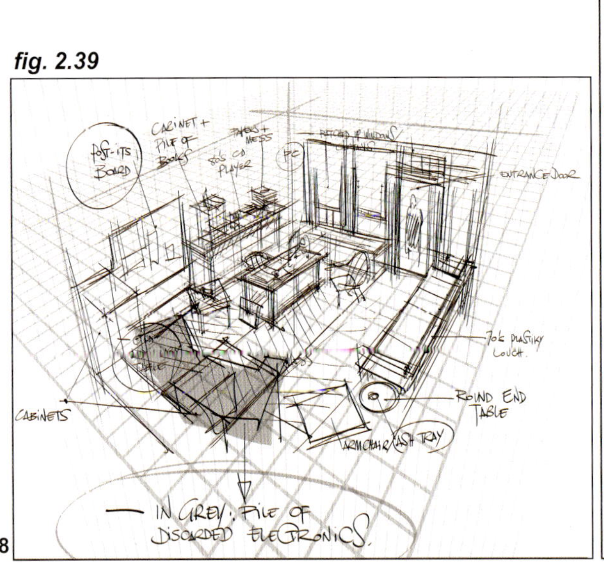

fig. 2.39

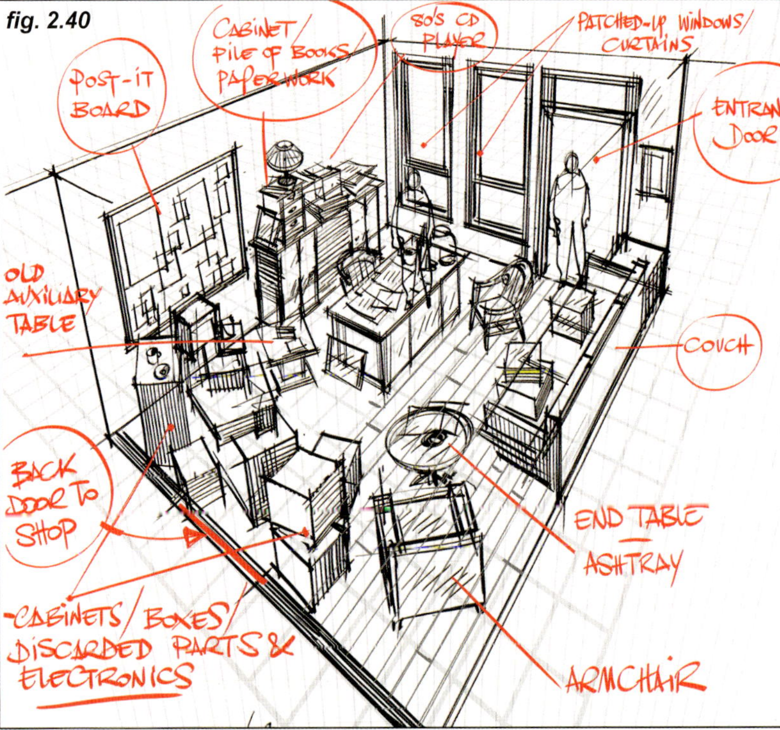

fig. 2.40

To further investigate how to group all these elements in a compelling way, the best approach is often to alternate between **line sketches** and a **grayscale lighting tonal.**

Lighting tonals unify all the elements and props within a location—treating them not as individual, scattered parts that happen to occupy the same area but bundling items together as graphic shapes of light and dark that make for nice compositions, leading the eye around in an orderly manner, using lighting to create spotlights and shadows and integrating smaller shapes into larger, more graphic shapes. (See Chapter 2 of my first book, *Framed Ink.*)

So with all these in mind, let's read a more detailed description of Johnny's office from our imaginary script:

". . . a somewhat dark space with interesting light coming through the windows that overlook the back alley (the one where Sidney parked her car). As mentioned, the office is outdated, feels a bit 'greasy,' has a desk with some computer monitors that clearly need to be disposed of and updated, piles of pending paperwork, and 'Grandma's desk lamp.' Johnny's chair is there, as well as another one for a guest, a dusty leather couch with a small end table next to it right behind the door, some lamp stands, and a boom box that belongs back in the late '80s. Filing cabinets here and there and a pile of cardboard boxes containing all sorts of merchandise and auto parts block the entire back wall of the office, including the door that leads to the shop downstairs."

Fig. 2.41: In this tonal image the desk is hit by light while the pile of boxes behind it becomes one major shape integrated with the other elements in the atmospheric background. Using light, **these disparate items and shapes combine as masses that work well together, creating interesting overall silhouettes.** (See the chapter on rendering grayscale artwork in the book, *Framed Drawing Techniques.*)

Once the grayscale works well, a line drawing can be reverse-engineered by tracing the outlines of everything in the tonal.

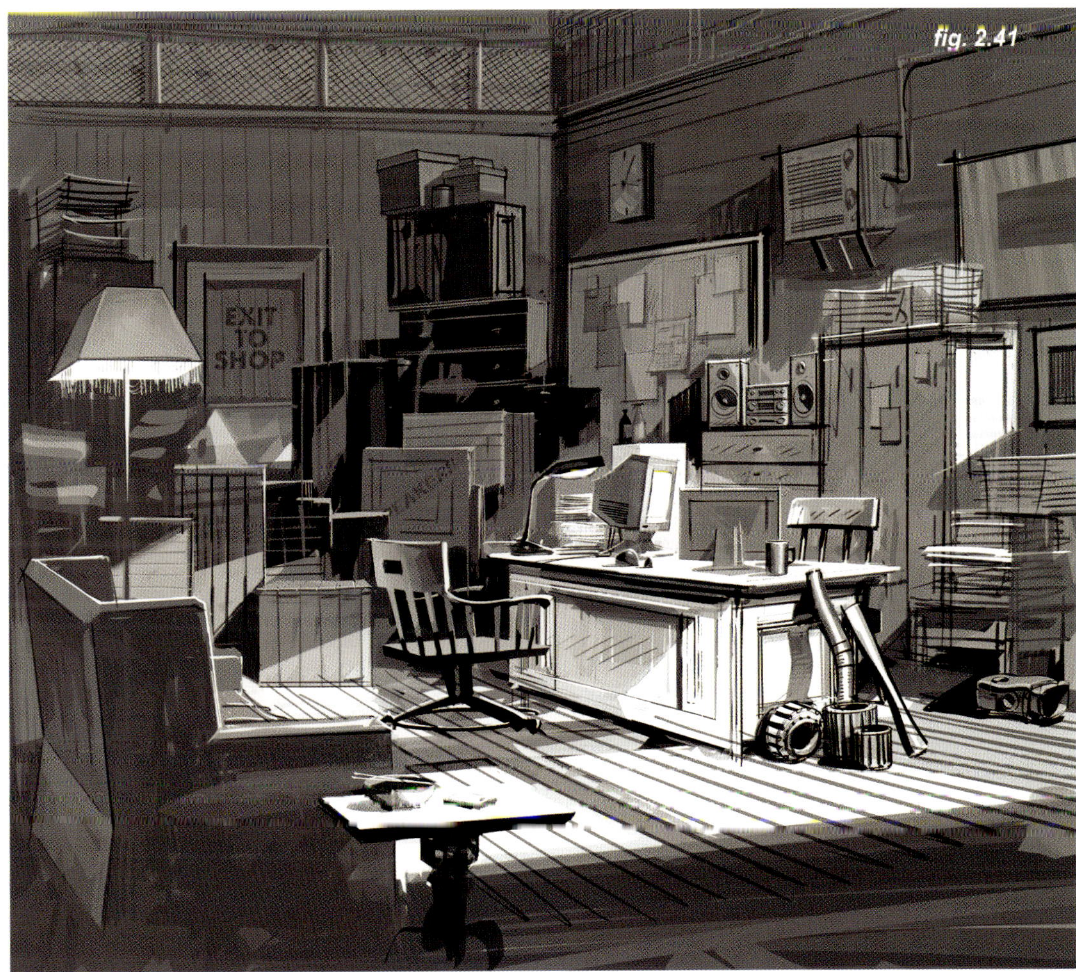

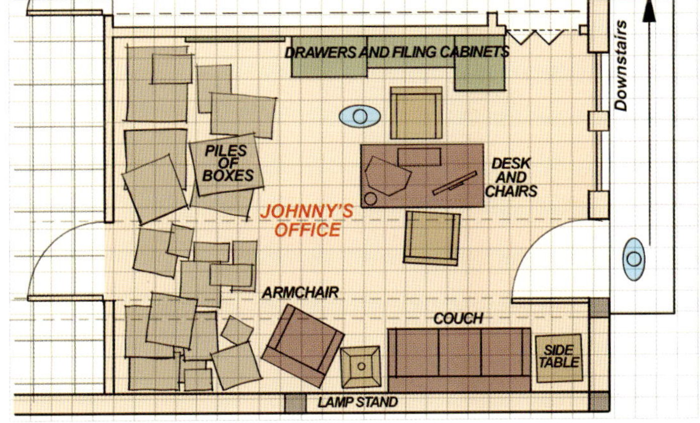

fig. 2.42

Fig. 2.42: With everything in place, it is time to create a final map of the location. This map includes a grid where each square represents 10 square inches and the blue ovals represent characters.

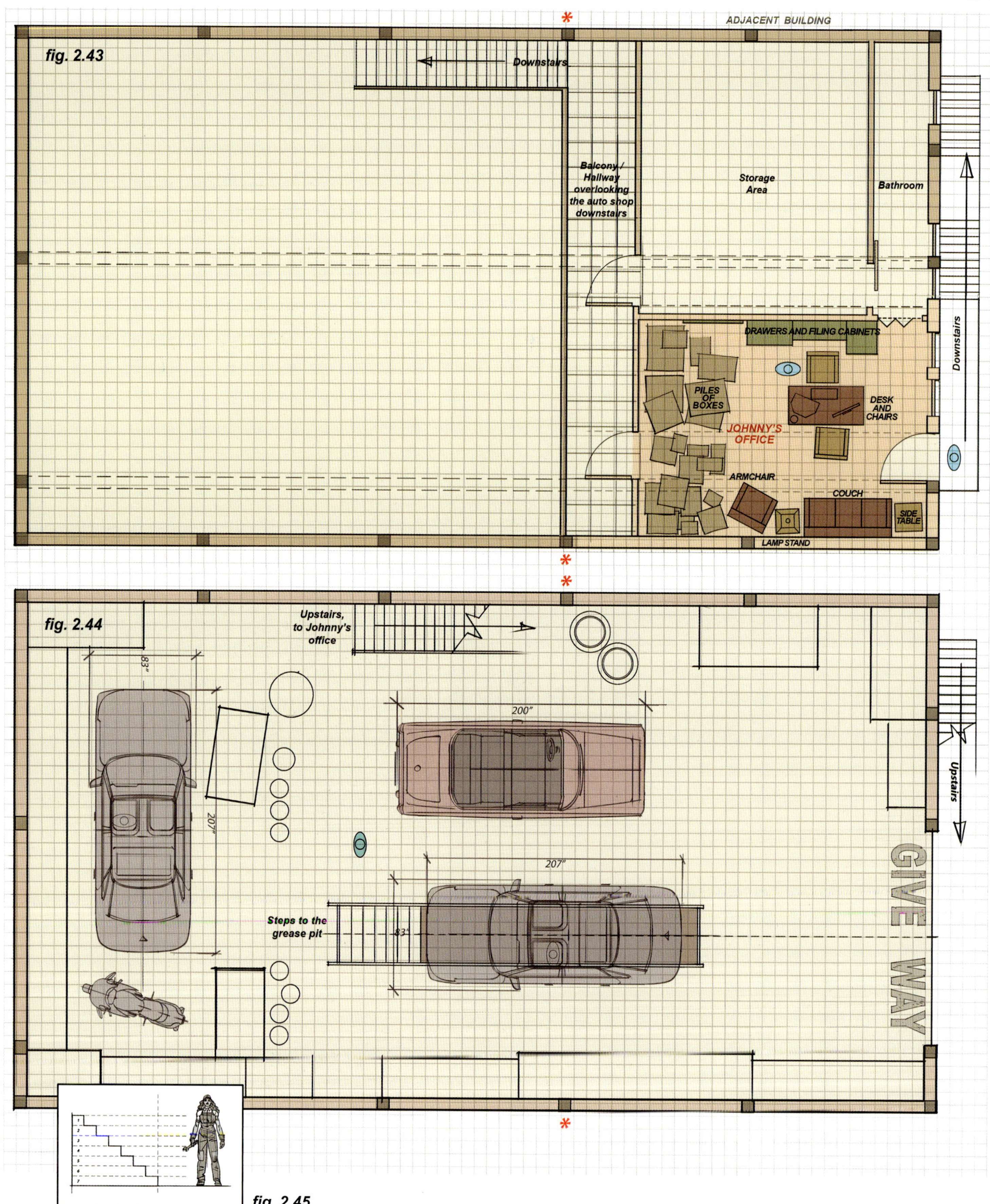

fig. 2.43
ADJACENT BUILDING
Downstairs
Balcony / Hallway overlooking the auto shop downstairs
Storage Area
Bathroom
Downstairs
DRAWERS AND FILING CABINETS
DESK AND CHAIRS
PILES OF BOXES
JOHNNY'S OFFICE
ARMCHAIR
COUCH
SIDE TABLE
LAMP STAND
fig. 2.44
Upstairs, to Johnny's office
83"
207"
200"
207"
83"
Steps to the grease pit
Upstairs
GIVE WAY
fig. 2.45

Figs. 2.43, 2.44: These are the final plan views (top views) for both floors of the auto shop, **based on previously developed concept sketches of the building's exterior and interior.** This is the part of the process when the artistic design and the technical, structural vision **continue to inform each other,** until both make sense as one. So, starting from the script's description of the locale, we move on to quick perspective sketches (see pages 040–041, 048–049) to work out the overall and coherent sense of scale, proportions, and volume, including the height, width, and depth of the buildings. Then we create grayscale tonal views (page 010), making sure the exterior and interior match and correlate.

We are now prepared to finally develop a **technical view** of the space in question. There are a number of things to take into account when developing these. First, **always include a measuring square grid** (in this case, each little square represents 10 square inches in reality) **and a character or characters** (here in blue) to keep track of a realistic scale.

This being a garage facility, another must-have are top views of cars, drawn to scale. These were added making sure their measurements are realistic and match the overall setup and sense of space.

Looking at the first pass of the plan view, I had the impression that the resulting width of this diagram might not be enough for the characters to walk around the vehicles comfortably, nor match the look and feel of the main perspective drawing on pages 046–047. So, once I had this draft on paper, I decided to have a **real-world experience** about the feel of that overall area. I got out of my studio, went to a relatively long hallway, and stood on a spot that we will call point **A.** I looked toward the end of the hallway and—imagining I was up against one of the walls of our imaginary garage—**I determined with my naked eye about how far away the opposite wall (point B) would be, so that it would feel realistic and comfortable.**

Once I visually determined point B, I grabbed a measuring tape, wrote down the distance between A and B, and went back to my computer. There I compared that measurement with the one on the existing view. I was happy to see that both were very close. At this point, I repeated the same procedure with **Johnny's office in mind,** and in this case realized I had to push the background wall a bit in order to make the space deeper.

The pillars holding the structure (the small, dark squares within the walls) are **evenly spaced** and coincide with the beam that holds the interior balcony (marked with a red asterisk). In fact, when I determined I had to push the far wall of the office back a bit, that required adjusting the positioning of the pillars so that **they would still coincide with the beam that supports the balcony** overlooking the auto shop downstairs.

When designing a building where pillars and columns are an important part of the construction, make sure that these elements are positioned not to interfere with windows or any other holes on the walls, since obviously a pillar would be compromised or collapse if it were cut (see also, a discussion of pillars on page 081).

Now for some other measurements. The interior staircase that goes up to the second floor has **the same number of steps** as the main perspective view on page 046. These always need to match. This number was already calculated when doing the perspective view by positioning an average-height **character** (about 5'8") right next to the staircase and taking 7.5 inches as the standard height of a **step.** This calculation determined there should be 22 steps in order to reach the already established level of the balcony or hallway that overlooks the interior of the shop. (For further details on how to technically work out this perspective, see Chapter 7, pages 124–125 of my book *Framed Perspective, Vol. 1.*)

Next, the **exterior emergency staircase** facing the back alley needs to be consistent with this. Therefore, the number of steps (counting the landings) is also 22. Sure, it is possible that since they are different types of staircases, the steps may be different heights, but for the sake of this example, they are the same.

Fig. 2.45: The same measuring system was applied to the steps that go down to the bottom of the grease pit. There's Sidney, for scale.

As always, there are instances in which it is okay that the exterior and interior do not match perfectly. For example, if exteriors were shot at a real location and the windows of that façade were of a certain size—then when building the set for the office interior on a soundstage it becomes clear it would look more dramatic if the windows were bigger than they are in real life—it would be okay to build somewhat bigger windows on the soundstage, as long as the discrepancy with the real ones is not so obvious as to be noticeable to the audience and take them out of the story.

Next up, the façade's elevation drawing.

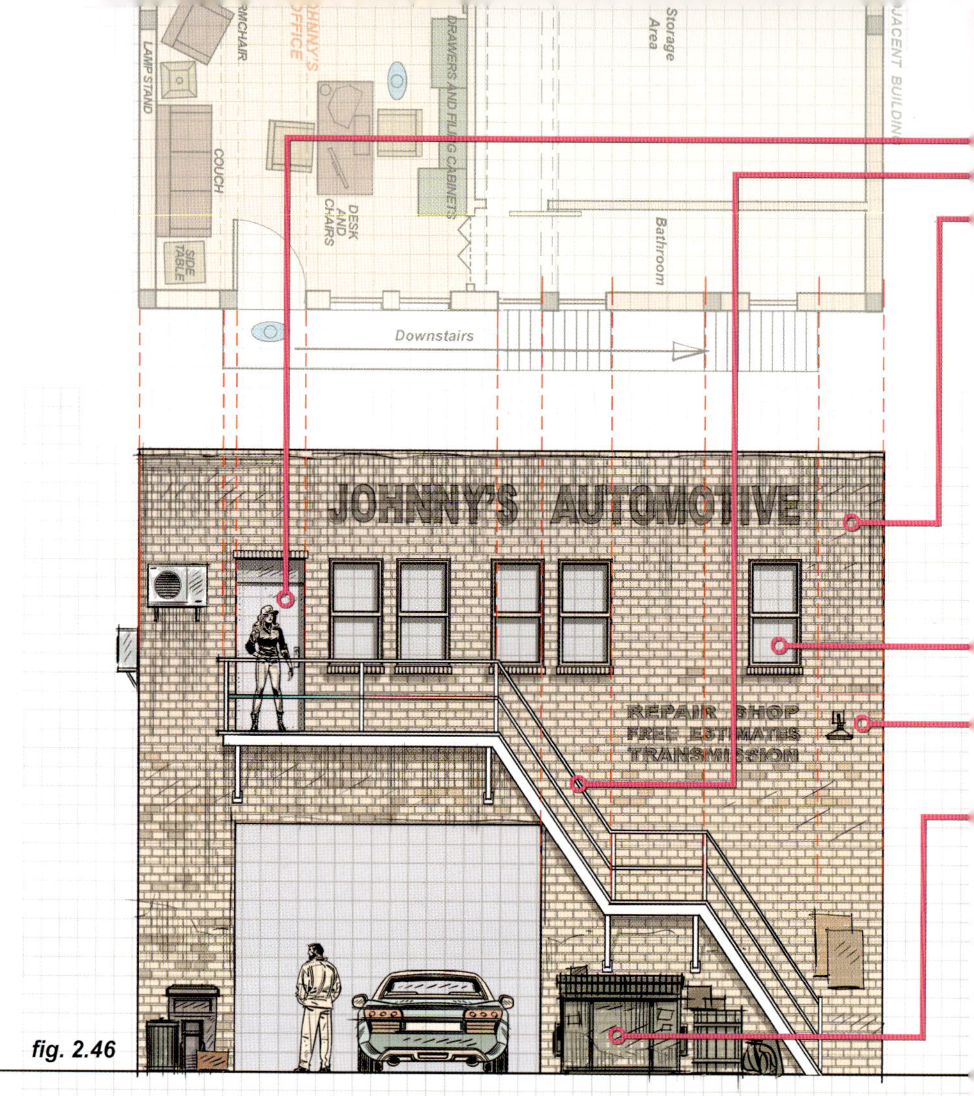

Fig. 2.46: Elevation view of the front of the building.

Whether designing for a 3D animated movie or a live-action feature in which actual, physical, life-sized sets need to be built, or for theatrical productions or even graphic novels in which a location's accuracy and detail can be essential, it is always recommendable to draft the necessary views so that the environments can be properly built or represented.

The same way that the two floors of the building had to make architectural sense together, in that they both have the exact same size and proportions, and the pillars are aligned in the exact same placement, **the floor plan (top) view and the façade elevation (front) view must also match perfectly.**

DESIGNING THE PROPS

Figs. 2.47–2.49: Most items and elements included in this location will need to go through a similar process, and there will be plenty of them. Between the office and the shop there are desks, chairs, light fixtures, boxes, CD players, bulletin boards with documents pinned on them, filing cabinets, all sorts of additional furniture and props, as well as cars, tools, cabinets, posters, and many more items in the downstairs shop.

Eventually, each item's design is presented in detail—not just its **shape** but also its **materials, texture,** and **stylization details.** In a process called **packeting,** this information is collected in a number of additional reference documents, which are sent to the departments in charge of building each and every item that will ultimately be part of the movie.

Figs. 2.50, 2.51: Image callouts like these are part of this packeting process, all with the unified look of a template that also includes the artist's name, date, and any additional notes needed to execute the piece.

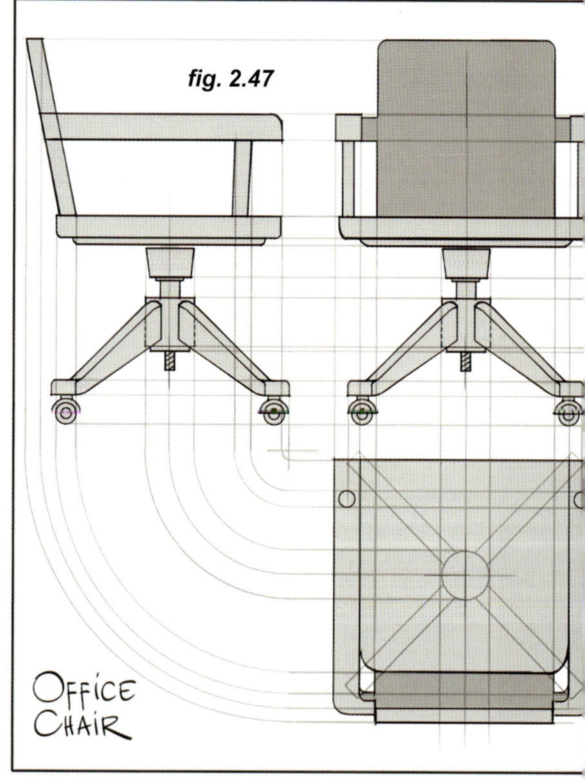

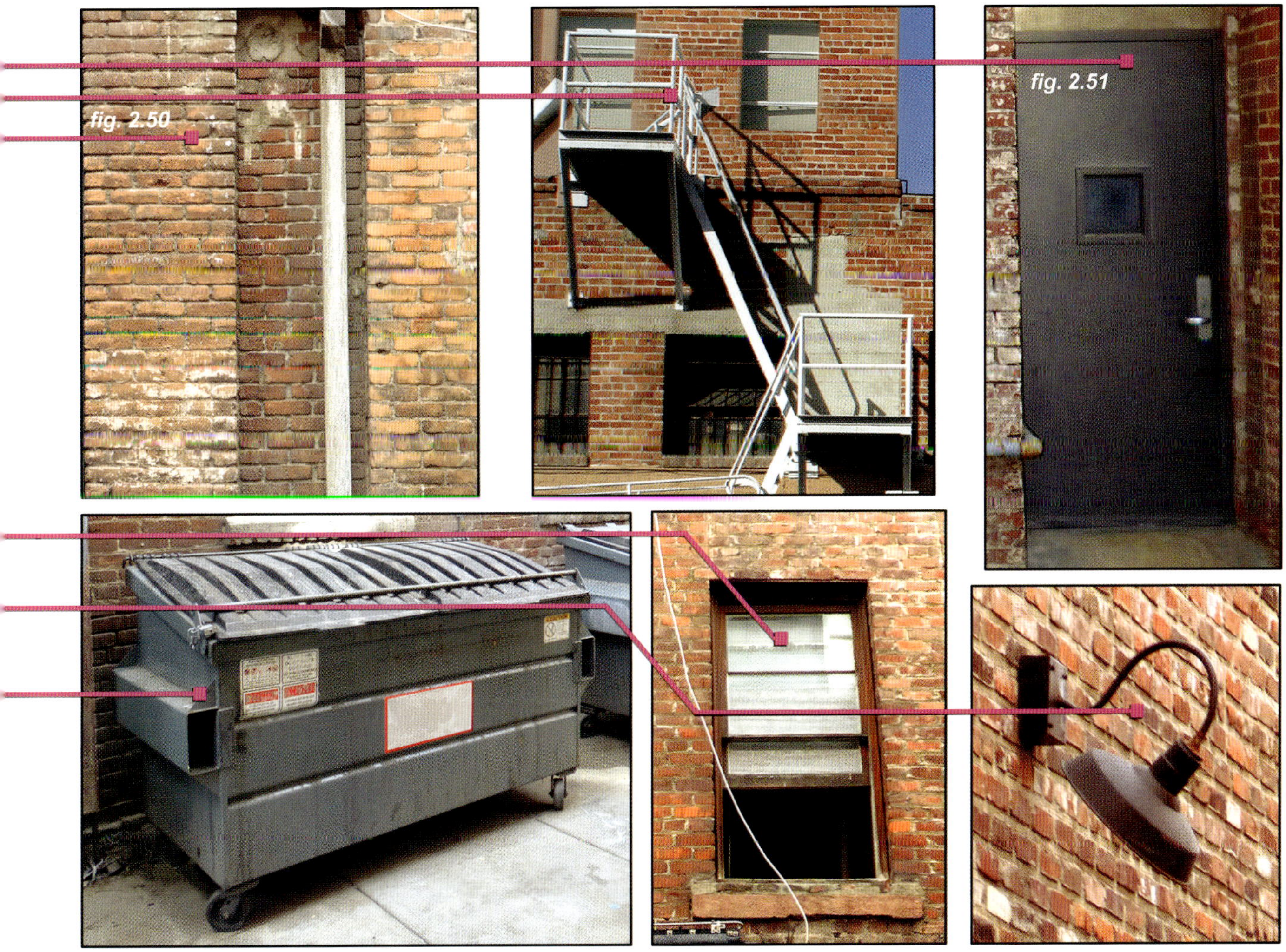

fig. 2.50
fig. 2.51

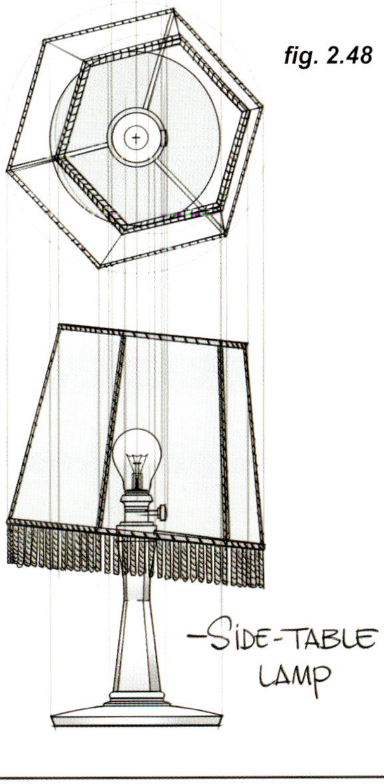

fig. 2.48
fig. 2.49 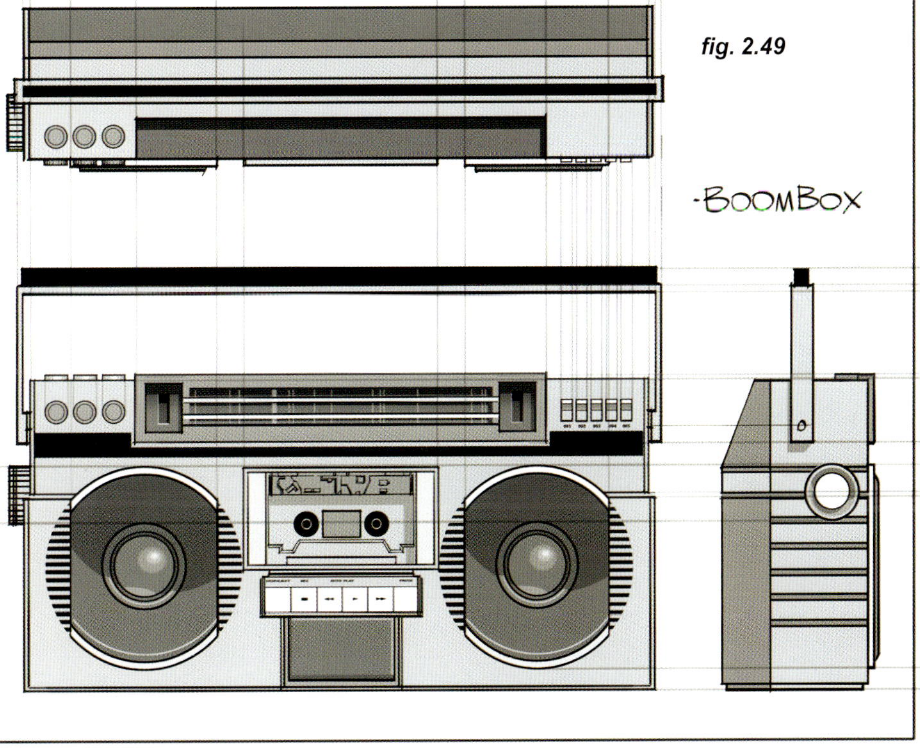
-BOOMBOX
-SIDE-TABLE
LAMP

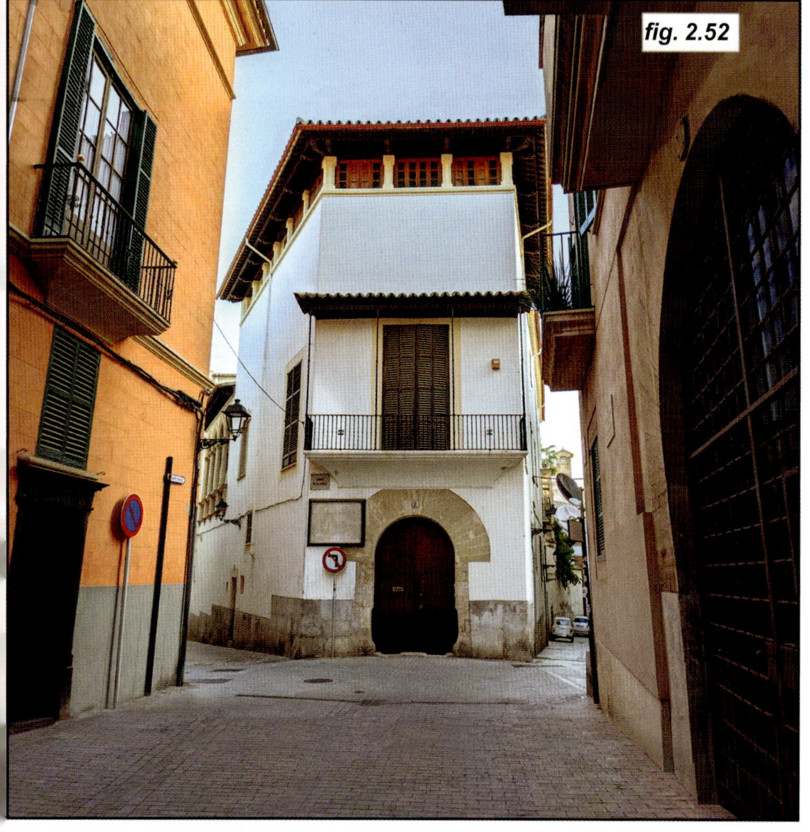

fig. 2.52

ORIGINAL IDEA AND PRELIMINARY SKETCHES

Besides the details that make a location special, the first thing to pay attention to is **the overall signature look** that will differentiate the location very **distinctively** from any other place in the story.

Fig. 2.52: After a lot of photo research, the concept of the auto shop occupying an old building that splits a street in two, creating a fork, did the trick. There are a good number of instances of this setup in ancient Mediterranean cities, like this example in Palma de Mallorca.

Once this decision was made, it was time to start a long sketching session. Different options were explored, including not only this central, iconic building but also the surrounding ones, so that the whole area started taking shape with its full look and flavor. Observe that part of this special look is the fact that big, bolder round shapes and curves are brought in extensively compared to Johnny's location.

Figs. 2.53–2.57: Next are some of the sketches and preliminary studies, including my **thought-process notes.**

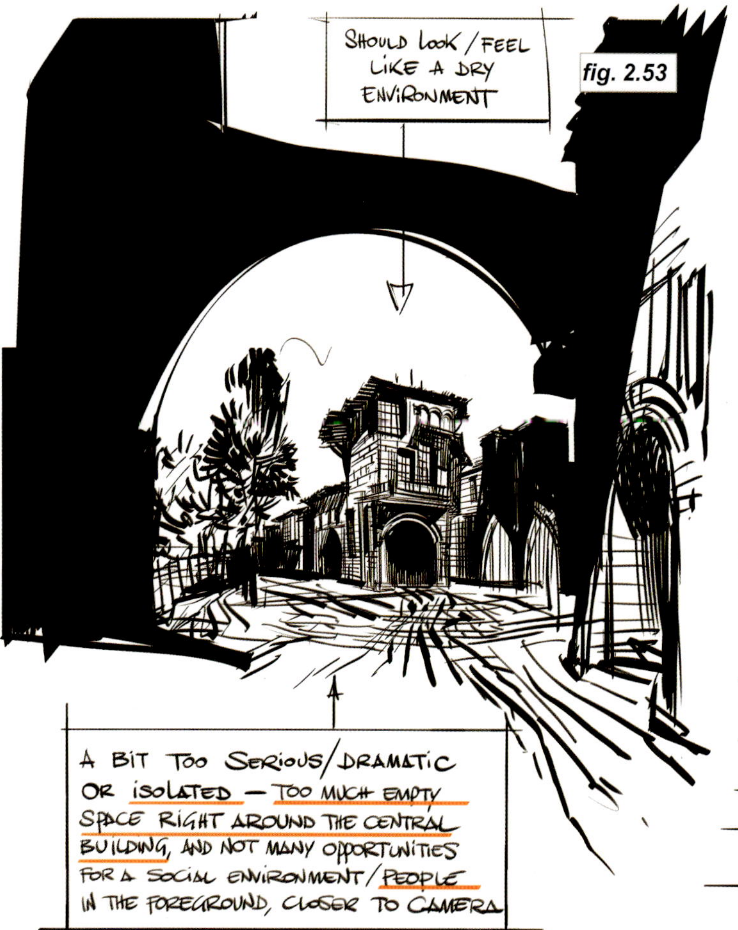

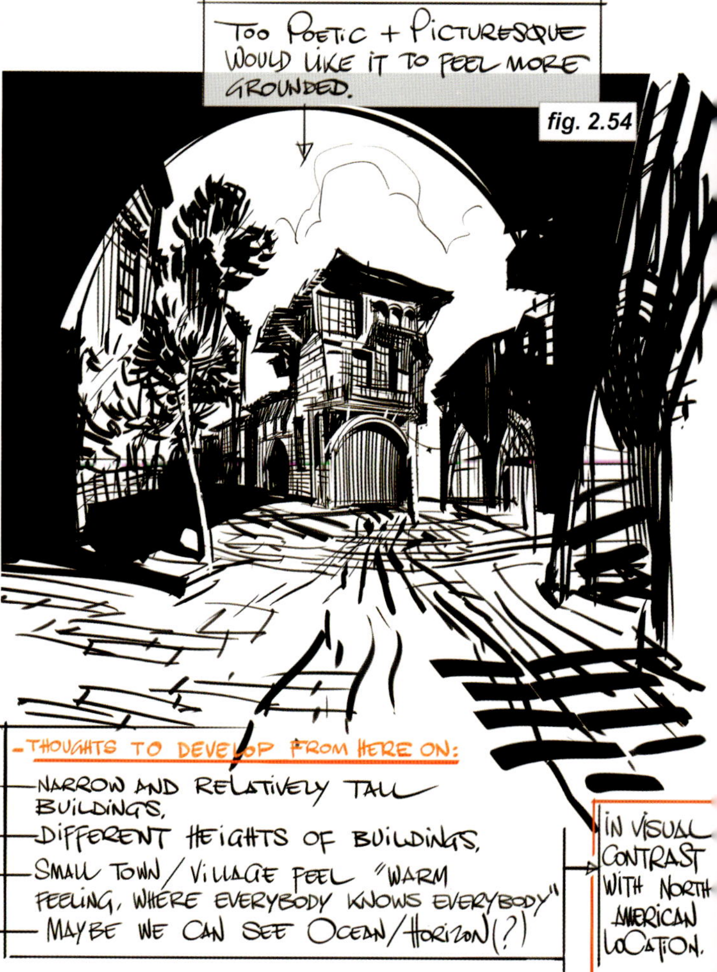

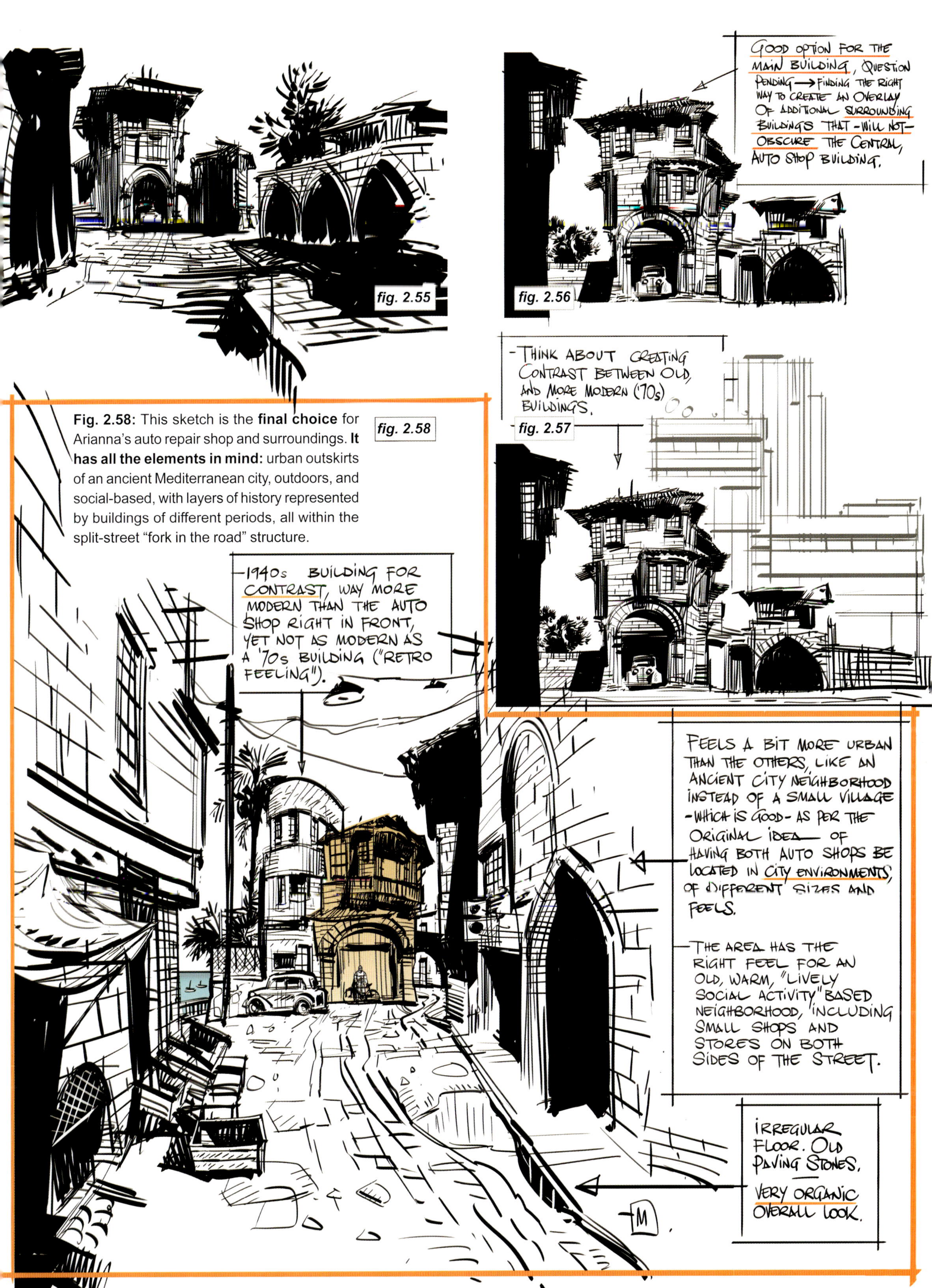

Fig. 2.58: This sketch is the **final choice** for Arianna's auto repair shop and surroundings. **It has all the elements in mind:** urban outskirts of an ancient Mediterranean city, outdoors, and social-based, with layers of history represented by buildings of different periods, all within the split-street "fork in the road" structure.

fig. 2.58

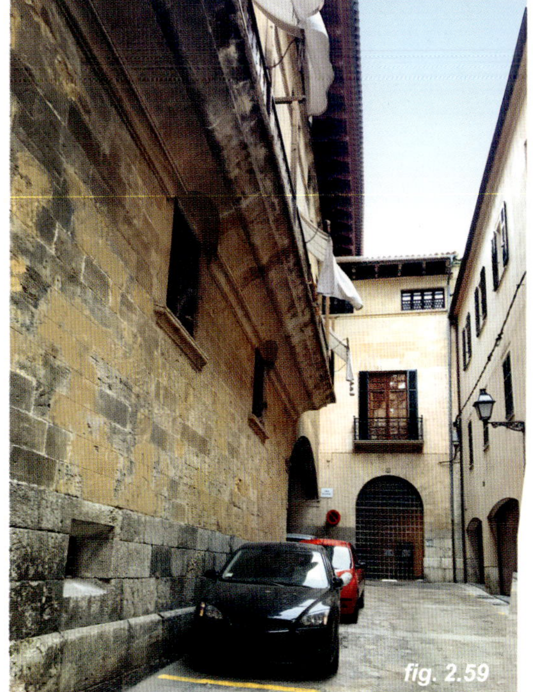

Figs. 2.59–2.63: As usual, the location starts taking its final shape with the help and inspiration of the references previously gathered for this work.

Fig. 2.64: As we sketch **the street,** focus on finding the right balance and proportion between its width—narrow enough to summon this "centuries-old construction" feeling, yet wide enough to offer a clear view of all the elements and a sense of open air and nature.

One feature helpful for this purpose is to establish arches and **openings on the side** so that we can see sky and ocean through these gaps, enhancing the contrast with the more claustrophobic look of Johnny's industrial location.

An accurate perspective underlay makes it easier to draw freehand for a look that is irregular and organic, while at the same time credible and solid.

fig. 2.59

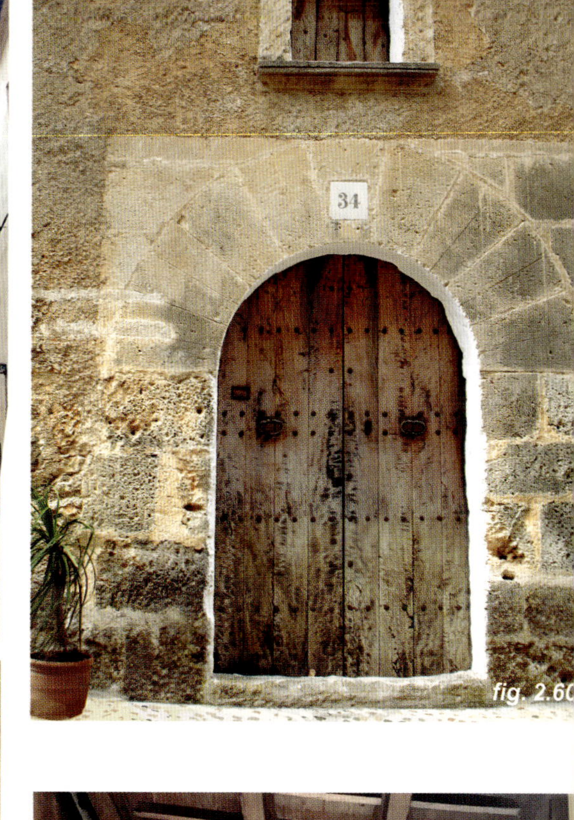

fig. 2.60

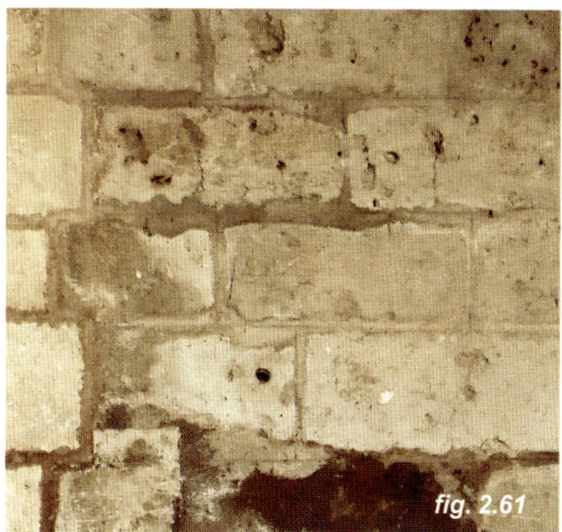

fig. 2.61

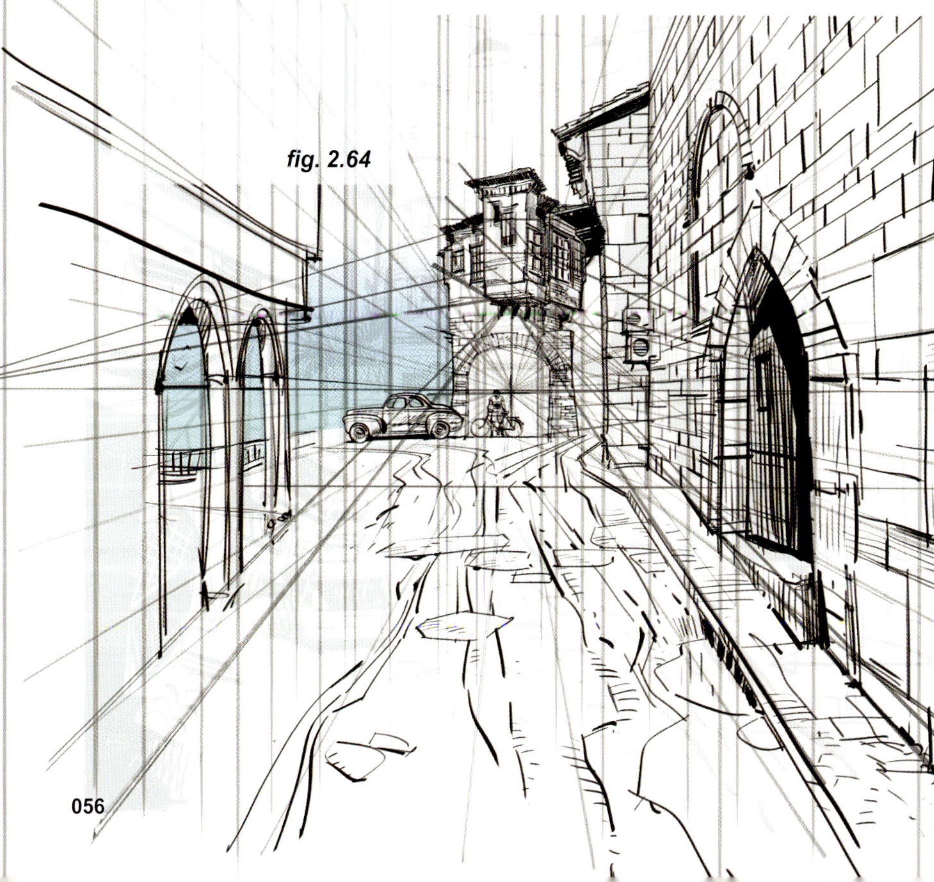

fig. 2.64

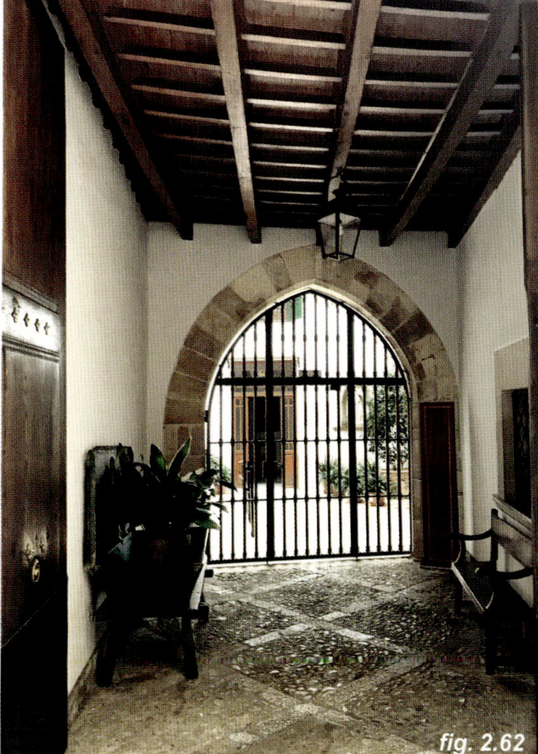

fig. 2.62

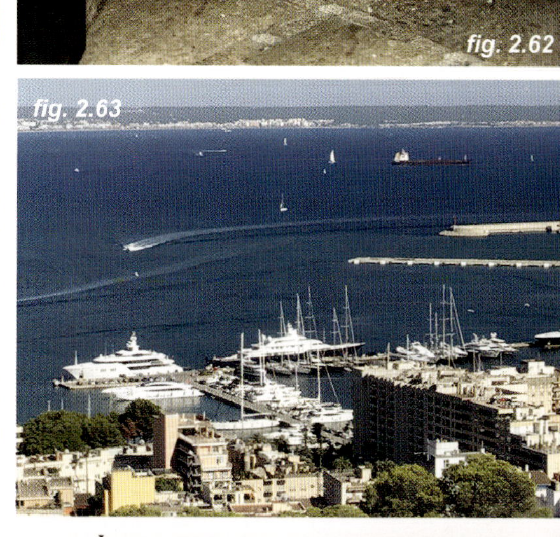

fig. 2.63

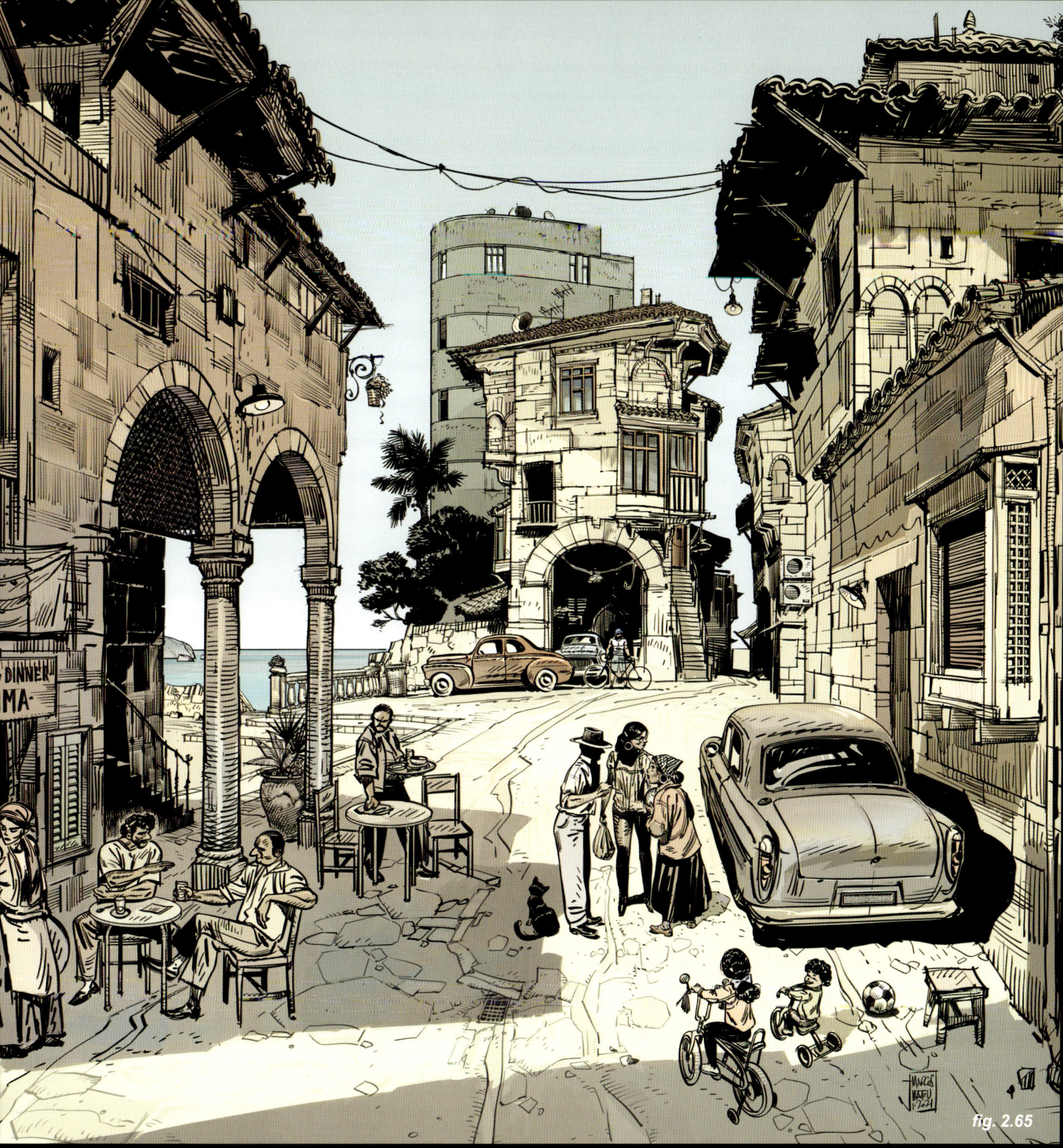

Fig. 2.65: Summing it up, this final design shows a vibrant social scene that portrays the outskirts of an ancient city with rather contrasted patches of lights and shadows, irregular constructions, and buildings that have been added to the place organically throughout the centuries, including a tall, green, Bauhaus-style building in the background and cars of older decades. The open arches to the left really emphasize a sense of air and layers of space all the way to the horizon line, in contrast with the wall and the tall underpass at the end of Johnny's alleyway.

Arianna's auto shop itself follows this same philosophy, as a centuries-old building that has had additions and repairs ever since, with a more straightforward entrance to the second floor, yet with both open and enclosed balconies that protrude at various angles and face in slightly different directions, like a gracious architectural puzzle that indicates the interior might also look somehow like an organic labyrinth.

Just like for Johnny's garage, once we have decided on a look, volume, and proportions, it is extremely helpful and informative to draw plan (top), side, and elevation (frontal) views of the building or buildings. These can be drawn by hand from different angles or built as a 3D model. Further ways to use these drafts, like drawing a full and accurate three-quarter architectural view of the design, were explained in detail in Chapter 9 of my previous book, *Framed Perspective, Vol. 1.*

Fig. 2.66: In this specific technical drawing of the front of the house, it appears to be a wider building than in the artistic representation on page 057.

This optical effect occurs because, in this elevation view, the front and the sides of the building appear to be completely compressed within a single, flat plane, just like they would look using an extremely long lens (see "A Quick Word on Lenses," *Framed Perspective, Vol. 1,* page 028). Whereas, the artistic view on page 057 more clearly shows the depth and perspective effect of the building, visually separating front and sides from each other.

Fig. 2.67: This difference in widths is shown by the orange lines measuring the front of the building and the blue lines representing the width of the whole construction.

Please note that all these views should include elements that give a proper and accurate sense of scale. The blue rectangles represent the correct dimensions of a car, although the most obvious and standard way to communicate scale is to add a human figure.

Fig. 2.68: The side elevation of Arianna's auto repair shop includes a properly detailed side view of a car, matching the dimensions of the blue rectangle in fig. 2.67.

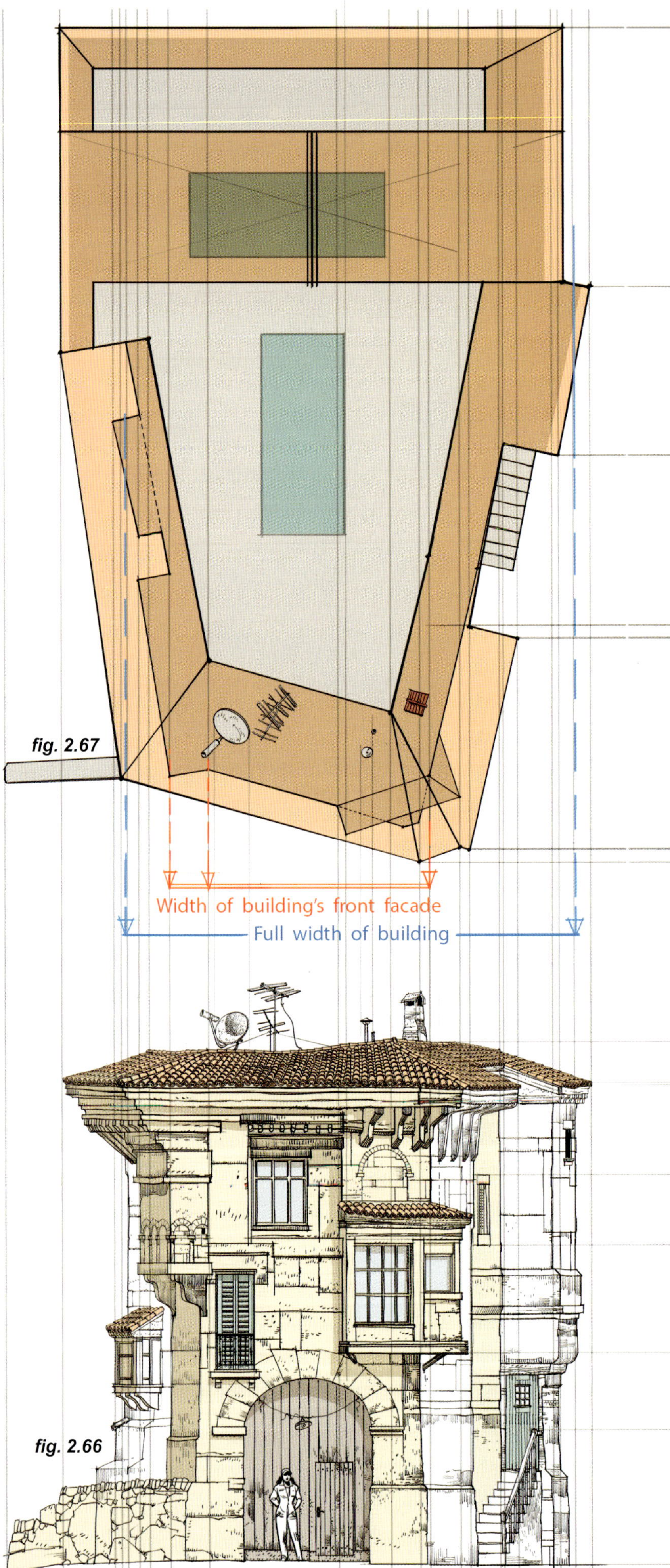

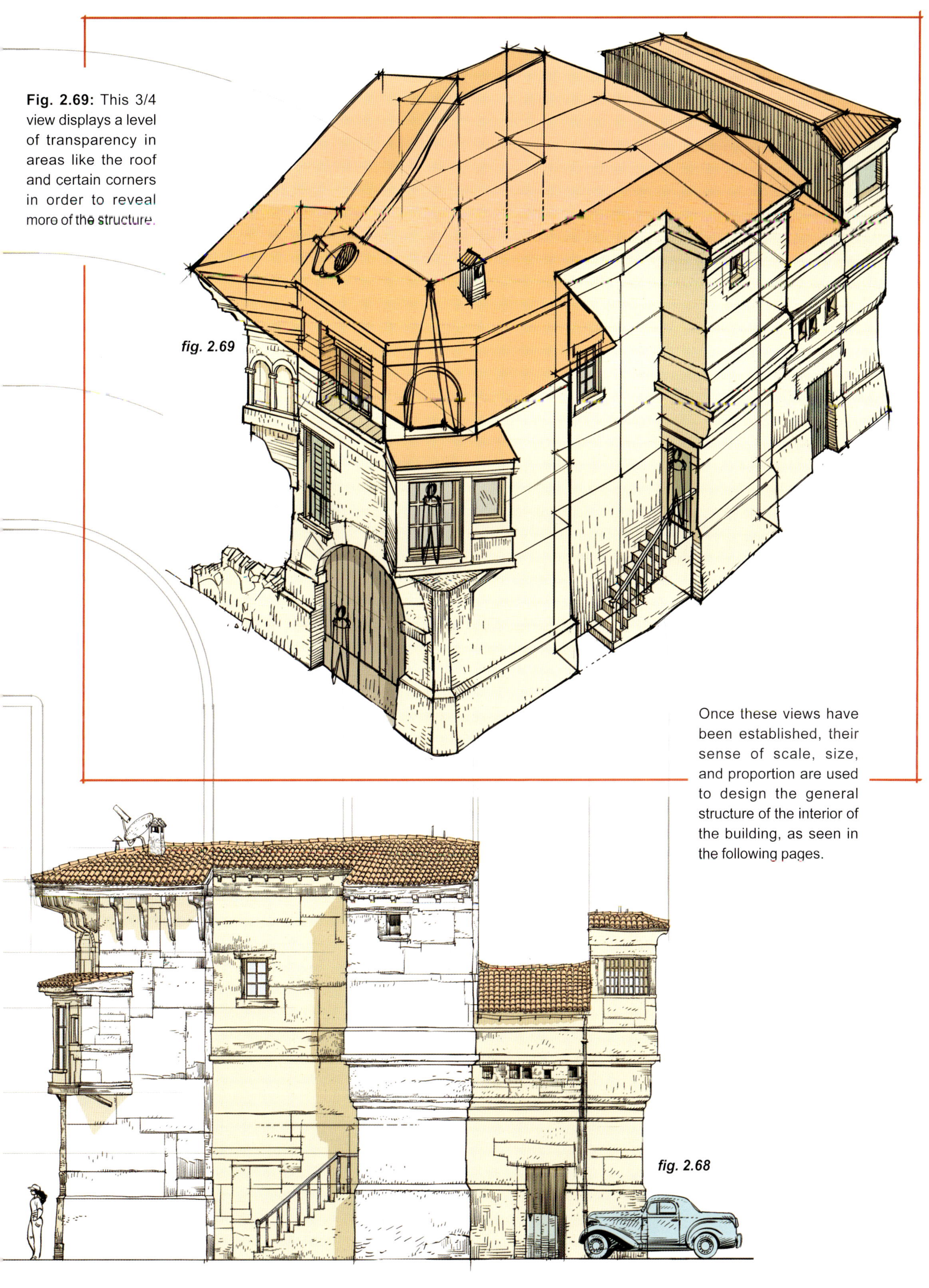

Fig. 2.69: This 3/4 view displays a level of transparency in areas like the roof and certain corners in order to reveal more of the structure.

Once these views have been established, their sense of scale, size, and proportion are used to design the general structure of the interior of the building, as seen in the following pages.

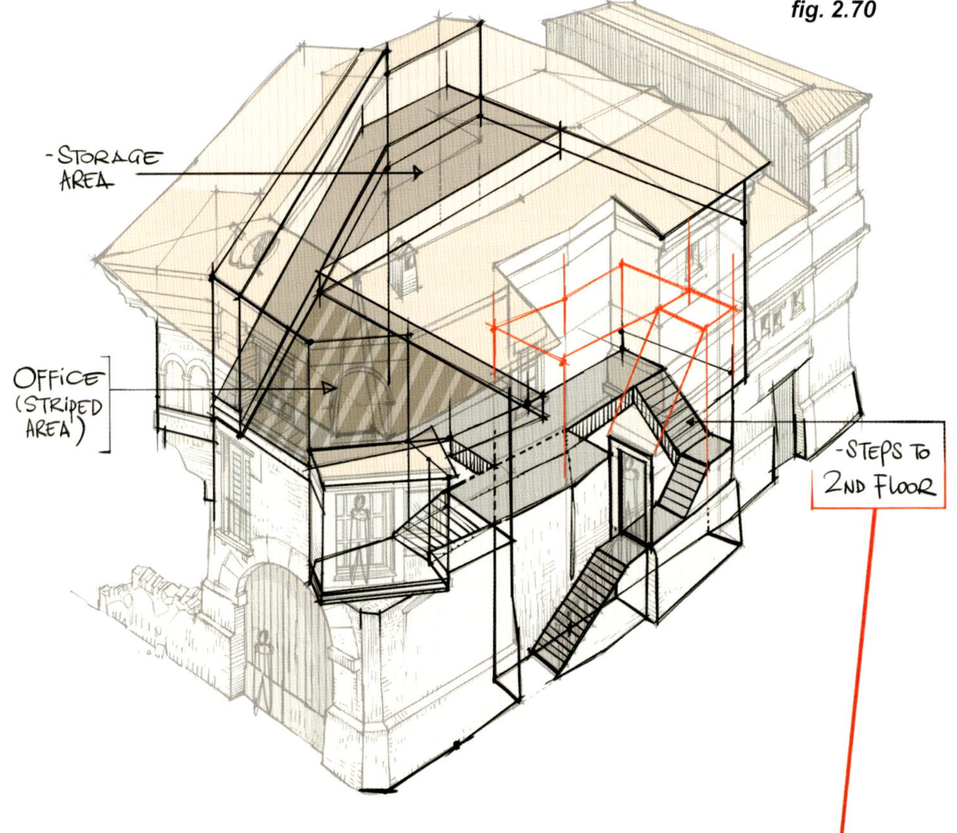

Everything will be worked out so that the **interior** design matches the space that was already created for the **exterior.**

Reminder, the interior and exterior can be made to match exactly or can be fudged a little as long as they both make overall sense together. It is okay to cheat—up to a degree—in order to maximize the visual appeal of the two designs, interior and exterior, as separate items, as long as they do not distract the audience by not looking feasible or not belonging within a consistent, cohesive reality.

Fig. 2.70: Basic design of the interior space and structure that matches the organic shape language established by the lighting and volume study in fig. 2.71, a study that allowed us to reverse-engineer the space, which is the base for this technical approach to it.

Fig. 2.71: This **grayscale lighting tonal** shows a rough, shape-based view of the interior, as seen from the front entrance looking in, and a sense of atmosphere.

An environment begins to grow primarily from a general sense of shapes and atmosphere that make sense in terms of the design brief, **before nailing down specific architectural lines and styles.** Rough tonals can be *very* helpful and informative at this stage.

Formalization of these masses of lights, darks, and shapes comes later when making structural and architectural sense of them through the specific use of line work and textures, yet **the starting point can, in most cases, essentially be dictated by gut instinct** as to what fools right.

Again, aiming to contrast with Johnny's location, Arianna's features vertical shapes as opposed to horizontal, and round shapes as opposed to rectilinear. Also, the lighting is more organic. Natural sunlight shines through the upper windows, creating a visual distinction between the hot outdoors and the much cooler indoors.

fig. 2.72

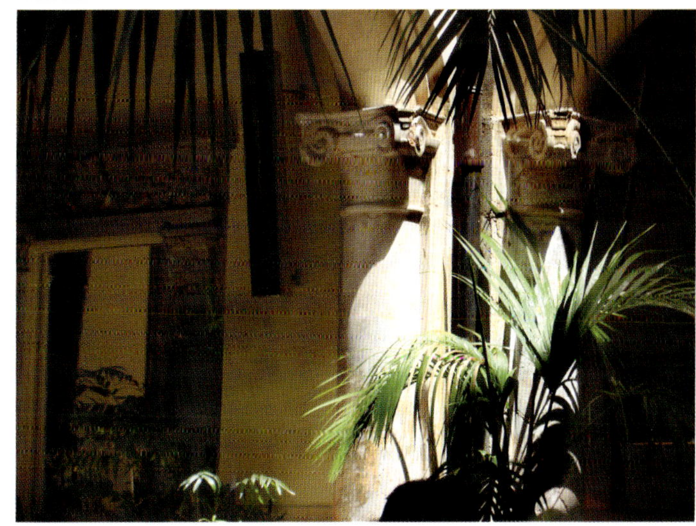

fig. 2.73

Heading into the final lap, it is important to have a clear vision not only for the atmosphere of this interior but also of the architectural details and props that will enhance the flavor of this part of the story.

Figs. 2.72, 2.73: Photo references have been gathered for a sense of lighting based on soft spotlights.

Figs. 2.74, 2.75: These sketches were rendered as studies for the weathered props in the set.

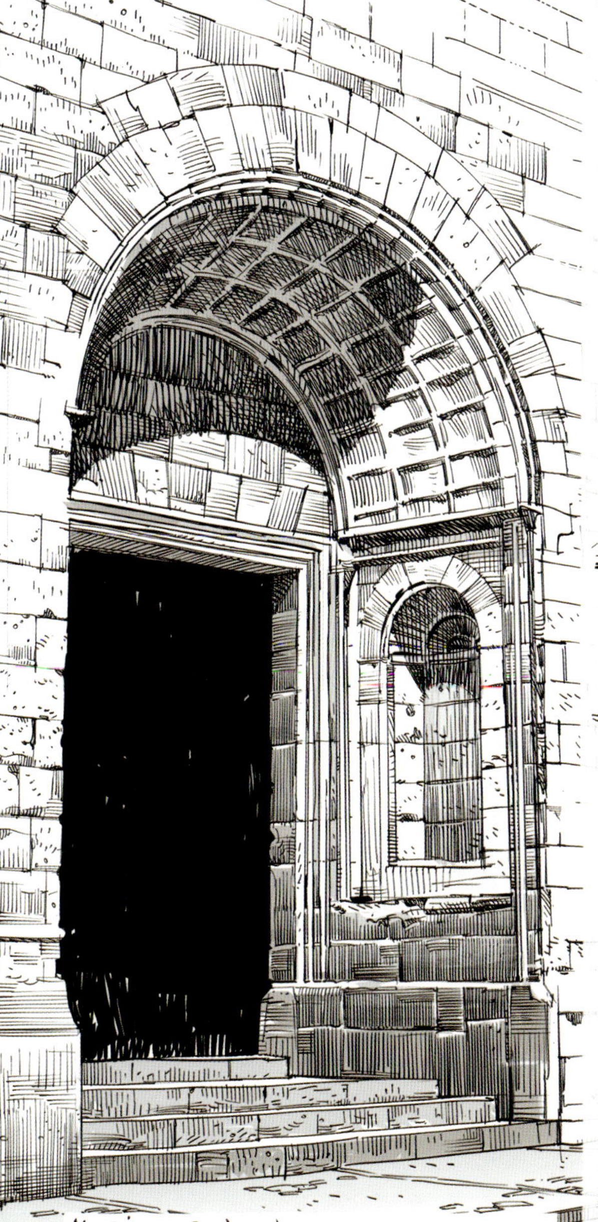

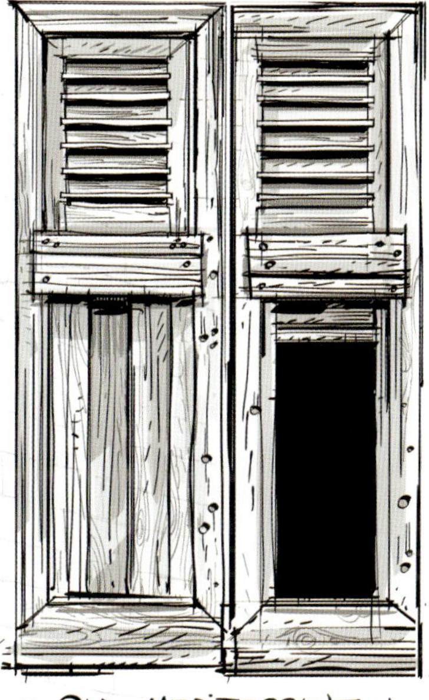

fig. 2.74

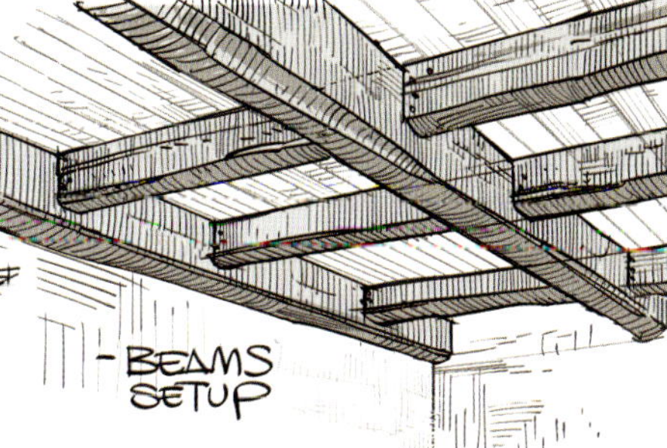

fig. 2.75

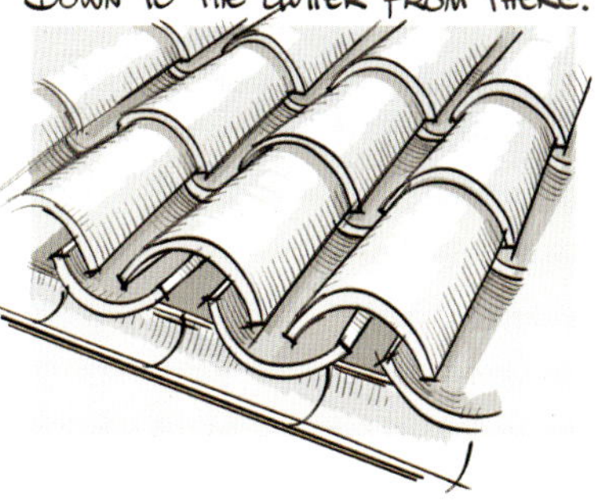

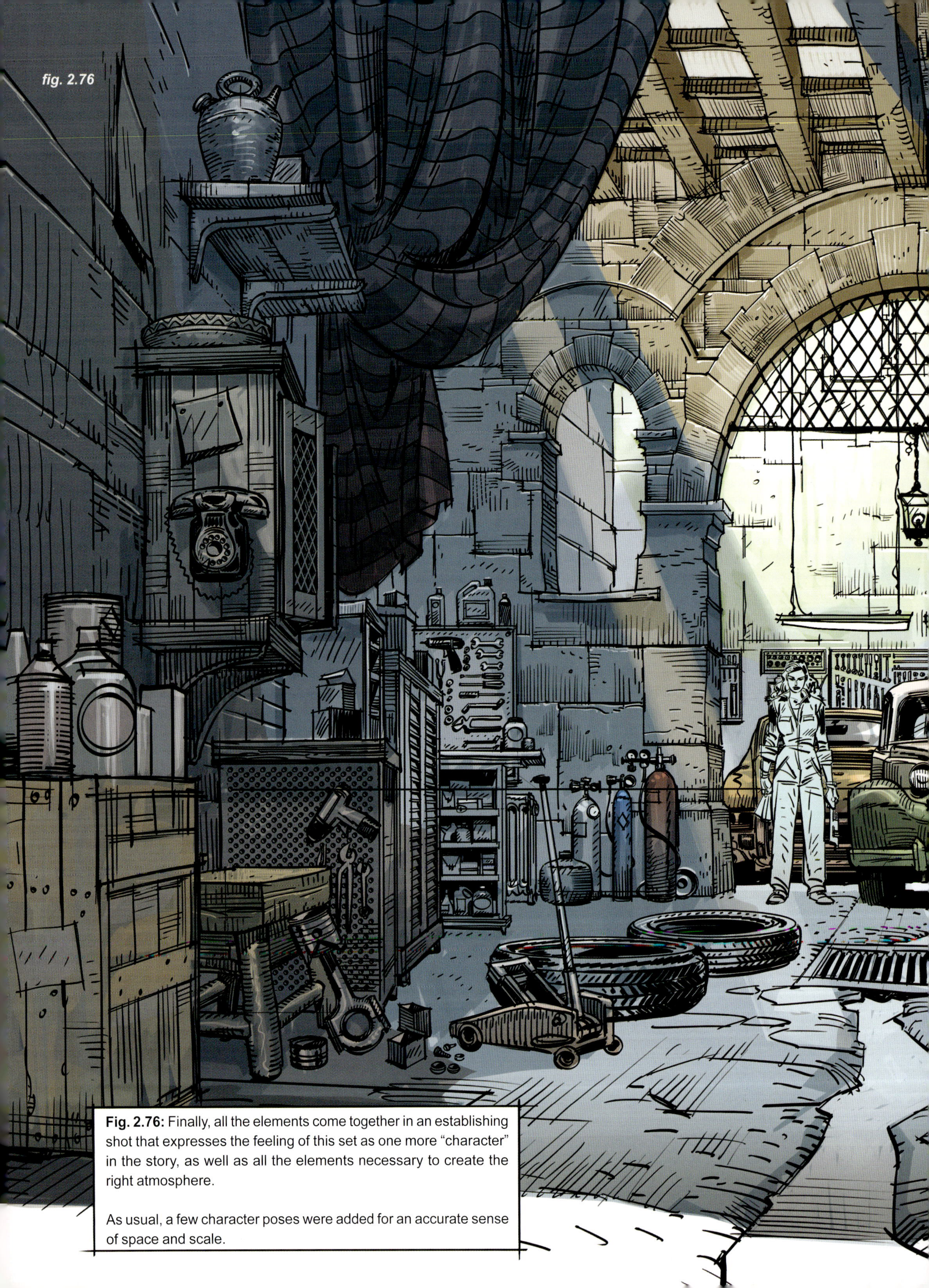

Fig. 2.76: Finally, all the elements come together in an establishing shot that expresses the feeling of this set as one more "character" in the story, as well as all the elements necessary to create the right atmosphere.

As usual, a few character poses were added for an accurate sense of space and scale.

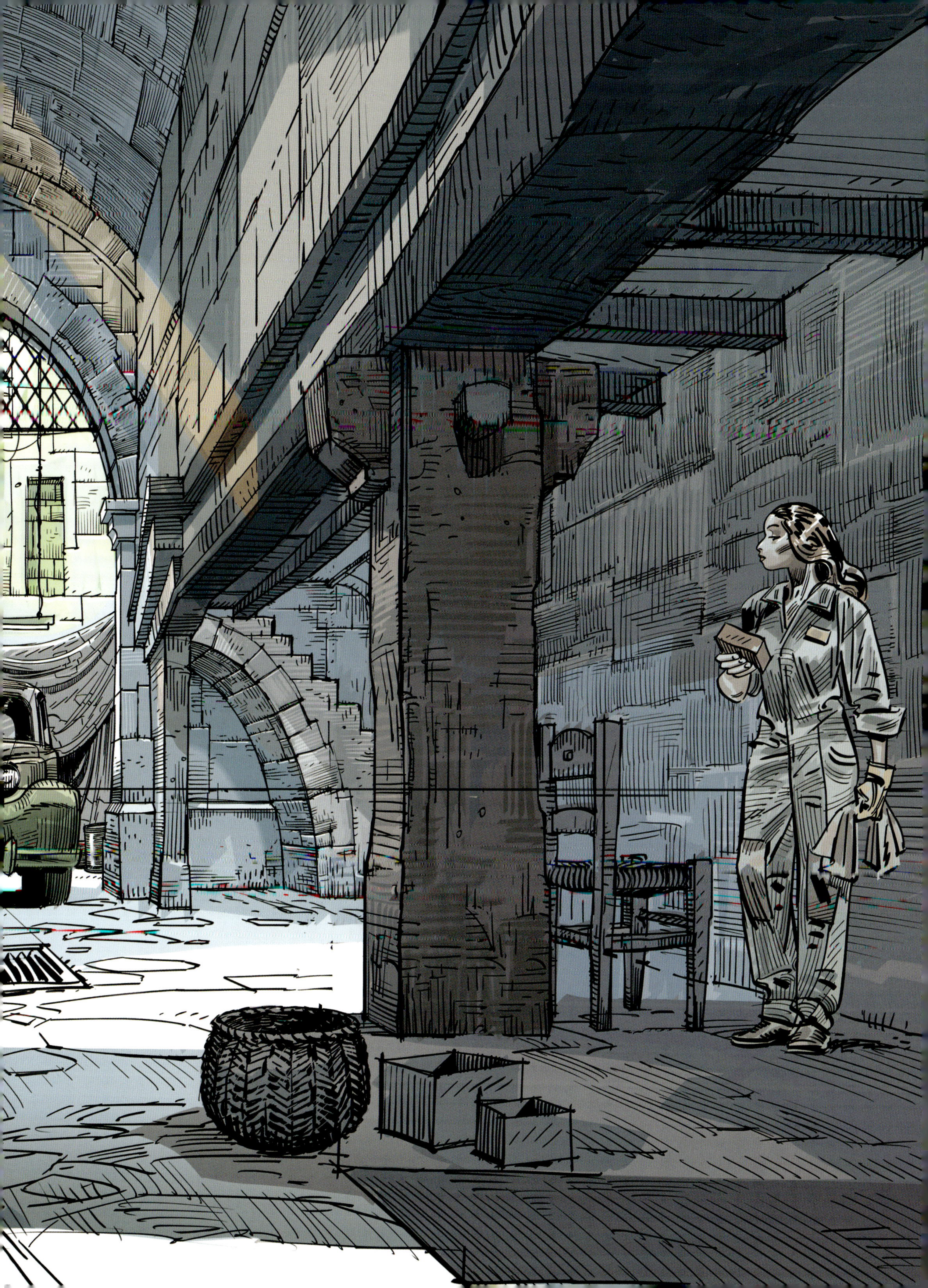

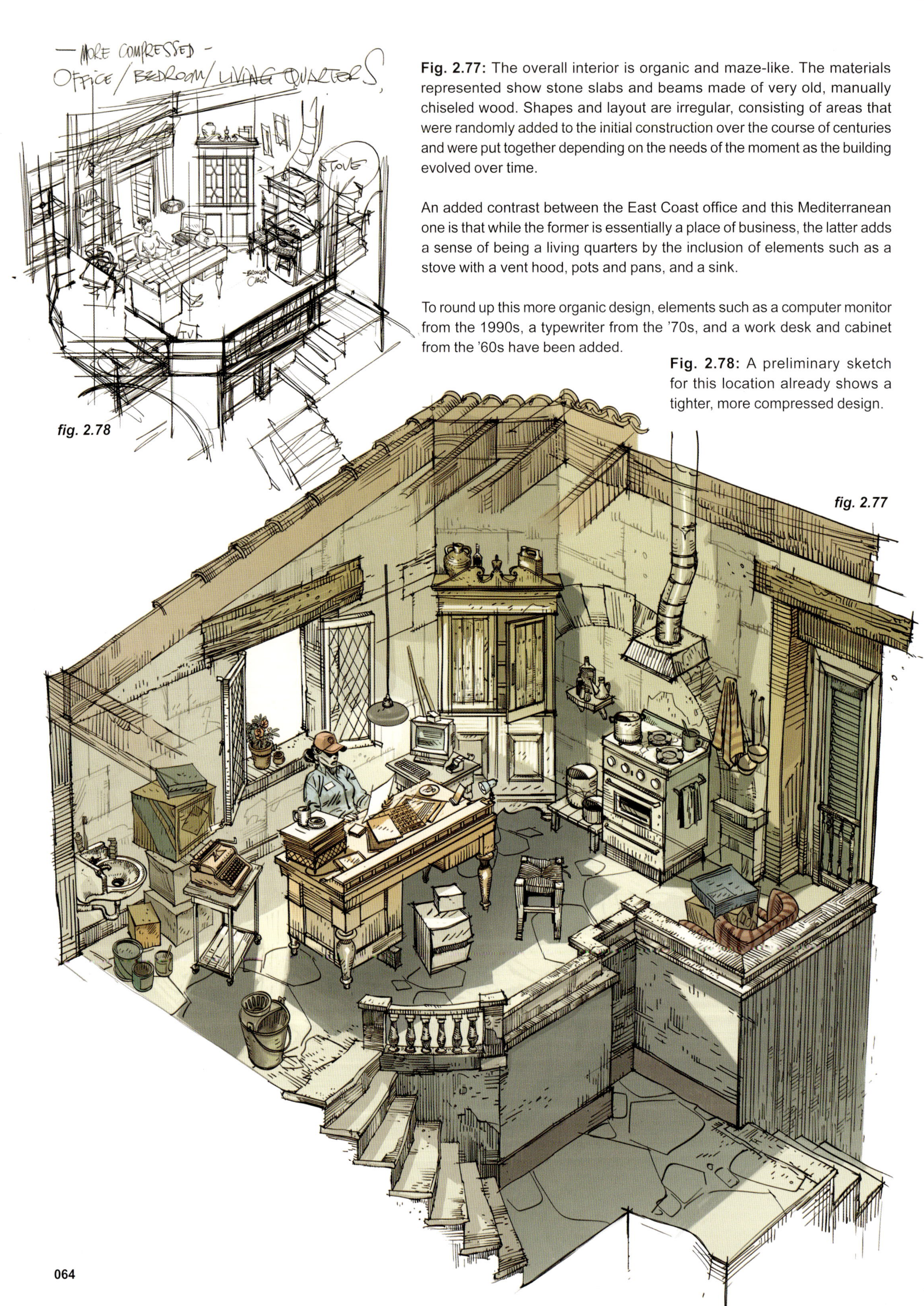

fig. 2.78

Fig. 2.77: The overall interior is organic and maze-like. The materials represented show stone slabs and beams made of very old, manually chiseled wood. Shapes and layout are irregular, consisting of areas that were randomly added to the initial construction over the course of centuries and were put together depending on the needs of the moment as the building evolved over time.

An added contrast between the East Coast office and this Mediterranean one is that while the former is essentially a place of business, the latter adds a sense of being a living quarters by the inclusion of elements such as a stove with a vent hood, pots and pans, and a sink.

To round up this more organic design, elements such as a computer monitor from the 1990s, a typewriter from the '70s, and a work desk and cabinet from the '60s have been added.

Fig. 2.78: A preliminary sketch for this location already shows a tighter, more compressed design.

fig. 2.77

BUILDING UP TO A HISTORICAL EPIC

We know **contrast** is one of the main tools to create drama and interest at many different levels. This and many other devices will be applied to this new case, the development of a **historical epic.** This type of story allows us to explore several different aspects of life in a human settlement through its many social levels.

So, let's consider the fascinating civilization of ancient Egypt, and its various social and environmental strata, to develop a number of locations and how we can visually make the most of them.

First up, a humble area in a small town in ancient Egypt 4,000 years ago, with a population of hardworking farmers and artisans, where the architectural elements are of relatively basic construction laid out with regular geometric shapes and volumes. Then we will explore richer, more elaborate and grand areas of town that will make the journey of our characters and the process of the story captivating.

AN ANCIENT EGYPTIAN SETTLEMENT / PRELIMINARY RESEARCH

Here is a brief overview of how this society worked, felt, and looked.

Figs. 3.1–3.3: Based on research from multiple sources, an average "working-class" building was made from mud applied onto basic structures that consisted of intertwined branches. But because they kept being swept away by the floods . . .

Fig. 3.4: The method evolved to form mud bricks with the help of ladder-shaped molds. Wood—being a more scarce material—was reserved mostly for beams and doors.

Some of these construction techniques, like mud applied to a wooden structure or adobe bricks made of clay and straw, are still being used in parts of the world today in a process that has not changed much in 5,000 years. So, there are current color photographs or even online video of this process, which can be of great help in the development of these designs.

According to general archaeological research, the basic layout of this **modest type of house** had a rather rectangular design and would usually have an entrance room that contained an altar, then a central room with a central column to support the roof where the family or families living there would get together to eat (see pages 076–077 for an example). Other rooms surrounding the main one, also mostly of rectangular design, would serve different purposes, from sleeping quarters to storage of tools or grain. Beds were either raised off the ground as a simple structure with a mat on top made of threaded hemp, or the mat might simply be placed directly on the floor.

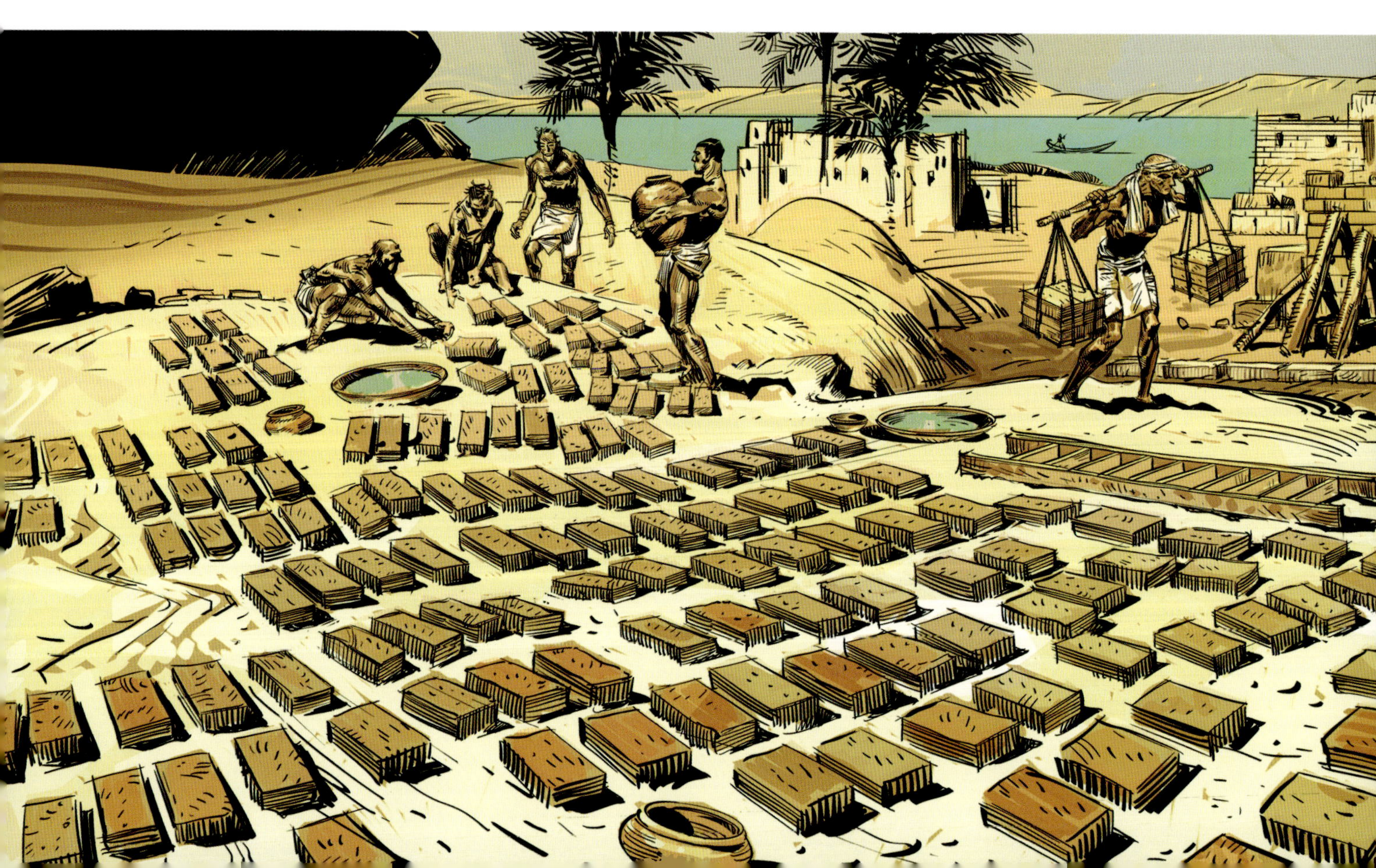

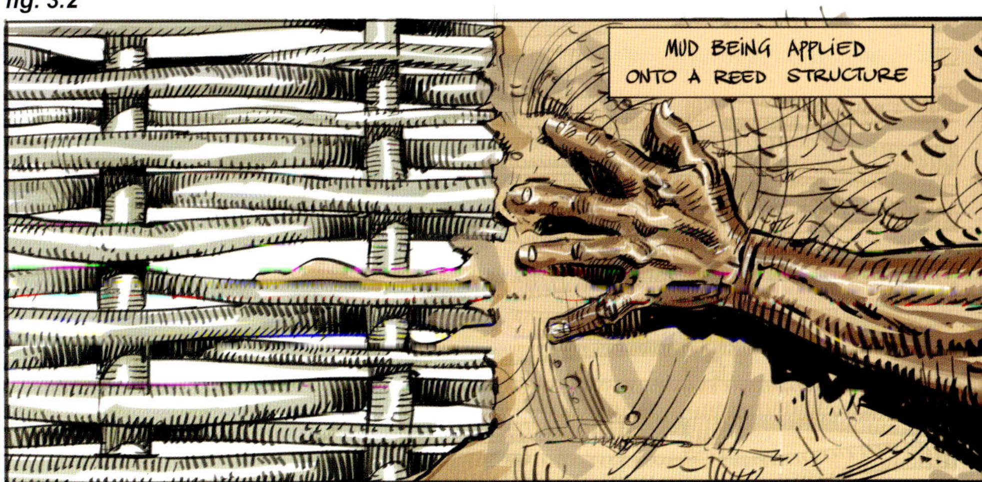

Domestic animals lived in a backyard space. Since bathrooms were nonexistent, waste and trash were, for the most part, disposed of outside, either in the backyard or taken out directly to the street. Water for different household uses was brought from the nearest spring.

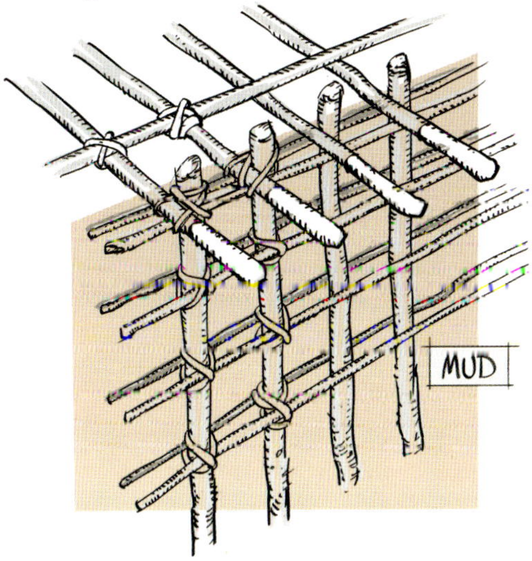

Normally a house had a raised entrance door, accessible by a ramp or steps, to reduce the amount of sand and dust blowing into the house. Windows were on the higher part of the walls to prevent animals from walking in.

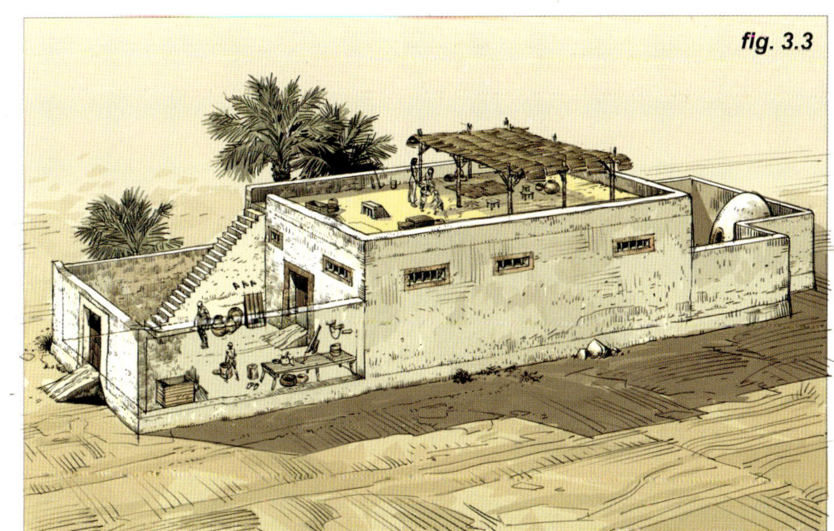

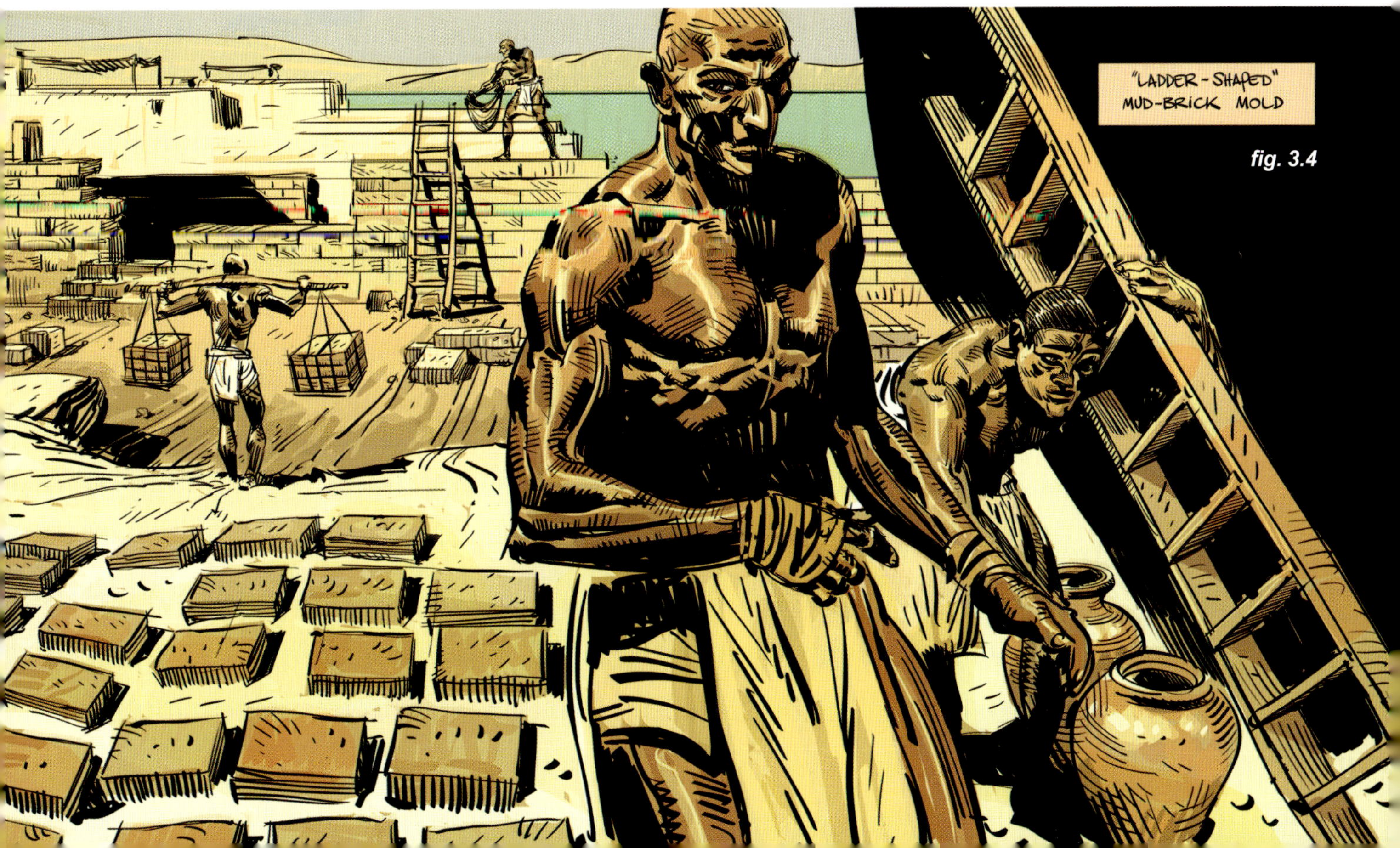

Fig. 3.5: These homes had flat roofs, usually with a straw-covered pergola on top to help cool down the temperature of the house. The roof was accessible by a ladder or staircase, and its inhabitants would spend the warmer nights there.

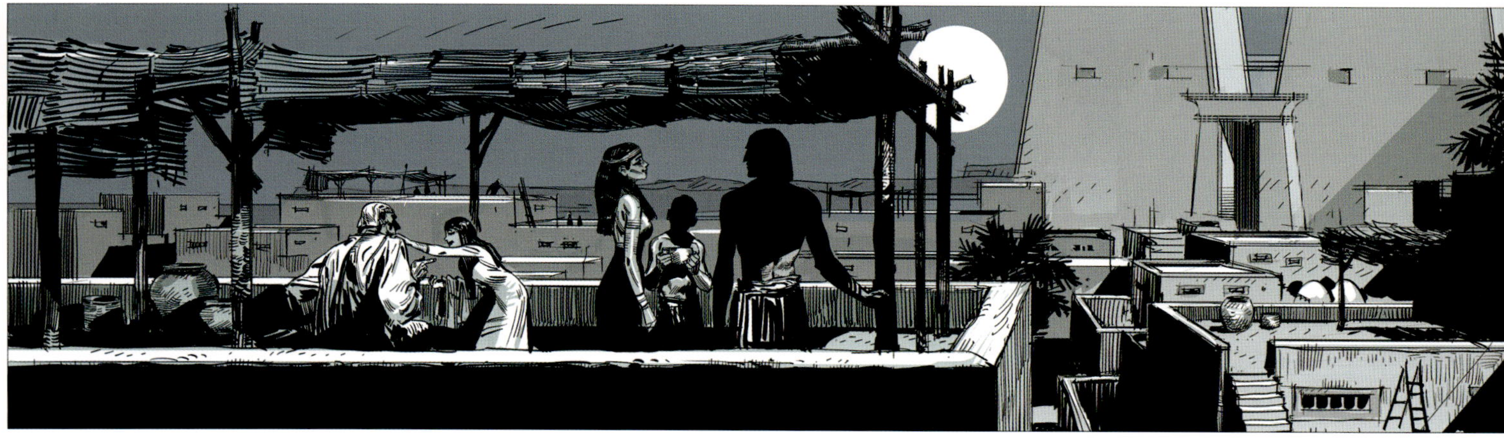

Figs. 3.6, 3.7: For the most part, when closer to rivers, houses were more loosely laid out on the land. When in more congested urban areas like a city or village, these houses would be built back-to-back within a much tighter grid of smaller parallel streets that would lead to a main one, as in a fishbone layout. Sometimes walls would be knocked down to connect two houses in order to create a bigger property. *These images are directly inspired by actual archaeological research and maps.*

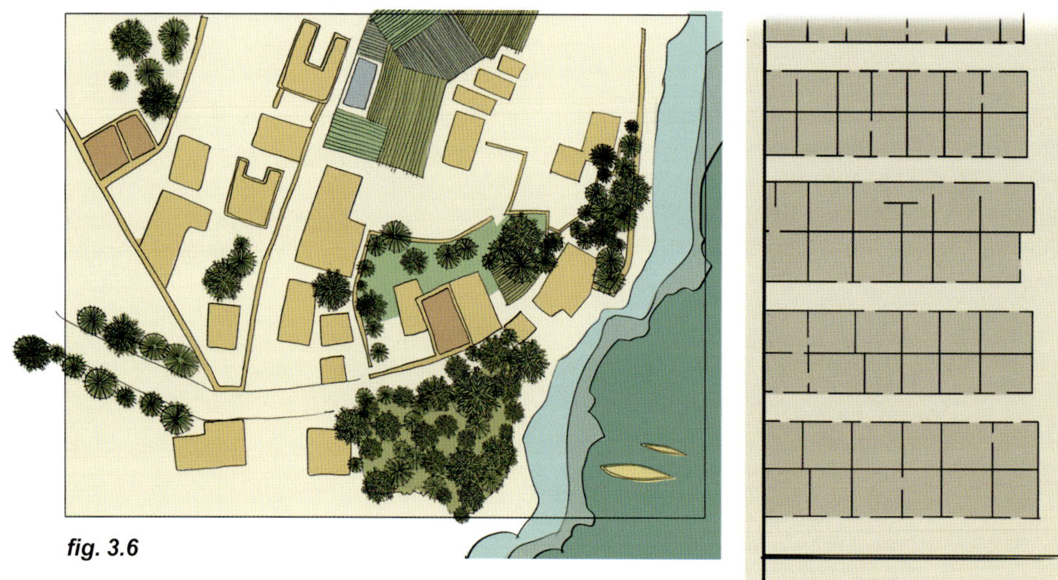

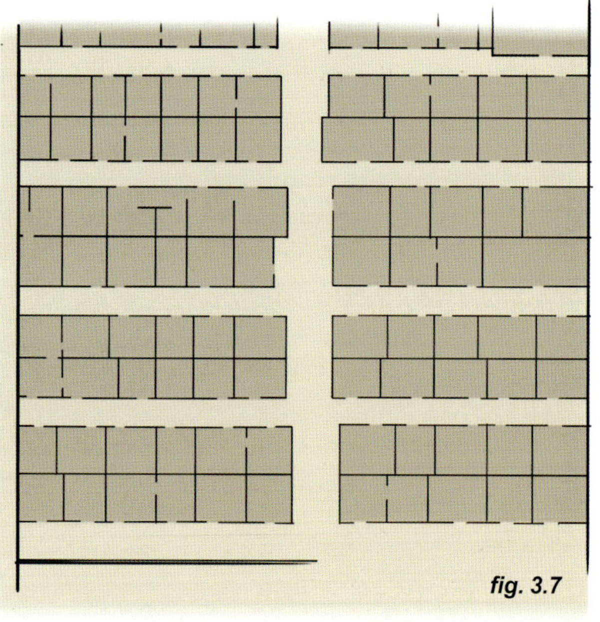

As much as they would take care of their homes, at any given time a number of them would be **under repair,** as the brick walls could partially crumble and need patching work. Most of these constructions were whitewashed in order to reflect the hot sunlight and keep the cool in, a technique still used in many hot climates of the world. These details (and many more that might be discovered during the research process) are important because when these objects and activities are visually represented, it makes the locations and societies in our designs **come alive.**

As a side note that would not really apply to such an early civilization as ancient Egypt, but thinking back now on the Washington, DC anecdote from page 028, this concept of change and evolution is something that we should keep an eye on when designing worlds in which different moments and periods in history can be present at once. Obtaining references only for the specifics of what an age is known for and making it look like **that's all** there is to it is rarely a realistic approach. It is **especially noticeable** in more recent periods of history. For example, more cars being driven on the streets during the 1950s would be from that decade, but many others would still be around from the '40s or even '30s. The same usually goes for architectural styles throughout history and even items of everyday use.

We can still find examples of wonderful, traditional old villages in the northeastern region of the African continent that retain a similar look and feel to the ones described here. They are not archaeological reconstructions but, in fact, still standing to this day. Access to references like these is invaluable, as they show the real visual essence of these types of locations as actual places.

Figs. 3.8, 3.9: Here are some sketches based on a variety of photo references of existing places. These are very useful for getting the "hand-to-brain" connection ready for the moment we put it all together to get the story going.

fig. 3.8

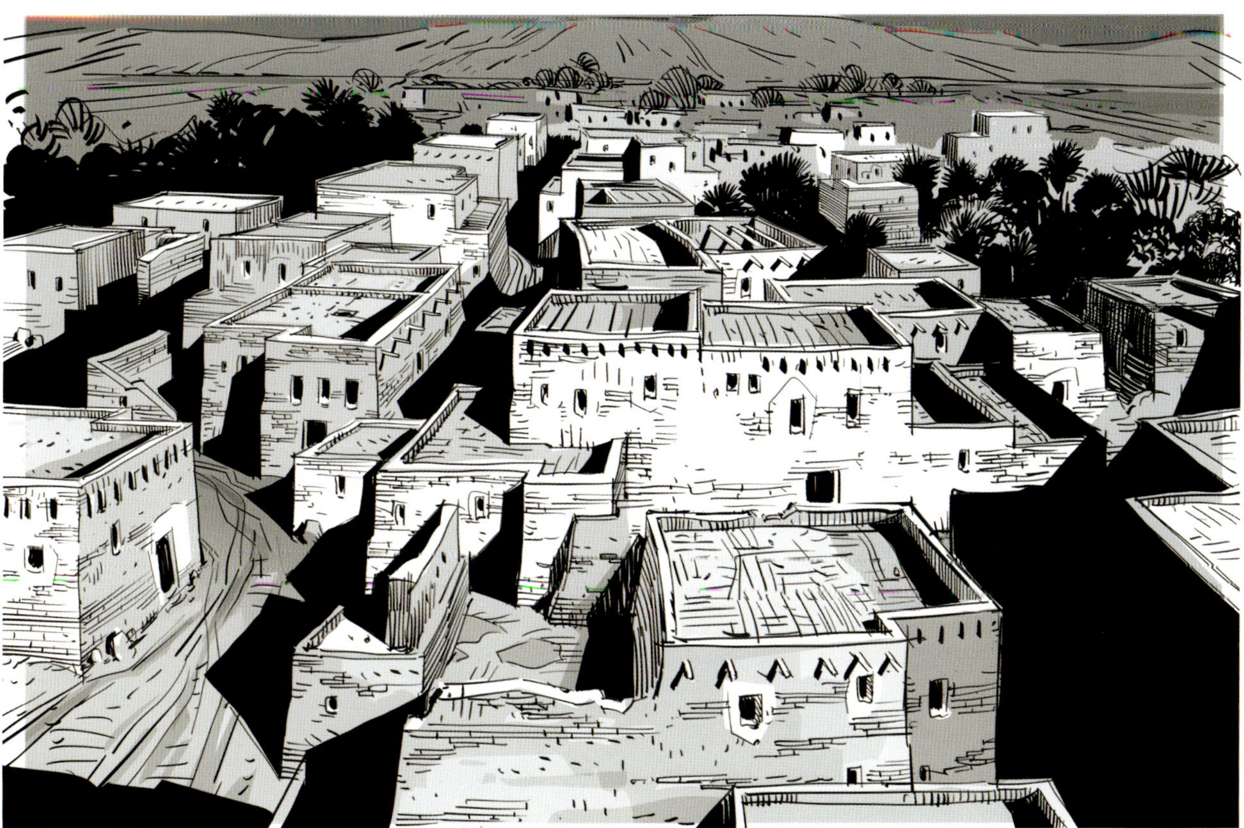

fig. 3.9

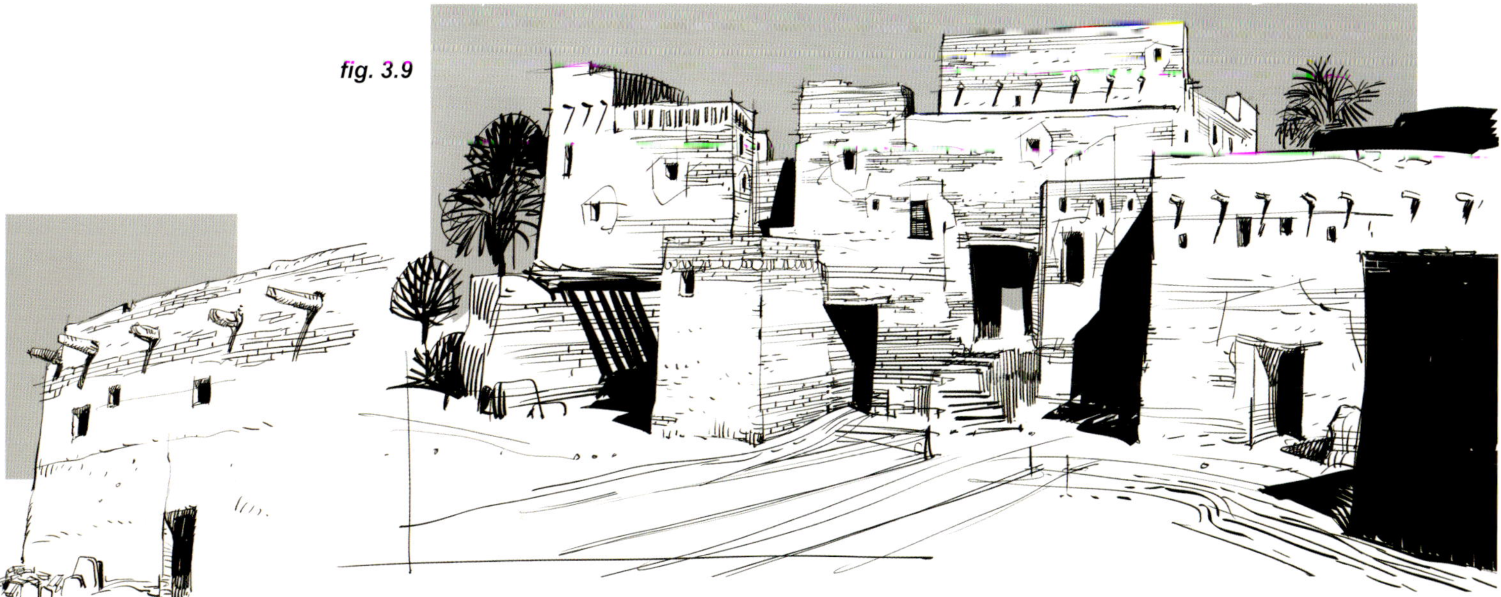

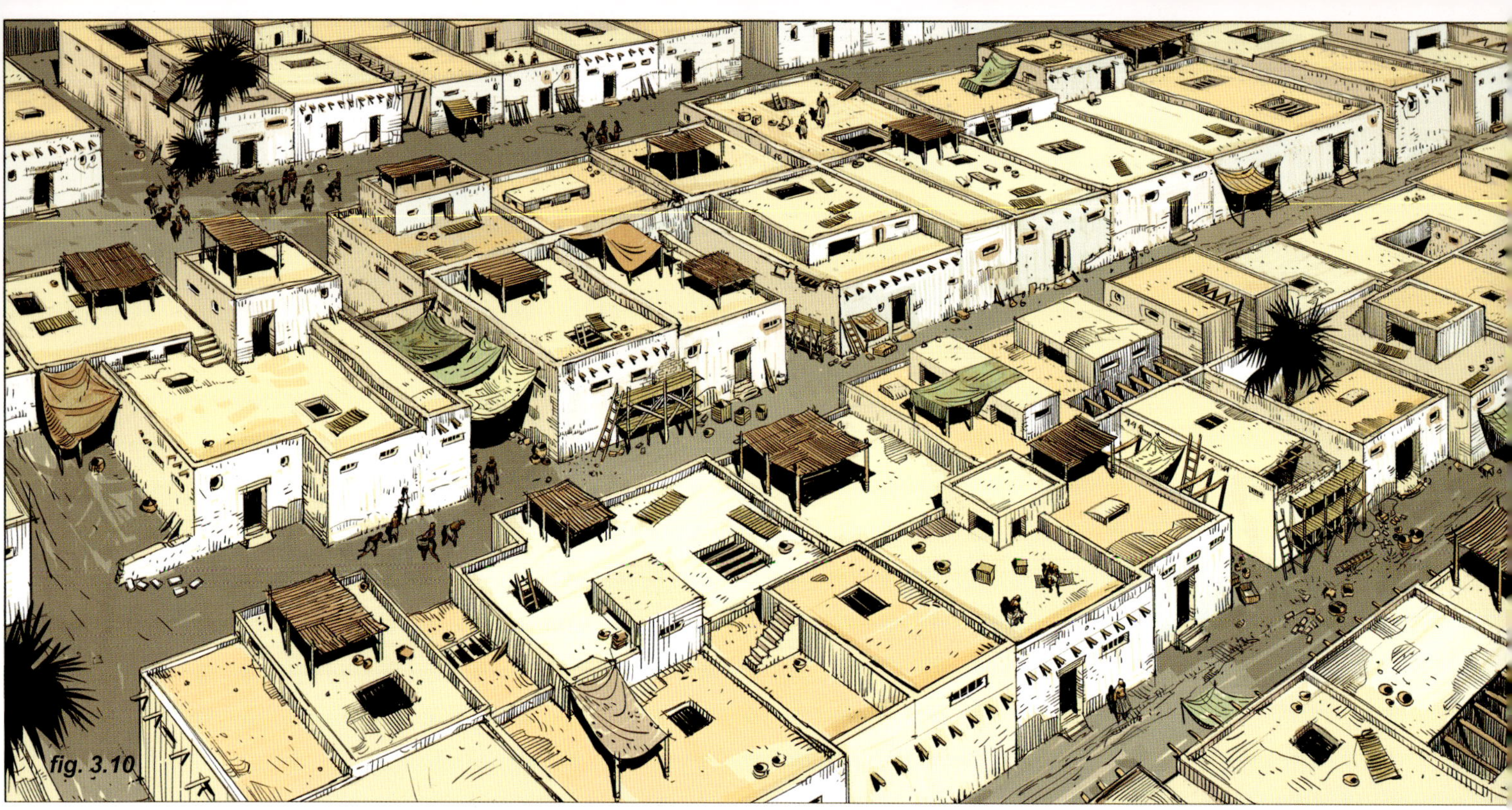

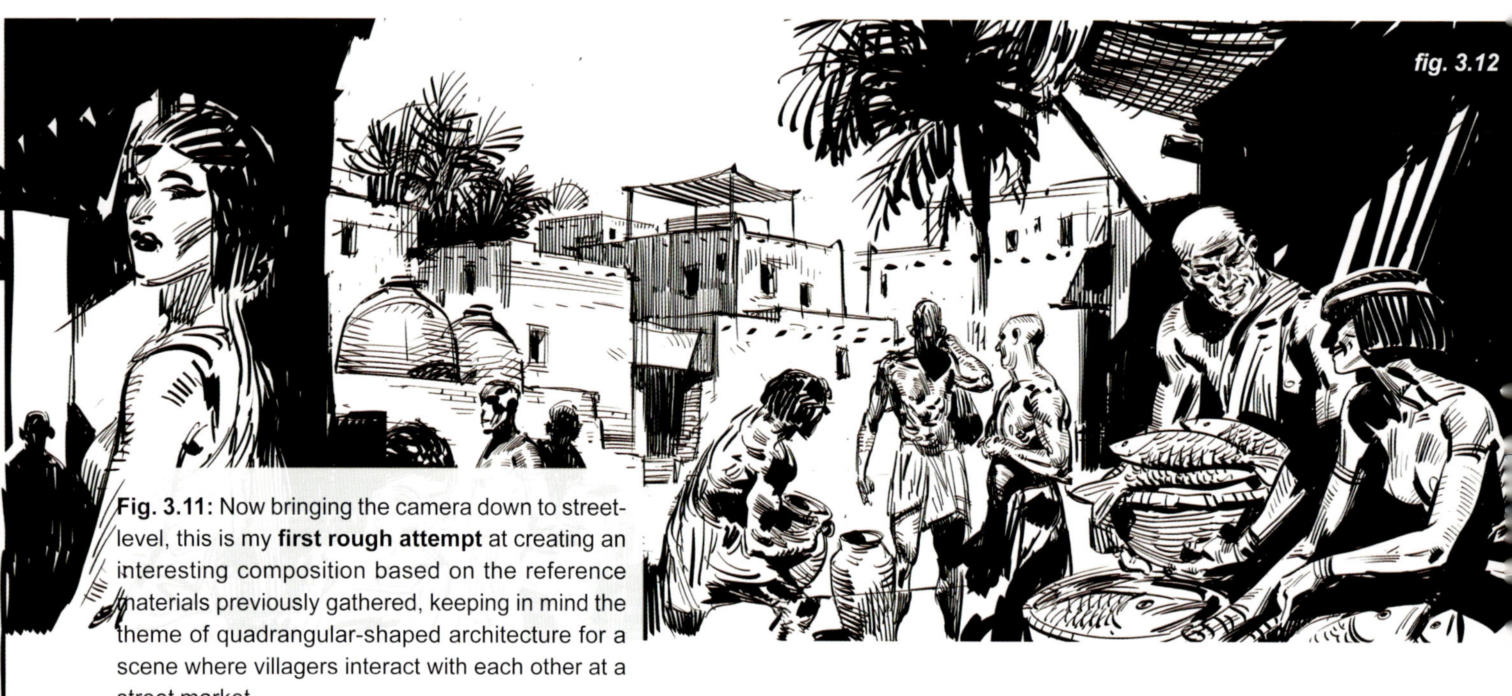

Fig. 3.10: This design shows what a neighborhood could look like when arranged in a grid with homes side by side and sharing walls. There is life in the streets, pets and farm animals with their owners, additional straw roofs and awnings to further protect from the sun, and staircases and ladders leading up to the roofs. Holes in the roofs and the high, narrow windows protected by wooden bars provide good ventilation to the houses. The constructions tend to have rectangular shapes, and some of them have scaffolding up against their walls while in the process of either being constructed or repaired.

Fig. 3.11: Now bringing the camera down to street-level, this is my **first rough attempt** at creating an interesting composition based on the reference materials previously gathered, keeping in mind the theme of quadrangular-shaped architecture for a scene where villagers interact with each other at a street market.

It works, but **overall feels generic** and does not make a proper **stylistic use of the elements** I could be playing with.

Fig. 3.12: So, I kept searching for a visual and graphic philosophy that would make this representation more unique.

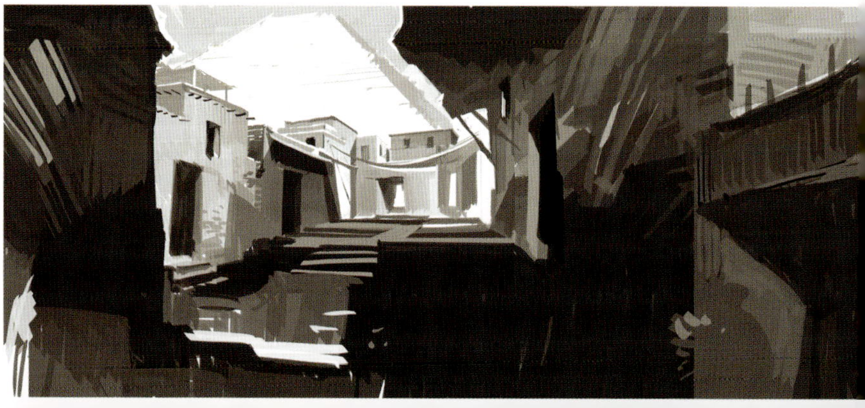

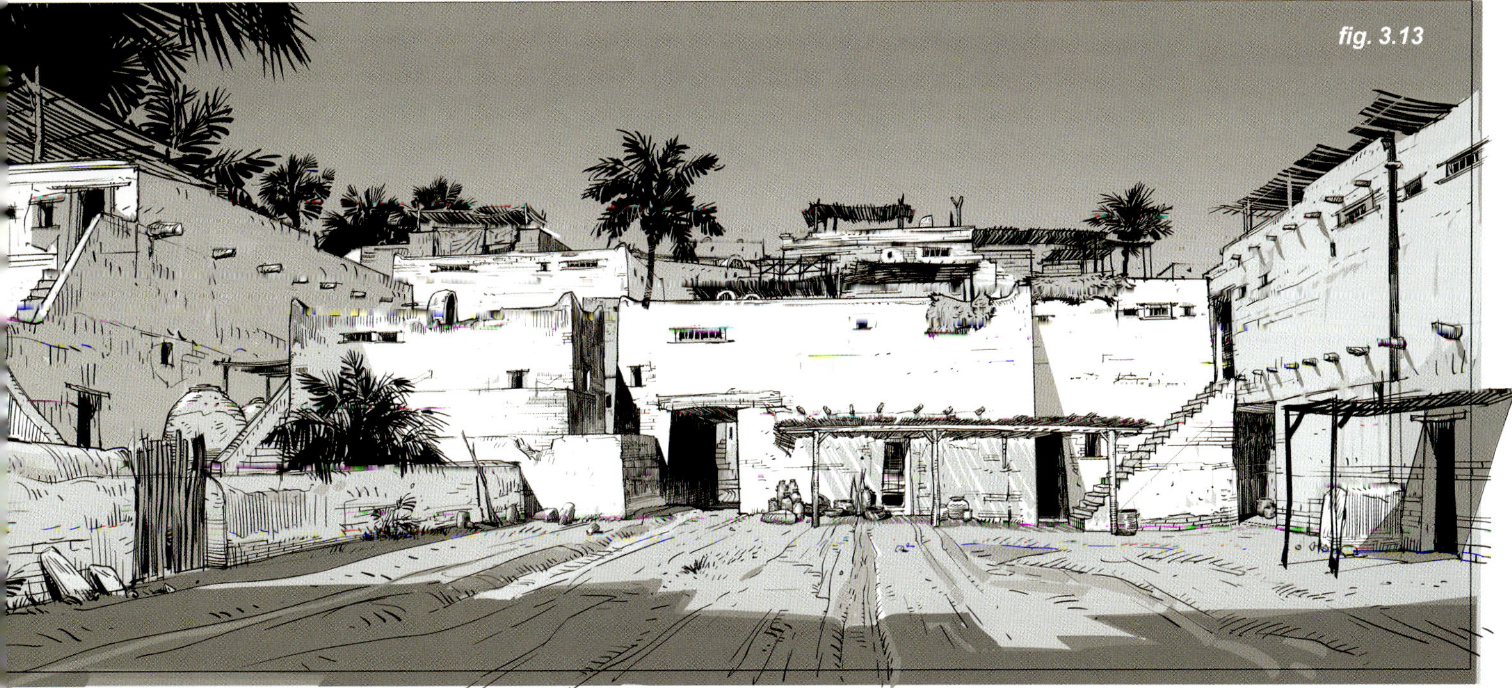

Fig. 3.13: The image above shows a choice in visual philosophy. Normally, when it comes to reading a line of lowercase text, we are able to do so even if only the top half of the words are visible, but not so much if we see only the lower half, because the top half of the letters are more easily identifiable. With a similar idea in mind, a decision was made to show just the tops of the buildings in the background, right above the ones in the foreground. The depiction of these flat roofs, with their flat reed canopies, concentrated at the top portion of the frame further emphasizes the squarish, geometrical look of these constructions. The same pattern has, in general, been applied to the façade of each building by showing the majority of windows and openings on the upper part of each house while leaving mostly flat wall in the lower portions. Altogether the result is a look with personality. It is a pattern that can be systematically applied throughout an entire frame, sequence, or movie, creating a unique style with a purpose.

Fig. 3.15: Diagrams of the above concept.

Fig. 3.14: The drawing below shows a more finished version of the previous village-square location with the addition of a marketplace in the foreground, where characters sell their goods at their stands in the shadows, away from the hot North African sun.

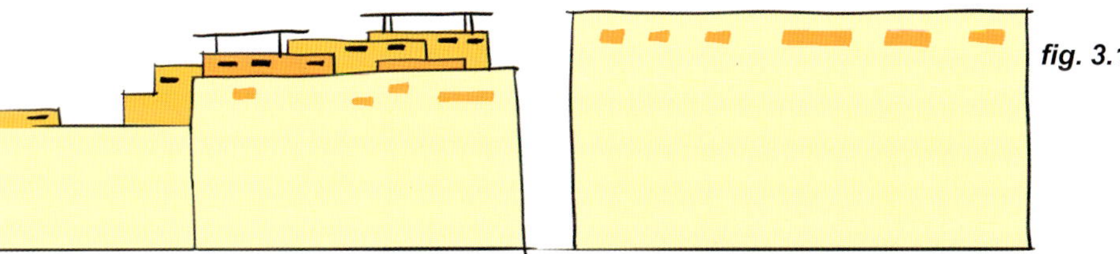

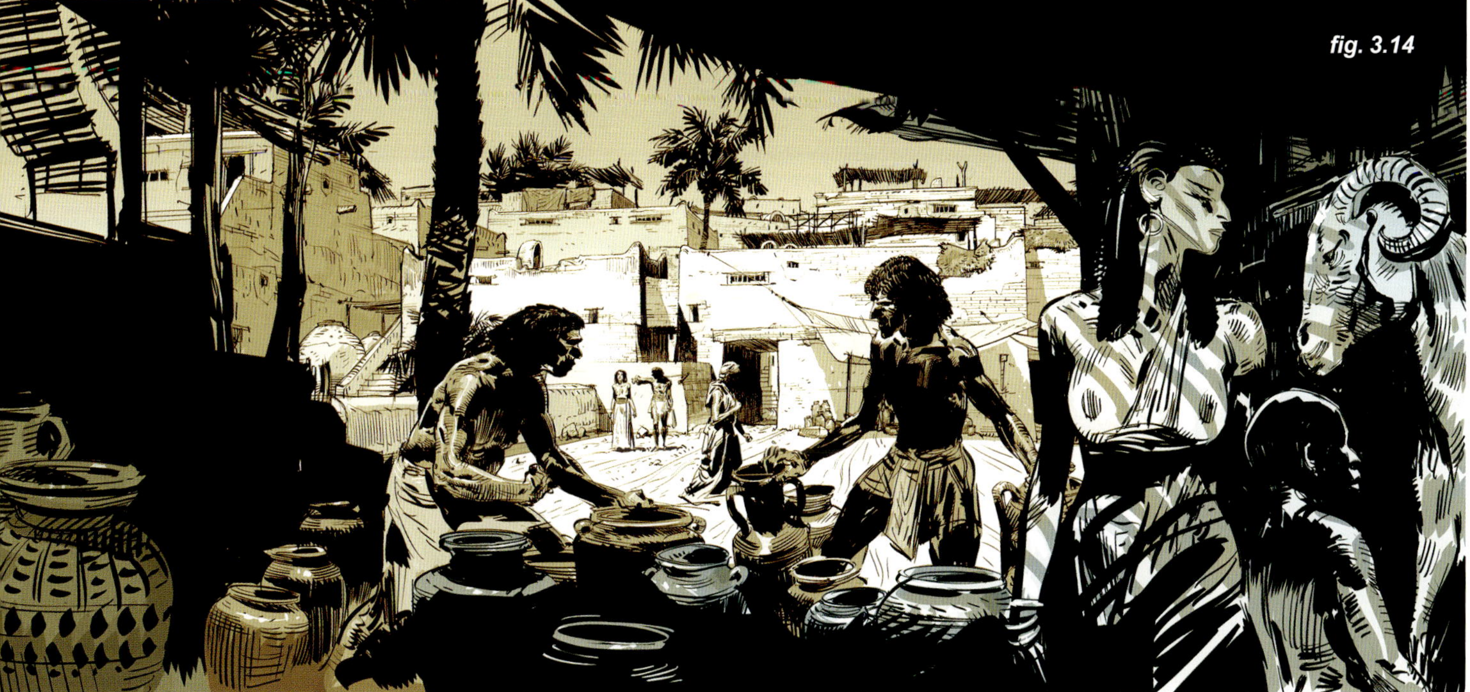

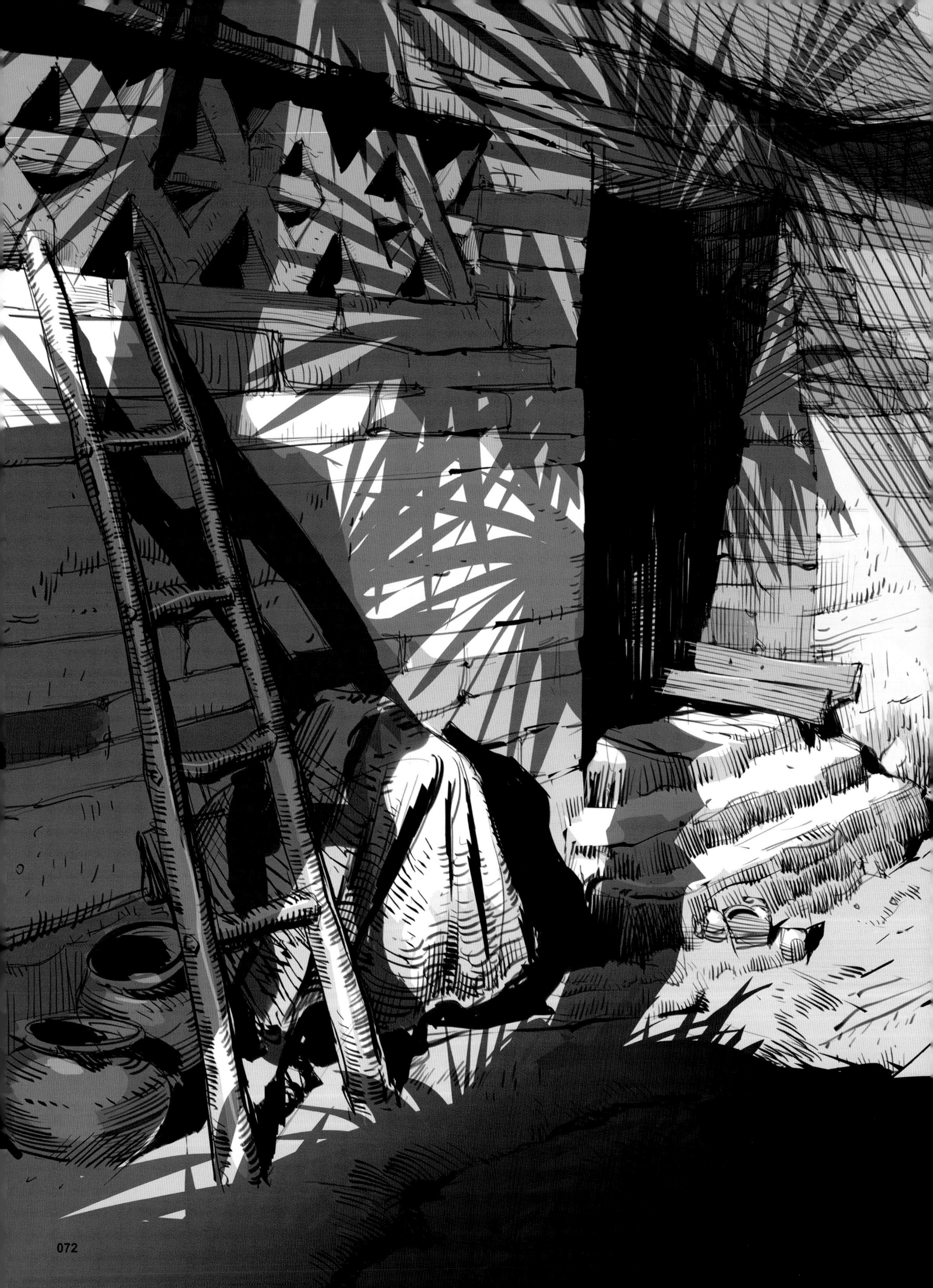

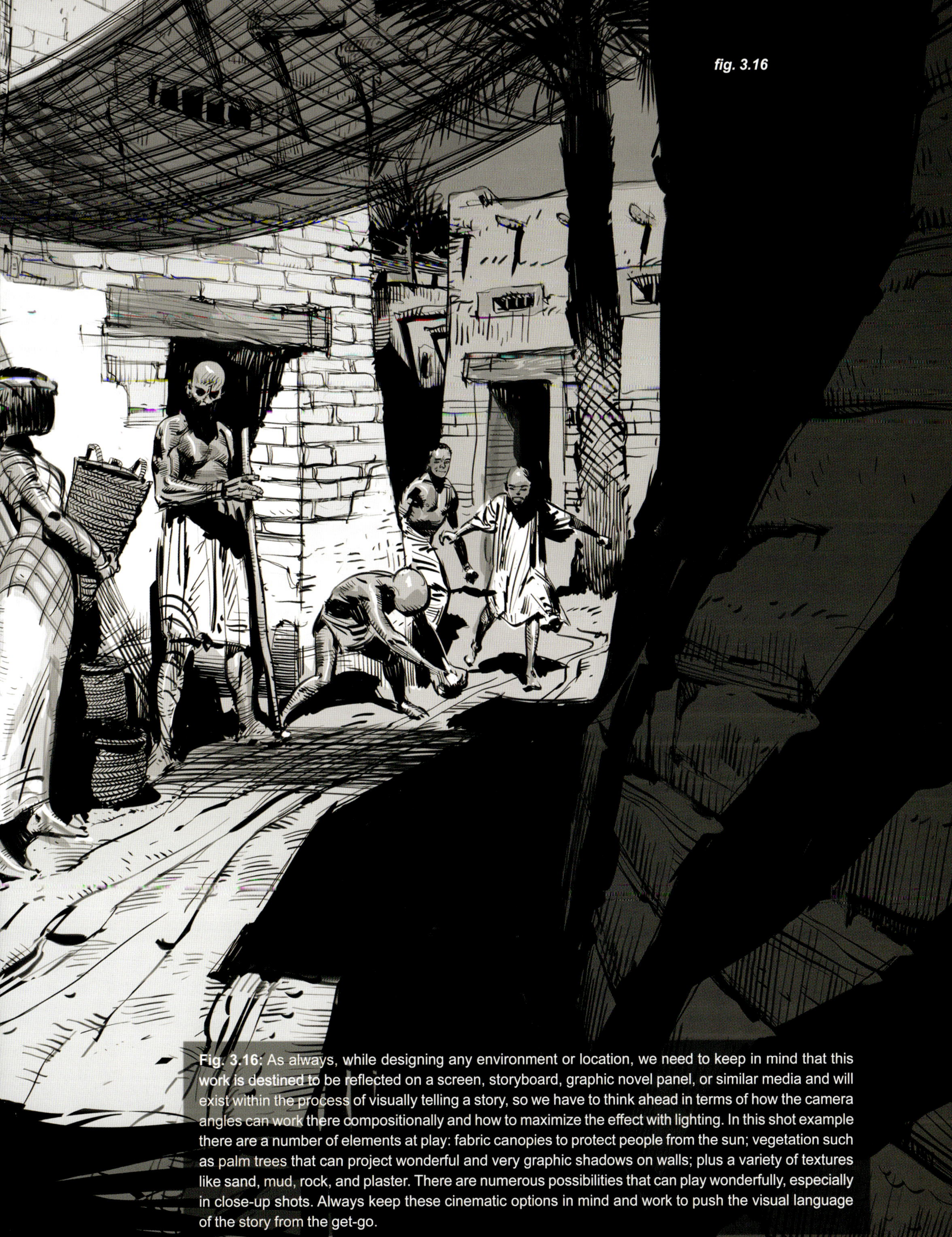

Fig. 3.16: As always, while designing any environment or location, we need to keep in mind that this work is destined to be reflected on a screen, storyboard, graphic novel panel, or similar media and will exist within the process of visually telling a story, so we have to think ahead in terms of how the camera angles can work there compositionally and how to maximize the effect with lighting. In this shot example there are a number of elements at play: fabric canopies to protect people from the sun; vegetation such as palm trees that can project wonderful and very graphic shadows on walls; plus a variety of textures like sand, mud, rock, and plaster. There are numerous possibilities that can play wonderfully, especially in close-up shots. Always keep these cinematic options in mind and work to push the visual language of the story from the get-go.

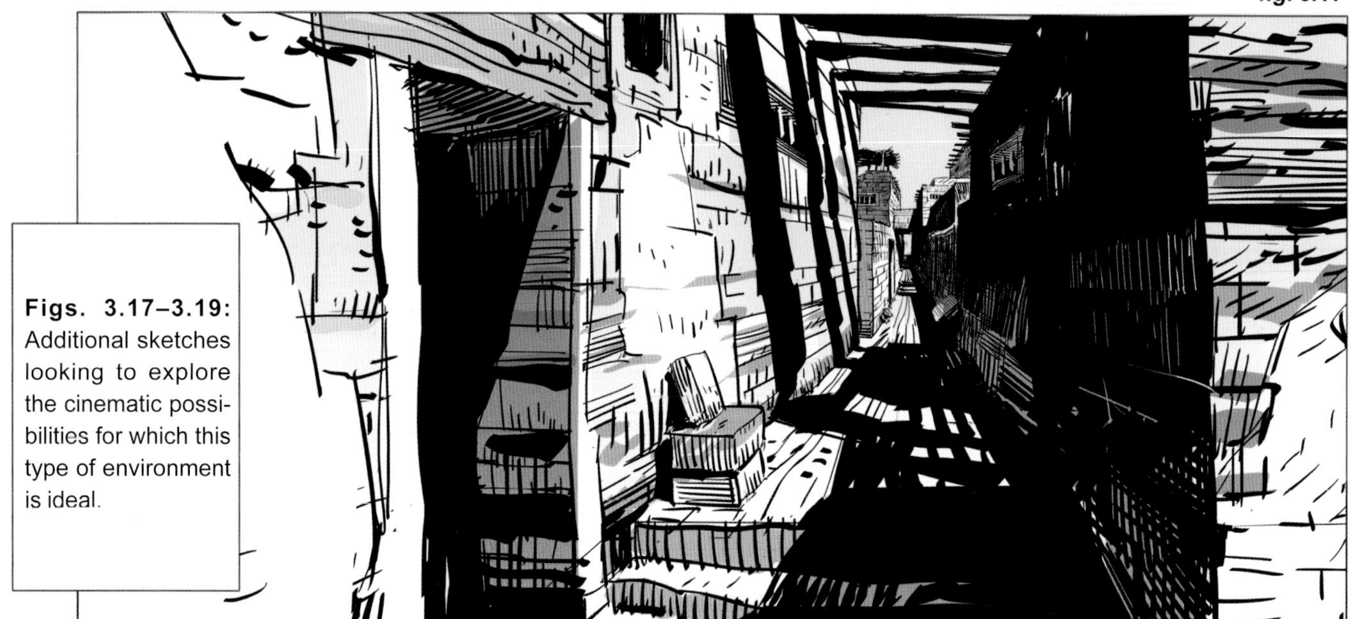

Figs. 3.17–3.19: Additional sketches looking to explore the cinematic possibilities for which this type of environment is ideal.

fig. 3.18

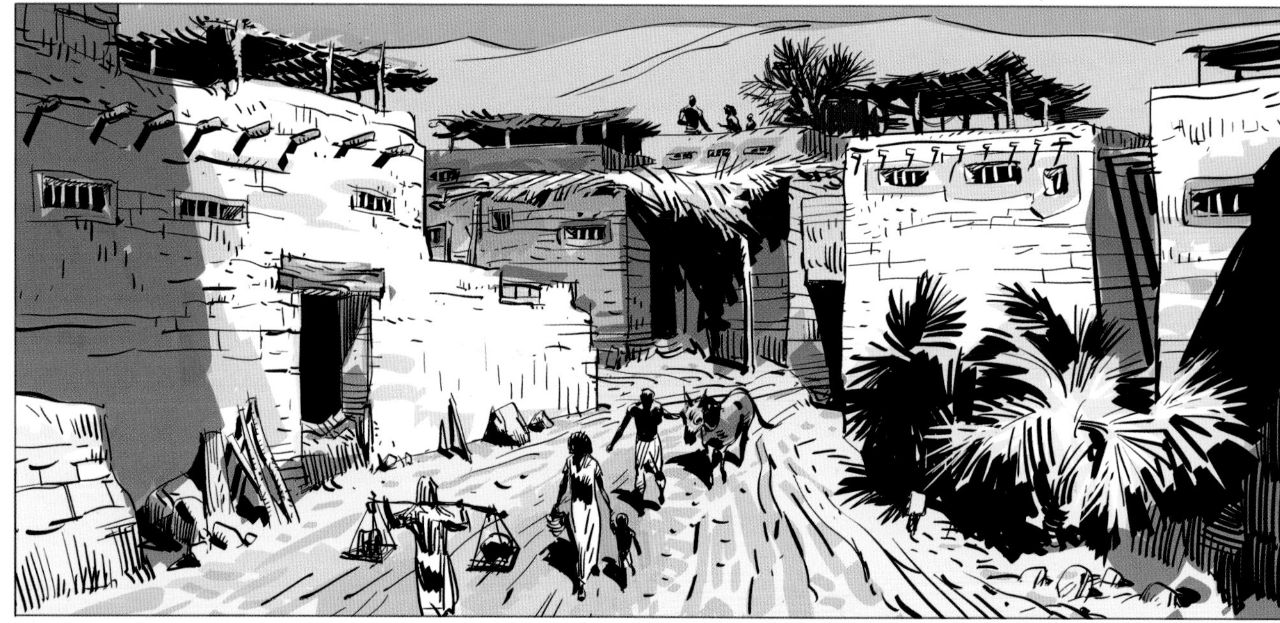

fig. 3.19

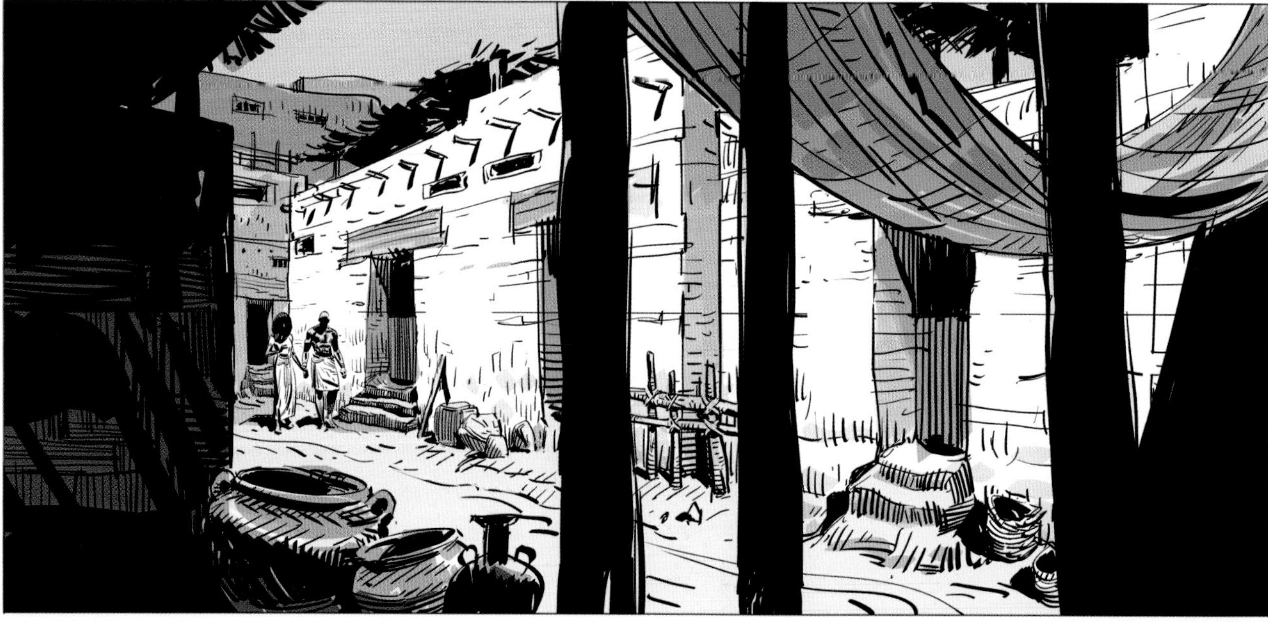

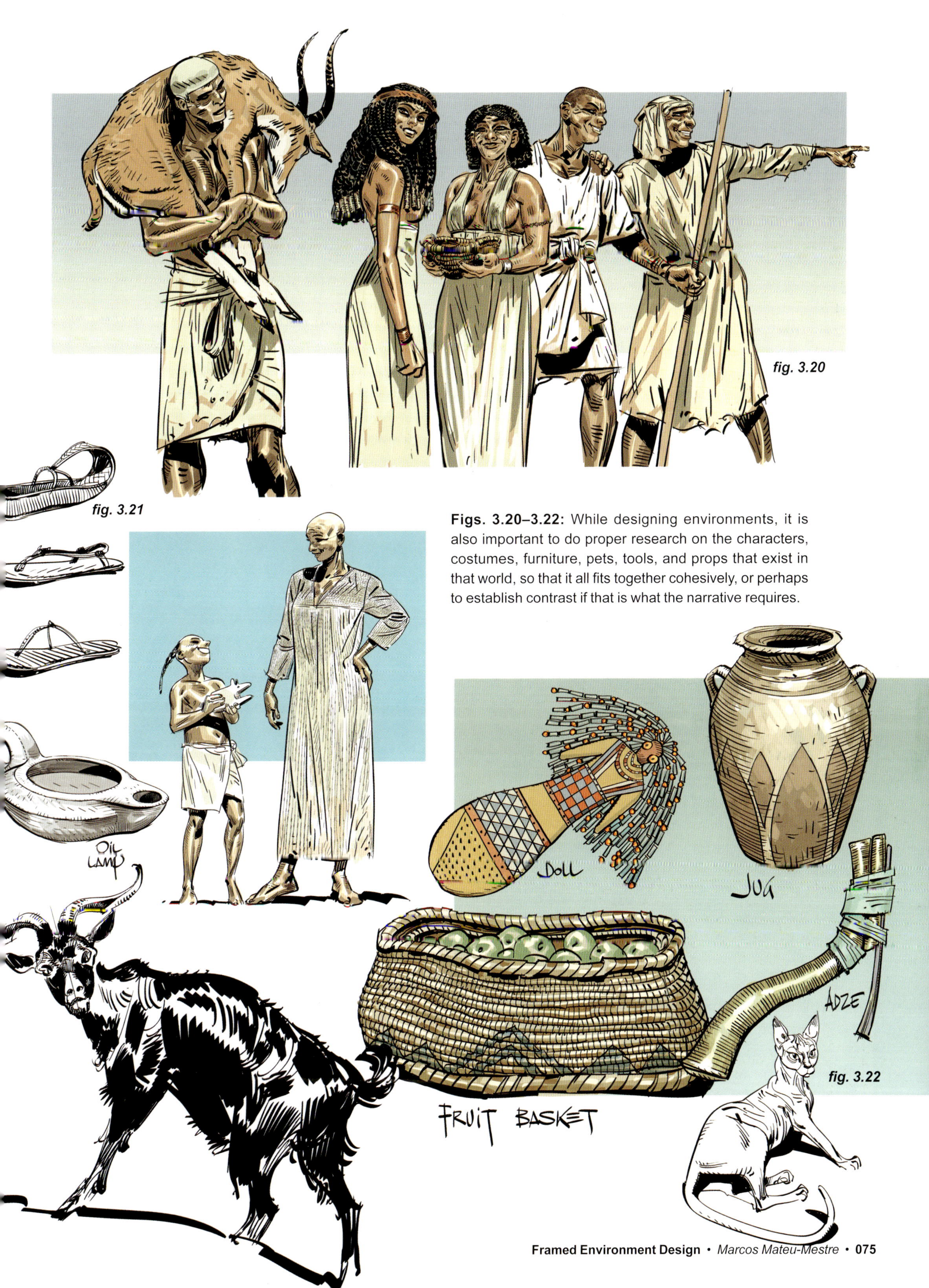

Figs. 3.20–3.22: While designing environments, it is also important to do proper research on the characters, costumes, furniture, pets, tools, and props that exist in that world, so that it all fits together cohesively, or perhaps to establish contrast if that is what the narrative requires.

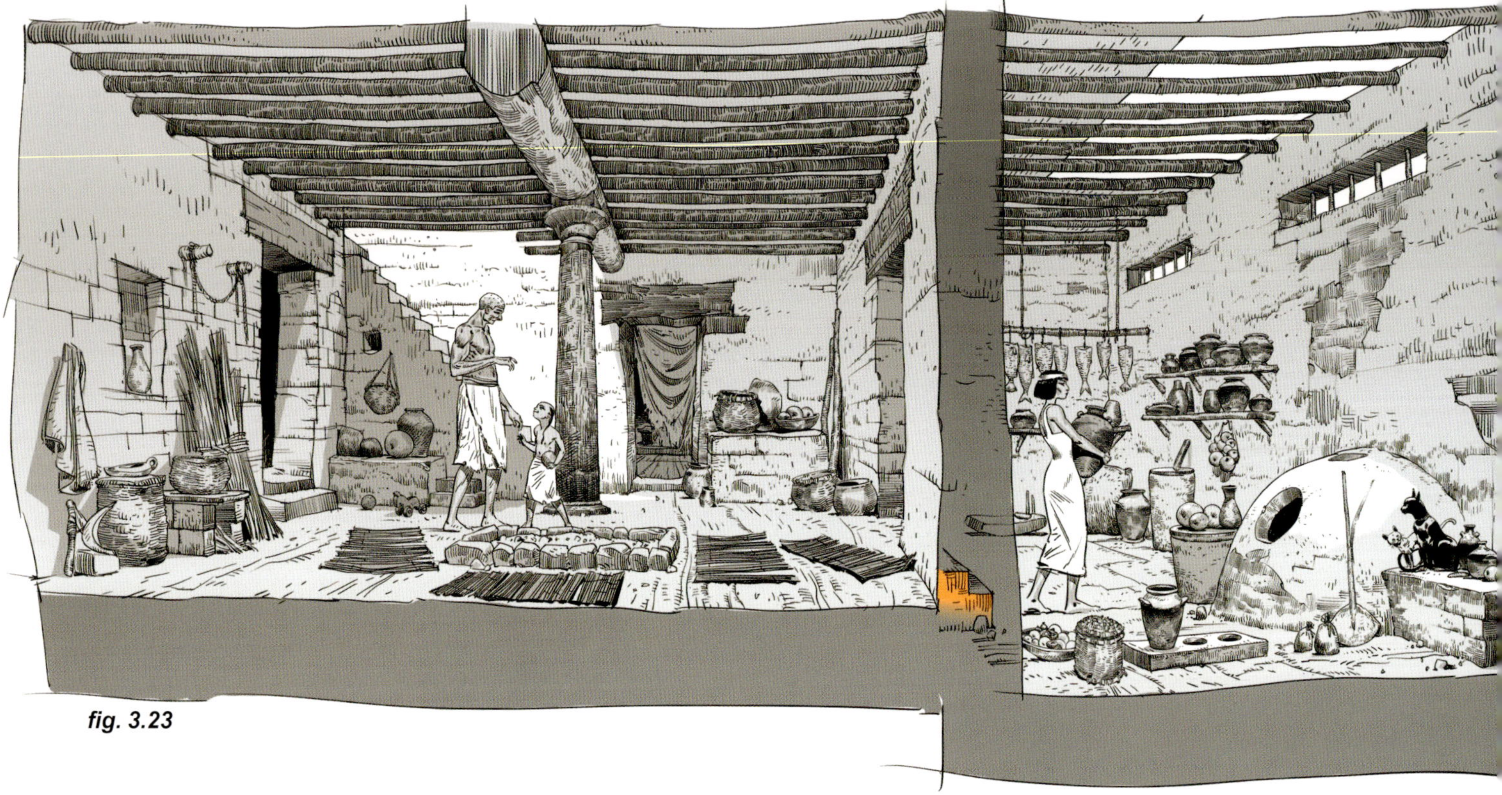

Fig. 3.23: This cross section of a worker's house interior shows two connected spaces, the central main room and the kitchen, which is accessed by going down two steps (in orange) from the main level. To make this simple environment feel lived-in, there are items scattered around, like containers (jars, straw bags), reed mats on the dusty floor to sit on, a bordered area in the center to set up a fire, a staircase up to the roof, an oven in the kitchen, some basic shelves, and baskets with fruits and cooking ingredients. Bundles of straw against the far wall are leftover from a recent patch-up job on the roof.

Fig. 3.24: This **grayscale lighting tonal** uses light coming through openings in the kitchen ceiling and from the rooftop access atop the interior staircase. This light bounces back up in the dusty air, creating a glaring effect in certain areas, adding a realistic texture to this hot location. (See Chapter 4 of *Framed Drawing Techniques* for the grayscale rendering process.)

Figs. 3.25, 3.26: Details of the same scene.

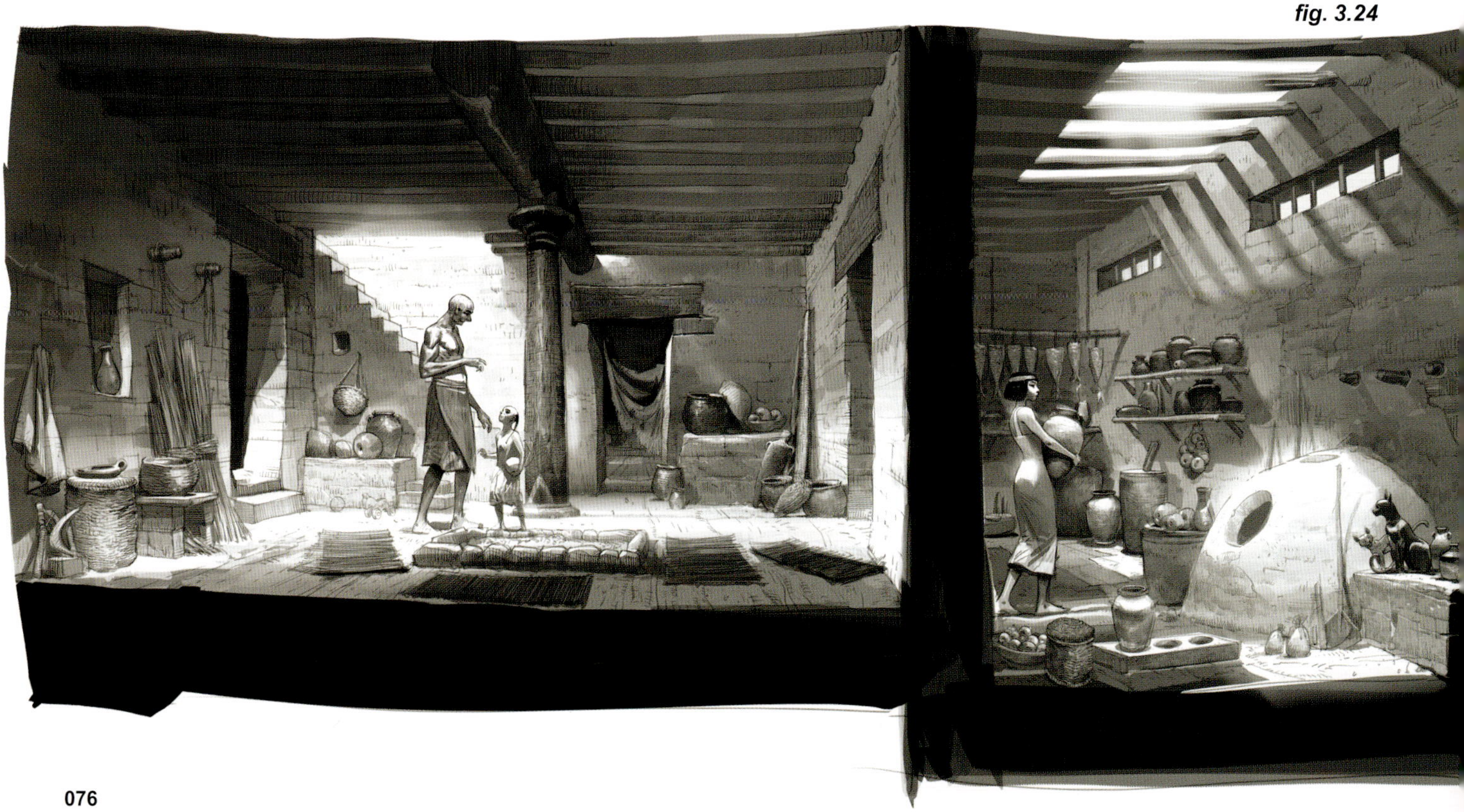

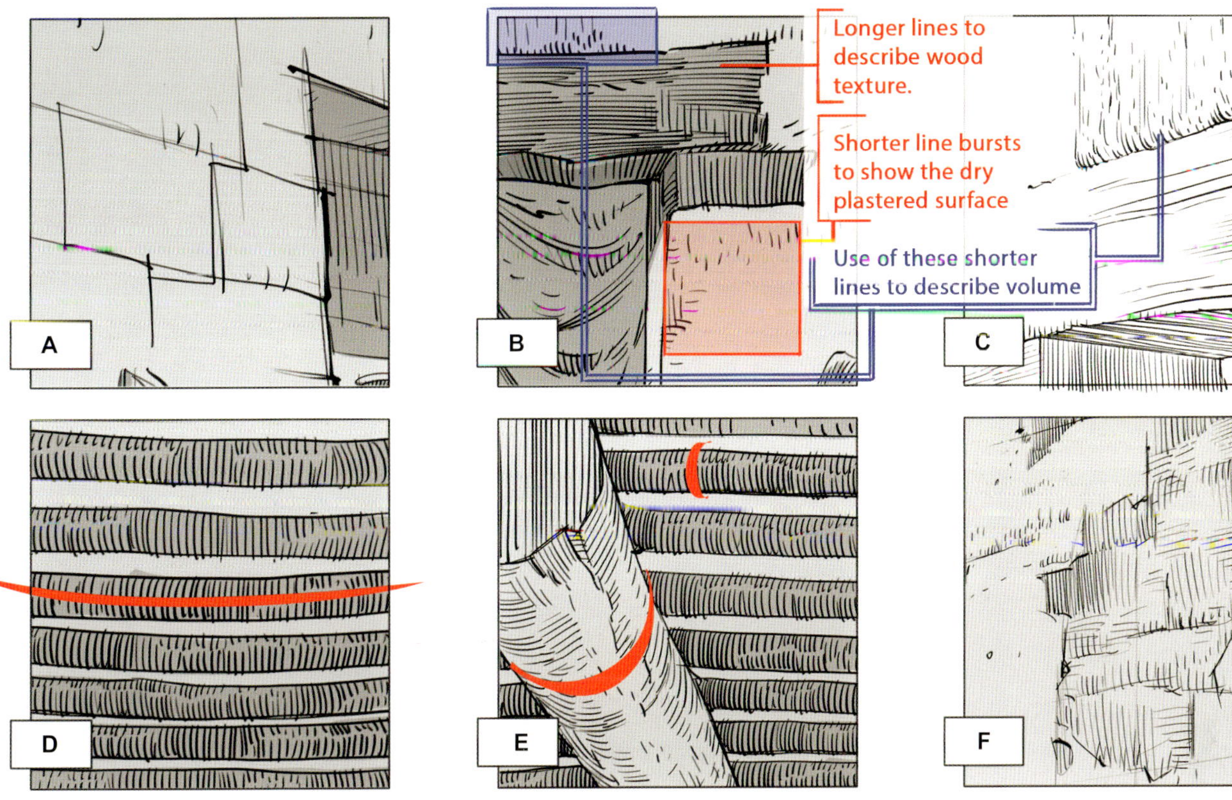

The above magnified details out of fig. 3.23 show (A) how to indicate brick texture in a simple way; (B and C) different line techniques to demonstrate types of construction materials, like wood or plaster; (D) the slightly warped beams under the weight of the roof to show a level of precariousness and the passage of time; (E) a sense of volume in elements like the round beams with the use of lines; and (F) the plaster covering the mud bricks being chipped and damaged in certain areas.

These elements help inform the audience of more than just a pure design or description of a space but also as a place where family life exists and evolves.

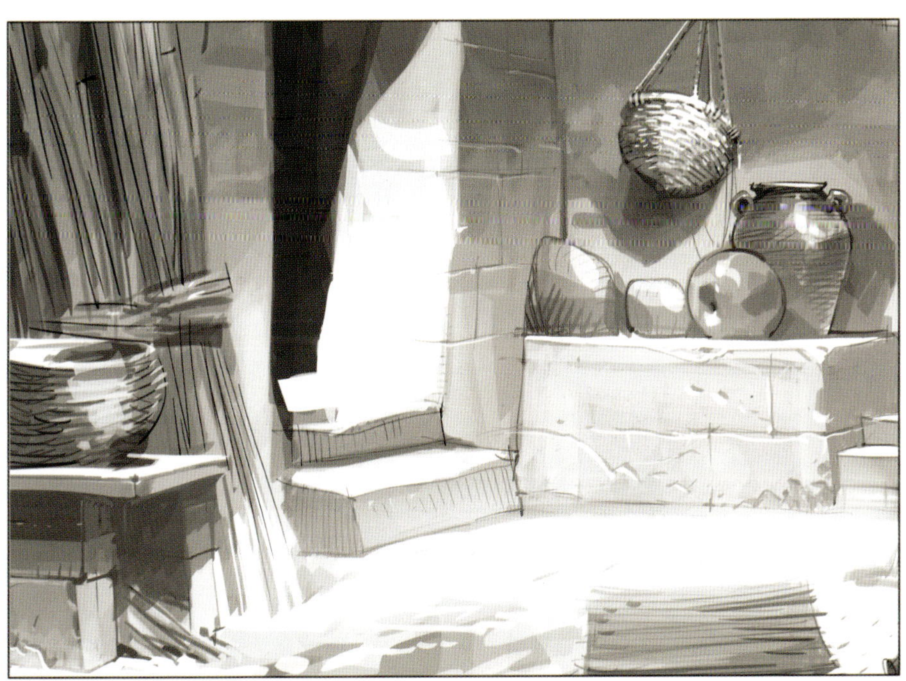

fig. 3.25

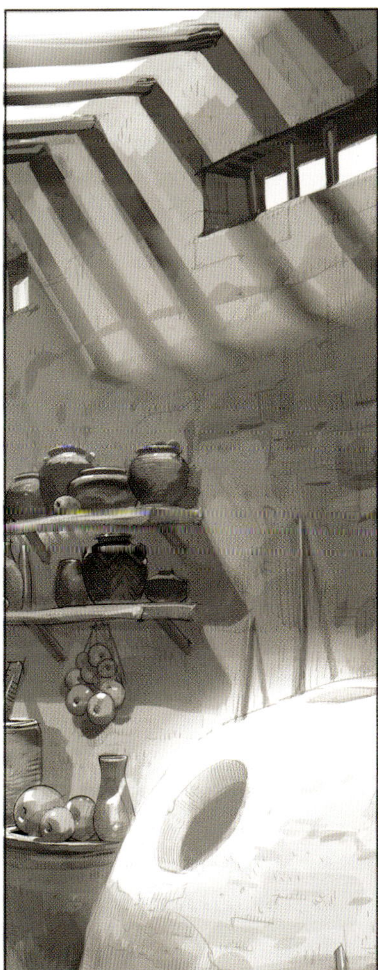

fig. 3.26

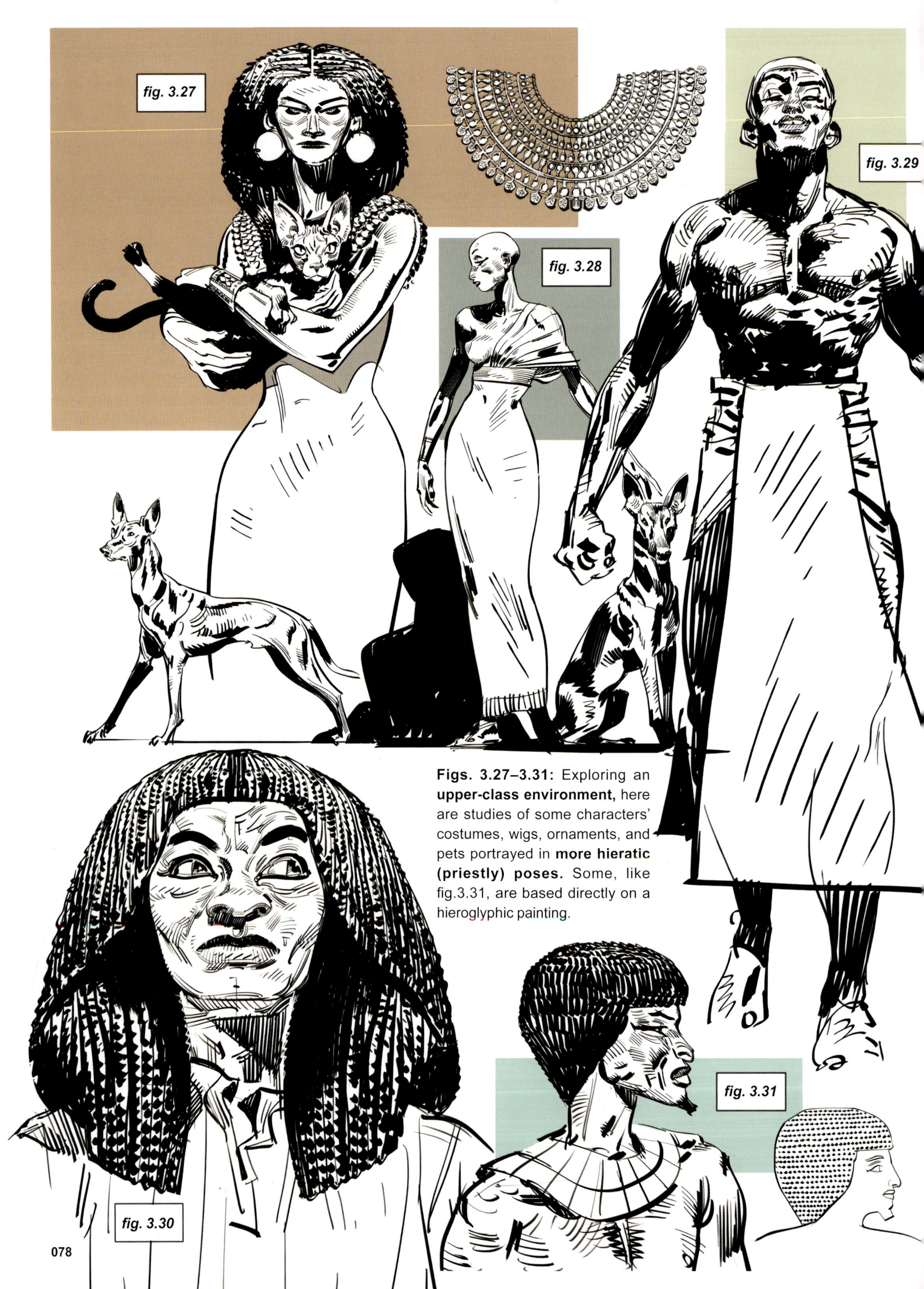

Figs. 3.27–3.31: Exploring an **upper-class environment,** here are studies of some characters' costumes, wigs, ornaments, and pets portrayed in **more hieratic (priestly) poses.** Some, like fig.3.31, are based directly on a hieroglyphic painting.

Fig. 3.32: Upper-class homes were located in the higher-elevation parts of town. Larger in size, more comfortable, and separated from the surrounding houses (emphasizing a sense of independence and power), they still adhered to this overall rectangular design in their modules, normally accommodating a pool and a garden. Some elements that make this location distinctive are: bigger size, additional floors (which could also be found sometimes in more simple constructions), servants working around the silos, a garden, and farm animals. All of this contributes to a feeling of a self-sufficient life in the senior house.

Fig. 3.33: Here is the **top-down plan view (floor plan),** detailing the areas where the action will take place. This sense of orientation and geography will be indispensable when blocking the scenes (choreographing the movement of the performers and camera). Also, establishing the four cardinal points (north, south, east, west) communicates the **angle of the sunlight** at any given time of day.

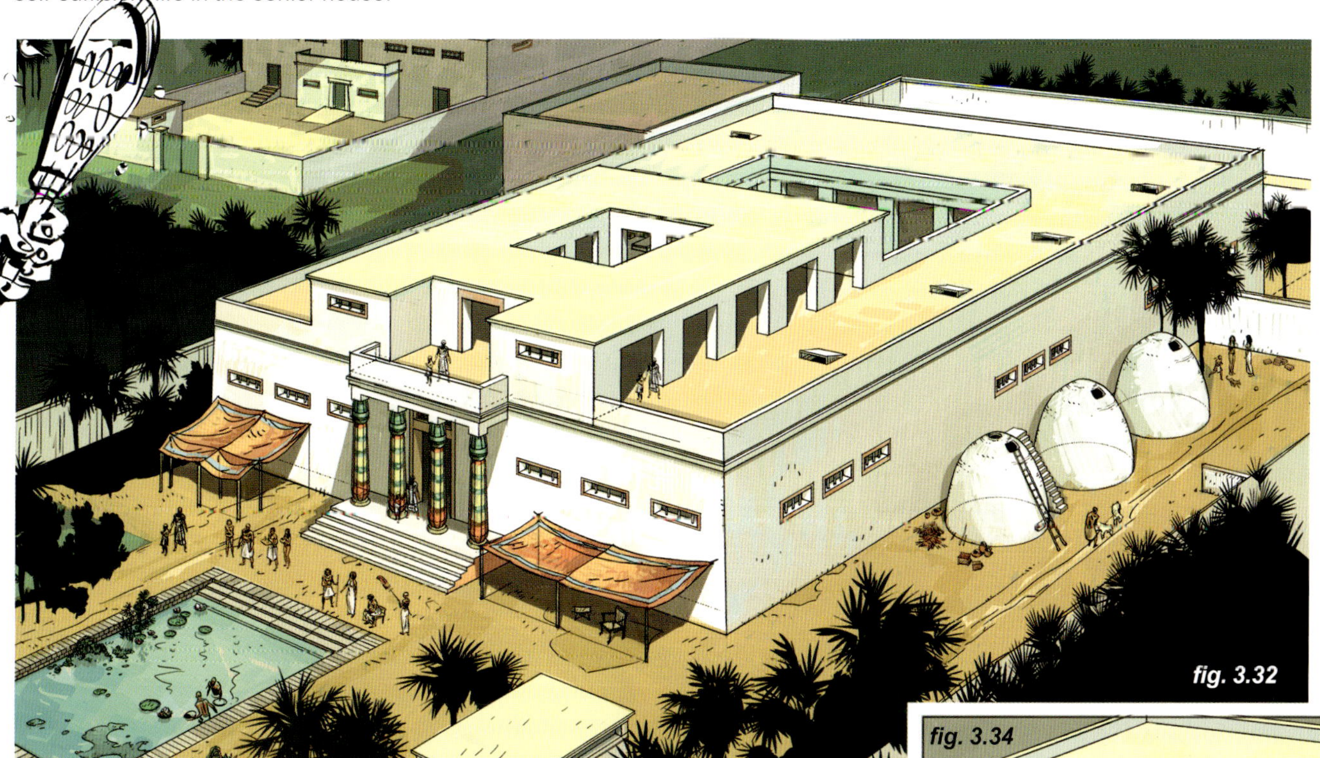

fig. 3.32

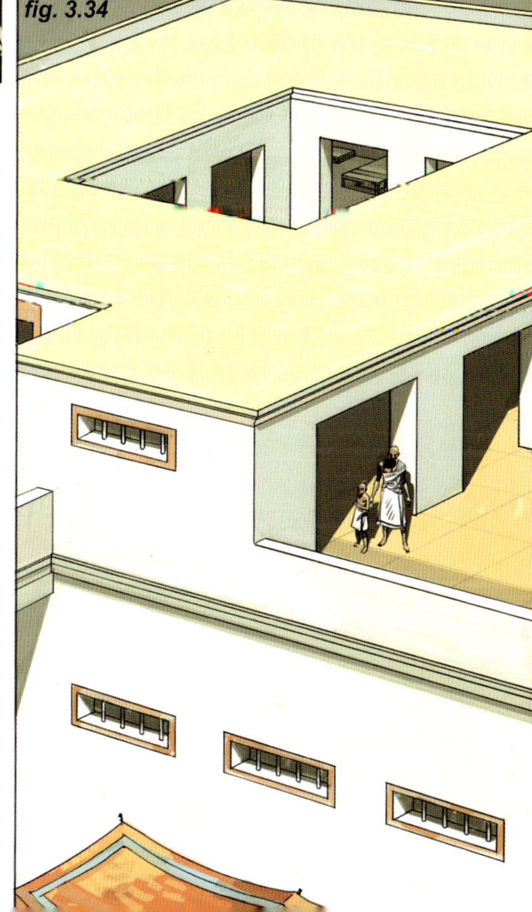

fig. 3.34

fig. 3.33

USING LINE QUALITY TO HELP DEFINE CHARACTER

Fig. 3.34: The chosen drawing technique adds to the overall feeling of cleanliness, structure, order, and grooming by using clean, straight lines most of the time, with just a limited amount of texture on the walls to indicate some level of the organic nature of the materials. This communicates the amount of care, wealth, and power of the family that lives there.

Inclusion of characters in the designs from the very early stages establishes a proper sense of scale.

Figs. 3.35, 3.36: Moving to an interior view, the central patio would be the hub of everyday life in the house. These sketches are based on reference research, trying out different solutions for size, proportion, number of floors visible from that area, design and type of columns that support the structure, and use or not of canopies and fabrics that help create interesting shadows or pockets of light, always considering how all these visual elements will play within the context of the story—bright vs. dark, opulent vs. moderate, etc.

fig. 3.35

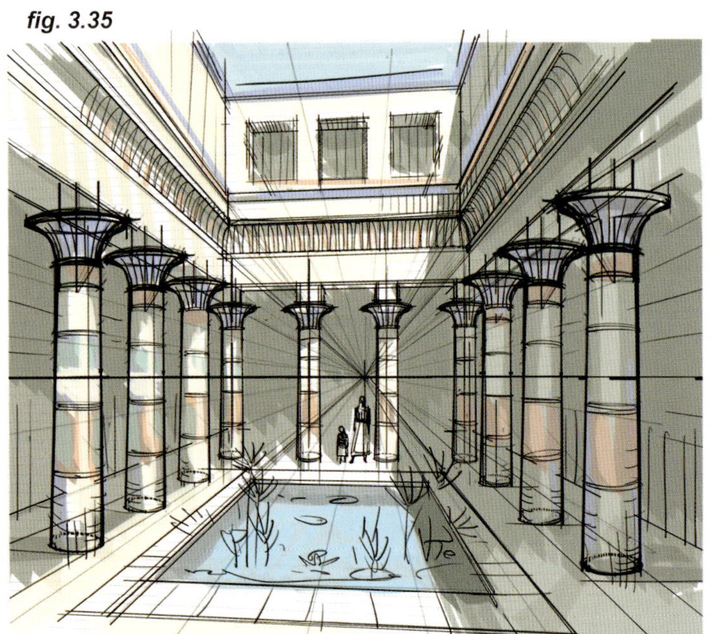

fig. 3.36

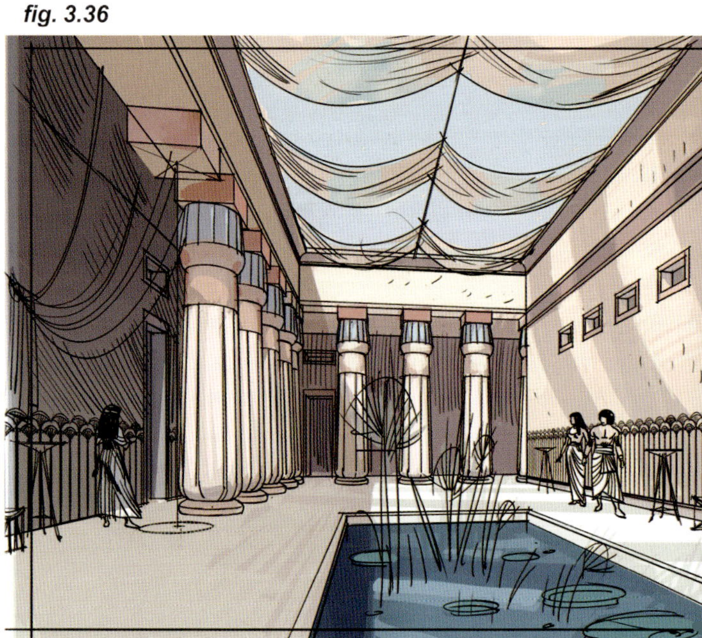

Fig. 3.37: Items, props, and details that might be found there that could be integrated into the general environment.

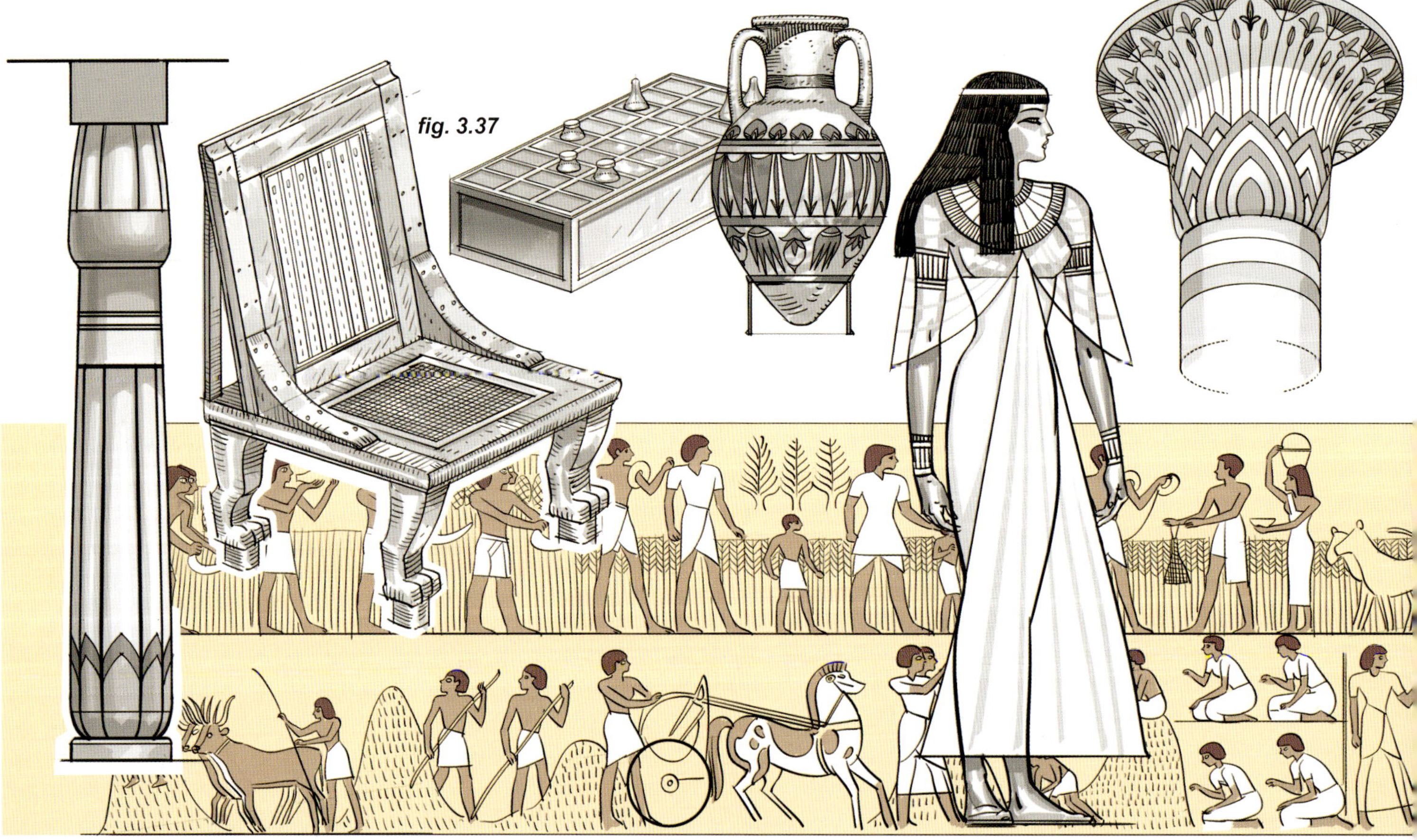

fig. 3.37

Fig. 3.38: Next, it is time to take a first pass at the location while keeping in mind the tone of the story, the character of the people living in it, and the context of this moment in the narrative. If there is a plan for some "visual fireworks" later in the story at another location that needs to be even more impressive, like a grand finale at a colossal temple that is one of the most incredible examples of architecture ever created, then at this point, and within the magnitude of this noble house, it is prudent to hold back a bit.

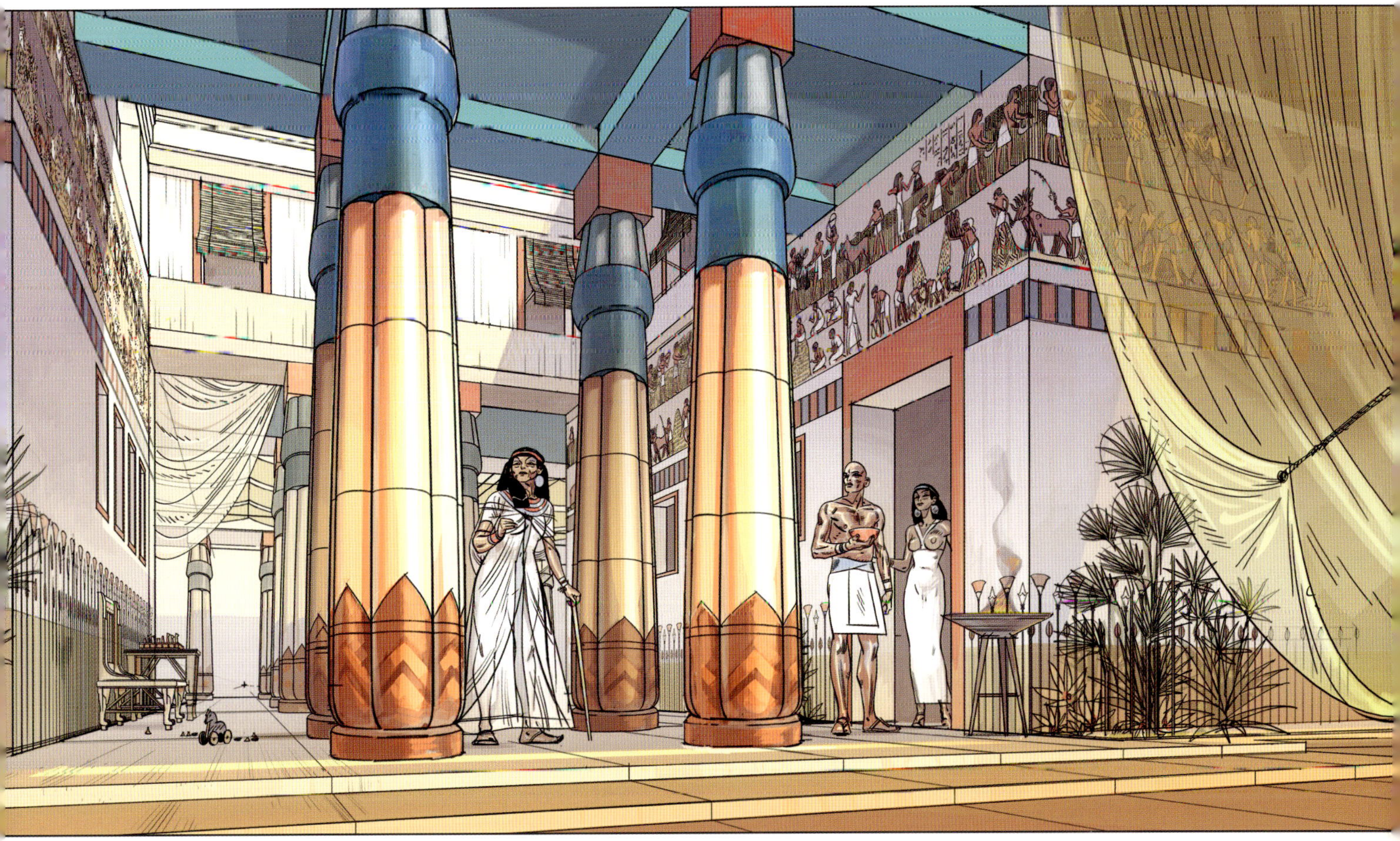

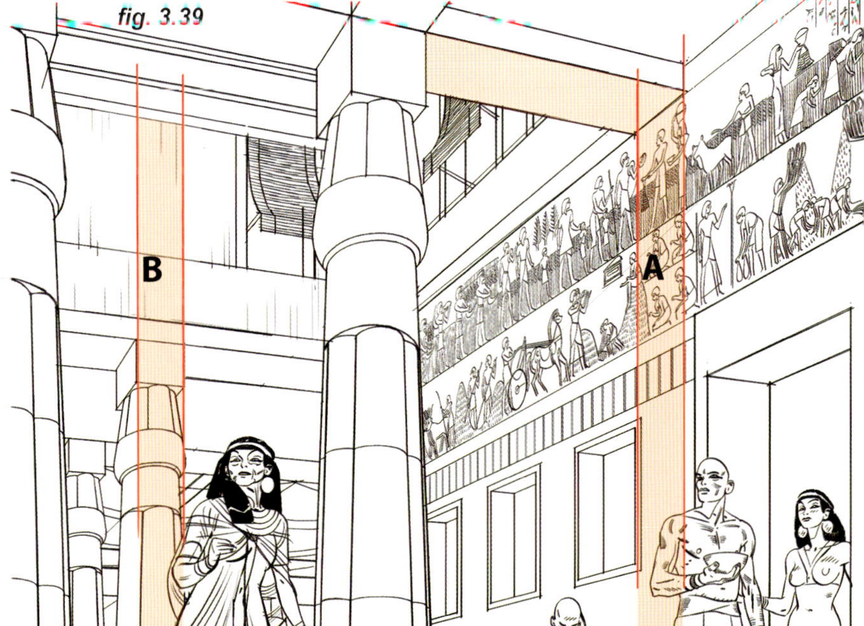

To keep it slightly less over-the-top, the decision was made here to use the papyrus bud design for the columns instead of the bell capital or palm capital, as seen in fig. 3.37. This shot requires a **more collected feel,** so the papyrus bud design seems to better project that.

As far as ornamental elements, the **murals** representing reeds throughout the lower part of the walls were originally designed as a taller pattern, but then they were shortened, as they might **interfere** with the audience reading the characters and actions well. Best to avoid the potential for a tall reed pattern to visually overwhelm, or "drown" if you will, the drama of a scene or the characters in it.

Fig. 3.39: Architecturally, notice that there are no openings (doors, windows) right underneath the main beam **(A),** as it would be supported by a vertical column or a solid part of the structure all the way down. This principle applies going upward as well **(B),** as one column would possibly support another one located directly above it (also discussed on page 051).

Hieroglyphic murals have also been included as powerful accents within the context of an overall more muted general color scheme. Other elements here, like big drapes, furniture, and reeds, can provide excellent opportunities to be used as interesting framing and cinematic devices, as we will explore more later.

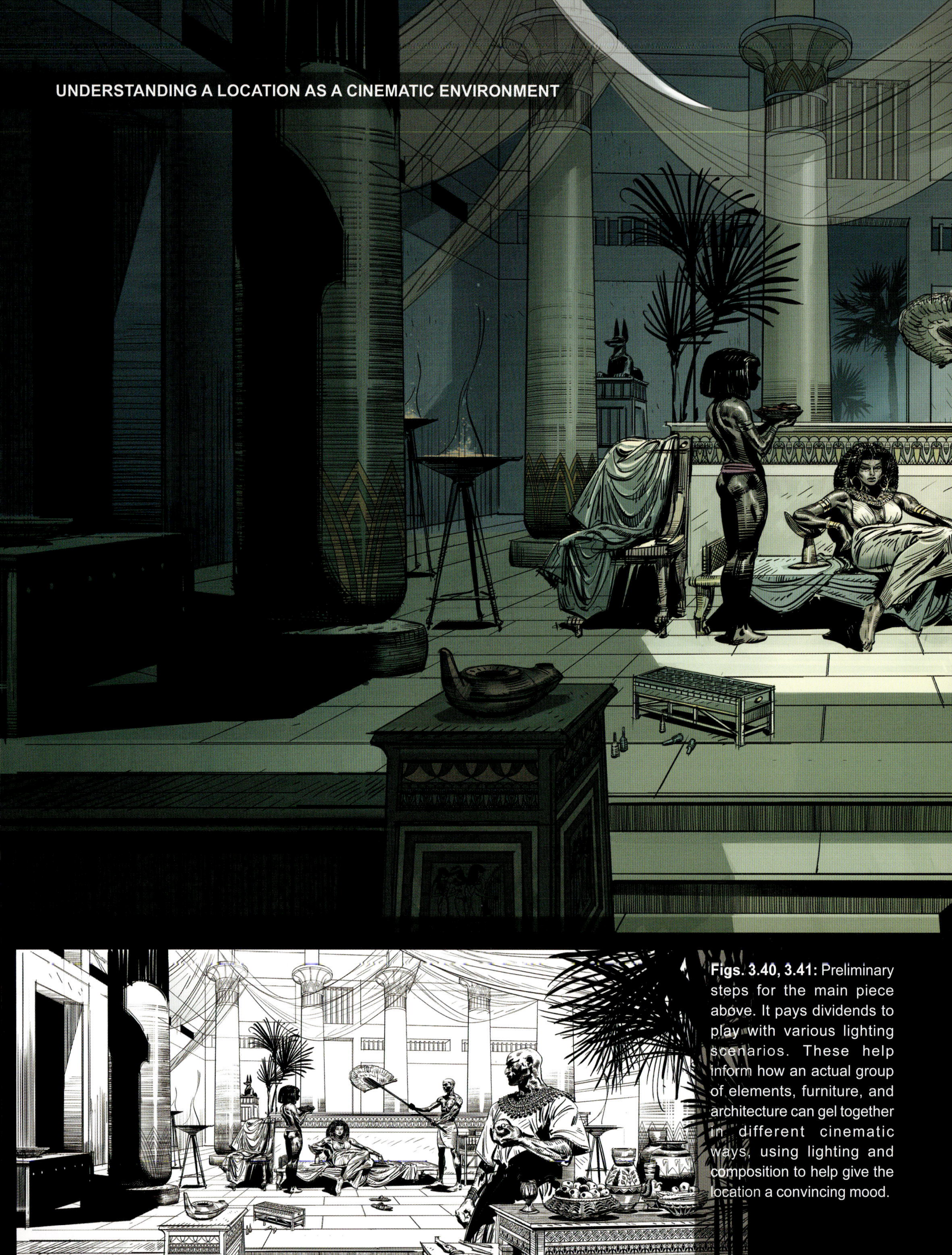

Figs. 3.40, 3.41: Preliminary steps for the main piece above. It pays dividends to play with various lighting scenarios. These help inform how an actual group of elements, furniture, and architecture can gel together in different cinematic ways, using lighting and composition to help give the location a convincing mood.

fig. 3.40

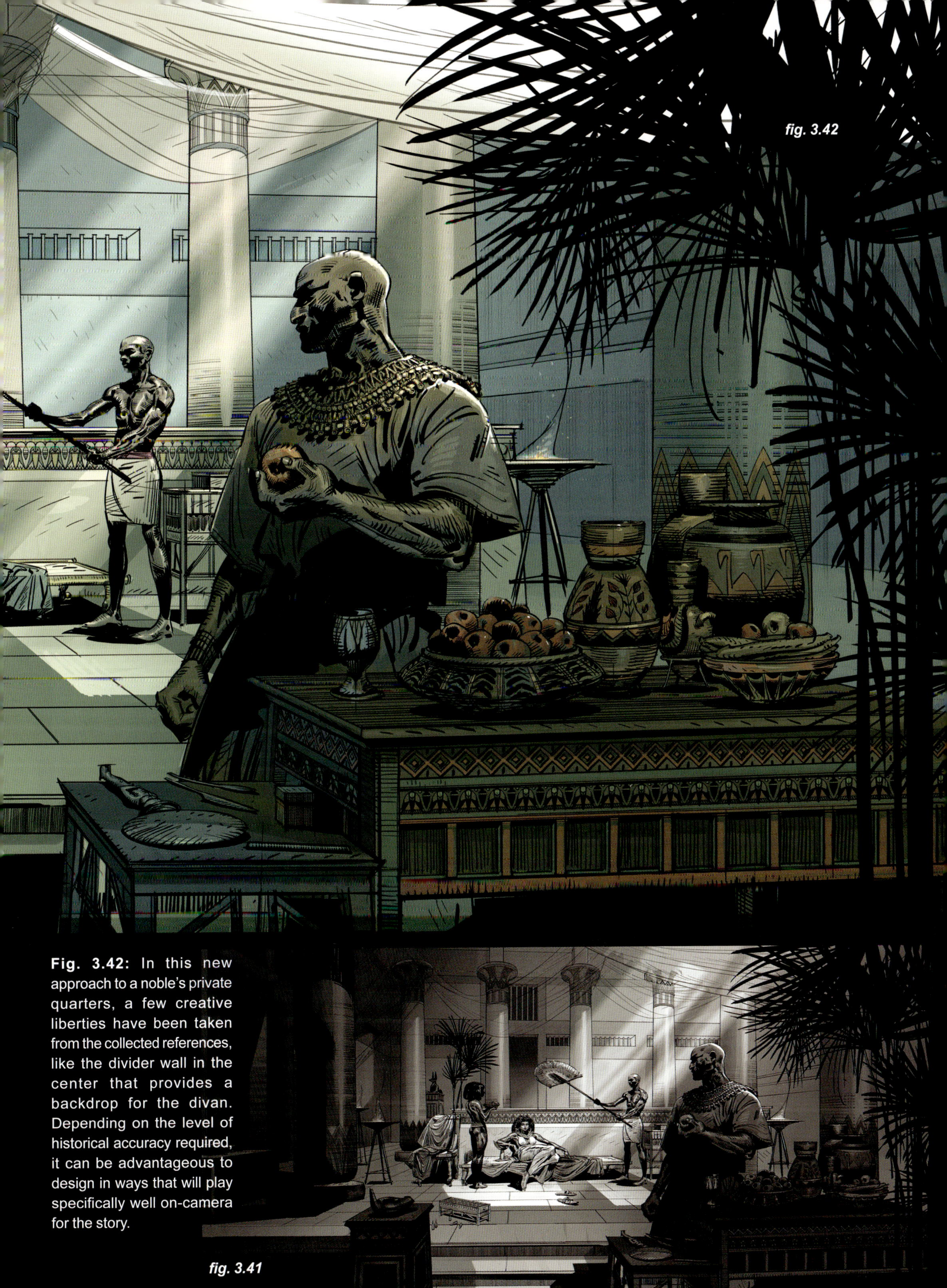

Fig. 3.42: In this new approach to a noble's private quarters, a few creative liberties have been taken from the collected references, like the divider wall in the center that provides a backdrop for the divan. Depending on the level of historical accuracy required, it can be advantageous to design in ways that will play specifically well on-camera for the story.

To **visualize a set's cinematic potential,** think about how its space works and how the camera might frame areas from different angles to make the shots visually interesting, perhaps featuring foreground, mid-ground, and background elements that could help the environment appear more rich and complex, together with a good sense of lighting solutions.

Fig. 3.43: This schematic of the **courtyard design** from page 081 shows how to have **a blocky and very basic version of the location in mind** while continuing to refine the design.

Fig. 3.44: Regarding **lighting**, fig. 3.33 on page 079 already included a compass rose, which indicates that the house's façade points west-northwest, and its back points east-southeast.

Knowing the direction of the sun is key in order to light a location and its surroundings in a realistic way. Because the sun follows an east-to-west path during the day, and Egypt is in the northern hemisphere, the sunlight is always slightly angled from the south. This informs which walls of the building are in light or shadow during the day. This can be important because it helps the audience make sense of the visual and geographical links between different areas and locations in the story, through the direction of the sun and its projected lights and shadows. (Relates to "Establishing Geography on Paper," page 011.)

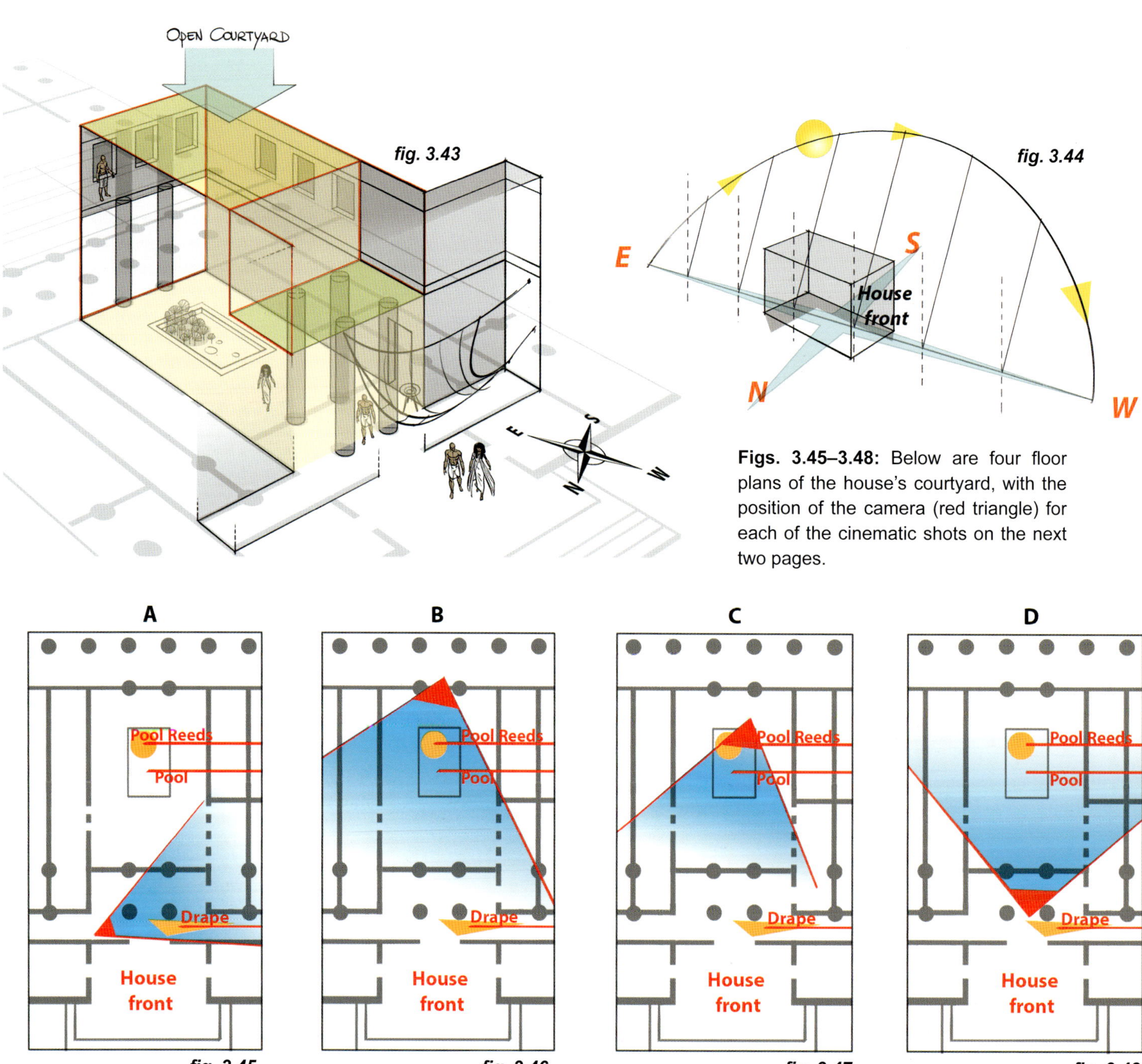

Figs. 3.45–3.48: Below are four floor plans of the house's courtyard, with the position of the camera (red triangle) for each of the cinematic shots on the next two pages.

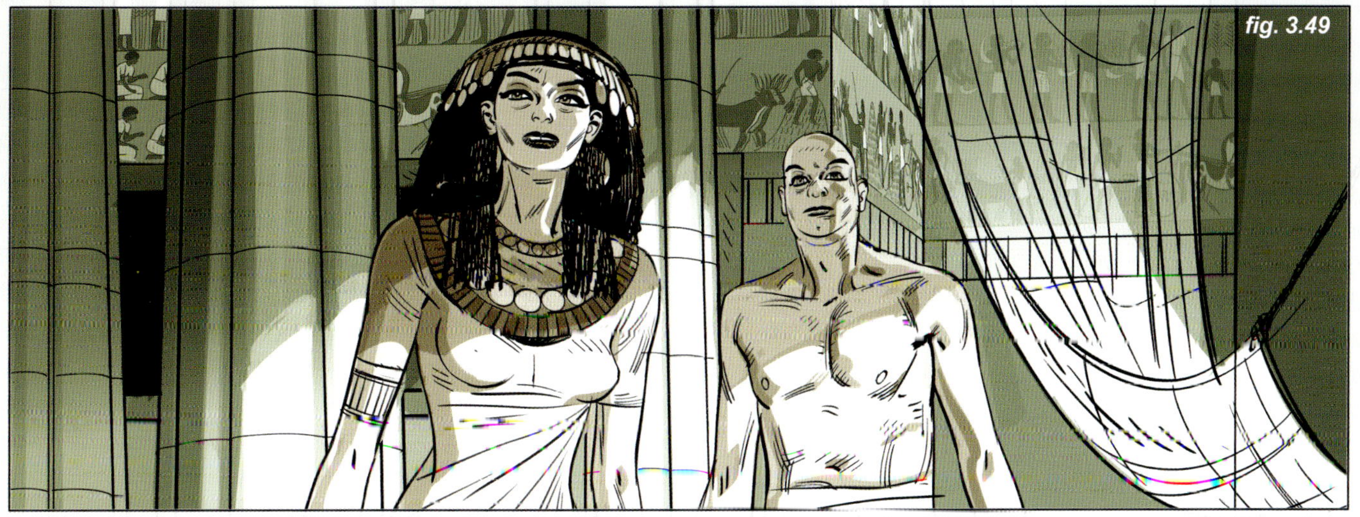

Fig. 3.49: Example **A**. Low camera angle, mostly focused on the characters' expressions and with a limited view of the background. Columns, drapes, and the mural under a lower, sunset lighting make for an interesting setup.

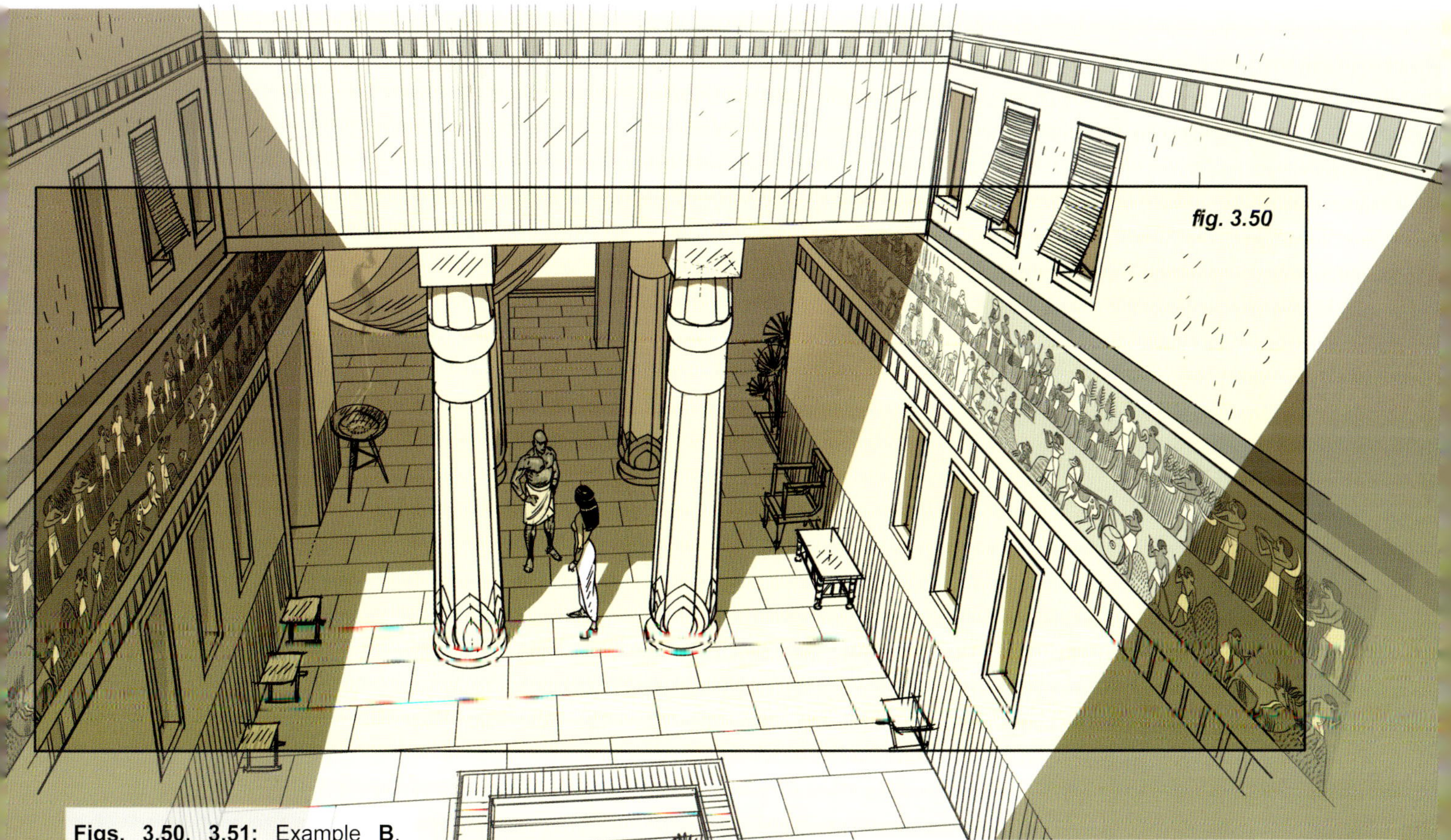

Figs. 3.50, 3.51: Example **B**. Implied point of view of someone from a room on the upper floor looking down on the courtyard. The complex environment with columns, hallways, patios, murals, lights, and shadows could definitely make for a mysterious, conspiratorial location.

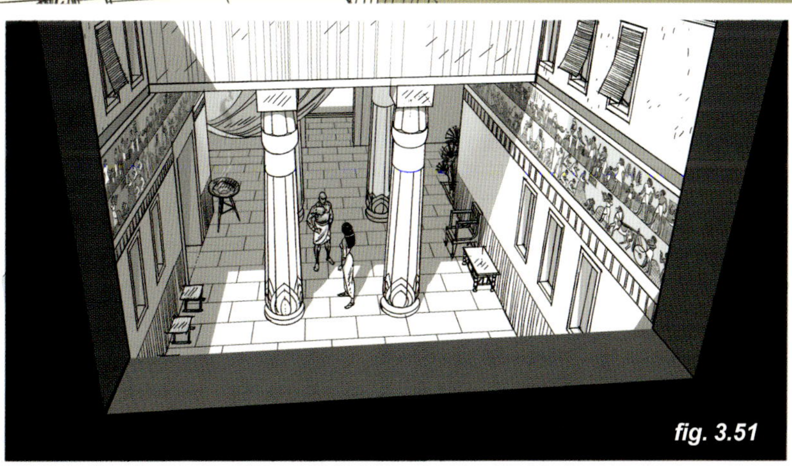

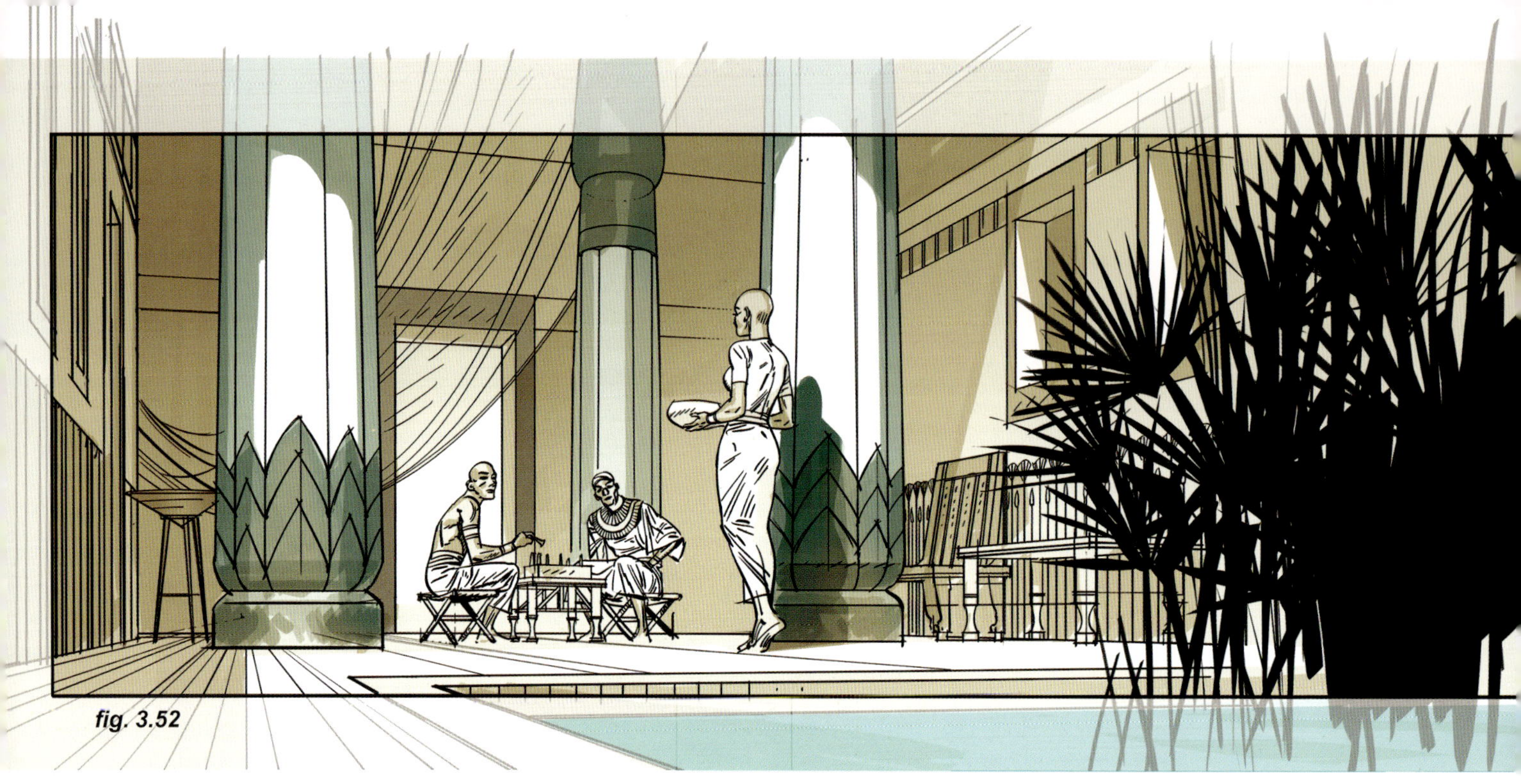

fig. 3.52

Fig. 3.52: Example **C**. This camera view creates an interesting visual: a small frame (entrance door, back wall) within a larger frame (between the two main columns) within the largest frames (foreground reeds, and the movie screen itself).

Fig. 3.53: Example **D**. The columns in the foreground, together with the silhouettes of the two people discussing some shady business in the middle of the night (point 1) then lead the eye directly to the window from where they are being observed (point 2) and then to the back patio with the hanging canopies, all the way into the distance (point 3).

Observe that all of these shots display a strong **sense of depth and perspective,** as did the original color design (fig 3.38, page 081). Depth can be used as part of a **visual language** to create differences between the worlds of the higher and the lower classes in the social pyramid. In this case, our treatment might depict the **more humble areas of this city** with a **visually flatter look,** often with the camera positioned in ways that show **less perspective** while also using **longer lenses** to flatten the effect.

fig. 3.53

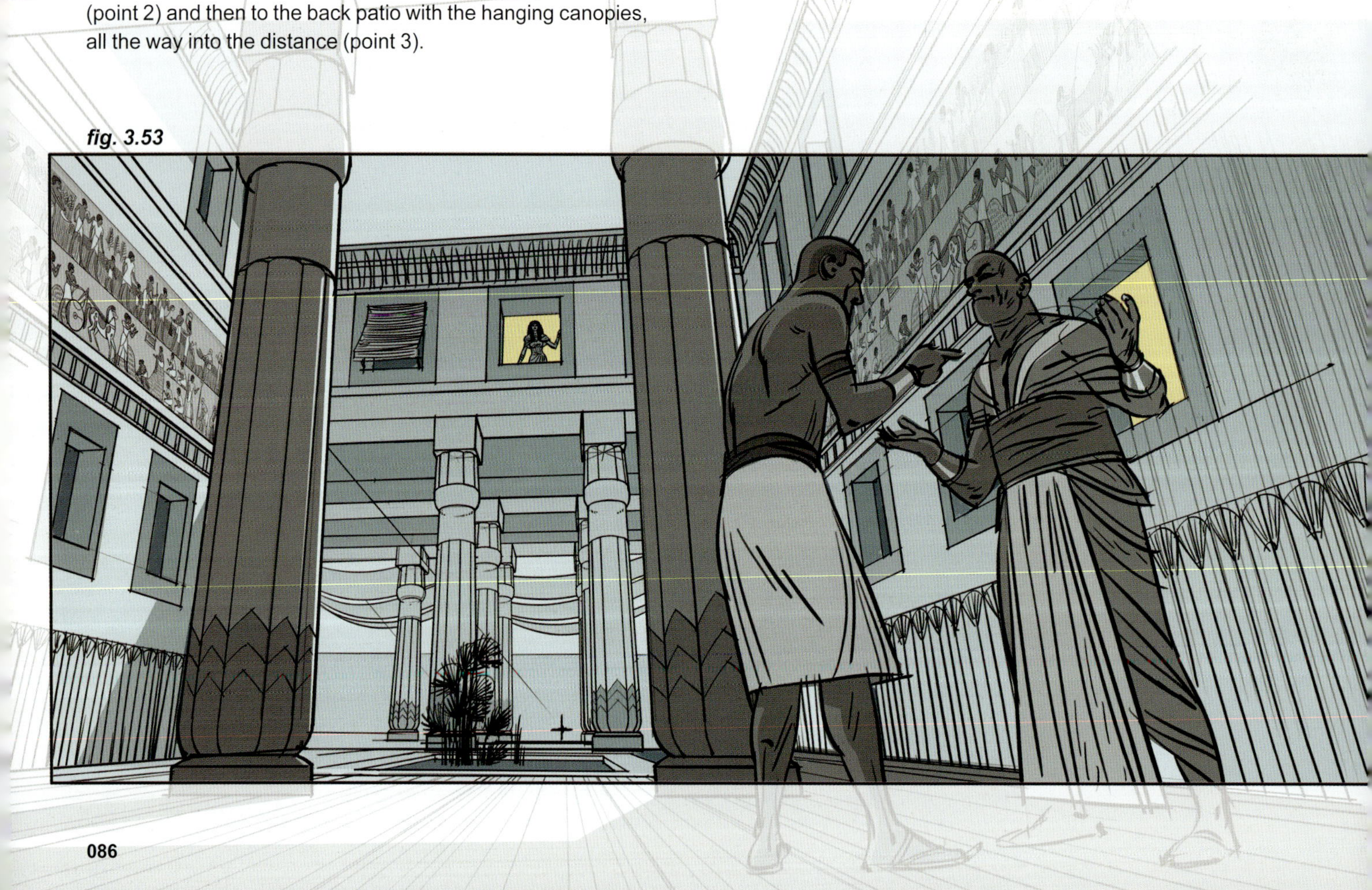

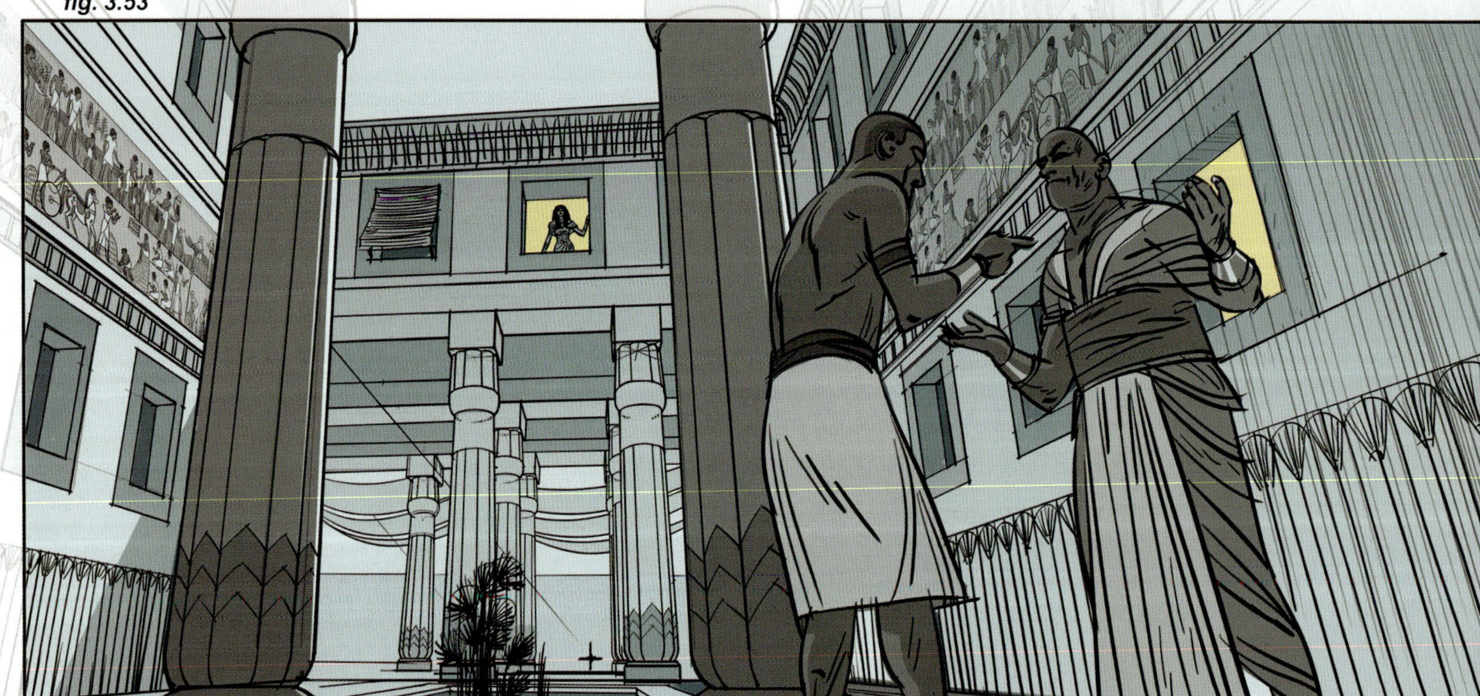

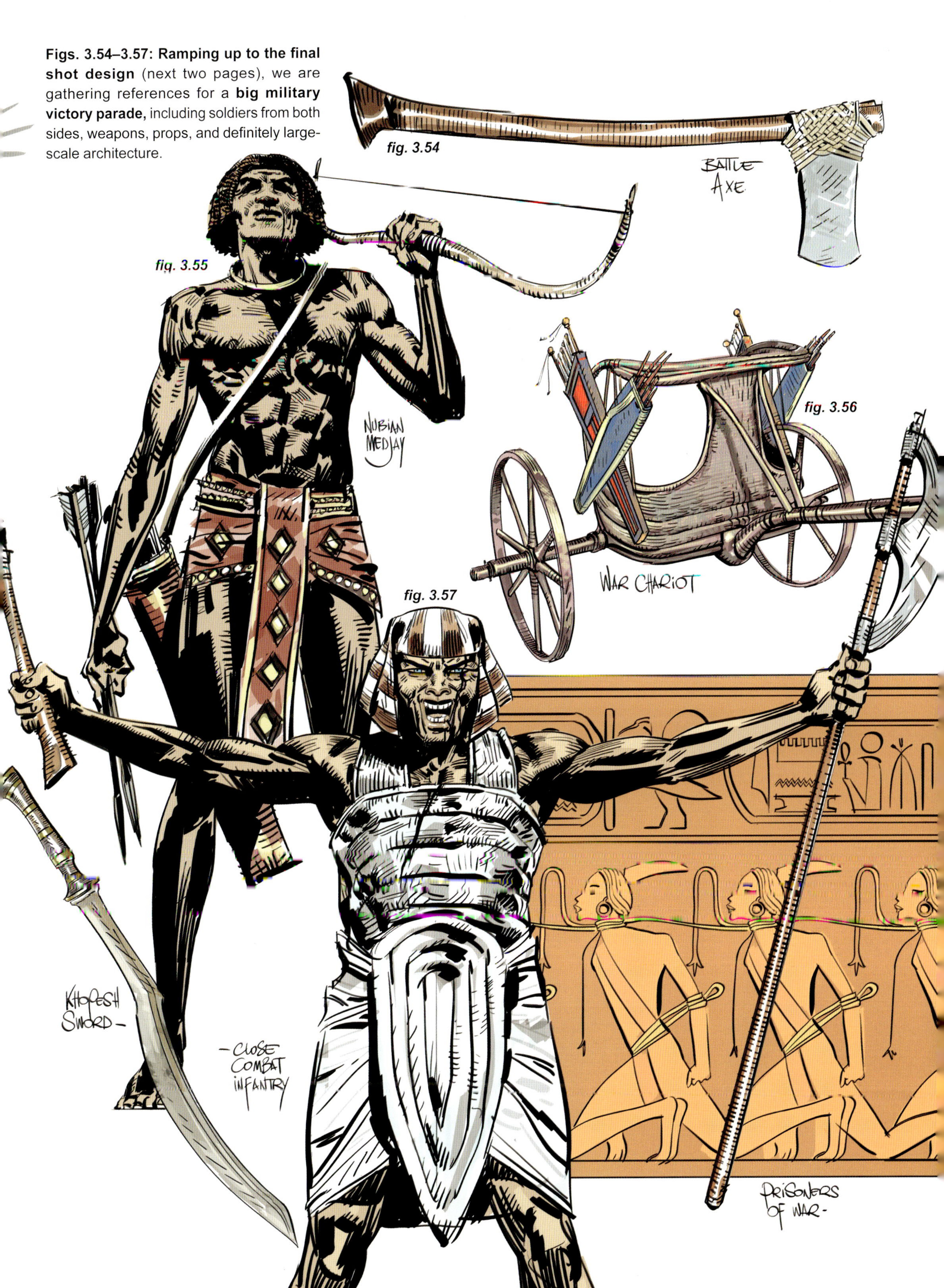

Figs. 3.54–3.57: Ramping up to the final shot design (next two pages), we are gathering references for a **big military victory parade,** including soldiers from both sides, weapons, props, and definitely large-scale architecture.

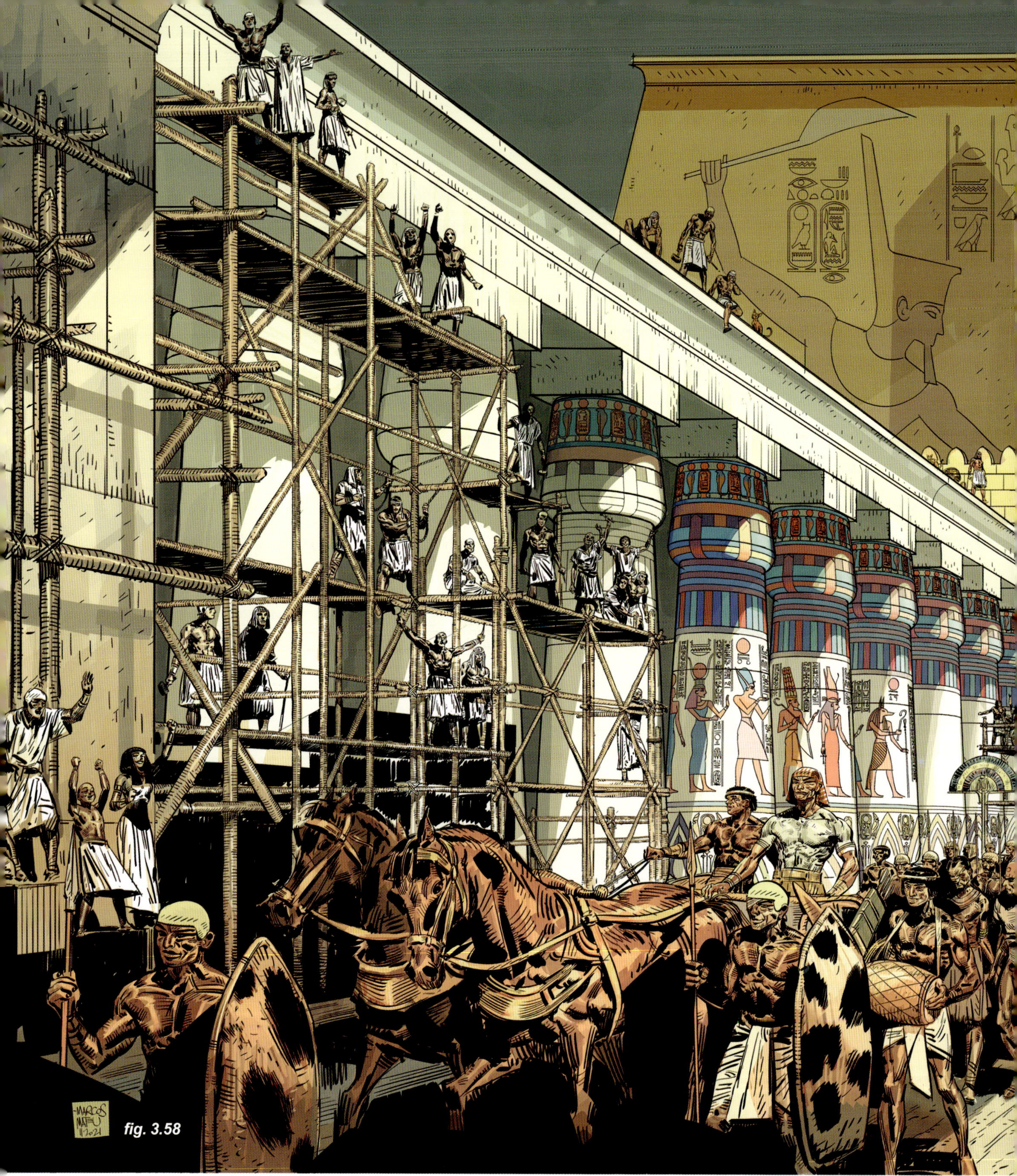

Fig. 3.58: If you recall the section on **scale progression** from my book *Framed Ink* (page 056), that is the philosophy at the essence of both the design and framing of this shot. In order to create this kind of scale we could, for example, start a scene with a close-up shot of regular citizens in the crowd talking to each other to then have someone call their attention to the parade that is about to start. At this point the camera would open up to a shot that reveals more of the crowd as well as workers on the scaffoldings so that the scale of the moment starts kicking in.

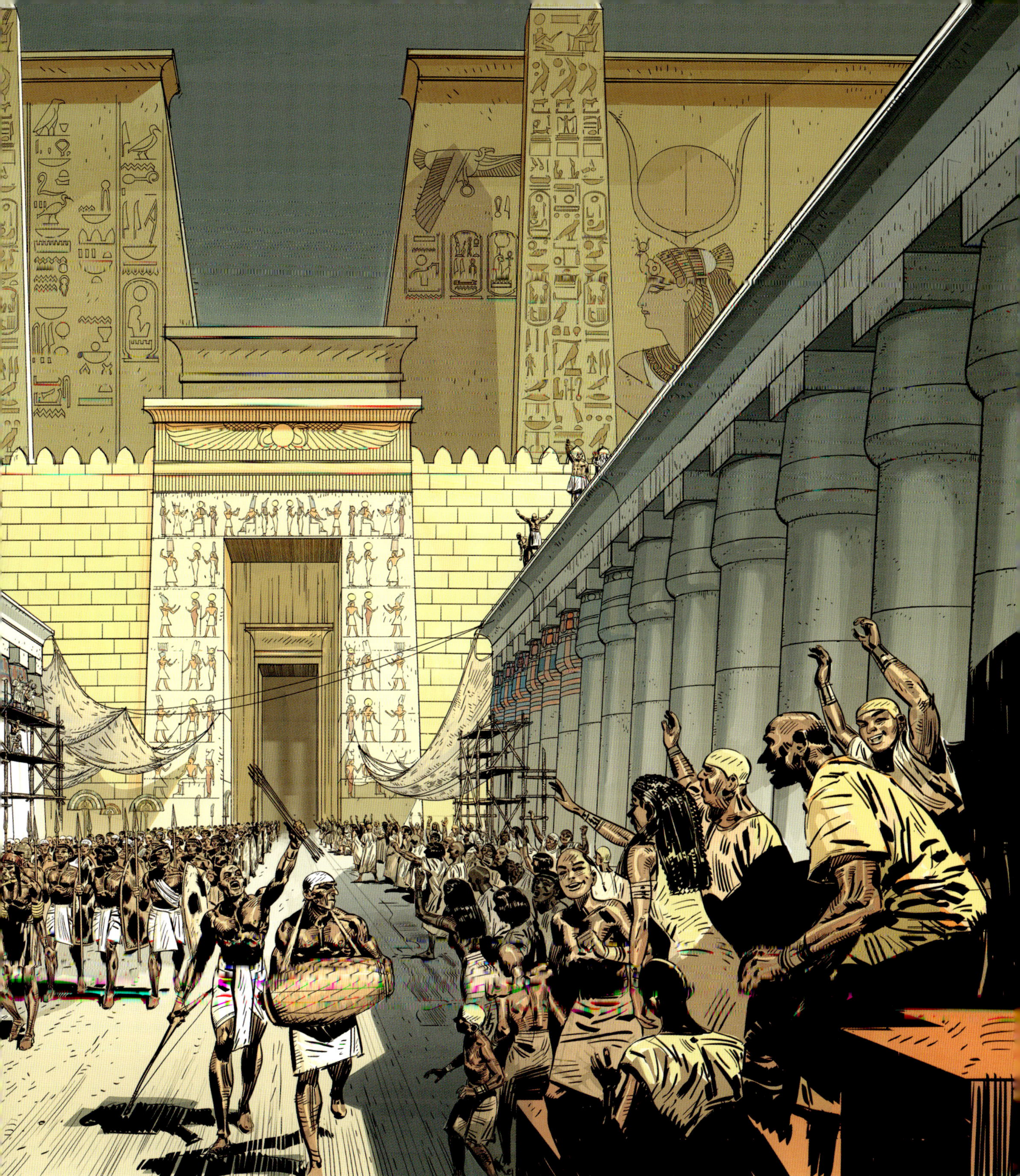

Then, further into the distance, as we keep widening out the shot, the architectonic **elements only grow bigger,** first with the colossal gate and wall on either side, to finally see the two front towers of the temple at the very back. The hieroglyphs help enhance this feeling of visual awe by making the larger shapes that enclose them appear even more fantastic by contrast.

On the next page are some enlarged details of this image, showing how scale was used to create an epic shot like this.

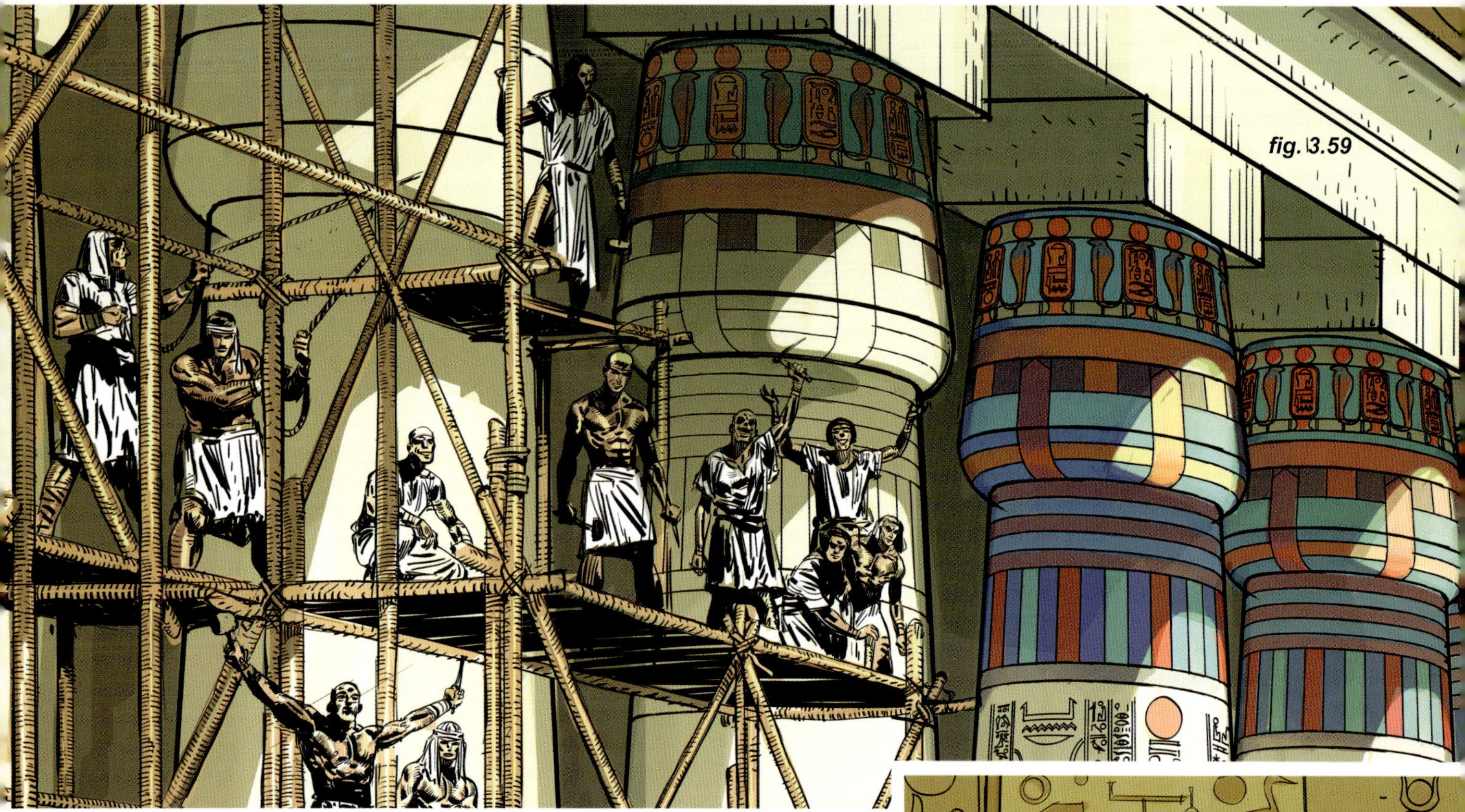

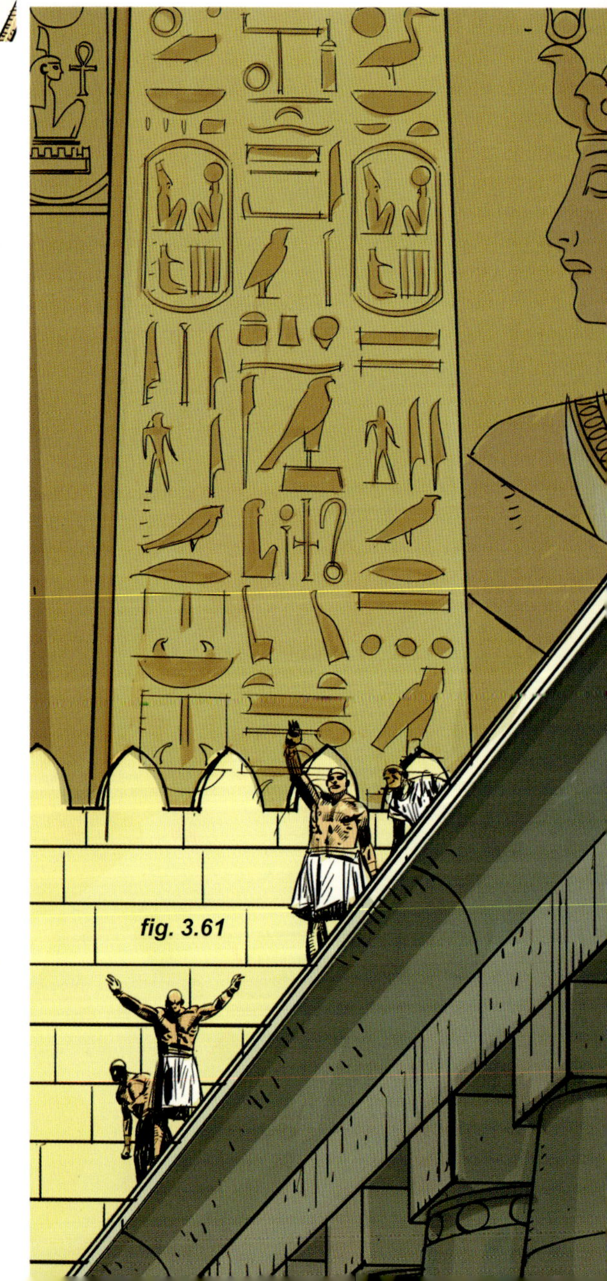

Figs. 3.59, 3.60: As discussed in the last paragraph on page 068, it is interesting to show locations "alive" at times of progress and evolution. Having artisans on the scaffoldings, with a view of the columns already built, but some not yet fully painted and decorated with hieroglyphs, indicates that we are witnessing part of a social process, including soldiers bringing back prisoners from a victorious campaign in an ever-changing world.

Fig. 3.61: Scale is enhanced by juxtaposing elements of extremely different sizes, such as the workers up against the constructions behind them.

fig. 3.60

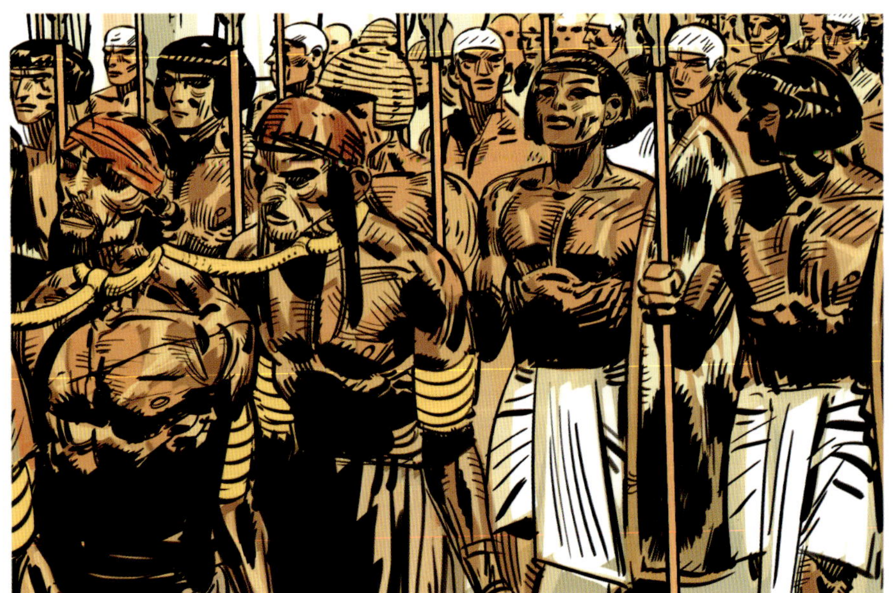

4

PUSHING THE SHAPE LANGUAGE

Within all aspects of designing an environment, let's now focus on **shape language.** This language is already an integral part of many aspects of our trade, like when working with light and dark in a scene and thinking about what graphic shapes these lights and shadows create. Or when designing a recognizable character, what are the key shapes that indicate who it is? The overall tone is influenced by incorporating shapes that are big or small, vertical, diagonal, or horizontal, smooth-flowing vs. broken up, and more.

To get started, as usual, consult references, not only architectural ones but also of natural shapes like mountains, plants, clouds… whatever gets your creativity going. Once general shapes are chosen, combine them with a sense of size, proportion, placement, and your overall instinct for composition. Also, consider camera placement, because shapes can look very different depending on where we see them from and through what lenses.

And in order to determine the storytelling validity of these shape languages, always think ahead: What tone will that location need to inspire in us? Will it benefit from a feeling of uniformity, or a variety of shapes to play up contrast? Does the story call for darker or lighter tones? Depending on those requirements, it might need a more enclosed area with more and taller walls, or on the contrary, bigger openings or no walls at all if the area will be flooded with light.

Here are some ideas to get us started.

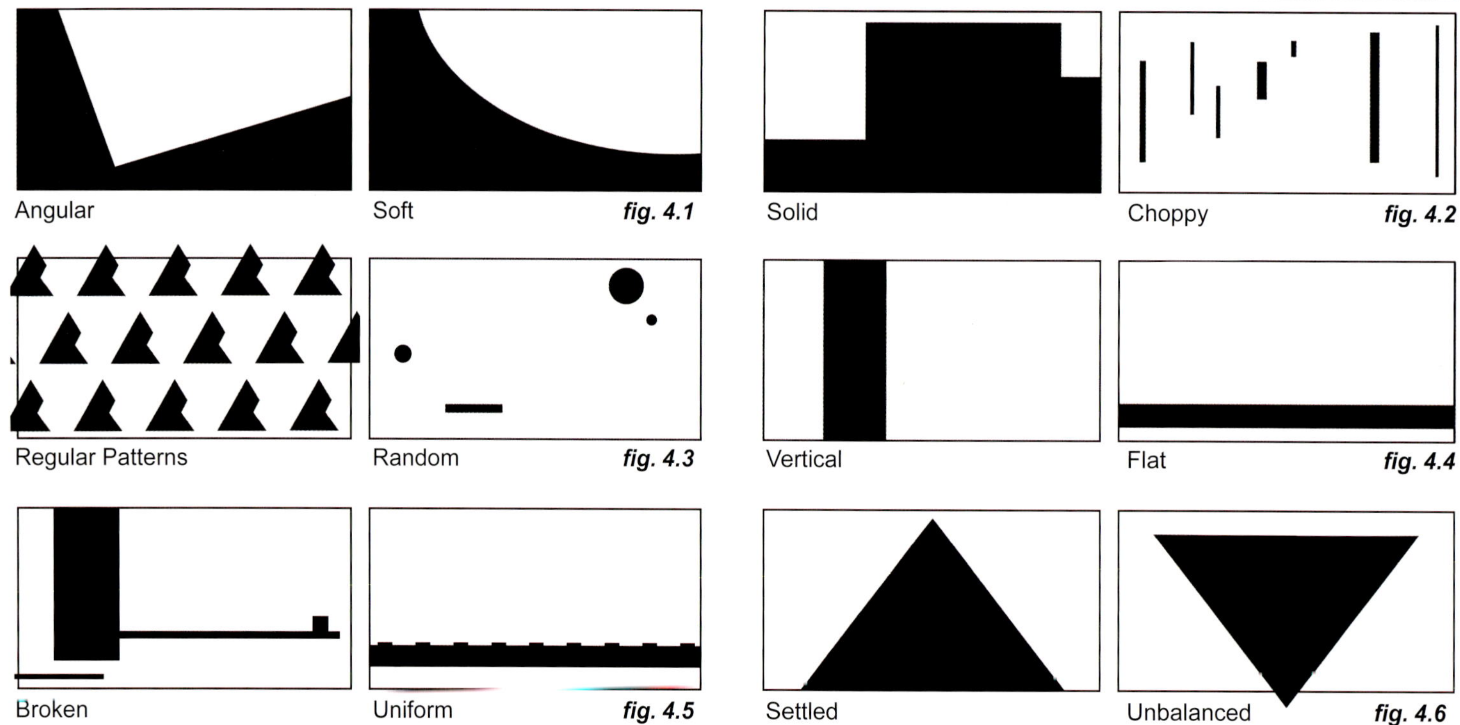

A BASIC CHECKLIST OF SOME AVAILABLE SHAPES TO PLAY WITH

Figs. 4.1–4.6: Any given shape can provide an array of perceptions in the audience, depending on the camera's point of view and framing of the shot.

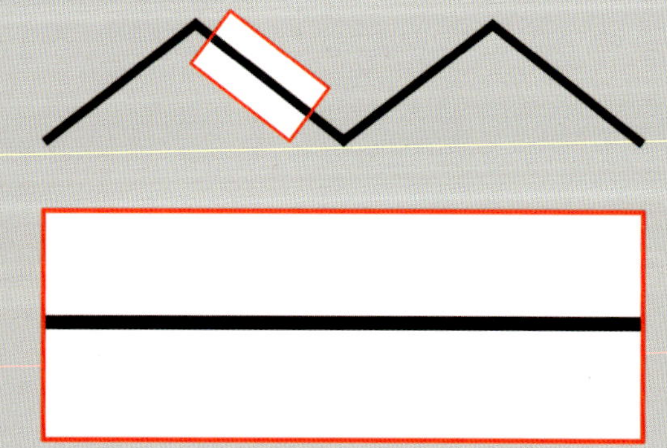

Say, for example, there is a dynamic, jagged line design, but at some point we need that design to feel passive and uneventful. The solution could simply be to position the camera to show only what we need to see to meet our visual needs (camera position framed in red, as opposed to framing the full jagged line).

And how do these shapes translate when applied to a practical location? Let's see how to work this out.

STRAIGHT AND EXTENDED VS. JAGGED AND COMPRESSED

The design of a location should always communicate something about the story and a particular moment in it. This can mean a part of the plot, a character, or the character's emotions in a particular scene. *Emotion is the key to storytelling,* from drama to comedy, from intense action to the dullest of moments, and everything else in between. These emotions do not often play in an isolated way but rather in *conflict* with each other.

Figs. 4.7, 4.8: Suppose there are two antagonistic characters with opposite personalities, one represents the good **(A)** while the other **(B)** is the twisted, dark element of the narrative. One approach is to identify **A** with an extended, horizontal, primarily more relaxed feel (I say "primarily" because, as just demonstrated, the camera can always alter the perception of things).

For contrast, **B** is assigned a more angular, dramatic type of line.

So, let's say we start by **designing their homes,** and we decide to do so based on these two very basic and abstract lines, which can later become a bit more elaborate within said simplicity. Remember, you'll always need a powerful, simple, and clear visual statement to go back to in this design business, so the more you simplify at the start, the (much) better off you'll be later on, as no matter how many subtle variations you can apply of the same shape, you'll still be clear on what your essential concept is.

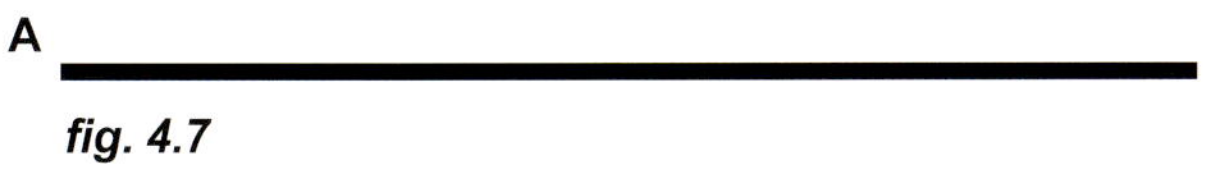

A

fig. 4.7

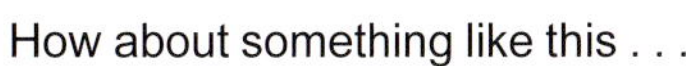

B

fig. 4.8

And now, how to translate these two lines into proper designs?

How about something like this . . .

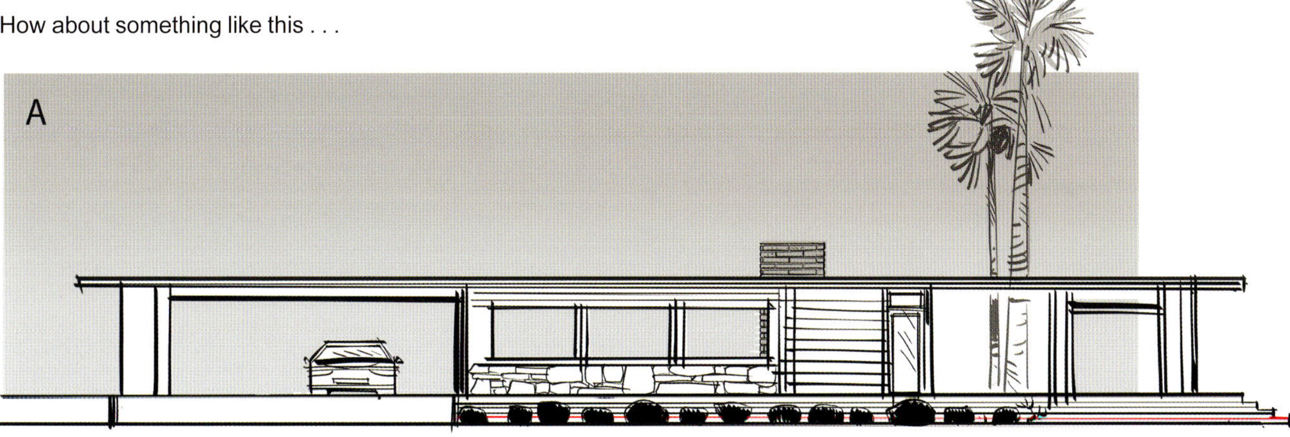

A

Once these visual statements have been established, how can the audience's perception of them be affected, depending on camera angle, framing, and composition?

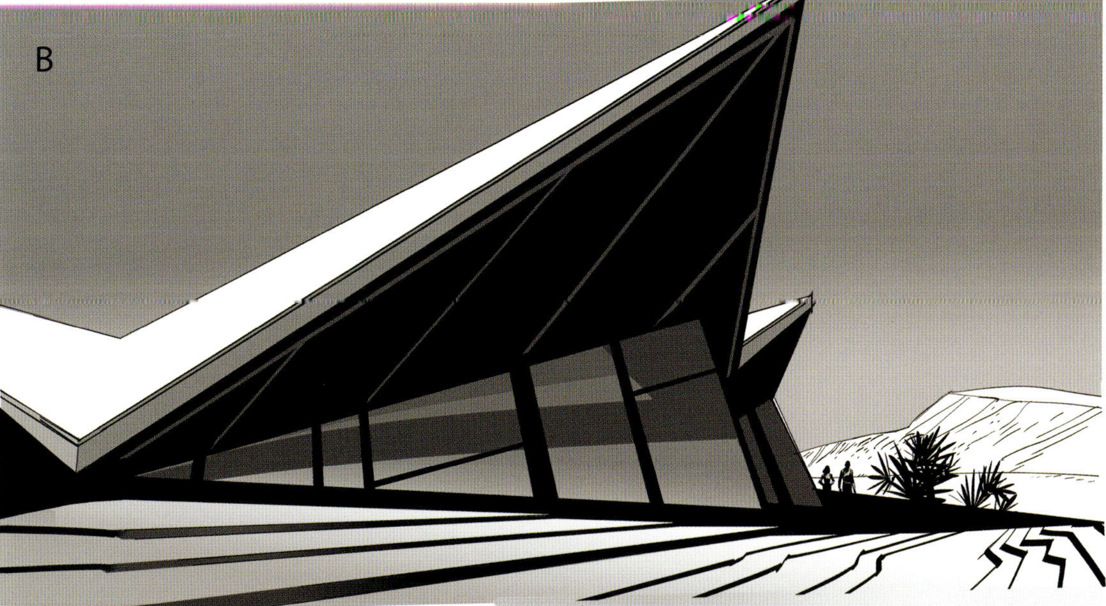

B

Even though a strong visual decision has been made, the characters are not emotionally black and white; there will surely be gray moments during their personal story arcs. We can represent these by moving the camera around and cropping the images as shown on page 092, figs. 4.1–4.6.

There will pretty much always be a number of ways to accomplish the same thing, but for now, imagine moving the camera to the right (like in example A2) so that the location is seen from a different point of view.

Figs. 4.9, 4.10: For example, imagine the character who is visually identified with straight and flat lines (A) reaches a climatic point that takes place in the "flat line" house. It will need to be spiced up a little as he or she starts showing more visceral emotions.

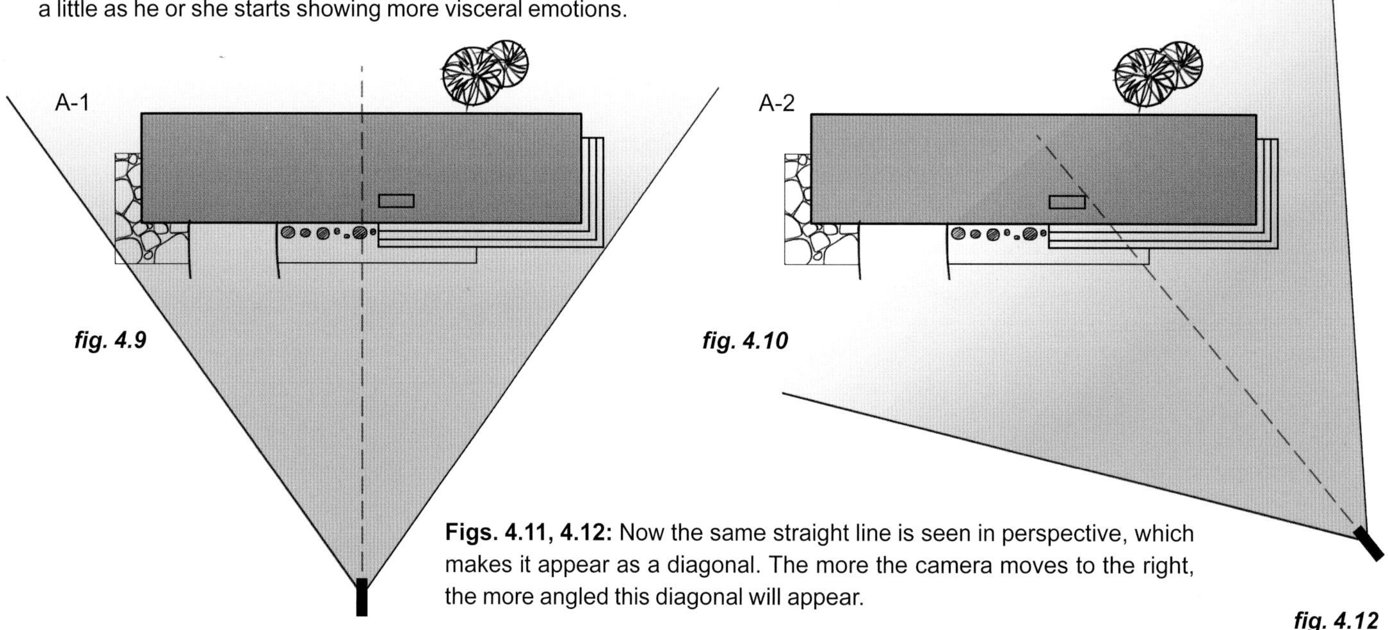

fig. 4.9

fig. 4.10

Figs. 4.11, 4.12: Now the same straight line is seen in perspective, which makes it appear as a diagonal. The more the camera moves to the right, the more angled this diagonal will appear.

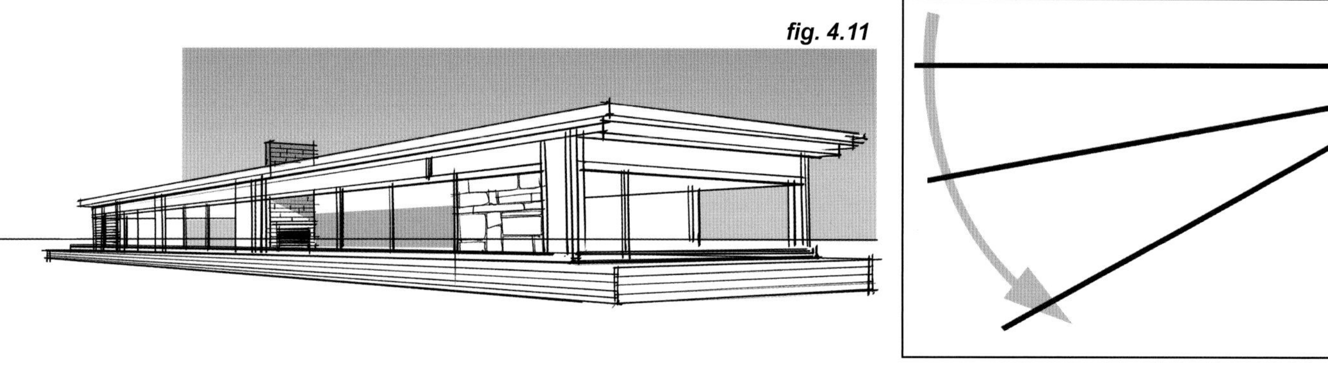

fig. 4.12

fig. 4.11

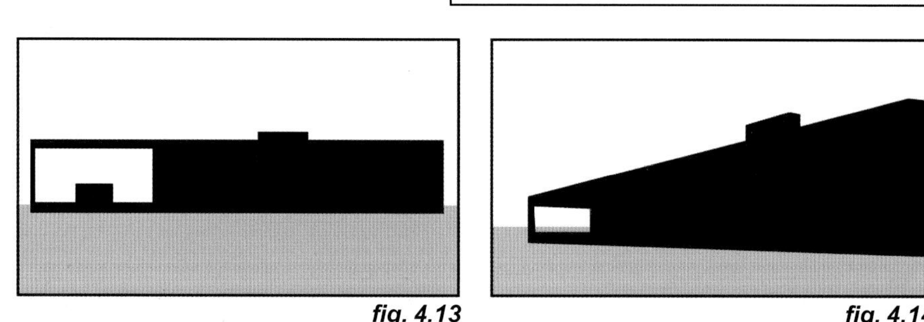

fig. 4.13

fig. 4.14

Figs. 4.13–4.16: This makes for a diversity of compositional solutions, as these abstract diagrams that represent the same location show.

Yet they all still have one thing in common: they are based on the straight-line motif that was created for character A.

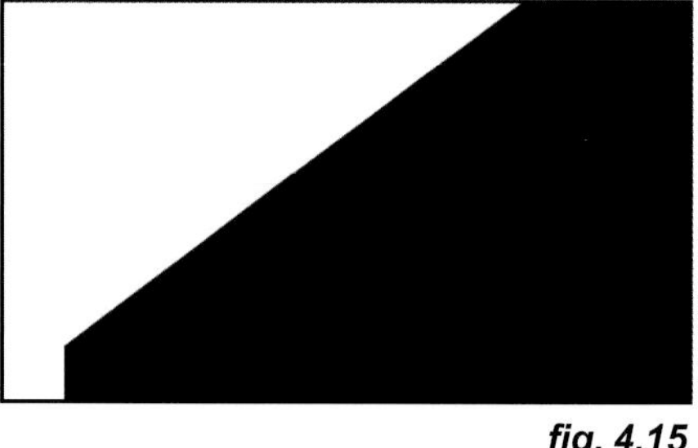

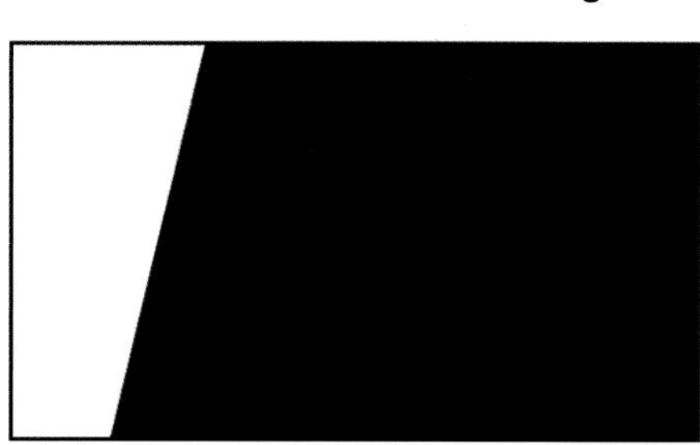

fig. 4.15

fig. 4.16

Figs. 4.17–4.19: These pushed examples indicate how accentuating the shapes of a more dynamically designed location can create extreme abstract patterns that will have an emotional imprint in our narrative world.

Figs. 4.20–4.22: Shape language can also be **applied to the characters** populating these worlds.

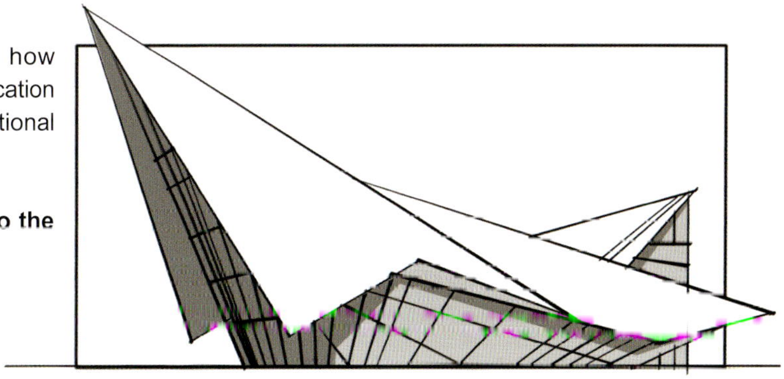

fig. 4.17

fig. 4.18

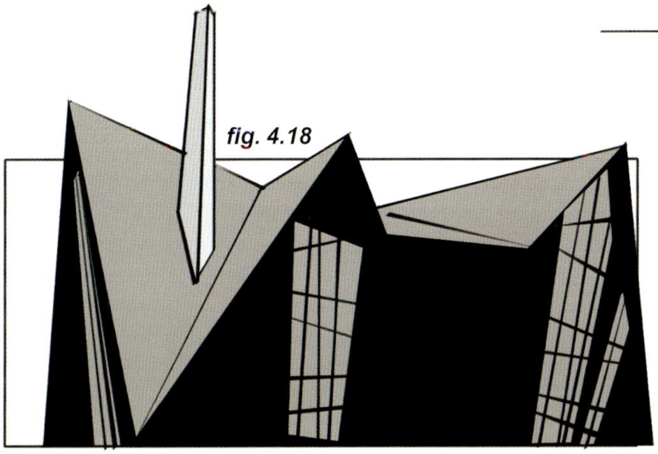

fig. 4.19

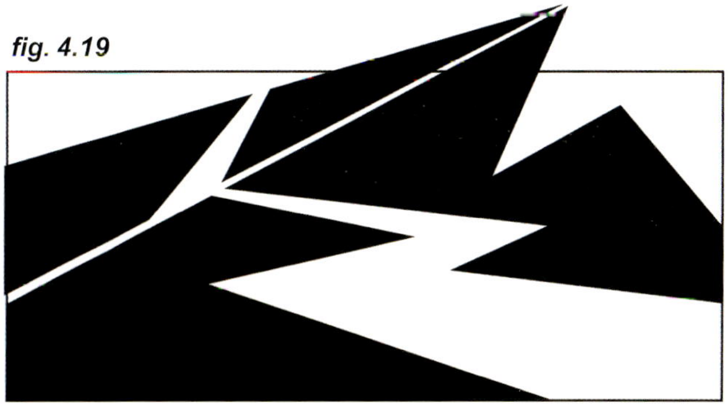

fig. 4.20

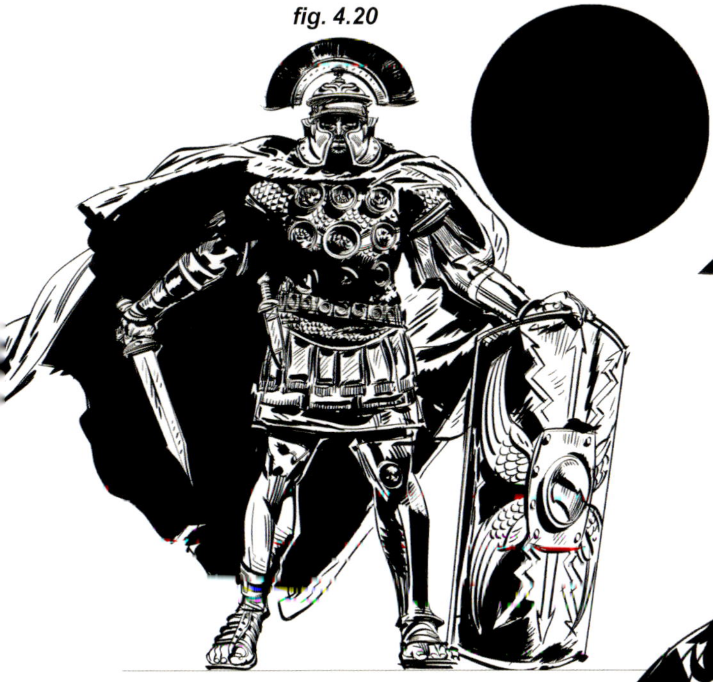

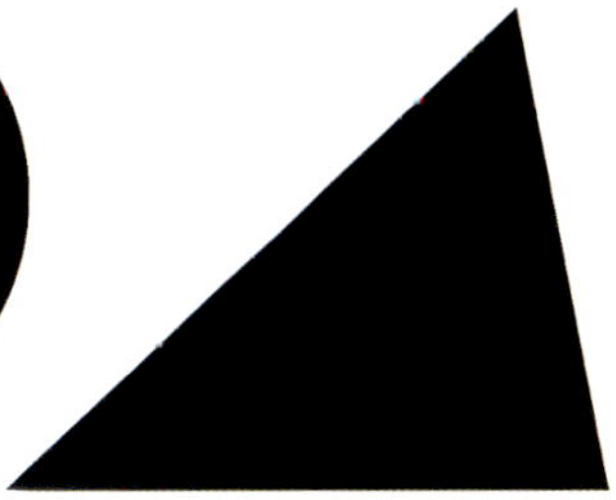

fig. 4.21

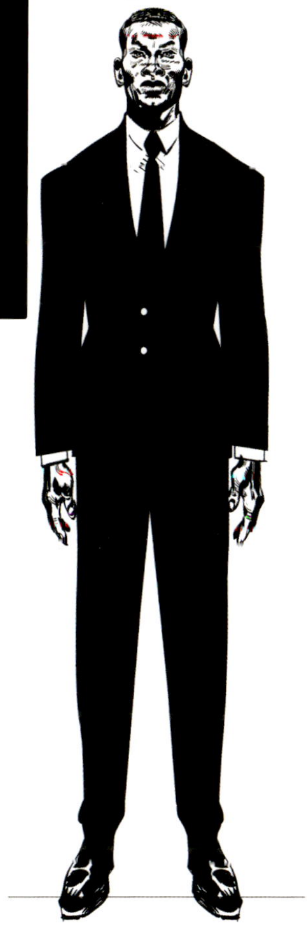

fig. 4.22

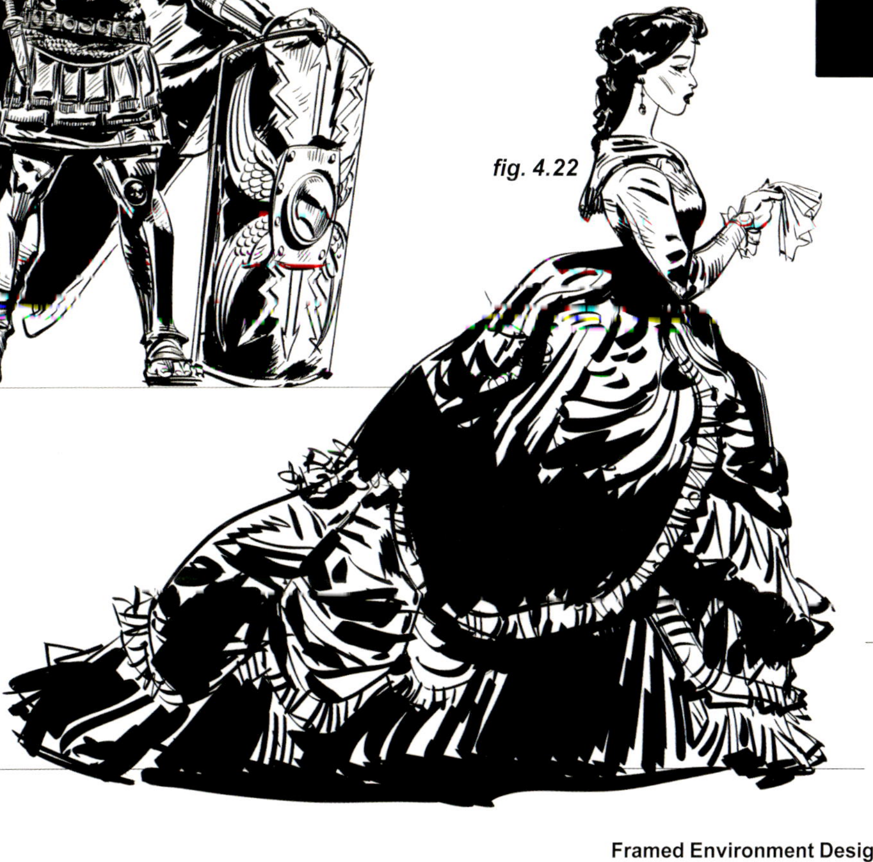

Following up on the previous points, let's dive into specific examples with two concepts in mind: developing designs based on angles and cubes first, and on curves and circles later.

ANGULAR, CUBIC SHAPES

Let's explore all options, from the most basic, simple cube to more elaborate ones, always thinking first of the look and feel of the shapes from a distance but also their possibilities for interesting close-ups. Let's imagine the assignment is to design a large building, a piece of experimental or futuristic-looking architecture with a cold, angular feel to it. We can go from a basic shape to a combination of them that will result in a more complex visual.

These first examples below play with elements such as balance vs. imbalance and larger vs. smaller volumes, making sure that such ideas are noticeable from a distance so that the building can be instantly recognizable.

Fig. 4.23: This is essentially a cube on a much smaller stand that narrows down toward the base.

Figs. 4.24–4.26: These follow a similar philosophy, combining bigger shapes (in reddish-brown) with smaller ones (in yellow-green), while still providing a sense of balance within the daring shapes.

Figs. 4.27, 4.28: These start exploring a look that would require really solid engineering in order for the structure not to topple over, pushing an uneasy sense of being off-kilter and dangerous that could provide the right tone for certain types of characters and action.

Getting inspiration from sources other than architectural ones can be a valid way to approach it. Notice how fig. 4.25 resembles the dynamic shape of an arrow's fletching (feathers), fig. 4.27 takes the shape of a stapler, and fig. 4.28 echoes the structure of a weather vane pointing in different directions. Since obviously this building will not spin with the wind, such rotational motion is insinuated by the floors pointing in different directions, almost as if various frames or poses of the weather vane were superimposed during a stretch of time.

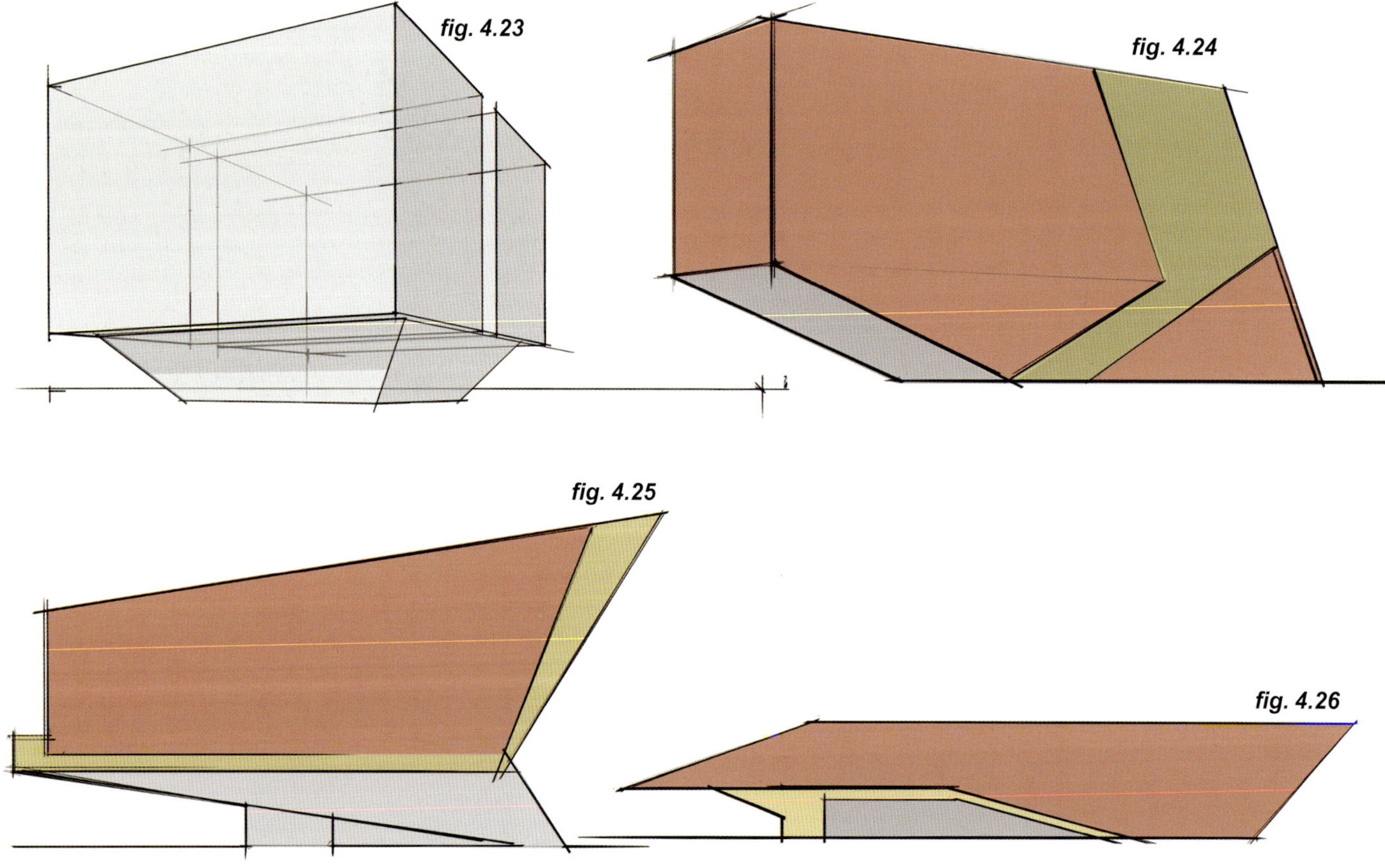

fig. 4.23

fig. 4.24

fig. 4.25

fig. 4.26

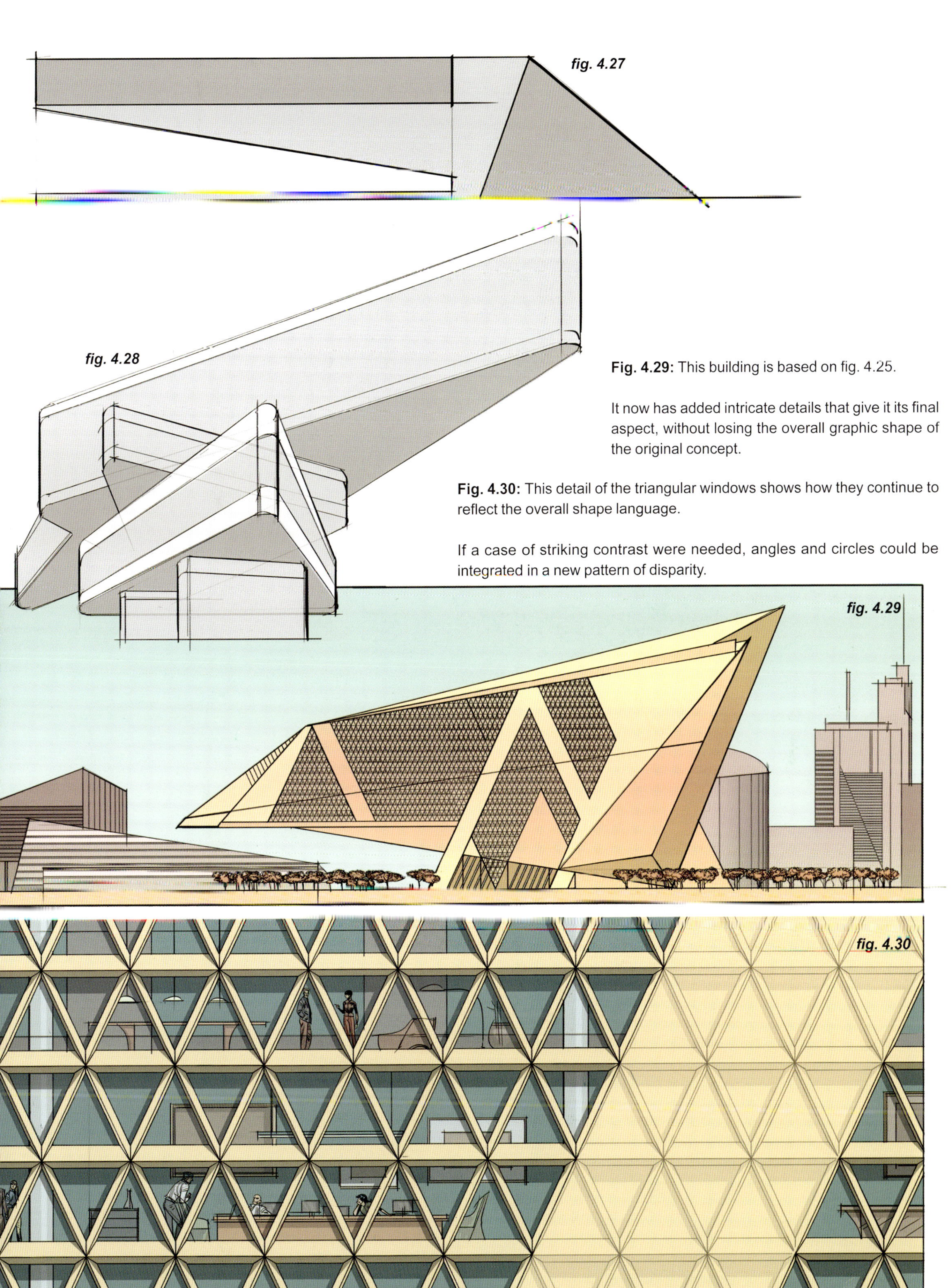

fig. 4.27

fig. 4.28

Fig. 4.29: This building is based on fig. 4.25.

It now has added intricate details that give it its final aspect, without losing the overall graphic shape of the original concept.

Fig. 4.30: This detail of the triangular windows shows how they continue to reflect the overall shape language.

If a case of striking contrast were needed, angles and circles could be integrated in a new pattern of disparity.

fig. 4.29

fig. 4.30

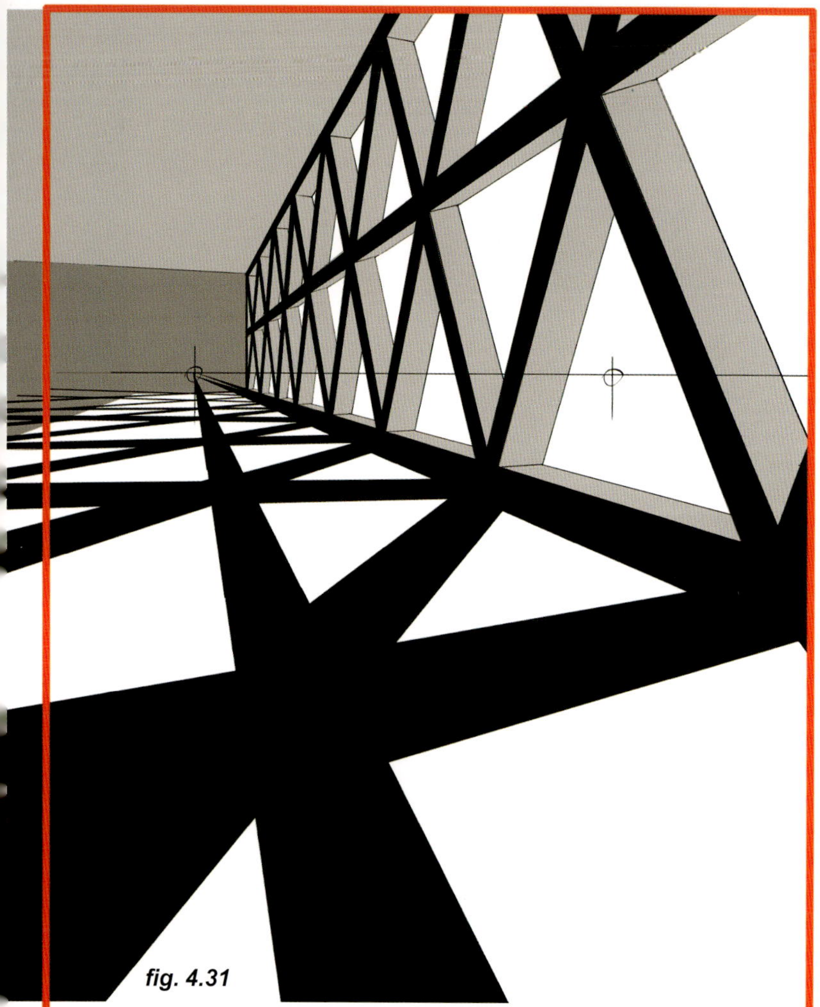

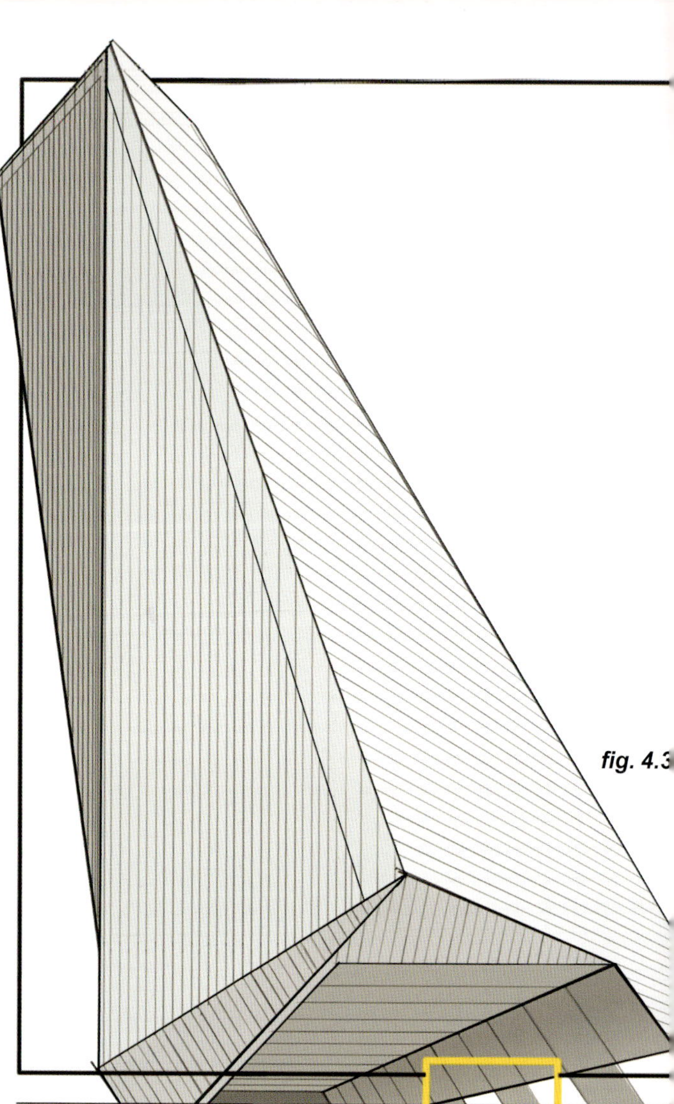

fig. 4.31

fig. 4.3

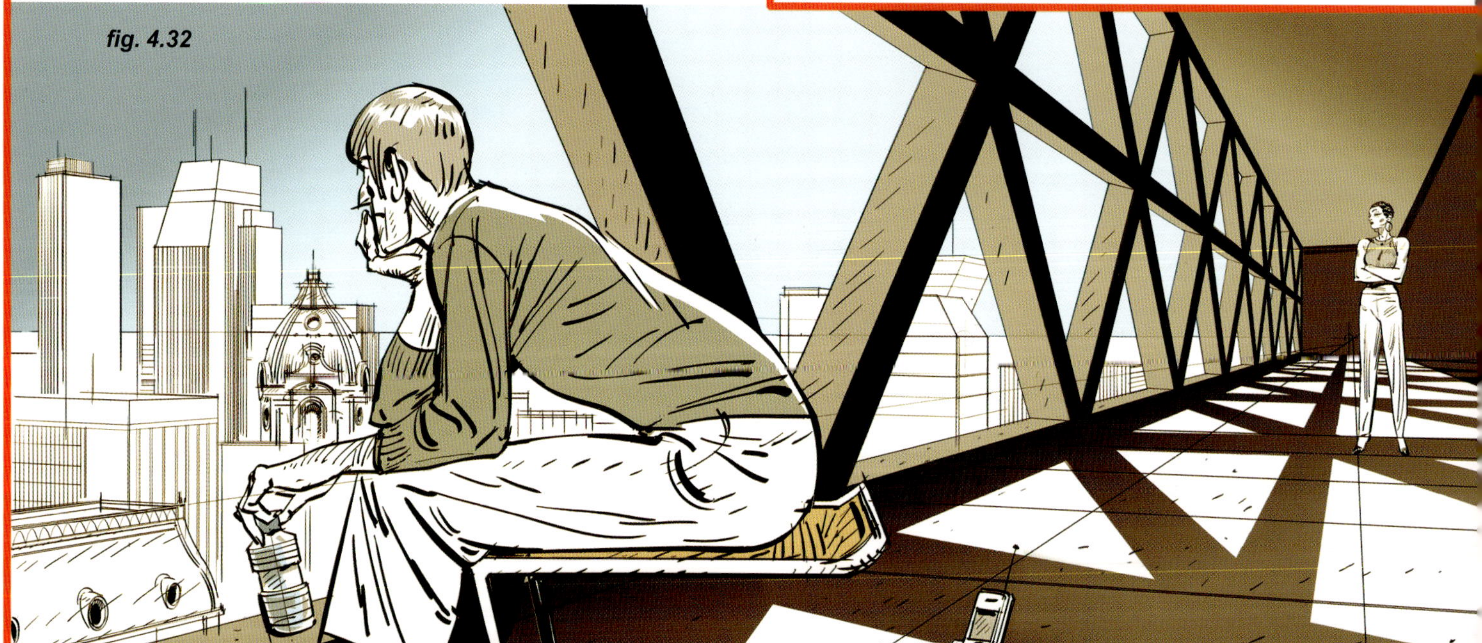

fig. 4.32

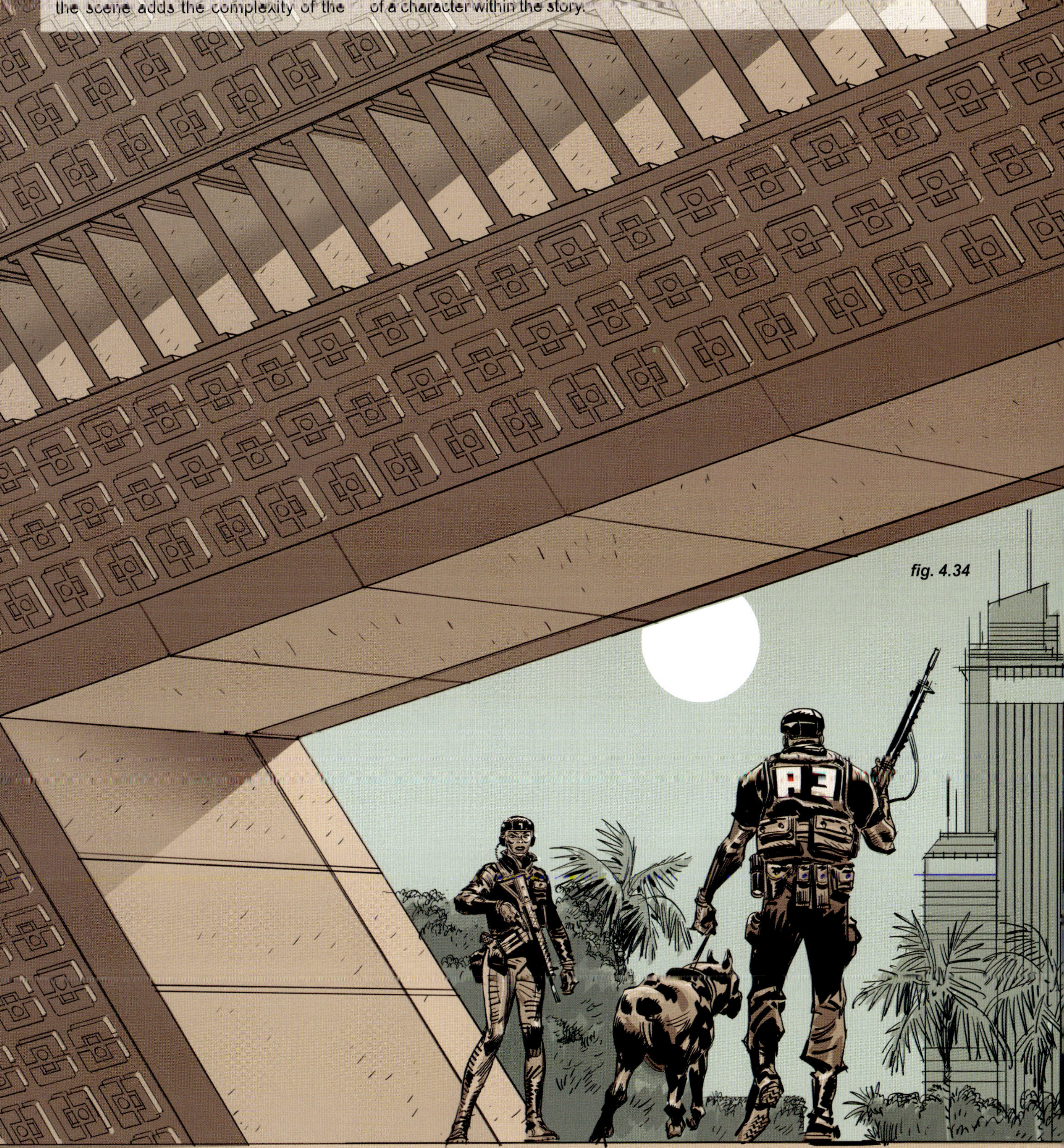

Figs. 4.31, 4.32: An interesting shape design not only brings a special feel to the structure of the environment but also creates opportunities for playing with composition, lights, and shadows.

Here the camera has been placed inside the building from fig. 4.29. **Backlighting** the scene adds the complexity of the pattern's shadows and using a wide-angle lens further enhances a sense of **depth and perspective.**

Fig. 4.33: Here is another example of a signature design that becomes easily recognizable from a distance, essentially giving the building the status of a character within the story.

Fig. 4.34: This detail of the area framed in yellow in fig. 4.33 shows how these architectural nuances follow the same strong diagonals concept that was established from a distance.

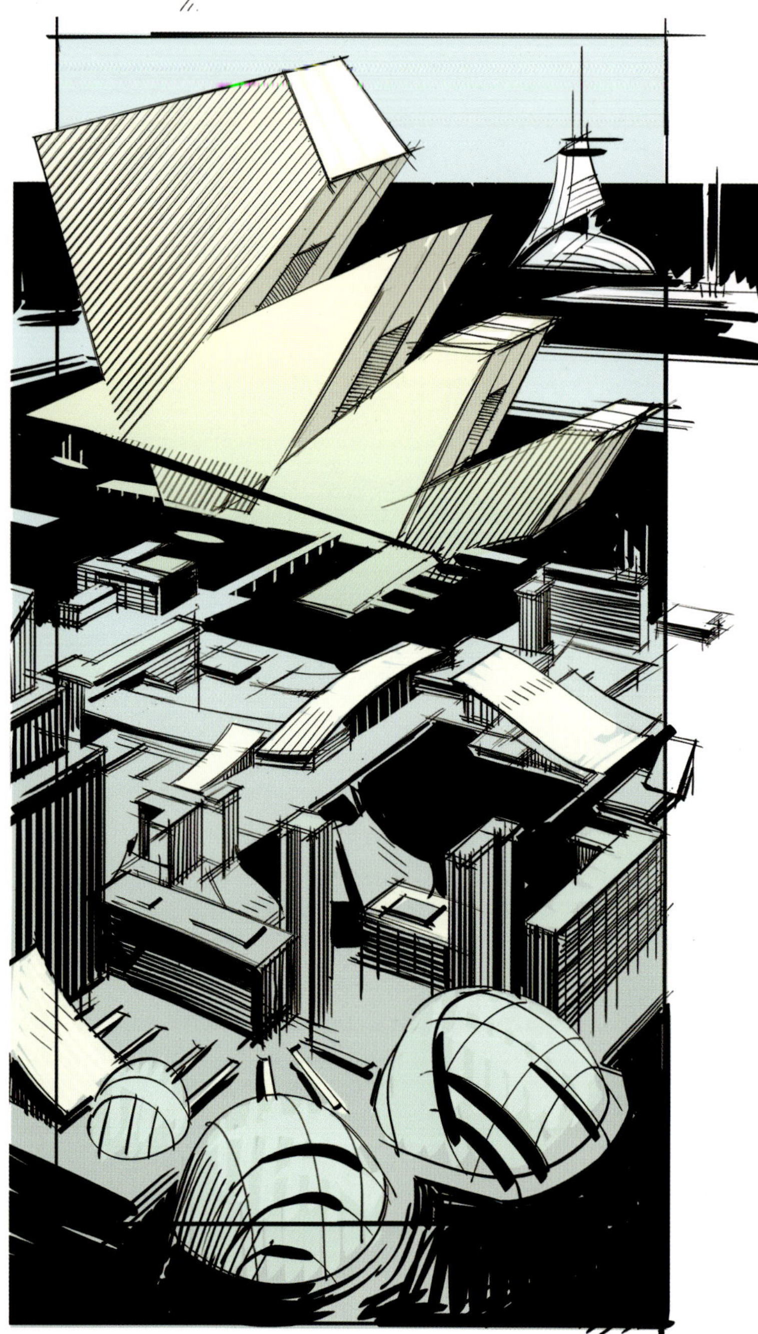

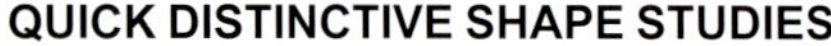

QUICK DISTINCTIVE SHAPE STUDIES

These **quick sketches of landmark buildings** are **distinctive** for a number of reasons:

Figs. 4.35, 4.36: One common factor is simply **size,** as these buildings are much bigger than the surrounding constructions.

Shape is another factor, as their designs make more of a **statement** compared to the more **predictably** and simply shaped neighboring buildings (in purple and green tones, fig. 4.36). How far we push the degree of contrast is dependent on the needs of the story.

Volume: Although sometimes these landmark buildings are subdivided into smaller volumes (orange areas in figs. 4.35, 4.36), every other piece of architecture around it is made of even smaller volumes, so the main building appears solid compared to the much more "'broken down" surrounding architectural landscape.

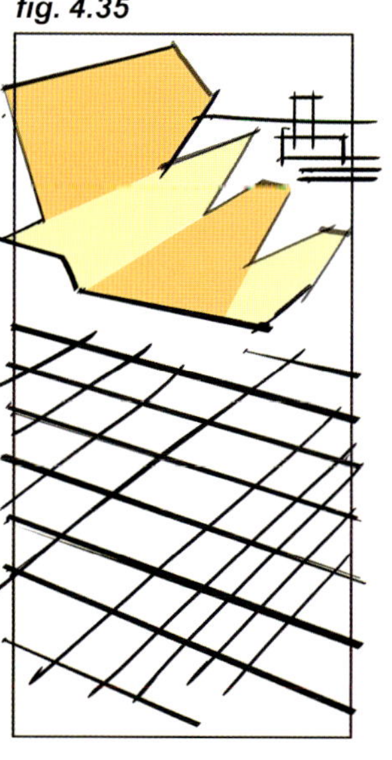

fig. 4.35

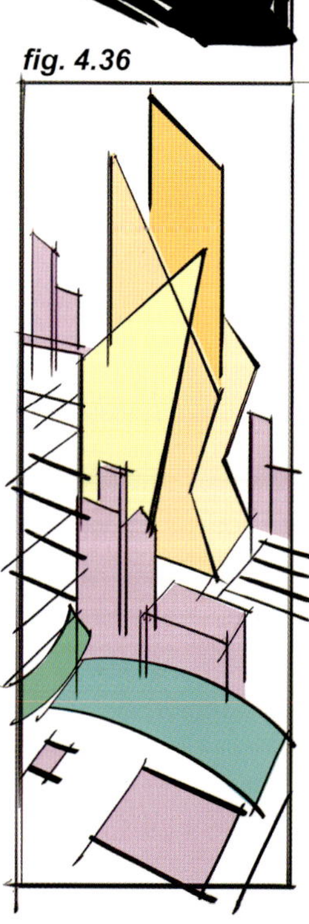

fig. 4.36

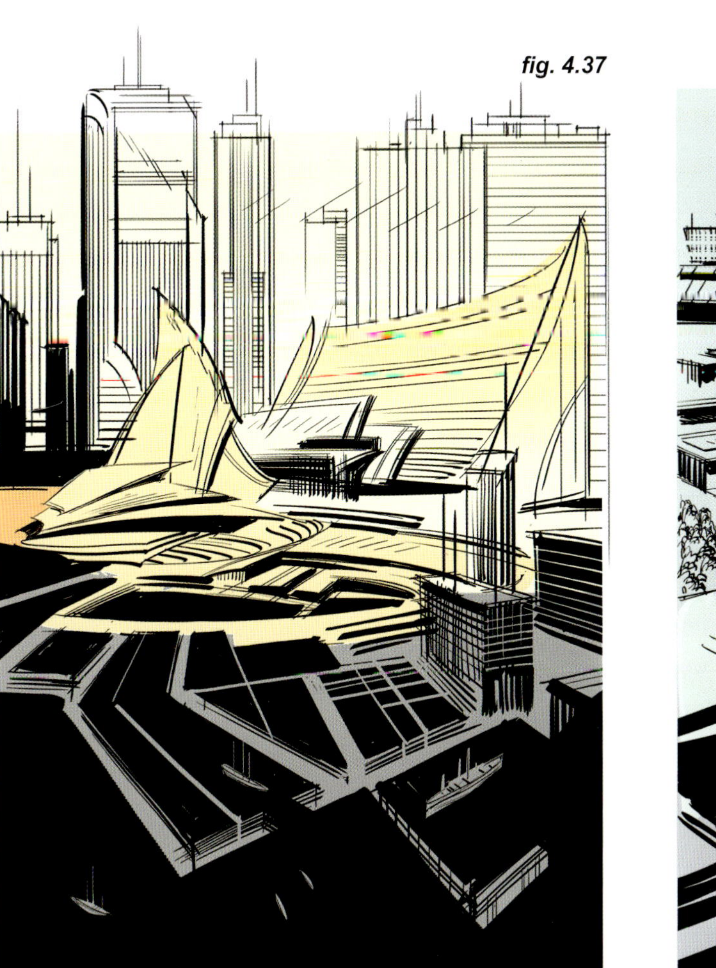

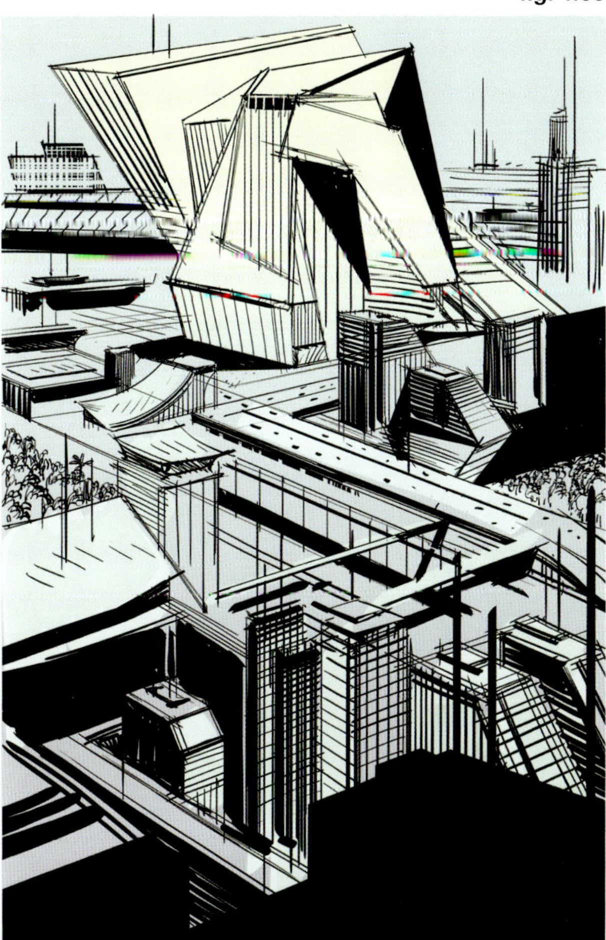

Fig. 4.37: This group of landmark buildings (darker yellow) are altogether smaller than the surrounding city, yet their **curved** shape language, and the fact that they are designed as **concentric layers,** creates a clear contrast with the more **rectilinear and blocky**-looking ones in the background (see fig. 4.40).

Fig. 4.38: The more predictable shapes in the lower part of the image put the spotlight on the building at top.

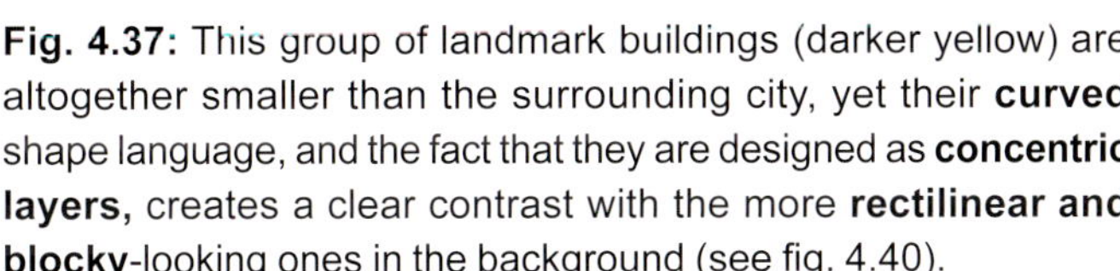

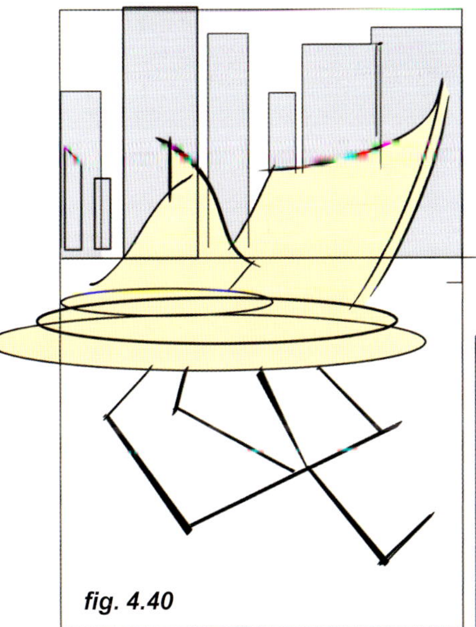

Fig. 4.39: The shape language contrast is extreme, with the foreground buildings inspired by purely natural and organic shapes. (Fig. 4.41, photo inspiration.)

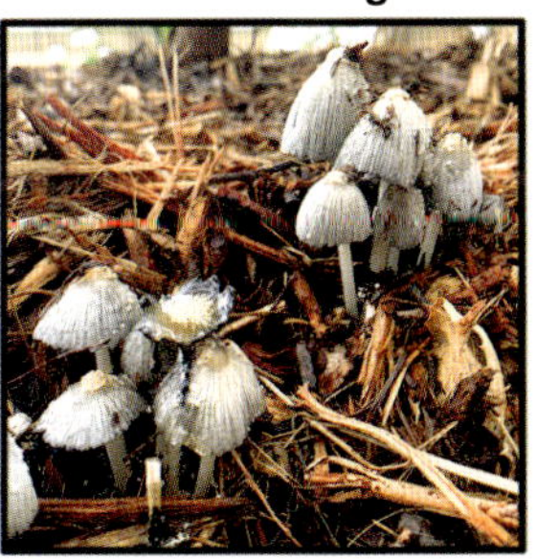

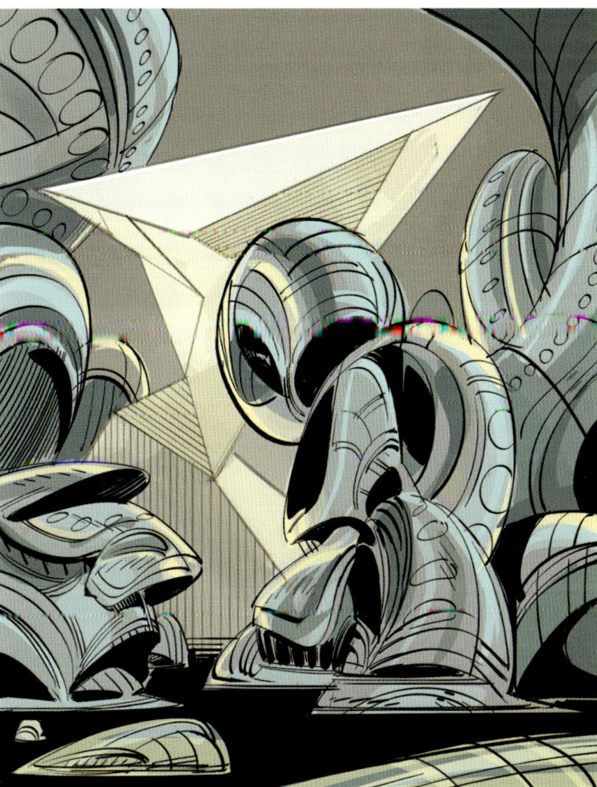

Having examined some general shape philosophies applied to exteriors, let's see how the same theories could be implemented in their matching interiors.

Let's get started with some basic exploration.

Figs. 4.42–4.44: Here are some hard, **angled geometrical spaces** for what could be the personal space of an **enigmatic character.**

These first "blue sky" passes are coming up grand and spacious, but let's say the script calls for a space that feels **tighter,** with a stronger sense of closeness that would make the story moment constricted in space and more **unsettling.**

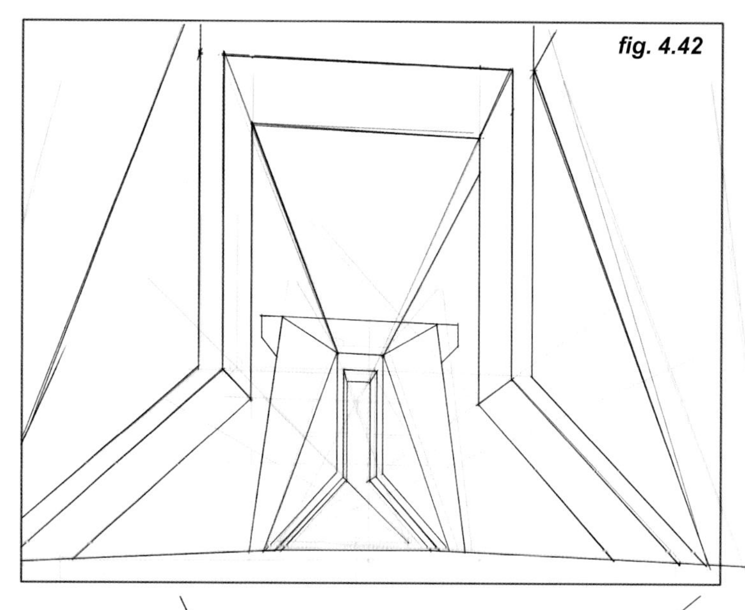

fig. 4.42

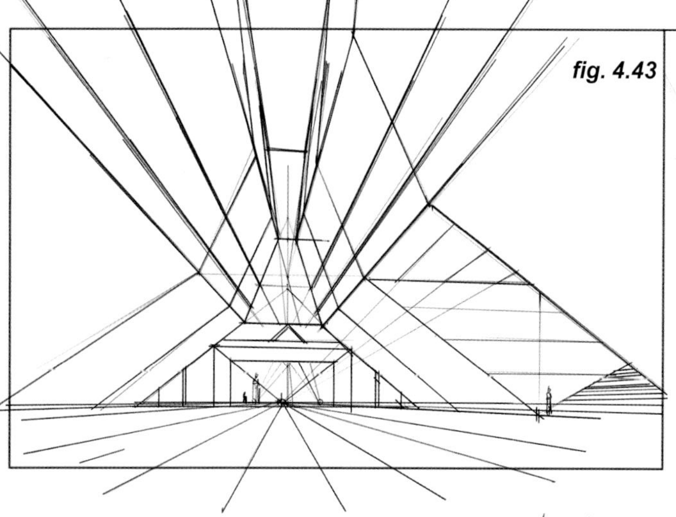

fig. 4.43

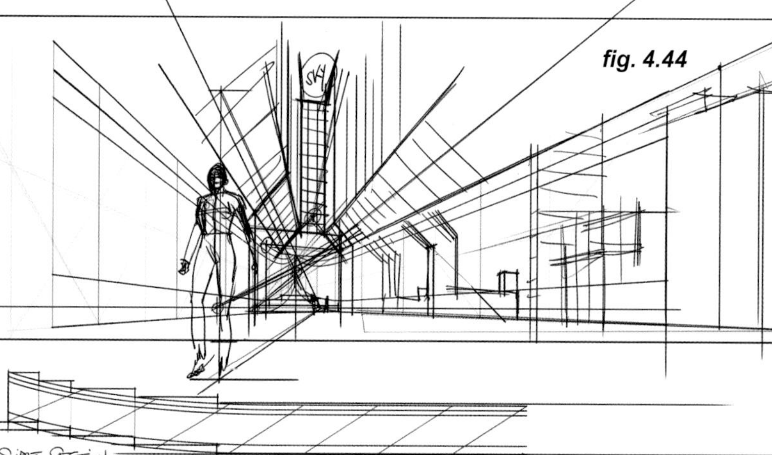

fig. 4.44

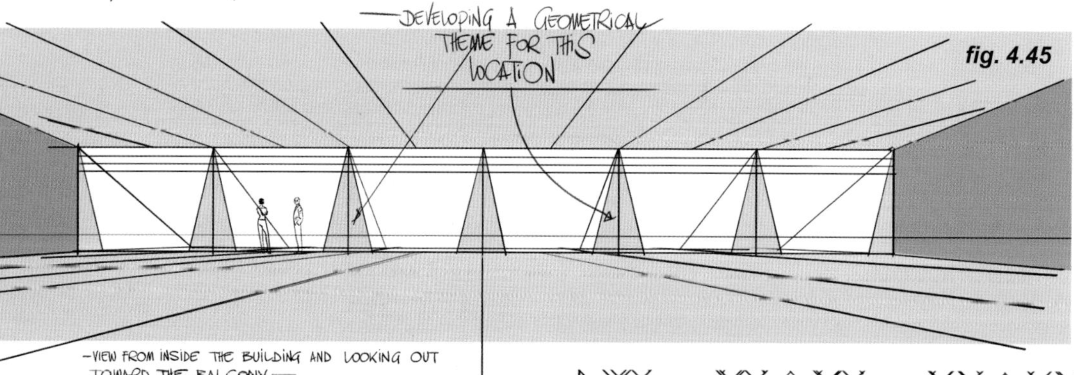

fig. 4.45

Keep exploring. At this point we are looking for **a feeling, a mood,** so it is fine to continue working at a very abstract level.

Figs. 4.45, 4.46: Now the look is being narrowed down to two interesting concepts: the angularity of the space and a closer, more human scale to it.

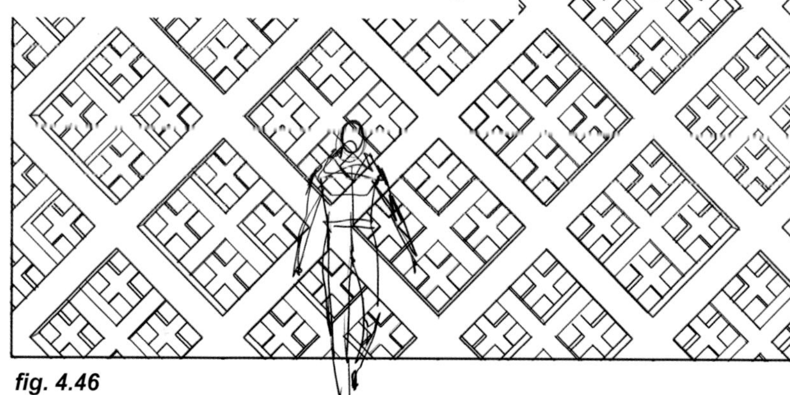

fig. 4.46

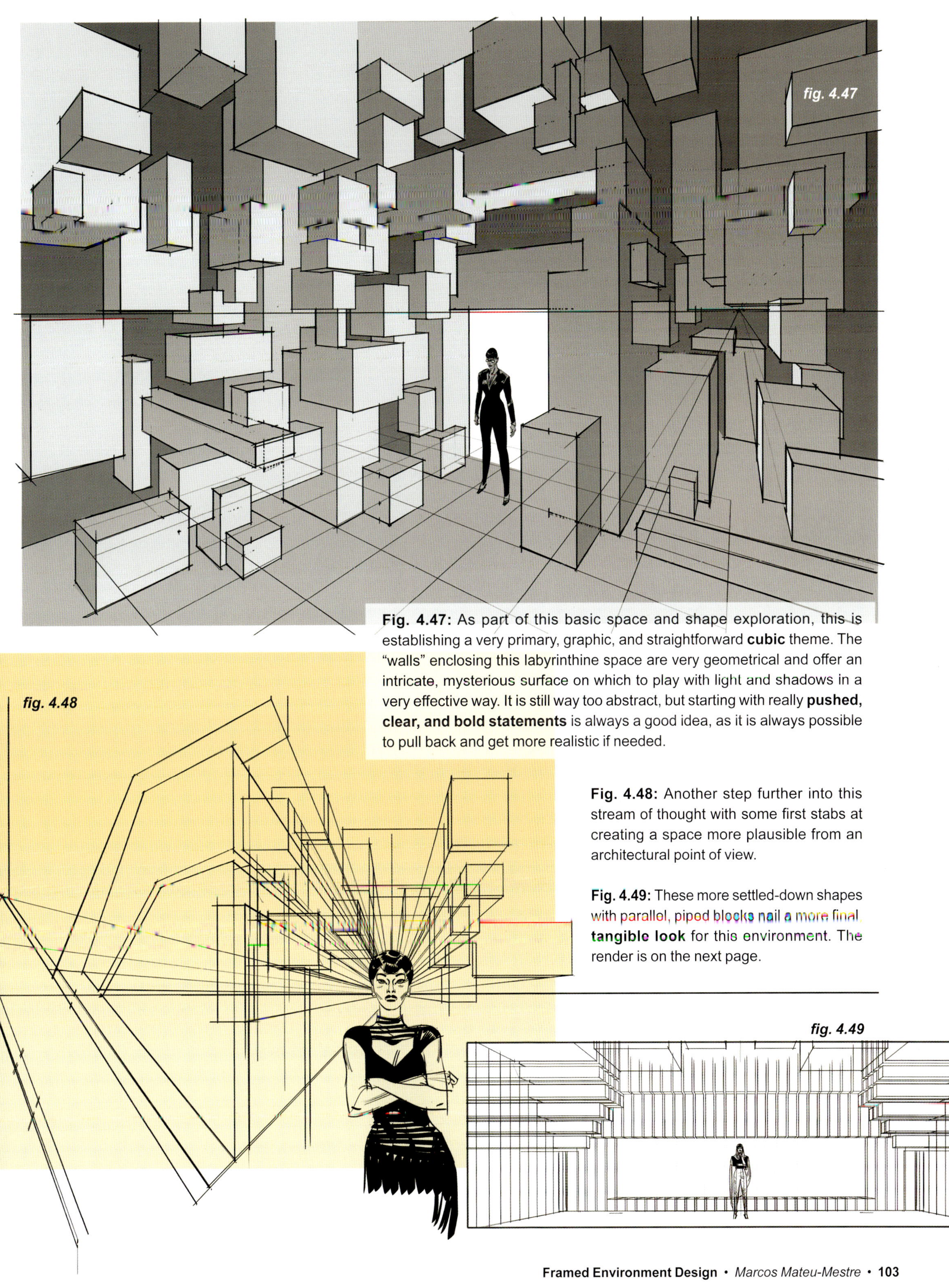

Fig. 4.47: As part of this basic space and shape exploration, this is establishing a very primary, graphic, and straightforward **cubic** theme. The "walls" enclosing this labyrinthine space are very geometrical and offer an intricate, mysterious surface on which to play with light and shadows in a very effective way. It is still way too abstract, but starting with really **pushed, clear, and bold statements** is always a good idea, as it is always possible to pull back and get more realistic if needed.

Fig. 4.48: Another step further into this stream of thought with some first stabs at creating a space more plausible from an architectural point of view.

Fig. 4.49: These more settled-down shapes with parallel, piped blocks nail a more final **tangible look** for this environment. The render is on the next page.

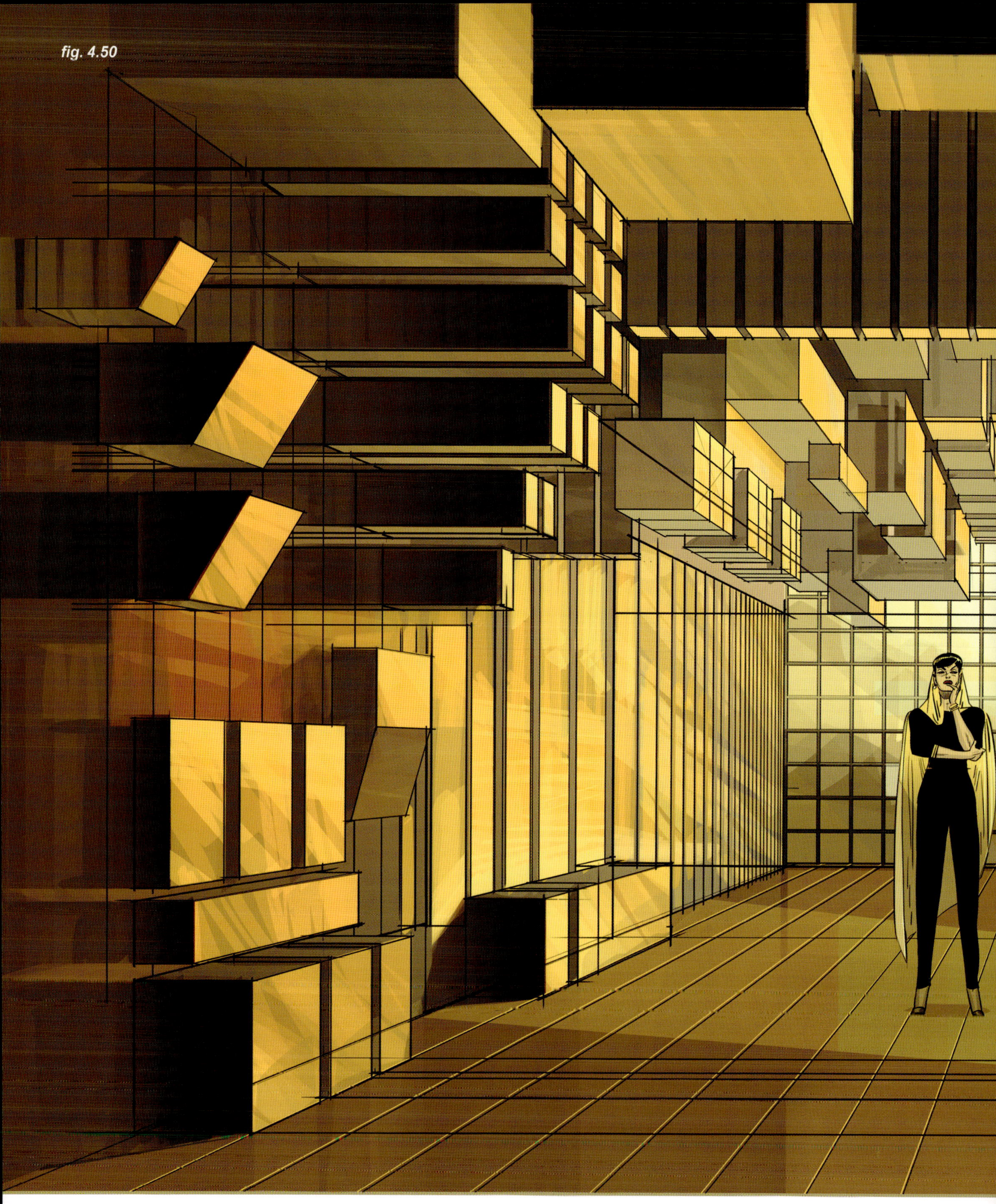

Fig. 4.50: The final execution includes a visual treatment of **intertwined beams and shapes** that give the impression of a solid structure and a sense of style. These shapes could be interpreted as structural beams or even gold bars with the proper colorization and **a reflective surface that plays well with any incoming light.**

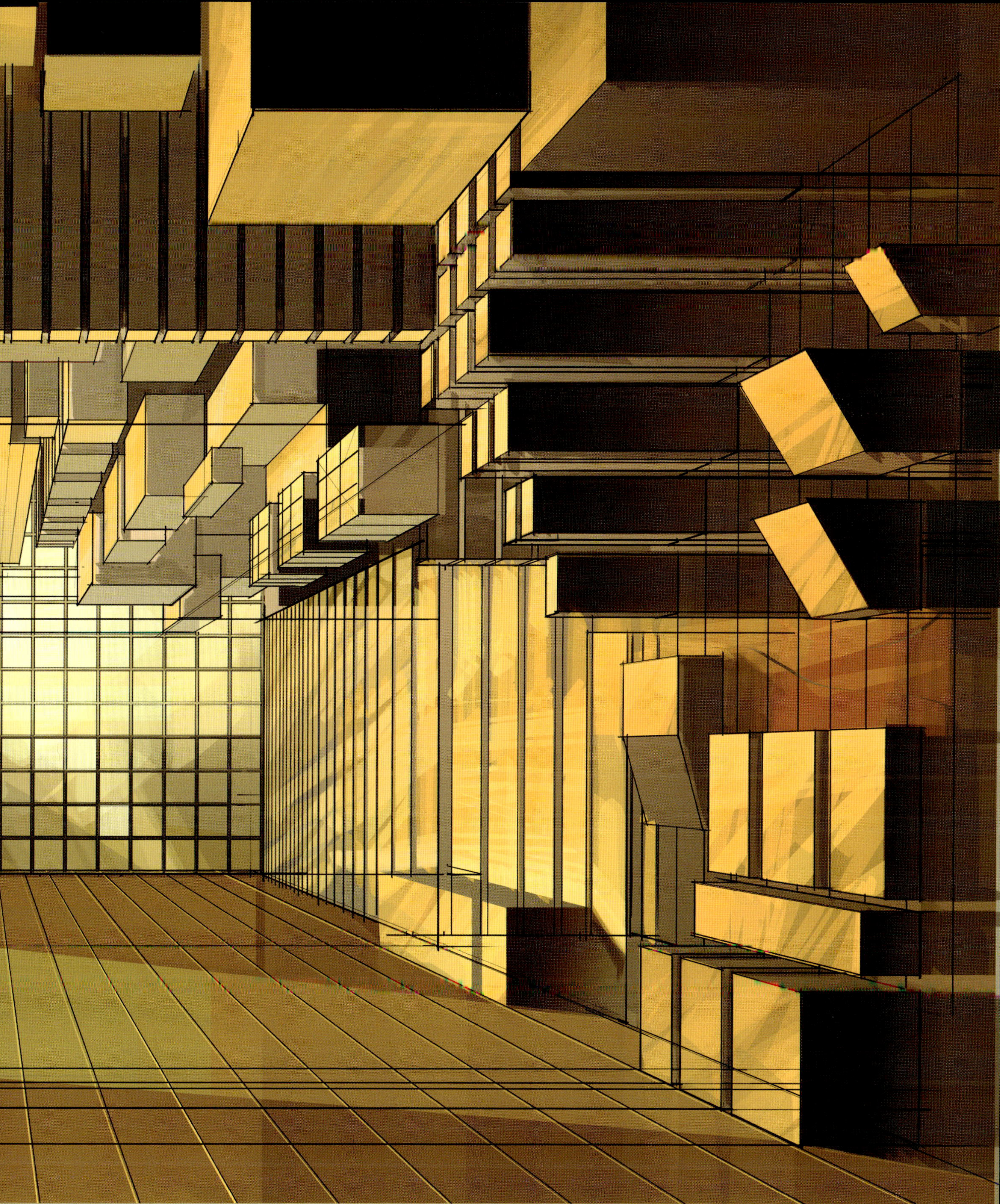

A visual vibe and inspiration I kept in mind during the final steps of this design was the metallic gears and components of the intricate machinery of an antique gold watch. Visualizing these types of references, and consistently reflecting back on them throughout the creative process, helps keep **focus and consistency** toward the design's final look.

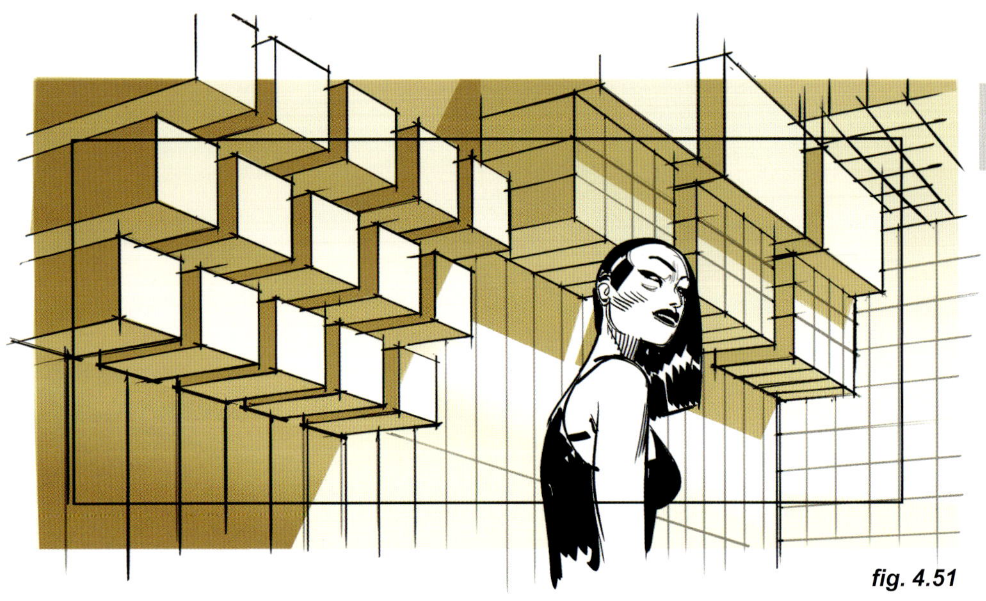

fig. 4.51

Keeping in mind an environment's potential to offer interesting camera points of view, these bold, angular shapes can bring a lot of game when composing shots.

Fig. 4.51: A low-angle shot of our character with a background that displays these rectangular shapes' strong sense of depth and perspective.

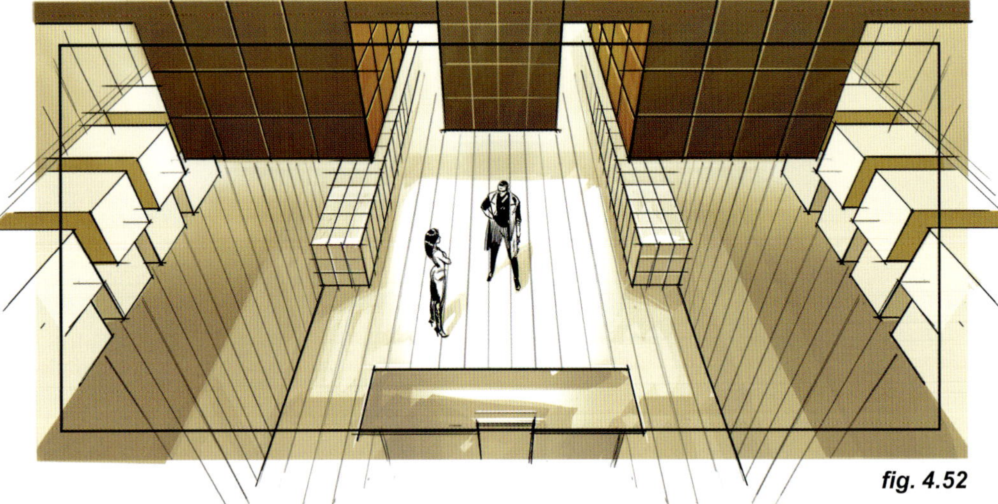

fig. 4.52

Fig. 4.52: A high-angle shot with the camera attached to the ceiling brings up the strong, backlit volumes in the top-foreground of the composition.

Fig. 4.53: This tilt-down shot starts on frame **A,** focusing only on the intricate and labyrinthine environment to establish a rather tortuous mood, which informs the relationship between the two characters as the camera lands on frame **B.**

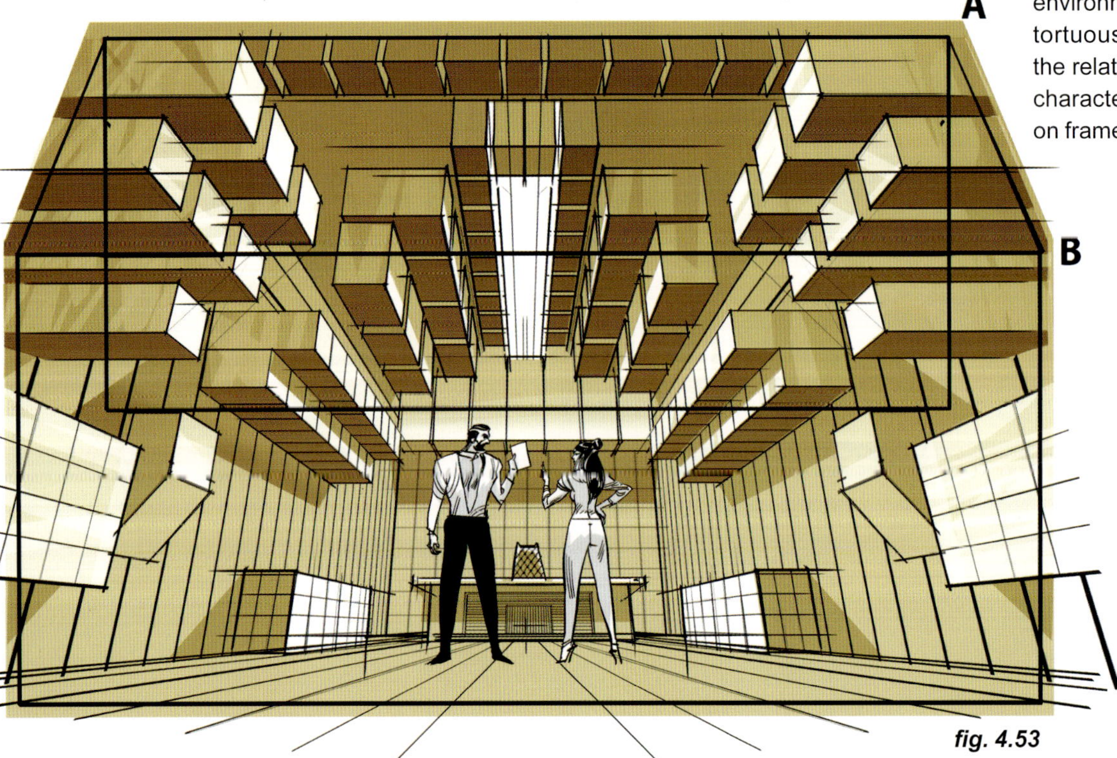

fig. 4.53

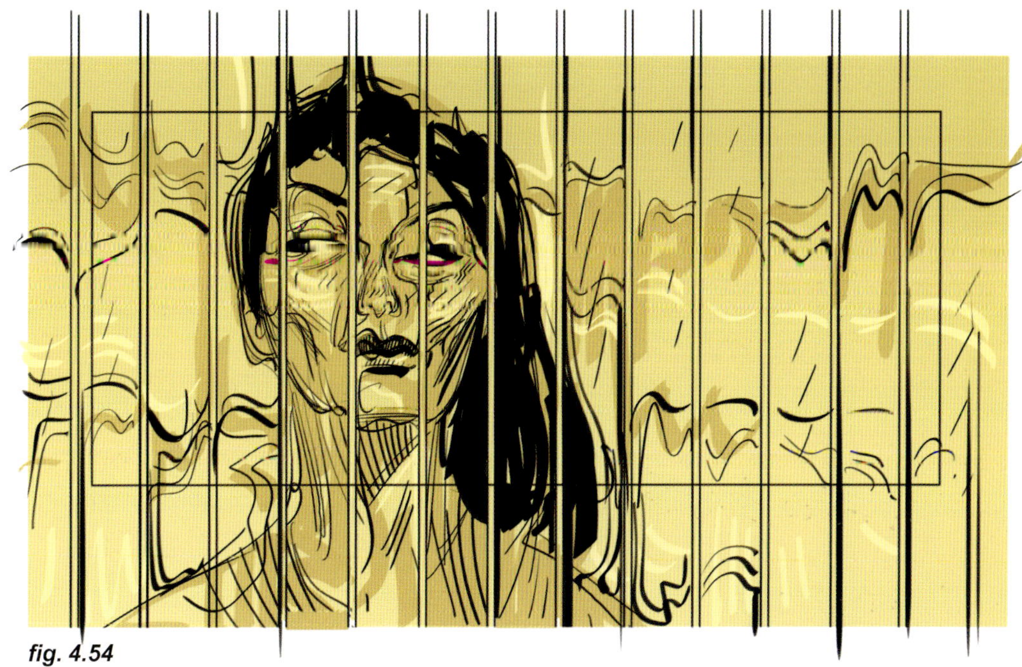

Fig. 4.54: Repetitive geometric blocks create a pattern on this wall made of reflective material. These individual blocks **distort the reflected image of the character** in a potentially unsettling moment in her personal story.

fig. 4.54

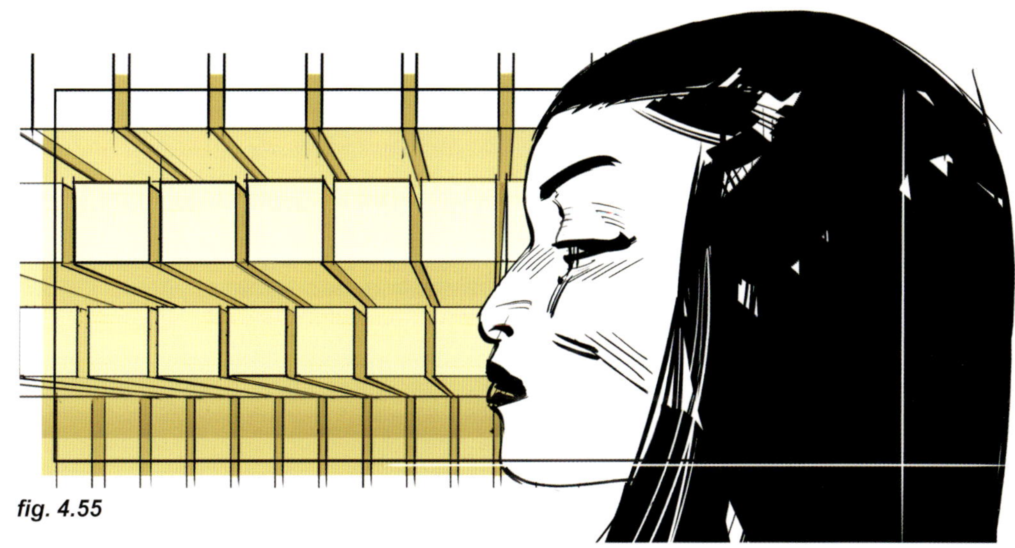

Fig. 4.55 A wide-angle lens can result in a level of visual distortion of the character's head in the foreground while the background shapes take on a very dynamic look. (See discussion on lenses in the book *Framed Ink,* pages 028–030.)

fig. 4.55

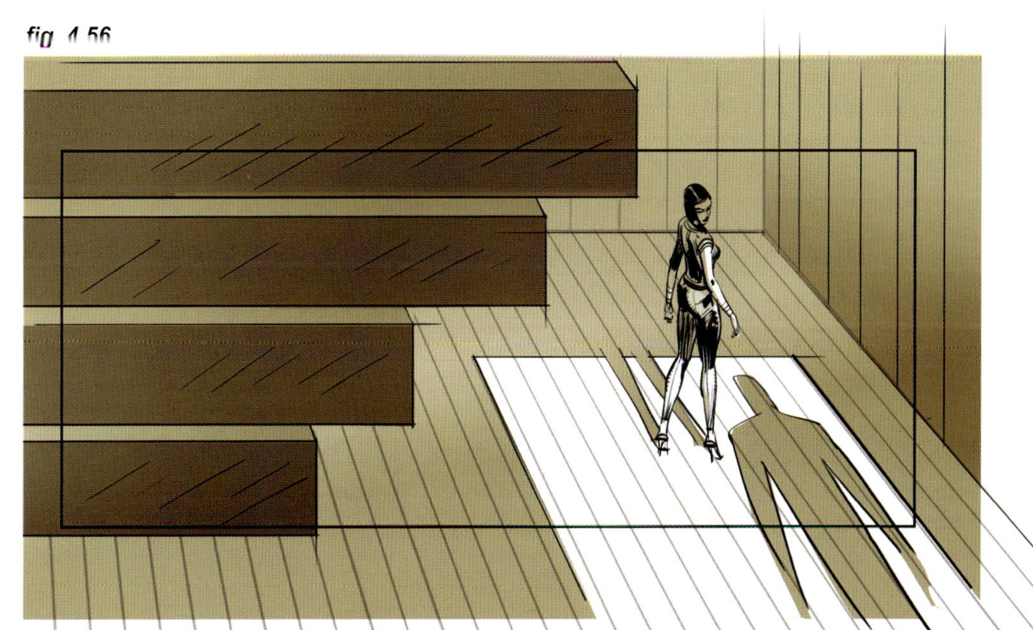

Fig. 4.56: The strong geometric shapes in the foreground visually press the character up against a corner, right at the moment an unexpected and unwelcome visitor shows up at the door (as the cast shadow on the floor indicates).

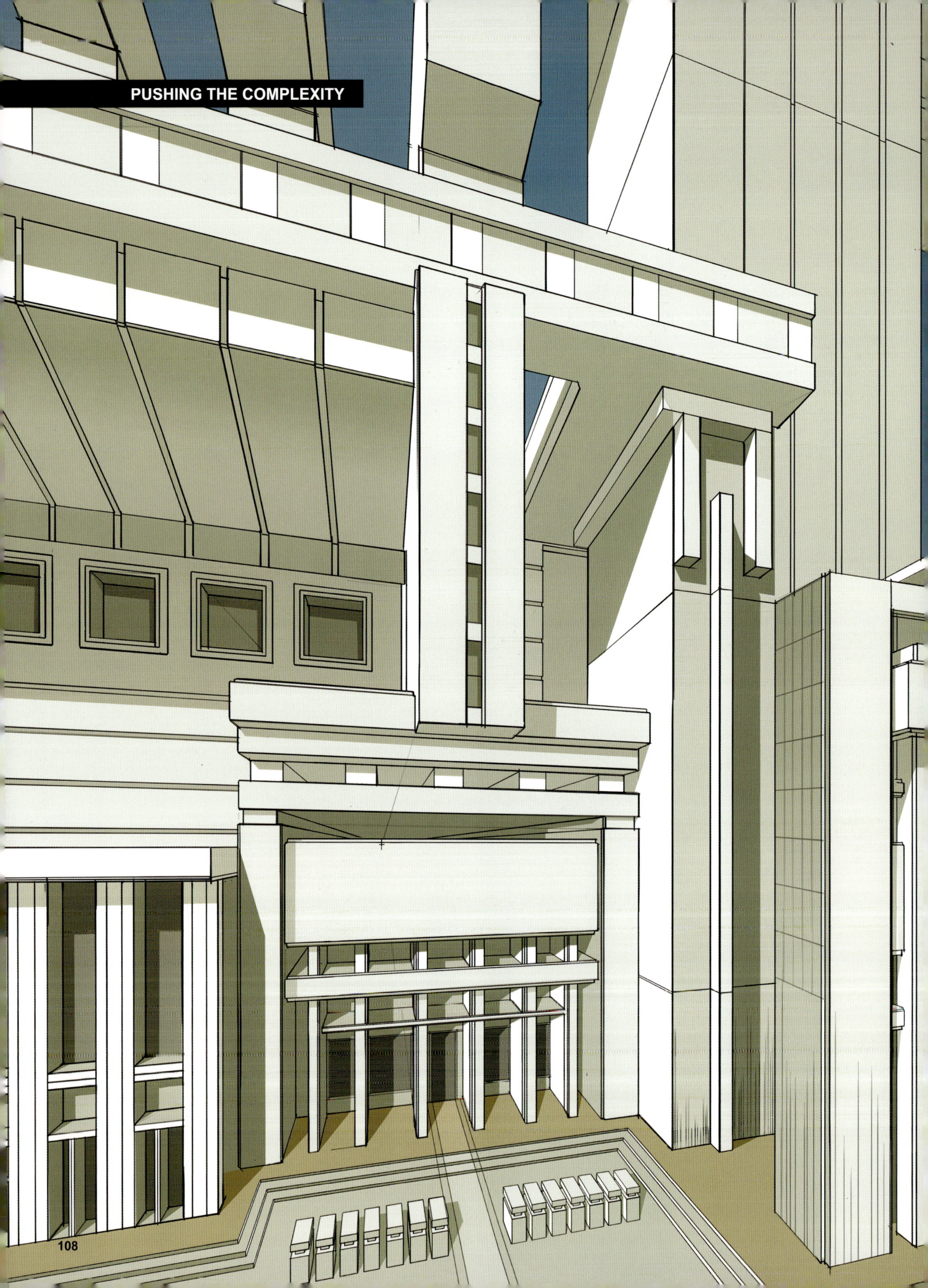

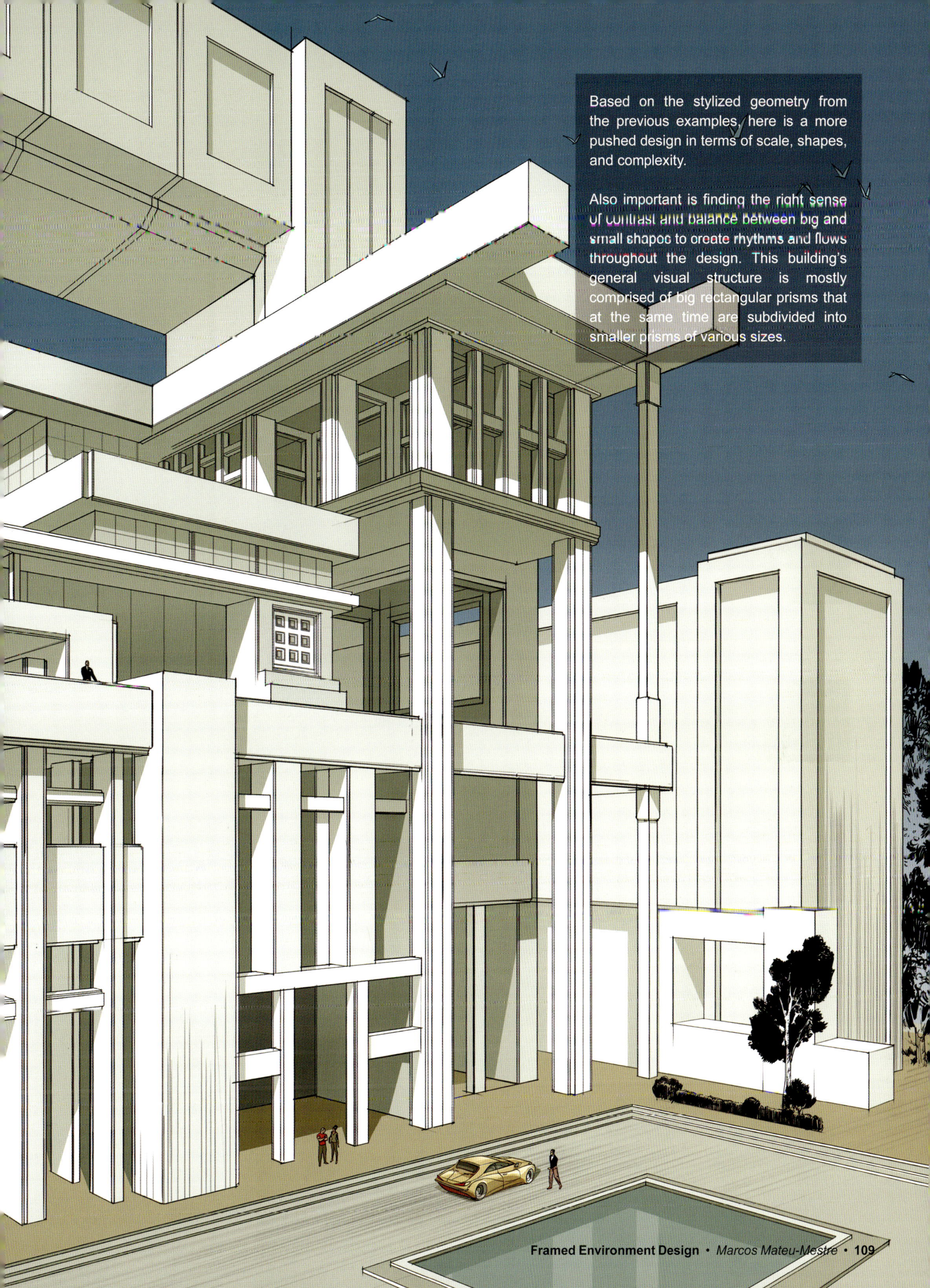

Based on the stylized geometry from the previous examples, here is a more pushed design in terms of scale, shapes, and complexity.

Also important is finding the right sense of contrast and balance between big and small shapes to create rhythms and flows throughout the design. This building's general visual structure is mostly comprised of big rectangular prisms that at the same time are subdivided into smaller prisms of various sizes.

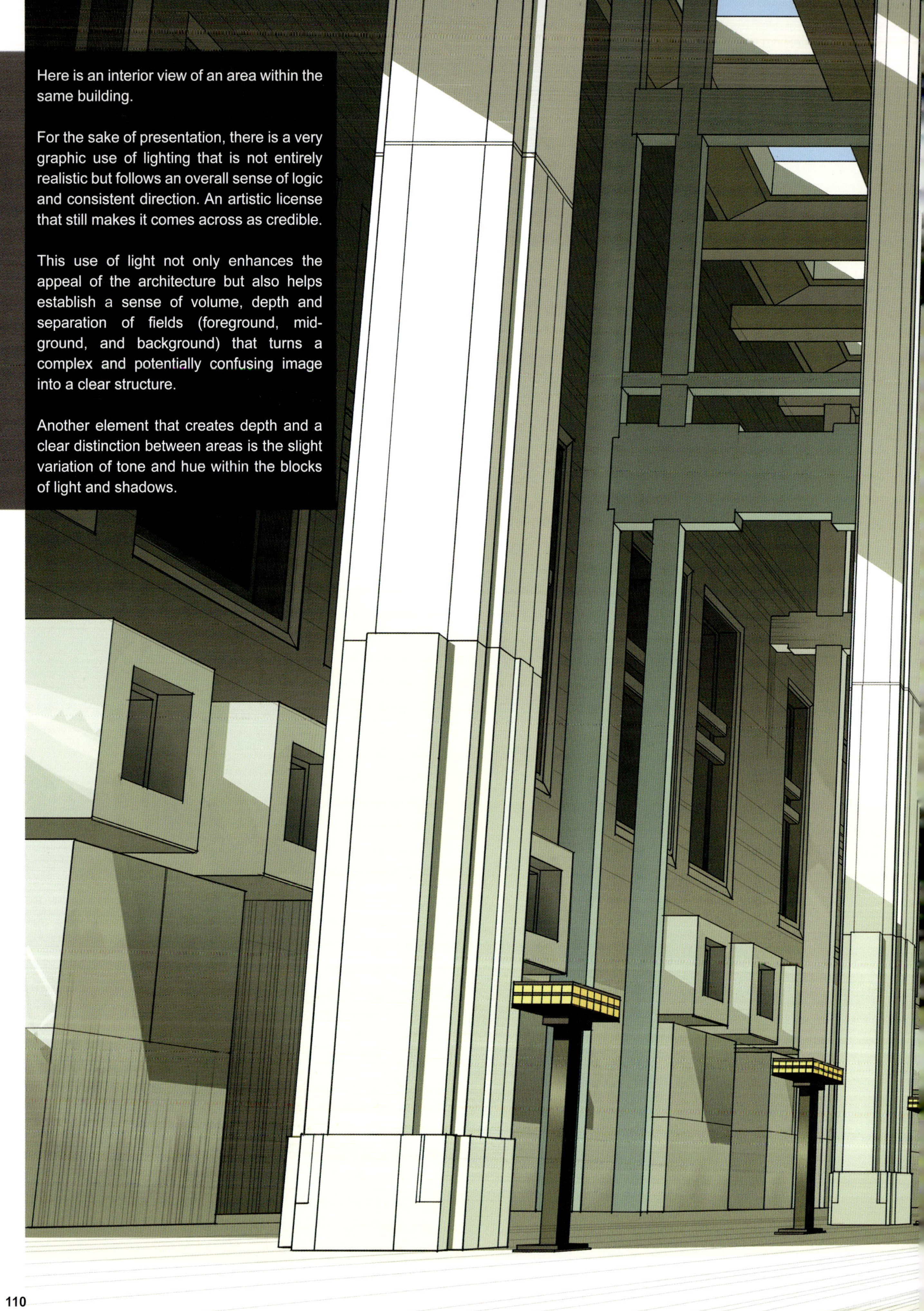

Here is an interior view of an area within the same building.

For the sake of presentation, there is a very graphic use of lighting that is not entirely realistic but follows an overall sense of logic and consistent direction. An artistic license that still makes it comes across as credible.

This use of light not only enhances the appeal of the architecture but also helps establish a sense of volume, depth and separation of fields (foreground, mid-ground, and background) that turns a complex and potentially confusing image into a clear structure.

Another element that creates depth and a clear distinction between areas is the slight variation of tone and hue within the blocks of light and shadows.

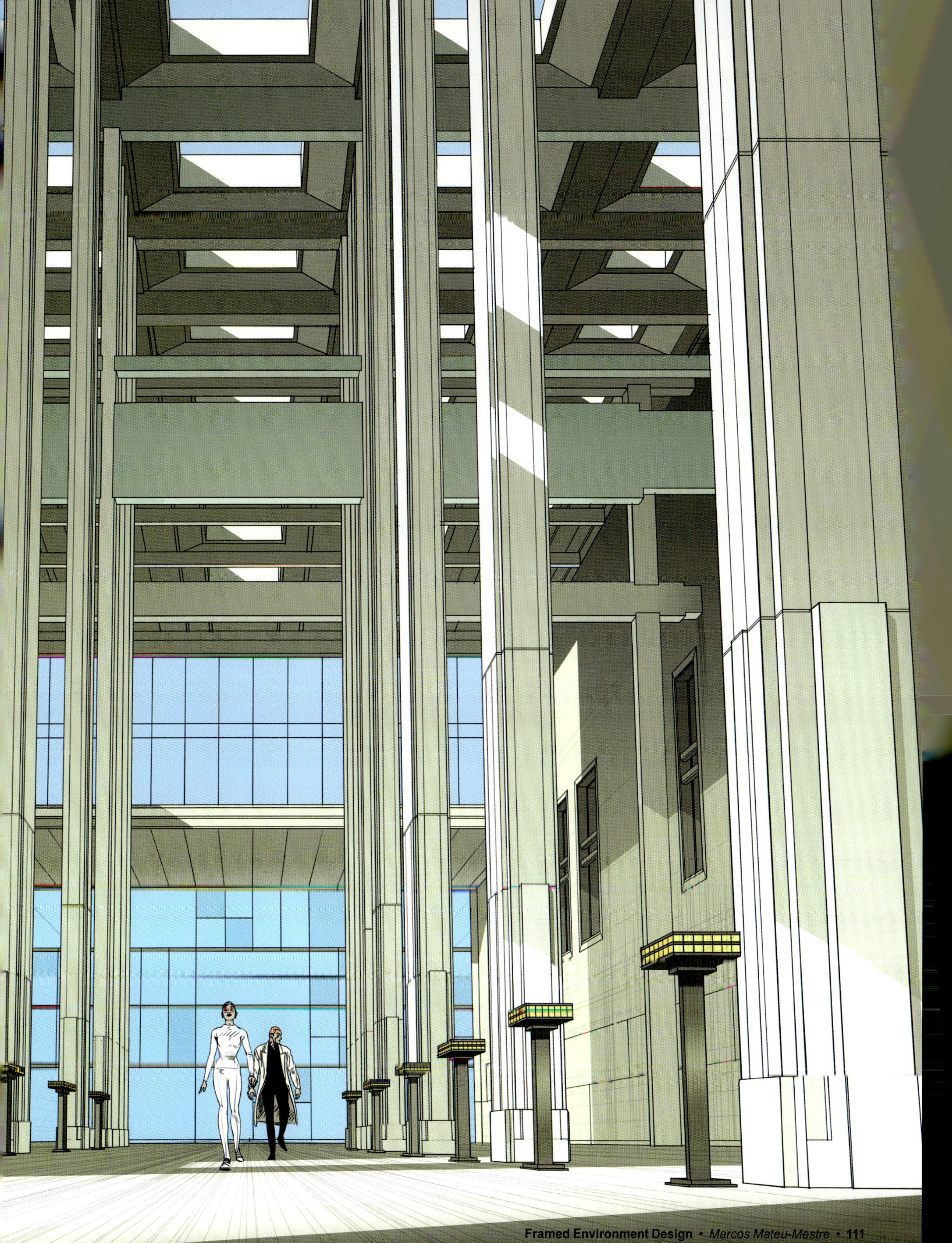

In general, curved shapes tend to look and feel very natural and organic, and because of that, inspiration can be gleaned from many commonplace forms and elements that surround us every day.

No matter how interesting an idea seems to be in our imagination, we cannot be sure we found what we need until we quickly visualize it as a sketch. It is by materializing something on a piece of paper, exploring what that design looks like from different angles and also surrounded by other elements of the environment, that we can confirm everything works well as a concept, both individually and in context.

Let's imagine a case now in which we want to develop strong, **unusual shapes**. Here are a number of sketches that push the envelope. Then, once we arrive at certain extremes, we can always pull back the intensity if that is what we think the project demands.

The reason why this is easier than starting off timidly and then trying to take it to the next level is because the first thing we need to try to figure out is, **"What makes this design unique and special?"** And that is what we should try to focus on from the start. Once we have established this element of "uniqueness," then we can do whatever is needed (push it further or pull it back), but now from a **position of clarity** of what elements must be preserved no matter what.

Fig. 4.57: A few examples of pushed exploration.

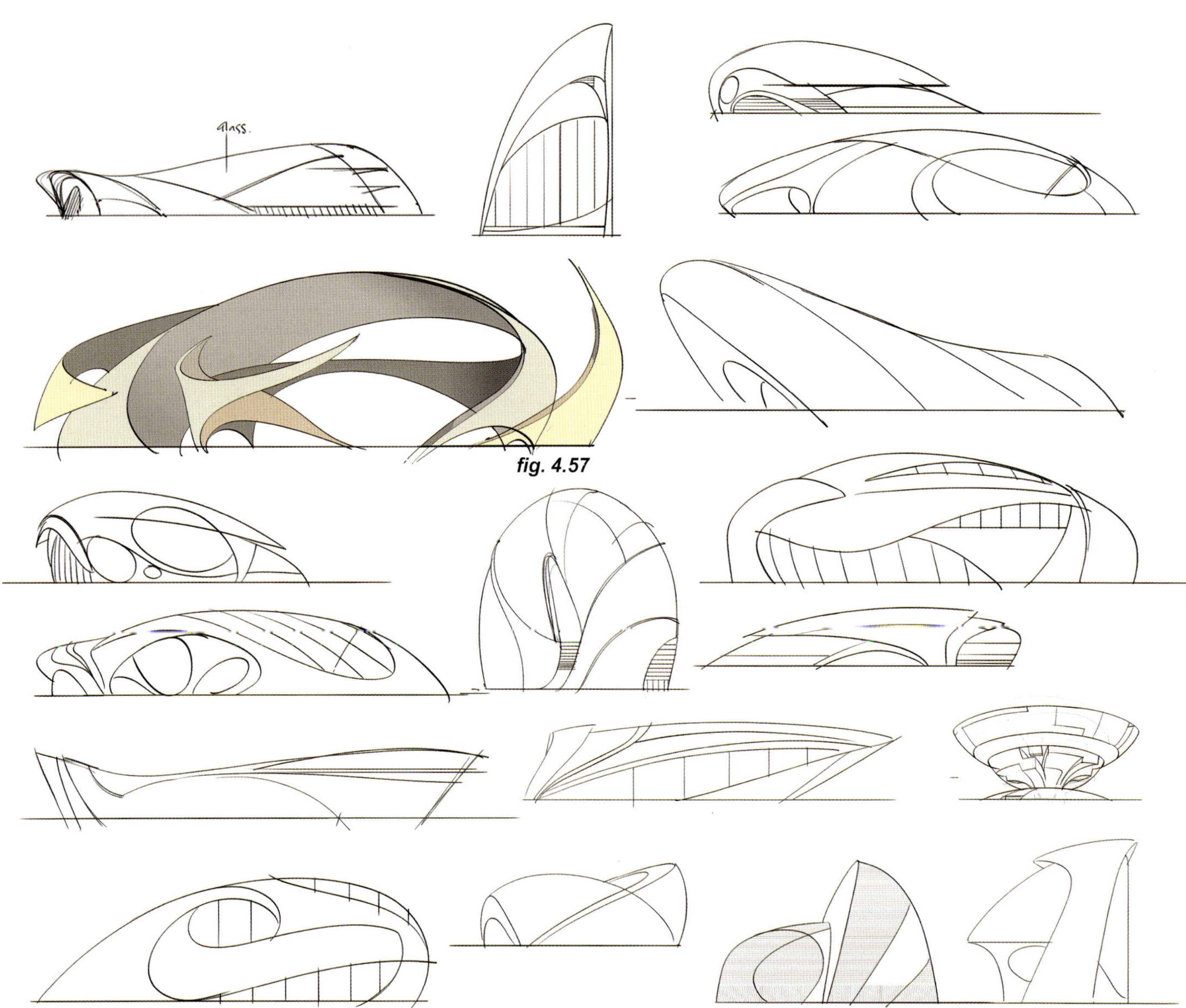

THOUGHT PROCESS

After having loosened up our hand and wrist with the previous sketches (similar to the exercise proposed in the book *Framed Drawing Techniques* on pages 016 and 074*)*, we can distill this flow of ideas down to a more grounded level and start designing buildings that would appear more plausible in the real world. This batch of concept sketches shows how ideas evolved.

Figs. 4.58–4.61: Playing essentially with curved lines and round shapes, these sketches went from a building inspired by the silhouette of a tall ship to one inspired by a football, to finally landing on a structure based on the idea of a pile of used tires.

Figs. 4.62, 4.63: From there the design evolved into further grounded ideas, like a solid structure with a distinctive look that could simply be described as a "horseshoe" or "concentric circles."

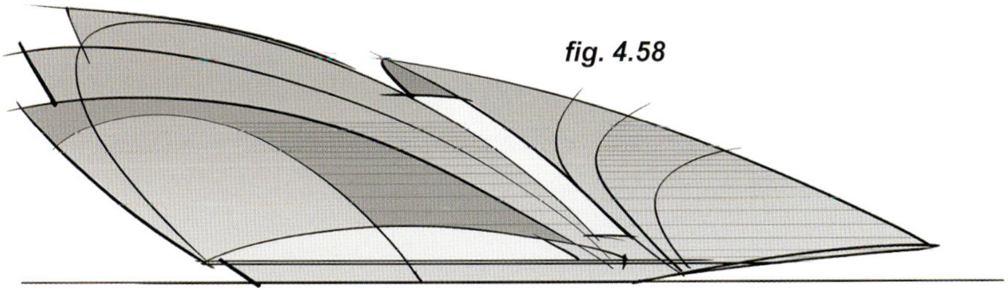

fig. 4.58

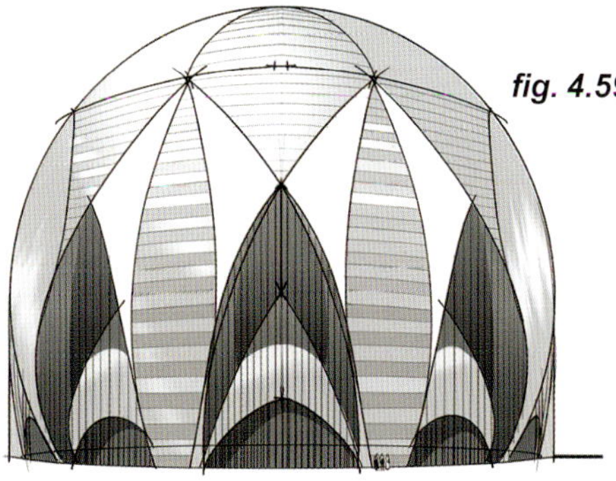

fig. 4.59

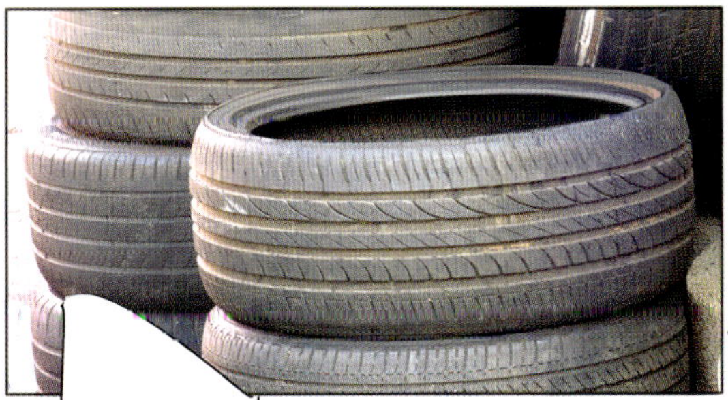

fig. 4.60

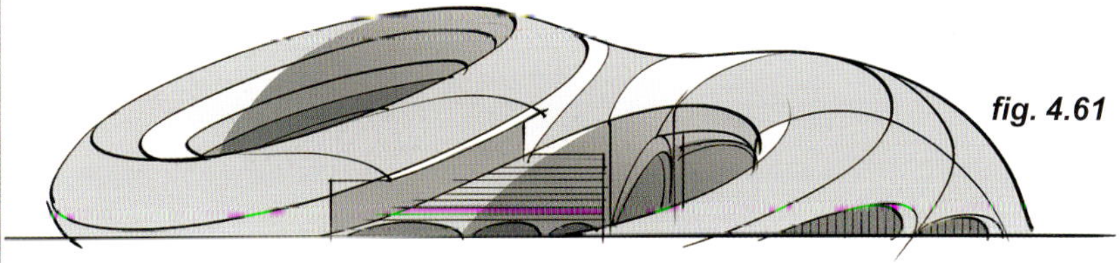

fig. 4.61

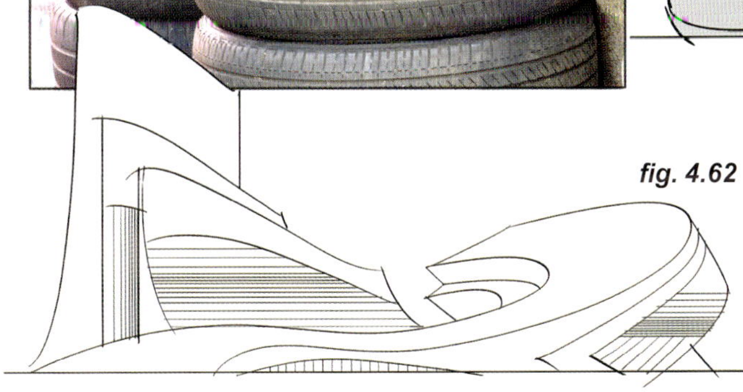

fig. 4.62

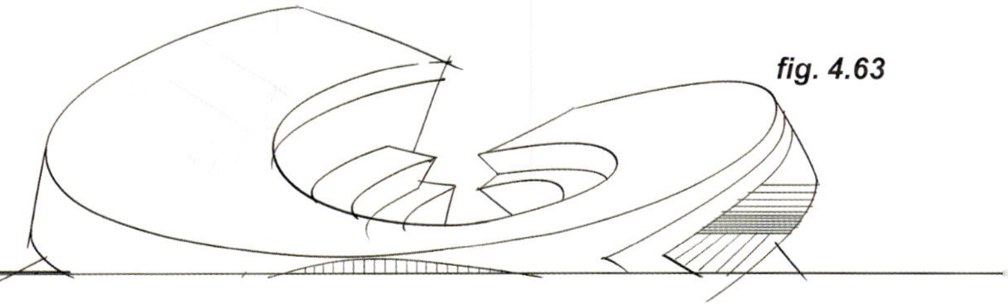

fig. 4.63

Figs. 4.64, 4.65: Taking off from these two horseshoe-like shapes we arrive at our next idea, with two U-shaped buildings forming an interlocking unit as they face each other—one (in orange) bigger than the other, engulfing the smaller one within its bigger shape in a way that is reminiscent of the layered petals of a rose. An interesting idea that merits its further development in the next pages.

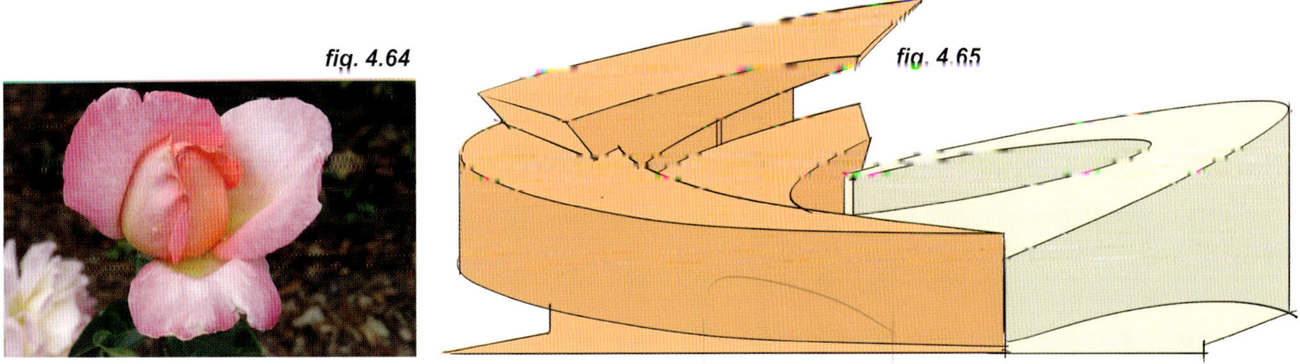

fig. 4.64

fig. 4.65

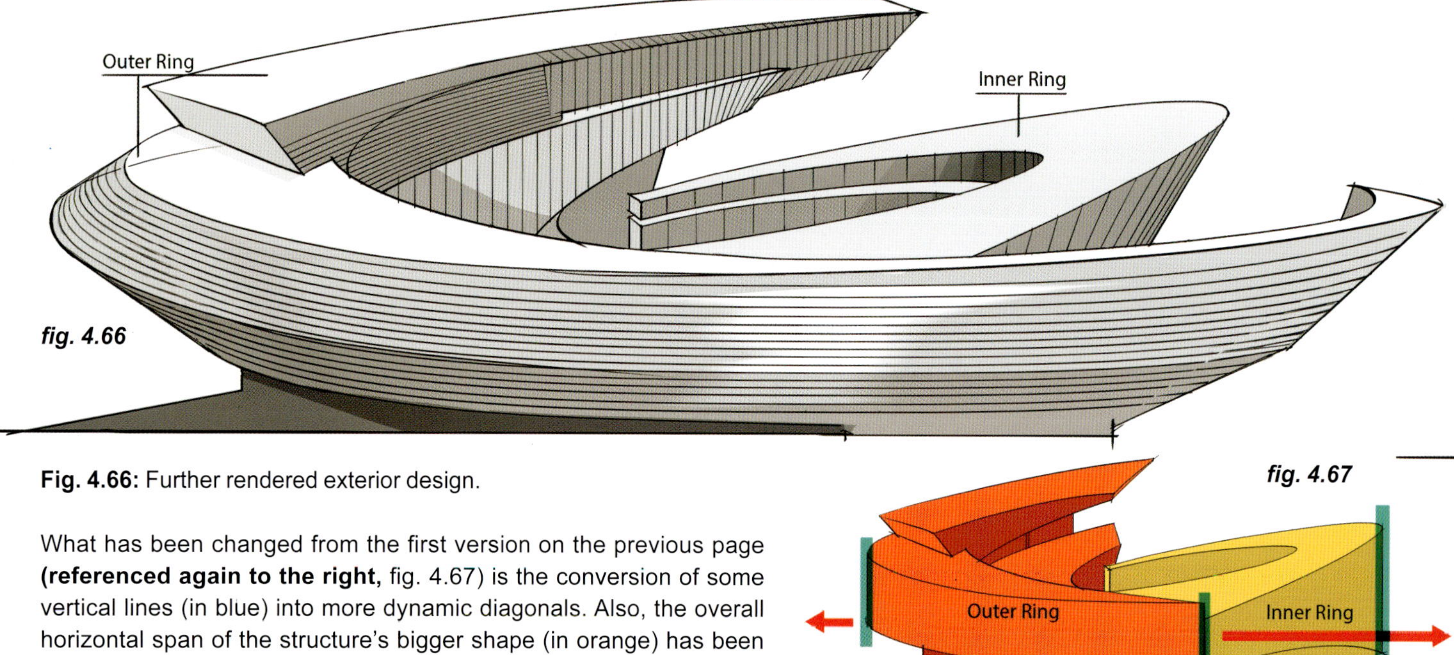

Fig. 4.66: Further rendered exterior design.

What has been changed from the first version on the previous page **(referenced again to the right,** fig. 4.67) is the conversion of some vertical lines (in blue) into more dynamic diagonals. Also, the overall horizontal span of the structure's bigger shape (in orange) has been stretched sideways (red arrows) so that it now further surrounds the smaller, inner one, creating a more dynamic and stylized look.

As a next step, we will start exploring design options for the inner courtyard of the building. How can we use these curved and round shapes with angled accents for its design?

Adding to the combination of these shapes, we will also focus on the distinctive look of two major and opposed curved structures evolving around each other, a peculiar look no matter where we view it from, inside or outside.

Normally we would build the edifice so that we could shoot exteriors and interior views on the same model, in that way all views would exactly match the structure. Yet, for some specific shots we might want to alter some of the views.

Let's say, for example, we build this as a 3D model that looks very dramatic from the outside, but when the camera moves inside, the views look too narrow and claustrophobic. Occasionally, we can consider the solution of creating a model for the exterior that feels good as such, and a second model for the interior which is the same but wider and more open.

In that case we would need to verify that the exterior and interior shots are not connected by any direct camera moves. The moment we shoot the exterior and then move the camera inside the building in continuity and without cuts, the transition between one and the other will most likely be impossible to execute if this change happens in real time and we see how things connect (or don't really connect!) with each other.

Fig. 4.68: Below, a first attempt at creating such a concept.

Predominant curves conform these three floors of staircases, stacked in a diagonal fashion (blue arrow) rather than straight up vertically, in striking contrast to the verticals and horizontals in the surrounding areas. (Note the human figures added for scale.)

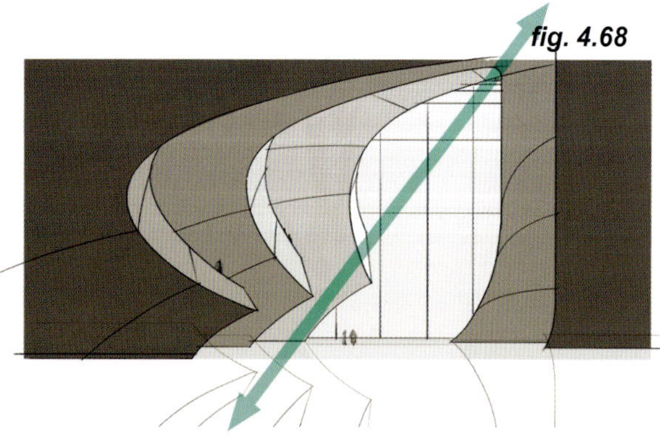

Fig. 4.69: As usual, the top-down view of a map will help our team clarify the flow of story events in a location, as well as the position of any potential camera shots.

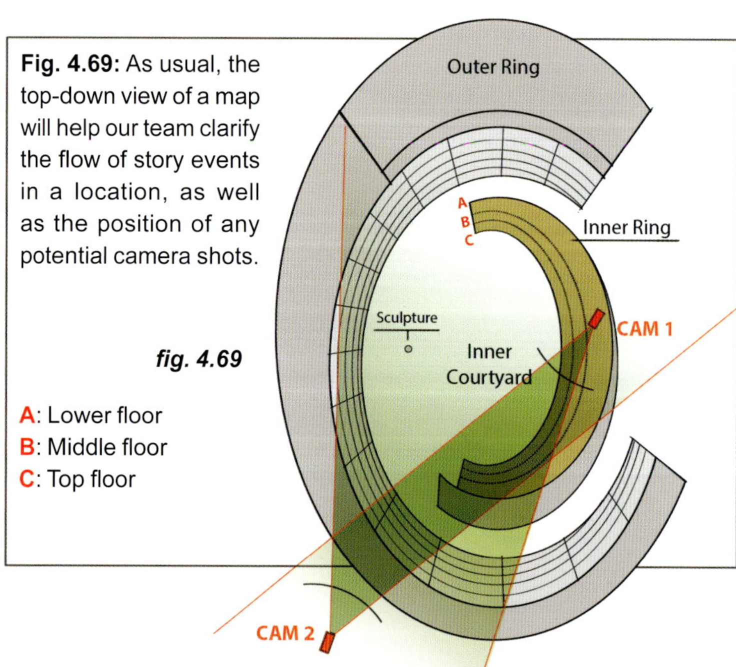

fig. 4.69

A: Lower floor
B: Middle floor
C: Top floor

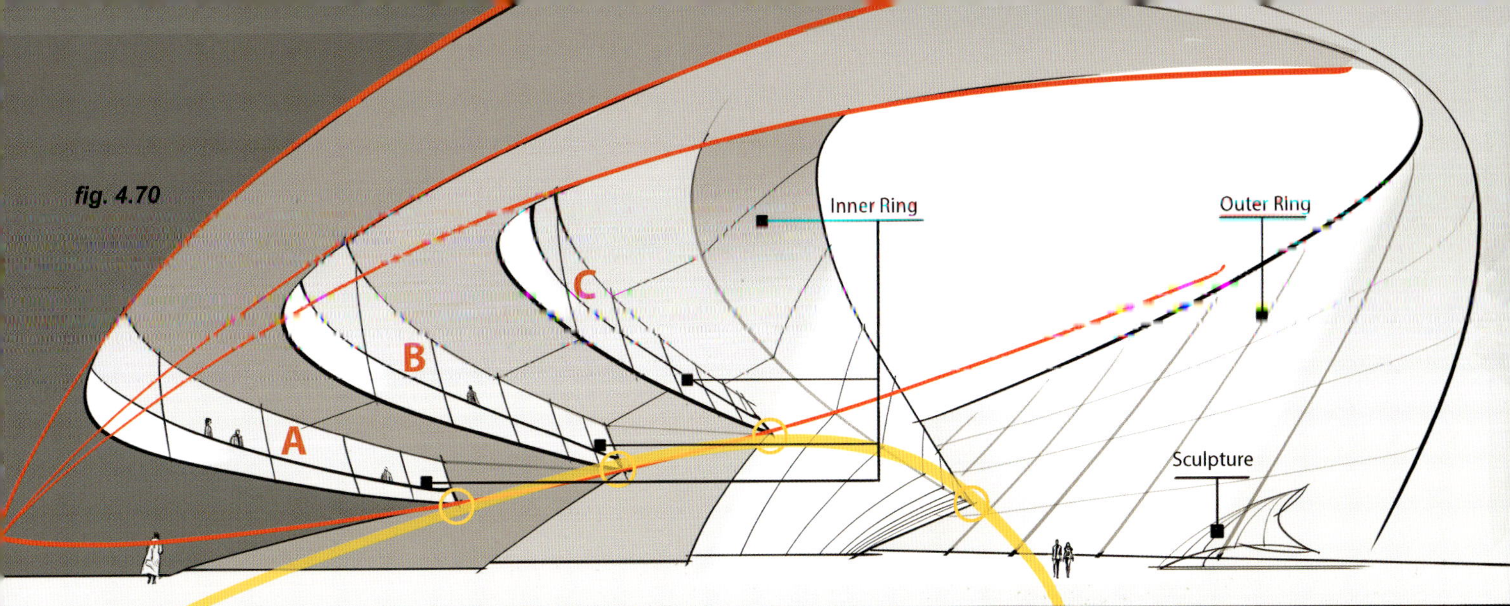

Fig. 4.70: An advanced version of the building's main inner courtyard with all the elements previously discussed, plus a pushed sense of dynamics and imbalance within a structure of flowing curves (represented by the red and yellow lines).

The three floors visible from this angle have been marked with the letters **A**, **B**, and **C**. As usual, the inclusion of characters to communicate the space's sense of scale is very important.

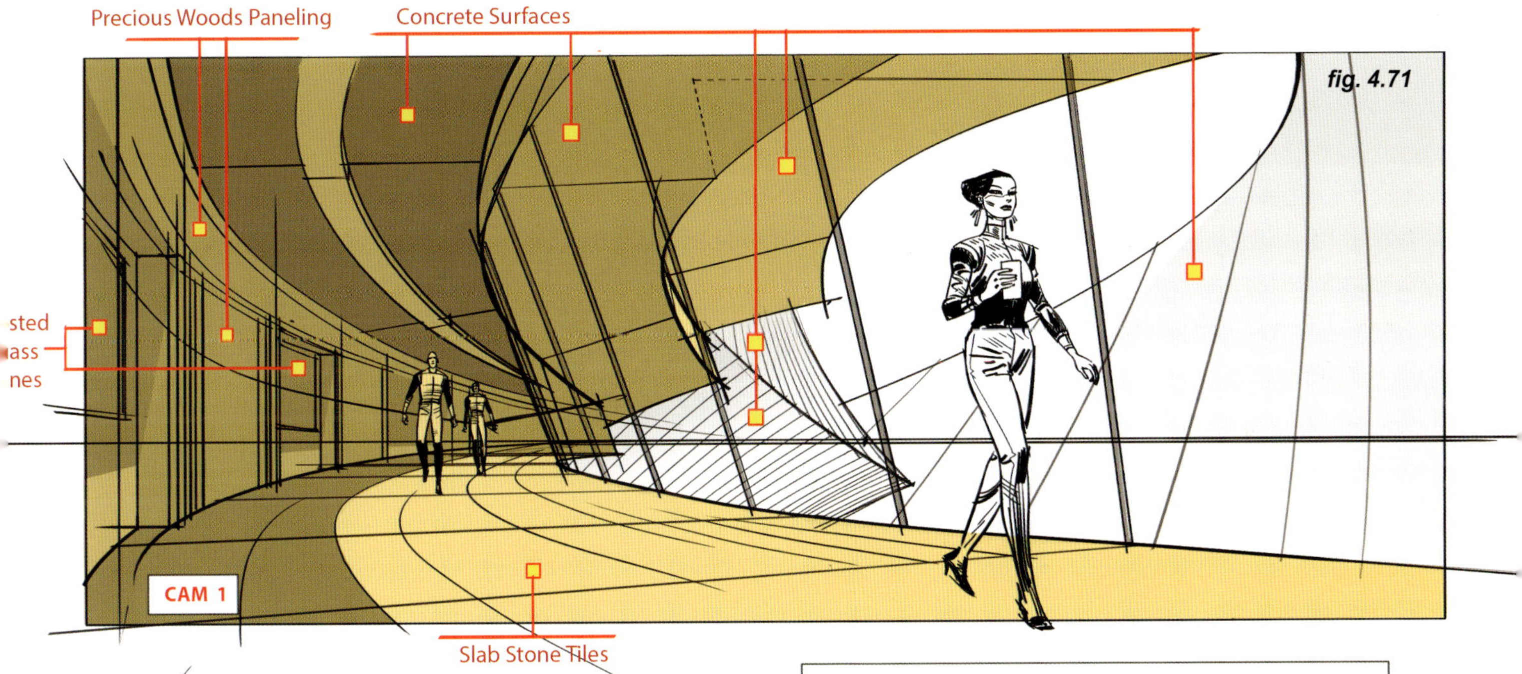

Fig. 4.71: Camera 1 view, located on floor A. (See camera position in fig. 4.69.) Notes have been added indicating the architectural materials and textures envisioned for this location.

Fig. 4.72: Reverse camera angle (Camera 2, fig. 4.69) this time from the ground floor.

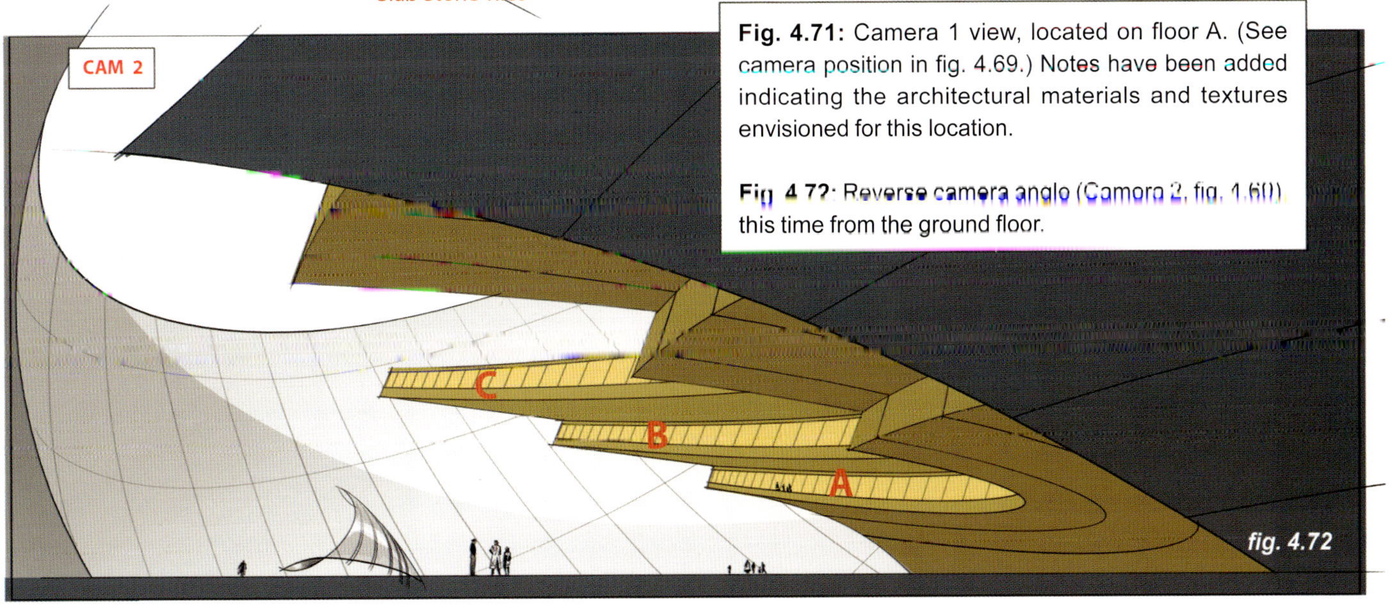

Fig. 4.73: While exploring interior spaces of this building, like apartments, offices, and labs, there are two very distinctive features available: the overall **curved** style of the construction and its **ascending** ramp design (see orange arrows).

Fig. 4.74: These ascending lines on the glass can be visually played against the verticals of the walls and the horizontals of the ground planes for contrast.

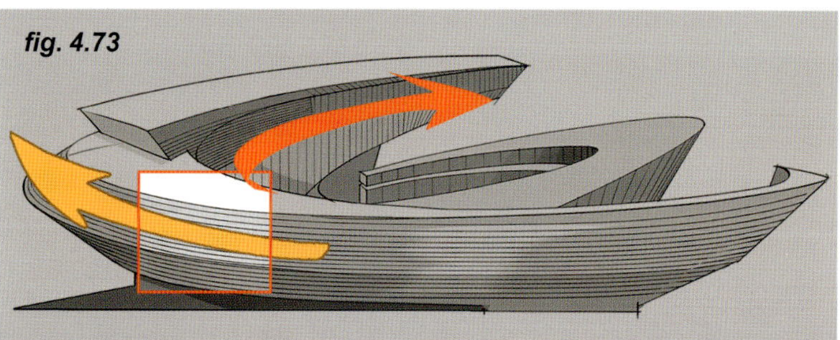

fig. 4.73

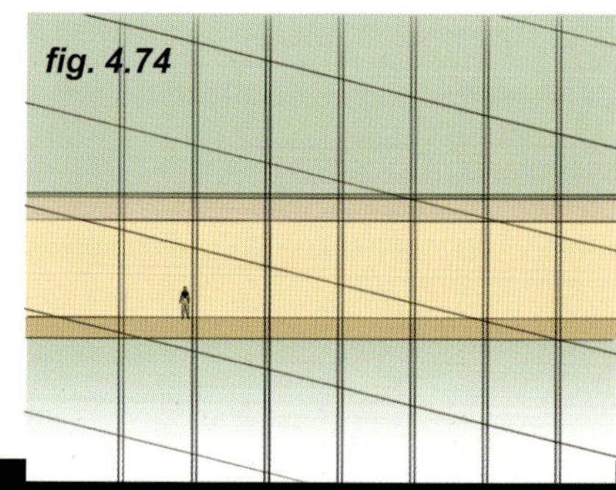

fig. 4.74

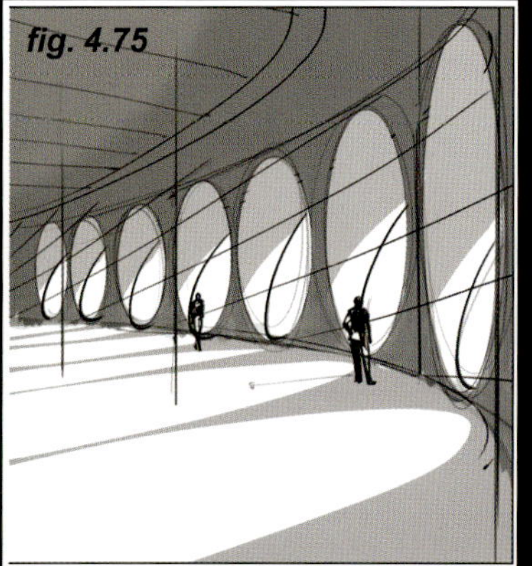

fig. 4.75

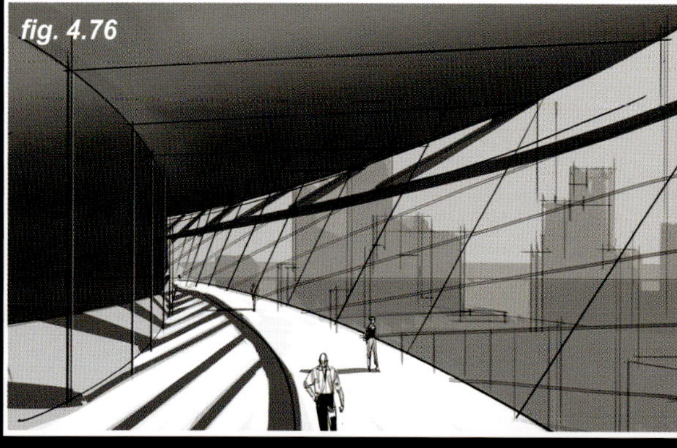

fig. 4.76

A number of preliminary sketches explore various options:

Figs. 4.75, 4.76: Searching for ways to introduce curves, diagonals, and their projected shadow effects before pushing the shapes further.

Fig. 4.77: Although the exterior of the building looks graphic and experimental, an interior design like the one in this sketch runs the risk of being too organic and not belonging to the same world. We have to find the right balance.

Figs. 4.78 , 4.79: Things are now becoming more feasible, with a sense of architecture that is daring yet more settled than fig. 4.76, making more sense for this case.

Figs. 4.80, 4.81: These start to emphasize the curves that were explored in fig. 4.79.

The area between the big arched glass window (in green) and the rooms in the round area to the left (in yellow) now becomes a very long hallway from which to overlook the city.

Fig. 4.82: We have decided to give the place a really pushed height for scale. That allows it to be subdivided into different levels (red area).

Fig. 4.83: Getting to a cleaner version of the concept that is almost ready to turn into a final design (*next pages*).

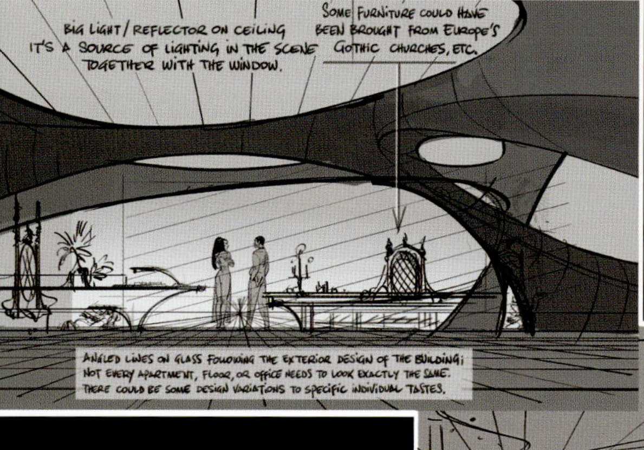

fig. 4.77

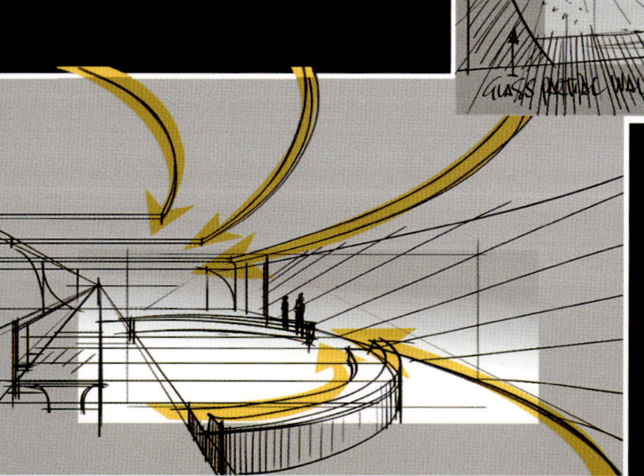

fig. 4.78

fig. 4.79

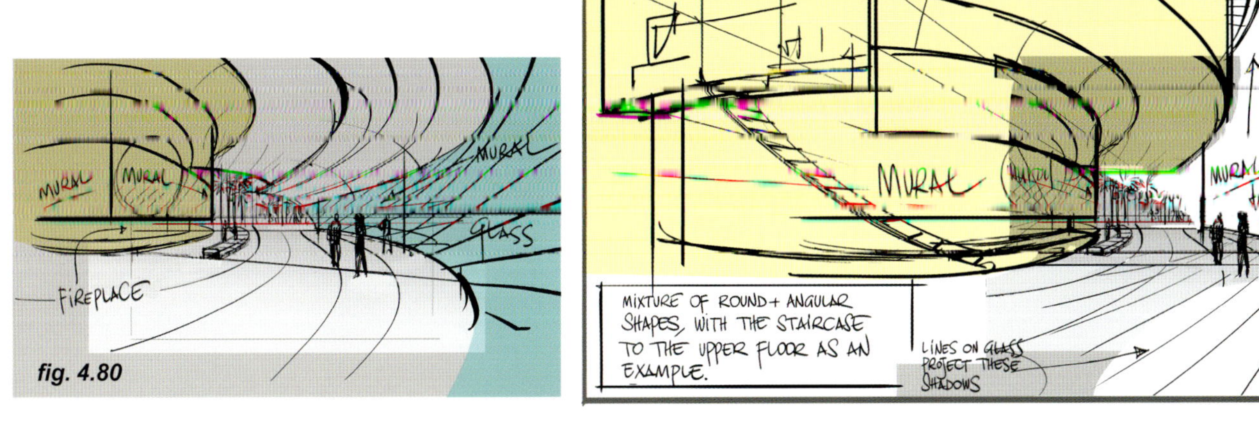

MURAL
MURAL
MURAL
GLASS
FIREPLACE
fig. 4.80
MURAL
MURAL
MURAL
GLASS
MIXTURE OF ROUND + ANGULAR SHAPES, WITH THE STAIRCASE TO THE UPPER FLOOR AS AN EXAMPLE.
LINES ON GLASS PROTECT THESE SHADOWS
fig. 4.81

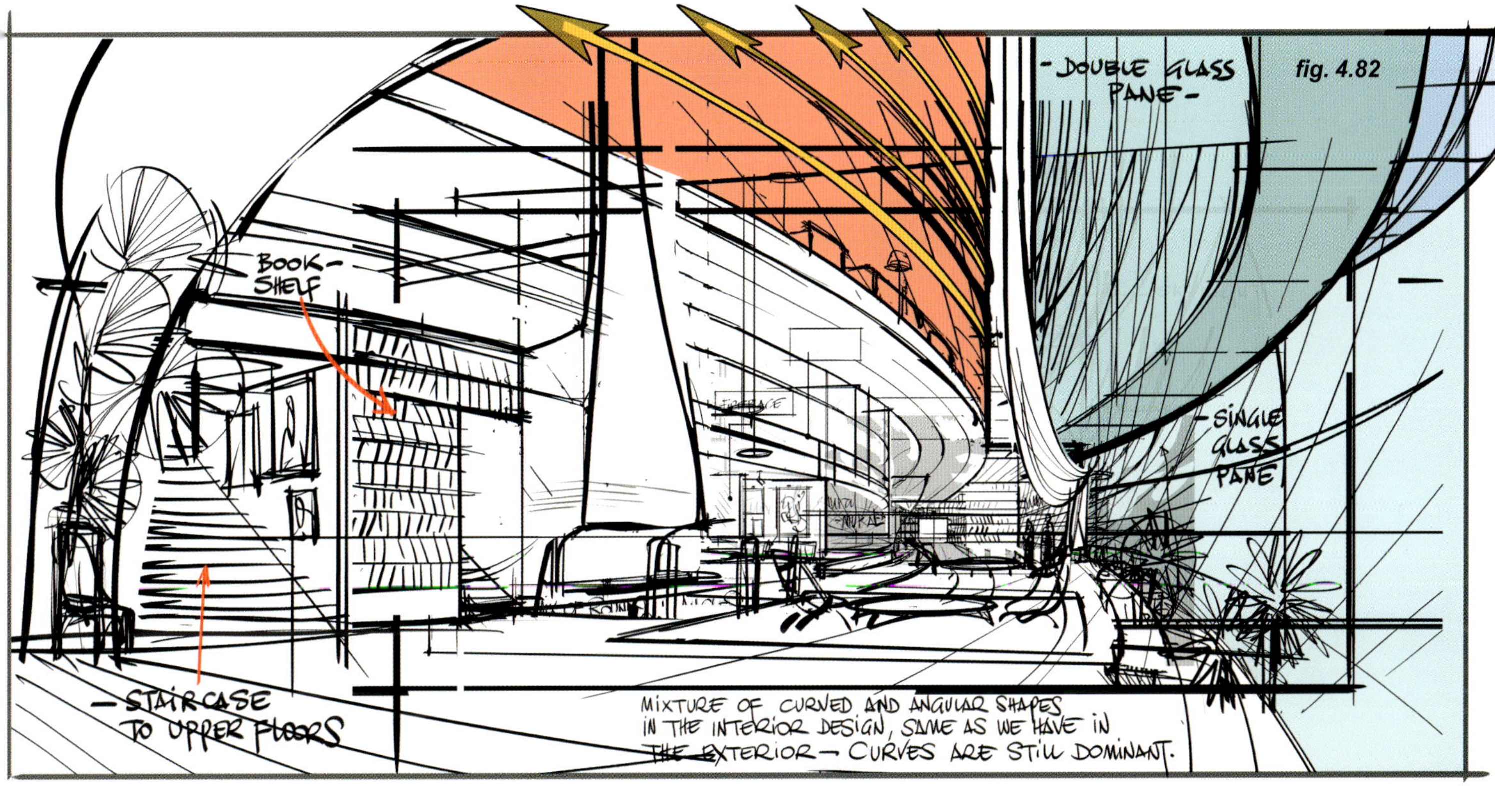

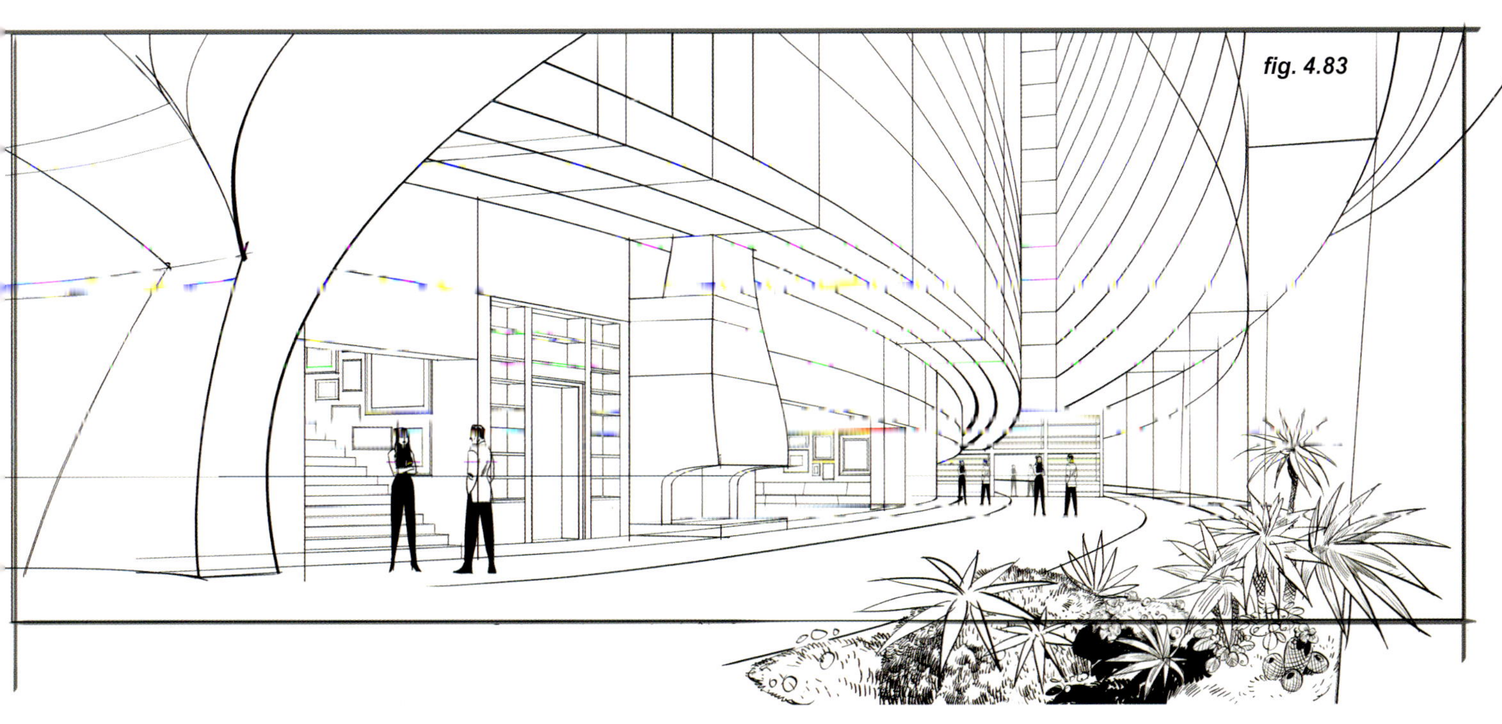

- DOUBLE GLASS PANE -
fig. 4.82
BOOK- SHELF
FIREPLACE
MURAL
SINGLE GLASS PANE
- STAIRCASE TO UPPER FLOORS
MIXTURE OF CURVED AND ANGULAR SHAPES IN THE INTERIOR DESIGN, SAME AS WE HAVE IN THE EXTERIOR → CURVES ARE STILL DOMINANT.
fig. 4.83

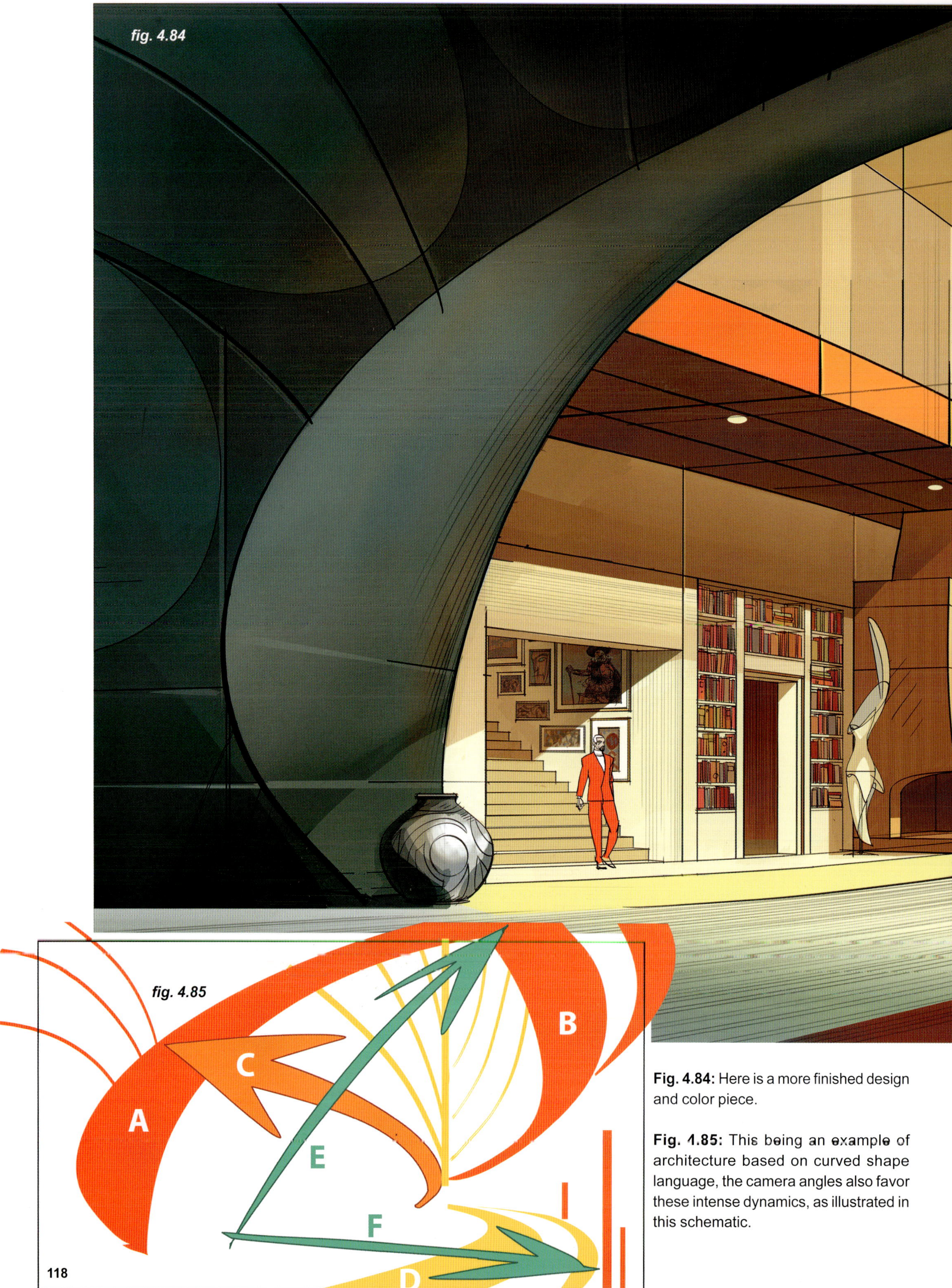

Fig. 4.84: Here is a more finished design and color piece.

Fig. 4.85: This being an example of architecture based on curved shape language, the camera angles also favor these intense dynamics, as illustrated in this schematic.

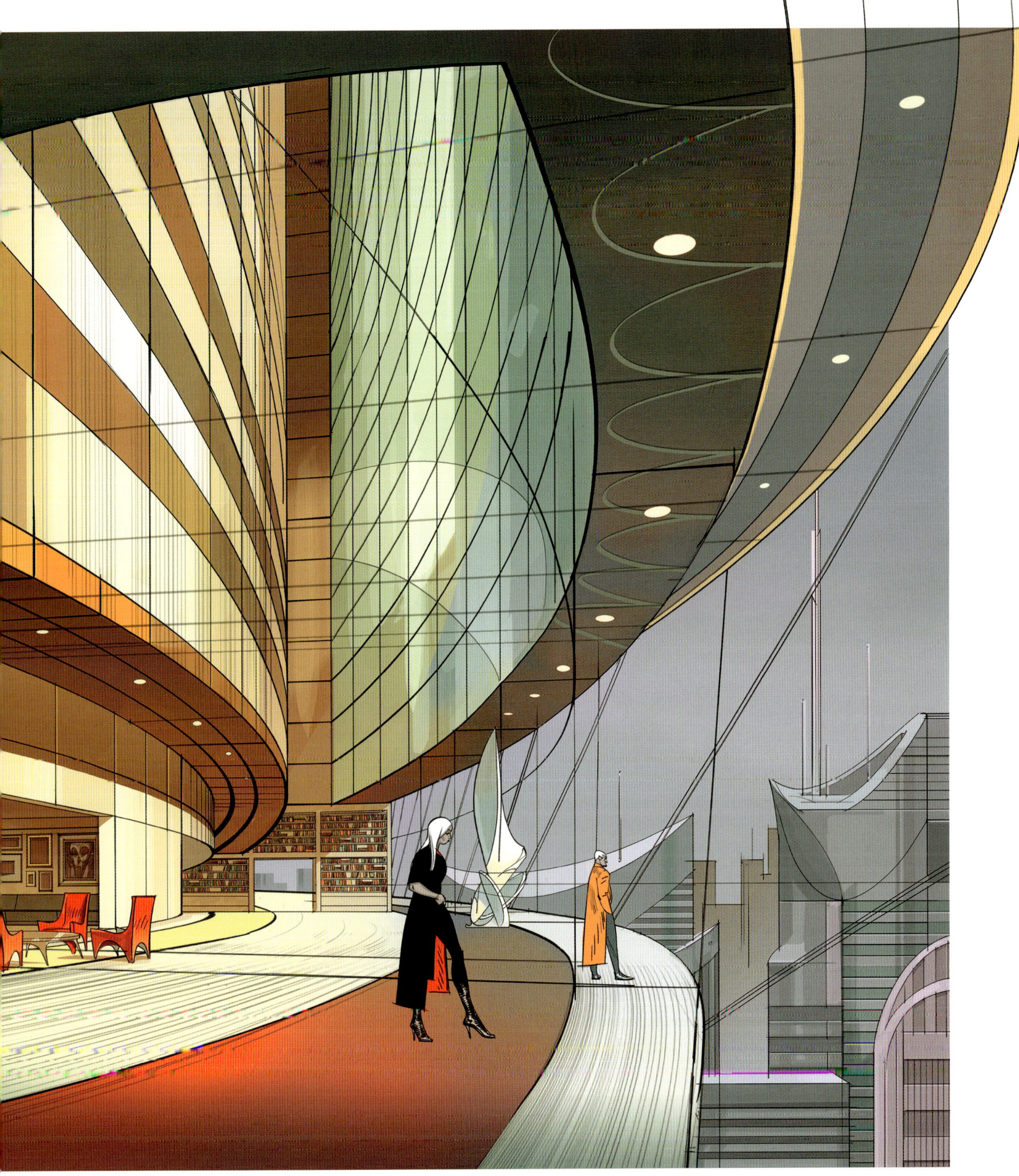

Lines **A** and **B** combine in a dynamic position that tilts to the right (see green arrow **E**), crossing the screen in a diagonal fashion while at the same time creating contrast with the strong verticals in the rest of the environment. The other curves of the structure almost mimic the motion of jet planes flying past, right above our heads.

To maximize the building's effect, all the surrounding skyscrapers are lower so that our central piece becomes even more imposing by contrast.

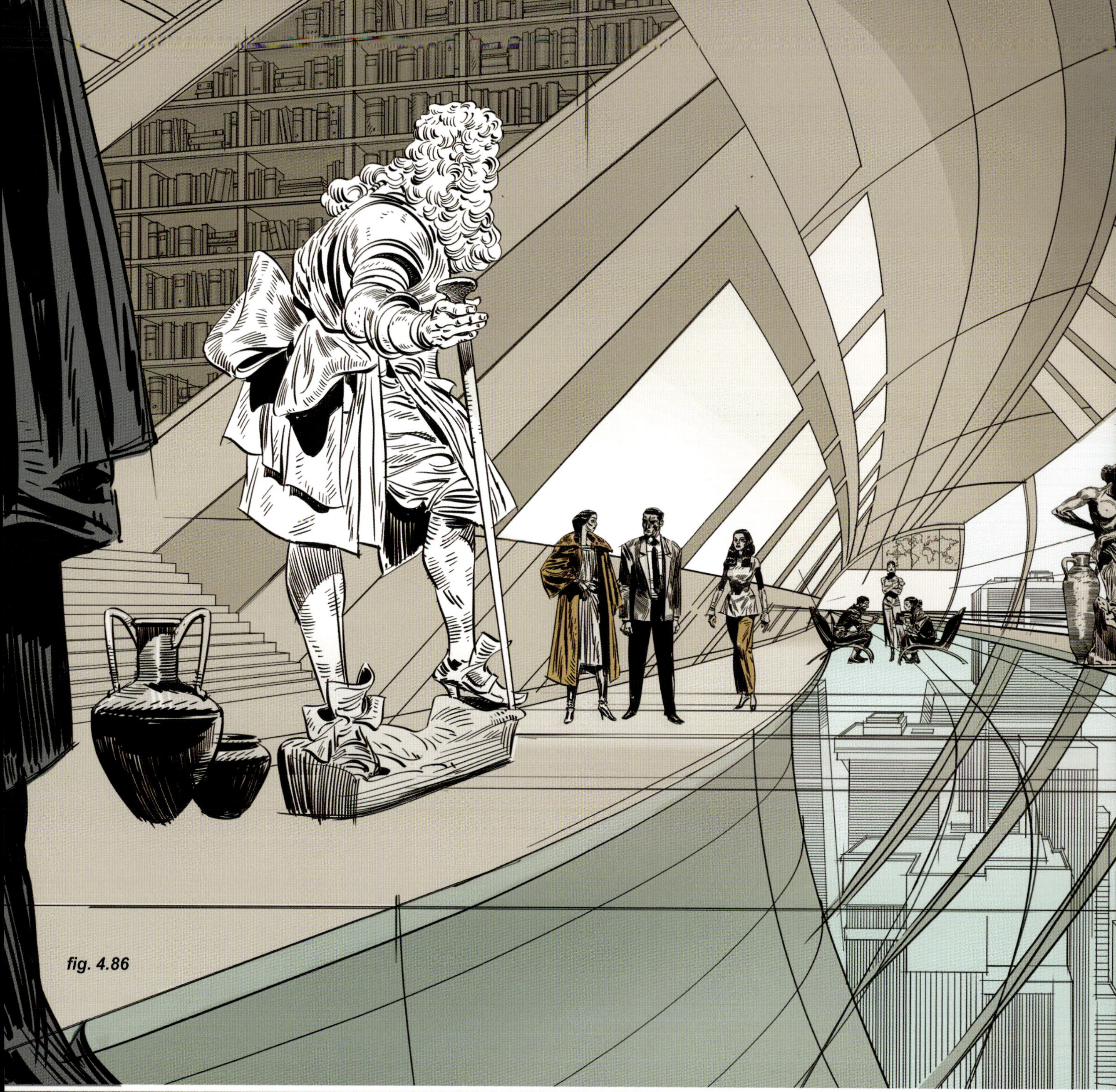

fig. 4.86

Fig. 4.86: The same basic idea can completely turn into a new tone and character with the appropriate changes or additions. What in the previous page's version could look more like an embassy or a political center of sorts, this new take turns more toward what we could expect from a museum or research center, including statues and other pieces of ancient art, as well as maximizing the impact of the space by bringing in a glass floor that adds an extra dimension as it allows us to see through it to the city below.

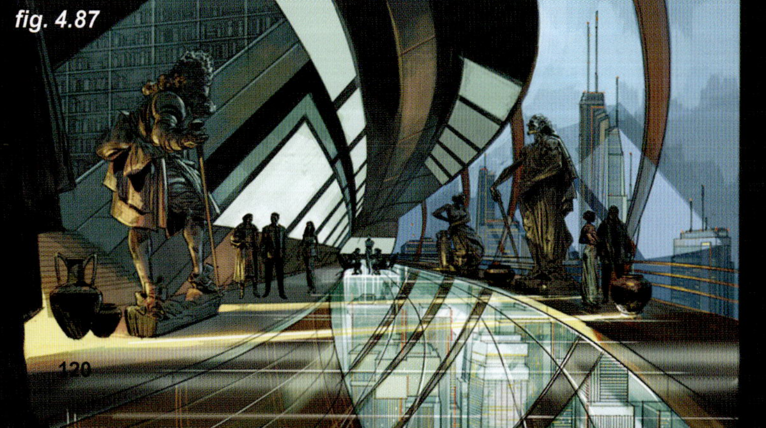

fig. 4.87

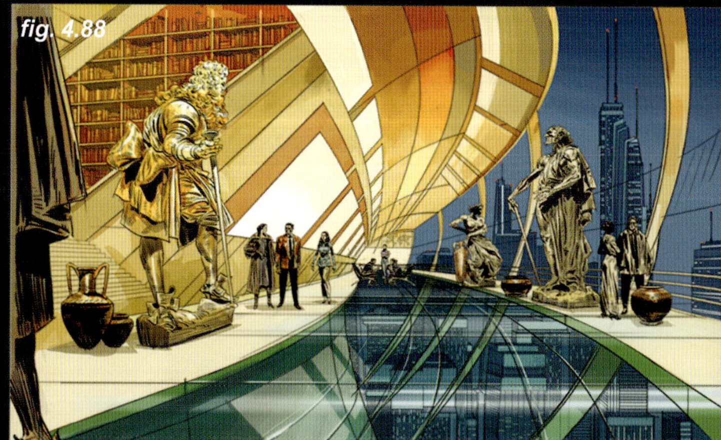

fig. 4.88

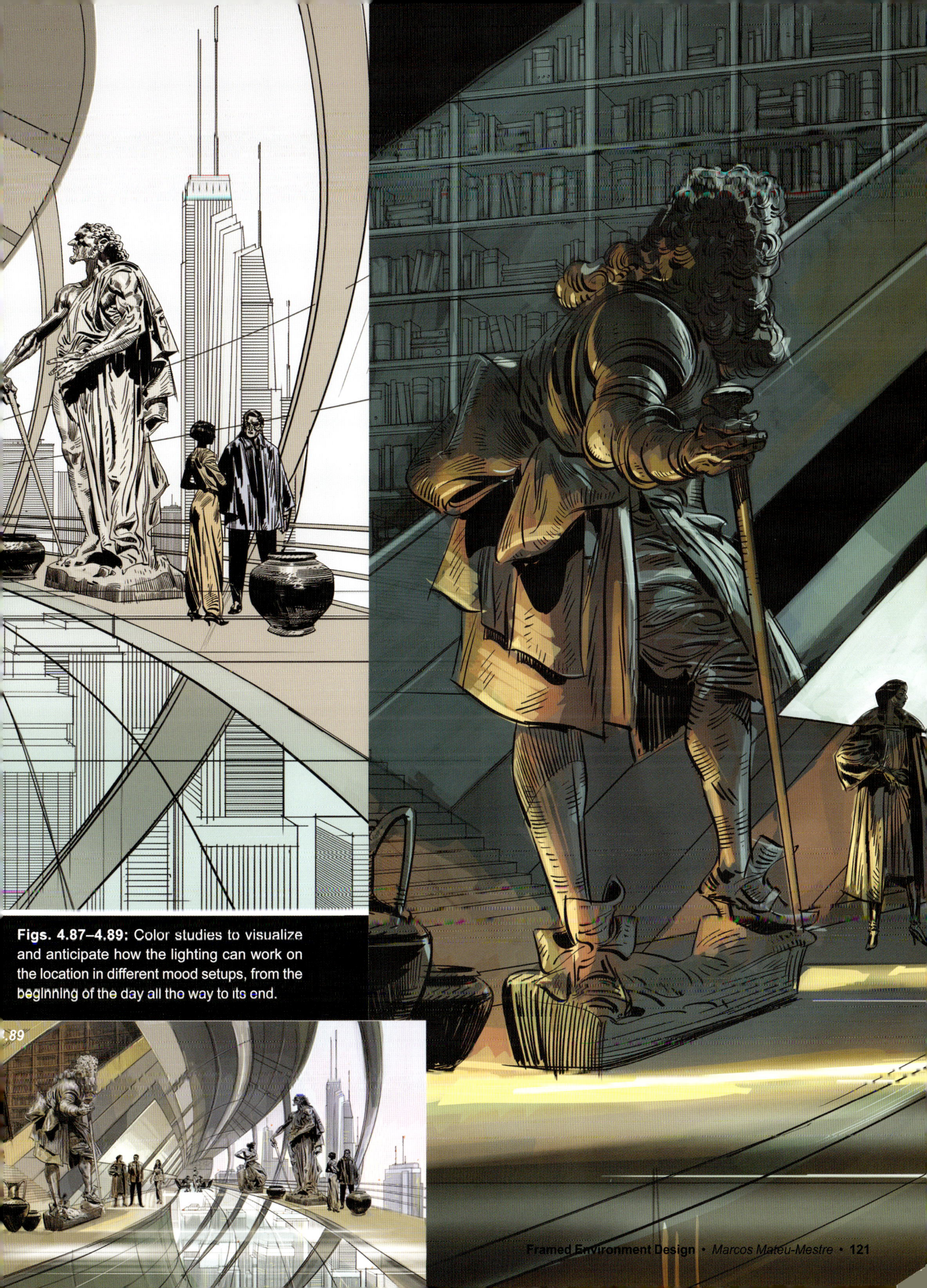

Figs. 4.87–4.89: Color studies to visualize and anticipate how the lighting can work on the location in different mood setups, from the beginning of the day all the way to its end.

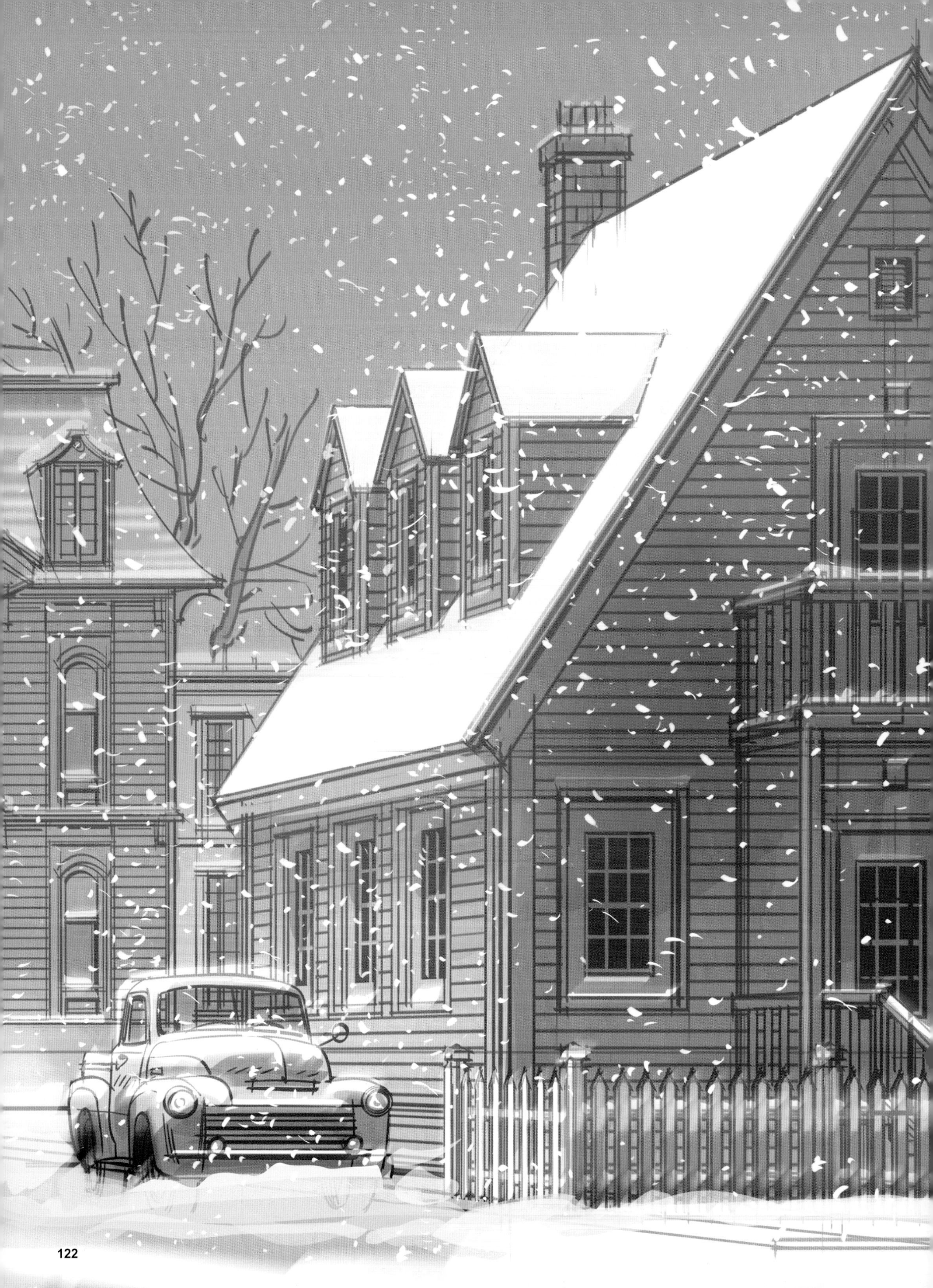

5

WEATHER, LIGHTS, CAMERA, ACTION!

During the environmental development process we aim at a number of visual and narrative goals, for example representing and emphasizing the personality of the character who lives in the location, the tone of a business or company housed in a building, a character's emotional state, or the meaning of an element within the context of the story. In general, this is at the essence of any design.

Yet if at any time a different perception of the place would better suit the story, the same exact environment can show completely different tones depending on how it is shot.

This chapter is dedicated to exploring how various light and weather conditions directly affect the narrative tone of any given location, looking at it as a canvas on which to "superimpose or paint the narrative tones" needed for our story moment. So, without further ado, let's get into it.

A HOME'S LIVING ROOM

Moving now to a quaint, small village somewhere in New England, with buildings that range from the American Victorian era to the 1950s, two characters are having a discussion in the living room of one of their homes. Let's explore some options.

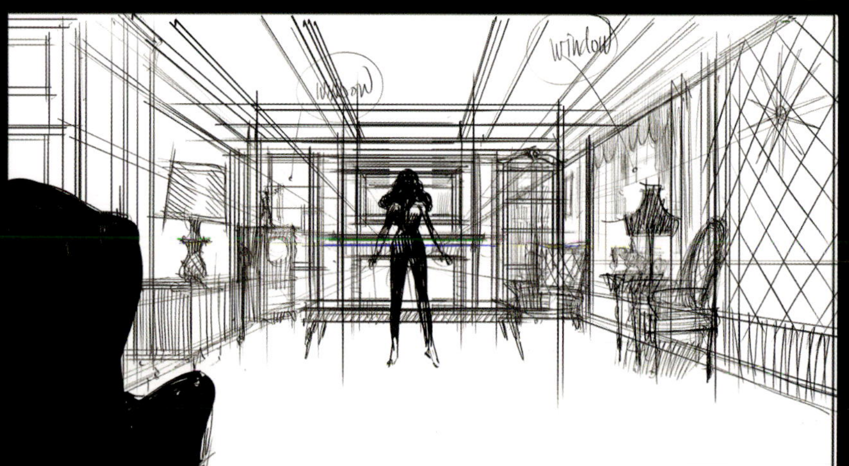
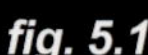

fig. 5.1

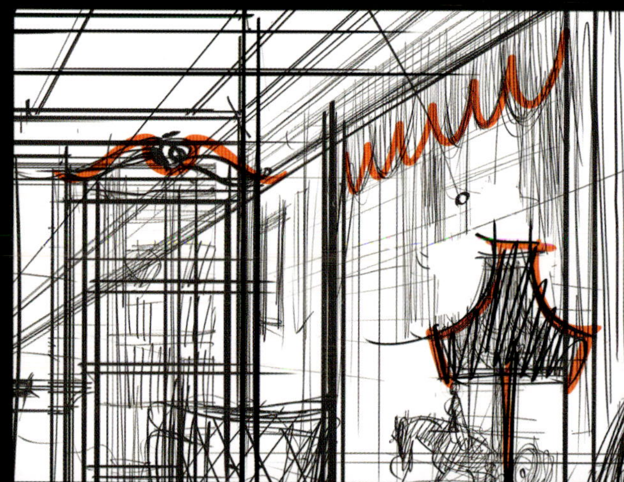

fig. 5.2

Fig. 5.1: A shot with one single vanishing point provides visual clarity as a way to introduce the location. The sketch includes some basic shape elements like lamp stands, armchairs, and windows with diamond-shaped glass, all elements of a house that could have been built around the 1940s.

In order to nail the time period, the characters will eventually need to dress accordingly, otherwise the furniture could be just the owner's personal choice at a later period. (The woman in the center of the room is only for scale purposes at this point.)

Fig. 5.2: This cropped image shows the shape language referenced above in more detail, through elements like the top of a bookcase (an imitation of a simplified Georgian or Sheraton style that was still around in the '40s), the lampshade near the window, and the cornice of the curtain. These are iconic shapes that, once in the mix, can play in ways so that they stand out, like backlit against the windows, to emphasize here and there

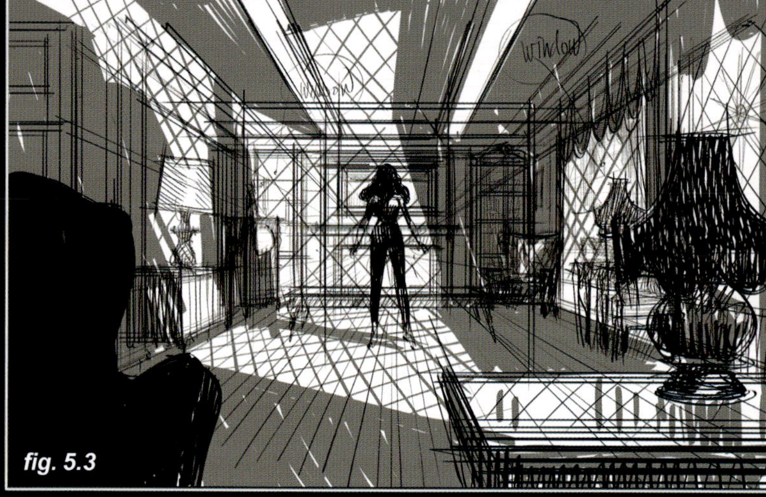

fig. 5.3

Fig. 5.3: Dramatic lighting as a first exploration of how certain types of lights and shadow

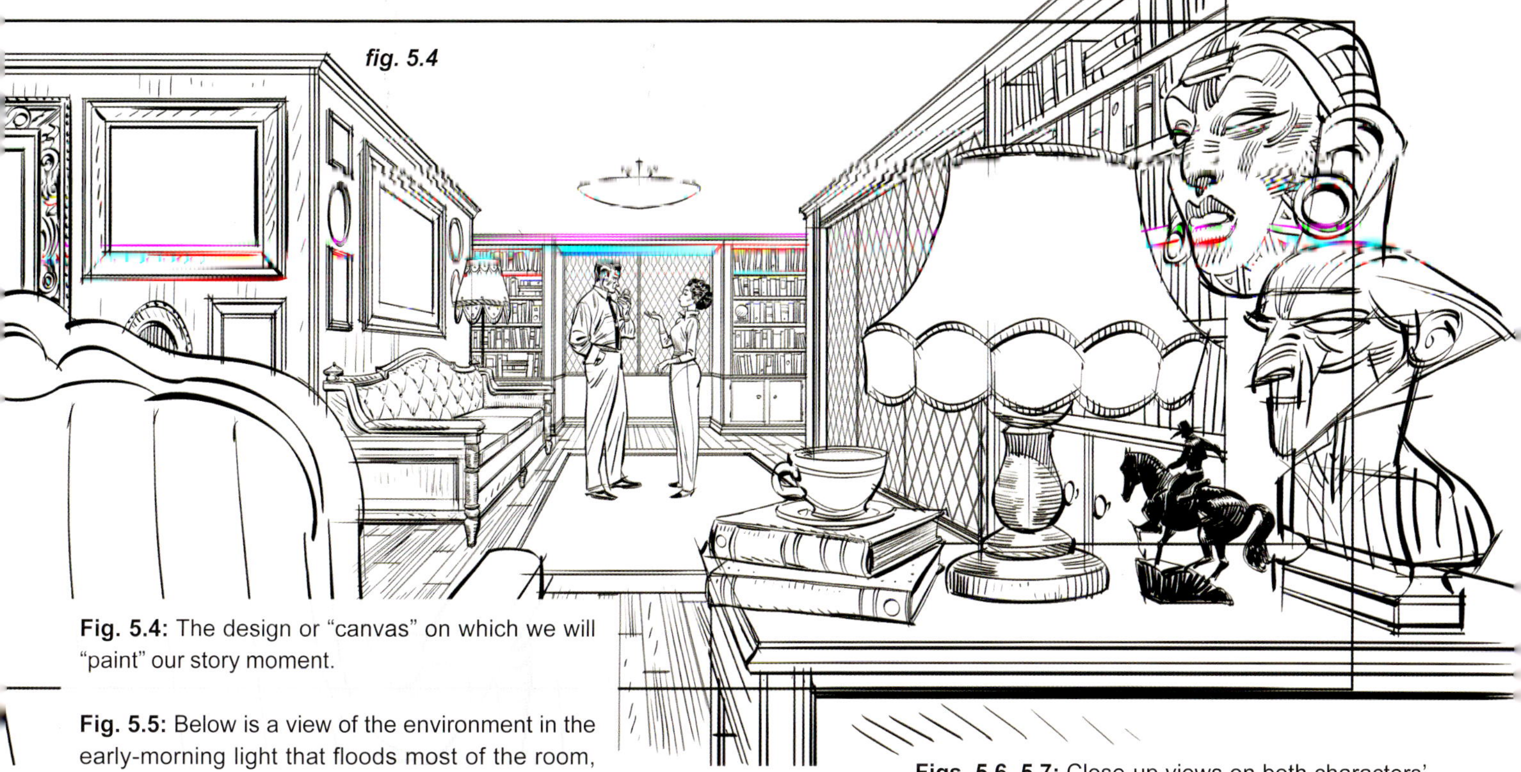

Fig. 5.4: The design or "canvas" on which we will "paint" our story moment.

Fig. 5.5: Below is a view of the environment in the early-morning light that floods most of the room, revealing most details with a combination of soft, direct light and some reflected light as well. It is inviting and welcoming.

Figs. 5.6, 5.7: Close-up views on both characters' faces and expressions in the same soft and balanced lighting quality.

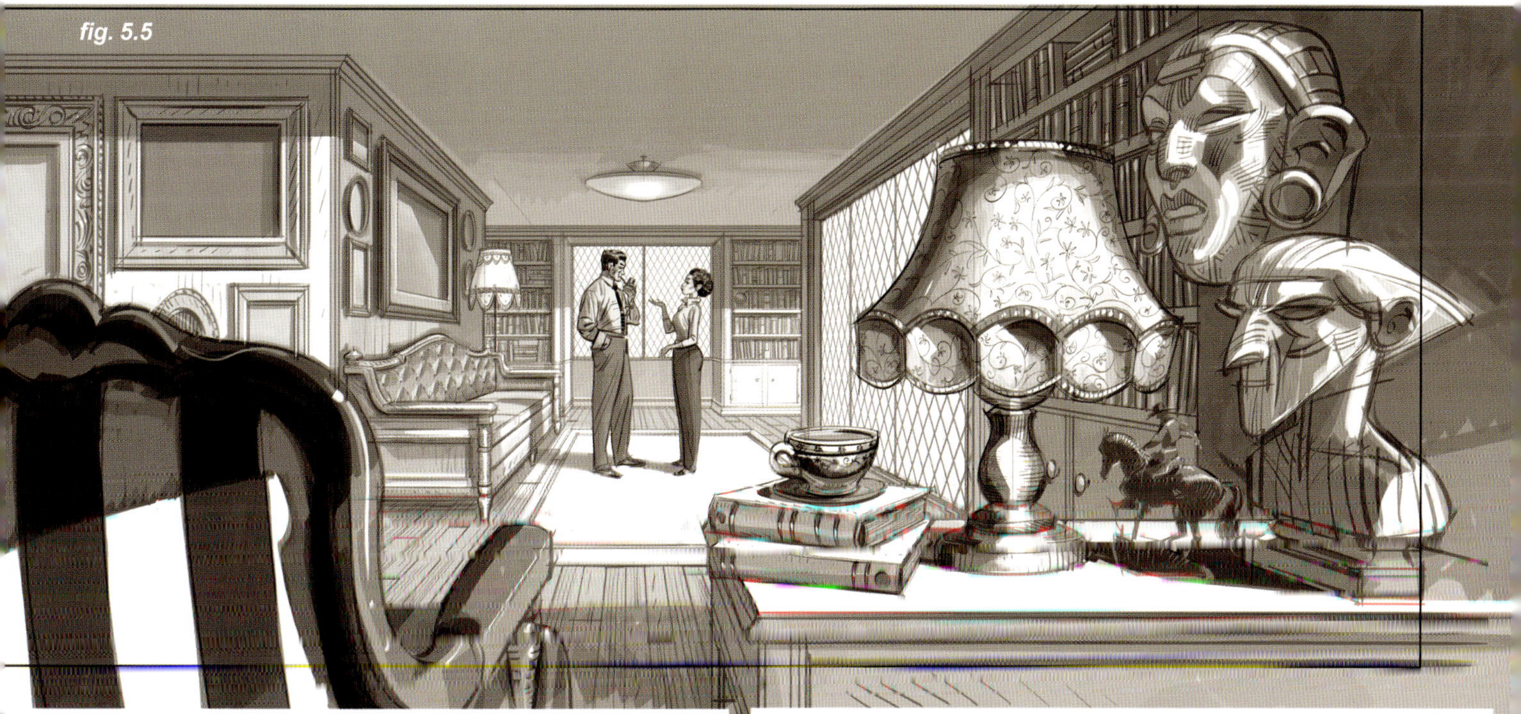

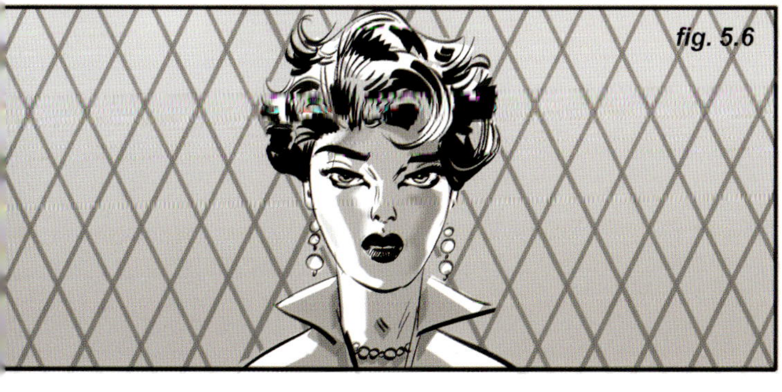

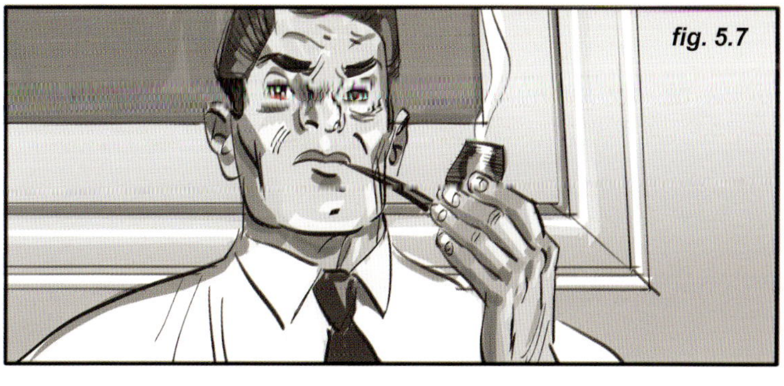

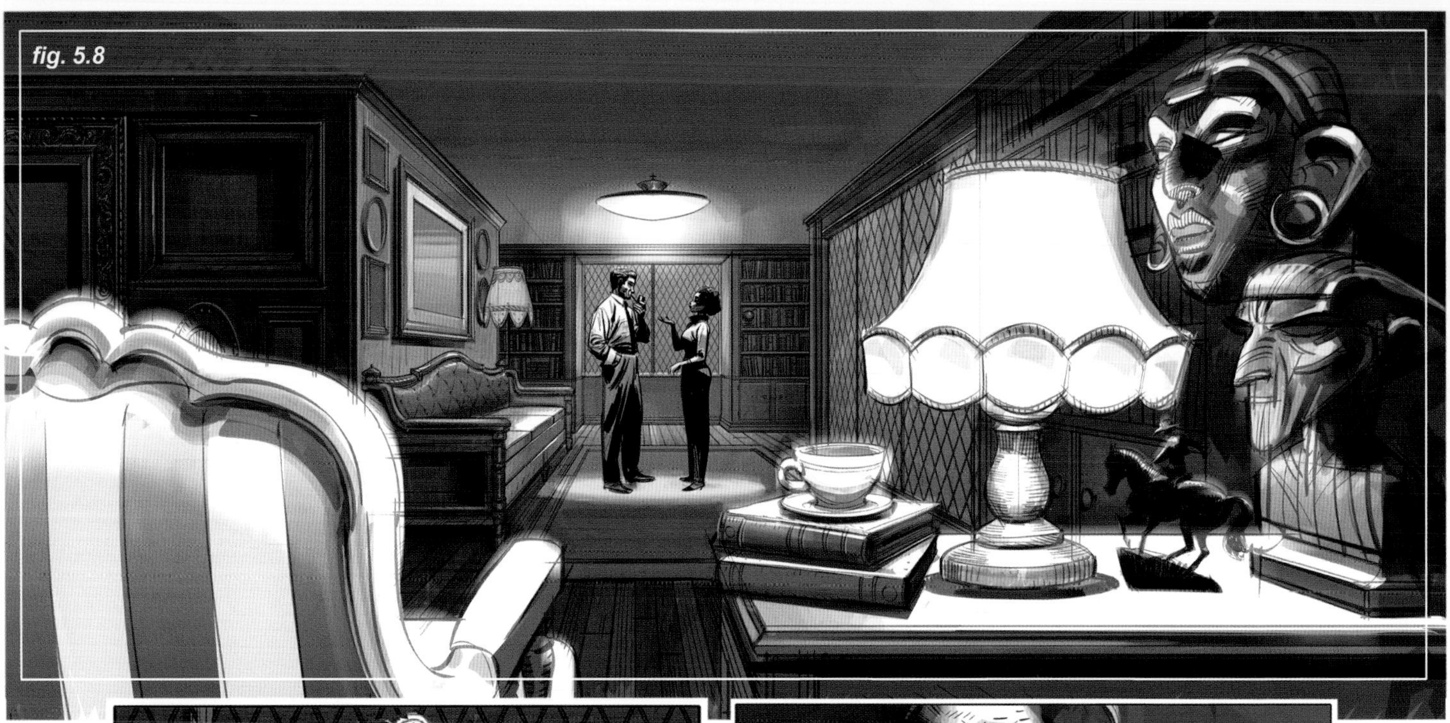

fig. 5.8

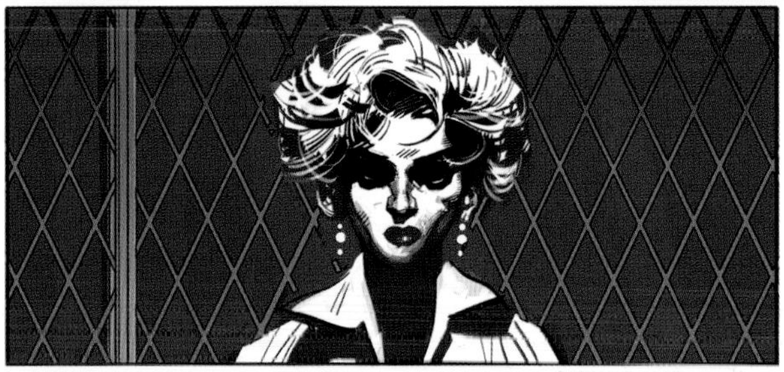

fig. 5.9

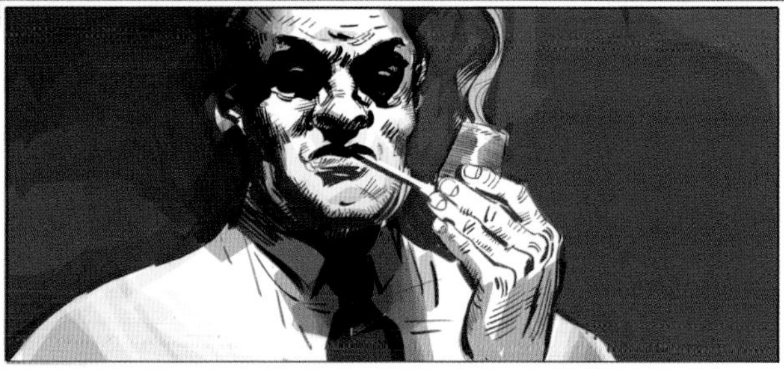

fig. 5.10

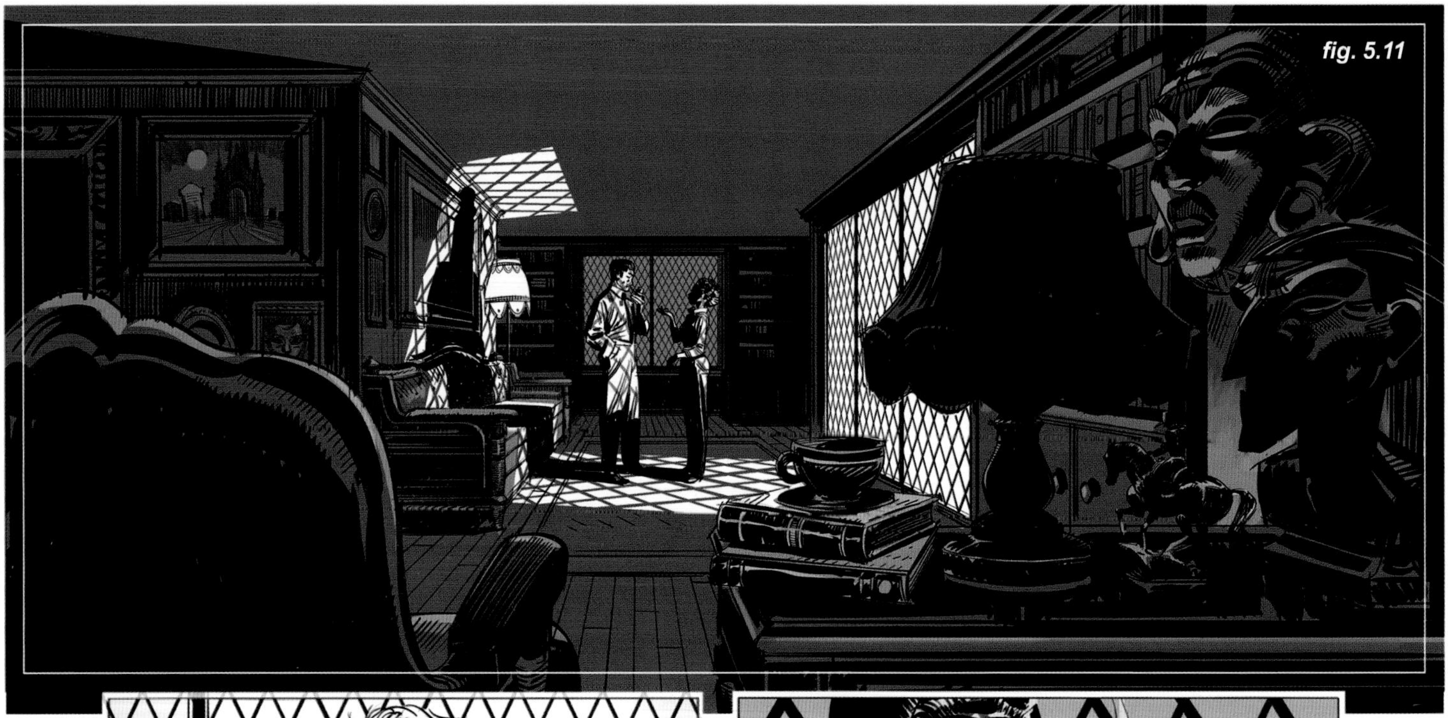

fig. 5.11

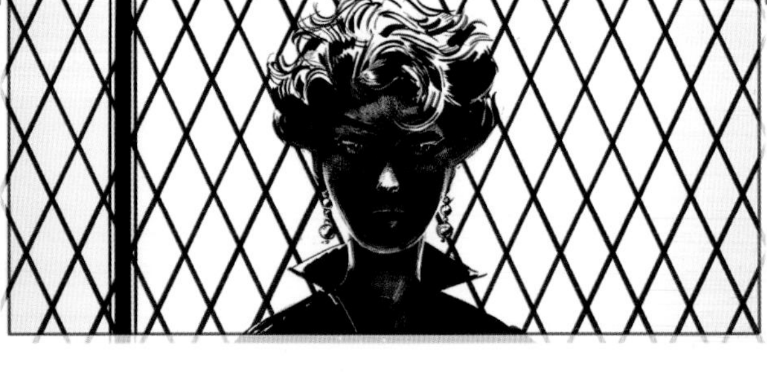

fig. 5.12

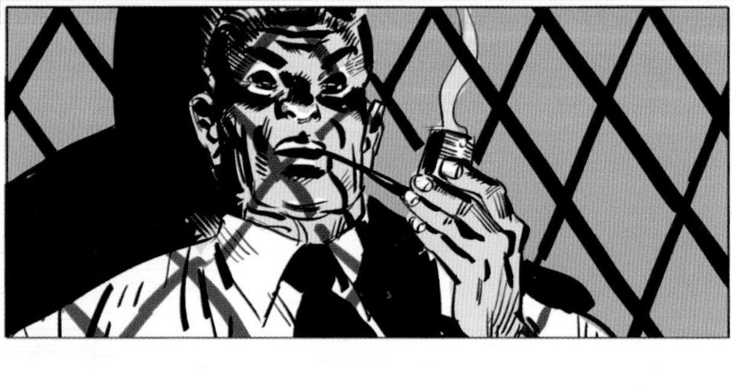

fig. 5.13

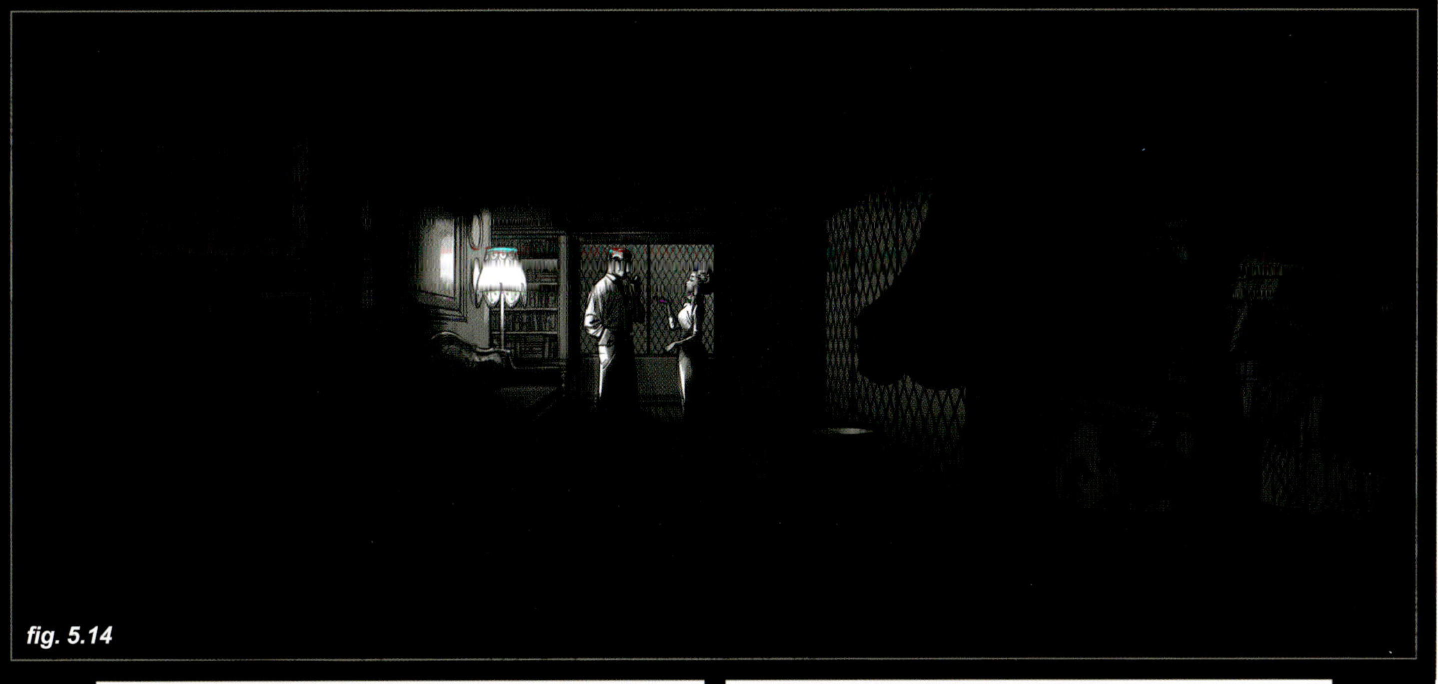

fig. 5.14

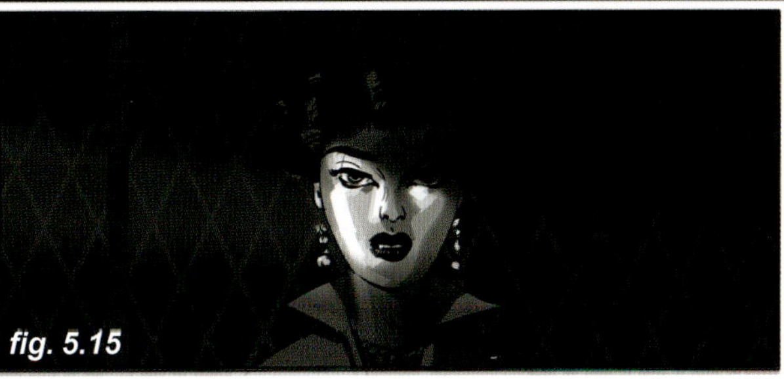

fig. 5.15

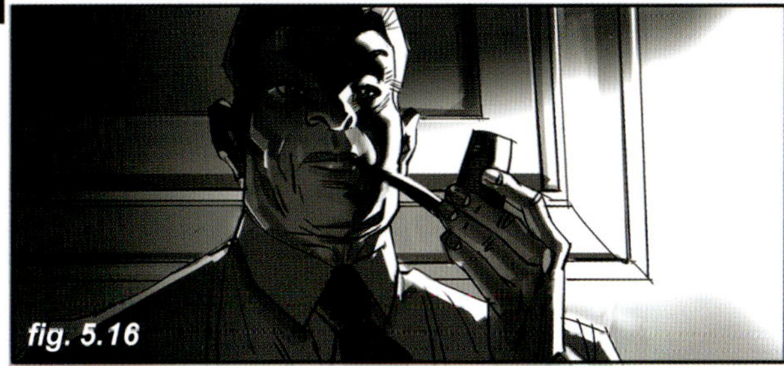

fig. 5.16

Each of these cases reflects a different emotional moment.

Figs. 5.8–5.10: While fig. 5.5 represents a calm moment, this lighting setup creates complexity and pushes contrast without getting to the point of hard drama. The characters are directly under a ceiling light fixture that creates a spotlight on them, as though they are standing on a theatrical stage in a reduced area of big, tonal contrast, immediately surrounded by a range of mid-tones. This setup is broken at the foreground, where another shaft of light hits all the elements that are close to camera.

So, the full lighting range of this shot goes, from foreground to background: light and contrast, then mid-tones, then theatrical contrast again right where the characters are, and finally mid-tones again at the far back.

It is clearly later in the day, so the light sources are artificial. Not having bright windows in the shot also helps keep the attention focused on the interior, creating a bit of a more confined feeling.

Fig. 5.11: The window and its diamond-shaped design project strong, surrealistic shadows around the room with the help of a really powerful light source outside the house. This might be a garden light with its intensity pushed to obtain this very stylized and distressing moment.

The light source could also be moving if it were coming from a car arriving at the house during this dark hour of the night. In this case, the projected shadows would also be moving across the room, hitting the characters for that brief second and revealing them to the camera in a dramatic way.

In this image the tonal blocks can be basically simplified as two: the projected pool of bright light and the rest of the room as a dark visual block.

Figs. 5.12, 5.13: Observe how this lighting scenario affects the characters' close-ups to increase the tension of the moment.

Figs. 5.14–5.16: This example is the darkest, most dramatic one where we almost have to figure out the characters and their acting in the dark, revealed only by the strong rim lights hitting them from the lamp at the far corner of the living room.

Still, the elements part of the design of this location (the paintings on the walls, the table lamp, and the head sculptures in the foreground) are just slightly visible, so we still get an idea of what is going on in the surrounding area.

Again, visible iconic shapes like the one of the lamp on the foreground side table help establish the characters and the time period of the story.

Weather can also radically change the narrative meaning of an environment. Let's explore this on a view of the village's Main Street where our two characters live.

PRELIMINARY SKETCHES

Fig. 5.17: This first sketch has a higher camera angle, closer to a standing person's eye level, and the houses all face Main Street. The overall silhouette is not very graphic, as the temple's steeple, the central tree, and the house at foreground-right all fight for attention.

Fig. 5.18: This sketch takes a bolder ink approach with no detail, using only shapes to make sure the overall silhouette reads well. The houses in the mid-ground and background face Main Street, but the ones closer to camera show their front. It can make for a more interesting design as they face a park, the open area where the camera is located. Taking all this into account, this design is the better option for our case.

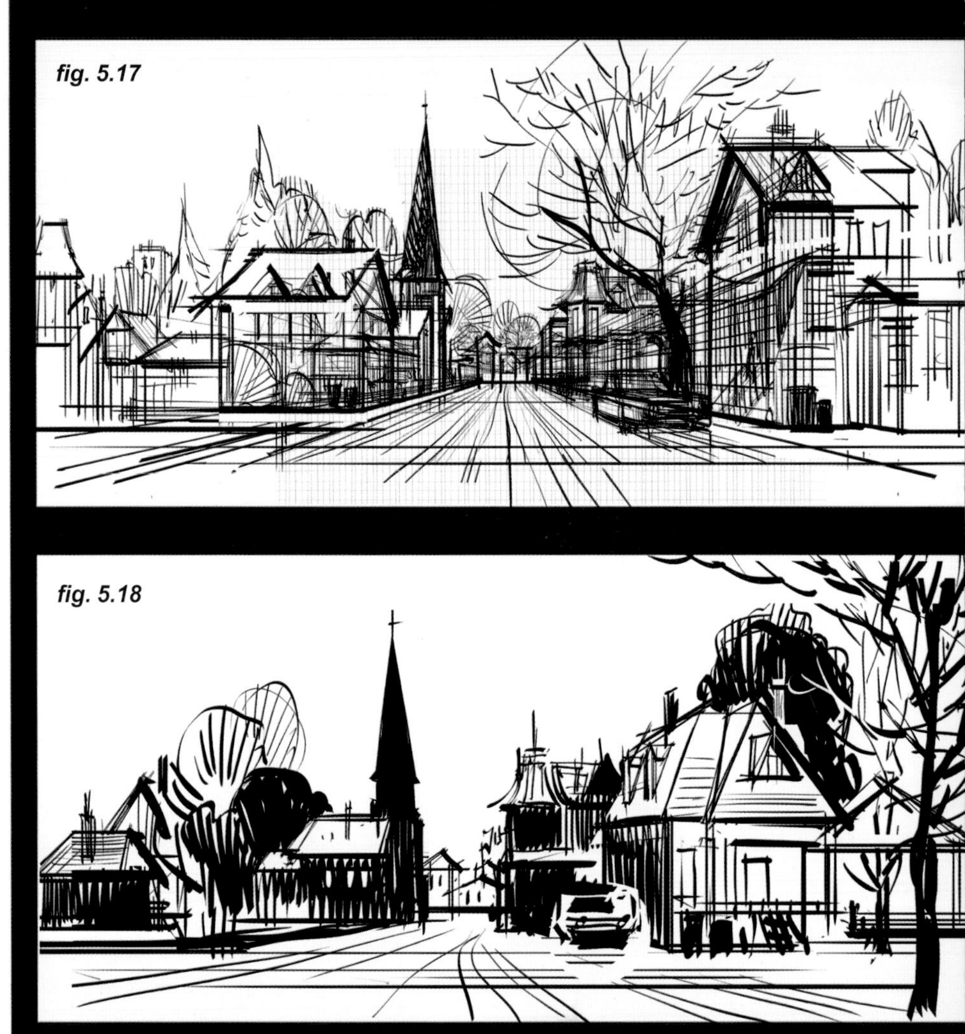

fig. 5.17

fig. 5.18

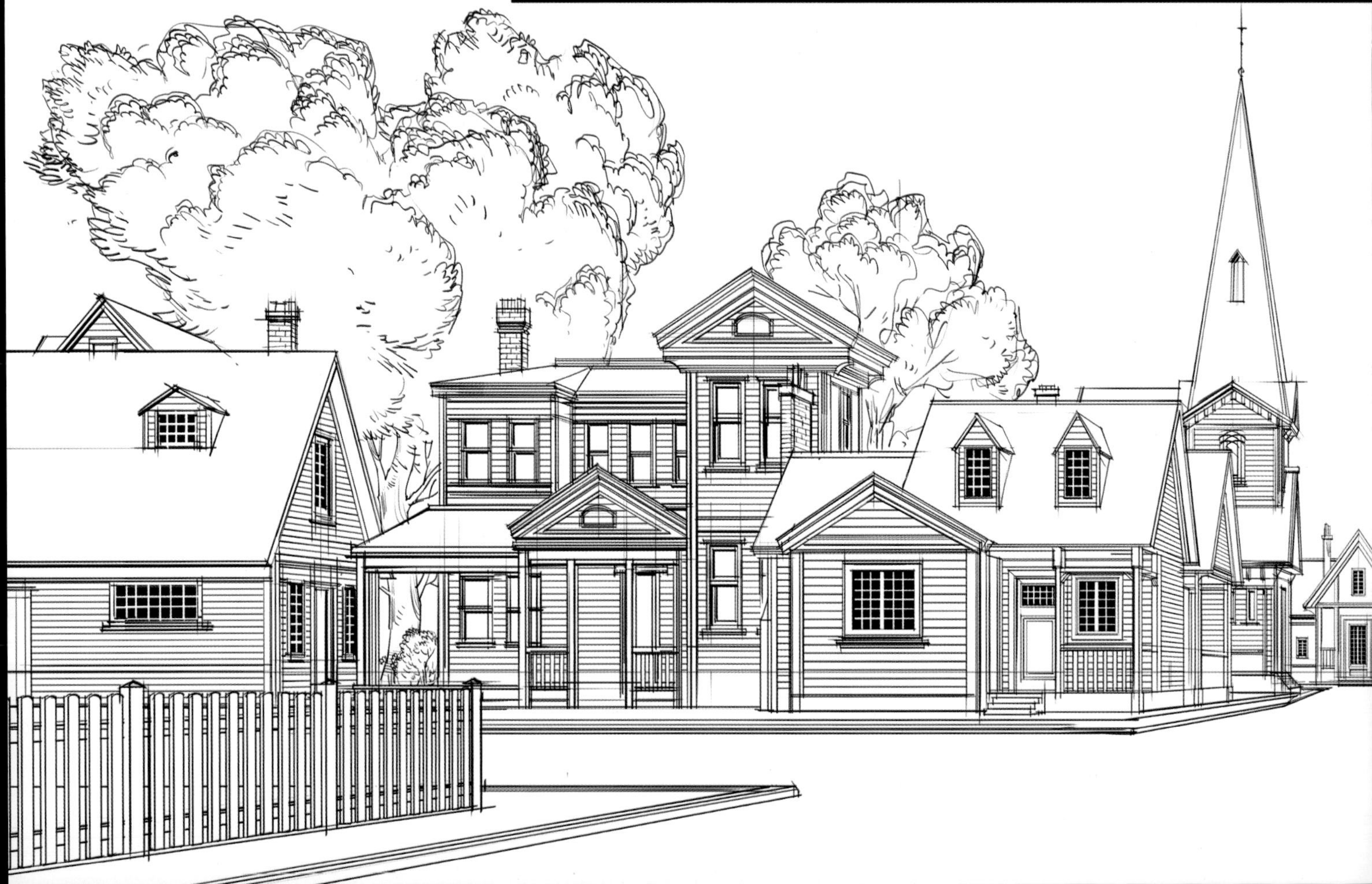

Fig. 5.19: As a result, we have an image with a clear and iconic focal point (the tall steeple) plus an interesting variety of buildings that range from American Victorian to 1940s, showing the passage of time and growth of this small village. Still, these architectural styles are conveniently scattered around the area rather than grouped separately, so that they blend in rather than creating specific groups of attention, which works well in this case.

Fig. 5.20: As far as church steeple designs go, the gathered references provided a wide variety of them. Many showed the overall structure broken down into interesting smaller sections like this one, but because the intent was to have this piece serve as a graphic focal point, a single-bodied structure with long and uninterrupted straight lines was definitely a prime option.

The trees add not only an interesting variety of shapes and a nice sense of "lived-in" atmosphere to the village. They also help frame the shot at its sides while allowing for an open sky at the center, having the pointier, more angular shapes of the rooftops clearly add to the visual texture of the moment.

Next step, let's now bring in the weather and see how things can change dramatically depending on how we work in this environment.

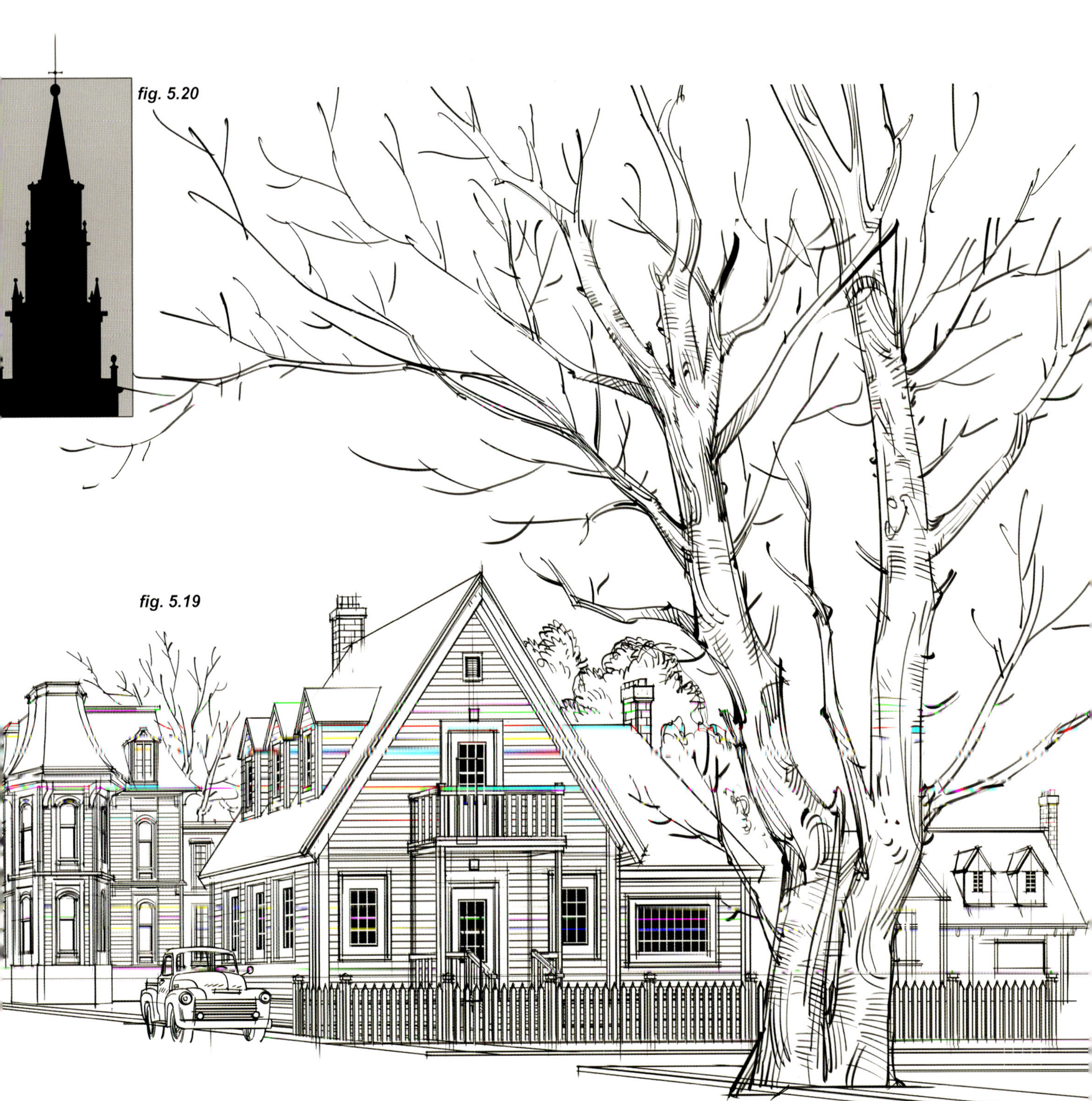

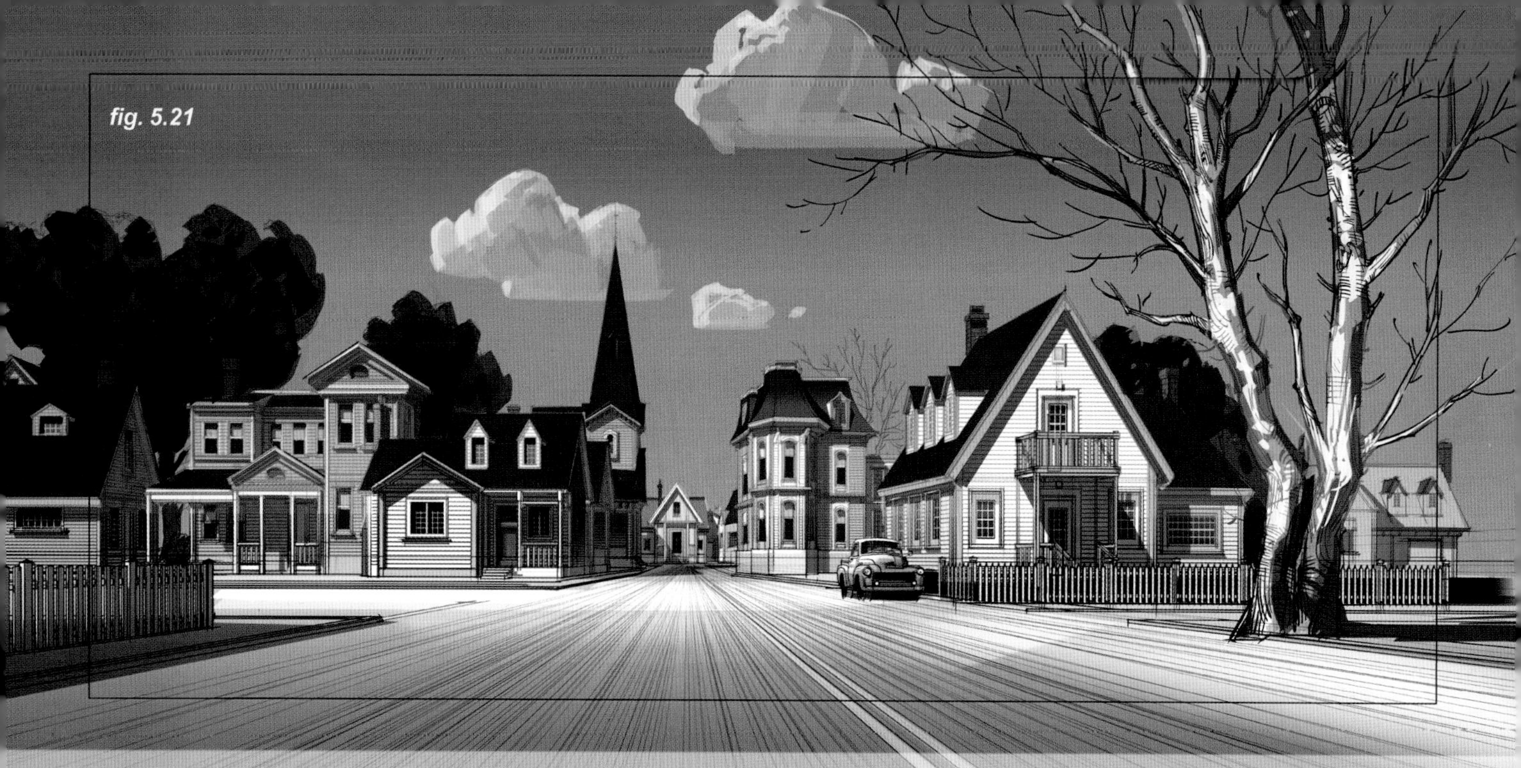

Fig. 5.21: "Typical" **beautiful weather,** a **happy day** in town to get this round started. Good lighting conditions offer a clear view of the subject through the contrast of light and shadow, with a crisp silhouette of the roofs' skyline against a bright sky, lighter walls of the homes, and a few puffy clouds for a picture-perfect moment.

Fig. 5.22: Rain lays a strong texture over this gloomy landscape. The day is cloudy and dark, and despite a level of contrast, details are becoming difficult to read within the shot. Also the tonal range is minimized, making for a "feeling down" moment.

The big puddle of water reflects the scene, creating a unique look.

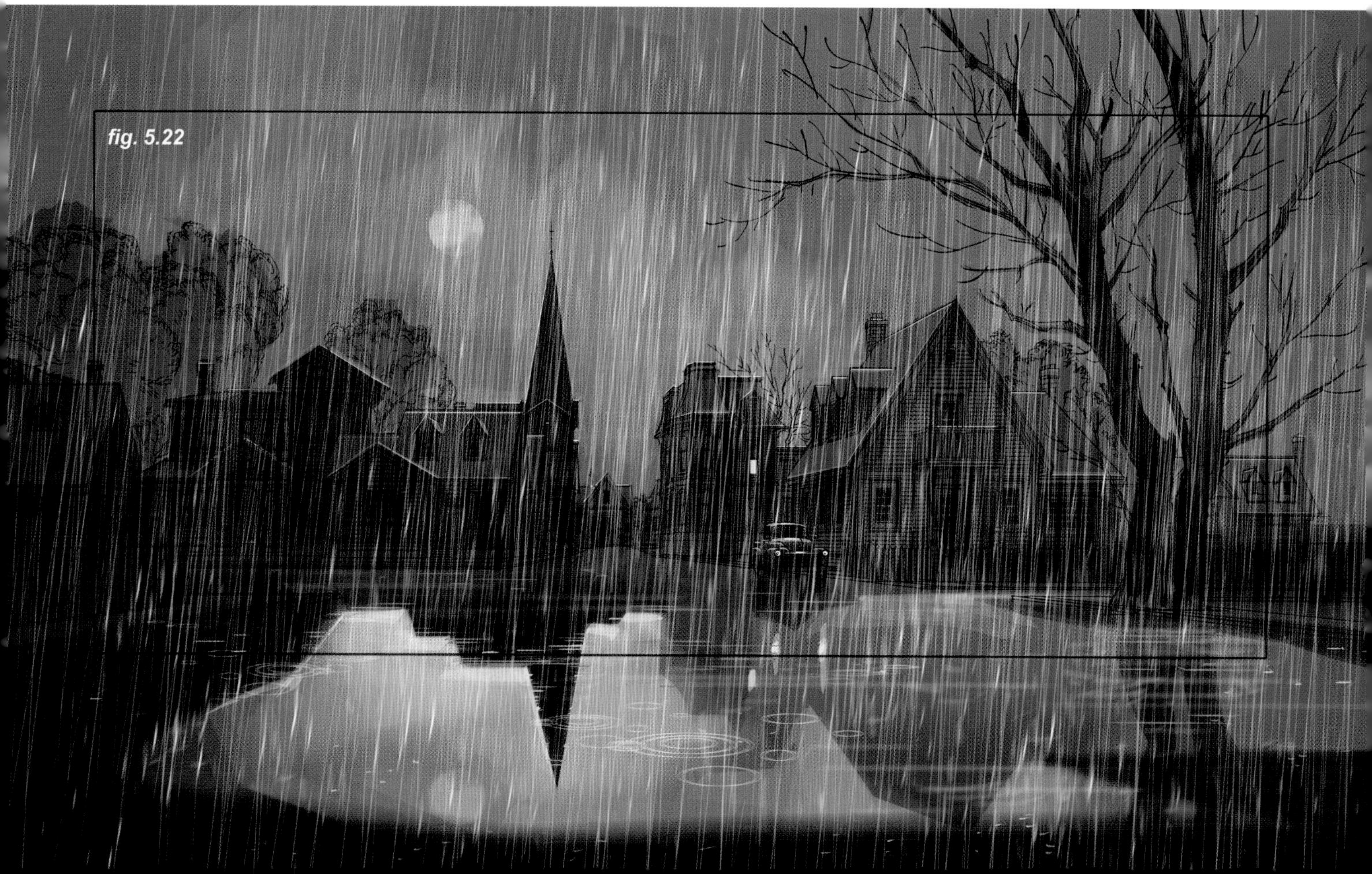

fig. 5.23

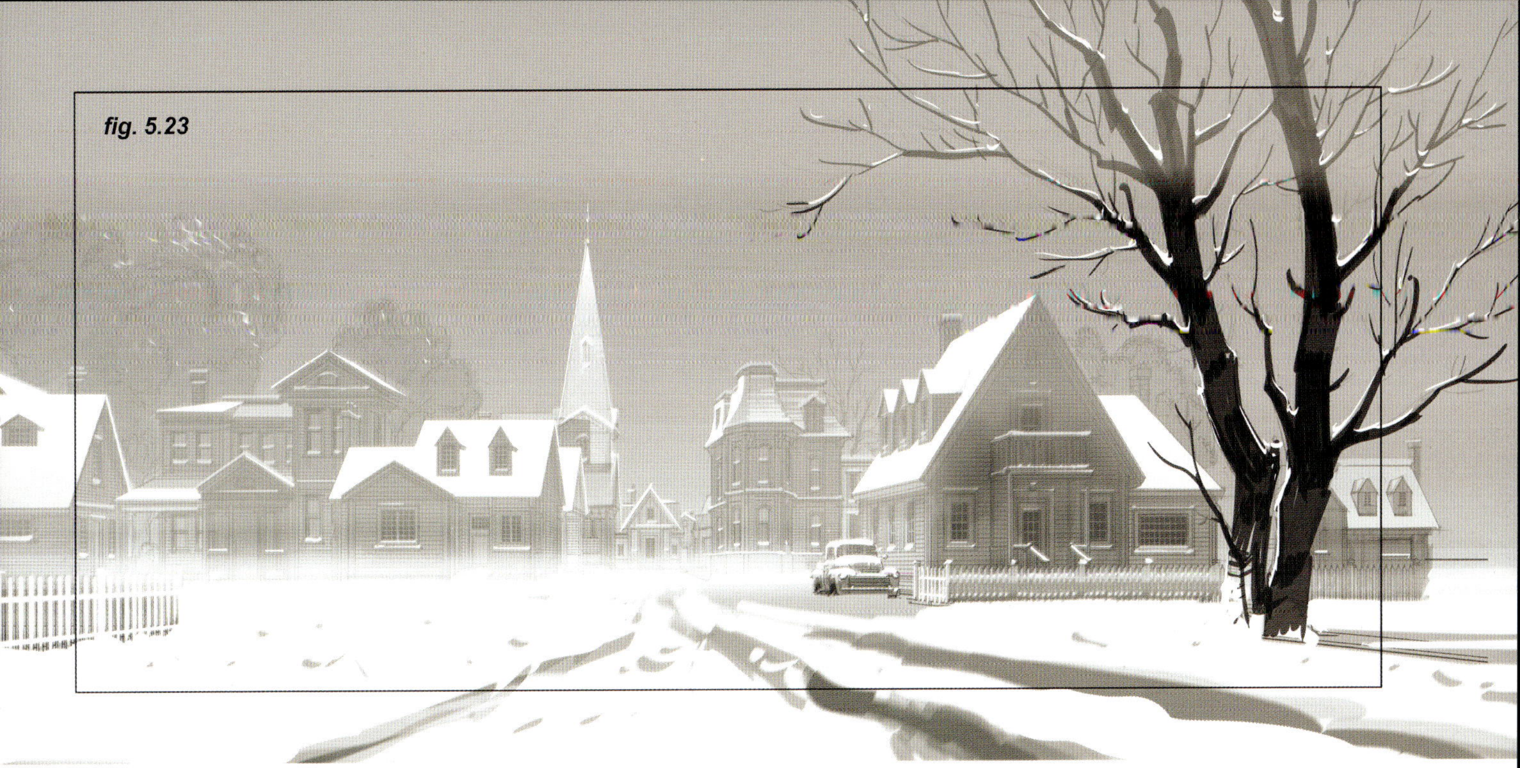

Fig. 5.23: A calm blanket of snow has just covered the village. The whole scene has now turned very atmospheric with a crisp foreground, a misty mid-ground, and an even foggier background. Contrast is overall dimmed except for the accents of the tree and the foreground snow. A sense of mystery and isolation is very present.

Fig. 5.24: Zombies and evil spirits might come out of this one any time now. Dark and powerful storm clouds brew in the distance. A dramatic spotlight emphasizes the shape of the steeple, the focus of the scene. Contrast is strongest at the center, and the farther we go toward the sides of the frame, the more everything drops in the shadows and the less we can figure out what is going on in this place.

These are just a small number of visual narrative options we can create by using **weather conditions,** but it shows how these can really seem like different worlds, "painted" on the same blank canvas.

These conditions will also inform the close-ups and **detail views** within the same sequence.

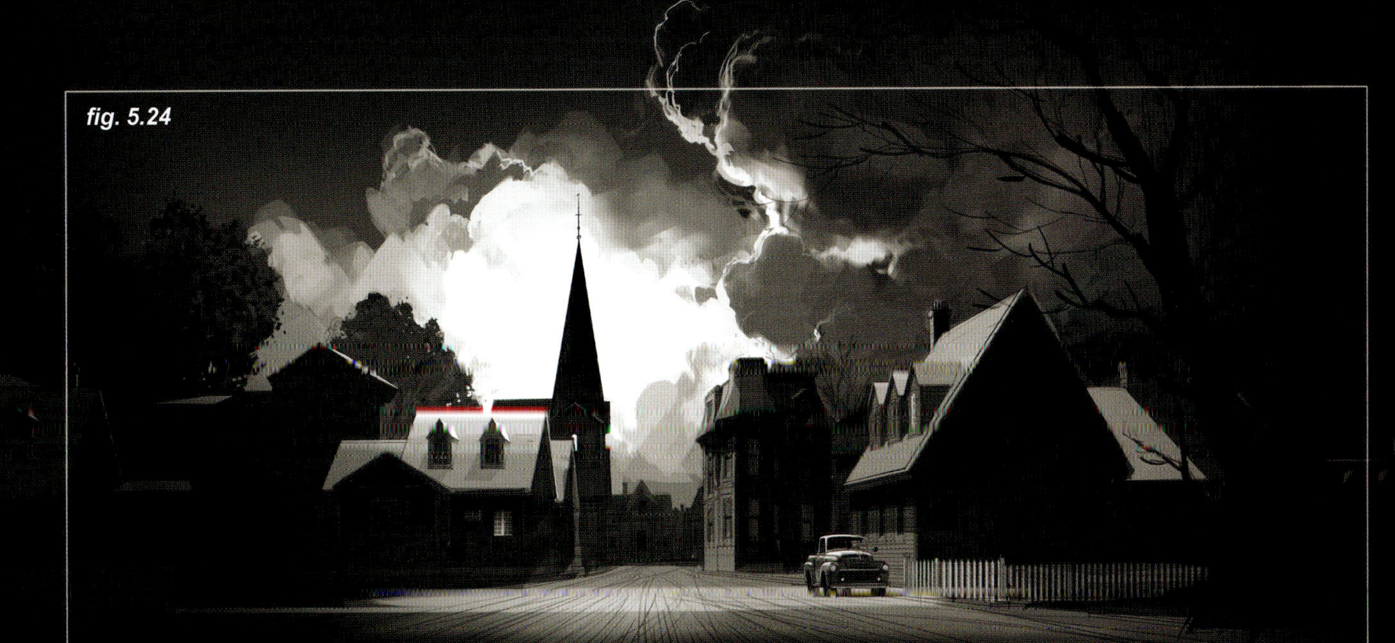

fig. 5.24

EXPLORING A FEW STORY MOMENTS

Whenever a scene has a strong visual personality to it, for the most part any fragment or snippet of it will reflect such spirit in order to exploit the potential of the established tone, as well as for continuity purposes.

Figs. 5.25–5.27: Referencing the sunny, clear day shown in fig. 5.21, these closer moments convey this idea. The beautiful weather makes for bright, high-contrast, high-energy shots, where things appear promising.

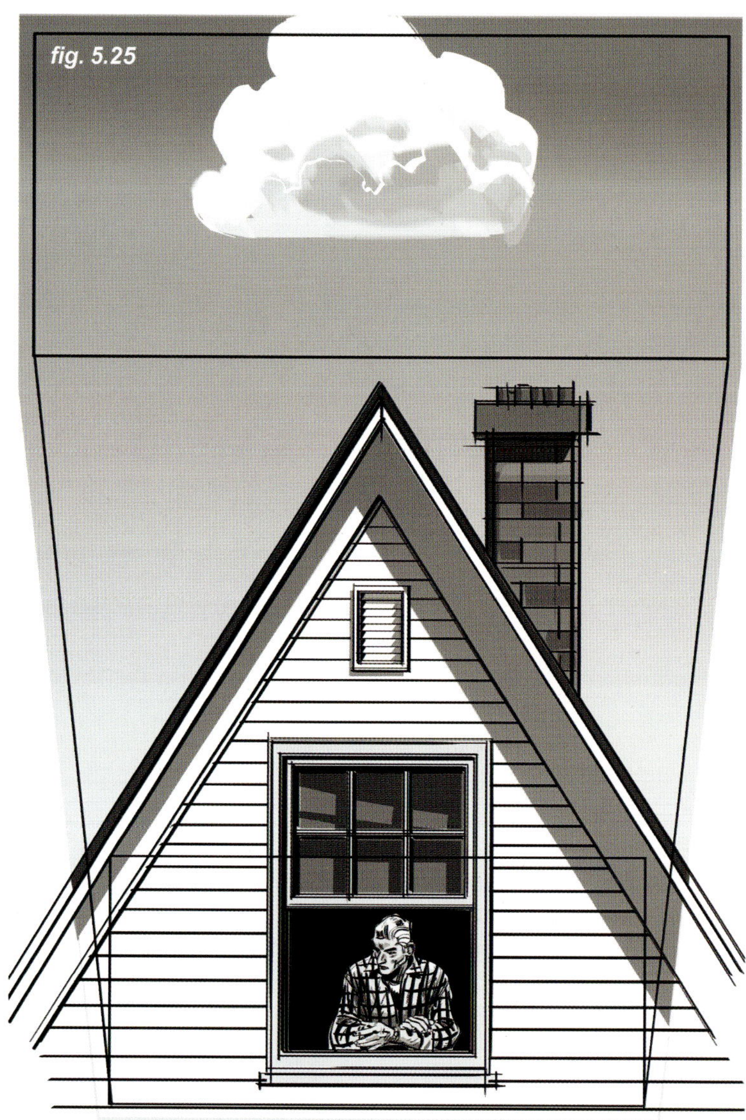

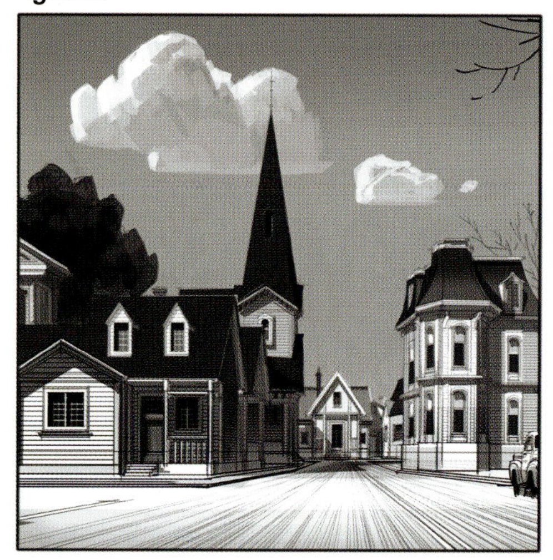

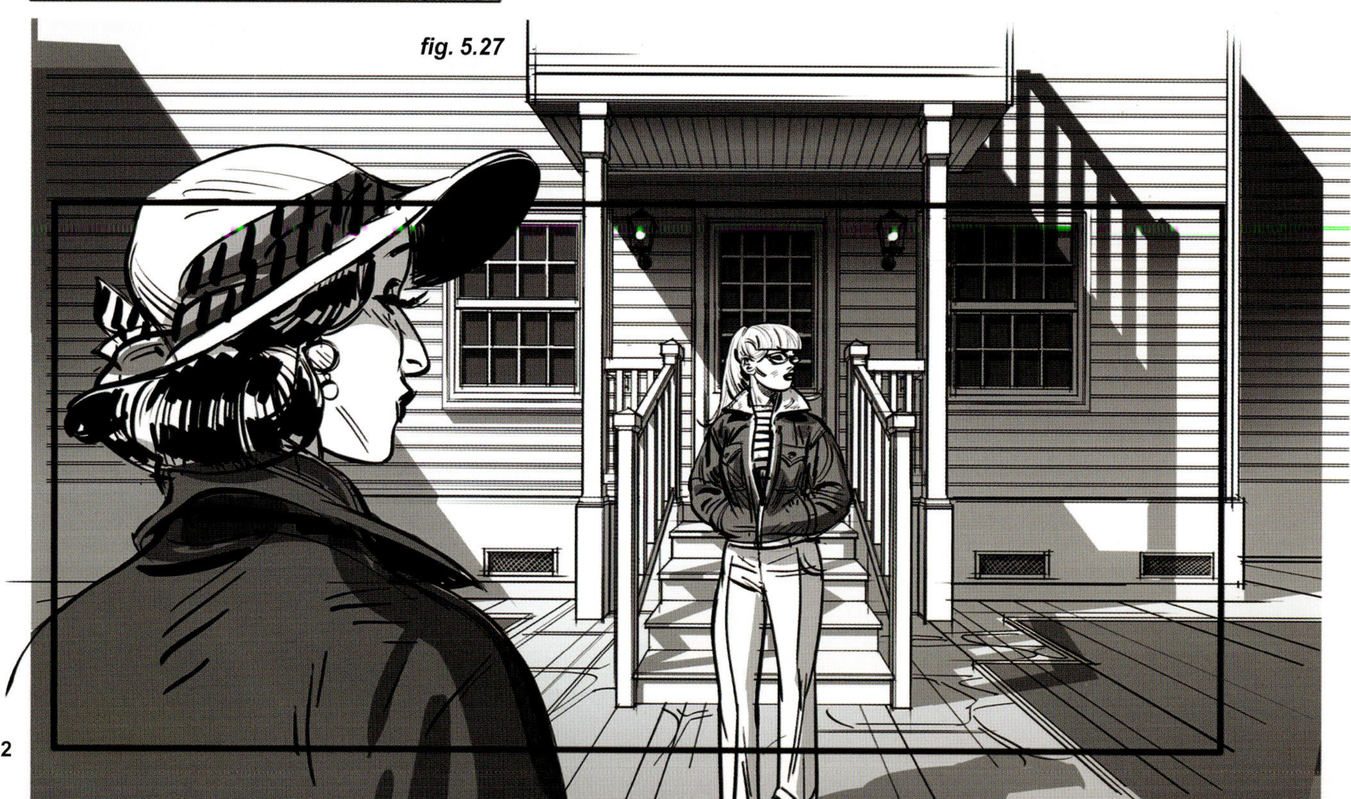

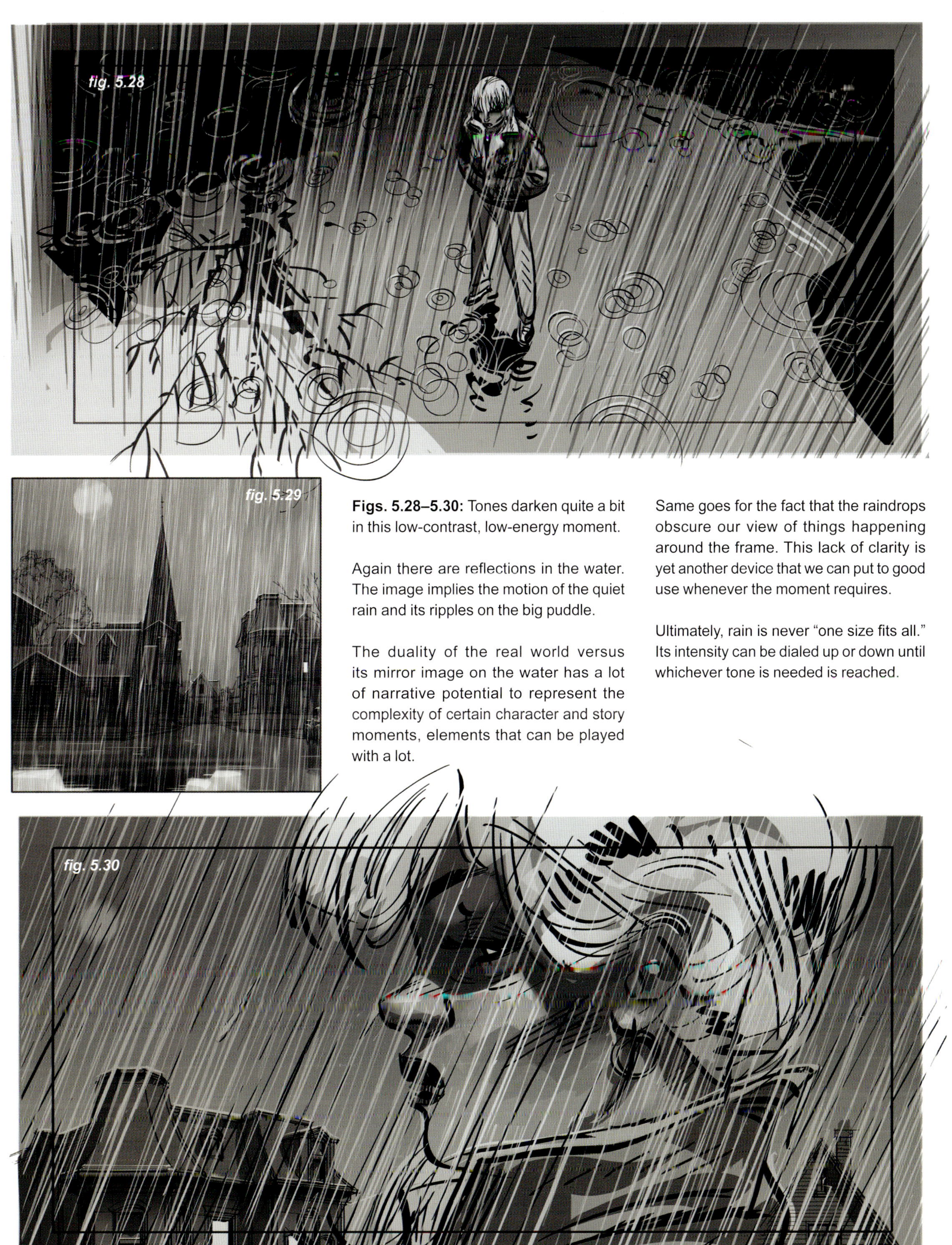

Figs. 5.28–5.30: Tones darken quite a bit in this low-contrast, low-energy moment.

Again there are reflections in the water. The image implies the motion of the quiet rain and its ripples on the big puddle.

The duality of the real world versus its mirror image on the water has a lot of narrative potential to represent the complexity of certain character and story moments, elements that can be played with a lot.

Same goes for the fact that the raindrops obscure our view of things happening around the frame. This lack of clarity is yet another device that we can put to good use whenever the moment requires.

Ultimately, rain is never "one size fits all." Its intensity can be dialed up or down until whichever tone is needed is reached.

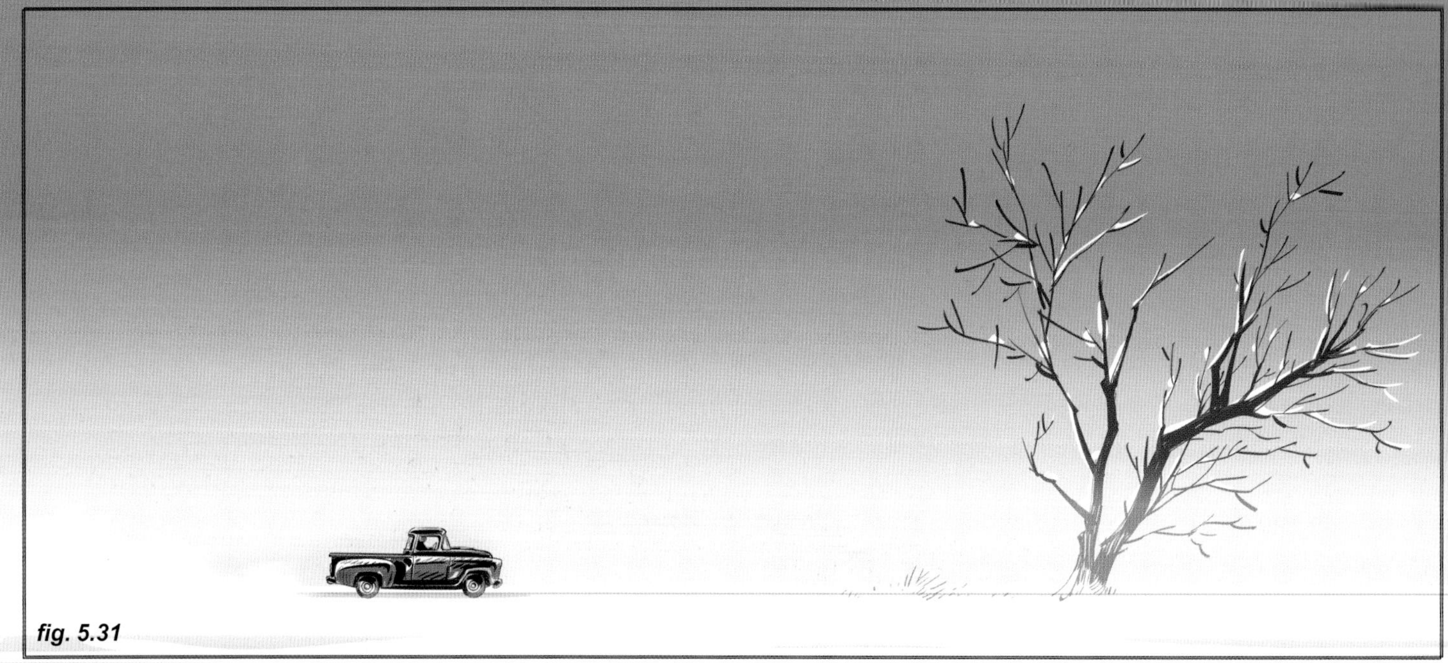

fig. 5.31

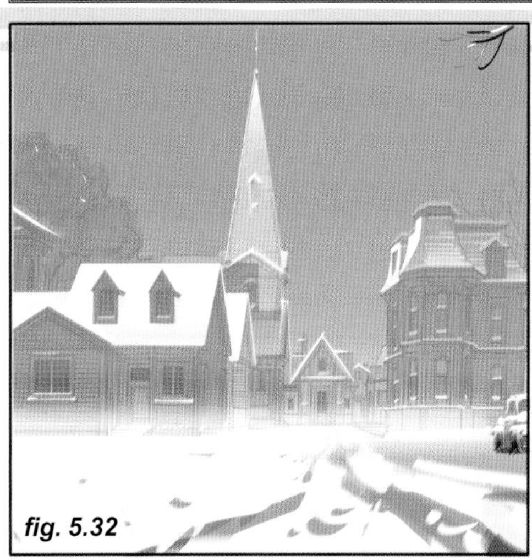

fig. 5.32

Fig. 5.31: If the moment calls for it, the clean, calm, and open nature of a snowy, foggy landscape can create a wealth of possibilities for the characters as they move through the story.

Figs. 5.32, 5.33: Or create an odd, eerie feeling with a diffused glaring light reflected on the snow, emphasizing an uncomfortable sense of solitude.

Figs. 5.34–5.36: These rather "film noir" style images give a lot of game for both black-and-white or color scenes.

When lighting is pushed to this extreme, it can establish great, suspenseful tones.

This contrast can be used strategically to set up good staging opportunities by clearly focusing attention on the main subject—or perhaps away from it, which would give a greater sense of mystery.

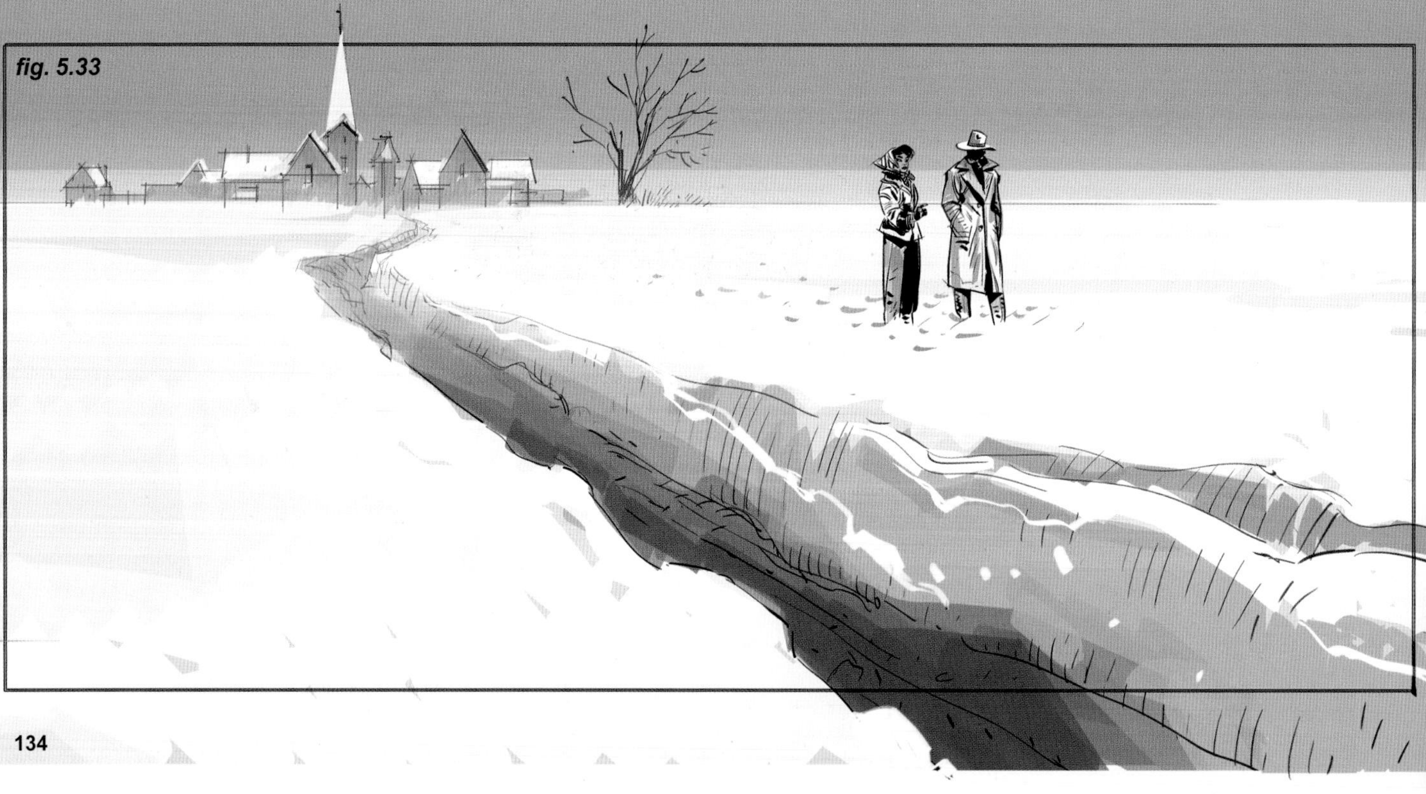

fig. 5.33

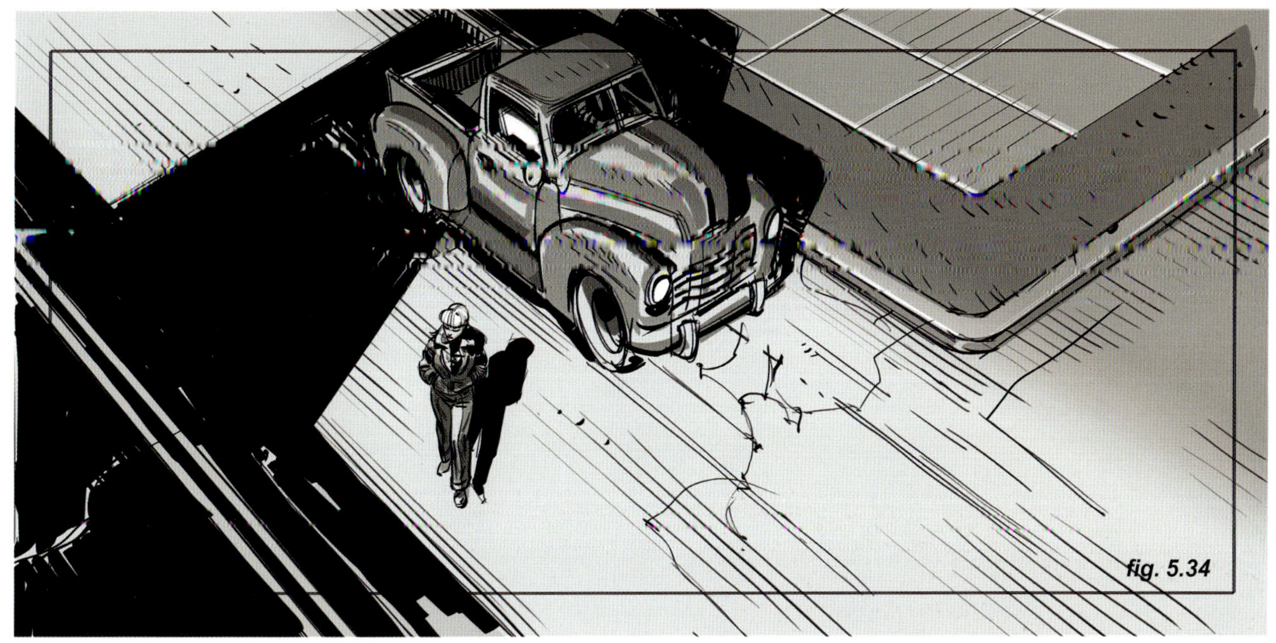

fig. 5.34

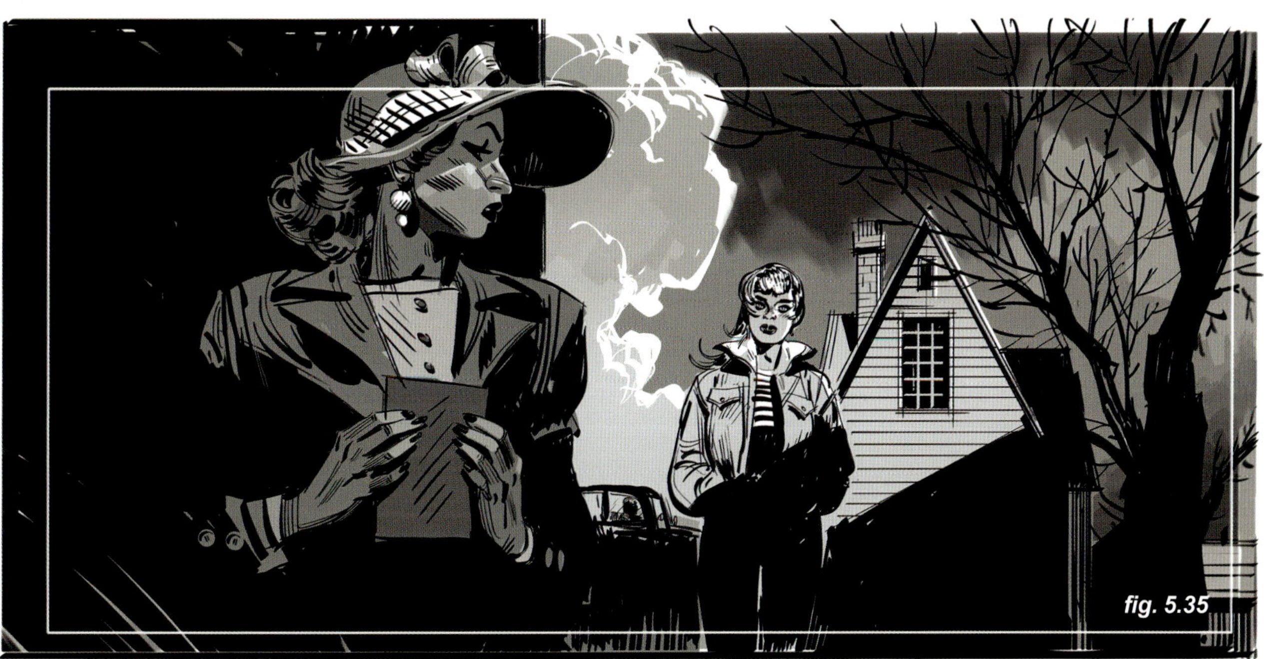

fig. 5.35

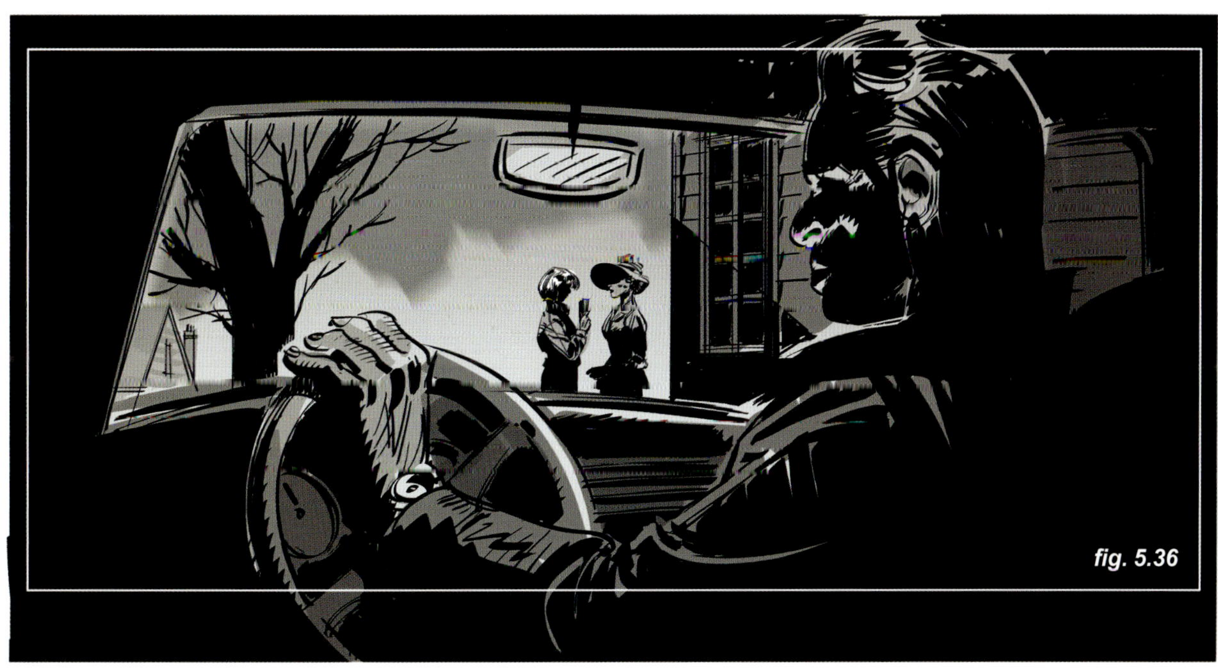

fig. 5.36

As needed, each element can be pushed to the limit, and then some. In the following cases, **lighting** the complex and intricate shapes of the environment's architecture can create unusual looks that may even feel surreal or expressionistic.

Fig. 5.37: Just to establish an overall sense of design, this fortress exterior anticipates the tubular-looking system of shapes that will be incorporated in the interior shots.

Fig. 5.38: This interior is loosely inspired by ancient Nordic construction. Complex systems of beams and columns incorporate straights and heavy curves as they interlock with each other, which helps frame the environment in unusual ways.

Fig. 5.39: A focused and explosive light source within a very dark environment shoots from the bottom up. This is an unusual light direction we are not accustomed to, as light sources are usually positioned above us.

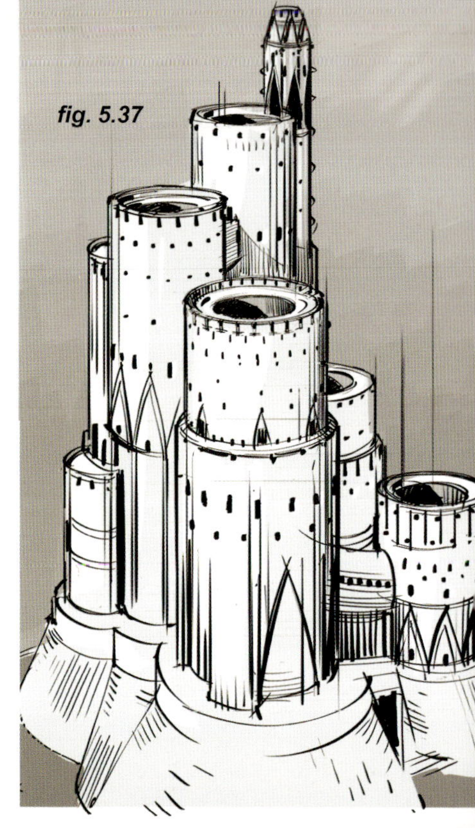

fig. 5.37

fig. 5.39

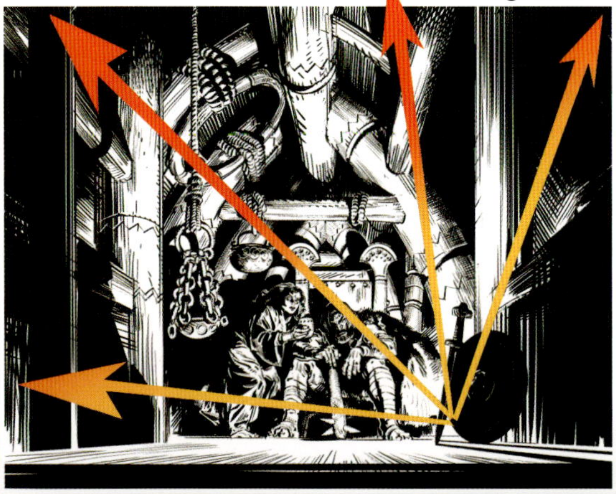

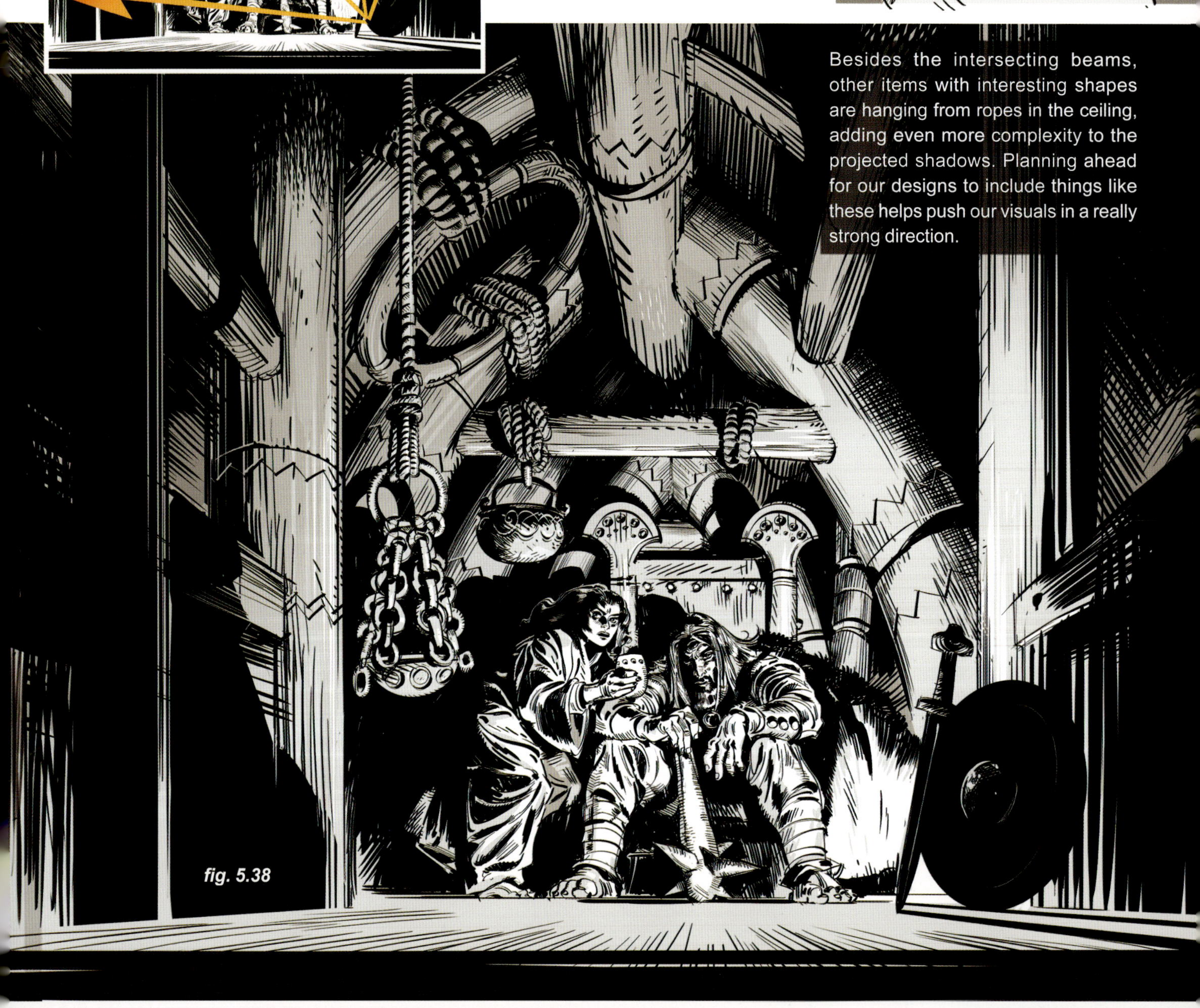

Besides the intersecting beams, other items with interesting shapes are hanging from ropes in the ceiling, adding even more complexity to the projected shadows. Planning ahead for our designs to include things like these helps push our visuals in a really strong direction.

fig. 5.38

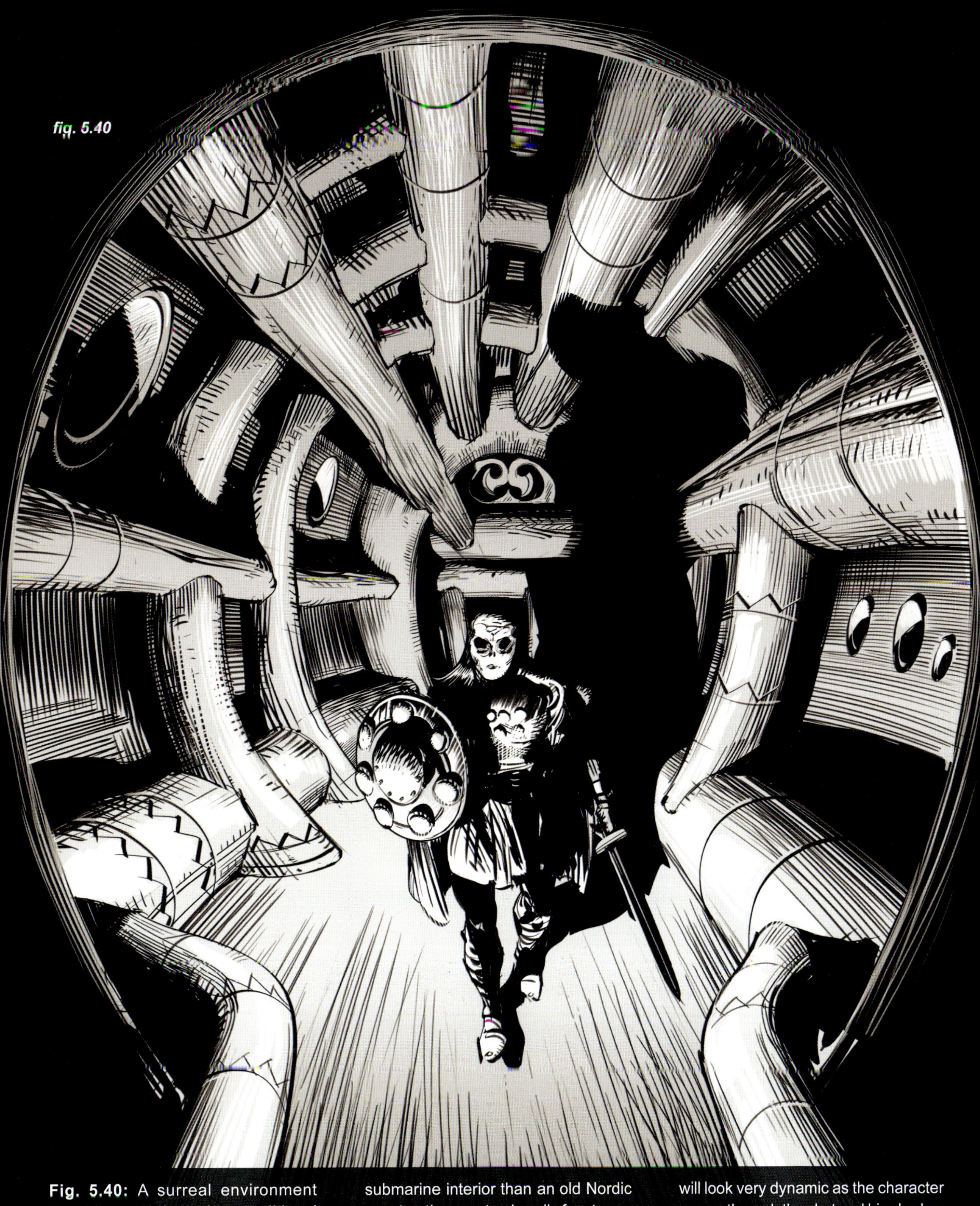

Fig. 5.40: A surreal environment like this one — that mixes traditional elements like carved wooden beams with a design that more resembles a submarine interior than an old Nordic construction—not only calls for strong, projected shadows on its heavily volumetric and irregular surface but will look very dynamic as the character moves through the shot and his shadow gets recomposed and rearranged with every step he takes.

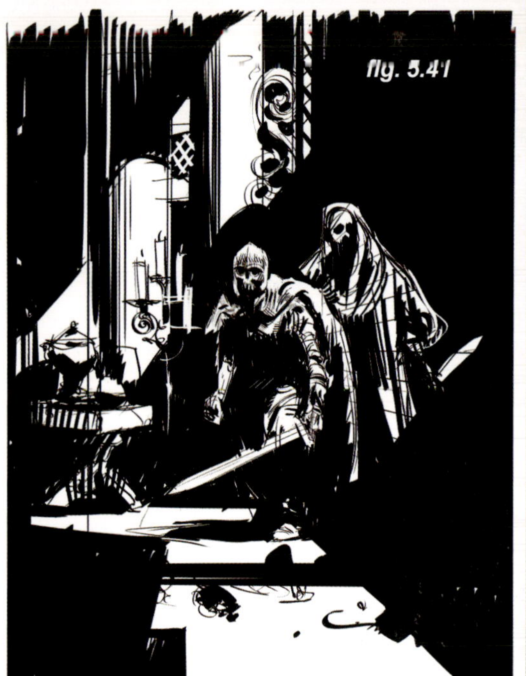

Fig. 5.41: It is important to consider the emotional moment first. At this rough-sketch stage there is not much concern for the proportions of the characters, the accuracy of their anatomy, or any of that. What matters is presenting them in a way that communicates the drama of the moment by enhancing the dynamic lines of their physical motions and facial expressions.

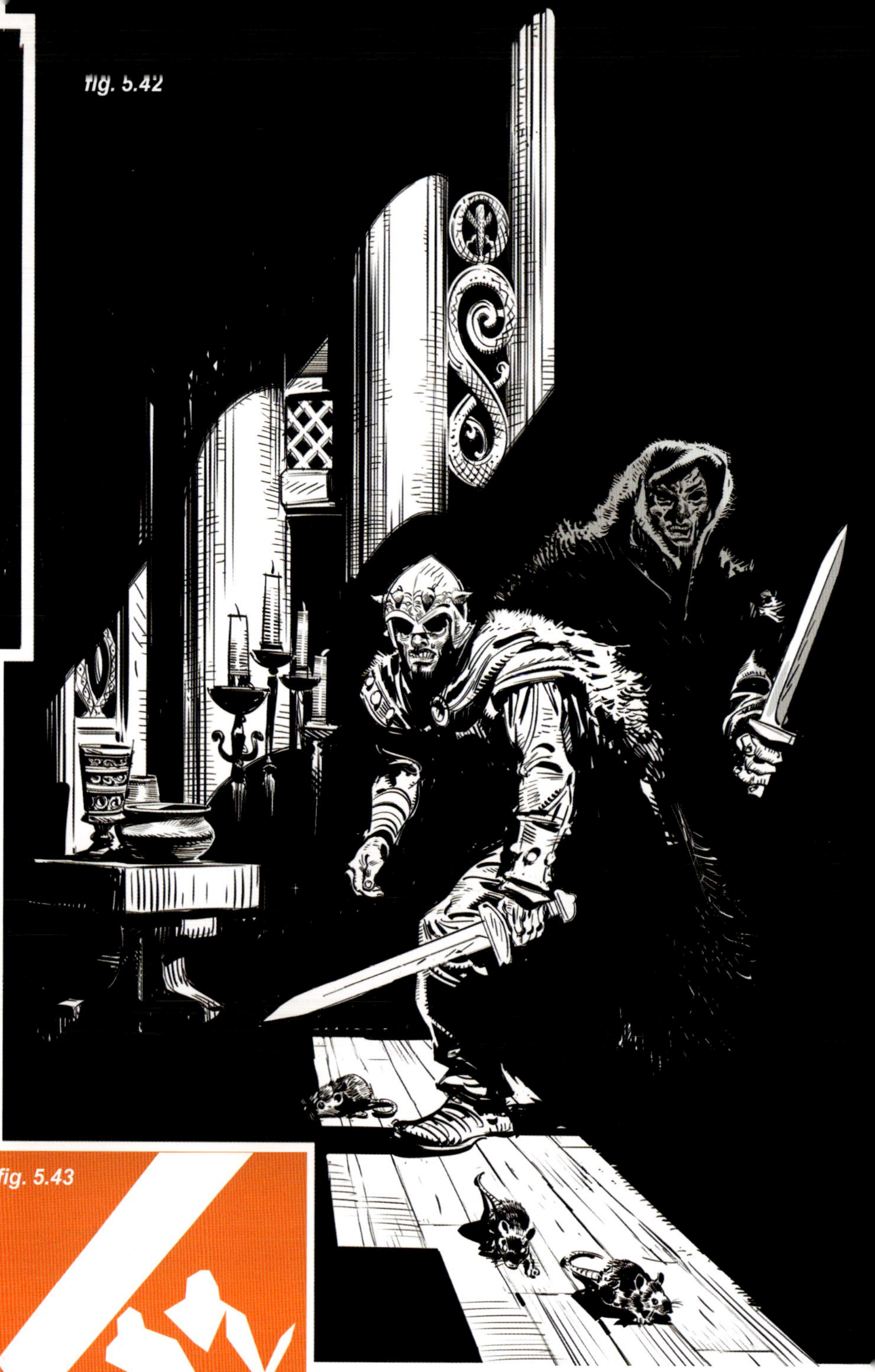

Fig. 5.42: In a very high-contrast case like this one, we can direct the light so that most of **the environment literally disappears** and the audience can only make out the details that we consider important enough to reveal.

Fig. 5.43: When light in an environment is so scarce, it is important to show details in a way that whatever needs to stand out does stand out—maybe it is the historical period, the tone of the building (calm, dramatic), or an item that will become key to the story. So think ahead how **to group certain items** so that with one ray of light, a lot is revealed.

Figs. 5.44, 5.45: Circling back to the use of weather, these two dramatic ocean shots show the potential of the ever-changing environment that is the sea; so dynamic in fact that contrast can be exploited by the juxtaposition of pretty much one frame to the next.

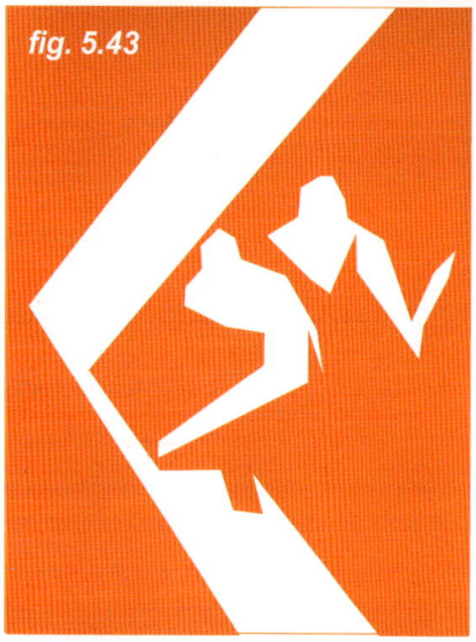

The long ship that dominates the first frame moves way down in the next frame so that both ships, the one in the foreground and the one in the distance, keep **alternating the balance of power** throughout the same scene as they rise and fall with the swell.

Figs. 5.46, 5.47: Observe how these compositions were born out of very clear visual statements, as seen in these quick sketches.

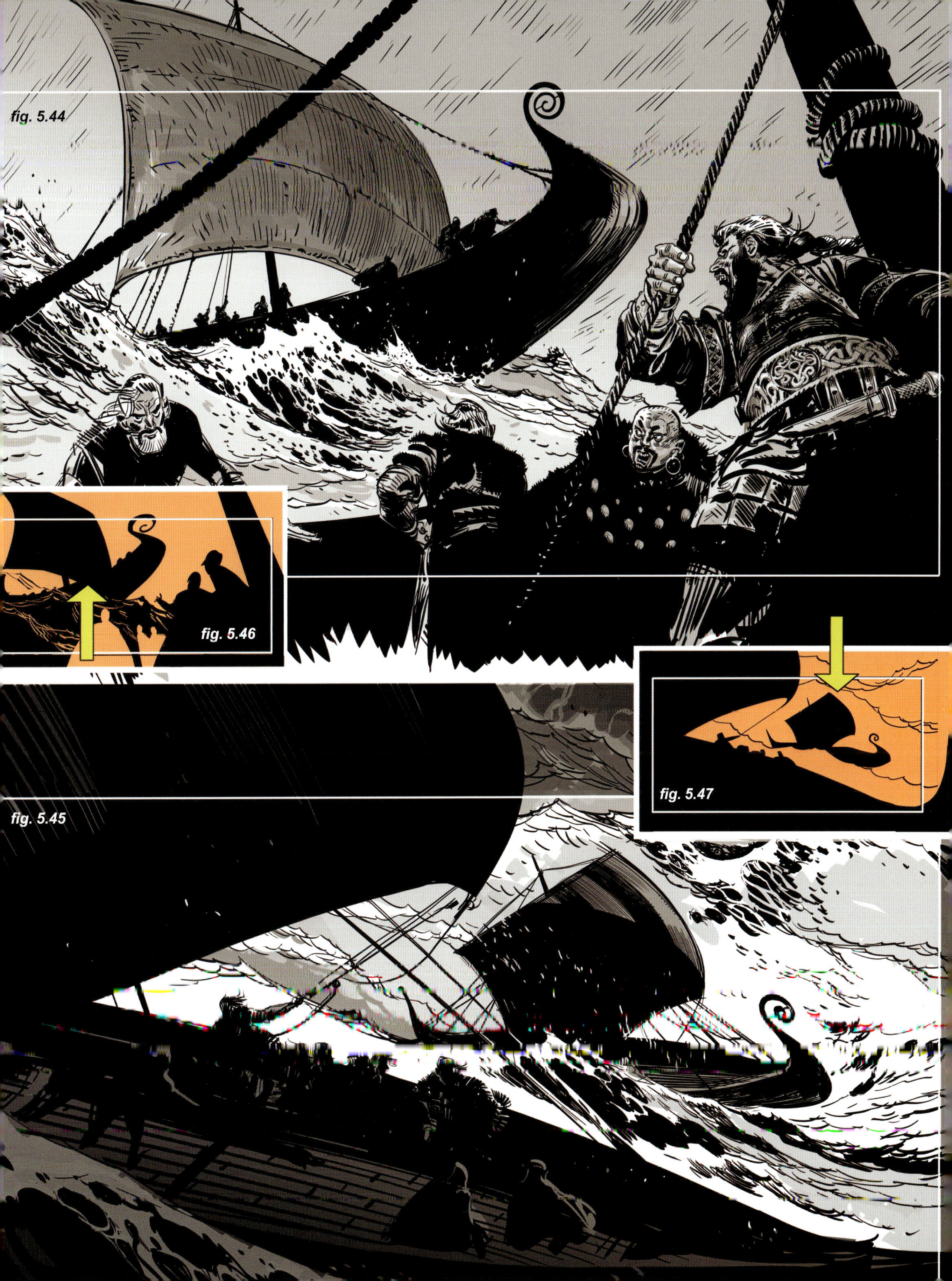

fig. 5.44

fig. 5.45

fig. 5.46

fig. 5.47

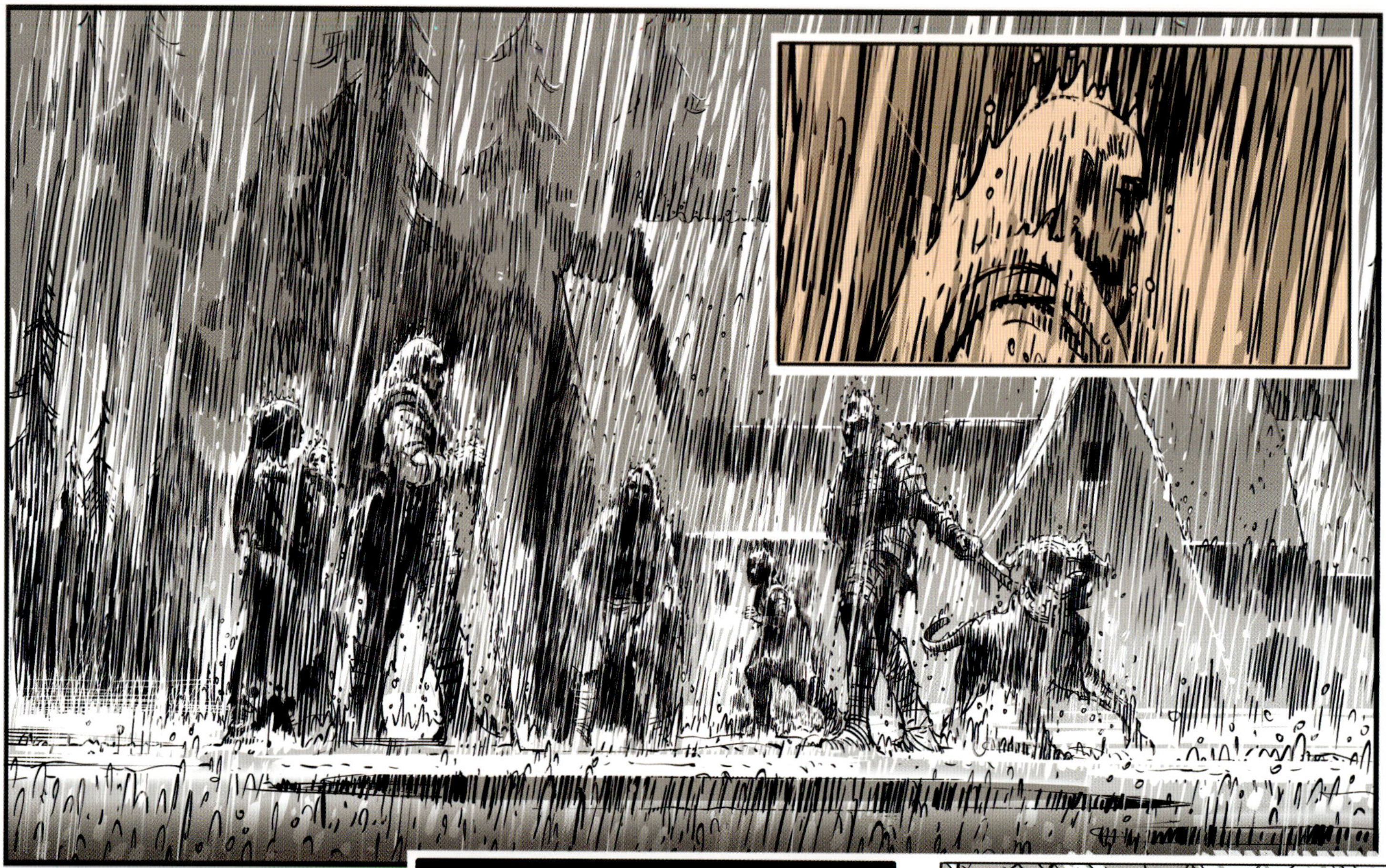

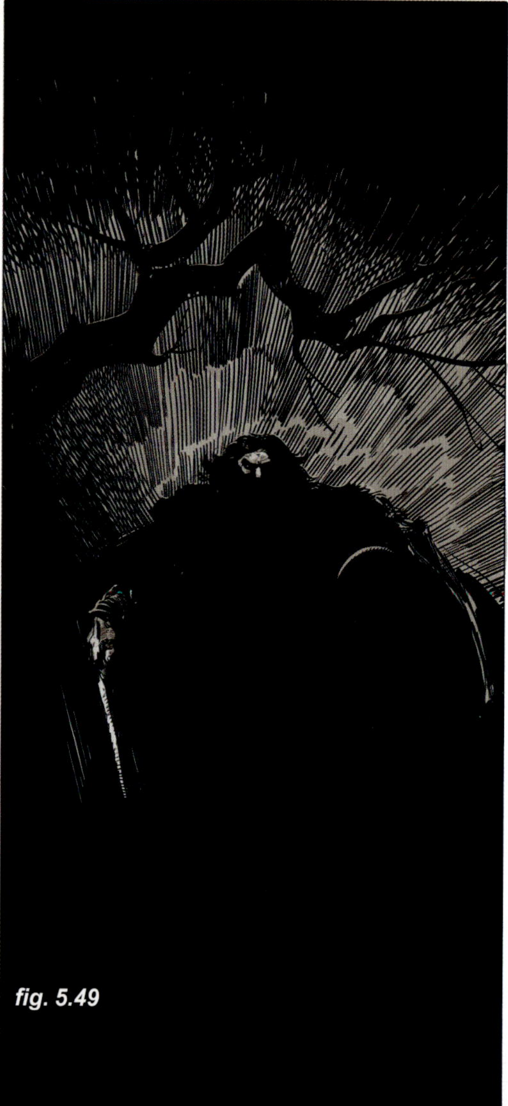

fig. 5.48

Fig. 5.48: Rain is another element that dramatically affects environments and can be dialed up or down as needed. In the image above, most of the details disappear and become visually transformed or irrelevant, just as lighting (or lack thereof) accomplished in fig. 5.41 on page 138. Rain can add a very strong, dynamic element to any environment.

Figs. 5.49, 5.50: These two final images show another example of revealing, concealing, or both simultaneously, through light and weather. In this case, it is lightning getting the job done by illuminating the scene intermittently.

Moving along in our journey, let's now get into how nature helps us tell our stories.

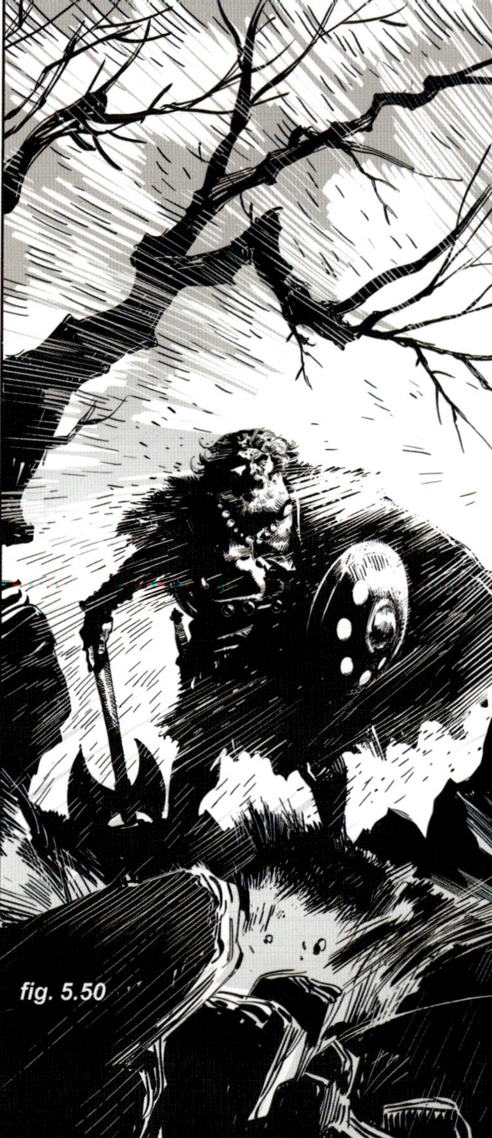

fig. 5.49

fig. 5.50

6

NATURE TELLS ITS TALE

Natural environments are composed of many different physical elements: trees, mountains, rocks, clouds, oceans, lakes, etc., that together with the use of light, camera choices, and weather form narrative visual units.

Each one of these elements can vary in shape, form, and size and can be designed and used according to the same philosophies already discussed for so many other elements, like architectural pieces and props. Combining them in various ways can produce soft flows, contrast, depth, monotony, dynamics, low tension, or whatever the story moment requires. This way, our natural landscapes speak to our audience and help give meaning beyond the dialogue.

Let's look at them as separate items first, and then through the staging and combining of many.

TREES

Through the most basic observation of trees, we immediately notice their variety of shapes and character. Some shapes look friendlier, some more dramatic, the sizes of some are imposing, or otherwise humble, or show harsh character, or are more decorative with flowers and gracefully shaped canopies. Depending on the season or time of year, some might be really bushy, portraying a look where energy and abundance of life is prominent, while at other times, like autumn and winter, they can appear drier and gloomier.

Let's see how reality can inspire us to build upon it. These are some reference pictures, together with the dynamic lines and sketches they inspired, for an insightful look at the visual opportunities these trees offer.

Figs. 6.1, 6.2: After a quick observation, it is clear the tree in this image stretches sideways, with elongated branches and leaves that contrast with the rounder, bolder-shaped trees around.

Fig. 6.3: This sketch pushes and stylizes these qualities to make a clear visual statement.

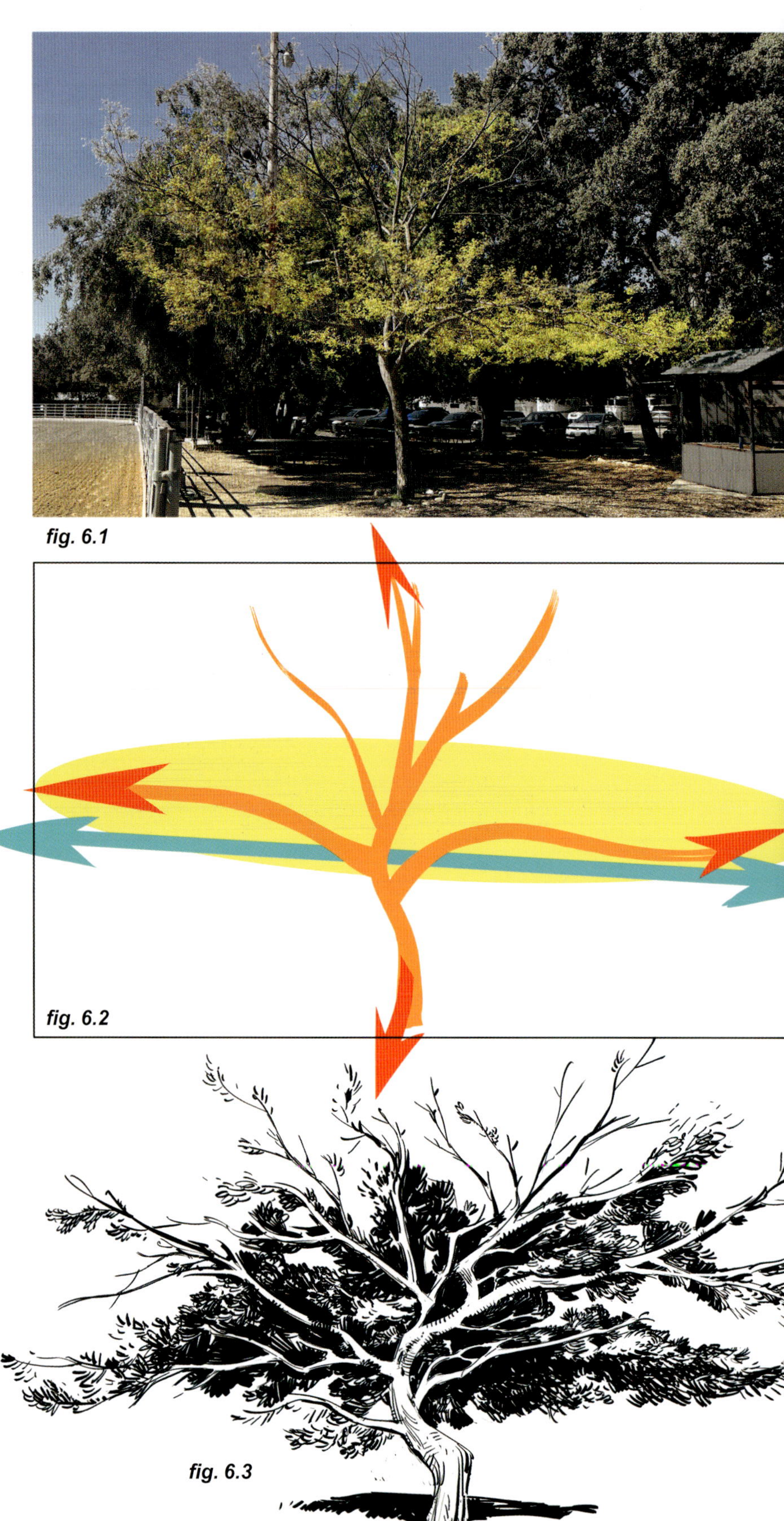

fig. 6.1

fig. 6.2

fig. 6.3

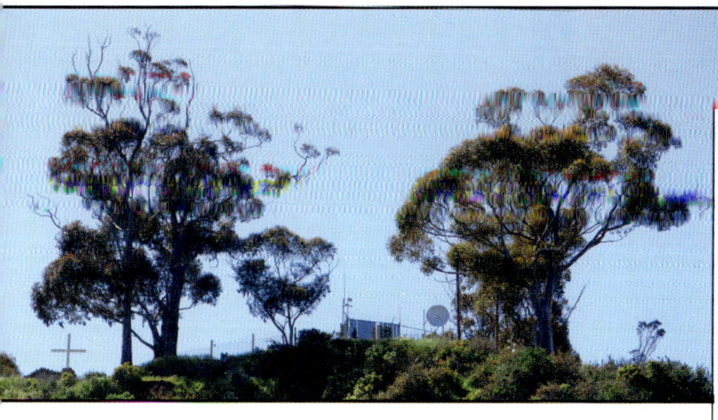

fig. 6.4

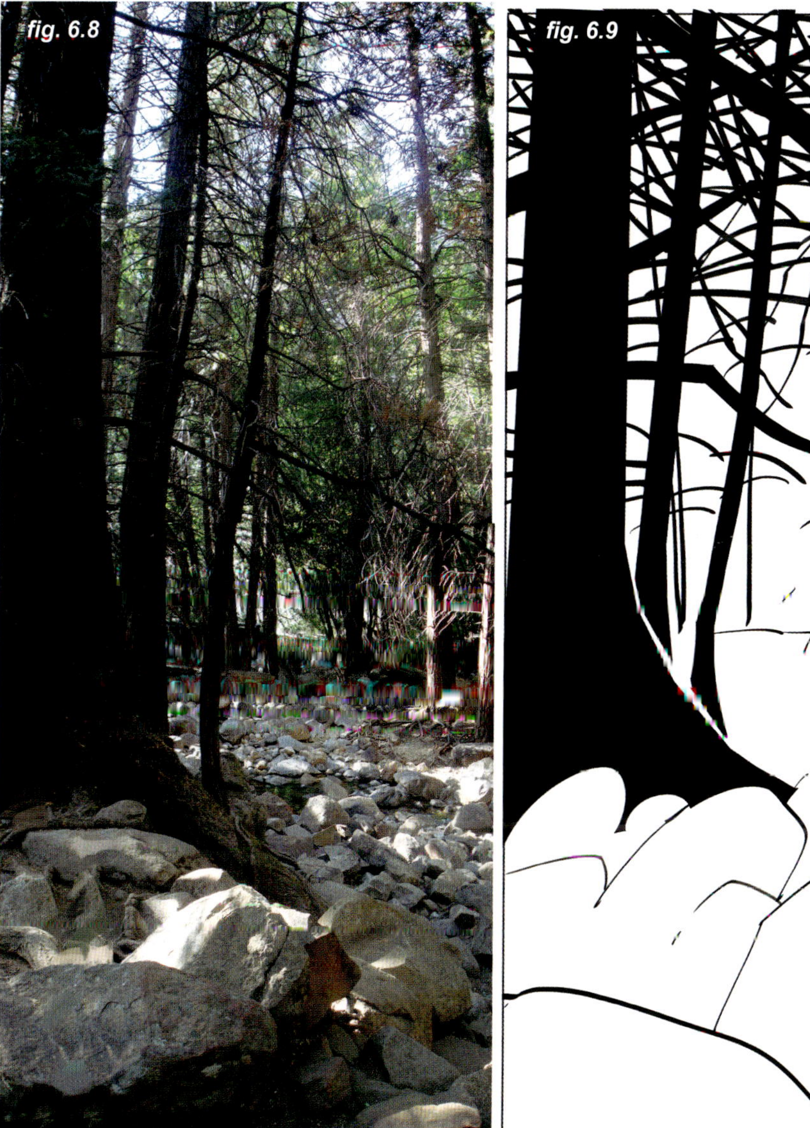

fig. 6.6

Figs. 6.4, 6.5: These two trees on a hill have a naturally graphic silhouette. If asked to make them strongly contrast with the golden-leafed tree in the previous example, we could push these dynamics in an even more upward, diagonal motion (red arrows) to further establish the difference.

Figs. 6.6, 6.7: Palm trees have an altogether different feel, tropical and explosive, like fireworks.

Figs. 6.8, 6.9: The combination of trunks and branches from different trees becomes a rather convoluted image, reminiscent of an entangled spiderweb.

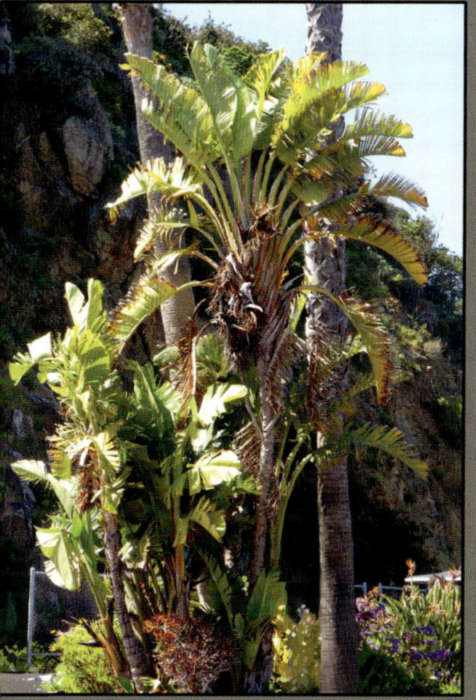

fig. 6.7

All of these elements and more can come into play effectively. Let's imagine a luxurious, finely designed estate where a character lives, in the middle of a natural, forested area, and we need to establish a unique, distinctive and exclusive feel to the place to make sure that when the characters walk from within its walls to outside, and vice versa, it is clear in both cases they are stepping into different worlds where different rules apply.

Fig. 6.12: (*Opposite page*) This illustration is visually pushed for the sake of the example. The outside forest is a chaotic and entangled natural environment, while all the greenery within the walls has been extensively manicured and domesticated so that a visual order rules. (These concepts echo what was previously explored in Chapter 4 on the use of geometrical shapes and volumes.) Texture-wise, both worlds are also at odds, with the forest trees appearing rougher and the hedges and topiaries seeming much smoother to the eye.

Fig. 6.10: Notice how the trees at the top have an angular style of line, with an abundance of zigzag diagonals and with the branches at the top opening up in a V-shape fashion (what we would call top-heavy), contrary to the hedges below, sitting upright and vertical, with curved shapes that tend to widen at their bases, in an A-shape fashion (that is, bottom-heavy).

Fig. 6.11: (*Bottom image*) As opposed to fig 6.12, in which the frontal, single vanishing point camera angle emphasizes a sense of symmetry and impactful graphic style, this image, even when using the same elements (manicured garden vs. natural forest), creates a lesser visual impression through a lower, three-quarter position of the camera.

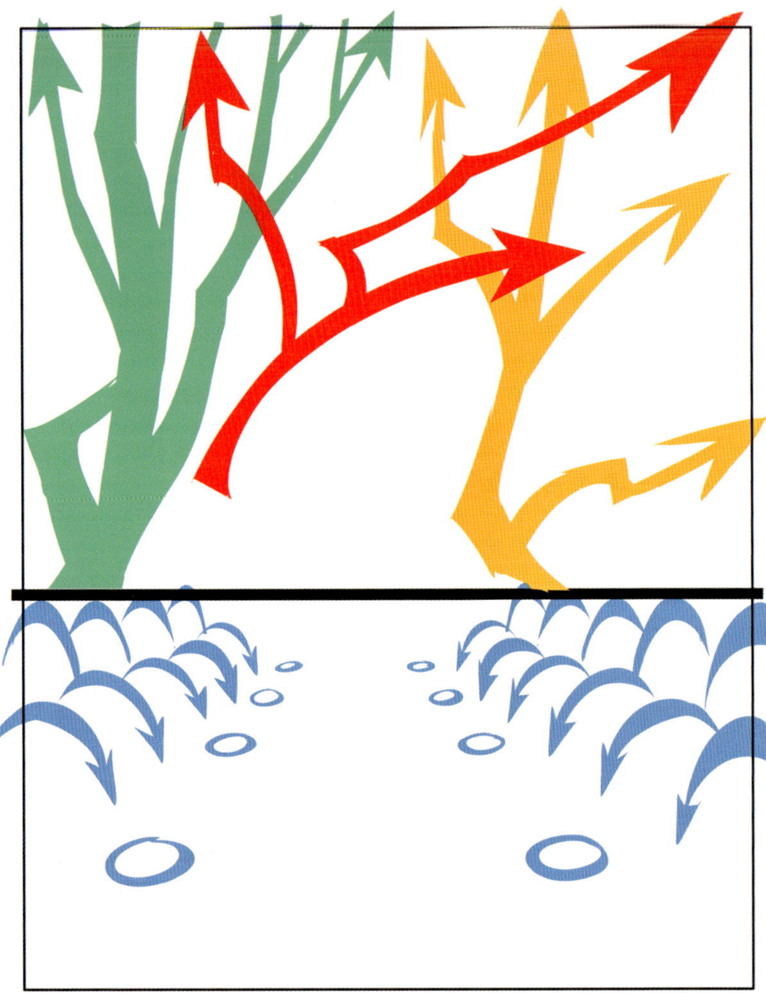

fig. 6.10

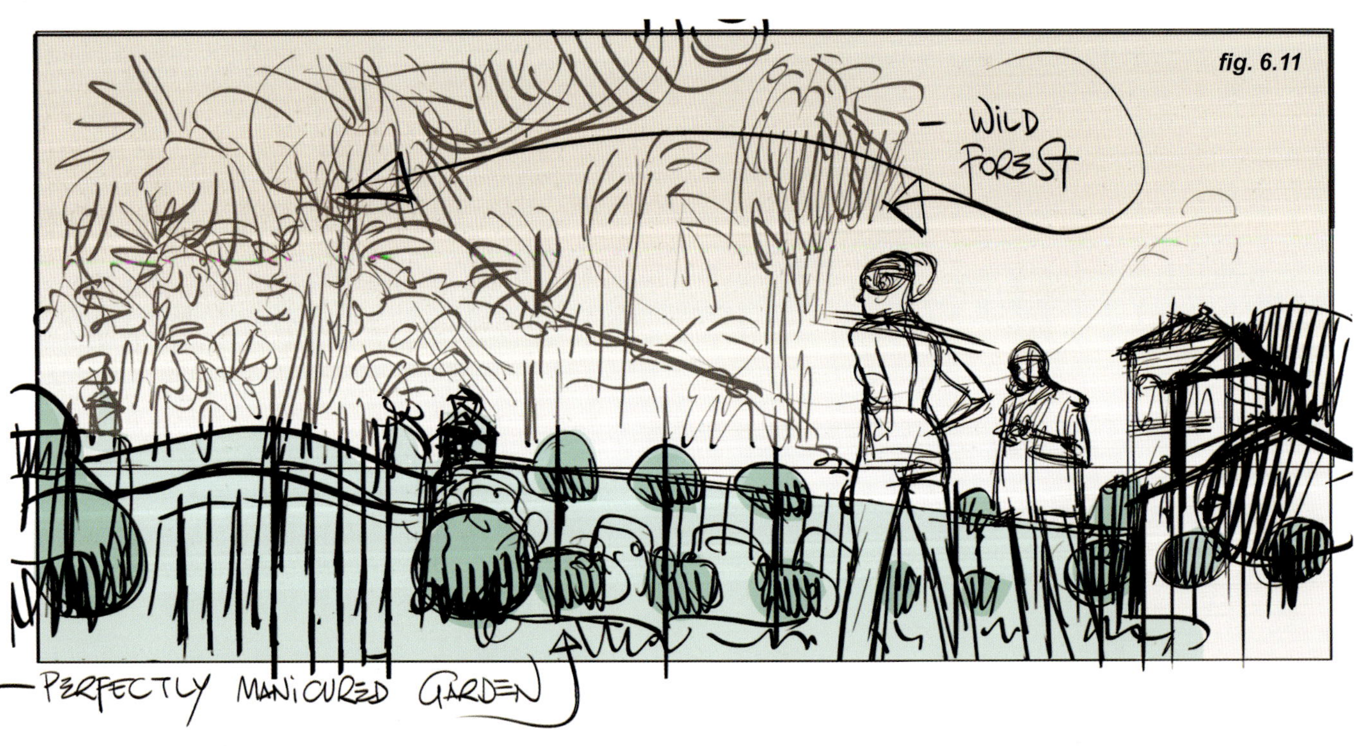

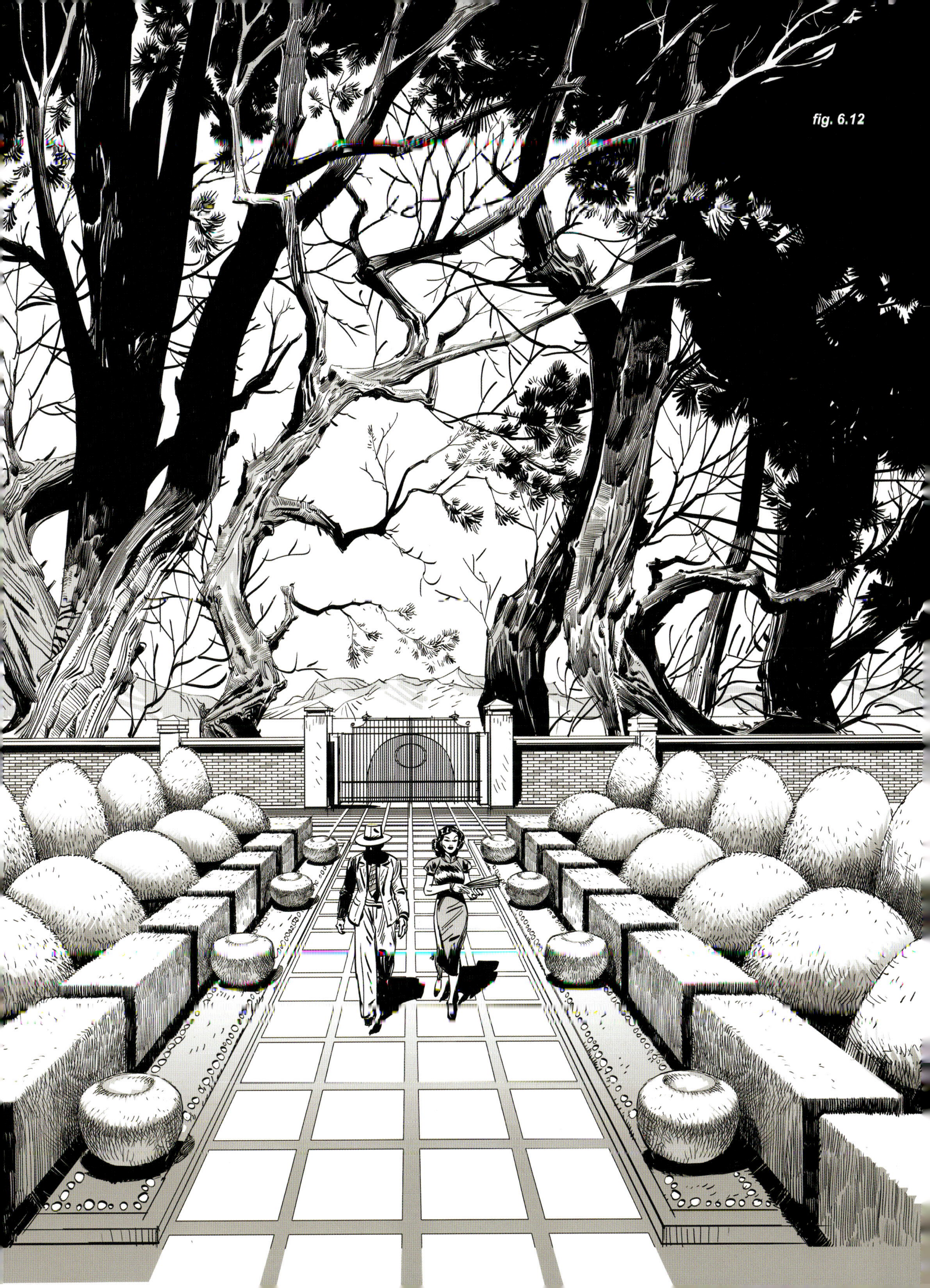
fig. 6.12

fig. 6.13

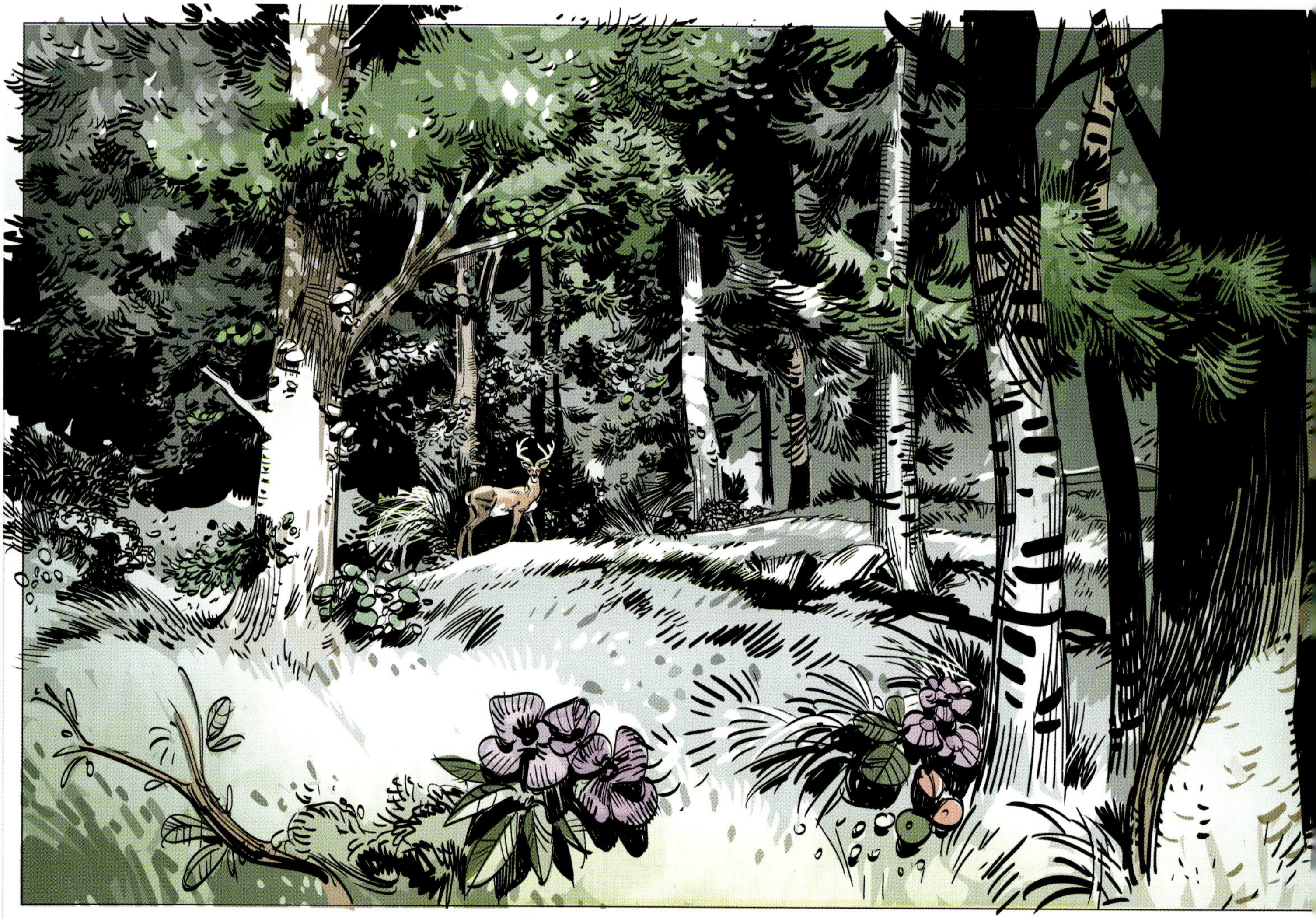

fig. 6.14

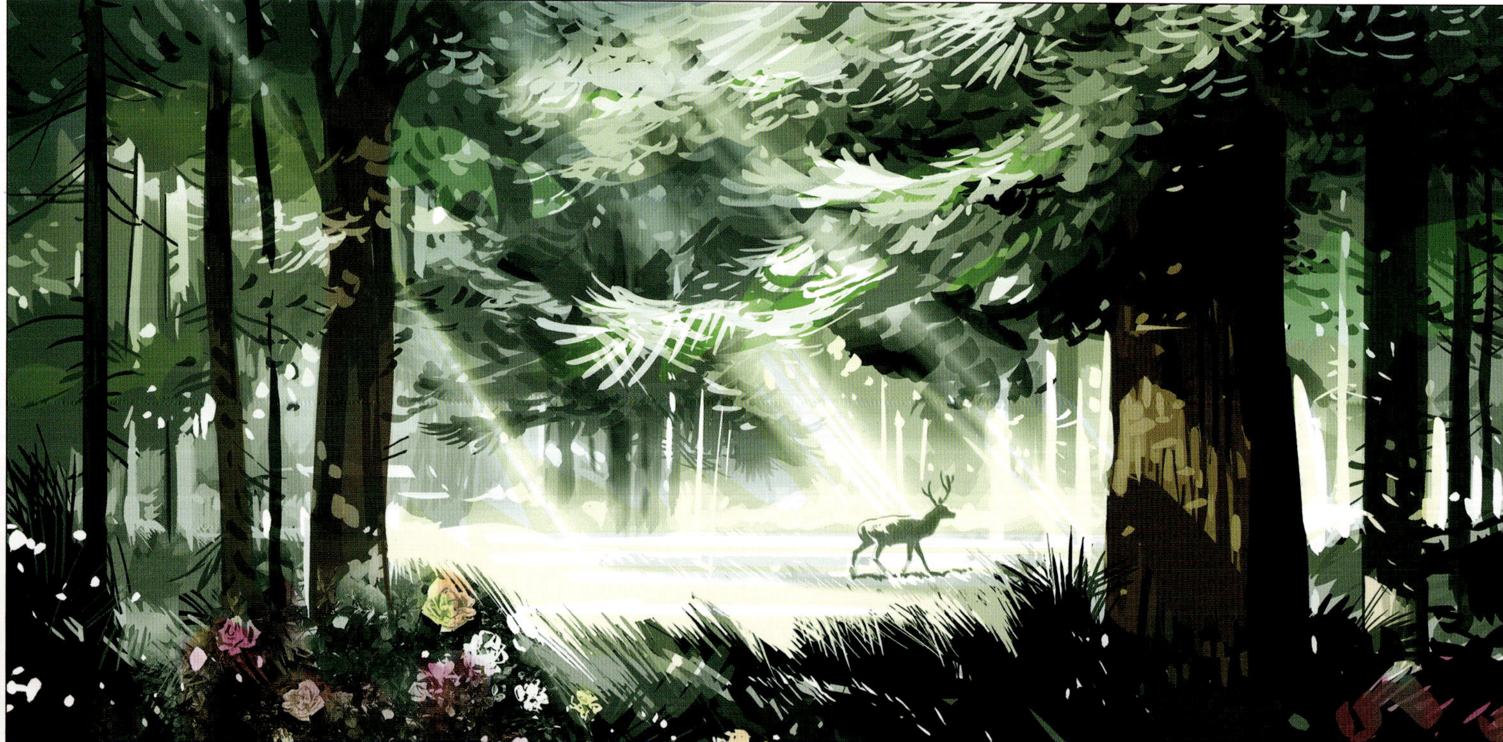

These two pages show how to use trees as a narrative tool throughout a full story.

Any visual element can be portrayed in a way that shows an emotional change and progression. In this case, it is trees within their natural context.

Here they take us from a quiet, idyllic moment to an intermediate, more unsettling one, finally landing in a really threatening place.

Take into account that these particular images are just that, examples, and that any element offering a visual progression can take many different forms, looks, and designs. Also, the progression could be reversed, starting at a point of discomfort and evolving to a final place of peace and calm.

Figs. 6.13, 6.14: These are two versions of a rather poetic forest. Let's analyze the elements that make them come across this way.

Fig. 6.15: (*Top graphic*) In this particular case, the calm is represented through the use of straight, vertical tree trunks with minor bends to emphasize a rhythmic sense of playful flow, all on top of a rather horizontal and calm forest floor.

Although a forest can be quite a dark place, given the limitations of light coming in, establishing clearings that allow for more sunlight to hit patches of flowers and grass allows for this peaceful visual moment we are aiming for.

Fig. 6.16: (*Top right*) This next step offers a more pushed view of the trees involved, as analyzed in fig. 6.17 (*middle graphic*). The overall design is more dramatic, playing with the ups and downs of the general terrain in a more vertical and wavy pattern. The trunks bend a bit more than before, and the branches are generally pointier and drier than in figs. 6.13, 6.14.

Fig. 6.18: The tree-trunk shape has now been taken to an extreme. Zigzagged, angular, pointy lines are predominant while showing this dead, dry, isolated fallen tree, as analyzed in fig. 6.19 (*bottom graphic*).

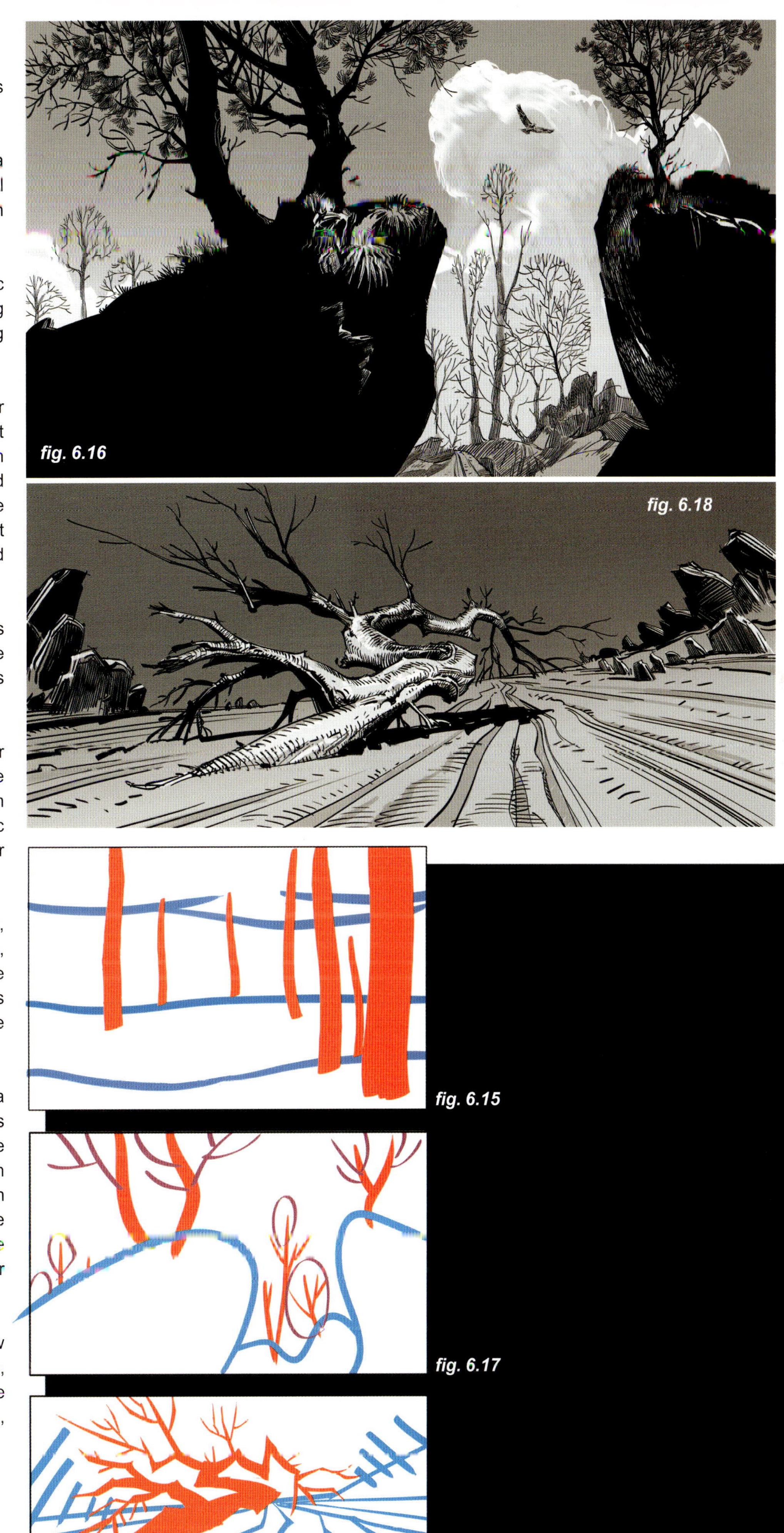

fig. 6.16

fig. 6.18

fig. 6.15

fig. 6.17

fig. 6.19

MOUNTAIN COUNTRY: SHAPE HARMONY VS. SHAPE CONTRAST

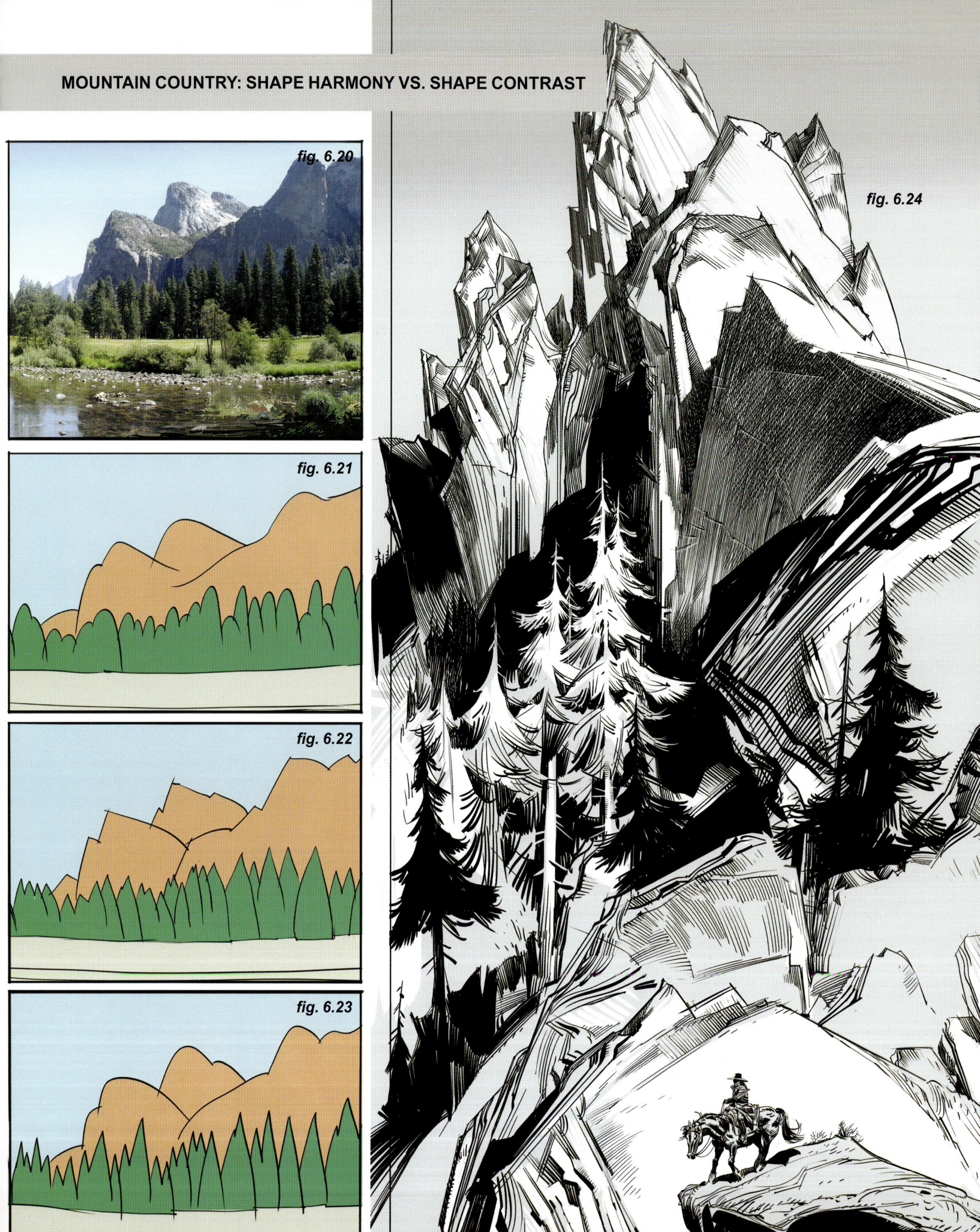

fig. 6.20

fig. 6.21

fig. 6.22

fig. 6.23

fig. 6.24

Fig. 6.20: This photo taken at Yosemite is an example of how we can find different types of line qualities in nature. The mountains favor wavy shapes, and the trees at the base are more pointy. From here we can decide which type of line to emphasize.

Fig. 6.21: If we favor wavy lines **on both** the mountains and the pine trees, it provides a sense of harmony to the overall landscape.

Fig. 6.22: Using a pointier or spikier look **on both** still provides a feeling of unity (yet a notch more energetic).

Fig. 6.23: Pointy trees at the base of curved mountains establishes a differentiation between foreground and background, creating more depth and a certain feeling of disassociation, like each are subtly representing a different world within the story.

Fig. 6.24: This illustration is an example of the hills and the trees being spiky and angular, which brings all shapes together stylistically and in harmony. Usually, angular shapes bring a certain sense of discomfort and danger, although there are always exceptions to any rule.

Fig. 6.25: This graphic shows the shapes of the three large areas that compose the illustration. They are overall triangular and go from the bottom all the way up in a series of zigzagged bursts of different lengths: short, long, medium (see arrows), which brings a level of balance to the image as one inclination counterbalances the others while still making it feel precarious given the differences in length.

Fig. 6.26: After the zone division, we consider the line dynamics. There is a big diagonal to the right, while from the center of the image, a number of rather explosive-looking lines point upward in a pattern that essentially conforms to the shape of a fan.

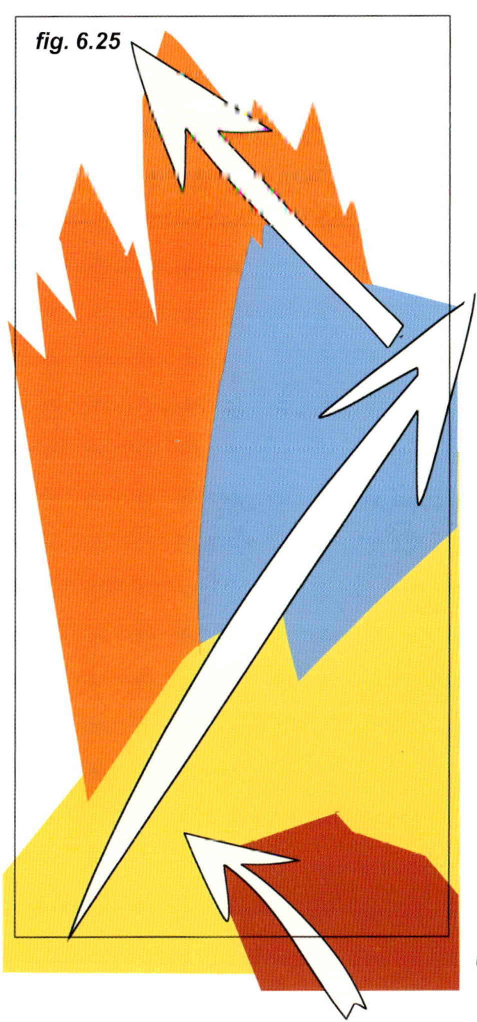

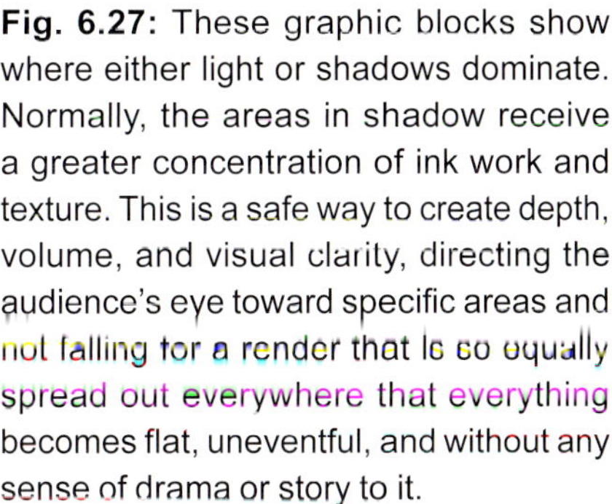

These lines create a design that feels very alive and dramatic by the use of opposed dynamic forces that contrast in length and area, mimicking a sort of house of cards that holds up solid yet is just a few moves away from crashing down.

Fig. 6.27: These graphic blocks show where either light or shadows dominate. Normally, the areas in shadow receive a greater concentration of ink work and texture. This is a safe way to create depth, volume, and visual clarity, directing the audience's eye toward specific areas and not falling for a render that is so equally spread out everywhere that everything becomes flat, uneventful, and without any sense of drama or story to it.

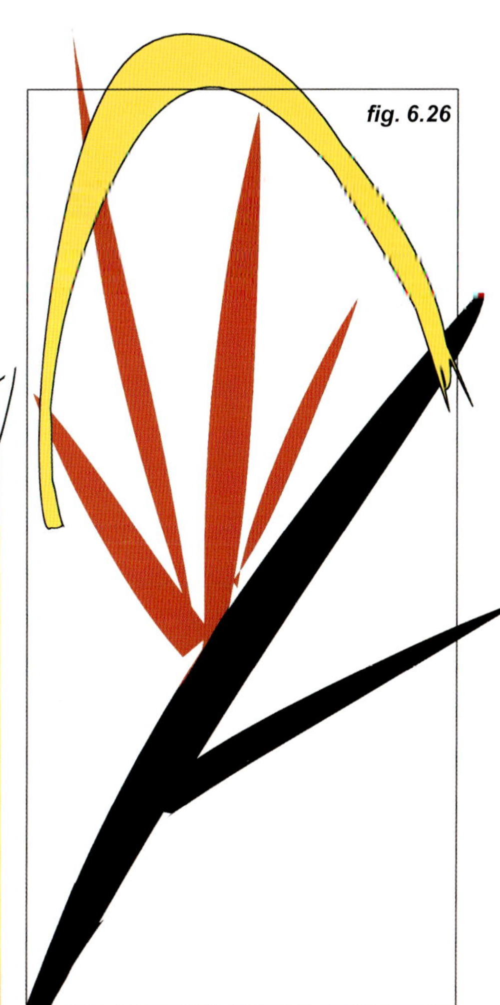

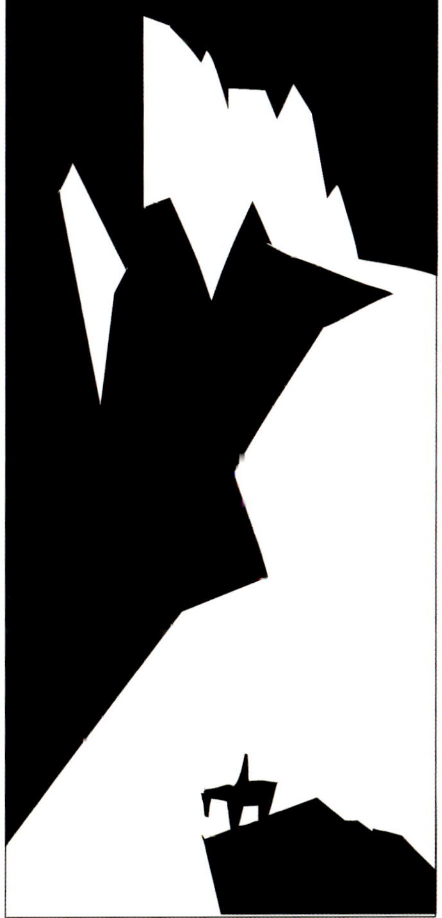

CHANGING THE SHAPE LANGUAGE

Fig. 6.28: As the story unfolds, changing the **shape language** can achieve a number of purposes. If the environment alters its character, it could mean that time has passed, or it can simply indicate geographical distance without a passage of time, as when cutting to simultaneous actions happening elsewhere.

If the environment shows a passage of time, it can have emotional connotations, as it is fair to assume that the character has now been through a number of adventures that have helped change their point of view.

Another layer to take into account is the **size,** scope, and magnitude of the environment. Shape language (rounder, angular, etc.) can also be combined with how grand or how small it looks in its design, bringing in a larger scope for more adventurous, epic moments, or simply scaling down for moments when everything needs to feel more personal or intimate, or when the character appears to be more in control of the surroundings.

Fig. 6.29: In the case of these shapes, the rounder lines are dominant, but it is a good idea to include a small percentage of straight or even angular lines, so as not to end up with a design that looks essentially too soft or just too obvious.

Fig. 6.30: Any line or shape quality that can be shown on grand and wide establishing shots can also serve its purpose in closer camera shots.

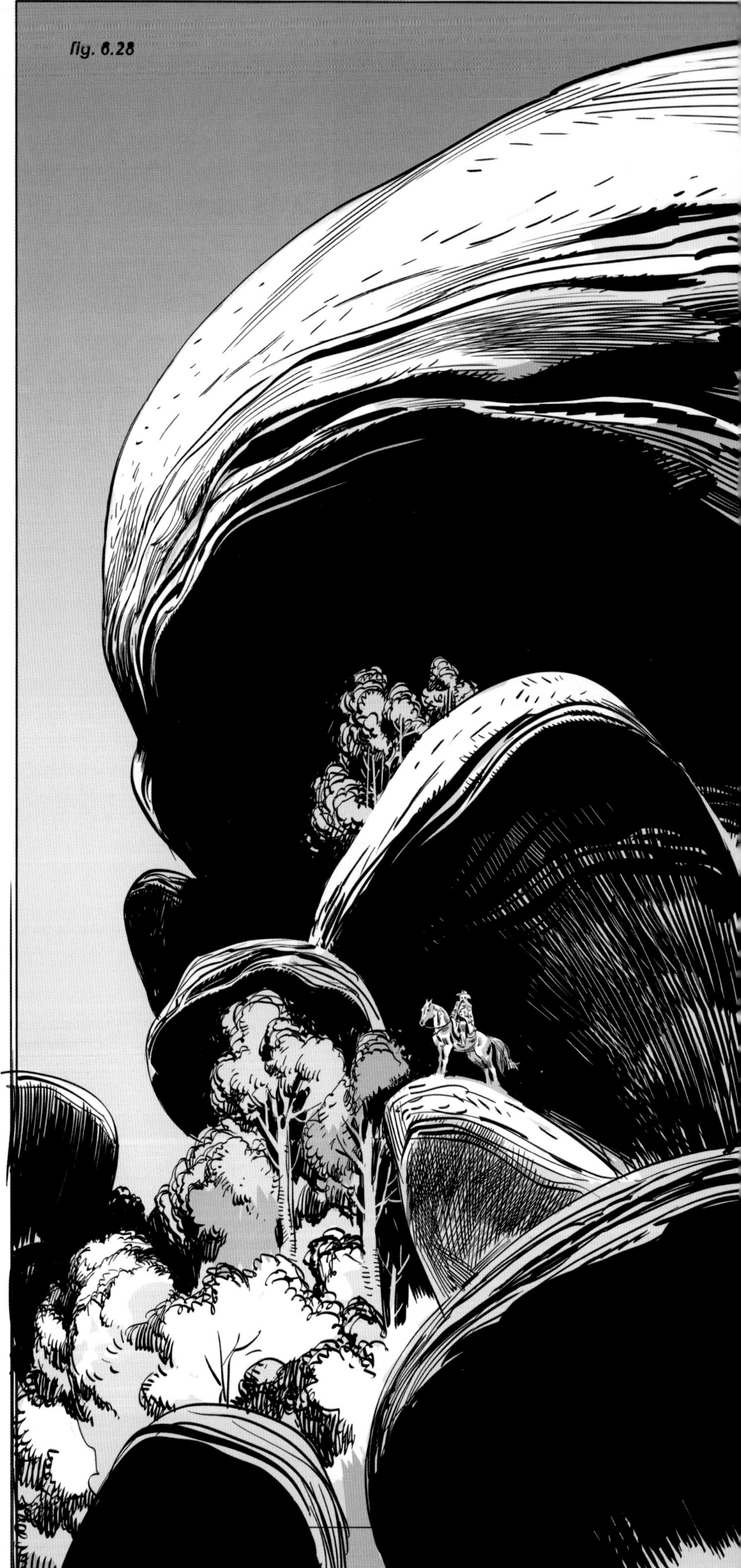

These two "graphic schematics" to the right show how the overall composition of the main shapes and dynamics of this environment work.

Fig. 6.31: Again, this illustration of the wide shot is broken into big, medium, and small areas.

As far as shape balance is concerned, the look of this environment is top-heavy, meaning the general perception is that of an inverted pyramid, expressing a rather unstable feeling.

Fig. 6.32: This "line dynamics" drawing shows a similar pattern to the ones explained in Chapter 3 of the book *Framed Ink, Vol. 2,* following the bouncing path an object would travel after being thrown around and just following the physics of the moment, becoming a visually structured and easy-to-follow route.

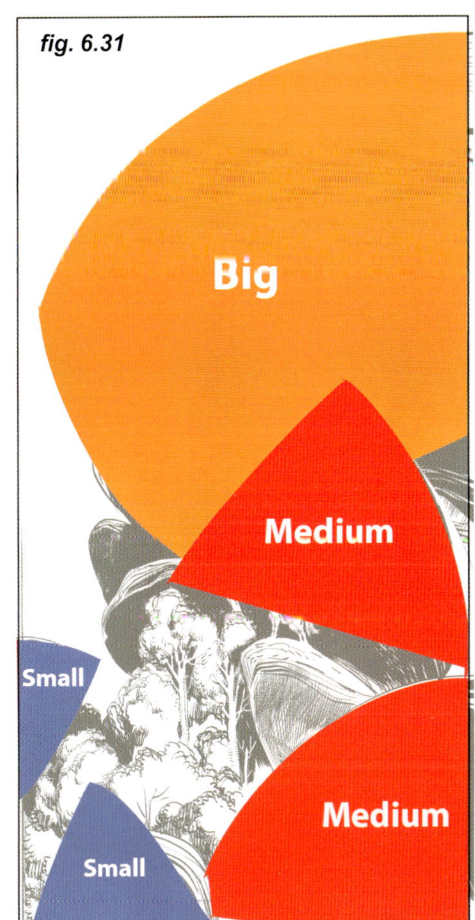

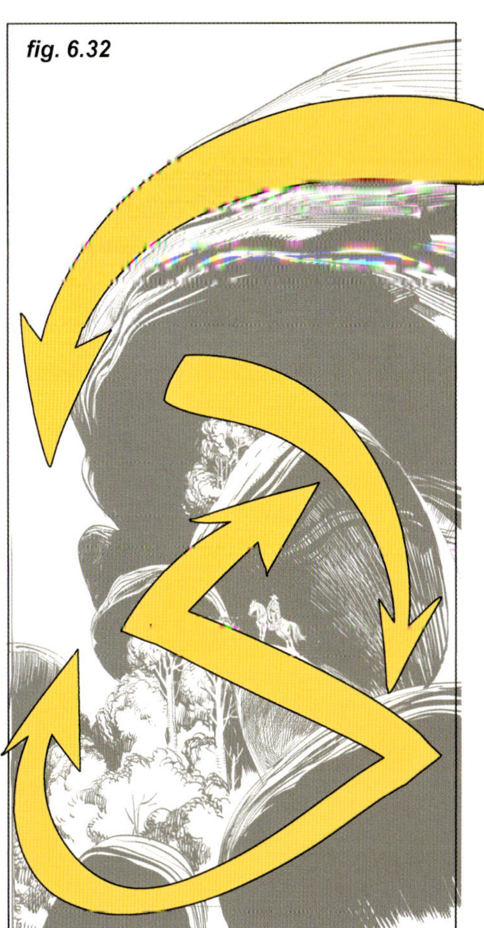

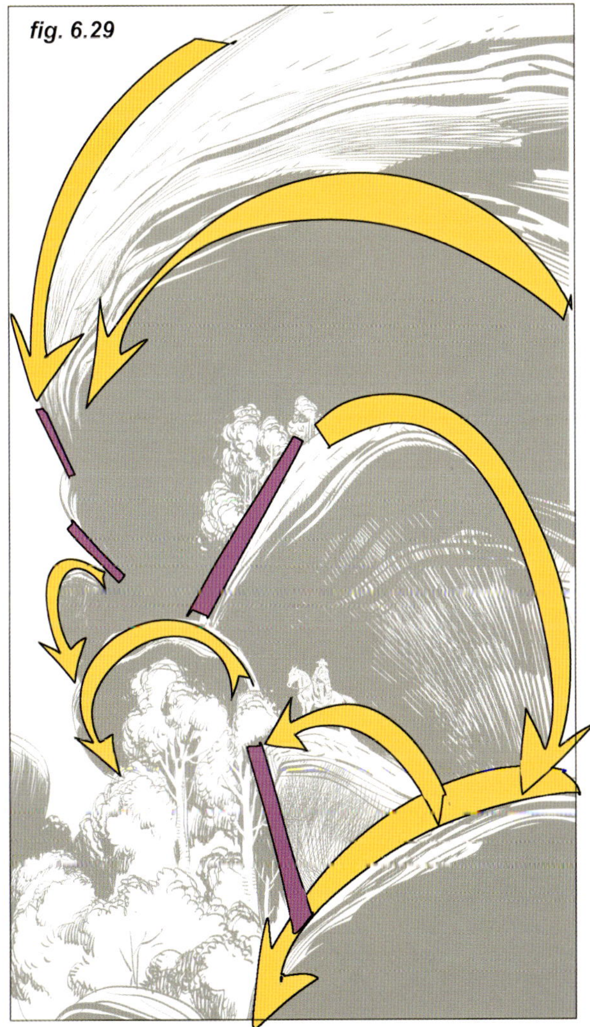

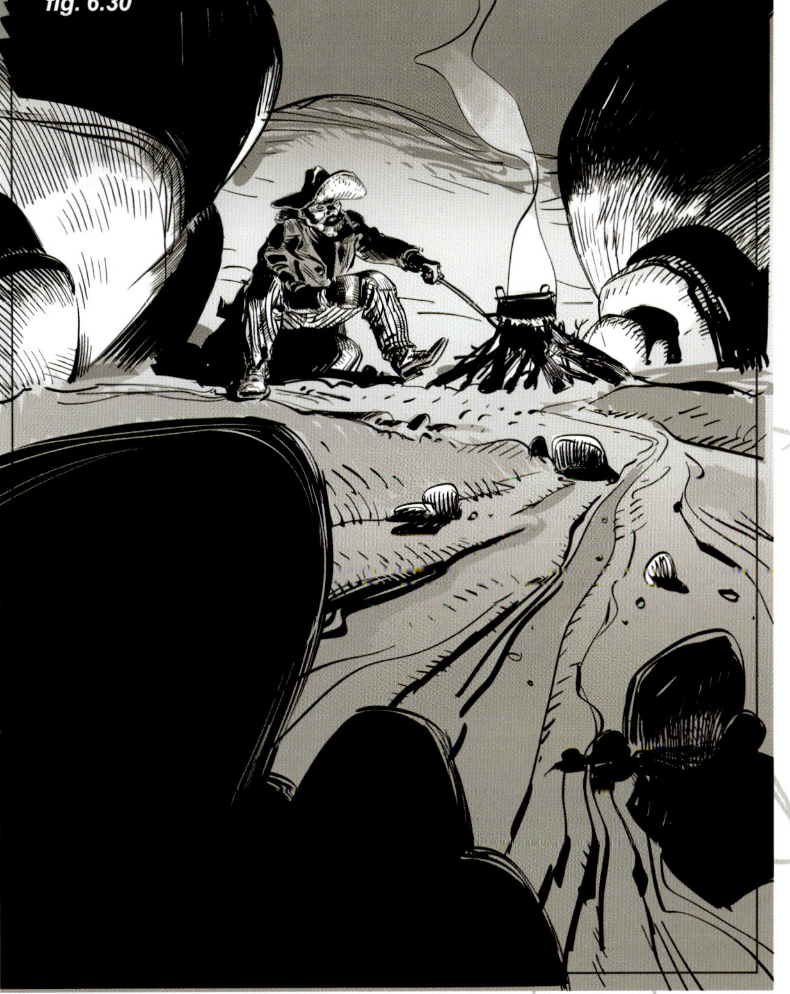

As in all things, the personality, scale, and atmosphere of a location is a factor that can be represented at many different levels of intensity. Separate environments can require different levels of energy, but even the same environment can sometimes require contrasting levels of impact if seen at different emotional moments in the story.

All this can be achieved within the same space or design by adjusting the camera angle and framing, as well as the choice of lighting options.

In this next example we will develop an extended, vast location. The different sections of its geography will help visually represent the consecutive stages of a long and emotional horseback journey by our character, Dakoda, with all its changes and ups and downs, starting at a green forest and arriving at an abandoned mining town in the middle of nowhere.

Fig. 6.33: We will think of the design globally, in continuity, as opposed to in disconnected fragments, so that everything makes sense within the flow of her story. Drafting a map showing potential camera angles helps guide us through the process.

We could first establish a grand, friendly, mesmerizing landscape around her, followed by a number of sections of land that keep getting drier, more dangerous, and hostile as a test to her endurance before she finally reaches her destination.

Figs. 6.34–6.39: These photographs can be a great source inspiration for this practical case.

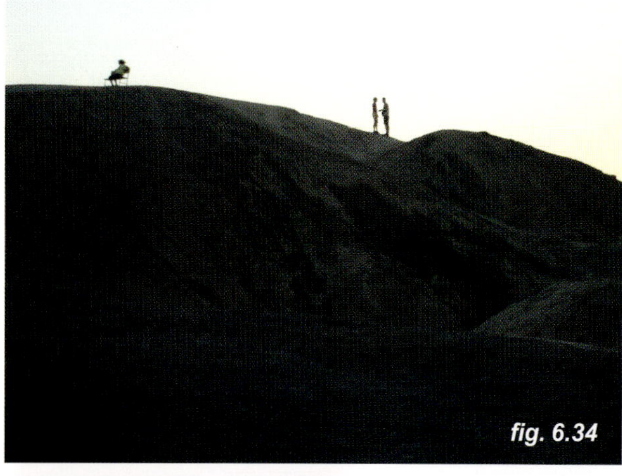
fig. 6.34

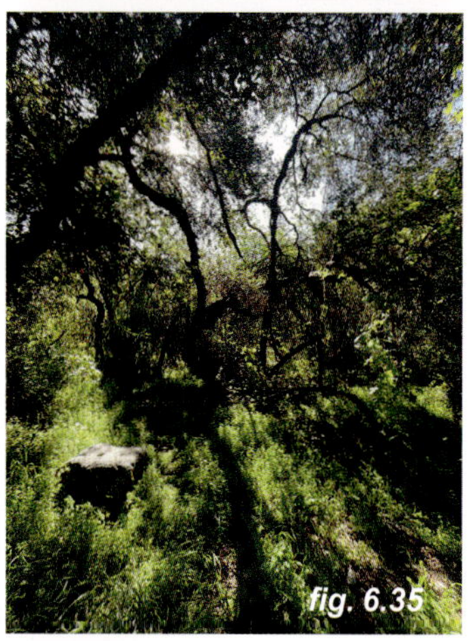
fig. 6.35

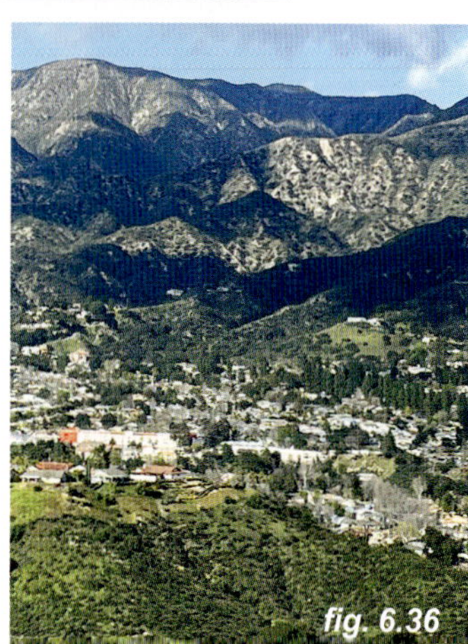
fig. 6.36

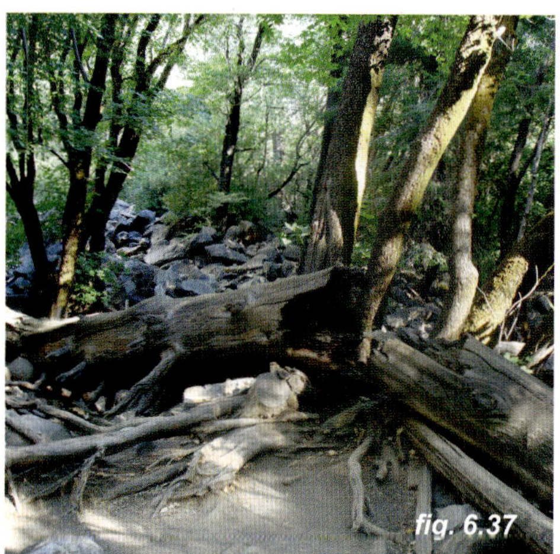
fig. 6.37

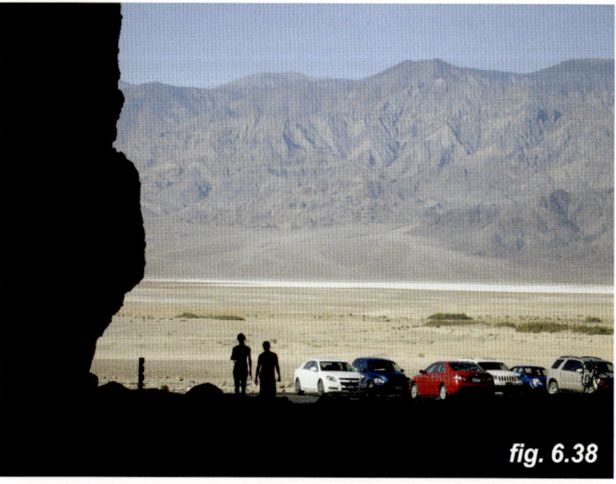
fig. 6.38

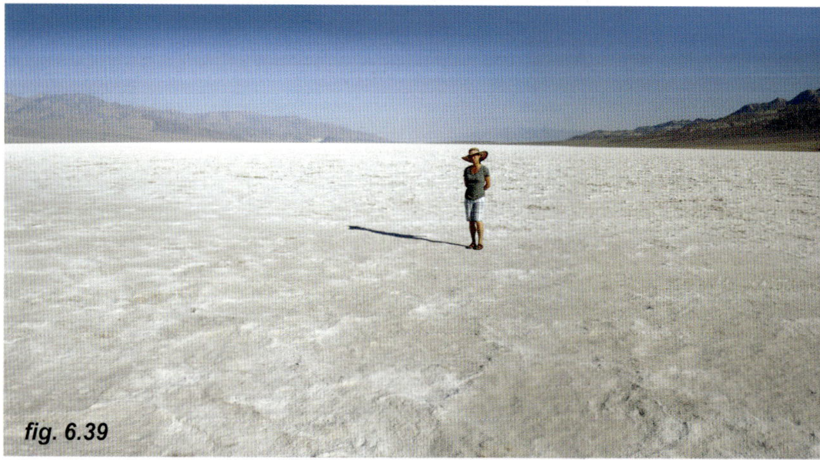
fig. 6.39

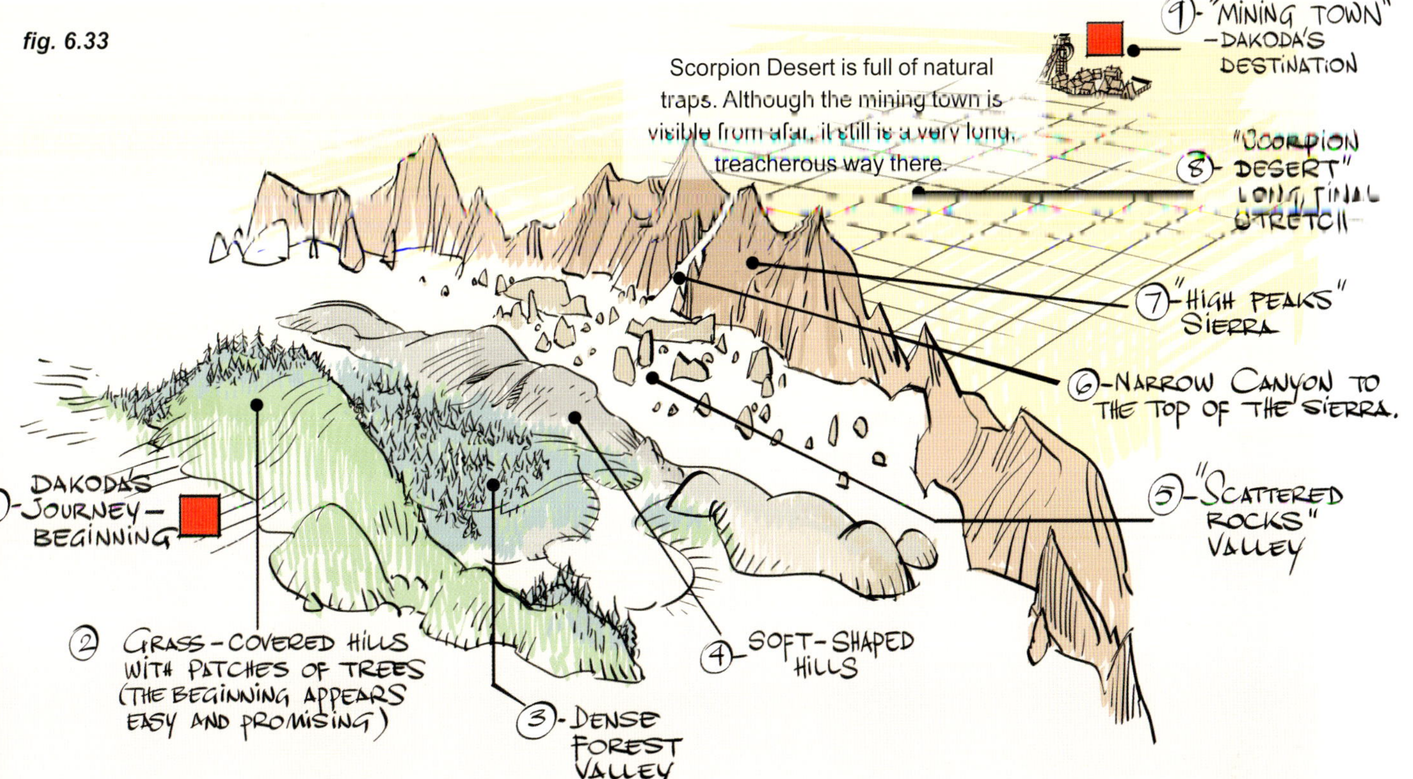

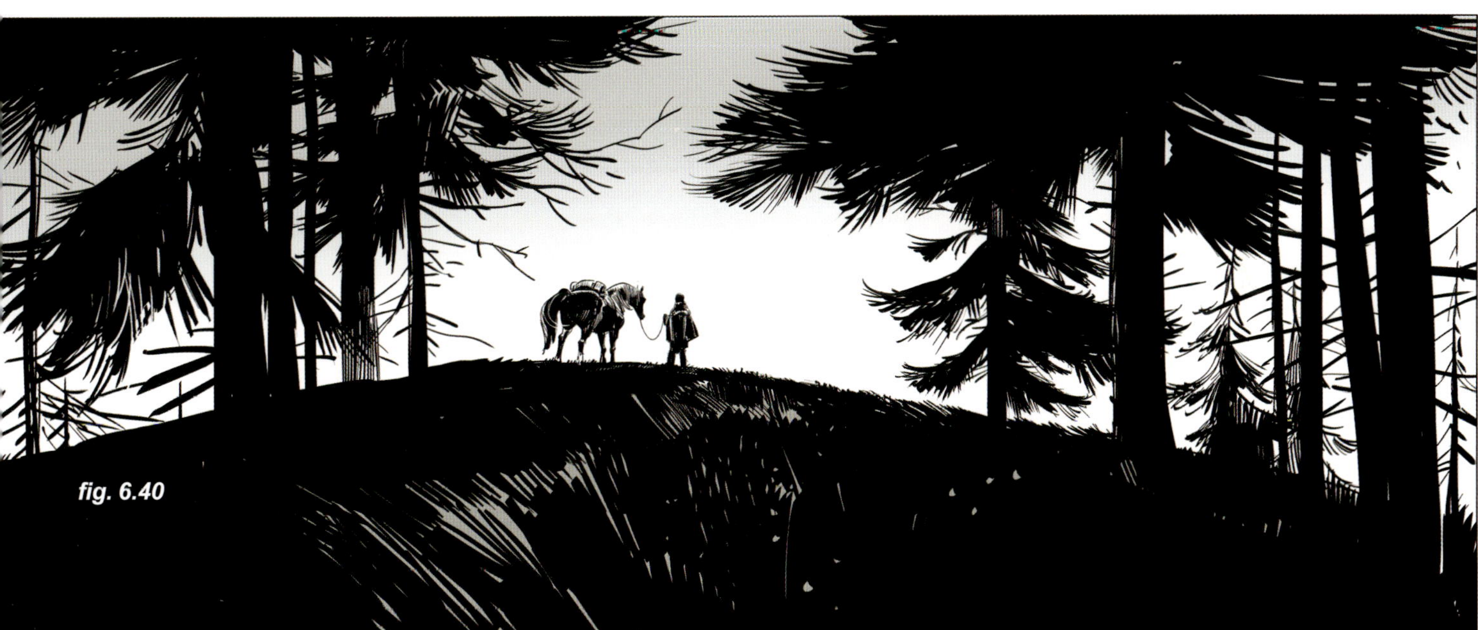

fig. 6.40

Fig. 6.40: This frame marks the start of Dakoda's journey, with an upshot pointing toward the top of the hill where she stands with her horse, next to a few majestic pine trees. The cinematic choice for this first frame is a very stark, cutout silhouette that establishes both character and landscape in a very clear read.

As far as visual language and its progression within the narrative is concerned, we have made a choice that the first shapes in this visual journey be basically **bottom-heavy** (pine trees) to eventually proceed and progress toward a **top-heavy theme** later on, when she gets to the Scattered Rocks Valley (see map, above).

Wanting a backlit image for this opening shot, the first step is to create a bold, graphic silhouette exactly as it is to be seen on-screen, rather than drawing the trees and the hill one by one, as individual items. Then, after making sure the composition works as a whole, we can design the trees by going over the silhouettes with pure line work if needed for production, knowing that once these line-designed elements are backlit, it will become the image that we need (meaning, we reverse-engineer the whole process). Otherwise, if the trees were designed as lines as the very first step, it would be impossible to predict exactly what they would look like once backlit for the shot.

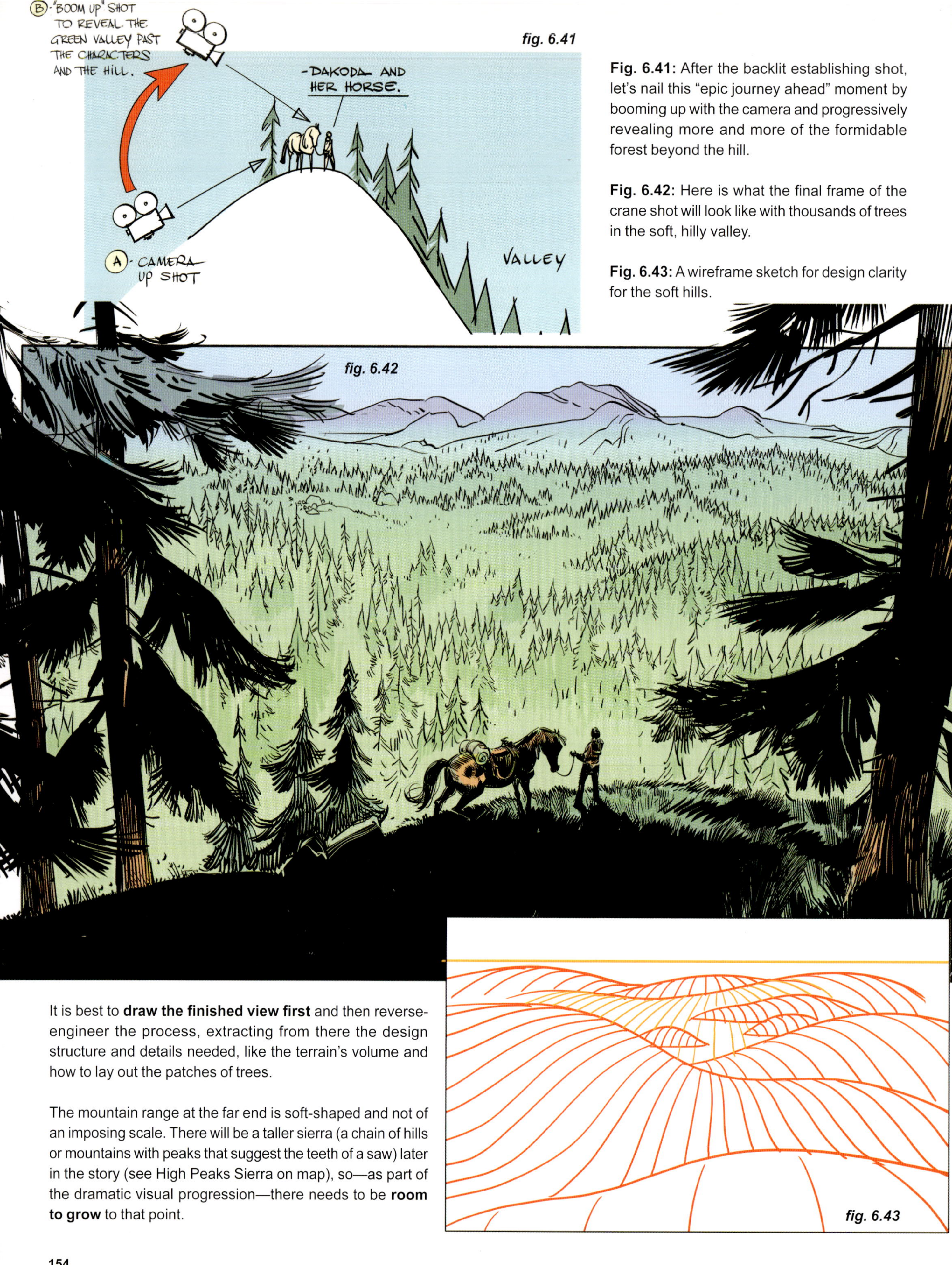

Fig. 6.41: After the backlit establishing shot, let's nail this "epic journey ahead" moment by booming up with the camera and progressively revealing more and more of the formidable forest beyond the hill.

Fig. 6.42: Here is what the final frame of the crane shot will look like with thousands of trees in the soft, hilly valley.

Fig. 6.43: A wireframe sketch for design clarity for the soft hills.

It is best to **draw the finished view first** and then reverse-engineer the process, extracting from there the design structure and details needed, like the terrain's volume and how to lay out the patches of trees.

The mountain range at the far end is soft-shaped and not of an imposing scale. There will be a taller sierra (a chain of hills or mountains with peaks that suggest the teeth of a saw) later in the story (see High Peaks Sierra on map), so—as part of the dramatic visual progression—there needs to be **room to grow** to that point.

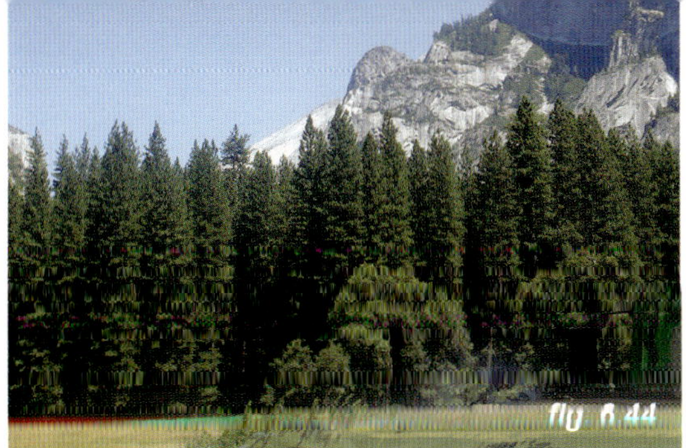
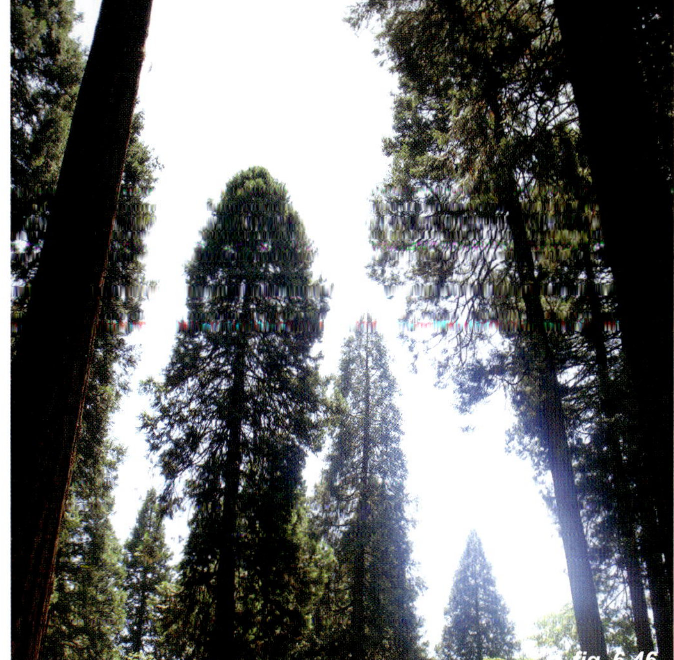
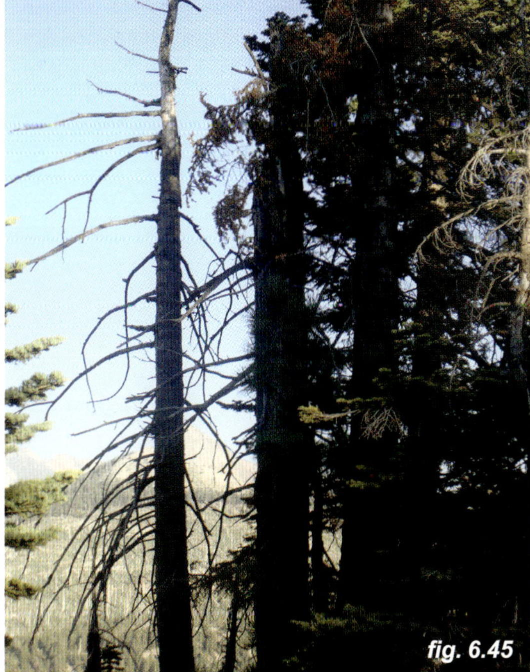
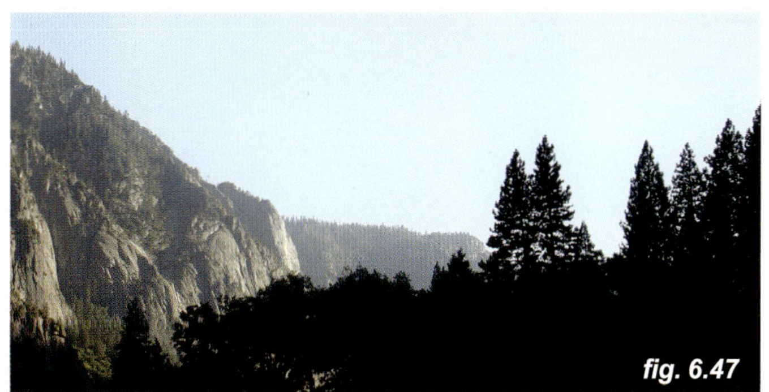

Figs. 6.44–6.47: Attaching photo references is important. Although our designs might be stylized, understanding where the shapes, lines, and volumes originally came from adds credibility to our work.

Fig. 6.48: As mentioned, a choice was made to start with overall bottom-heavy shapes and then make a dramatic change later on when we reverse the natural environment around our character, moving to straight-up verticals and lastly top-heavy shapes.

Fig. 6.49: We will also provide suggestions for the level of stylization and textures of trees, grass, rocks, and whatever elements appear in the scene.

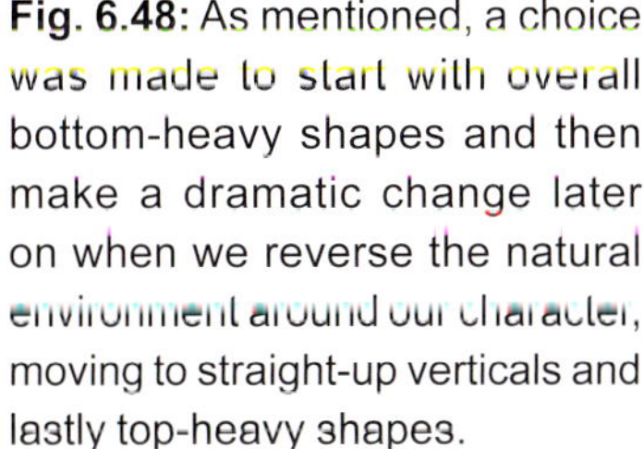

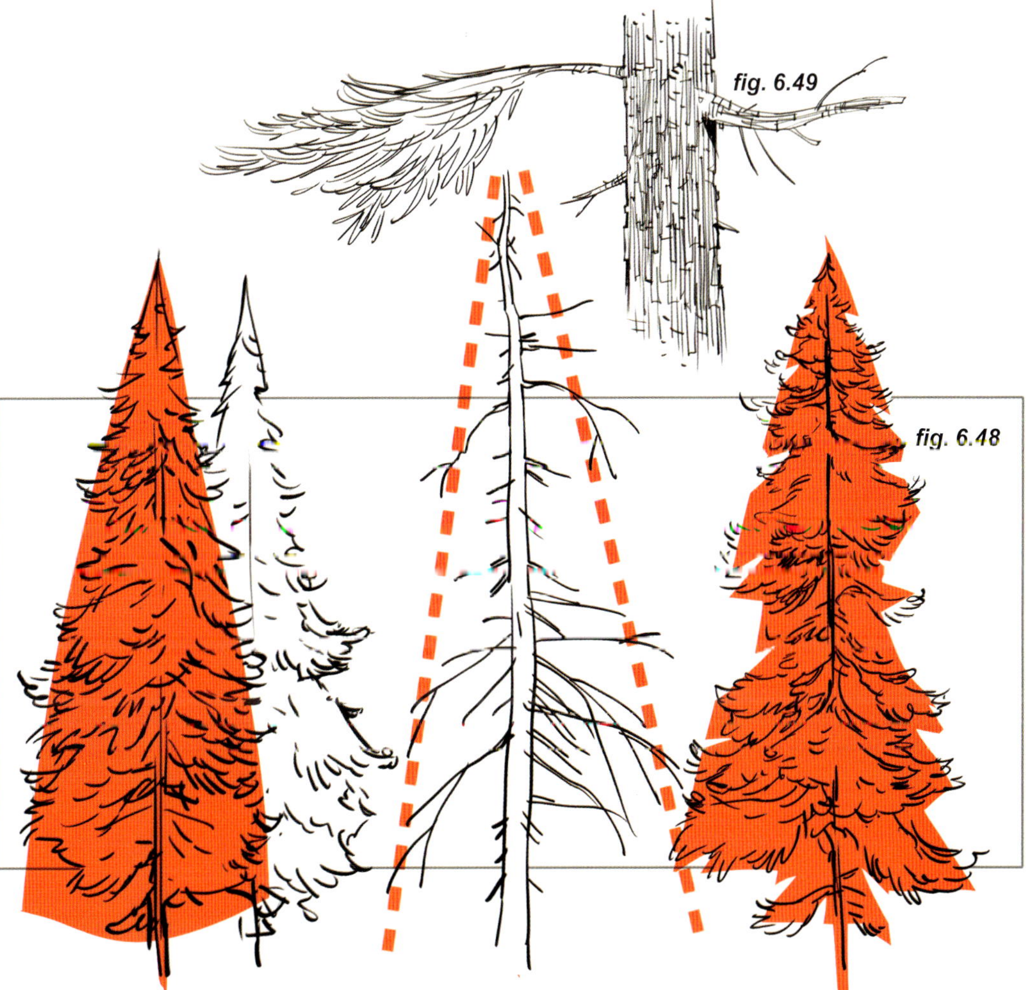

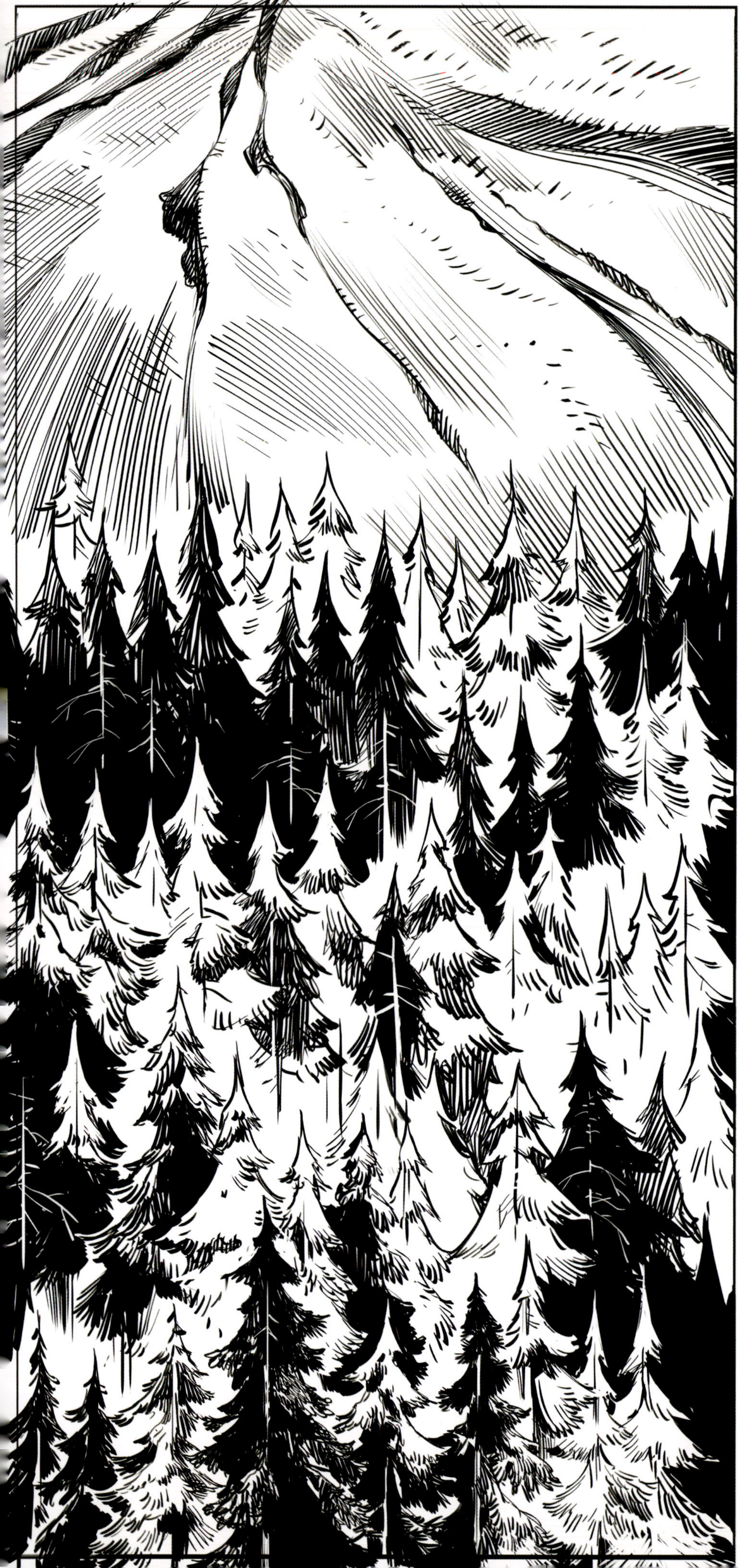

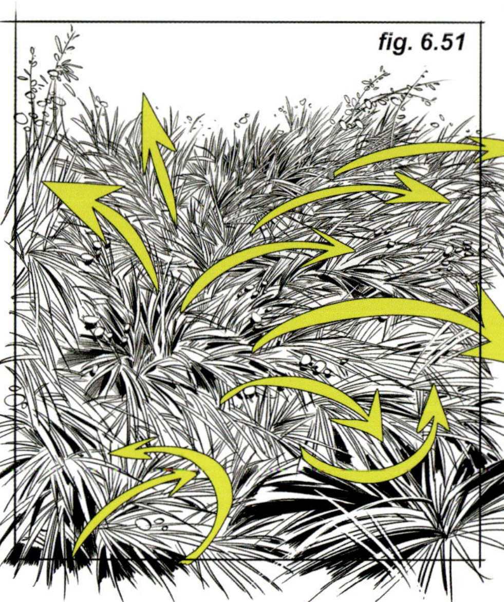

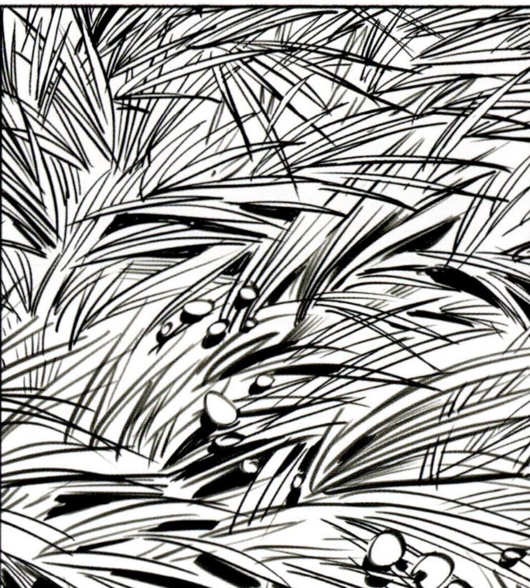

fig. 6.50

fig. 6.52

Figs. 6.50–6.52: Close-ups of the forest, mountain, and grass provide more orientation for a 3D environment-building team, in terms of design, texture, flow, and rhythm.

Any further design requirements (say, a branch with an eagle nest on it, or any specific story-moment need) should be designed with enough detail and additional notes to reduce any potential second-guessing in the future.

Design and style solutions can vary dramatically from one project to the next. These and all drawings developed in this book refer to the essential train of thought that keeps the ball rolling. The actual visual style possibilities these ideas can be converted into are endless.

SCATTERED ROCKS VALLEY

Fig. 6.53: And onto the next phase of Dakoda's adventure.

Beyond the forested valley and the soft-shaped mountain range, she crosses into a valley populated with scattered vertical rocks of all sizes.

In order to ramp up the intensity, we can start with smaller rocks and then increase their height as she gets closer to the other side of this new section of the environment.

Her geographical and emotional journey and our visual journey will unfold and evolve parallel to each other.

Fig. 6.54: The first section featured bottom-heavy trees. The environment now gradually evolves toward top-heavy shapes for these scattered rocks.

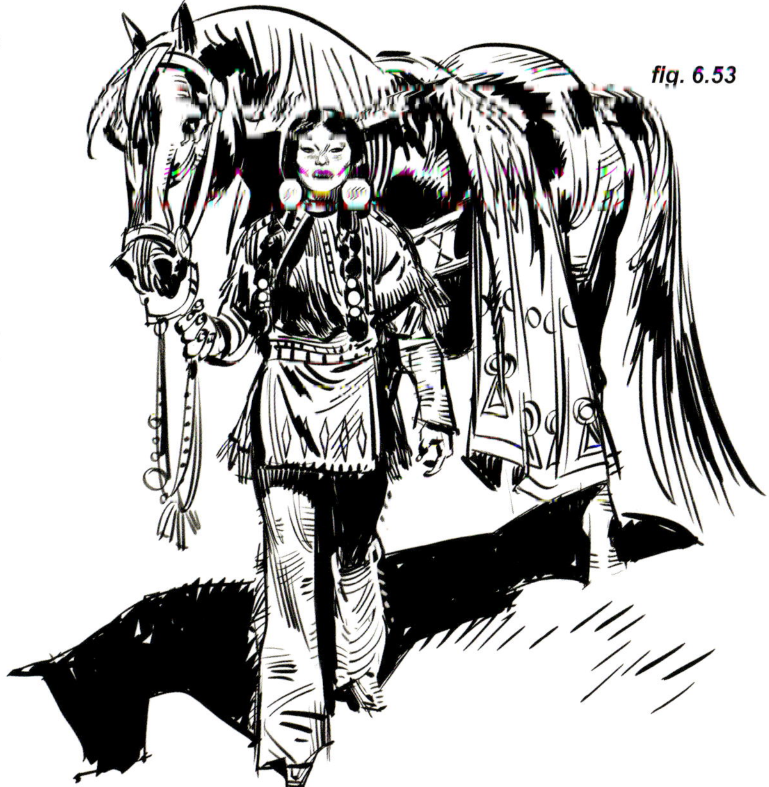

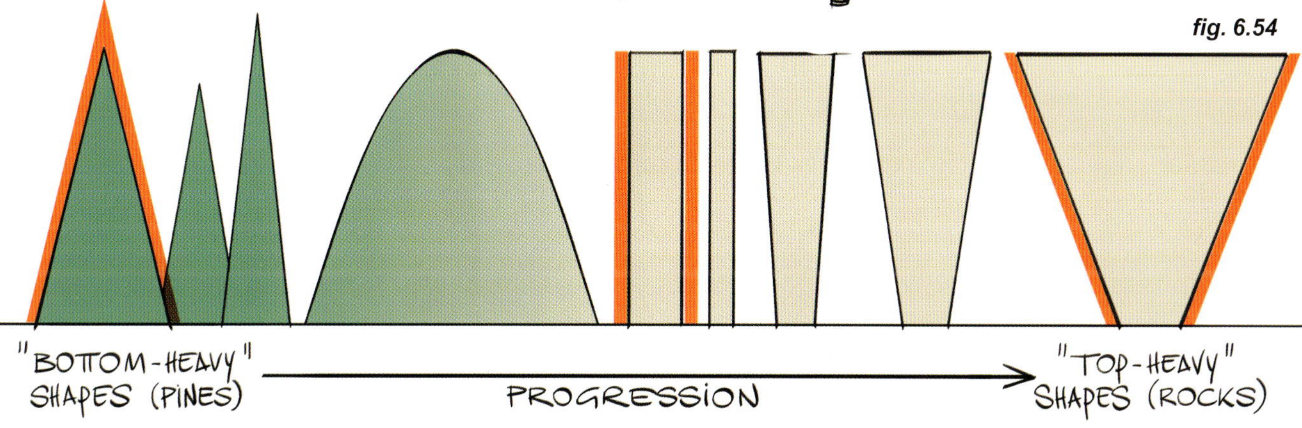

Fig. 6.55: This is a study of what these rocks will look like in the final version.

With the intention of playing the final Scorpion Desert right before the Mining Town as a very dry, sharp and angular place, these rocks here, for the most part, have a rounder look for contrast.

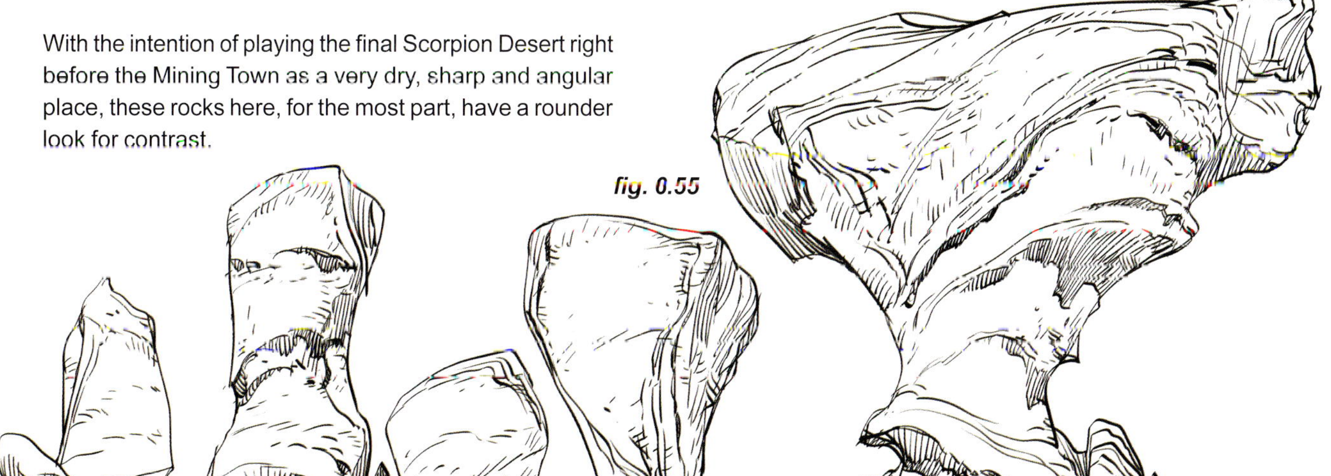

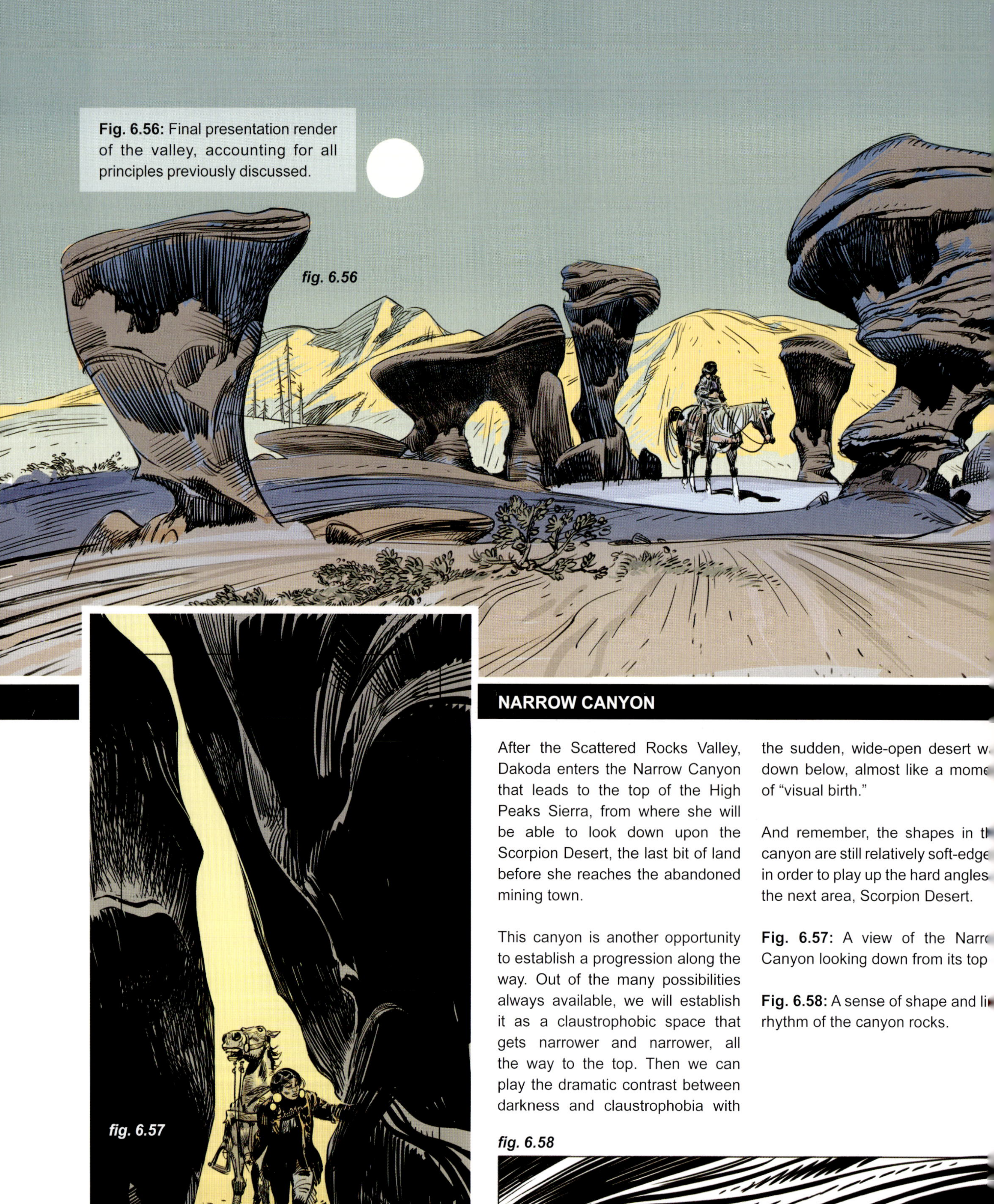

NARROW CANYON

After the Scattered Rocks Valley, Dakoda enters the Narrow Canyon that leads to the top of the High Peaks Sierra, from where she will be able to look down upon the Scorpion Desert, the last bit of land before she reaches the abandoned mining town.

This canyon is another opportunity to establish a progression along the way. Out of the many possibilities always available, we will establish it as a claustrophobic space that gets narrower and narrower, all the way to the top. Then we can play the dramatic contrast between darkness and claustrophobia with the sudden, wide-open desert w[...] down below, almost like a mome[...] of "visual birth."

And remember, the shapes in t[...] canyon are still relatively soft-edg[...] in order to play up the hard angles [...] the next area, Scorpion Desert.

Fig. 6.57: A view of the Narr[...] Canyon looking down from its top [...]

Fig. 6.58: A sense of shape and li[...] rhythm of the canyon rocks.

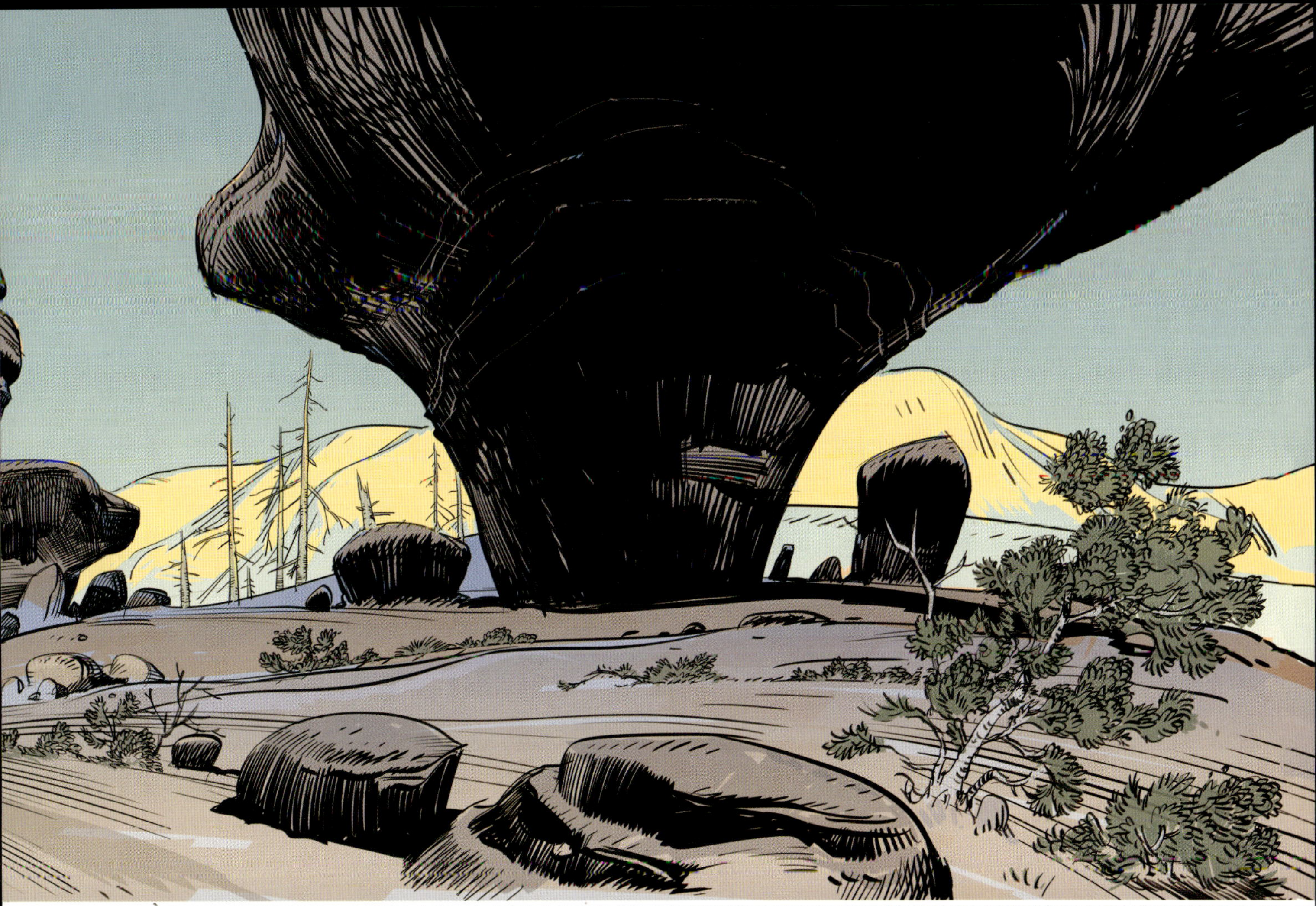

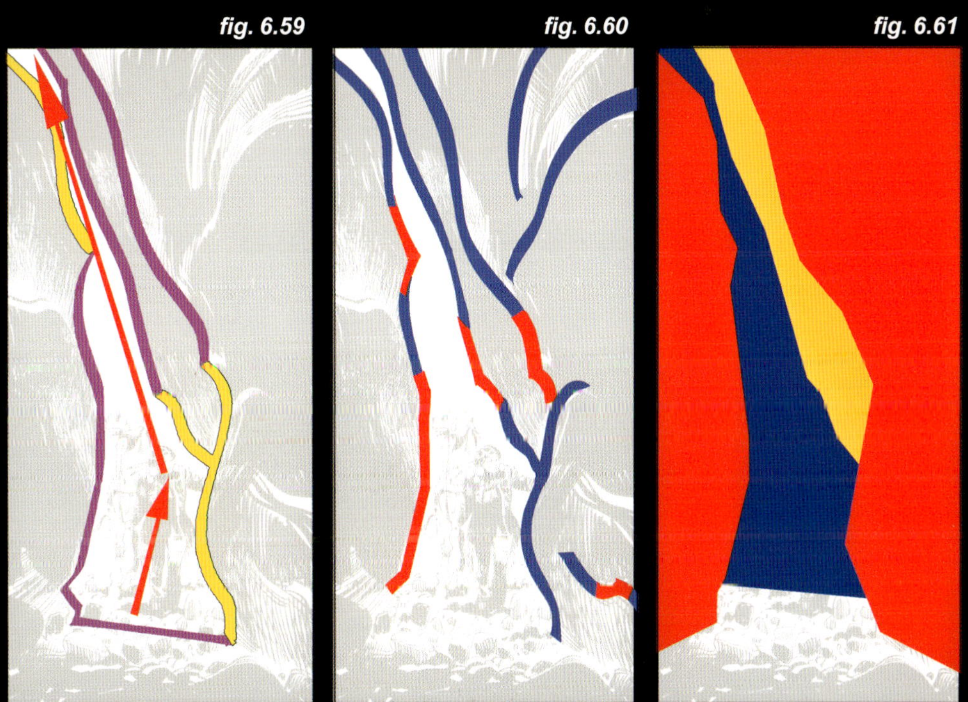

CANYON WALLS SHAPE ANALYSIS

As simple in shapes and composition as it might look, this environment follows basic ideas that make it feel interesting and appealing.

Fig. 6.59: The length of the main lines in its design varies, combining longer (purple) and shorter ones (yellow). The same principle applies to the length of the general angles into which it is subdivided (red arrows).

Fig. 6.60: Although its general shape language is curved (blue), adding punctual angular moments (red) helps anchor a sense of solidity in these rocky walls that might otherwise appear too wobbly.

Fig. 6.61: Providing variety by combining big, medium, and small masses gives the canyon a more vibrant appearance.

SCORPION DESERT:
THE FINAL STRETCH.

Drama by **contrast,** again.

Emerging from the very tight and almost vertical Narrow Canyon, we can now consider visually **dropping the environment** all the way down to sea level.

To augment this visual change, here is the place to use **the sharpest shapes of all.** This open, dusty surface might appear very flat from a distance, but on closer look we realize it is deeply irregular, full of dangerous gaps and holes in the rock, and with a surface-texture language that is much rougher than the previous canyon walls.

At the far end is a view of a distant mining town, right on the horizon, apparently just an easy ride away. Yet taking a second look, this final stretch of land is **filled with concealed natural traps and dangerous ground** that will turn it into a hell-like ride that seems to go on forever.

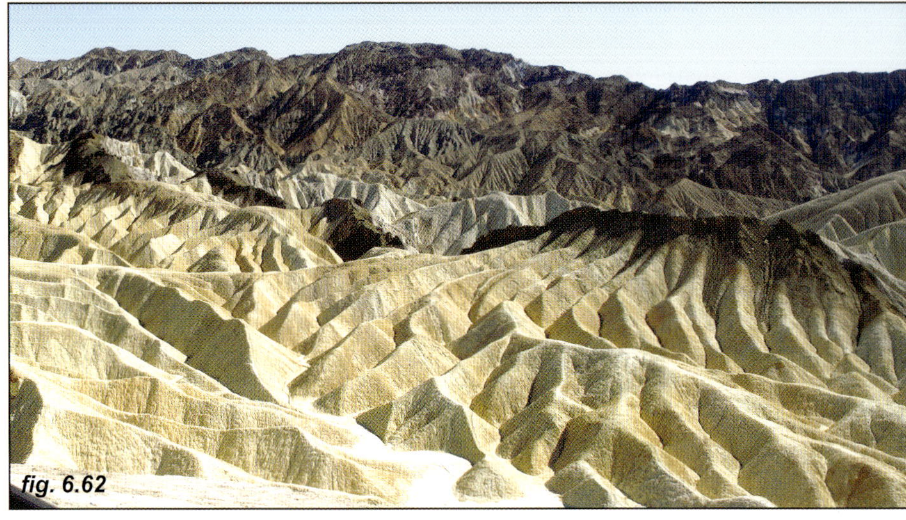

fig. 6.62

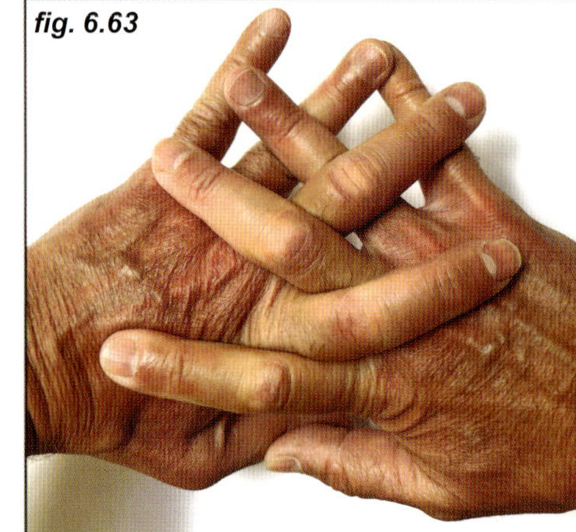

fig. 6.63

Figs. 6.62, 6.63: As an initial reference we can use this image of Zabriskie Point in the majestic desert of Death Valley, California. This is only a starting point, and we will visually push these rocky folds that seem to be "branching out" even farther, creating a **crisscross pattern** that resembles the shapes and gaps produced by intertwined fingers.

Fig. 6.64: A schematic, synthesized approach for the concept that will evolve into . . .

Fig. 6.65: The final design.

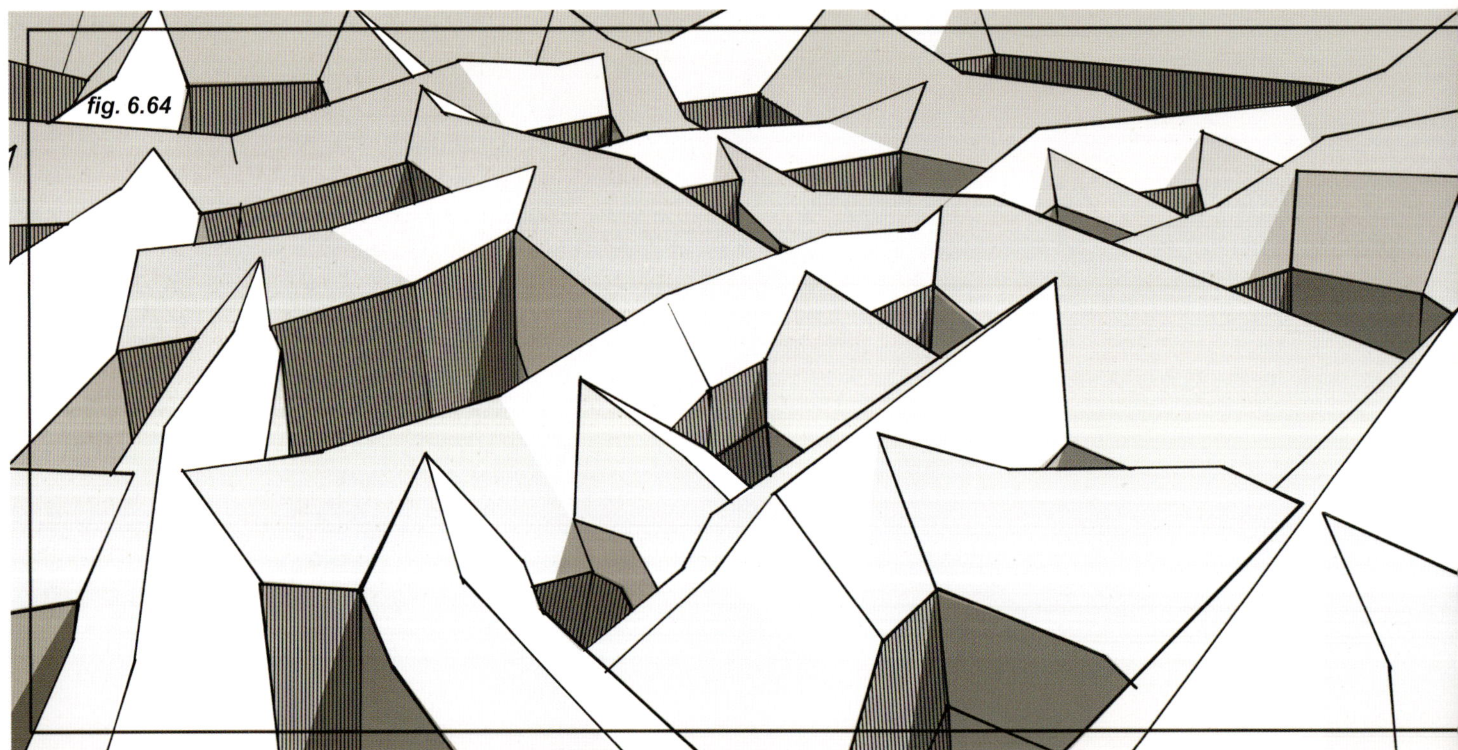

fig. 6.64

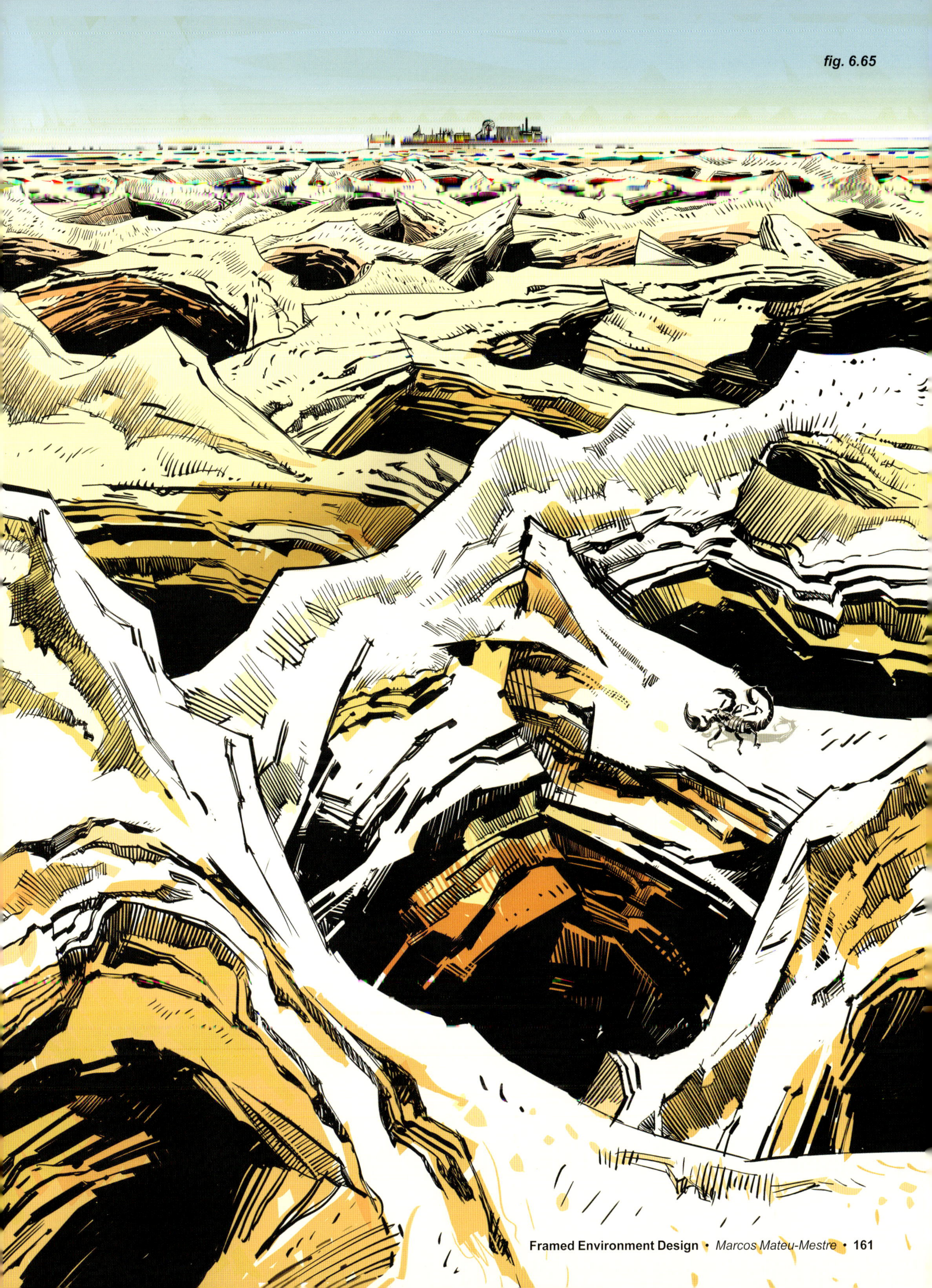

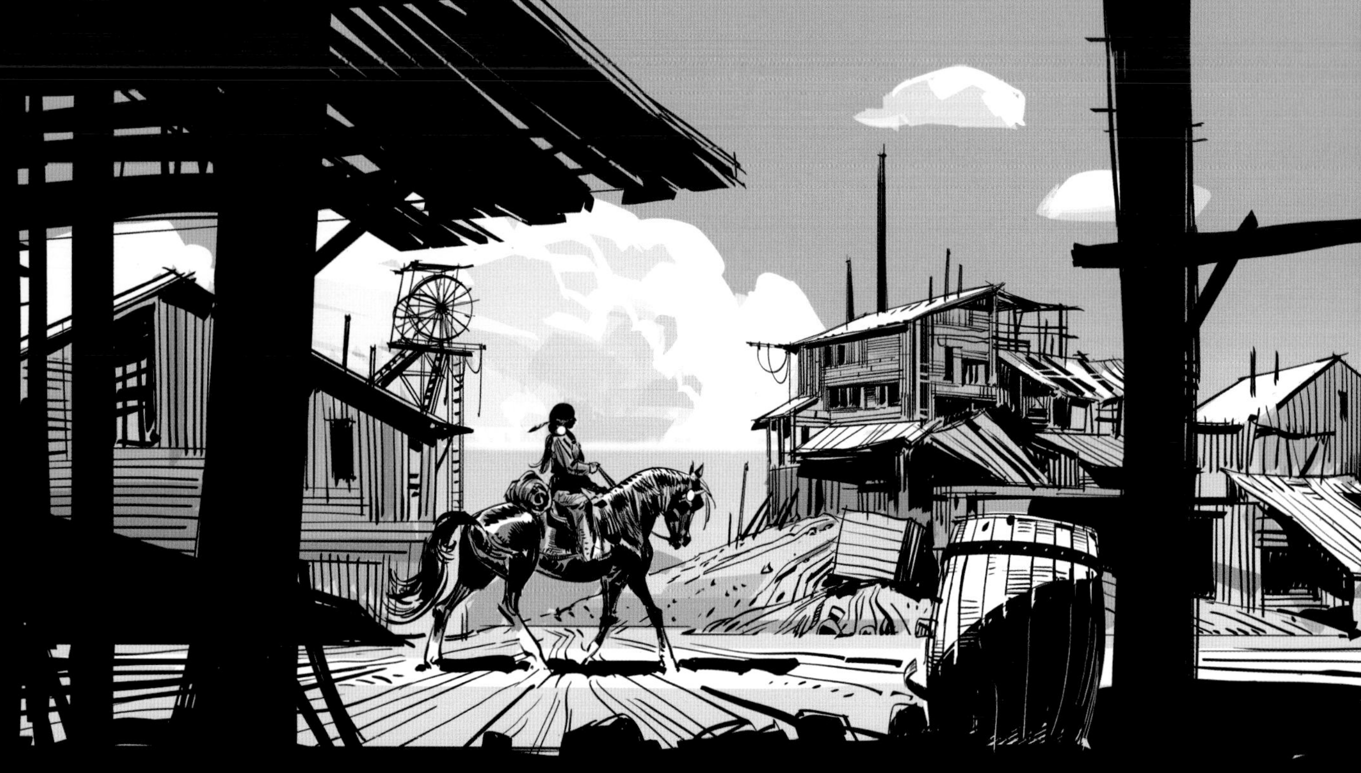

At last, Dakoda arrives at the mining town.

Let's not forget that environments—and the way we depict them through the use of cinematographic devices—are there to support the story and the characters' journey, every step of the way. The degree of intensity to which we push our designs and ideas depends on the tone we want to imprint on our story and the visual style we decide upon and commit to.

Now, what happens the moment our story goes beyond what we call "real world"?

What happens if we decide to explore a more fantastic vision while still trying to make it look plausible and somehow anchored in our earthly experience?

The purpose of this next chapter and its specific design example is to show how we can get to an imagined world of fantasy by starting off with real-world visual references, purely as inspiration, and then go through a process of pushing and stylizing these original ideas, taking them as far as we need to, in order to develop our personal visual concept for a story.

Notice that despite the use of real references, the imagined world ultimately portrayed in this next chapter does not represent any specific place or culture and is purely a fantasy. As we all have our own individual sense of what the concepts of "fantasy" and "pushing and stylizing" mean, it is up to each one of us to establish the artistic direction we want for these imagined worlds to evolve into.

A PATH TO FANTASY

THE CREATIVE THOUGHT PROCESS
PART 1

One of the recurring themes in film, graphic novels, video games, and illustration is the visual development and design of worlds that step into the realm of fantasy. It is about making environments believable, interesting, and appealing in the service of the story we are telling, no matter how different from reality they might look.

In most cases these worlds still have at least a vague connection with the things that surround us every day and that we are familiar with, even if just as a referential starting point, such as items that are part of our history or even still present in our lives and traditions.

For this chapter, we will be designing a location strongly integrated into a surrounding tropical environment.

For reference, we can **look at parts of the world where this sort of environment naturally exists,** starting with **Southeast Asia,** purely for inspiration and without specifically reflecting any of these cultures. This is a way to study how existing styles of architecture actually work, what materials they use, and how they are integrated into any structures. Then we can literally fantasize while taking this information as a starting point.

Since all possibilities are open at this point, the recommendation is to research not only architecture but also any sense of design they might apply to other aspects of their lives and traditions—such as woodcarvings, tools, weapons, costumes, and textiles—so that we broaden our options ahead.

1. STARTING THE PROCESS

Here are some of the sketches based on research from a number of sources. These shape and silhouette studies reflect the graphic qualities of vernacular constructions in Indonesia (fig. 7.1), South Sulawesi (fig. 7.2), New Guinea (fig. 7.3), and Sumba Island, Indonesia (fig 7.4, next page). The remaining sketches on the following page study the shape language and textures of a variety of traditional constructions in the Philippine Islands.

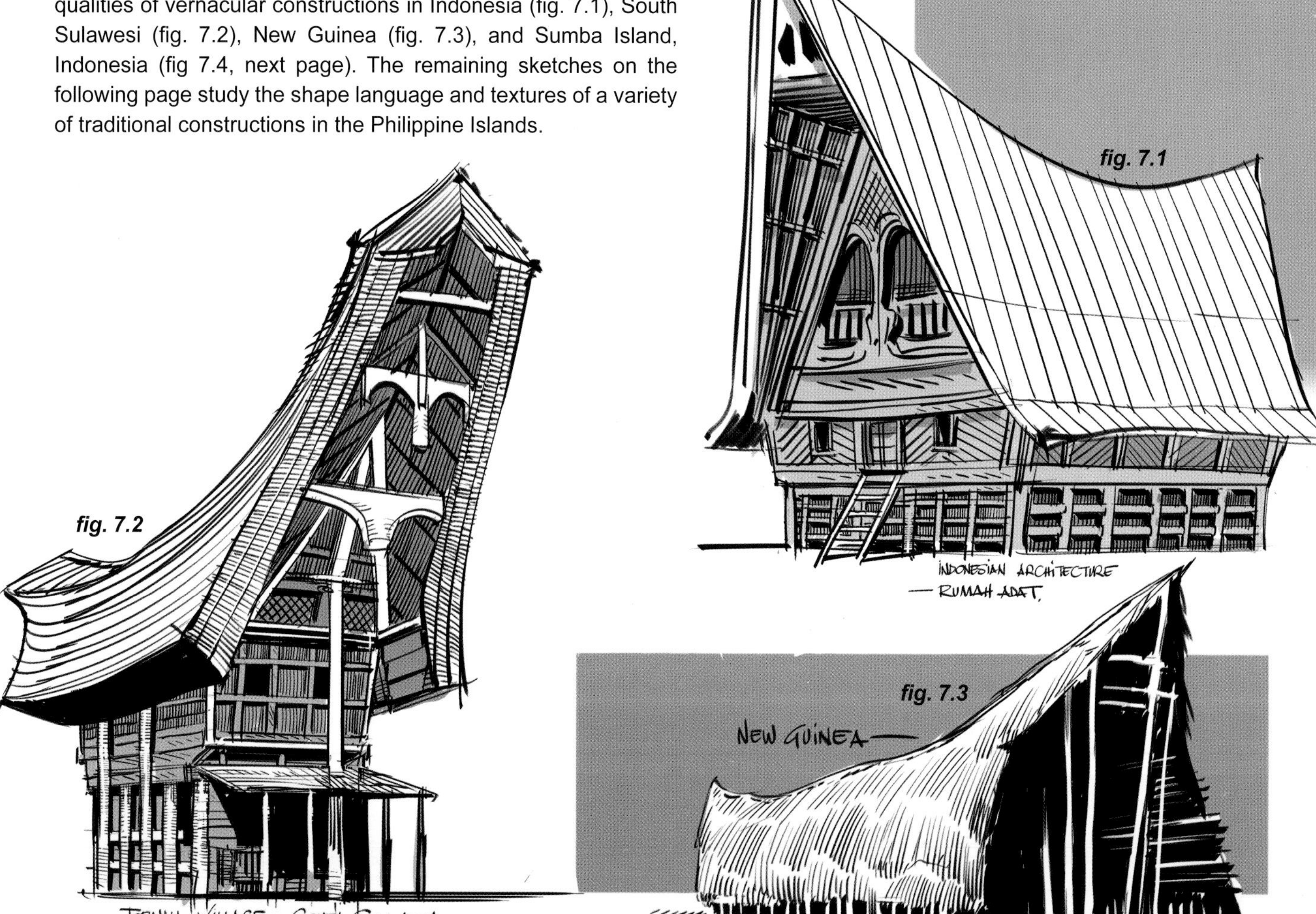

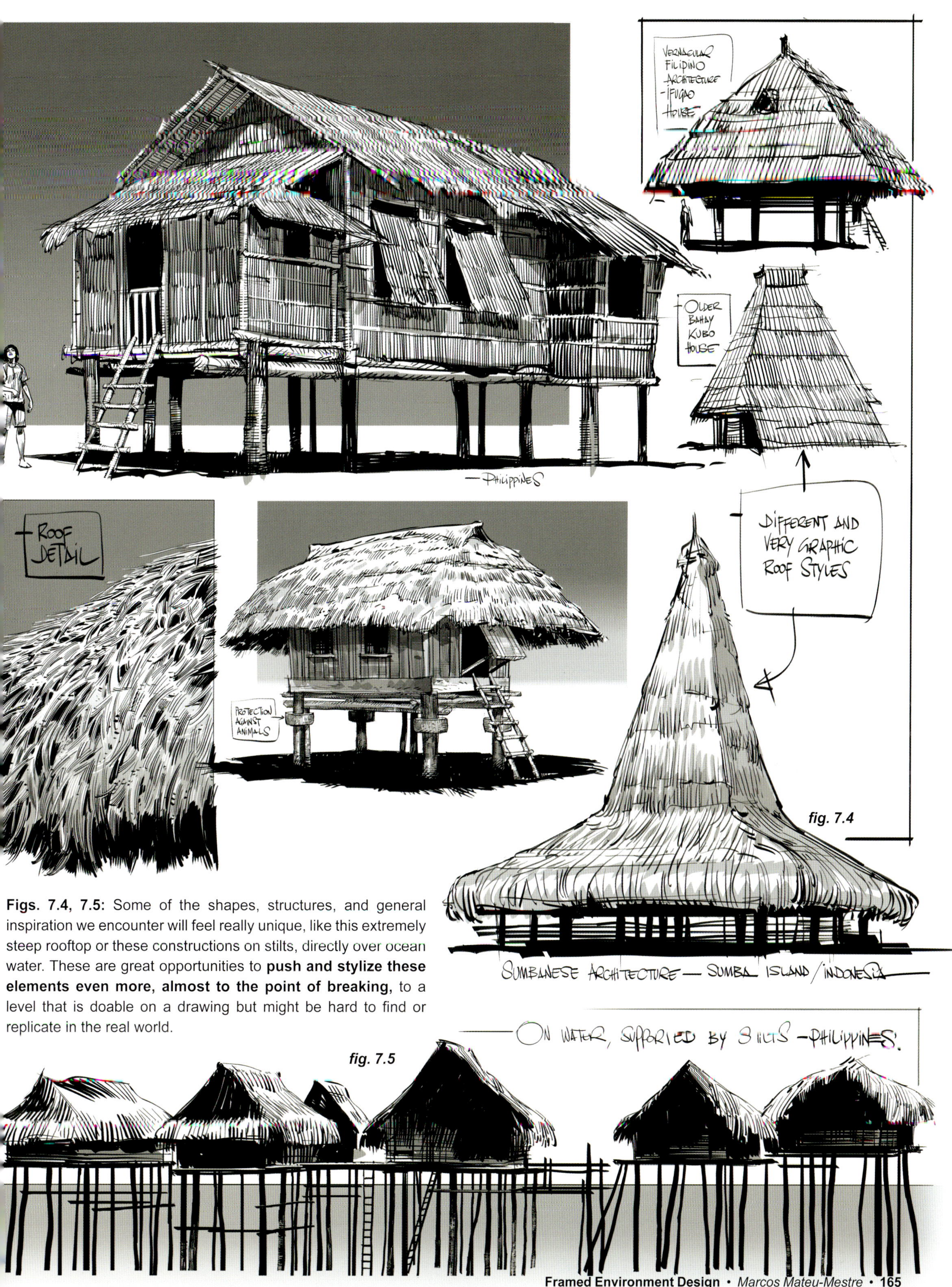

Figs. 7.4, 7.5: Some of the shapes, structures, and general inspiration we encounter will feel really unique, like this extremely steep rooftop or these constructions on stilts, directly over ocean water. These are great opportunities to **push and stylize these elements even more, almost to the point of breaking,** to a level that is doable on a drawing but might be hard to find or replicate in the real world.

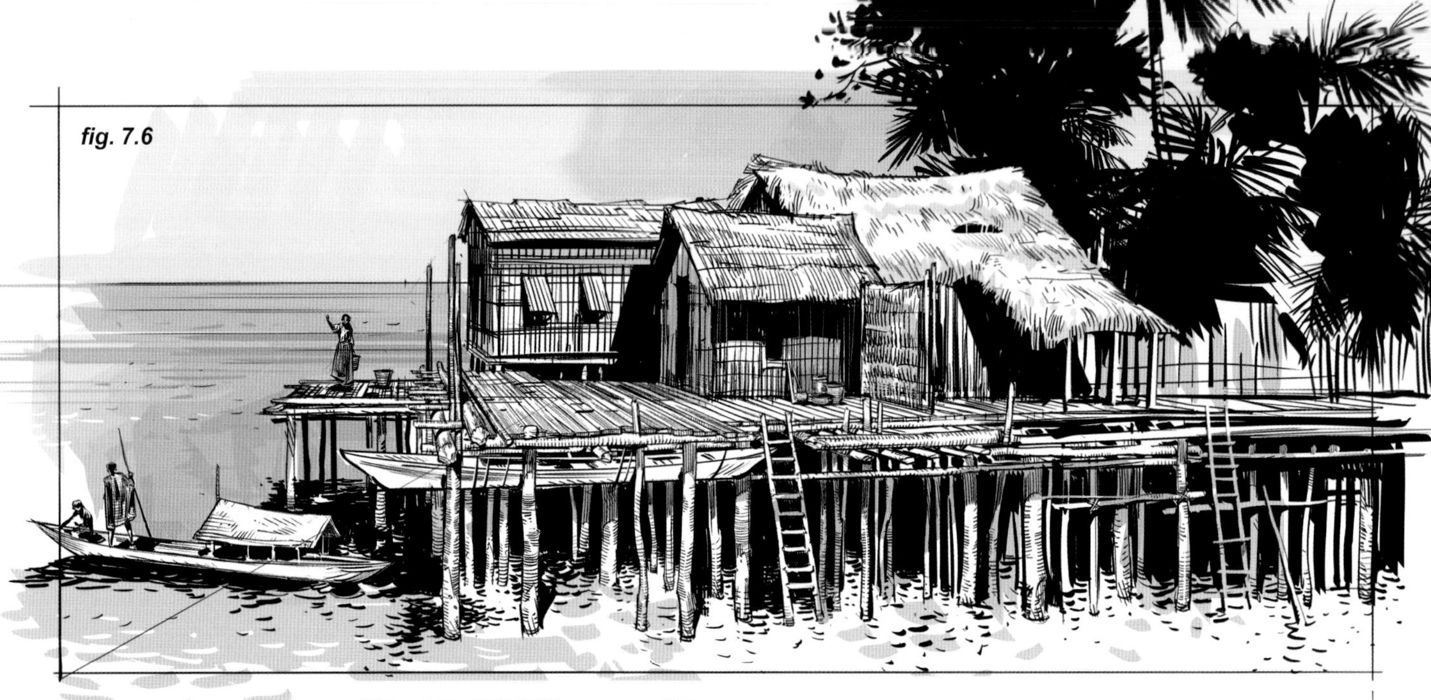

The research continues and eventually we run into more inspirational images.

Fig. 7.6: One of the interesting things about these types of structures is their level of visual complexity.

The supporting stilts are so numerous, and they feel so organic with their irregular shapes, that they come across like a forest of a thousand logs emerging straight out of the ocean.

It is really fascinating. Imagine shooting footage from underneath a similar boardwalk and among its numerous supporting pillars, especially if we push their design to be twice as tall, all in this semi-darkness and with the reflections of the scarce sunlight playing on the water's surface.

Fig. 7.7: This tree house based on photo reference is a whole world unto itself, creating a visual impact that makes one wonder how a structure like this was built and how life's everyday routines evolve in a location like this.

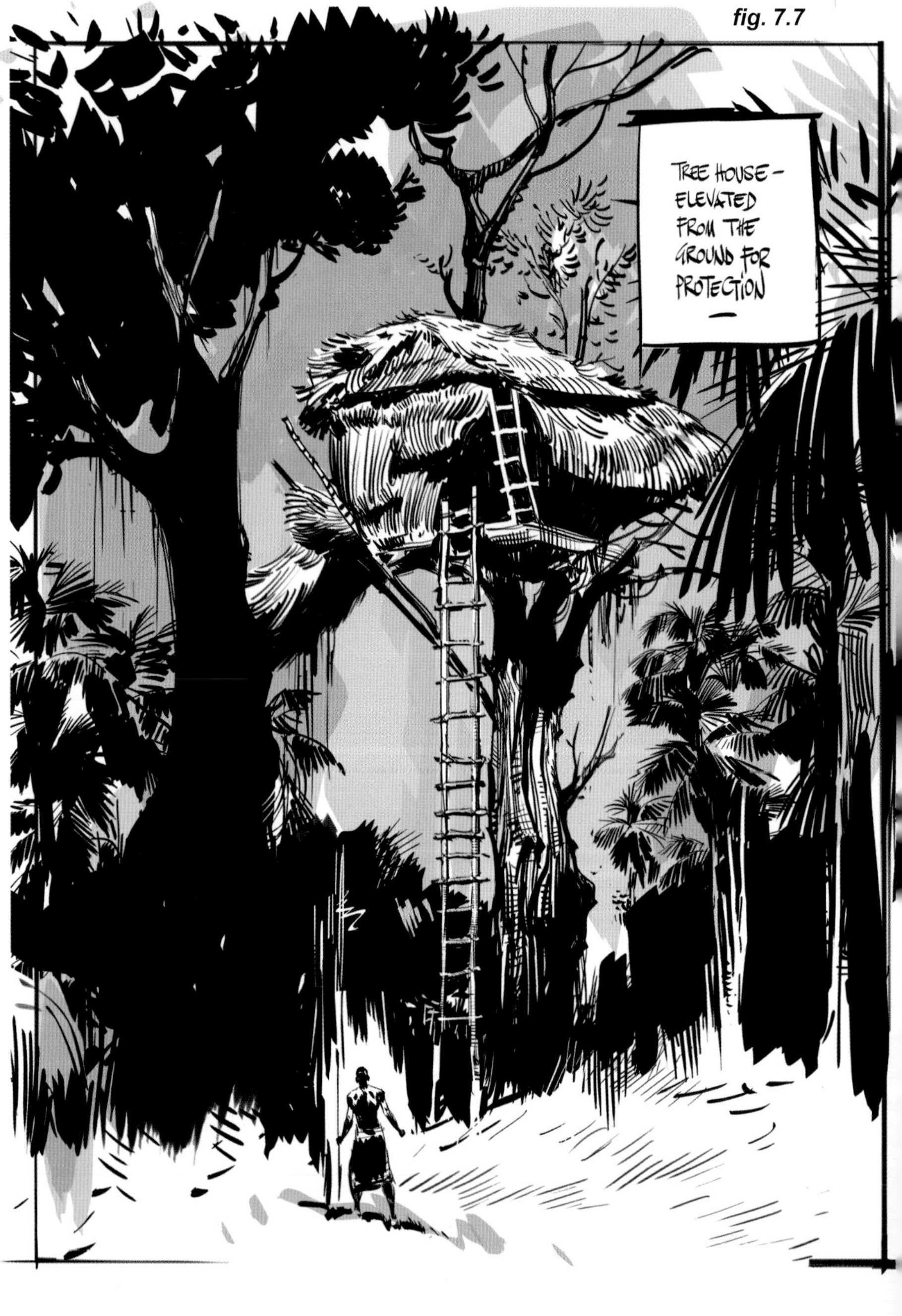

2. LOOKING PAST THE BIG SHAPES / ARCHITECTURAL DETAILS

While getting familiar with these wonderful constructions' general shapes, the nuances embedded in them also deserve attention.

Most images we see during this process will spark further curiosity in us. What do these constructions look like when taking a closer look? How are they actually built? What kind of engineering is required? How does it feel to live there? What sense of ornamentation is created that goes beyond the practicality of everyday duties and makes these spaces look really lived-in?

Figs. 7.8–7.12: These sketches were made as a result of this exploration, showing the kinds of details that keep us even more curious and motivated to dig deeper and deeper.

Next to the sketches, it is good to write down quick, informative notes as reminders of important or unusual details that add visual richness to the location.

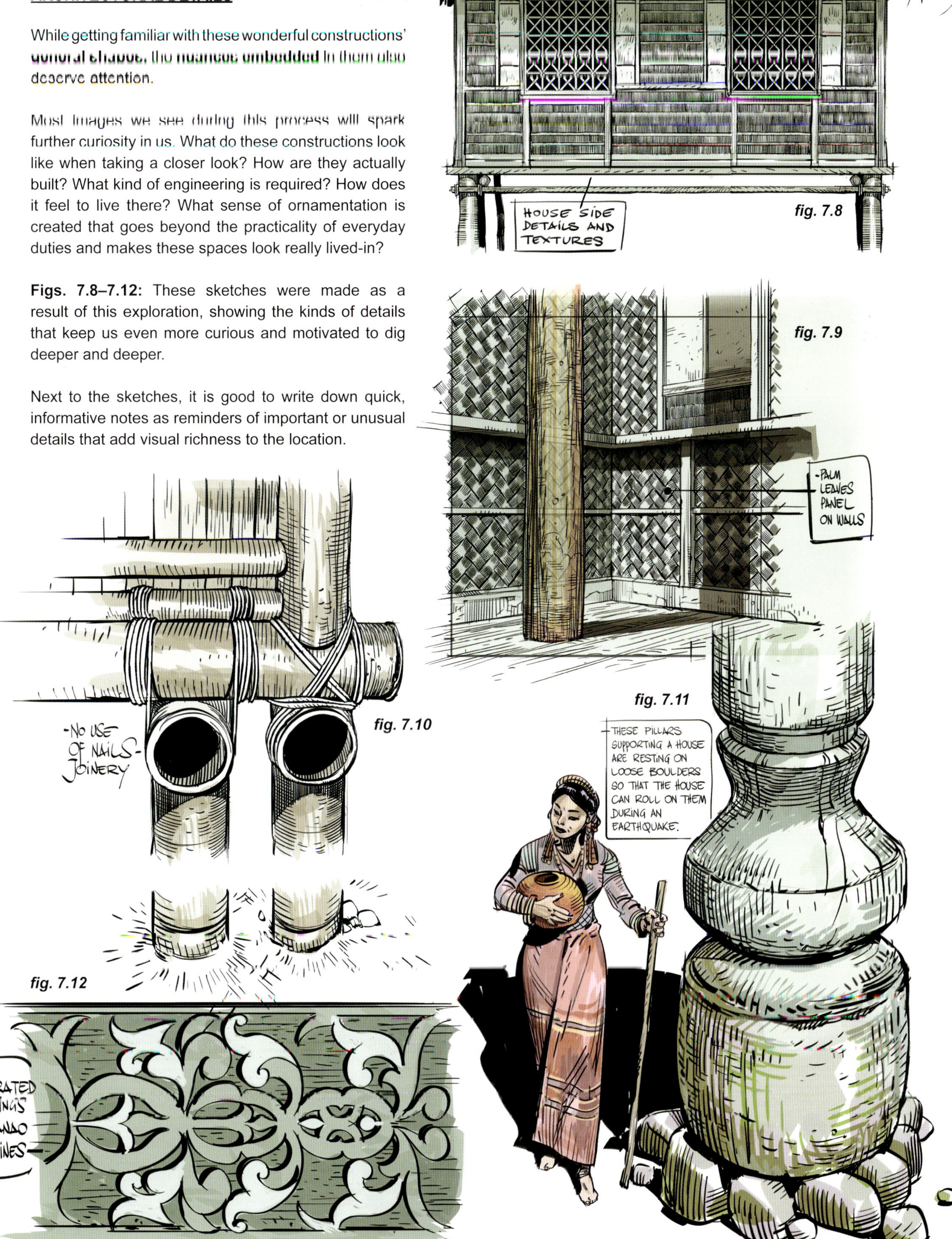

<u>**3. TESTING IDEAS / STARTING THE DESIGN PROCESS**</u>

At some point during the research it is time to start visualizing options and possibilities of how to create and develop the location for the project at hand. **Start testing the more or less vague, fantastic ideas in your imagination** by putting them "on paper."

One can never fully know one hundred percent how viable or effective these designs will be until they leave the world of the abstract and enter the physical, tangible reality of a drawing or a rough 3D model. So, while keeping the best references in mind and readily available, it is time to depart from them and to get the ball rolling.

fig. 7.13

Figs. 7.13–7.15: This first pass is about stylizing and recombining the shapes already explored through our research, pushing them to new limits by stretching them, making them much taller or wider, mixing big structures with smaller ones so that the village starts to acquire a strong and graphic appeal and a visual clarity from a distance. This allows the audience to better perceive a sense of depth, size, and proportion.

fig. 7.14

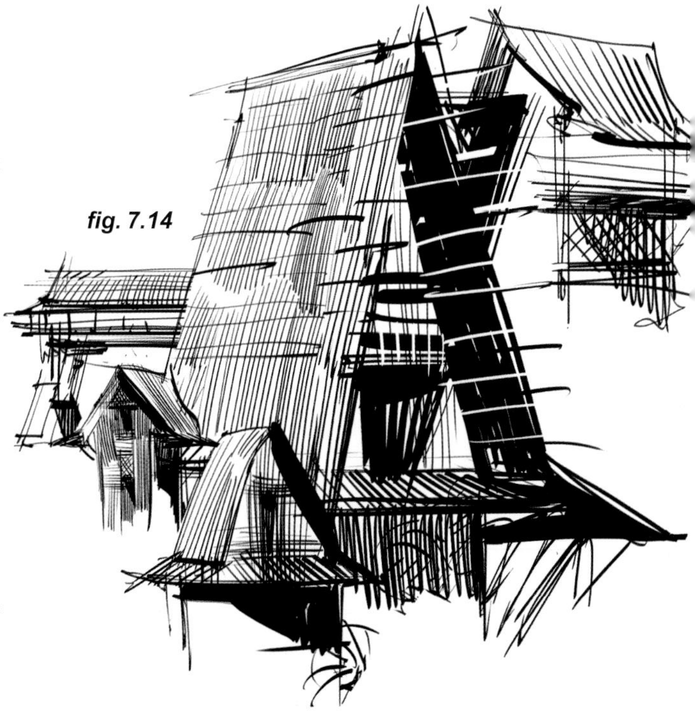

fig. 7.15

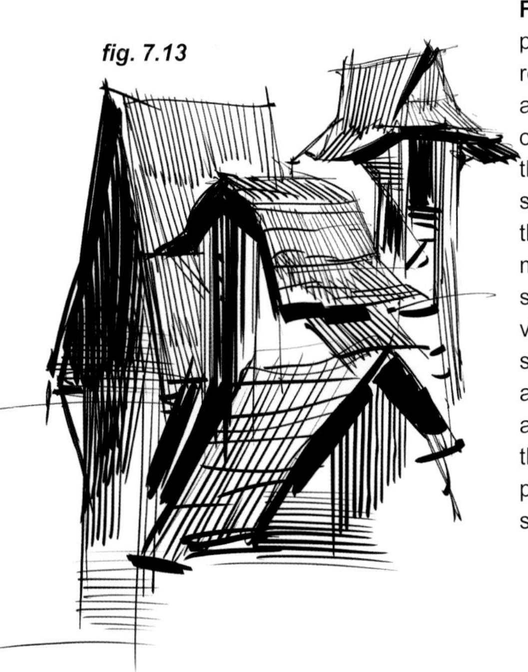

At some point in the process, I decided to explore an **overall vertical design for this location, attached to a rocky cliff rich in jungle-like vegetation.**

This natural backdrop should almost feel like "wallpaper" from afar, with the lush vegetation having the opportunity to visually interact and intertwine with the dwellings. That could also work very well when bringing the camera into pathways and secluded corners of the setting.

(As a side note, the sketches shown on these two pages are just a small fraction of the ones produced at this stage. The more we explore, the better.)

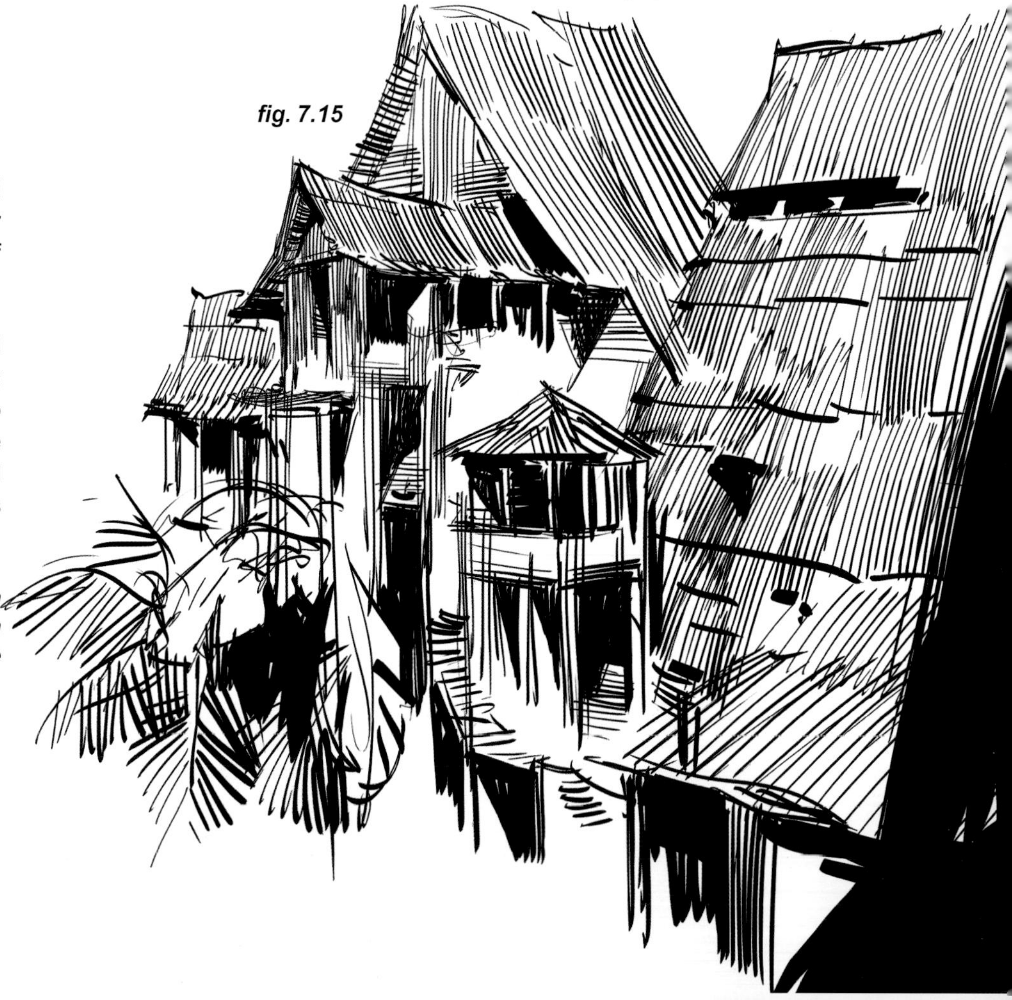

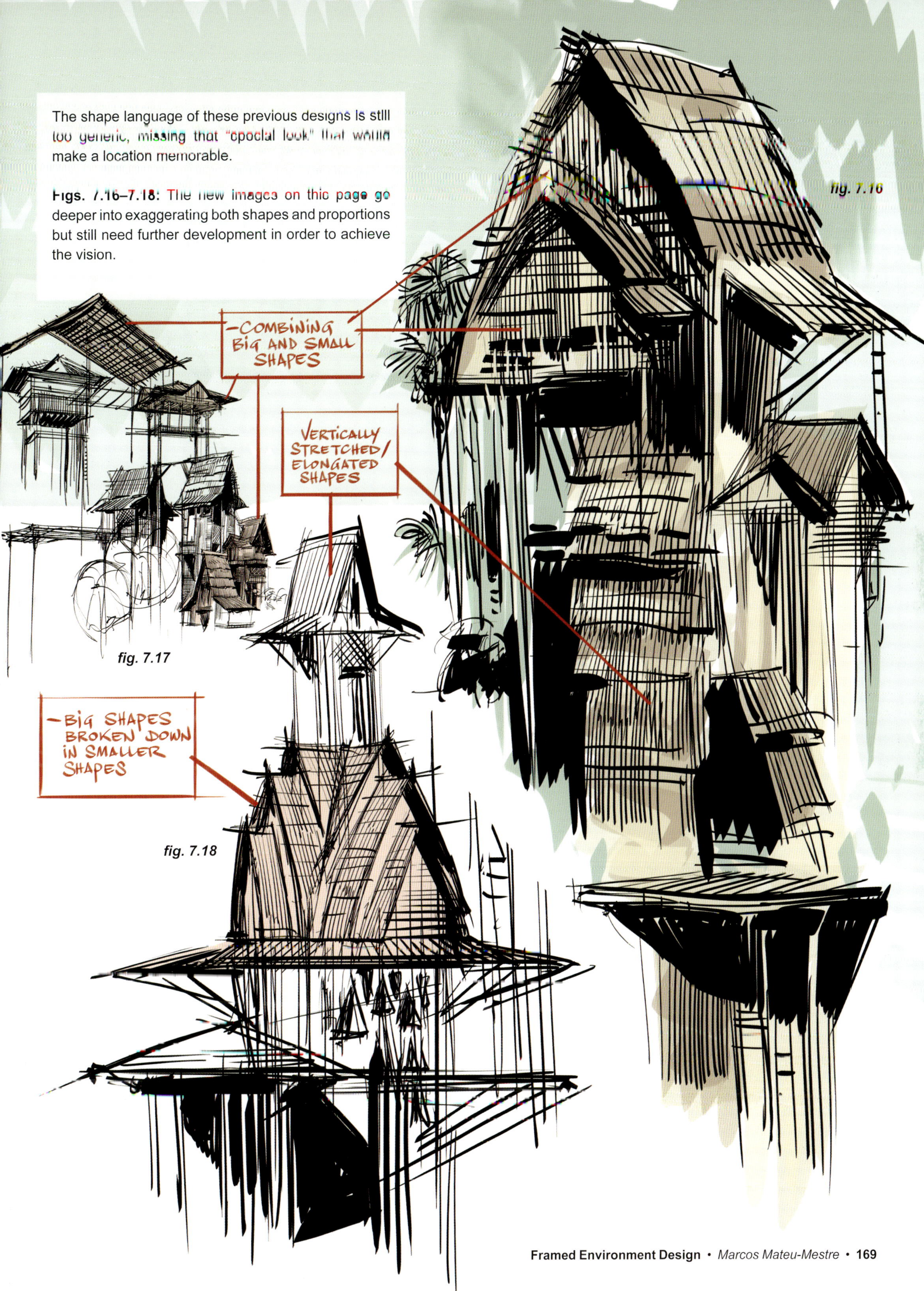

The shape language of these previous designs is still too generic, missing that "special look" that would make a location memorable.

Figs. 7.16–7.18: The new images on this page go deeper into exaggerating both shapes and proportions but still need further development in order to achieve the vision.

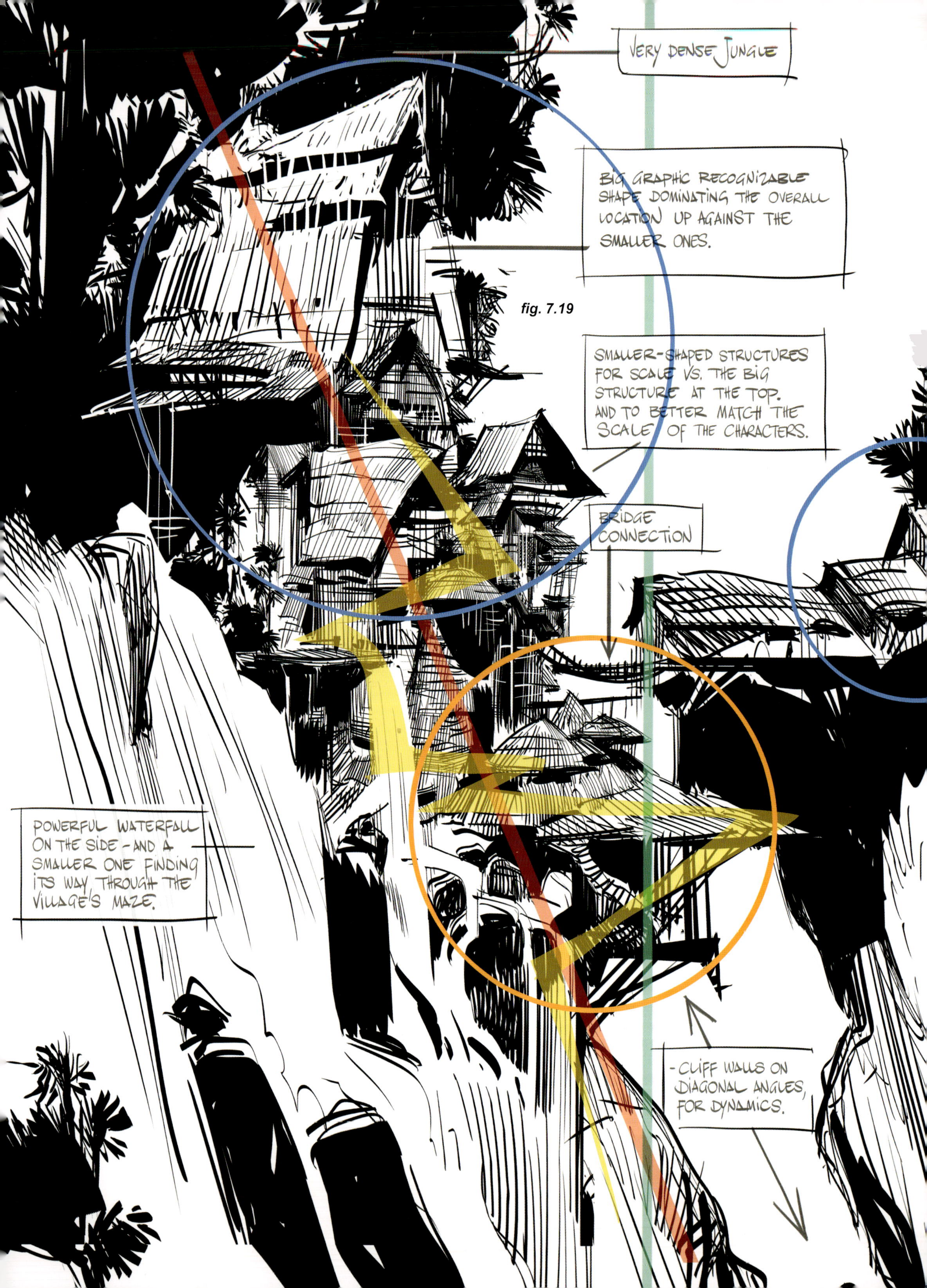

VERY DENSE JUNGLE
BIG GRAPHIC RECOGNIZABLE SHAPE DOMINATING THE OVERALL LOCATION UP AGAINST THE SMALLER ONES.
fig. 7.19
SMALLER-SHAPED STRUCTURES FOR SCALE VS. THE BIG STRUCTURE AT THE TOP. AND TO BETTER MATCH THE SCALE OF THE CHARACTERS.
BRIDGE CONNECTION
POWERFUL WATERFALL ON THE SIDE - AND A SMALLER ONE FINDING ITS WAY THROUGH THE VILLAGE'S MAZE.
- CLIFF WALLS ON DIAGONAL ANGLES, FOR DYNAMICS.

Fig. 7.19: This image "checks most of the boxes" we had in mind for this village: a visual piece loosely inspired by traditional architecture mainly from the varied Southeast Asian region, while **aiming at creating a distinctive fantasy world** with its own architectural and cultural rules:

1. The overall layout and distribution of **big shapes vs. small shapes** is starting to look good, as does the contrast between angular shapes (within the blue circles) and rounder shapes (orange circle), and how the **main area** (left of the green line) connects with a **smaller area** (right of the green line) through a bridge. All these contrasts and imbalances create an interesting visual texture, potentially favoring opportunities for character and story moments, with the inhabitants of the place having the chance to travel through **picturesque paths** and over **platforms and bridges,** with a **variety of backgrounds** that will give the **camera** plenty of juicy opportunities.

2. As mentioned, the overall layout of the village is a vertical one, although not just a straight vertical but with an overall **angle to it** (red line) and with a sort of **zigzag way down along this diagonal** (yellow).

3. Both **village and jungle interact** here and there, with no clear-cut separation between the two.

Eventually we will populate the place with balconies, ladders, scaffoldings, etc. This early version also shows the idea of a waterfall, as well as lush vegetation. But this is **only a second step** after the early research and initial sketches. So based on this new concept, let's push it further; **let's keep exploring** how to make this location a place of fantasy.

5. SHAPE AND DYNAMICS LANGUAGE: FURTHER RESEARCH

Now that the backbone of the village is in a good place, we can start thinking more about the specifics of the shape language within it, the details that can make it even more special. So let's return to actual Southeast Asian references to see if any visual design aspects from the region spark further ideas.

Figs. 7.20–7.24: Headpieces or hats are in fact a sort of roof, a surface that protects humans from weather, this region being too hot and sunny or cold and rainy, and there are very interesting shapes within this group.

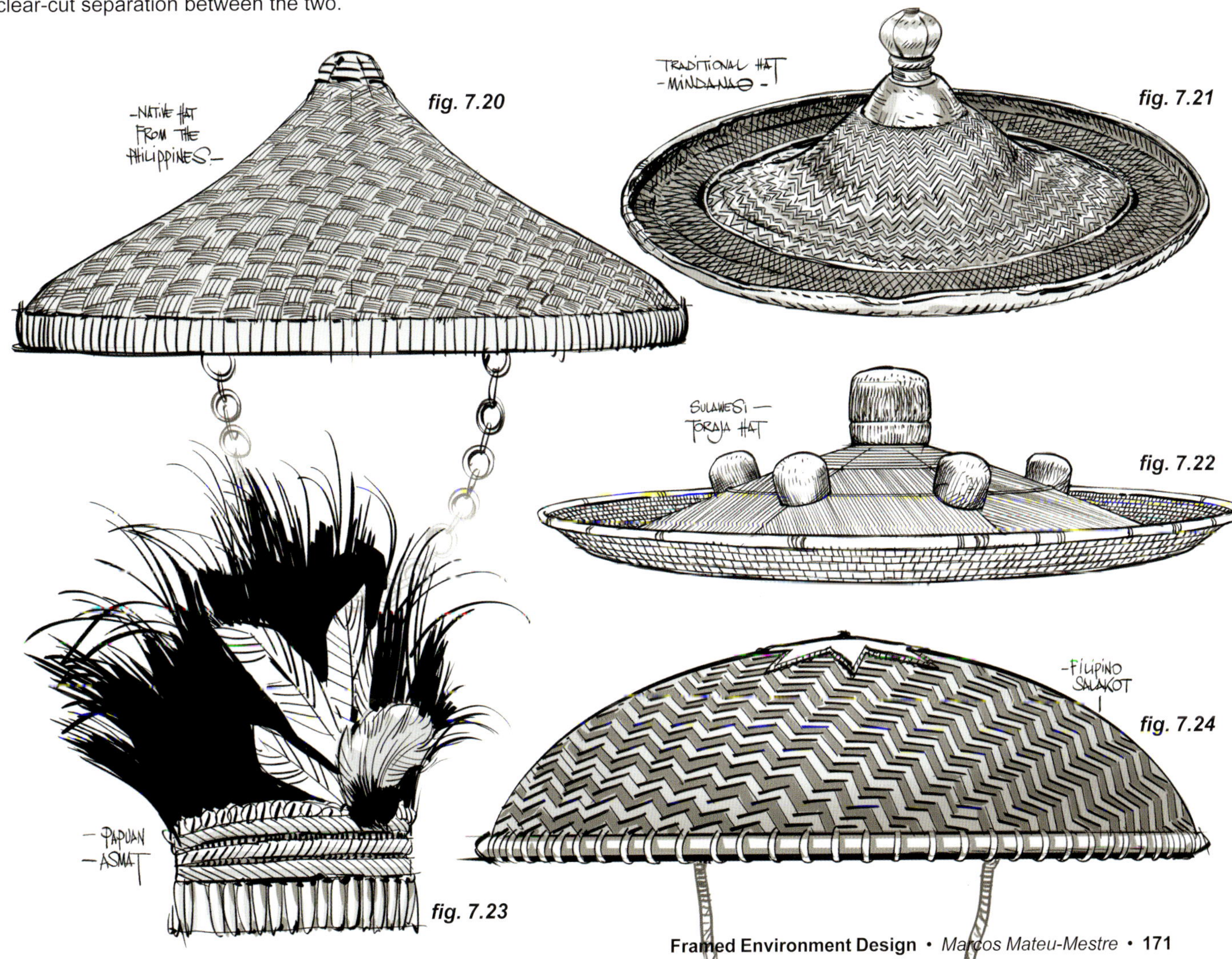

fig. 7.20

fig. 7.21

fig. 7.22

fig. 7.24

fig. 7.23

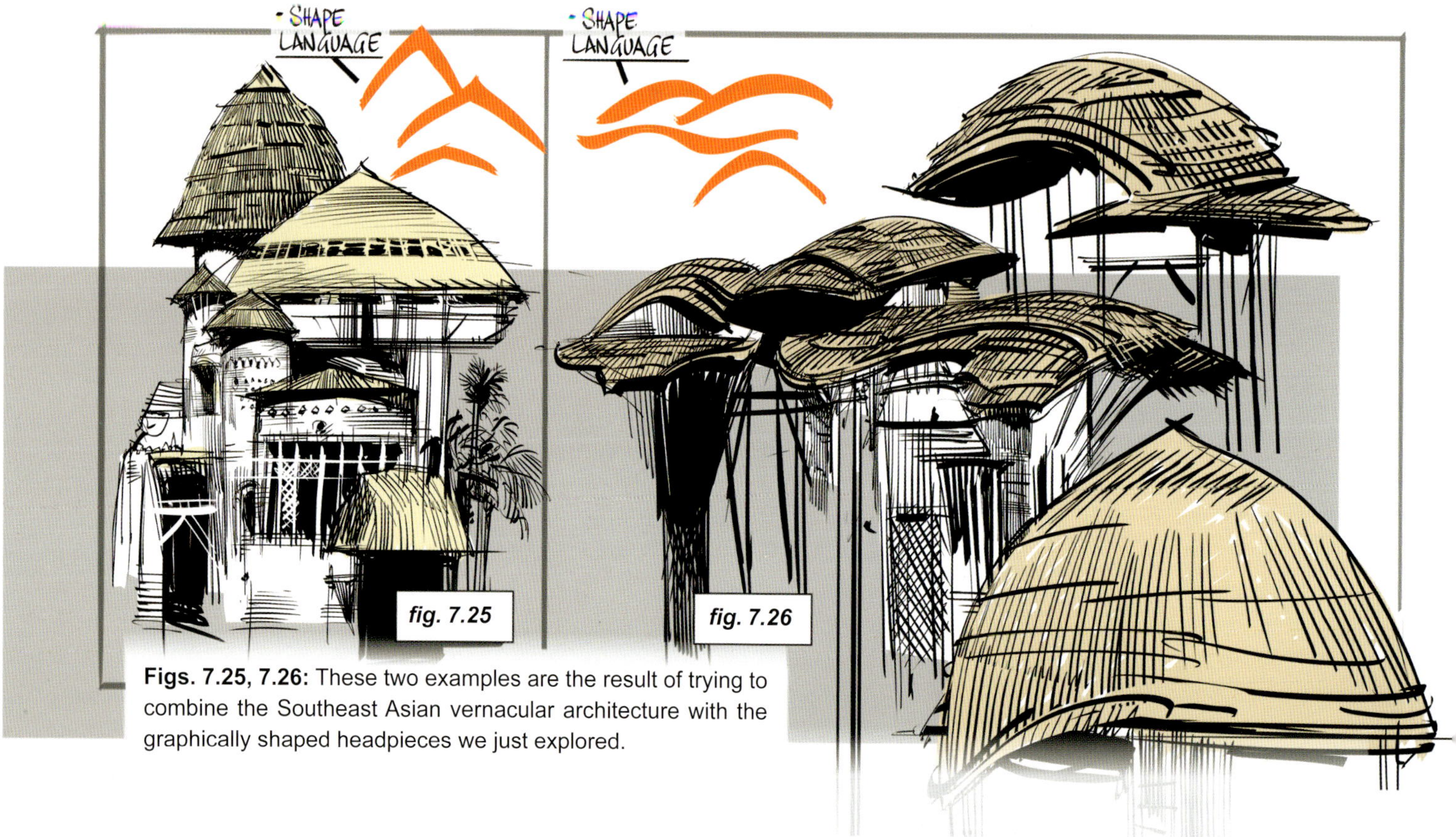

The two figures at the top are labeled:

Figs. 7.25, 7.26: These two examples are the result of trying to combine the Southeast Asian vernacular architecture with the graphically shaped headpieces we just explored.

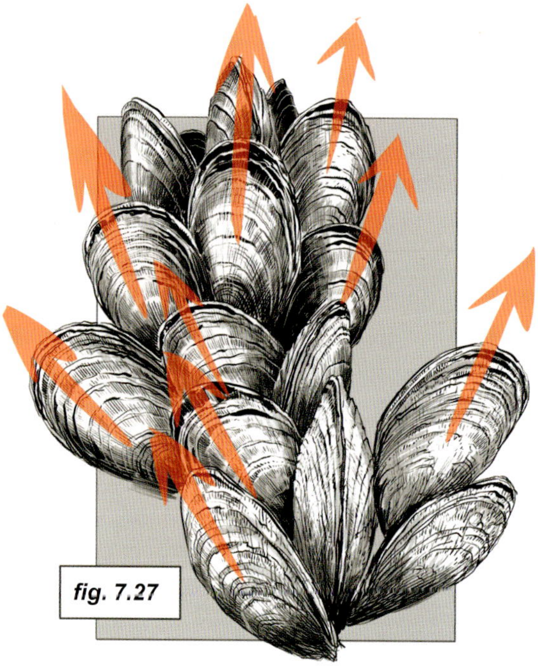

6. INTEGRATING ABSTRACT CONCEPTS SO EVERYTHING GELS

Sometimes incorporating external **abstract ideas** based on natural and organic references can be extremely useful. Here are two non-architectural concepts that can help combine the dwellings in this village in a structured, cohesive, and rhythmic way.

Fig. 7.27: The arrangement of these mussels **grouped on a rock** near the ocean offers a **sense of organic formation** that is varied in angles and direction yet retains a sense of purpose to it.

Fig. 7.28: Another thought comes to mind that establishes a wonderful **sense of direction, broken here and there by visual accents**. This **group of meerkats** watches over the horizon, most of them staring in a singular direction while a few heads point in different angles. This simple image has **so much rhythm and vibrancy** that can certainly be applied to the structural setup of the houses in our village.

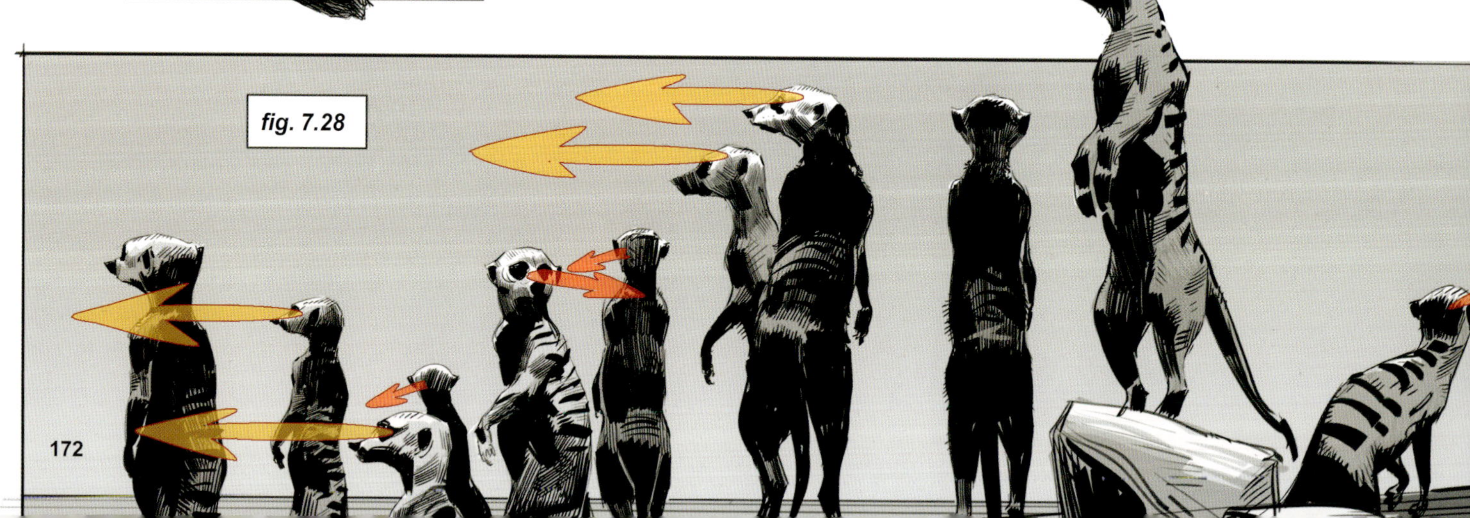

In addition to the immense wall the location rests on and connects and intertwines with, let's consider the other elements that need to be explored, such as rocks and the junglelike, lush vegetation.

Figs. 7.29, 7.30: Let's study the contrast between the thick trunks of the Balete Tree (Philippines) and the thinner branches that grow around them, reaching down to the ground . . .

Fig. 7.31: . . . the wide and lush-looking leaves of the banana tree . . .

Fig. 7.32: . . . and the Arenga Hookeriana in Thailand and Malaysia to get us started

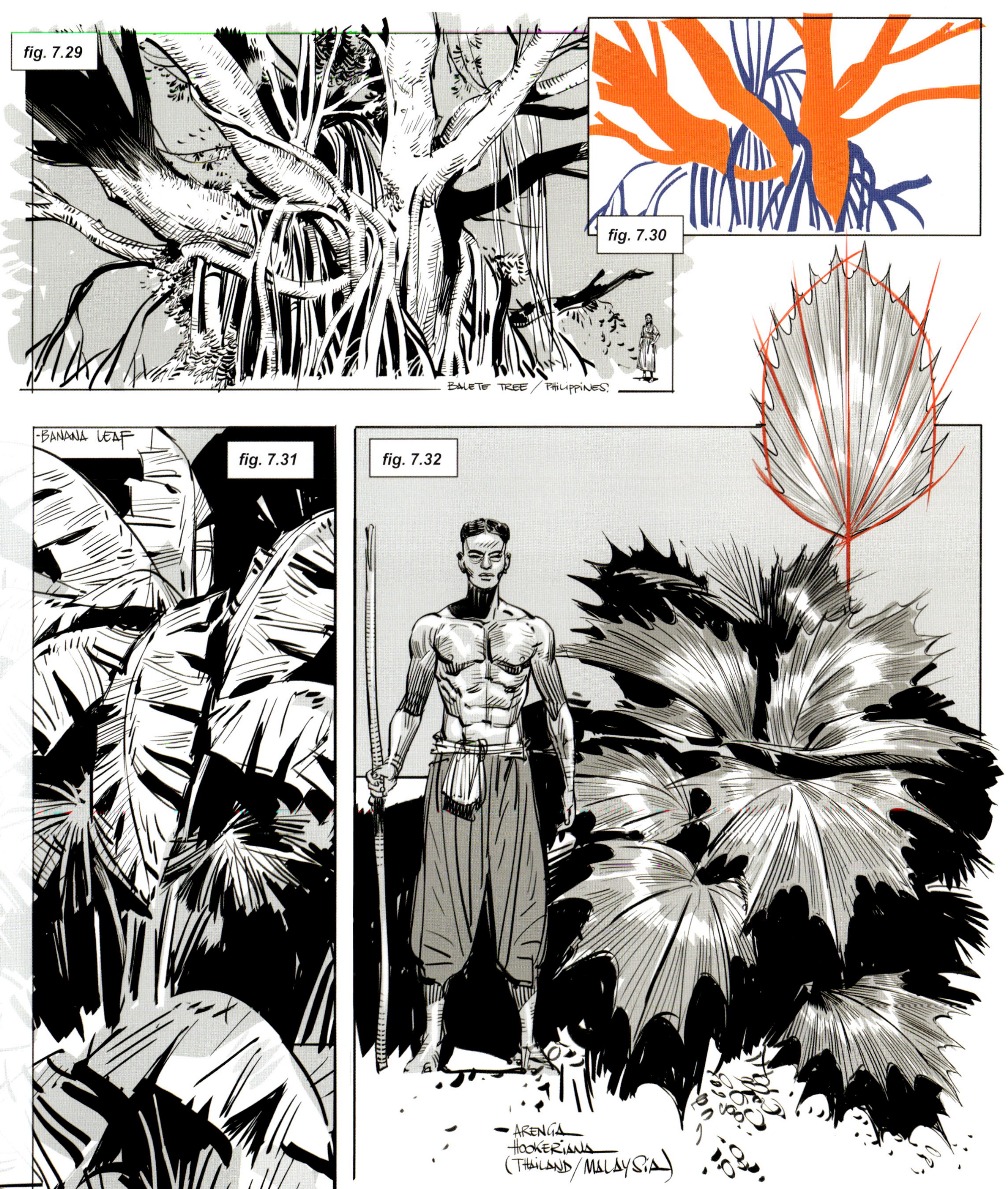

fig. 7.33

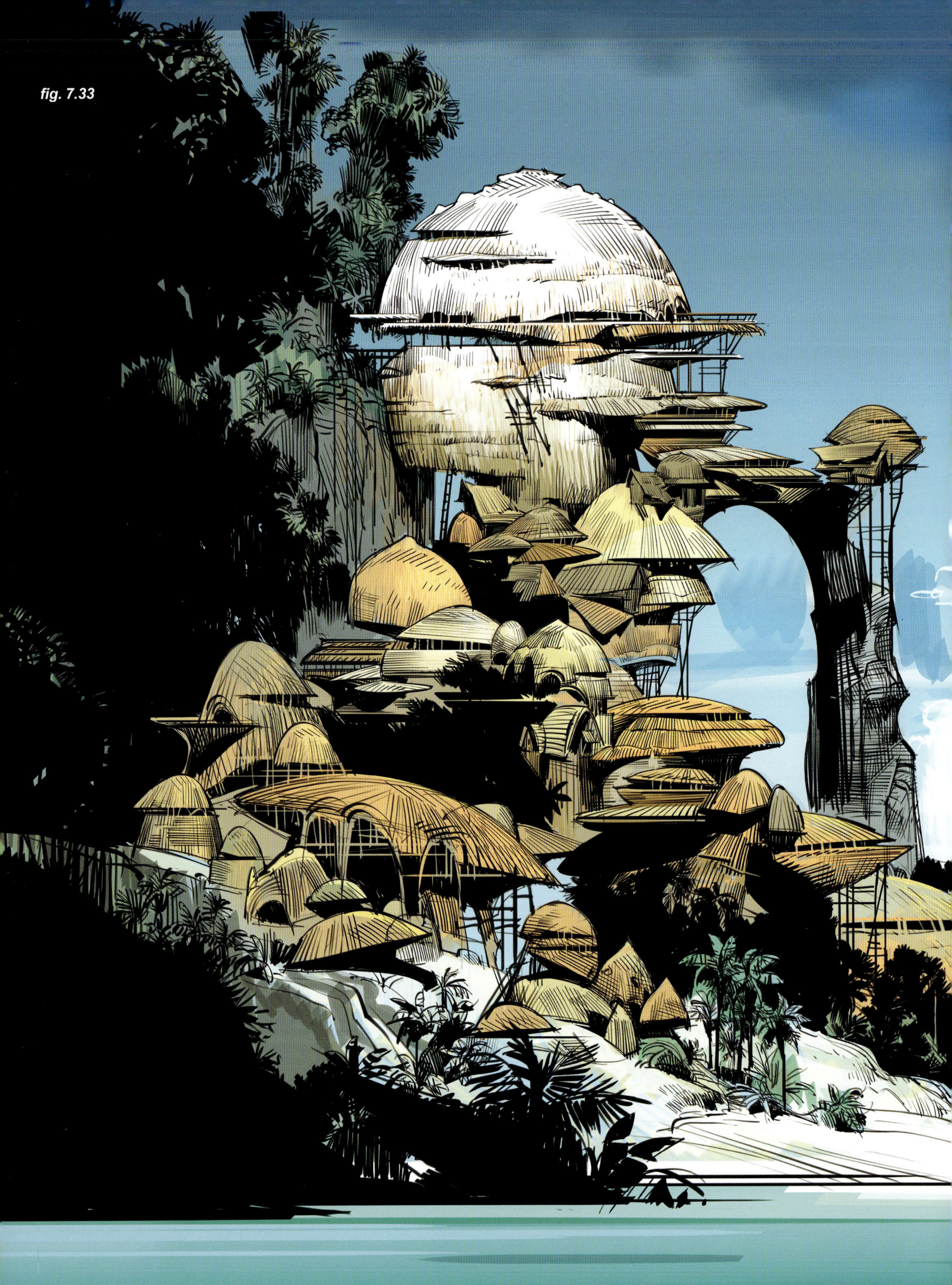

Finally, here comes a first serious pass at the village's overall design that has **all the basic elements we decided this environment would be about**, with a second (further pushed and developed pass) on the next two pages:

• Textures, colors, and materials **loosely inspired by vernacular habitat references of Southeast Asia**.
• The result of **translating** these references of **actual dwellings** and the more simple and streamlined shape of additional **designs from the same region** (like the headgear examples), and then **pushing** all these shapes and volumes **toward a fantasized version**.
• An **overall layout** and structure partly inspired by natural and organic concepts, like the **mussels attached to a rock** by the oceanside or the evolving motions of the meerkats' heads in the wild that tend to point in a consistent direction, only sporadically broken by some individuals in the group looking elsewhere, creating an interesting sense of dynamics.
• **Scaffolding and ladders** supporting and connecting different houses and areas, inspired by the **tree house** example on page 166.
• A diagonal layout that starts at the top and comes all the way down to sea level in a **zigzag path.**
• Adding to that, the full village setup **extends into the ocean** through the boardwalk at the very end.
• Part of the **jungle intertwines with the village,** something we will use in the more detailed frames to create interesting views in which both architecture and nature together create an inspiring language.

Also, this shot includes a distant background, a dramatic element made up of tall rocks rising up out of the ocean, resembling a gigantic monster's fingers, creating a sort of visual echo between these shapes and the village.

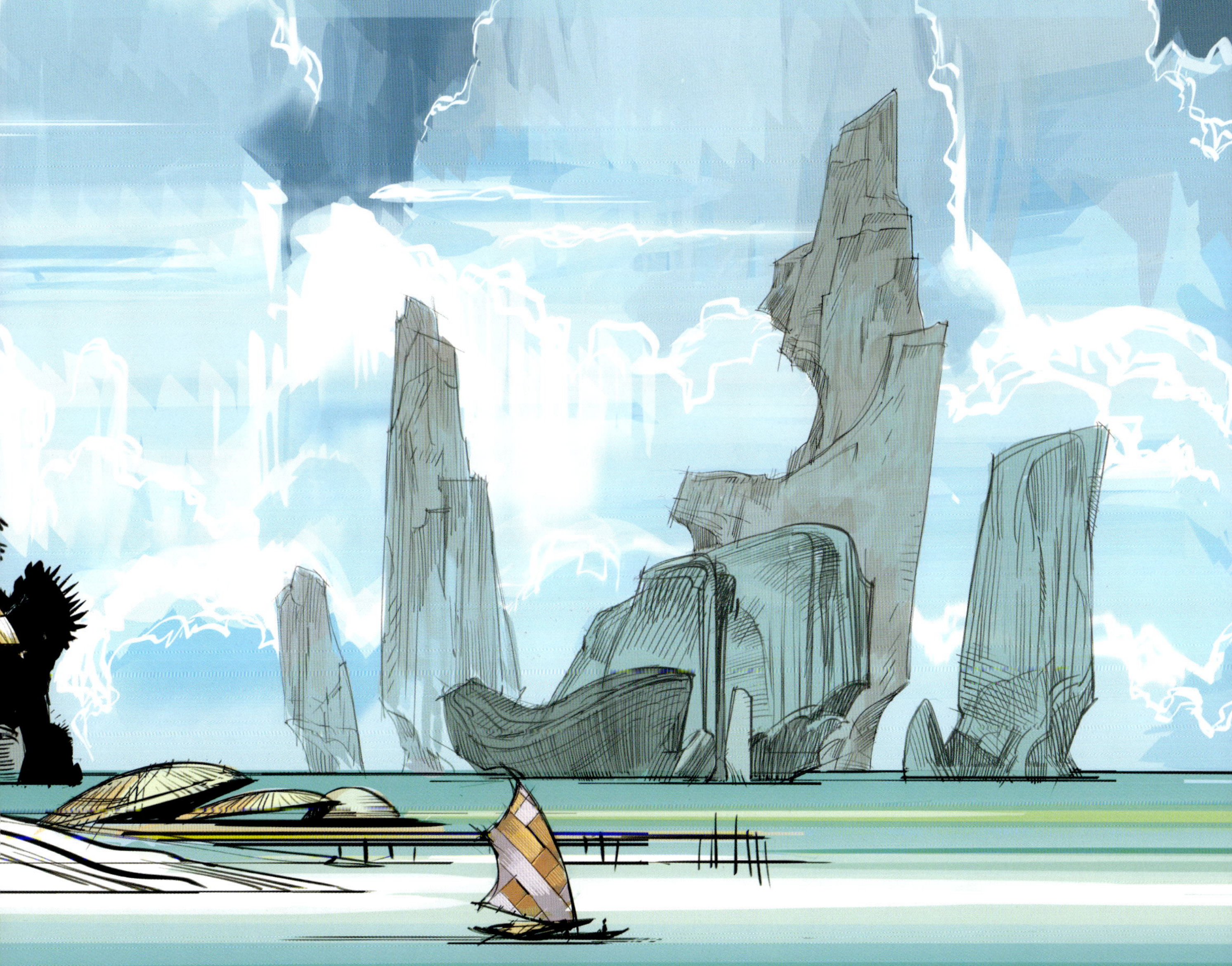

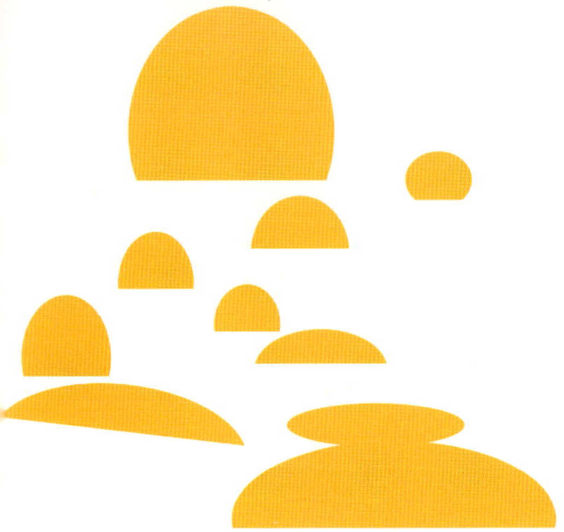

fig. 7.34

Fig. 7.37: This main illustration goes a solid step further than the previous illustration (page 174) by vigorously pushing its rounder and more even shapes into stronger dynamics and greater size contrasts.

Fig. 7.34: The schematic for fig. 7.33 (page 174).

Fig. 7.35: The schematic for fig. 7.37. Visually synthesizes this new **stronger contrast of size and shape** (more diagonals, verticals, horizontals, and pointier shapes).

Fig. 7.36: Focuses on the new, **sharper, more energetic angles** as well as the bent dynamics of the village.

Comparing both illustrations, this new one has a wilder, more anarchic feel than the more structured one (fig. 7.33), and while curved architectural shapes are still a dominant theme, this new design pushes things further until they appear a bit **off-balance,** with more **angled domes and rooftops,** some of which are now **stretched** in a way that seems to reach out toward the ocean below. Also, the supporting beams and stilts have gotten more intricate, mimicking the structure of the trees and branches supporting the tree house seen on page 166.

As this is all part of our exploration and experimentation, the choice of one design version over the other would depend on the visual needs of the story. However, we might decide to use both versions simultaneously in different areas of our village if that works better for the project.

Ultimately, our story needs and sense of design will have the final word.

fig. 7.35

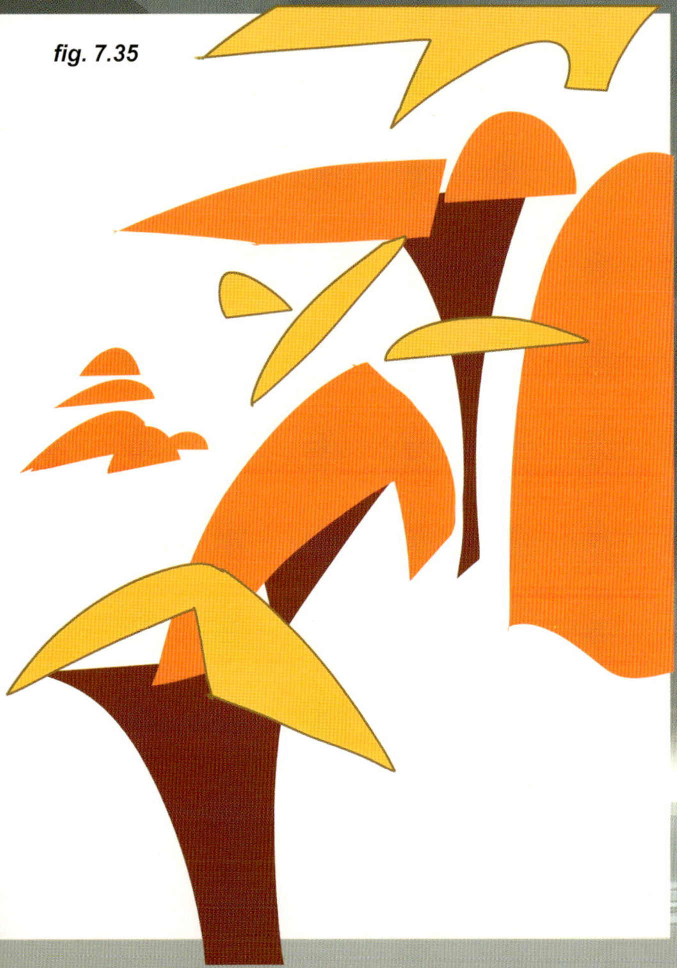

fig. 7.36

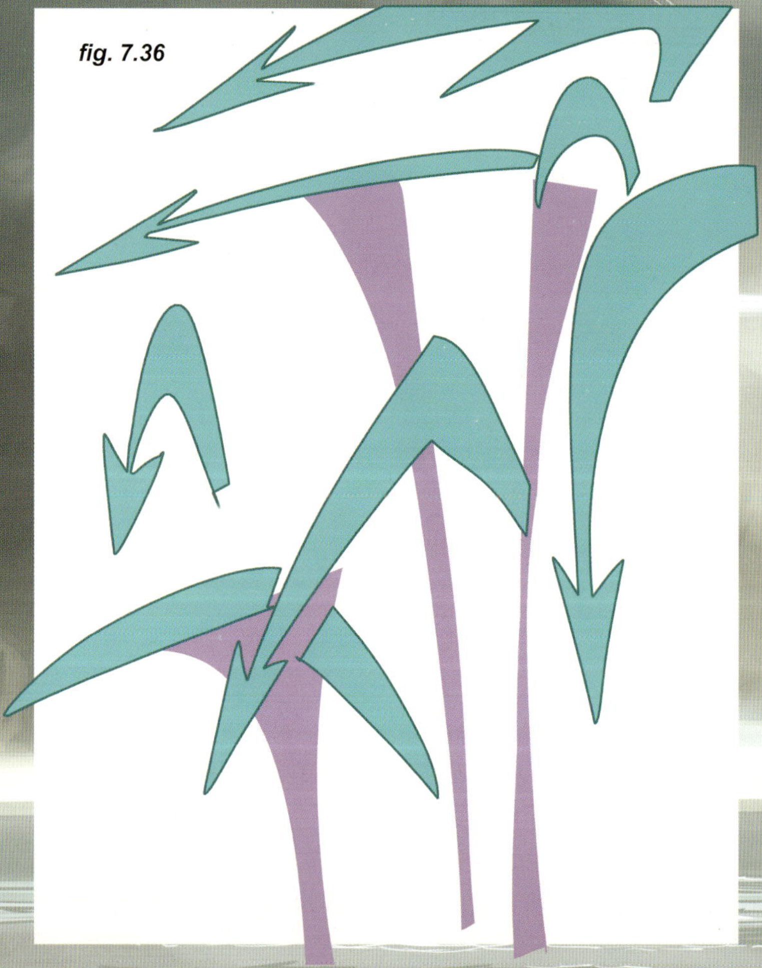

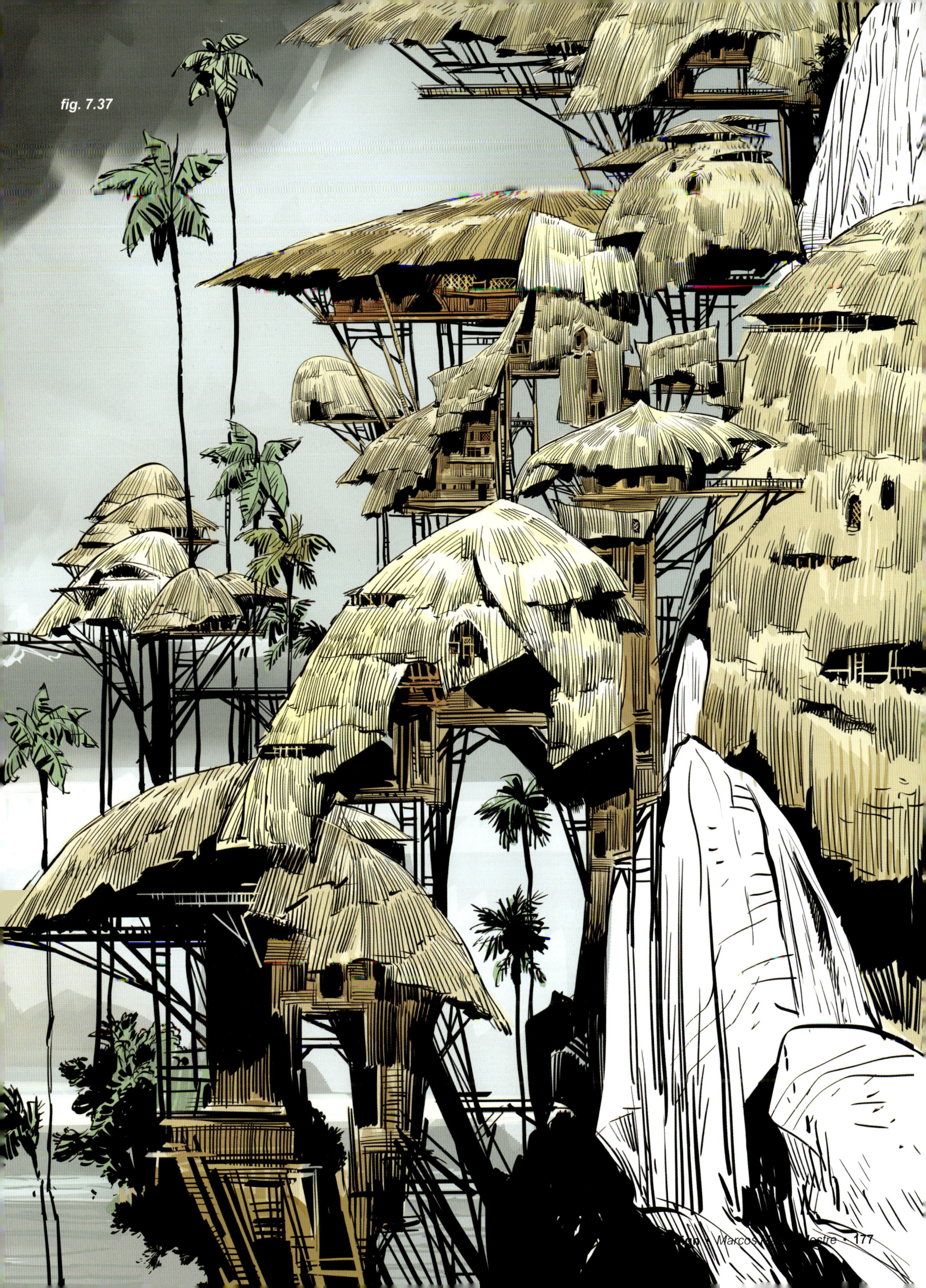

fig. 7.37

A PATH TO FANTASY

•LIVING IN THAT WORLD•

PART 2

GETTING INTO THE ACTUAL FABRIC

Time to make a decision.

For the sake of this example, let's go ahead and develop the earlier idea, the one from page 174.

That image established a general look and shape language for the village, and after this important first step, it is time to get into the second major phase, the details within the structure, the environment's inner fabric. This is analogous to writing a musical melody and then deciding which instrument will play what so that each and every part serves the overall theme that was already established.

And remember, we are creating a complex piece of information that will normally be passed on to a 3D modeler or designer. They should be able to take the data from our drawings without having to be too dependent on us to clarify things. Our work eventually needs to include a level of detail that supports this next step of the process.

Fig. 7.38: To get started, let's focus on a section of the overall exterior design (framed in yellow) to study the architectural shapes, textures, and design aspects of it at this point (no wall of rock or vegetation), keeping in mind it needs to feel like an actual livable space.

Now it is time to decide how the pieces of this puzzle will look and connect to each other, and how everything could work cinematically in front of the camera, while keeping the general flow that has been established. There is a balance between bigger and smaller shapes (as seen in the zigzag areas marked in green), establishing where "rivers" of smaller houses are "surfing" amongst the bigger shapes, to help create a richer visual texture, punctuated with accents (see red, orange, and blue color-coded annotations on the drawing).

As noted by the red circles, it is also important to pay attention to the **negative spaces** between dwellings, using breathers like bridges, arches, or pathways.

These auxiliary elements are as important as the houses themselves, therefore they need to have their own sense of size and proportion within the context, whether as narrow passages, wider streets, or boardwalks that can be anchored on the rock wall or just hanging from other structures.

These negative spaces help us properly organize the environment around them and are a way to ensure that there are working "arteries" through the "body" of the location.

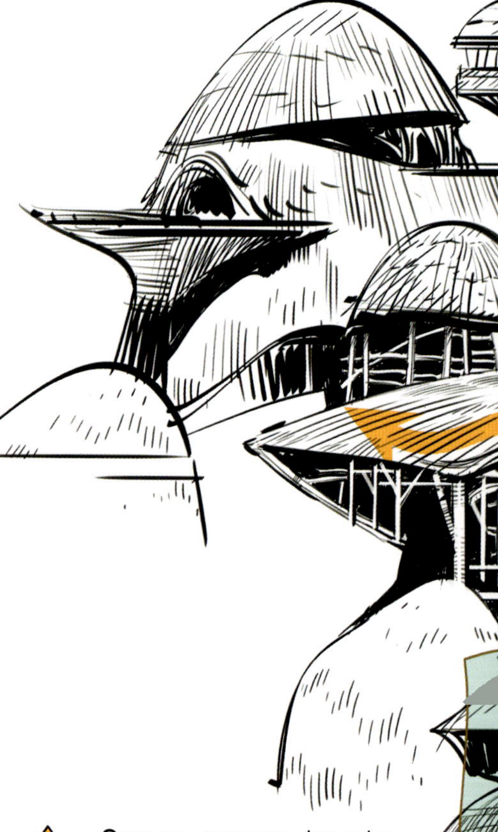

Orange arrows: Irregular-shaped arches.

Red circles: Arches, bridges, and passages as negative spaces to build around.

Blue squares: Some of the typical saddleback (steeply pitched) roofs are placed among the predominant domed or hat-shaped roofs as accents or variants.

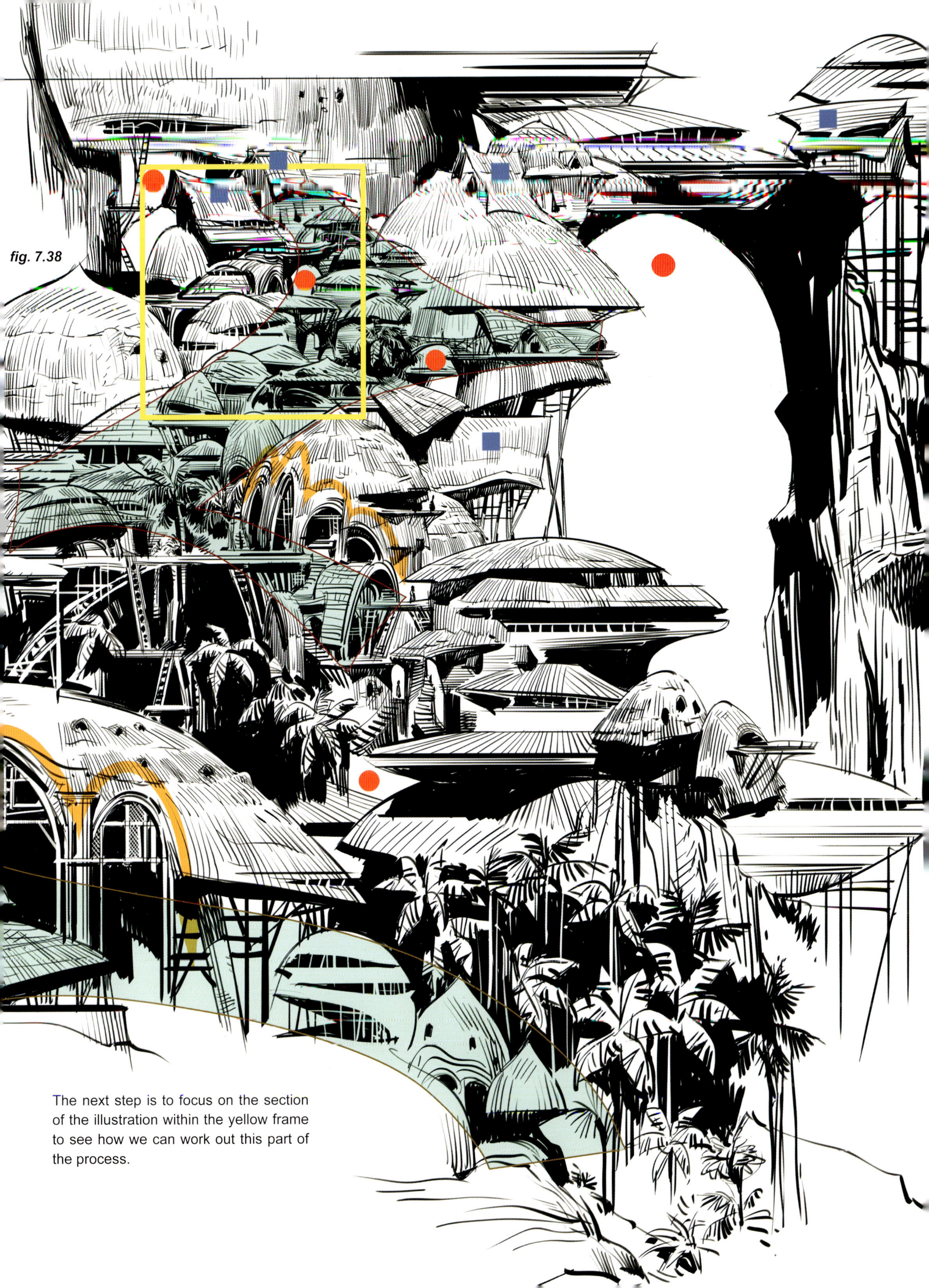

The next step is to focus on the section
of the illustration within the yellow frame
to see how we can work out this part of
the process.

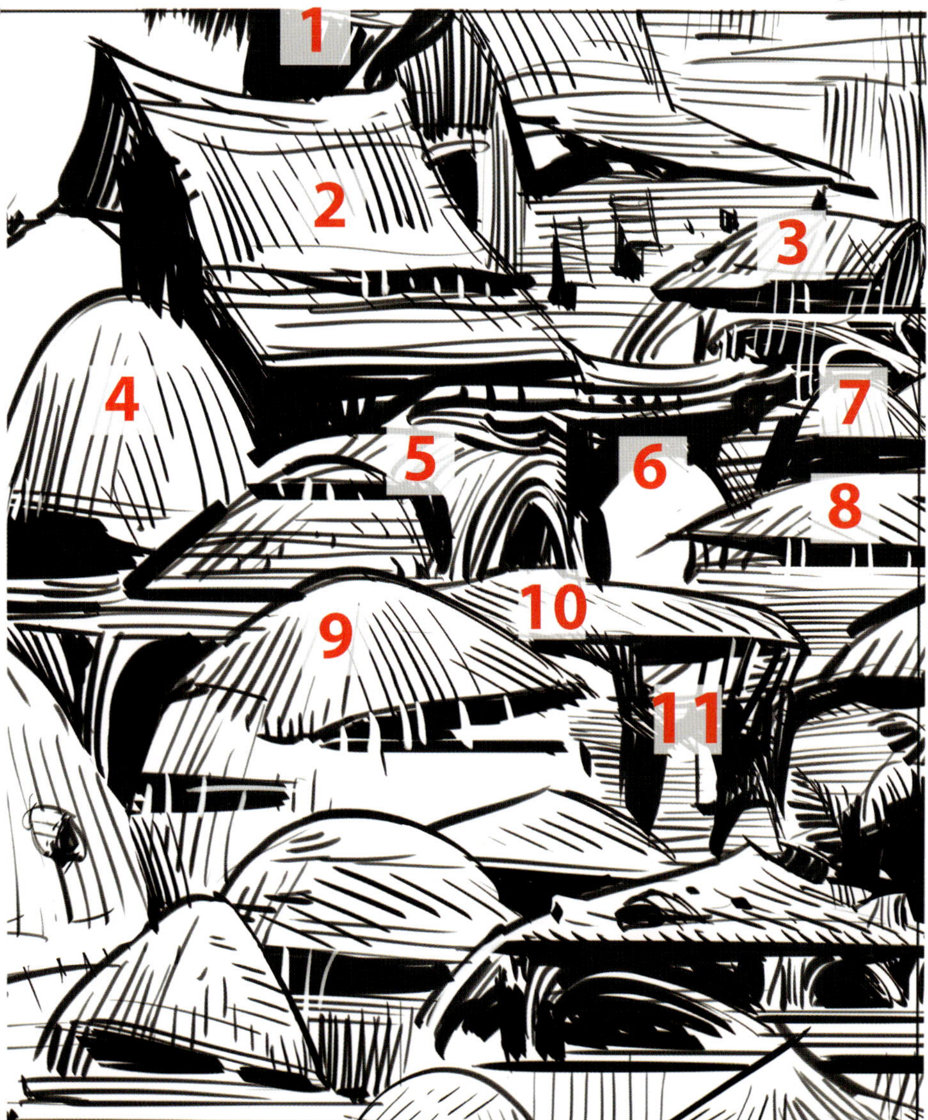

fig. 7.39

Fig. 7.39: As we keep enlarging sections of the preliminary design, it reveals just how much work still remains to be done.

Fig. 7.40: Further rendering the textures and materials like the bamboo beams, arches, and pillars, plus the straw and palm elements that make up the walls and rooftops.

At this stage, elements like palm trees and rock walls are just placeholders. In this particular case, we are concentrating on the architecture as the main focal point, to eventually work the elements of nature around it. A different project may require focusing first on vegetation and then adding buildings.

Note: The main structures in this section have been numbered so that we can clearly see the direct correlation between the "before" and "after" images. Also, standard characters are drawn here and there for clarity of size and proportion.

Fig. 7.41: Cropped frame, out of fig. 7.40, showing the level of detail depicted in this new render.

Eventually we will create even more nuanced renders of these in close-up images to better inform the 3D modelers.

fig. 7.41

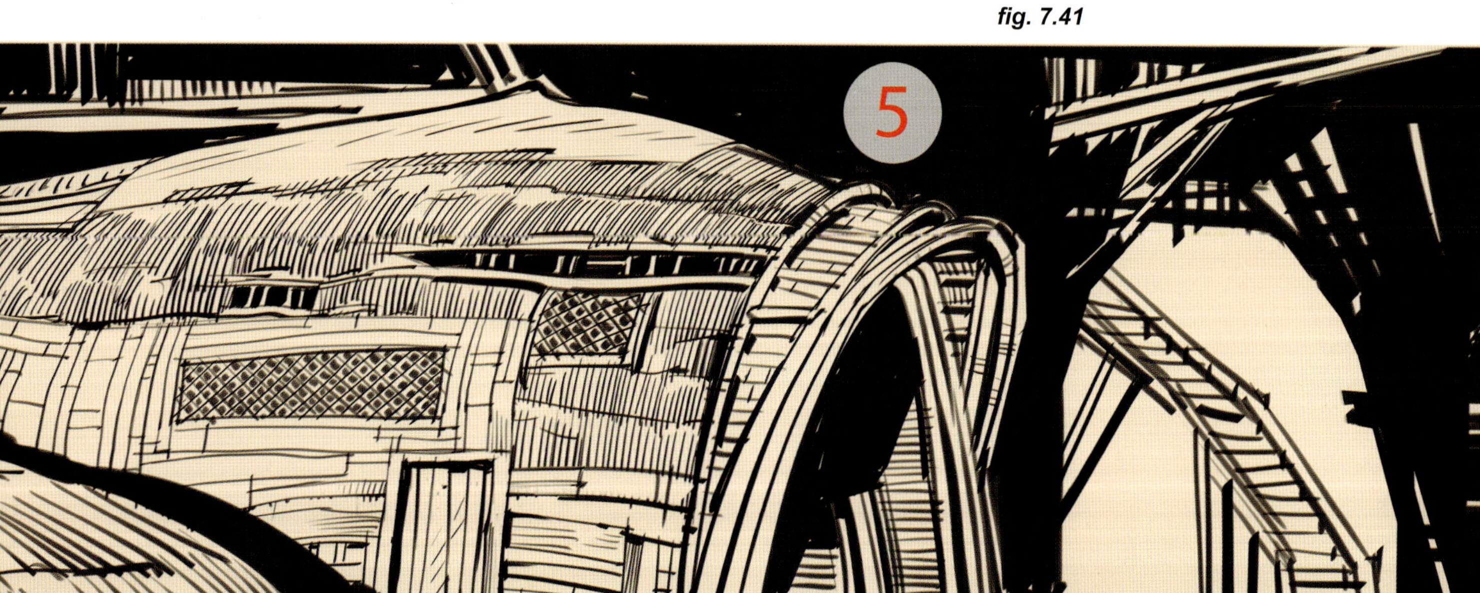

fig. 7.40

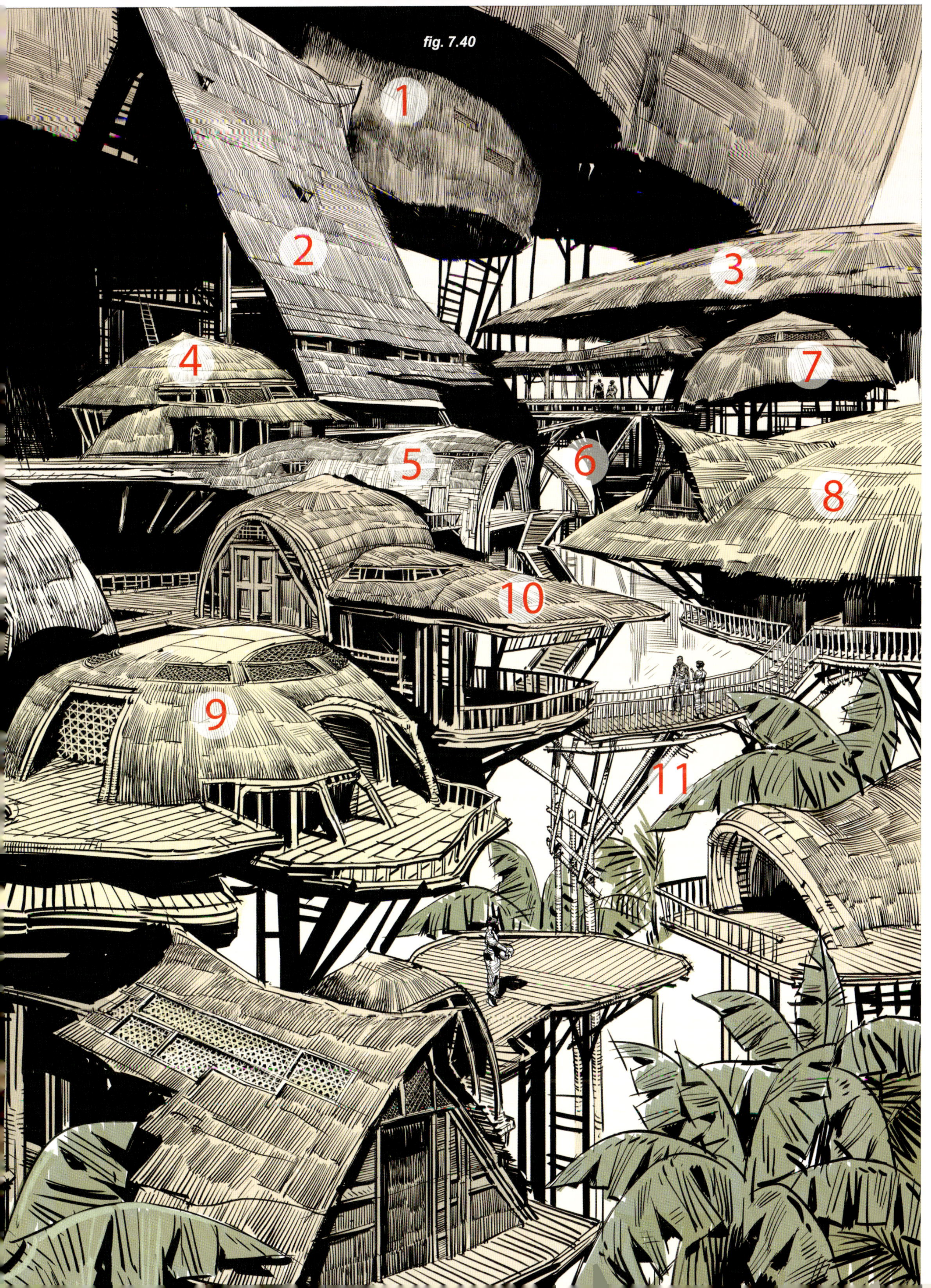

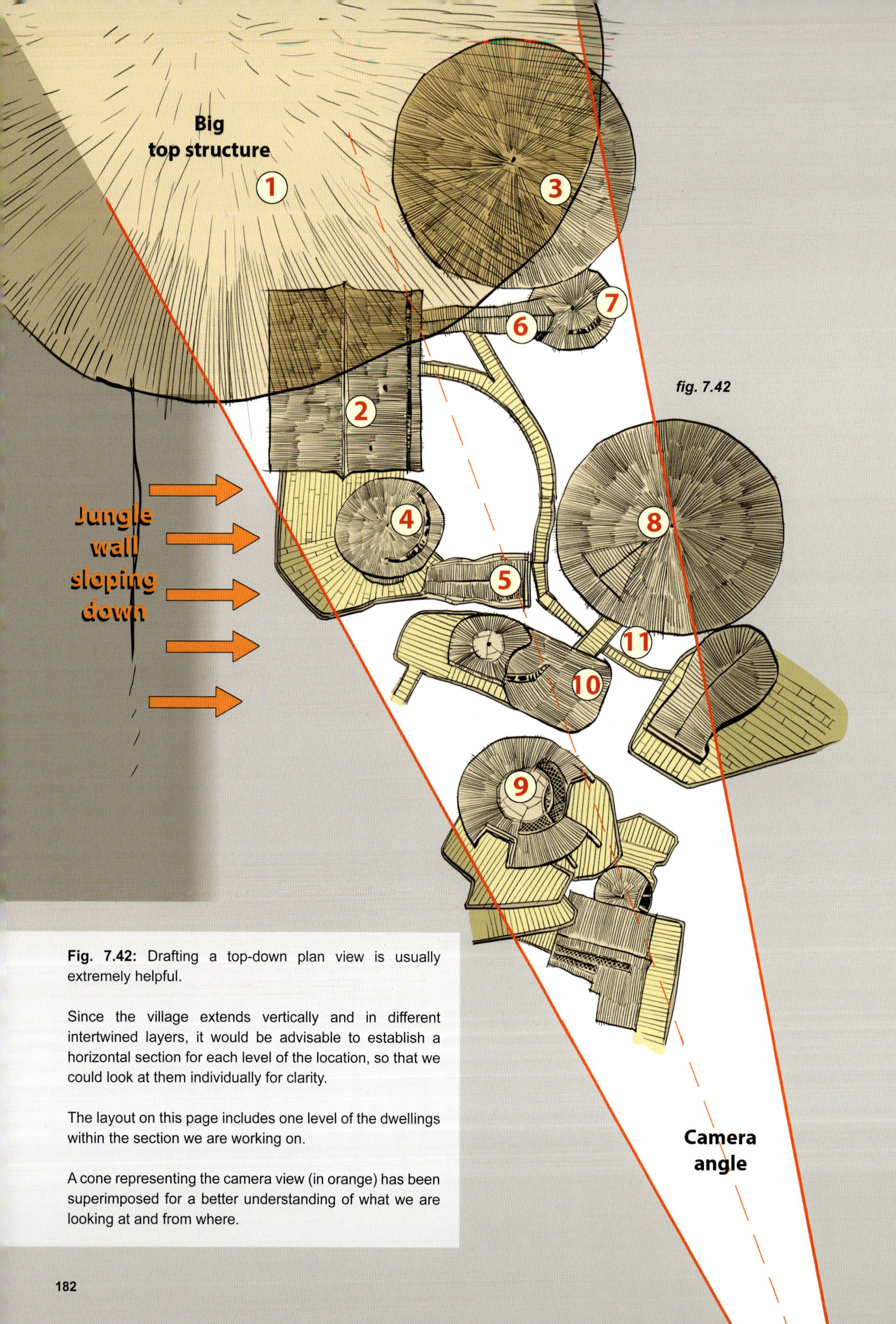

Fig. 7.42: Drafting a top-down plan view is usually extremely helpful.

Since the village extends vertically and in different intertwined layers, it would be advisable to establish a horizontal section for each level of the location, so that we could look at them individually for clarity.

The layout on this page includes one level of the dwellings within the section we are working on.

A cone representing the camera view (in orange) has been superimposed for a better understanding of what we are looking at and from where.

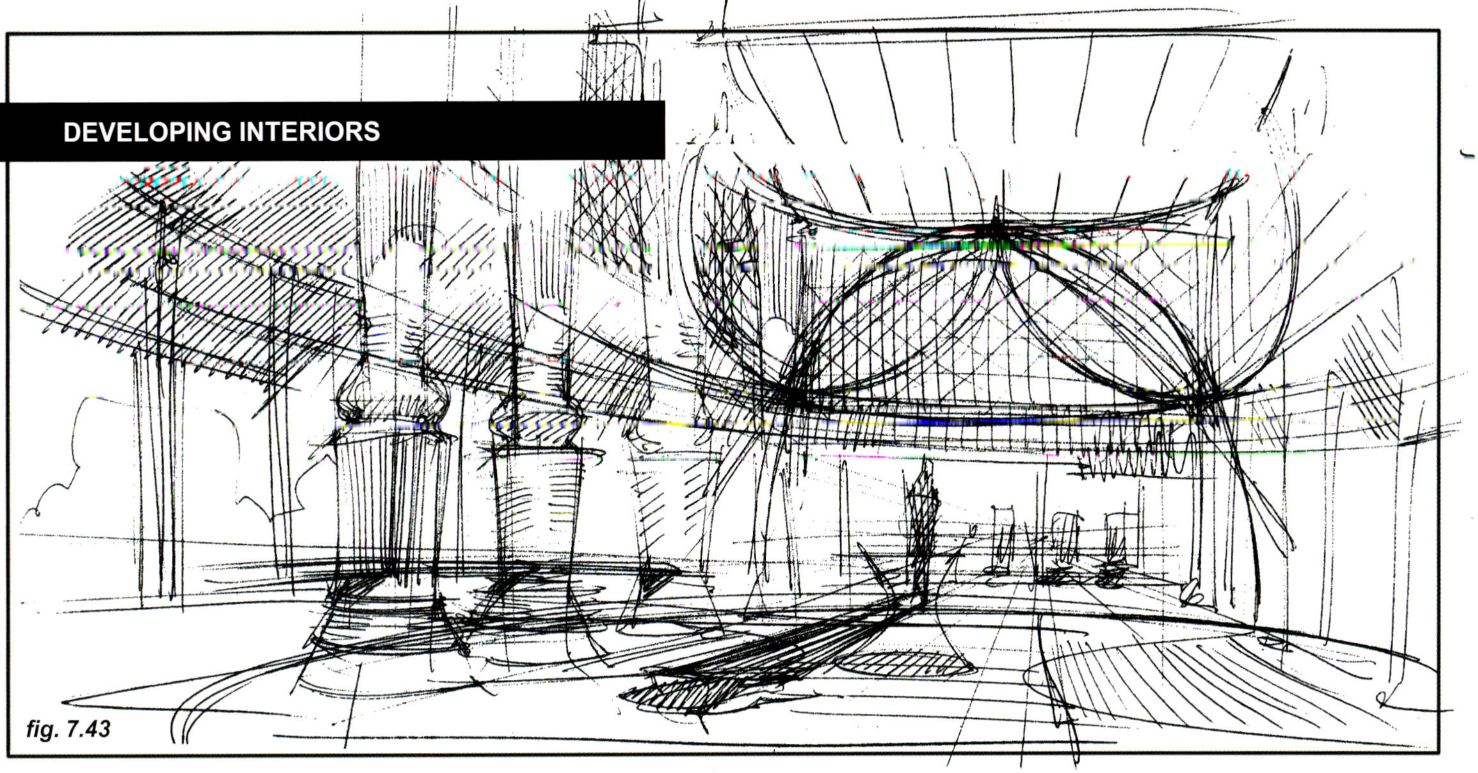

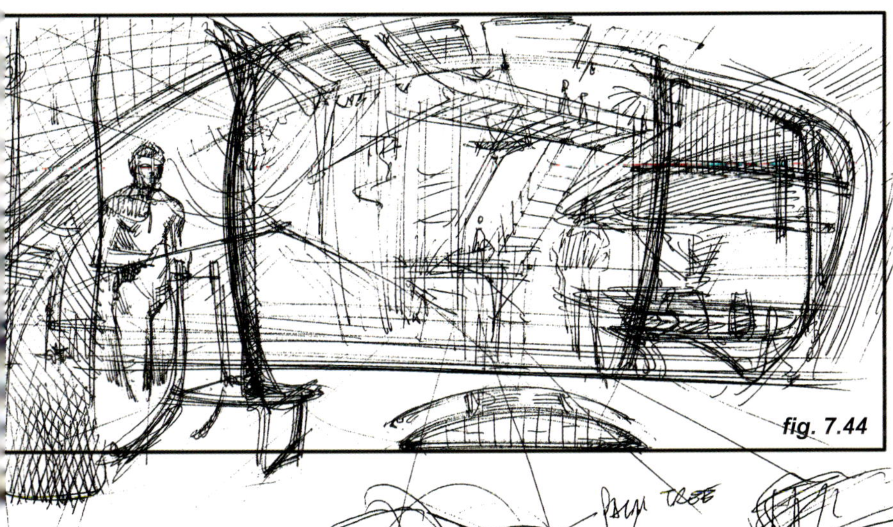

fig. 7.43

Now that we have come so far regarding the exterior of the village, let's go inside and draft some ideas for interiors and close-ups of the pathways.

Figs. 7.43–7.45: Here are three quick sketches looking for interesting points of view that would give a proper sense of the spaces and their details. Finding a solid base serves as a jumping-off point from which to flesh out proper design proposals.

fig. 7.44

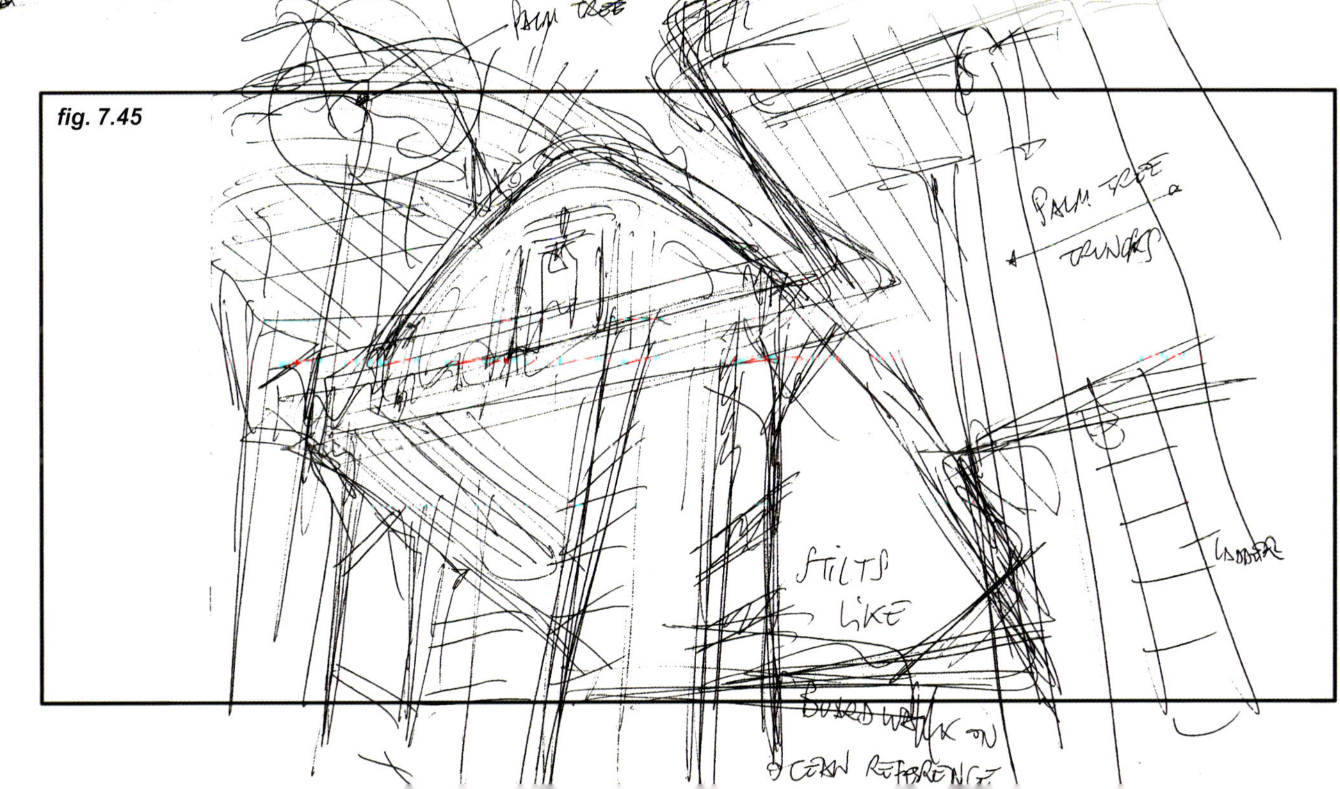

fig. 7.45

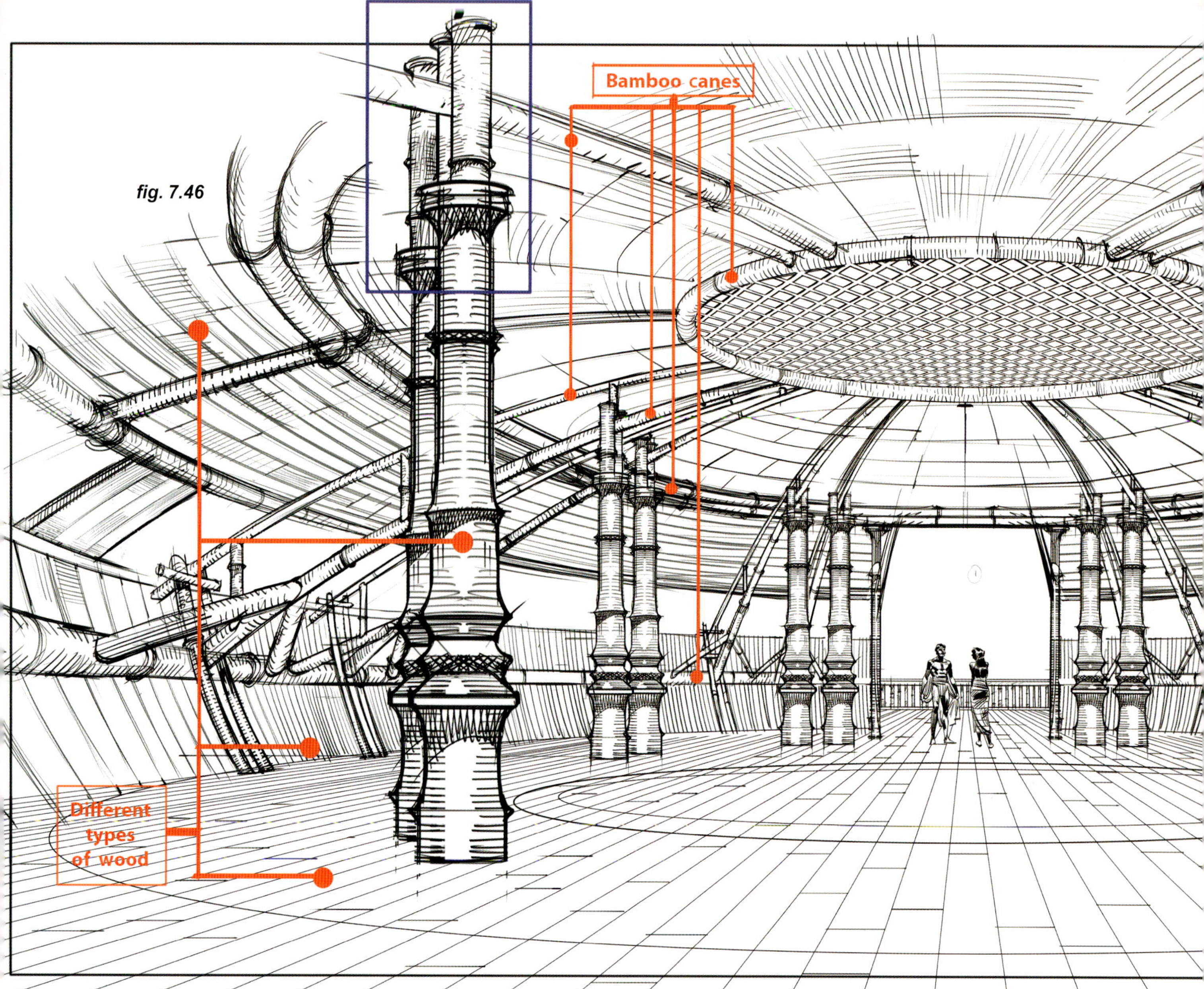

Fig. 7.46: Here is a clean-up pass on the previous page's first sketch (fig 7.43).

The design of this official **ceremonial hall** aims to echo the look of the exterior structures we have already established and be a believable interior to those. As a building of such dignity, it benefits from a level of complexity and intricacy that reflects such a hierarchy. This image is just a basic structure upon which many more layers will be added.

Main construction materials (annotated in red) are regular wooden planks, driftwood, palm leaves, and bamboo canes of various thicknesses. Notice that the pillars around the room's center, although made of solid wood, have been shaped and designed to be reminiscent of bamboo canes (loosely inspired by reference image fig 7.10, page 167), adhering to the surrounding natural environment.

Fig. 7.47: This is a detail of the area framed in blue, above. It is important to provide closer drawings for any design or architectural elements that might require further explanation.

Fig. 7.48: This color piece offers a view of how light can potentially work in this environment within certain circumstances and times of day. It also gives an approximate idea of the basic local colors of all the bare materials involved.

Fig. 7.49: As seen in previous examples, different section views (here top-down and side) of this Ceremonial Hall are important to understanding the space.

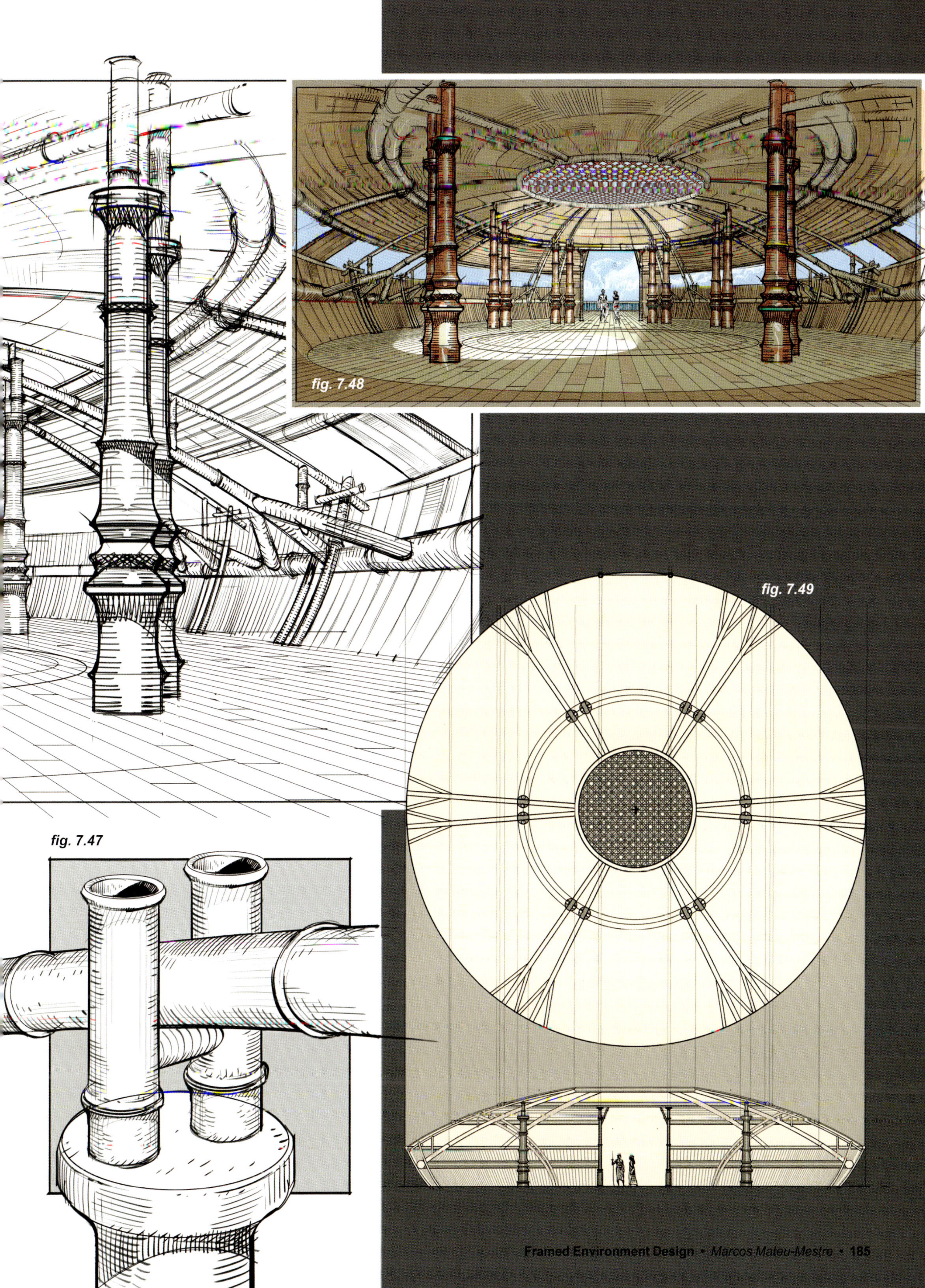

fig. 7.48

fig. 7.49

fig. 7.47

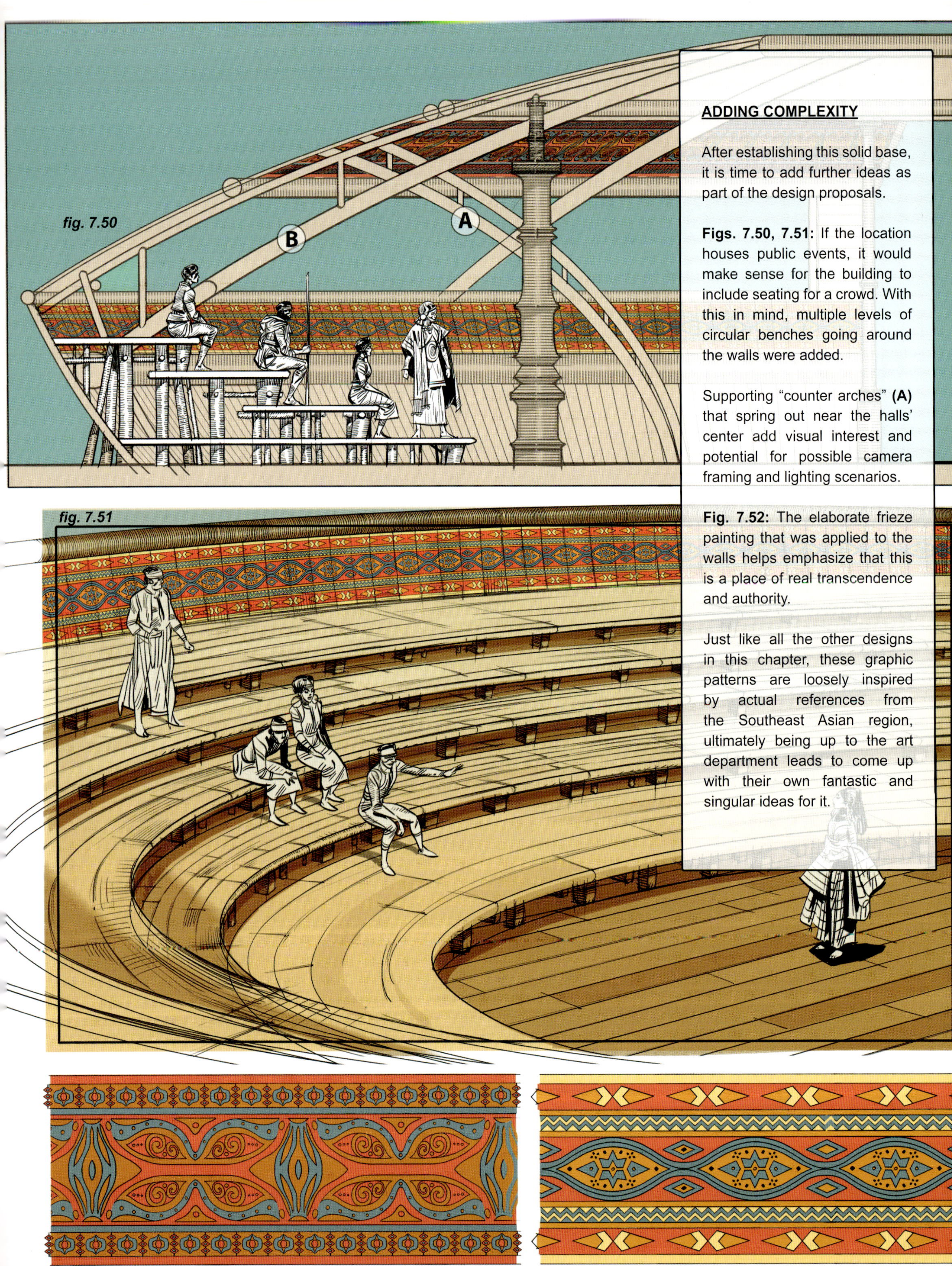

ADDING COMPLEXITY

After establishing this solid base, it is time to add further ideas as part of the design proposals.

Figs. 7.50, 7.51: If the location houses public events, it would make sense for the building to include seating for a crowd. With this in mind, multiple levels of circular benches going around the walls were added.

Supporting "counter arches" **(A)** that spring out near the halls' center add visual interest and potential for possible camera framing and lighting scenarios.

Fig. 7.52: The elaborate frieze painting that was applied to the walls helps emphasize that this is a place of real transcendence and authority.

Just like all the other designs in this chapter, these graphic patterns are loosely inspired by actual references from the Southeast Asian region, ultimately being up to the art department leads to come up with their own fantastic and singular ideas for it.

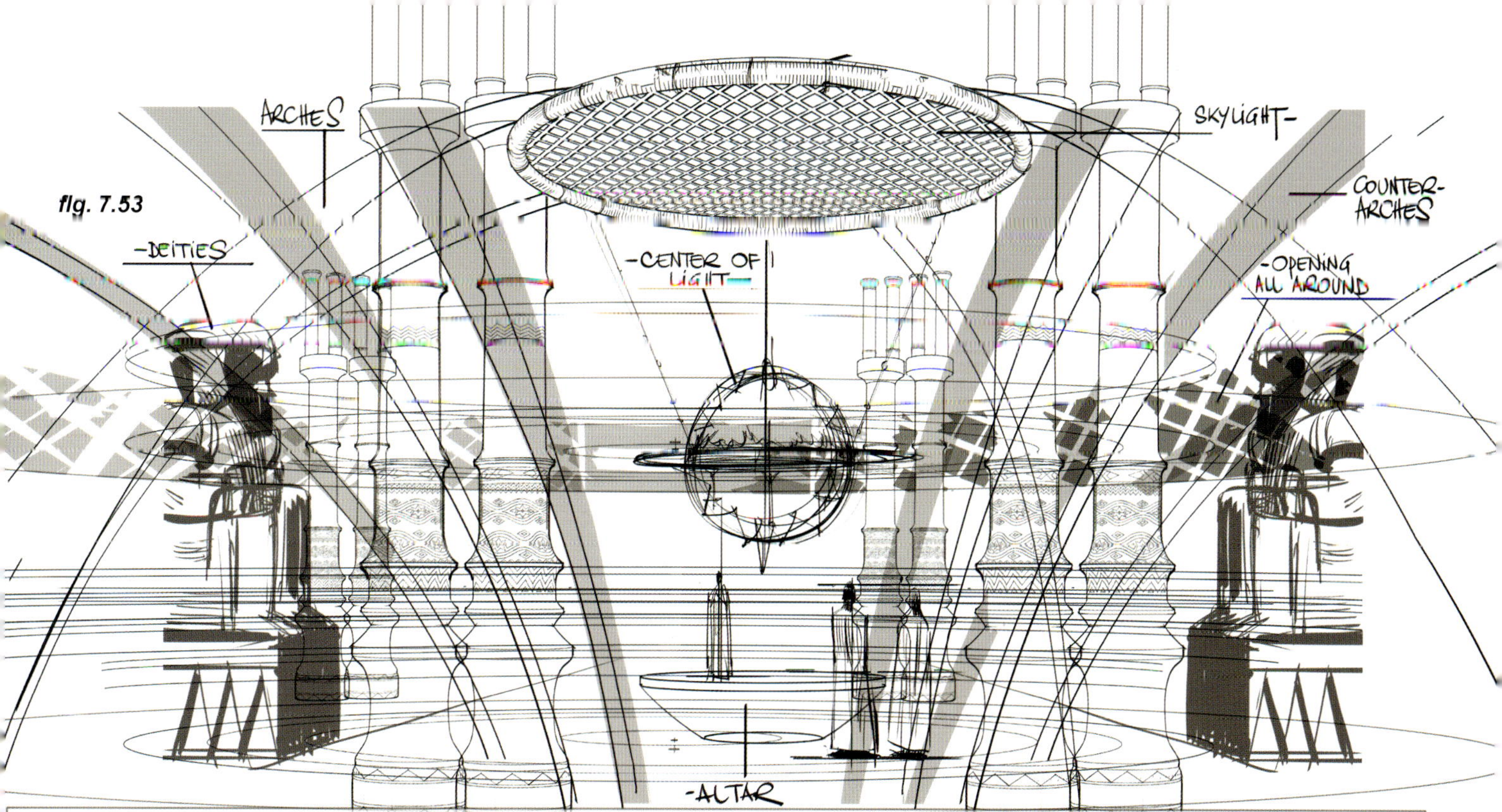

Fig. 7.53: In order to show the full potential of such a solemn location, a single vanishing point sketch was created to explore the possibilities of the entire framework and system of columns, and how the camera might look through them to enhance the cinematic experience.

Fig. 7.54: Final line drawing.

To bring in a further sense of fantasy, a mysterious glowing disc of light has been placed in the center of the room and will be the light source for the whole area.

And rather than overcrowding the place with characters that would obscure the design, only three of them were added for scale and basic atmosphere.

Fig. 7.55: Turn the page to see the final concept—including design, lighting, and color—of this ceremonial hall.

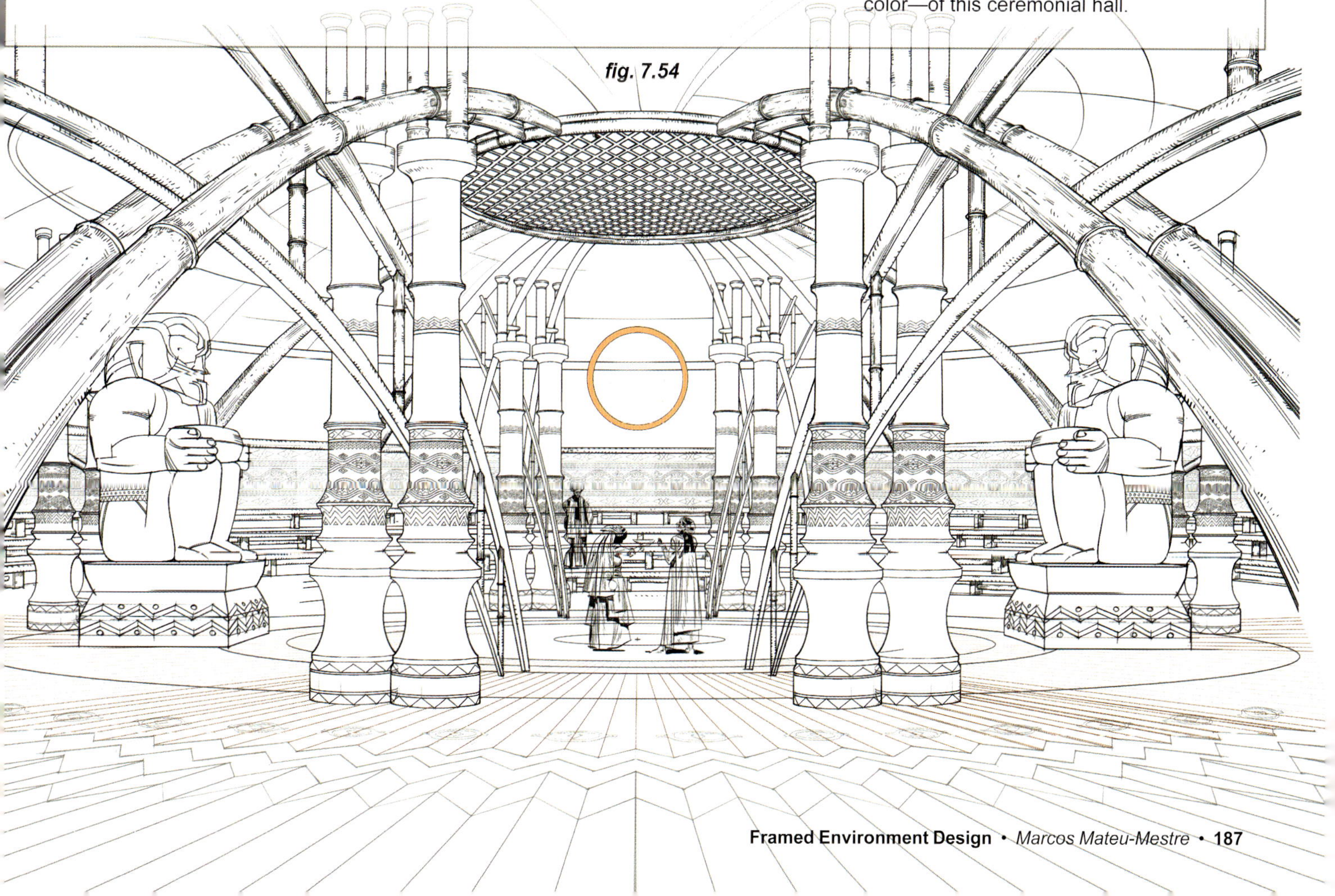

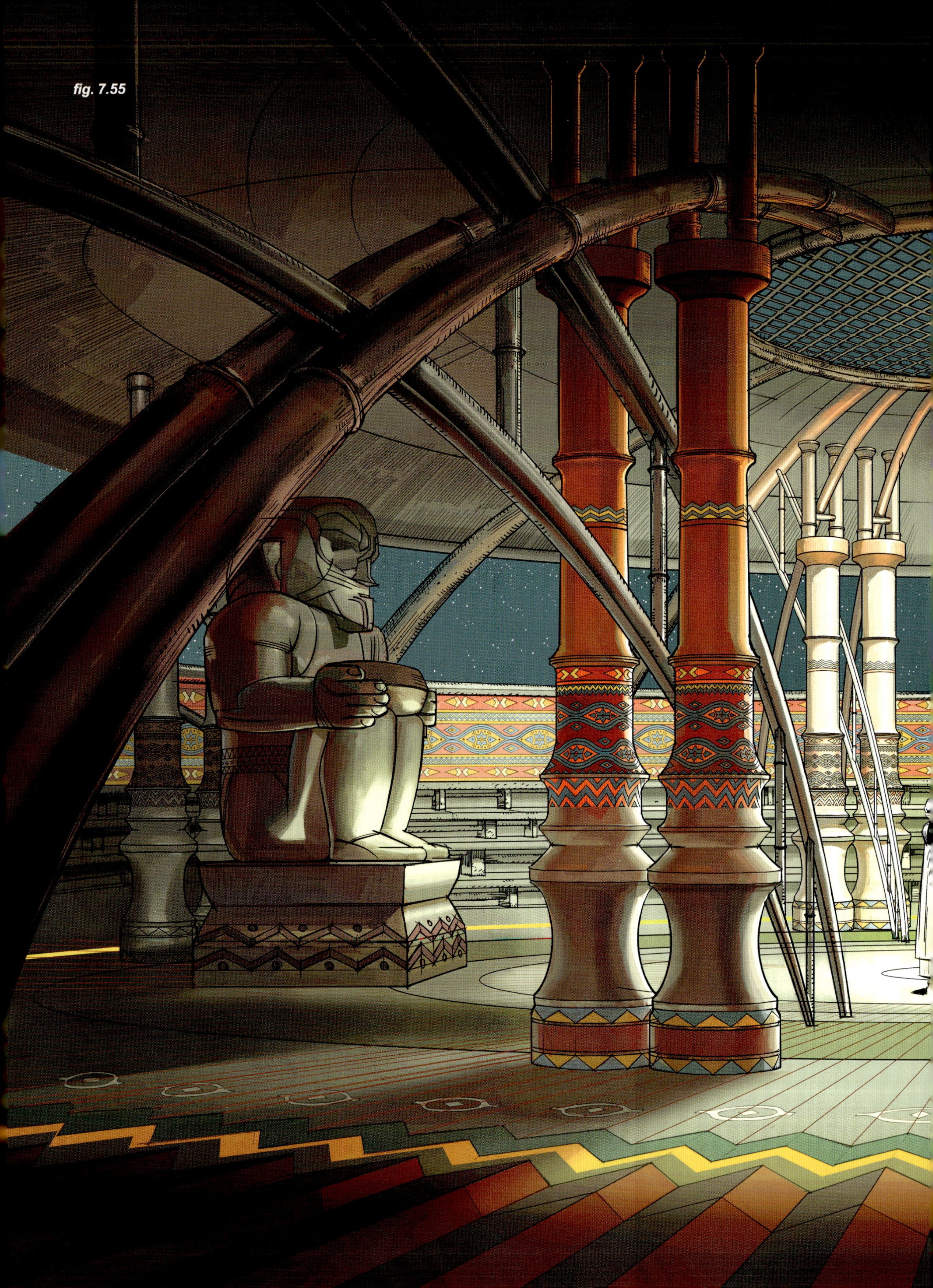
fig. 7.55

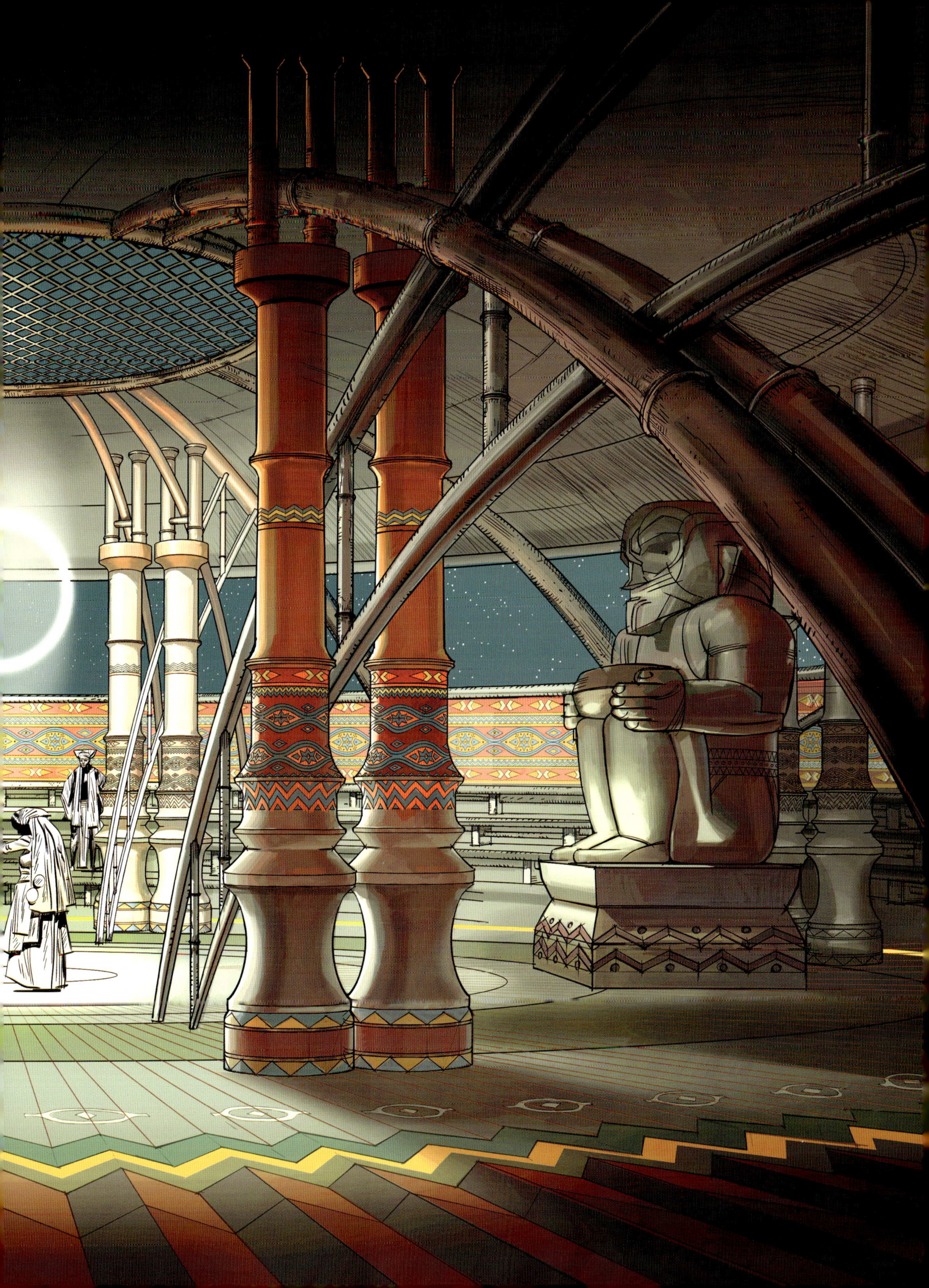

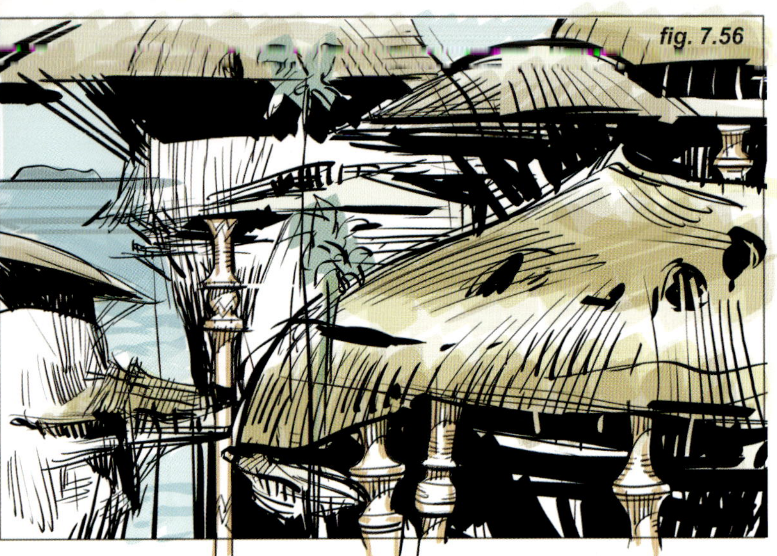

fig. 7.56

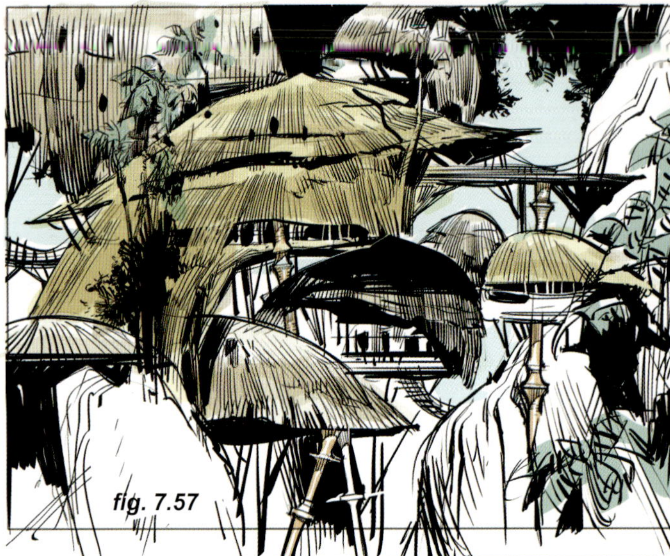

fig. 7.57

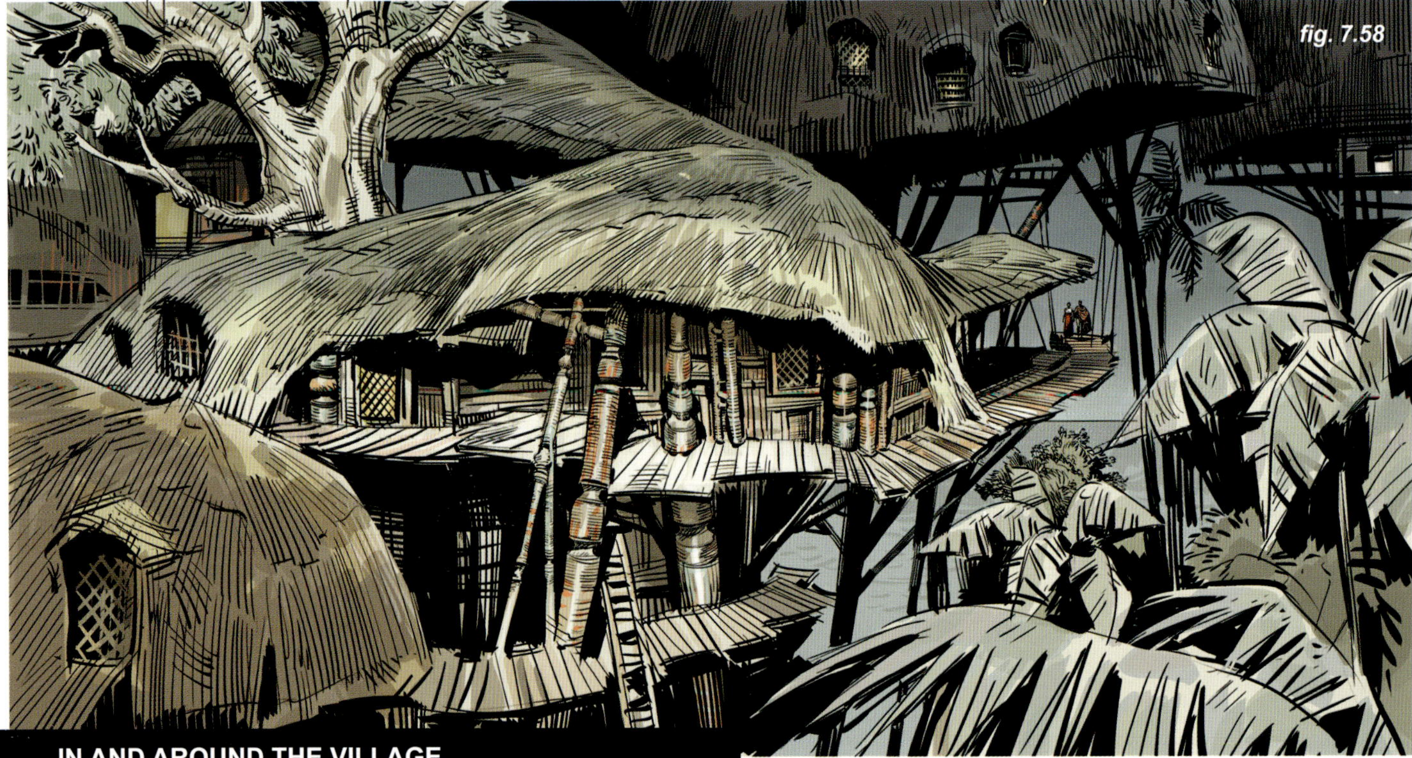

fig. 7.58

IN AND AROUND THE VILLAGE

Figs. 7.56, 7.57: Compositional ideas combining materials like straw, wood, trees, and negative spaces.

Figs. 7.58–7.60: Detailing a bit more now, bringing in vegetation as an element and playing with light and camera angles. Composing using the ideas of balance vs. imbalance and lines of tension, as explained in the book *Framed Ink, Vol. 2.*

Fig. 7.61: Interior view using a wide-angle lens of a big dome construction, grouping the structural elements, warping them, and decorating them, creating dynamics.

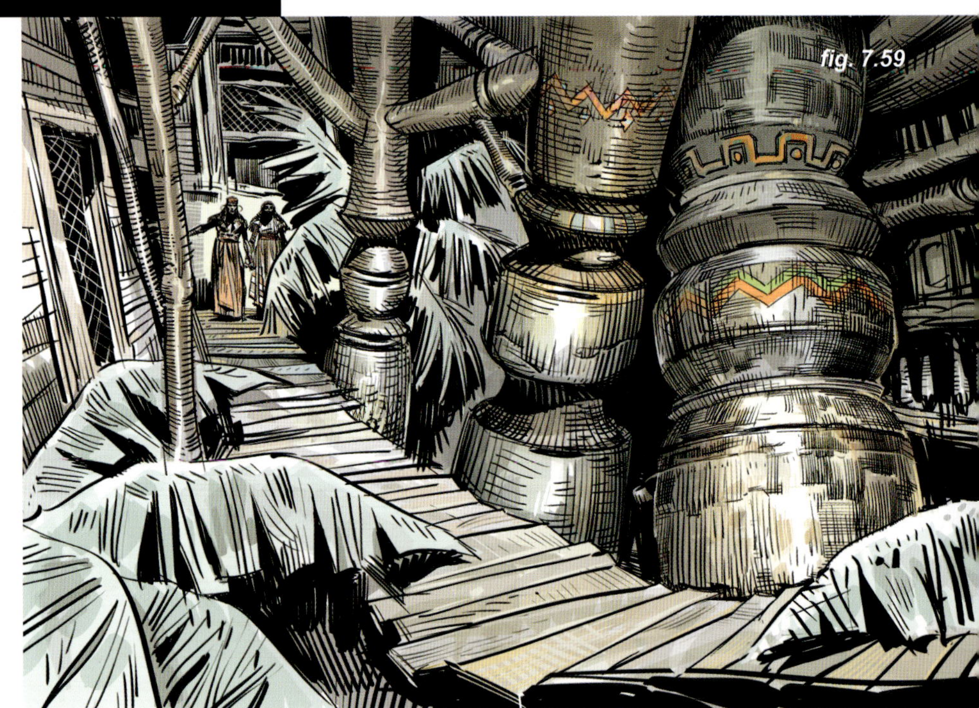

fig. 7.59

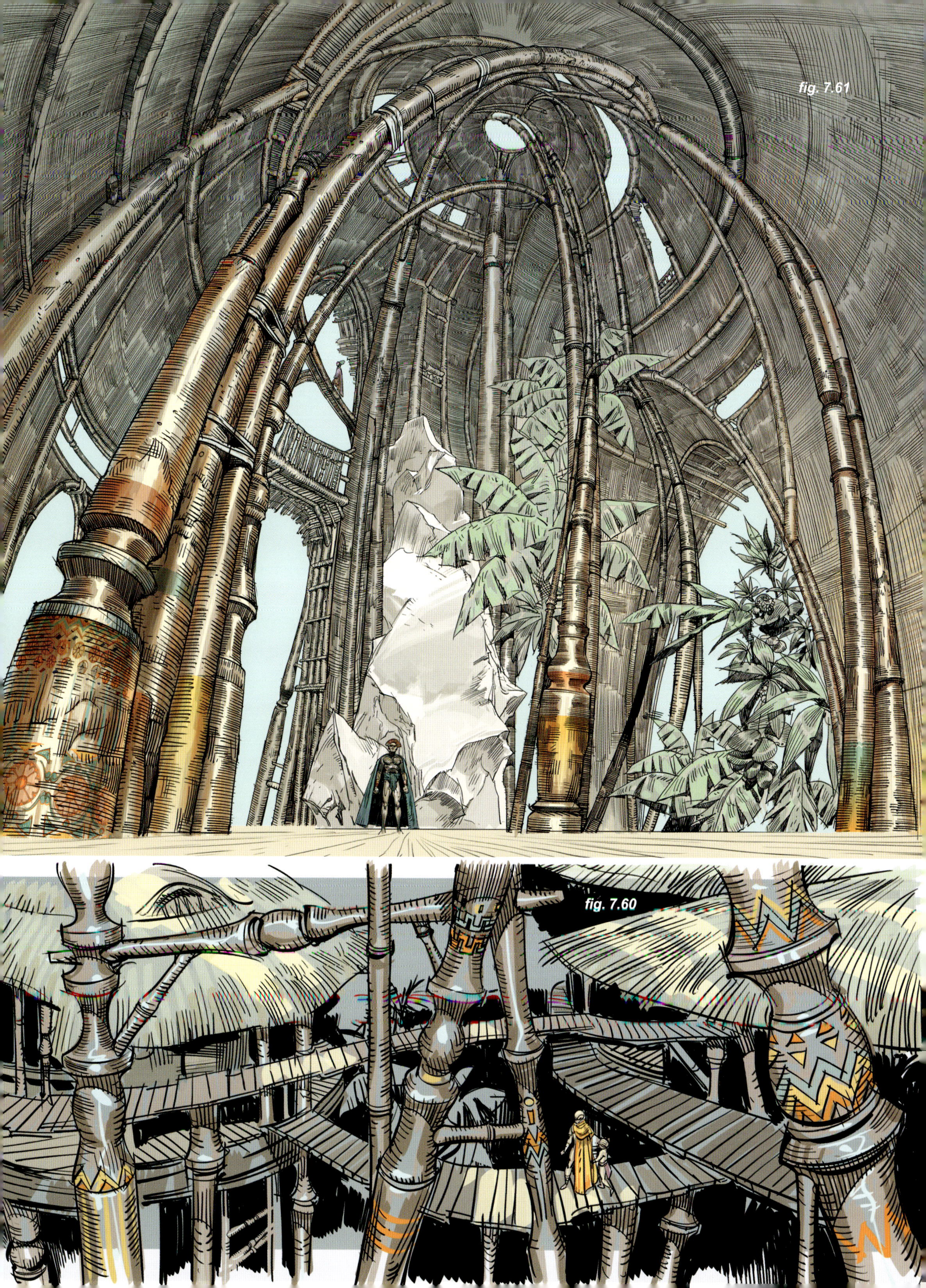

fig. 7.61
fig. 7.60

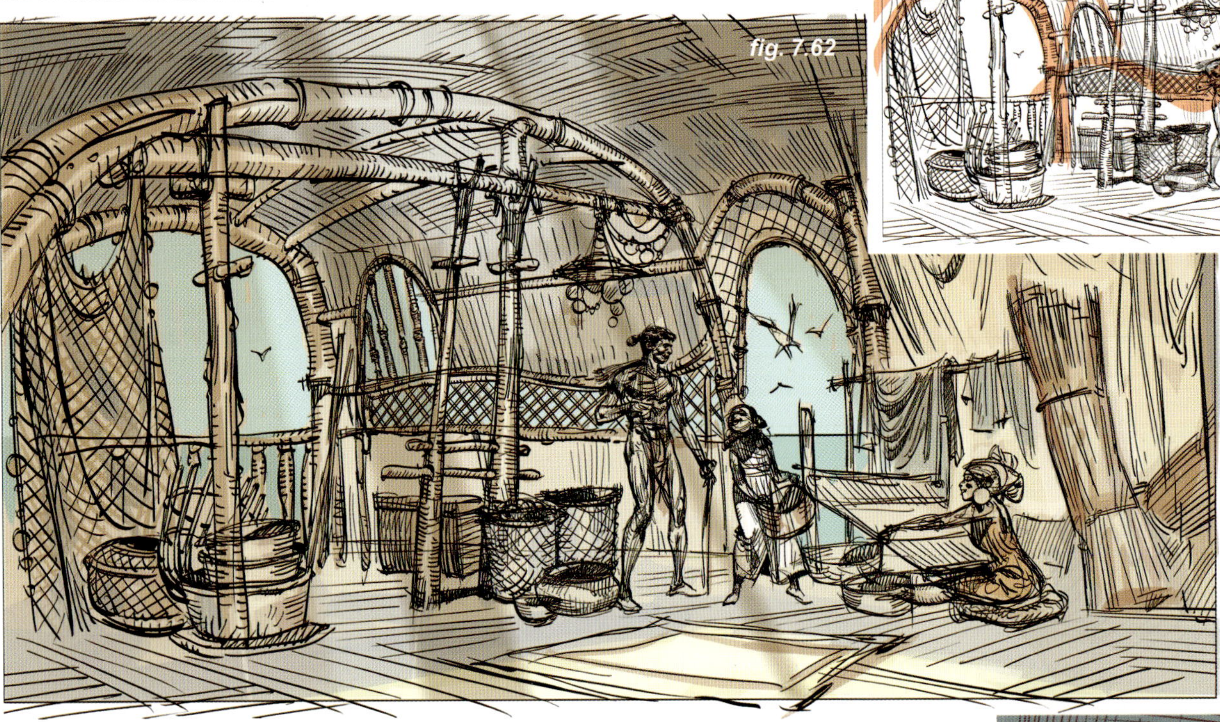

fig. 7.62

fig. 7.63

Figs. 7.62, 7.63: These first two studies for a humble fisherman's hut aim for a curvy shape language, as indicated by the red lines on the insert sketch. These shapes were already introduced in fig. 7.38 on page 179.

Figs. 7.64–7.66: Inspirational research was done for everyday tools.

Figs. 7.67–7.69: These sketches show a support structure that mimics the mechanism of an umbrella.

Fig. 7.70: The umbrella structure is represented in the final design.

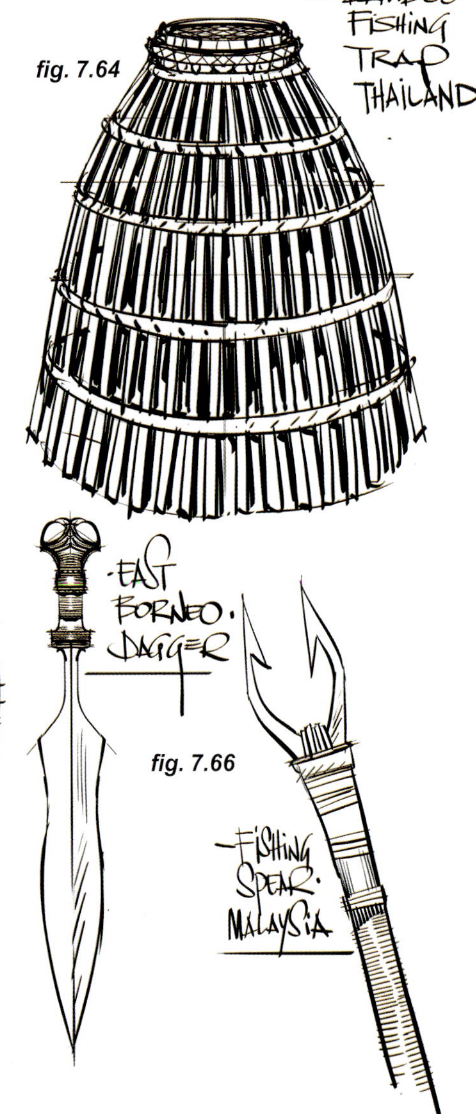

fig. 7.64

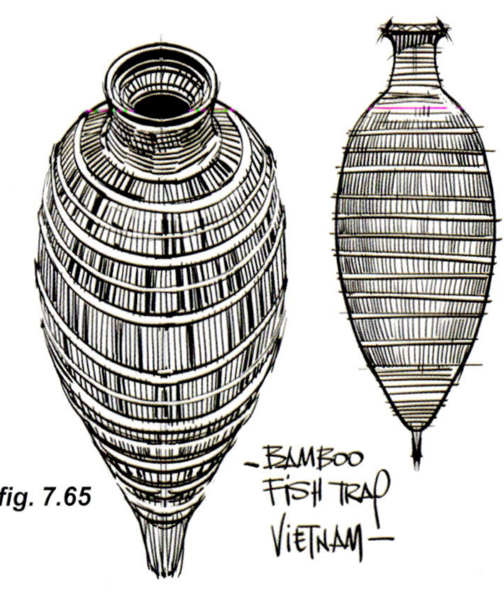

fig. 7.65

fig. 7.66

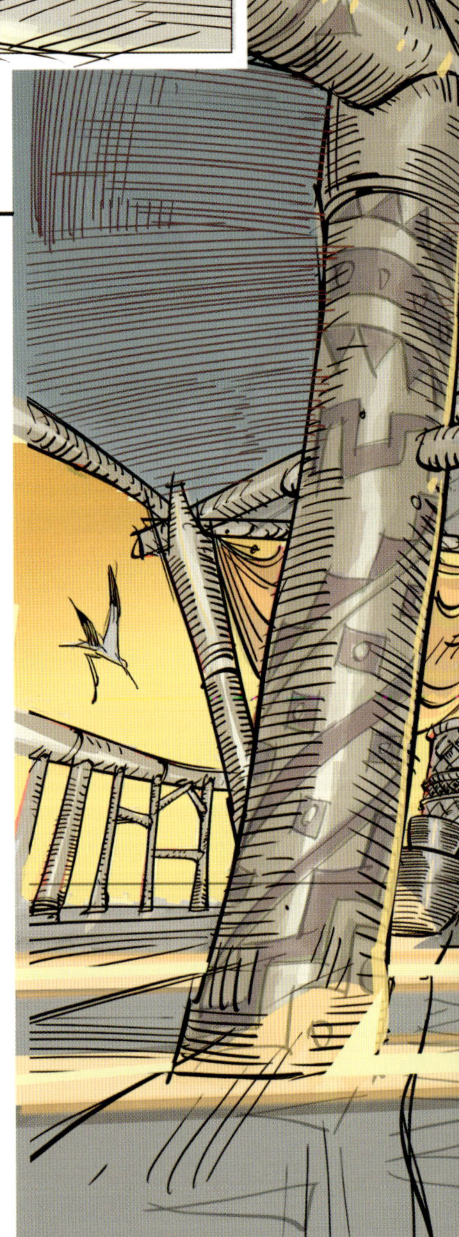

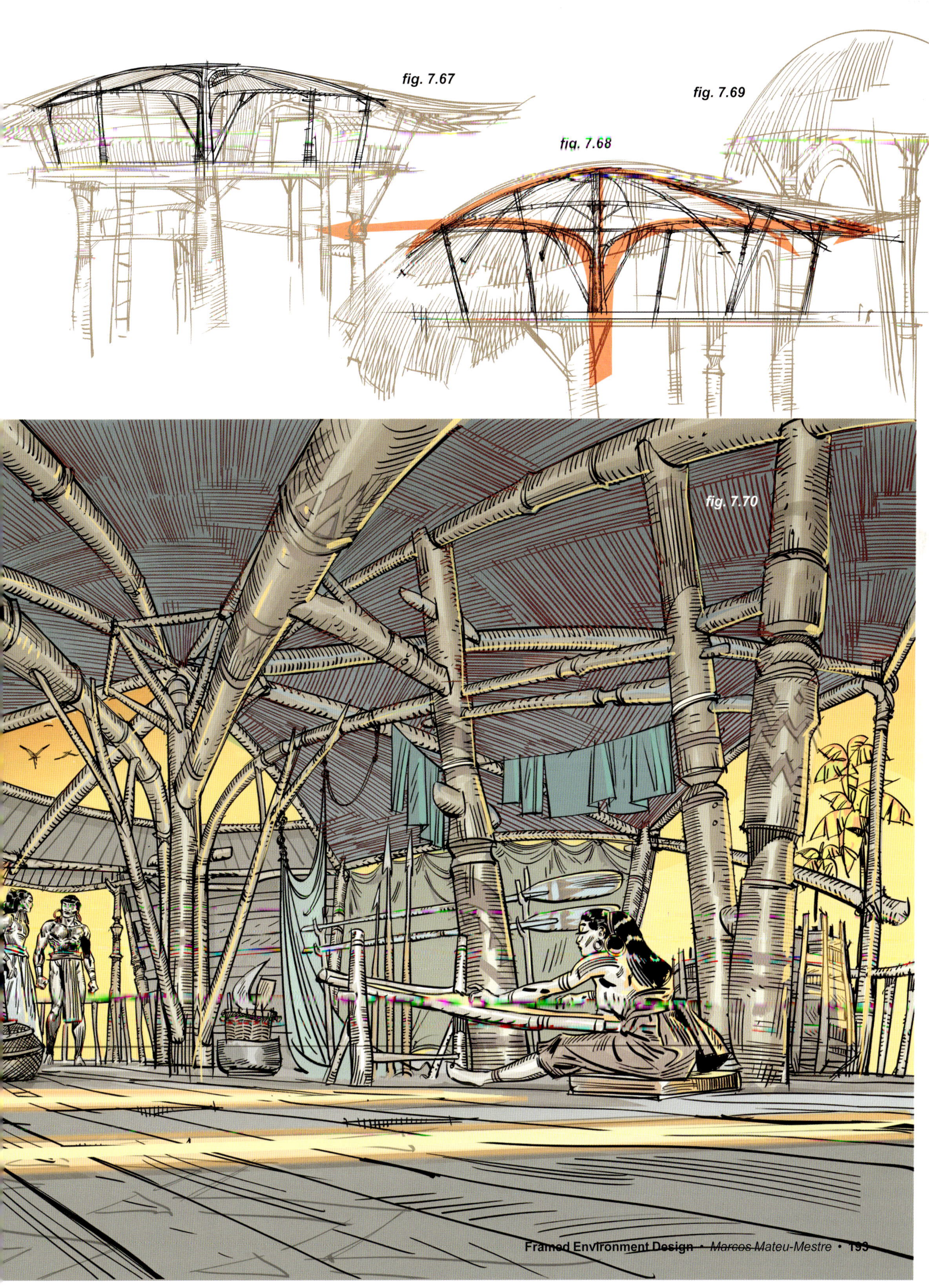

fig. 7.67
fig. 7.69
fig. 7.68
fig. 7.70

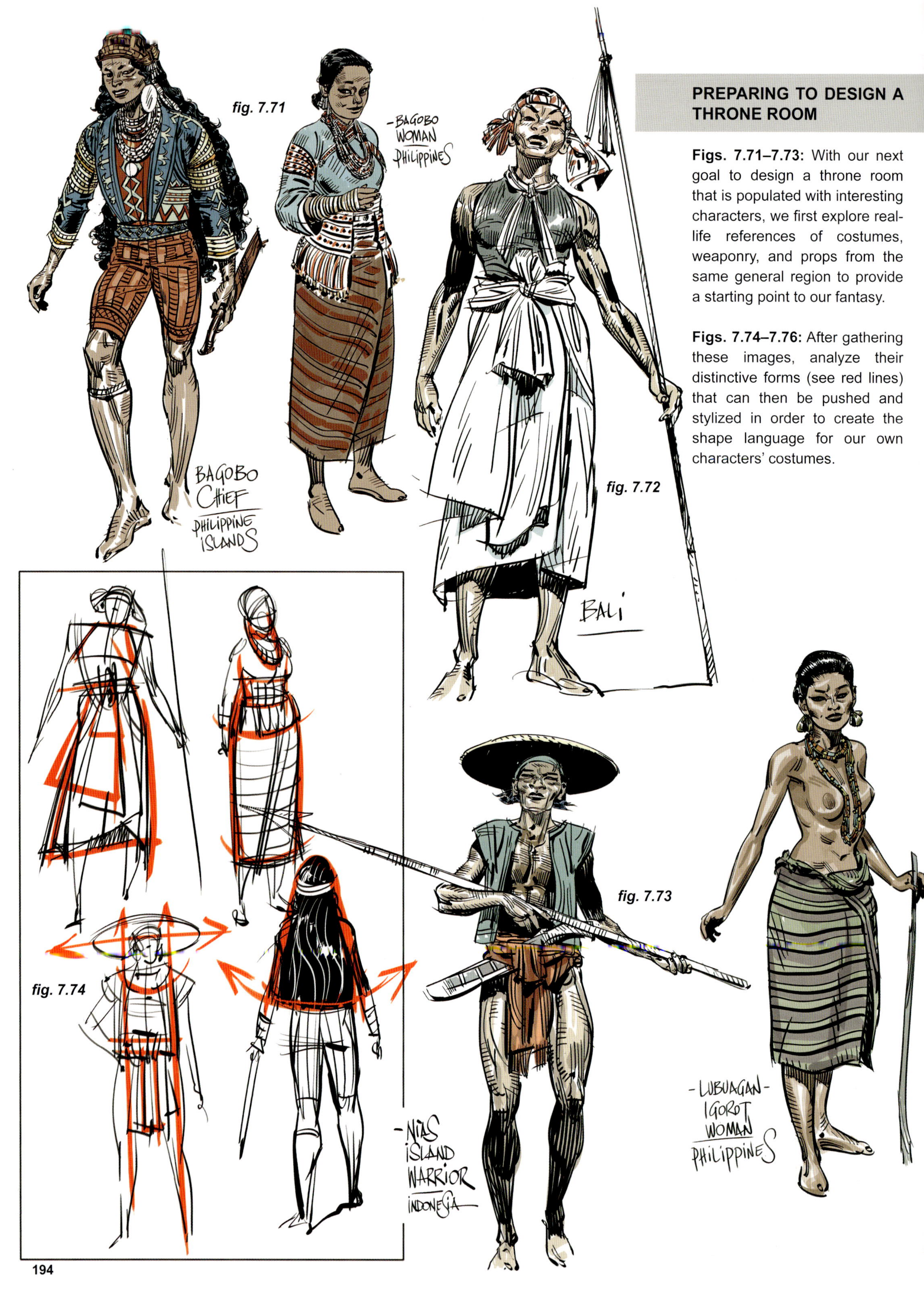

PREPARING TO DESIGN A THRONE ROOM

Figs. 7.71–7.73: With our next goal to design a throne room that is populated with interesting characters, we first explore real-life references of costumes, weaponry, and props from the same general region to provide a starting point to our fantasy.

Figs. 7.74–7.76: After gathering these images, analyze their distinctive forms (see red lines) that can then be pushed and stylized in order to create the shape language for our own characters' costumes.

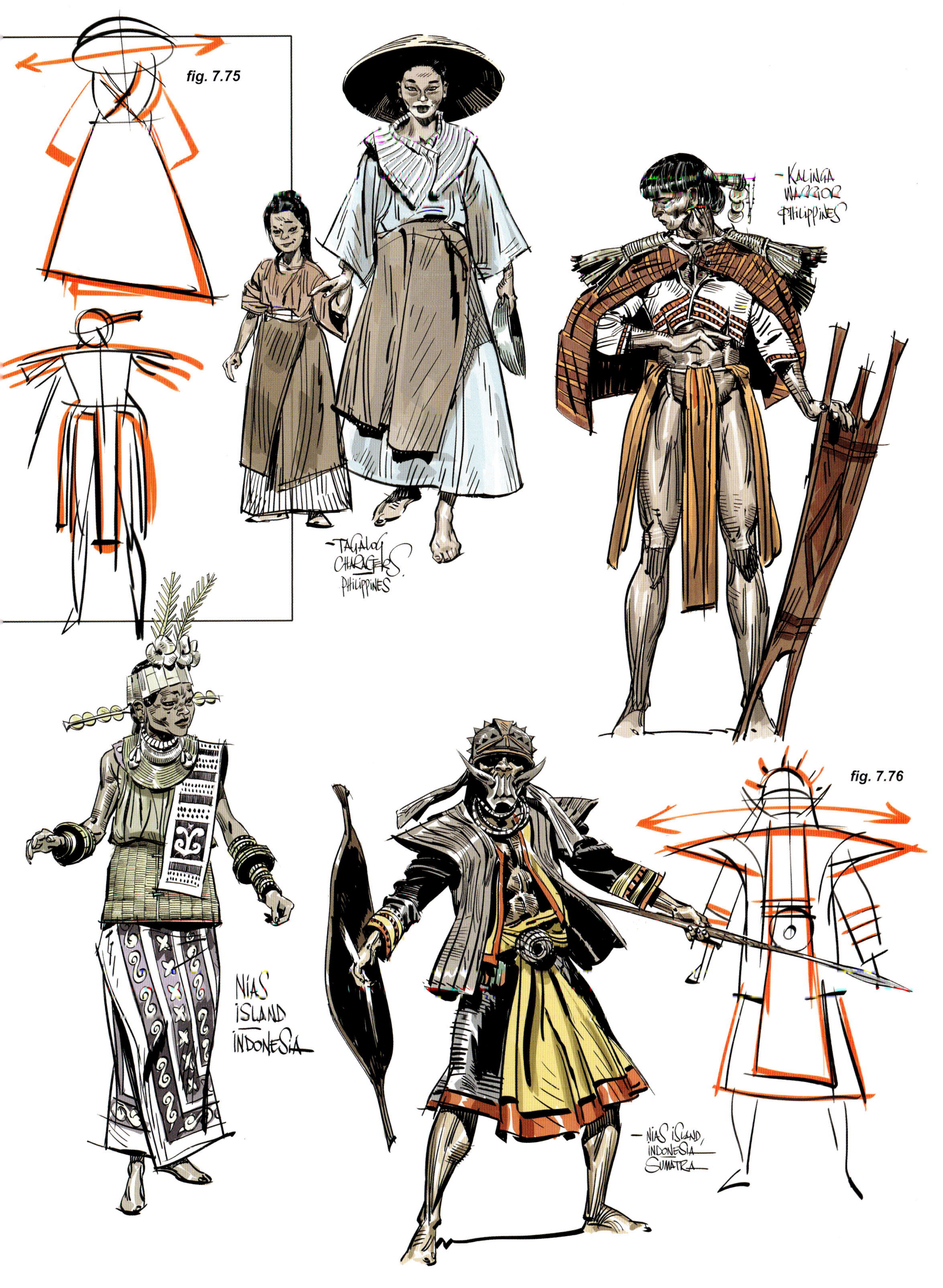

fig. 7.75
TAGALOG CHARACTERS. PHILIPPINES
KALINGA WARRIOR PHILIPPINES
NIAS ISLAND INDONESIA
NIAS ISLAND, INDONESIA SUMATRA
fig. 7.76

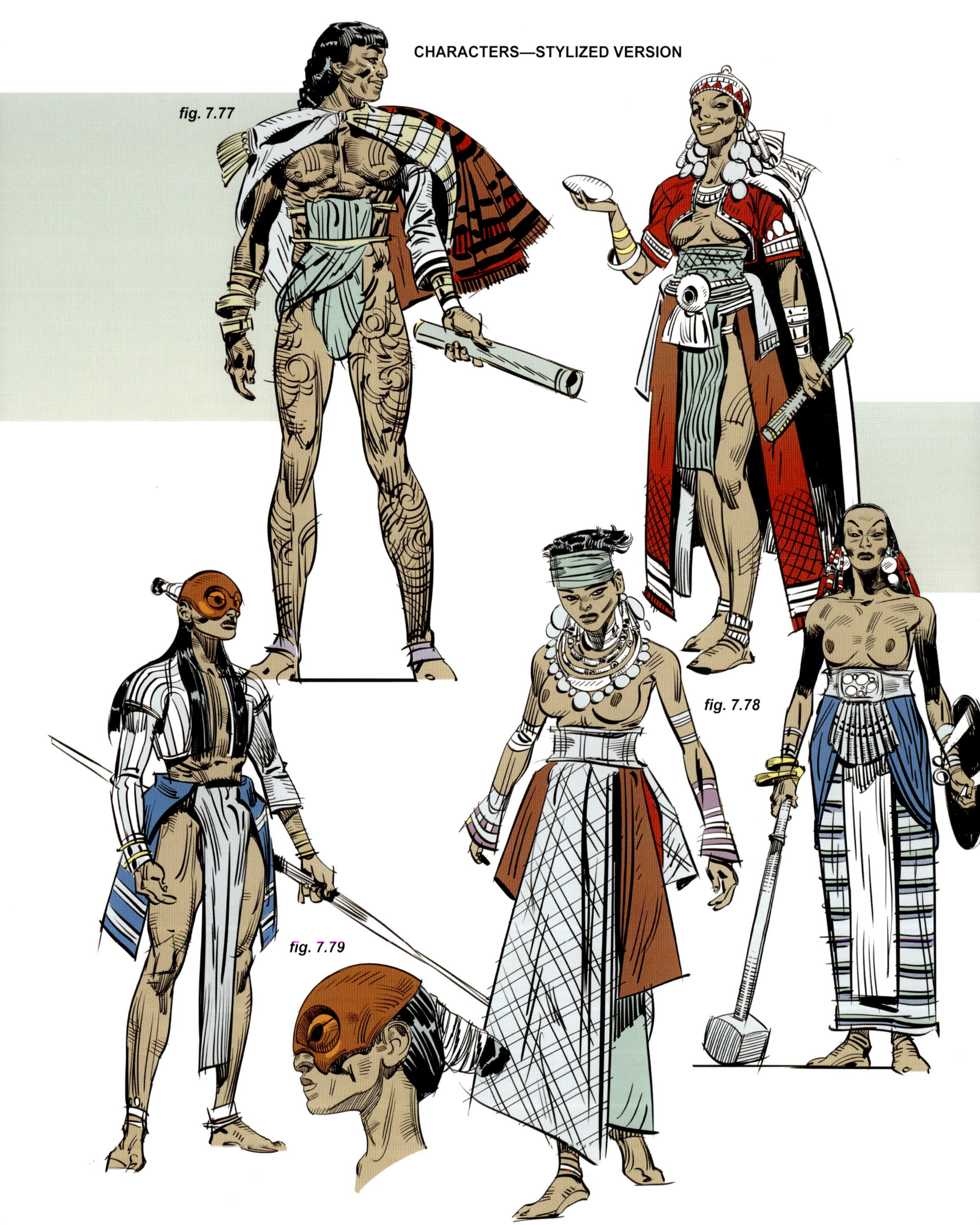
fig. 7.77
fig. 7.78
fig. 7.79

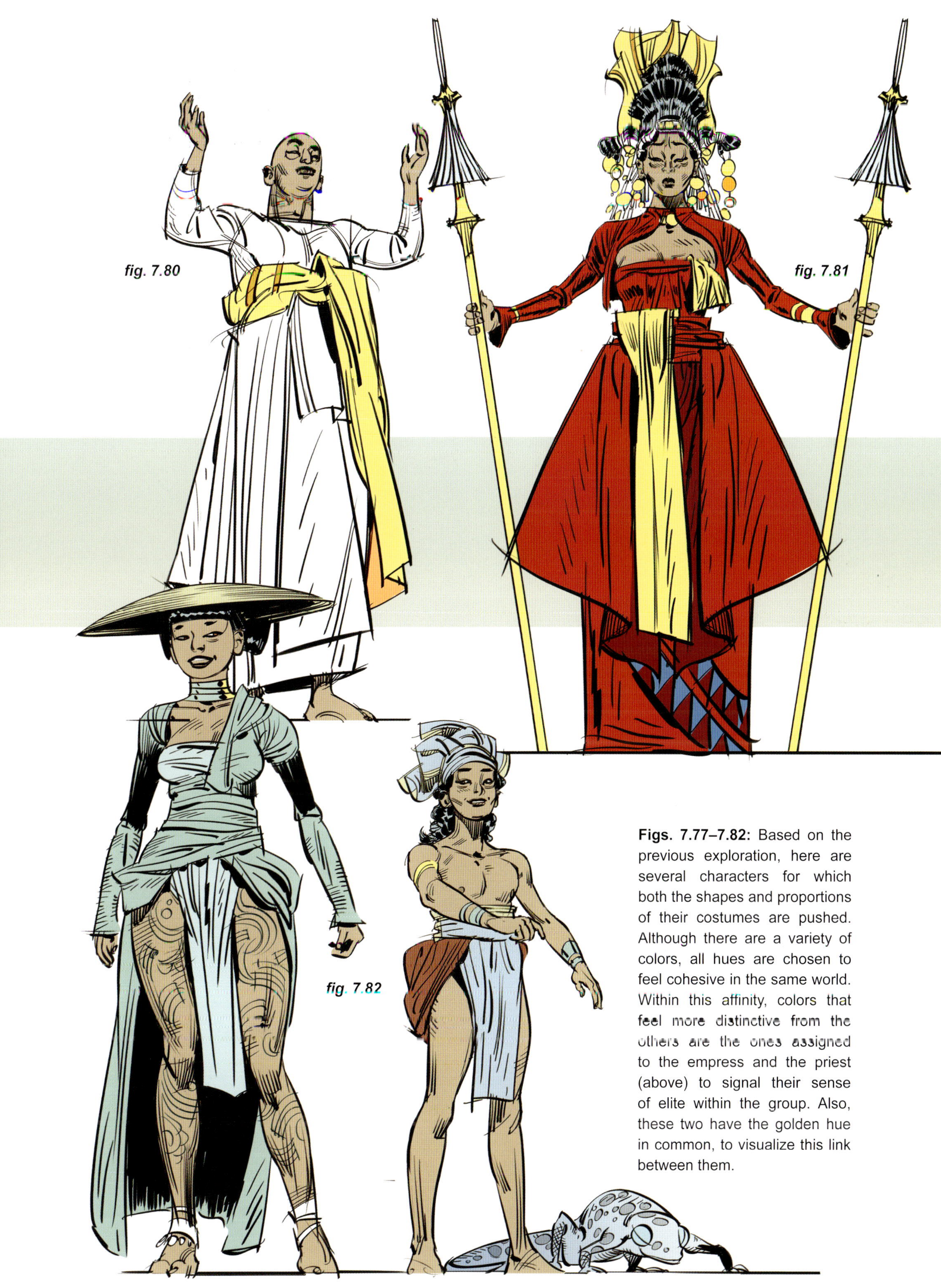

Figs. 7.77–7.82: Based on the previous exploration, here are several characters for which both the shapes and proportions of their costumes are pushed. Although there are a variety of colors, all hues are chosen to feel cohesive in the same world. Within this affinity, colors that feel more distinctive from the others are the ones assigned to the empress and the priest (above) to signal their sense of elite within the group. Also, these two have the golden hue in common, to visualize this link between them.

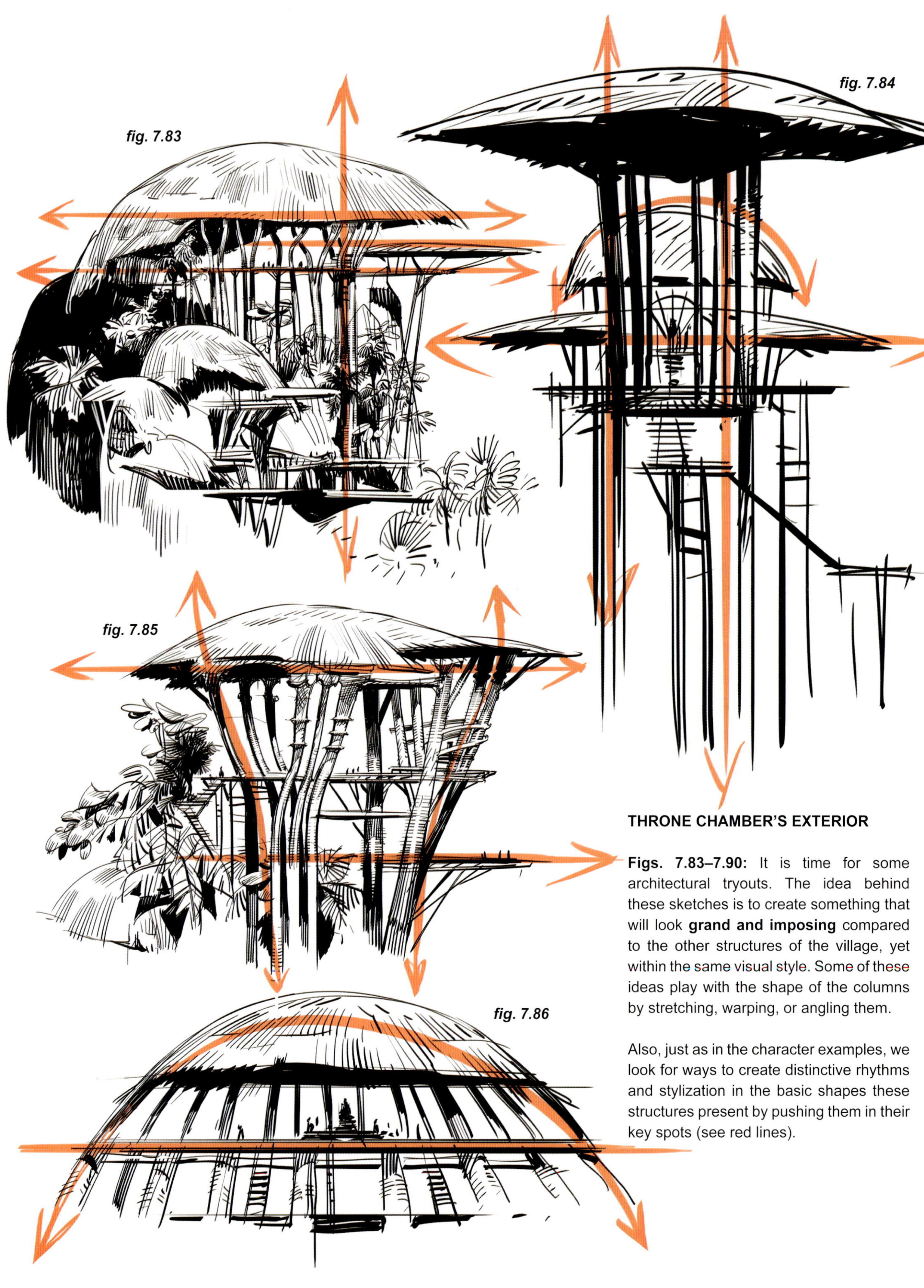

fig. 7.83

fig. 7.84

fig. 7.85

fig. 7.86

THRONE CHAMBER'S EXTERIOR

Figs. 7.83–7.90: It is time for some architectural tryouts. The idea behind these sketches is to create something that will look **grand and imposing** compared to the other structures of the village, yet within the same visual style. Some of these ideas play with the shape of the columns by stretching, warping, or angling them.

Also, just as in the character examples, we look for ways to create distinctive rhythms and stylization in the basic shapes these structures present by pushing them in their key spots (see red lines).

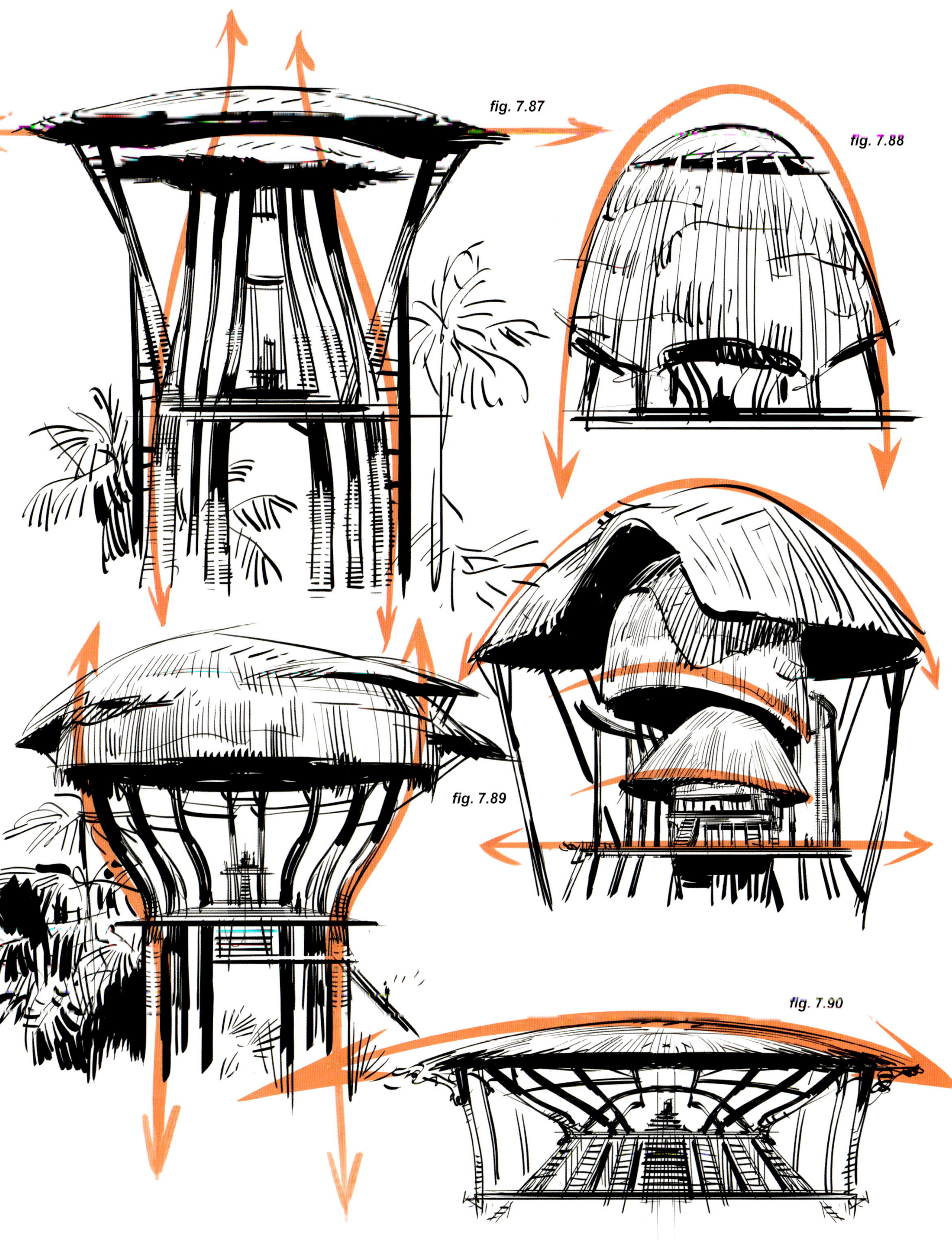

fig. 7.87
fig. 7.88
fig. 7.89
fig. 7.90

Figs. 7.91–7.94: More quick sketches for the same location, but this time studying the interior structure.

The concept is to have a building on an elevated spot within the village that has an elaborate and interesting structure of beams and columns, within the overall style we have already created, showing a level of solemnity appropriate for such a regal place.

The space will be grand, complex, and rich in detail, with a throne placed on an elevated platform.

This overall structure will support a dome-shaped roof and will have an opening all around, a sort of 360-degree window or balcony that will allow us to see the surrounding ocean and jungle from there, no matter what direction we are looking. This grand backdrop will give the whole site a very cinematic sense of space.

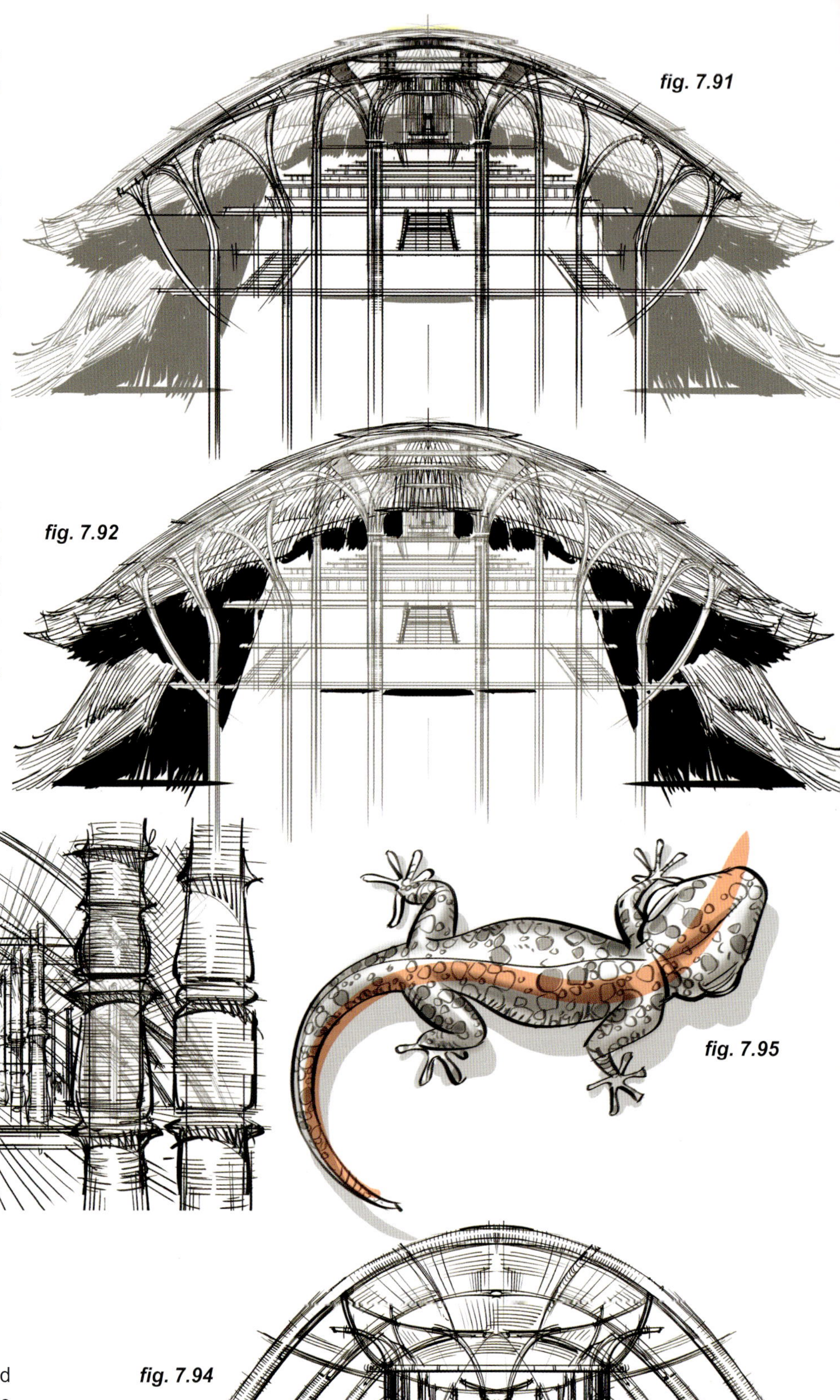

Figs. 7.95, 7.96: We have finally decided on a V-shape basic design with S-shape warped columns, to then build from there. These shapes make the structure appear more vibrant and interesting than other combinations. It is a design that can be linked, for example, to organic shapes such as that of a common salamander from the area (fig. 7.95), which, in our fantastical world, might have a special symbolism.

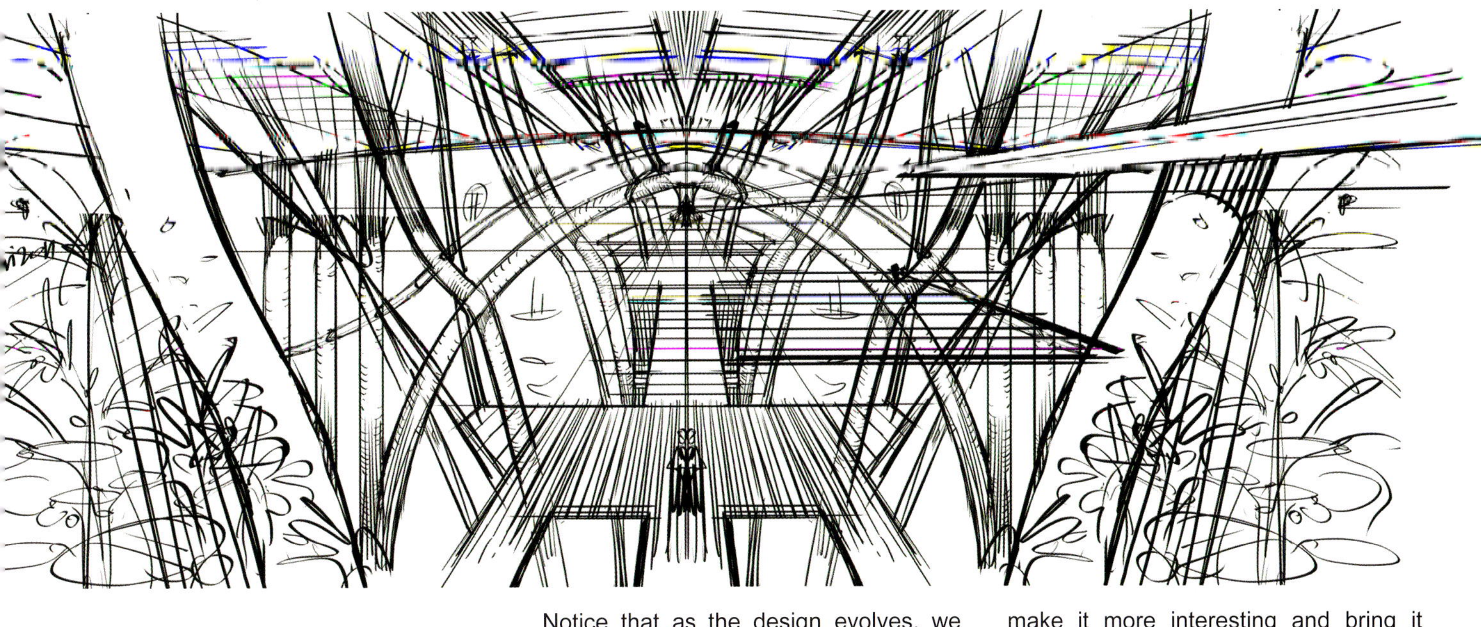

Notice that as the design evolves, we make sure to **break its symmetry** by including some straight, diagonal support columns in a variety of thicknesses to make it more interesting and bring it more toward the overall tone of its **wild and natural** surroundings.

fig. 7.96

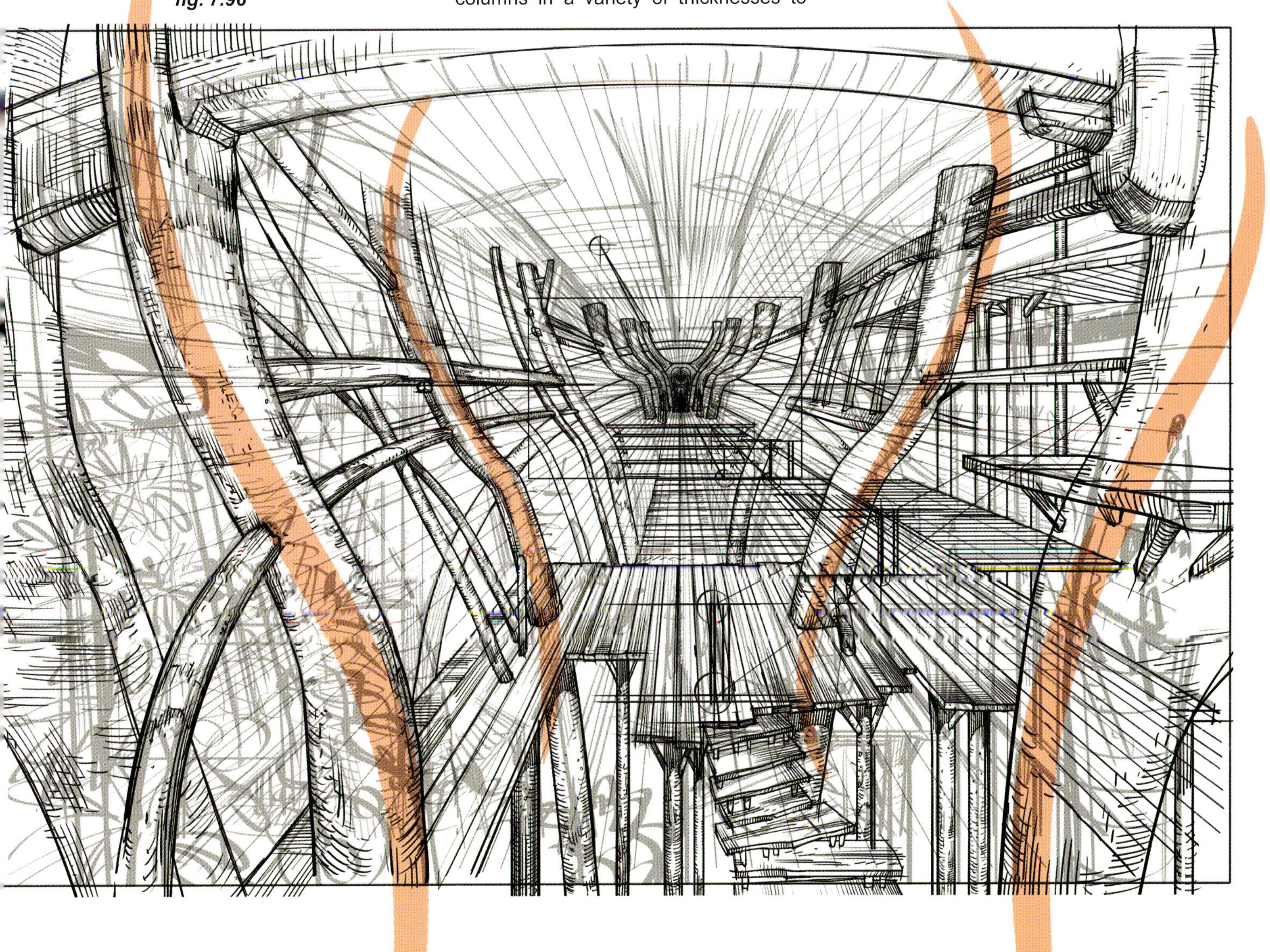

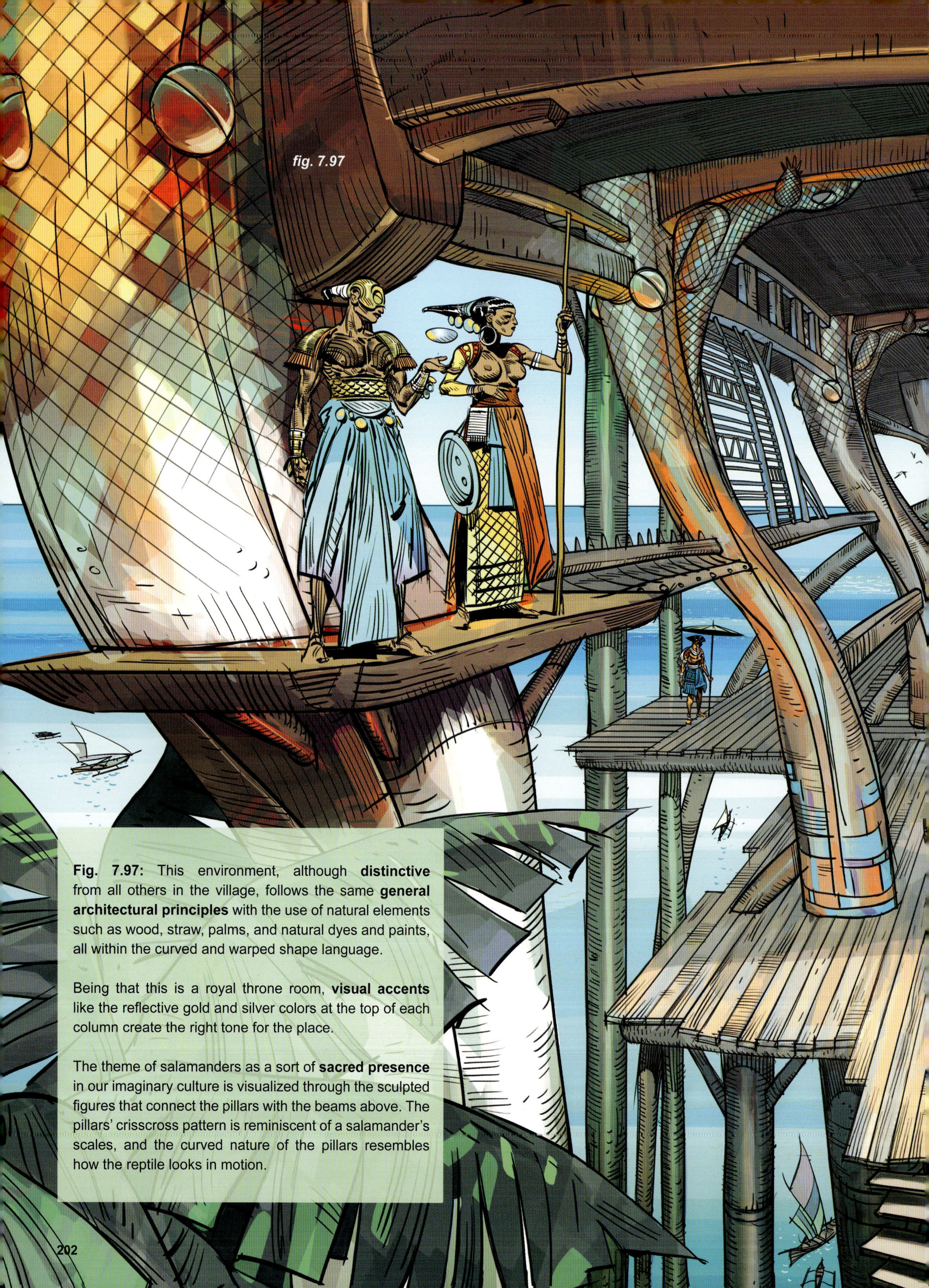

Fig. 7.97: This environment, although **distinctive** from all others in the village, follows the same **general architectural principles** with the use of natural elements such as wood, straw, palms, and natural dyes and paints, all within the curved and warped shape language.

Being that this is a royal throne room, **visual accents** like the reflective gold and silver colors at the top of each column create the right tone for the place.

The theme of salamanders as a sort of **sacred presence** in our imaginary culture is visualized through the sculpted figures that connect the pillars with the beams above. The pillars' crisscross pattern is reminiscent of a salamander's scales, and the curved nature of the pillars resembles how the reptile looks in motion.

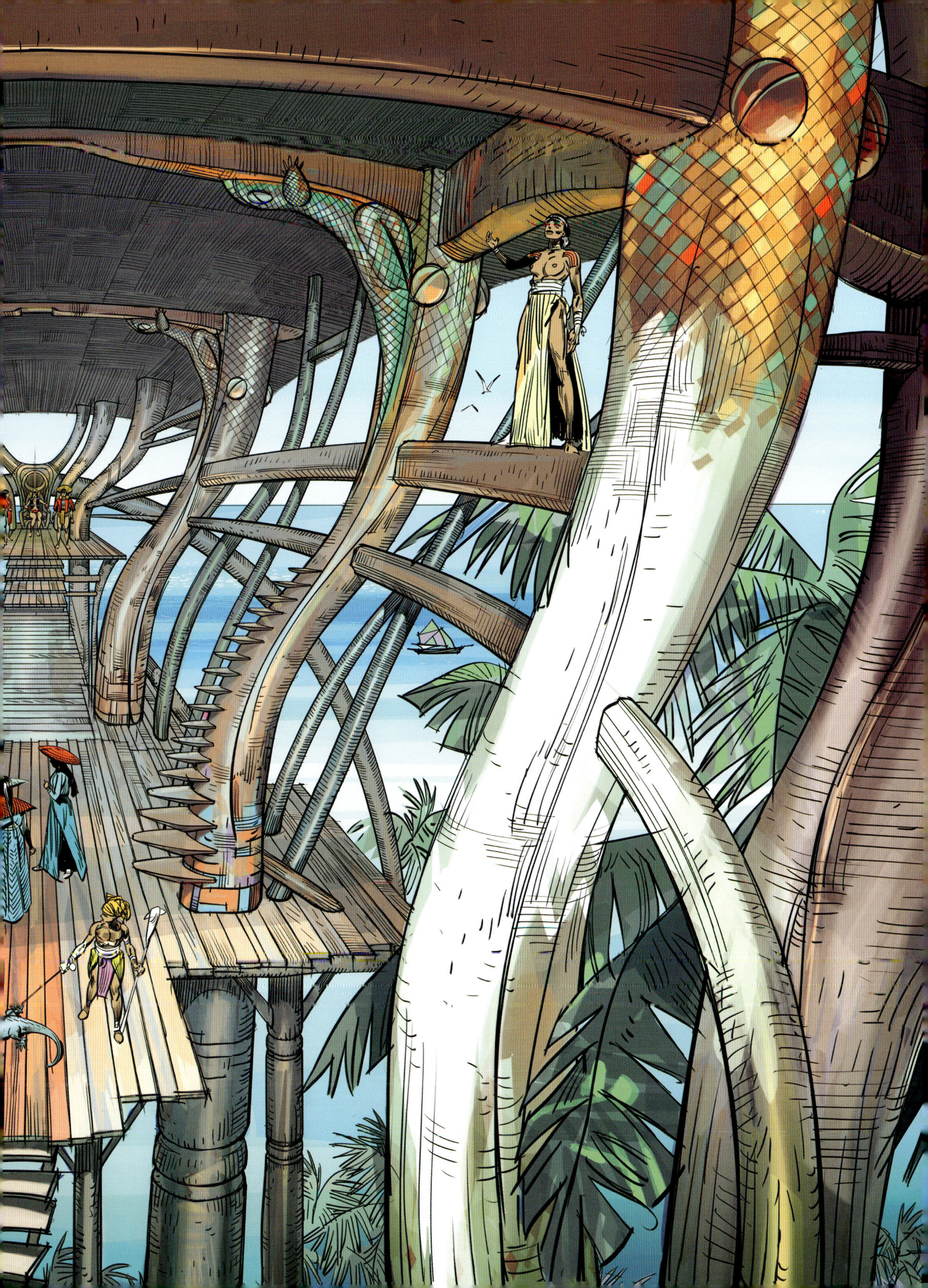

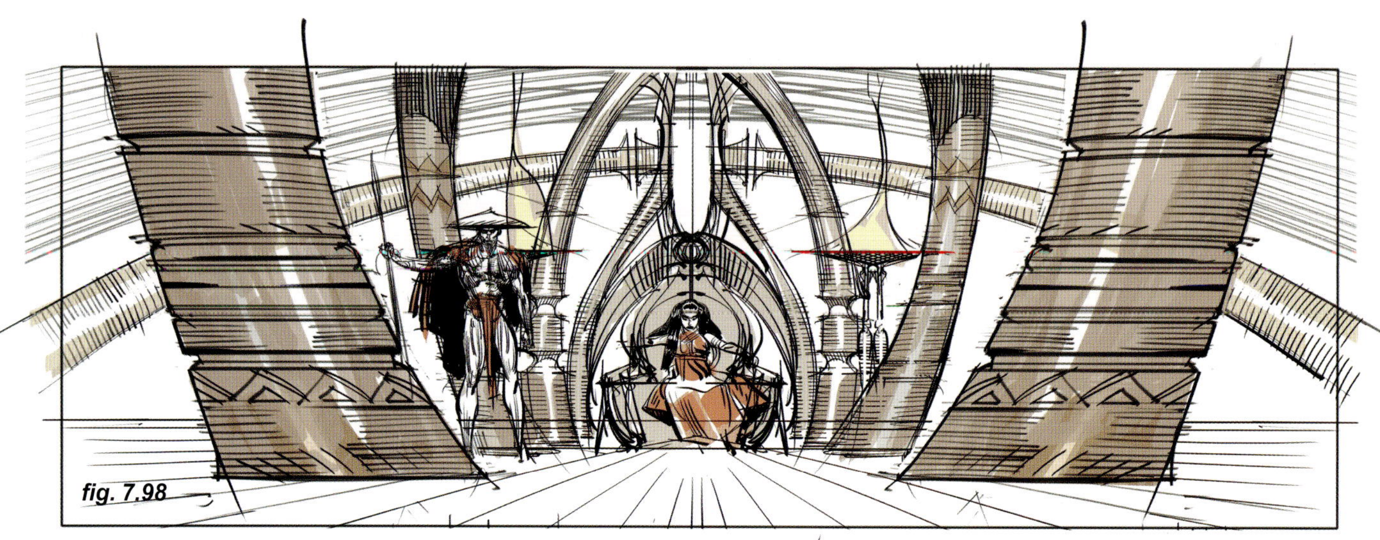

fig. 7.98

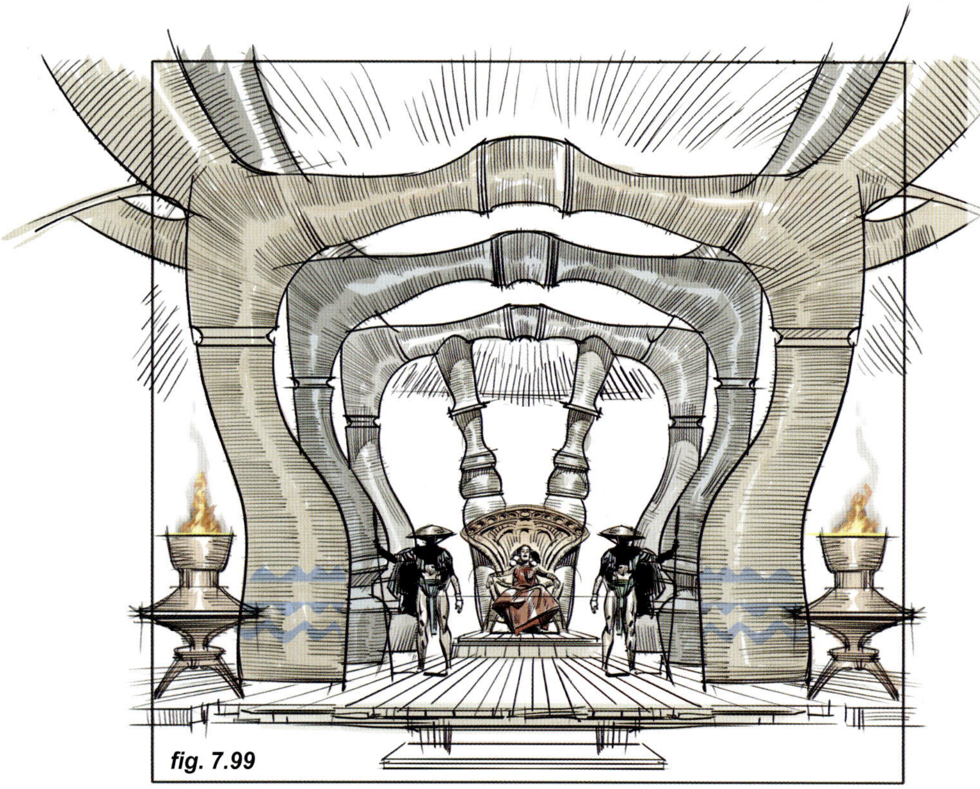

Figs. 7.98–7.100: Now that the general view of the throne room has been established, we focus on the main spot in the location, the throne itself, and start by doing several more detailed, "solemn-looking" sketches that set the proper tone, a few of which are seen here.

Fig. 7.101: The final decision was to go for a design closest to the one already defined in the general view.

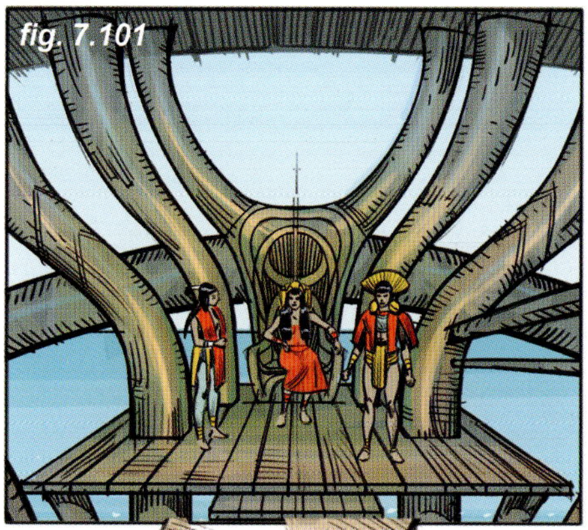

fig. 7.101

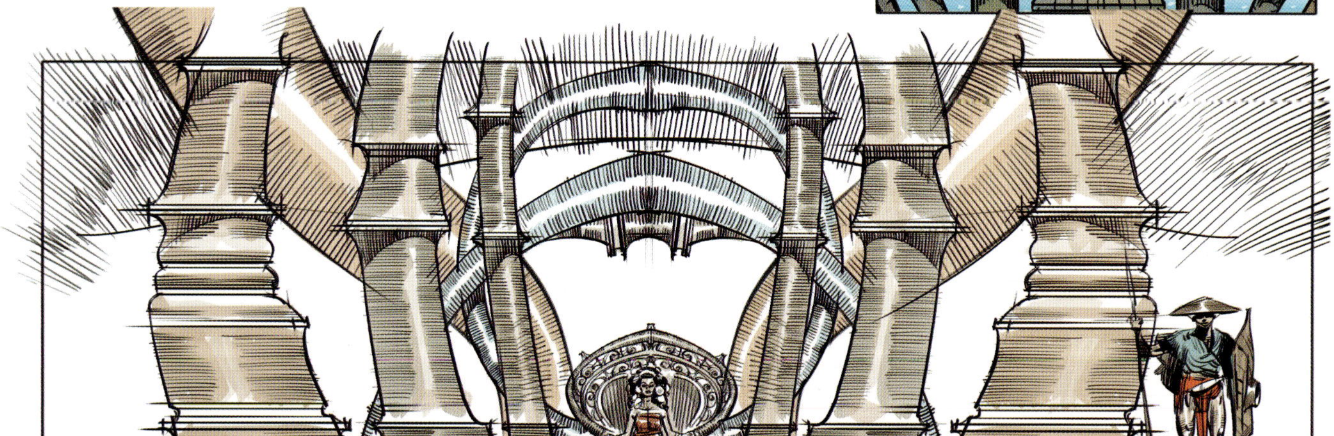

fig. 7.99

fig. 7.100

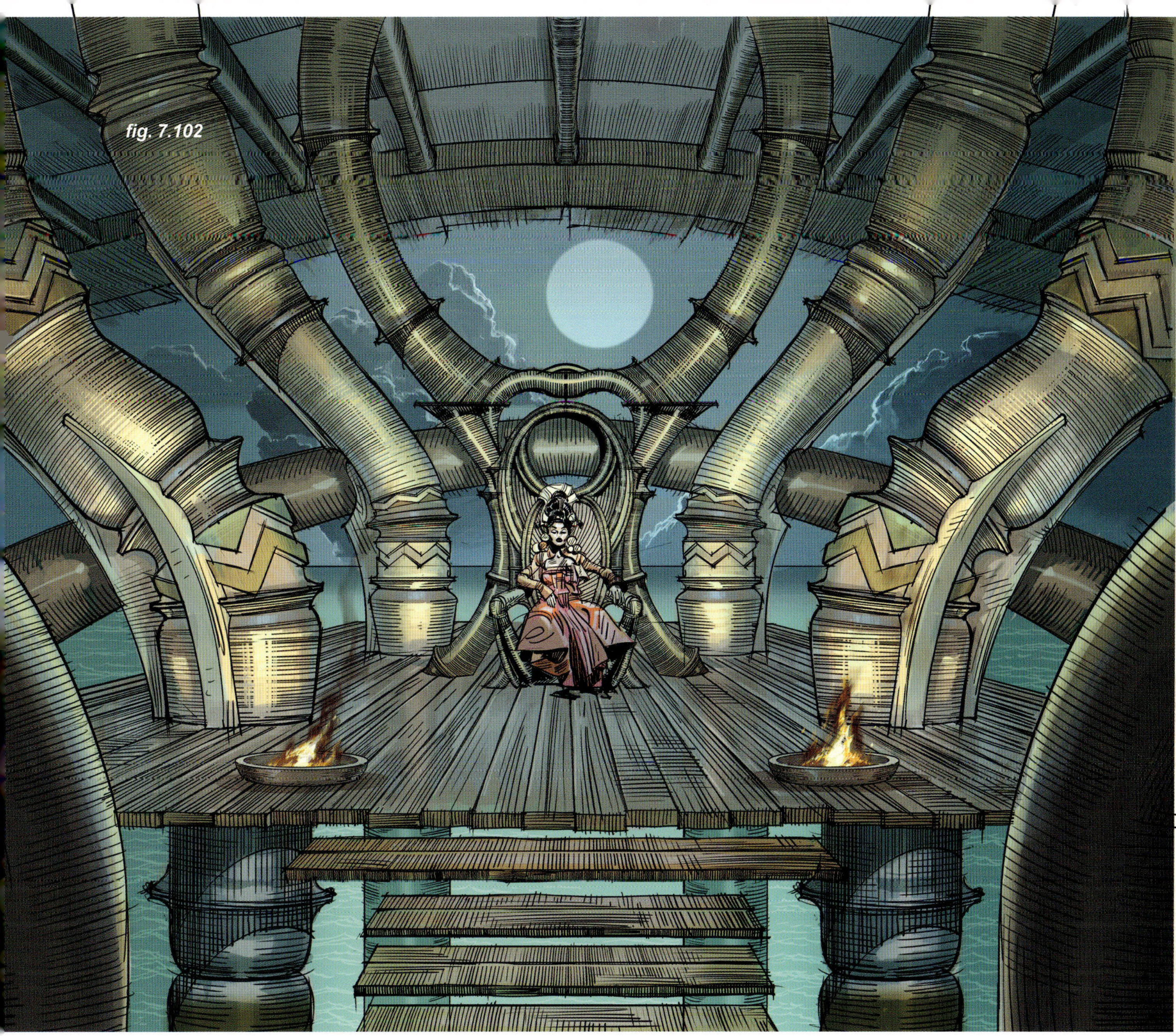

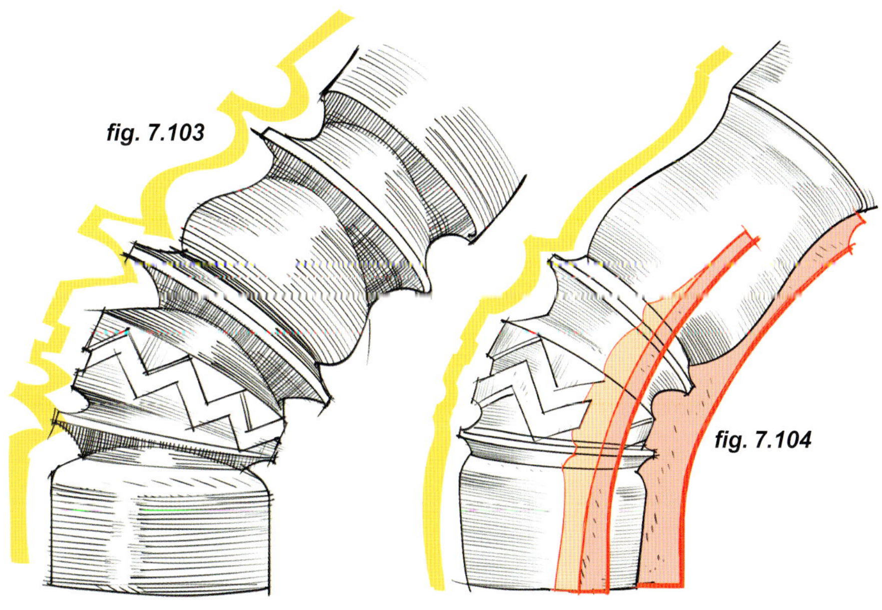

Fig. 7.102: In keeping with fig. 7.11's reference (page 167), carved and sculptural details were integrated into the S-shaped columns that surround the throne, just as they were with the design of the Ceremonial Room (pages 188–89.)

Fig. 7.103: In a first version, these shapes are so pushed they look like disconnected pieces of a beaded necklace, rather than a strong and stable support for an architectural structure like this.

Fig. 7.104: So, two changes were made. First, the sculpted shapes were softened and minimized (in yellow), and backbone-style supports were added to the sides of the columns (in red) for a more reinforced, solid look.

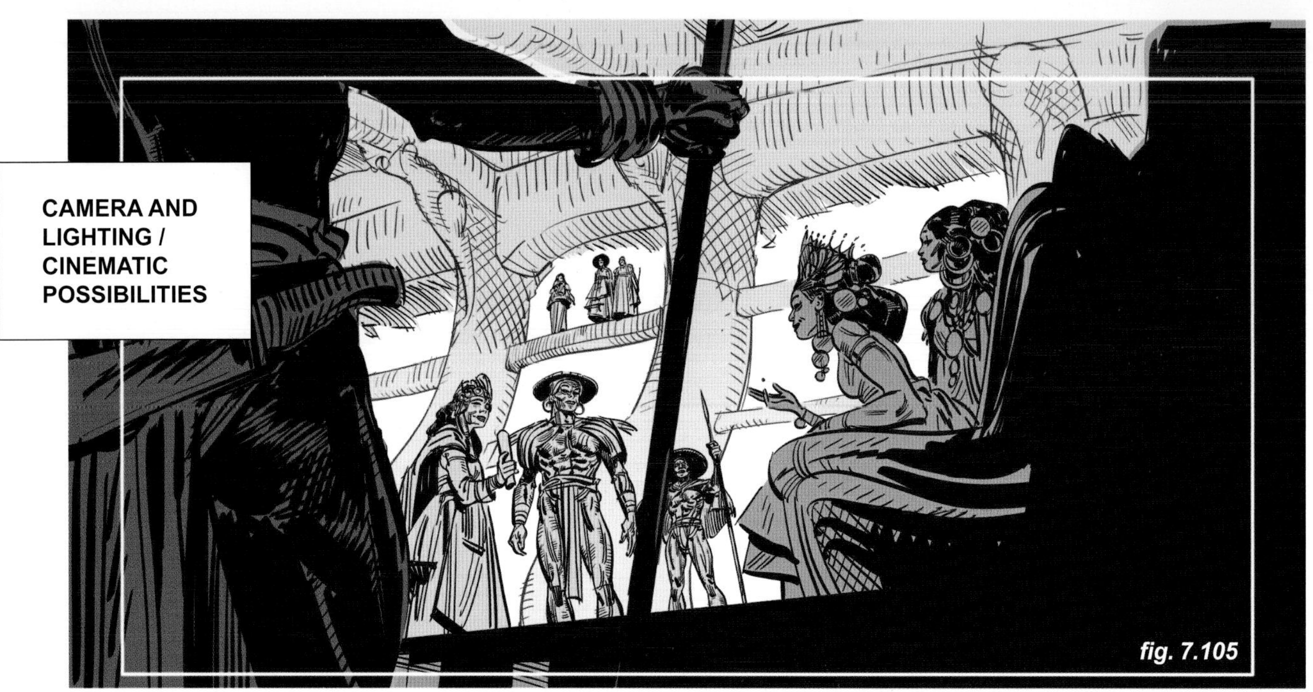

fig. 7.105

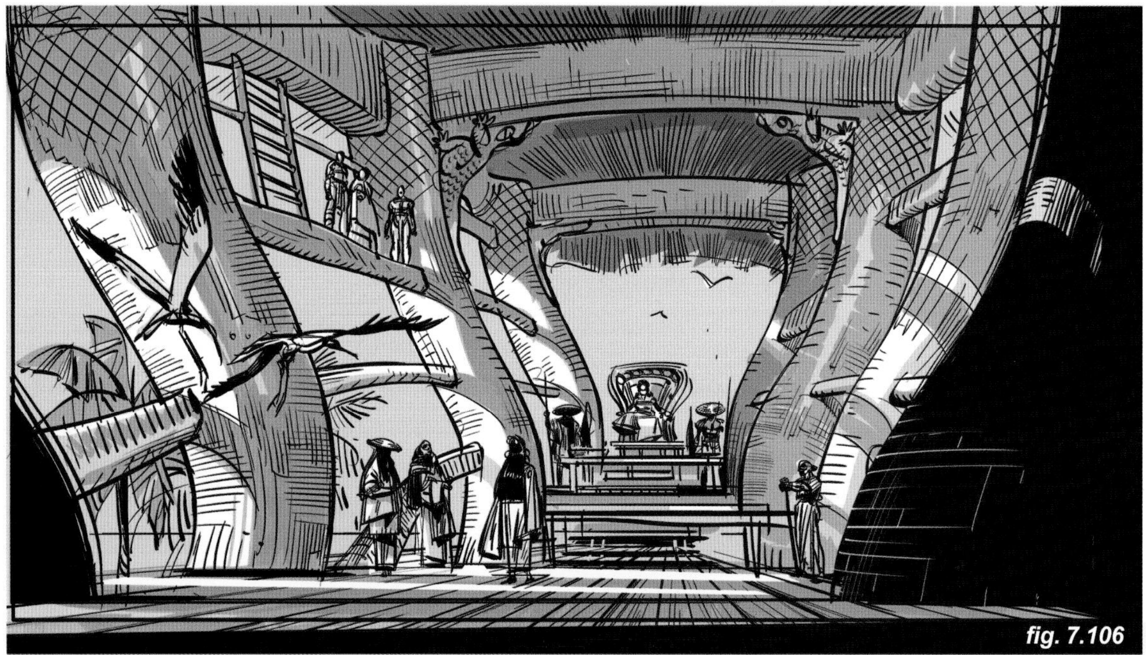

fig. 7.106

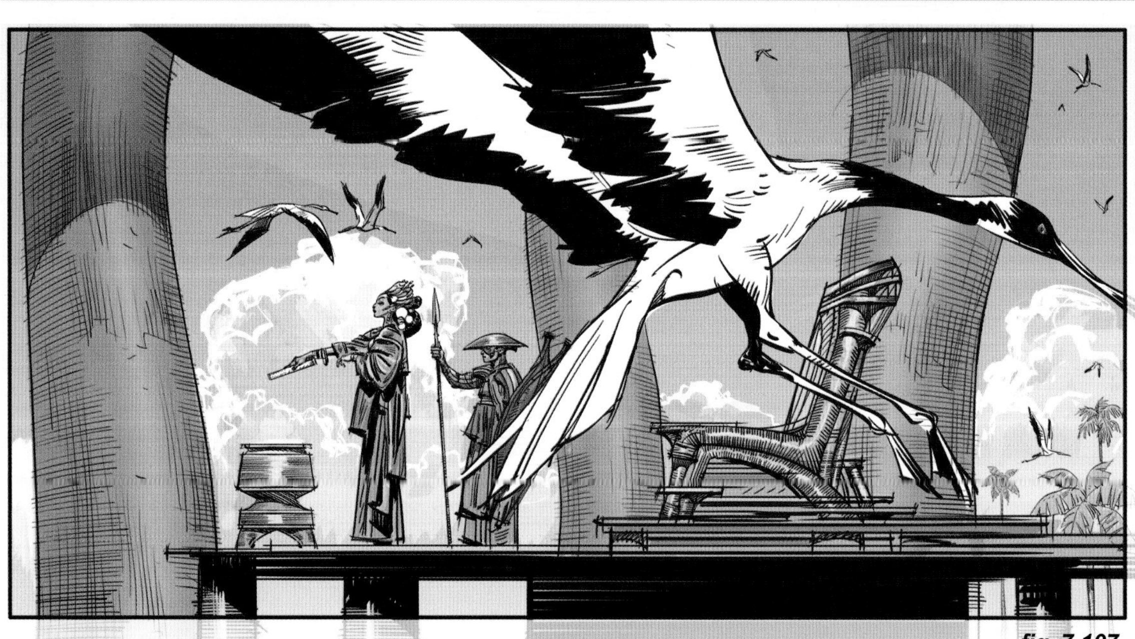

fig. 7.107

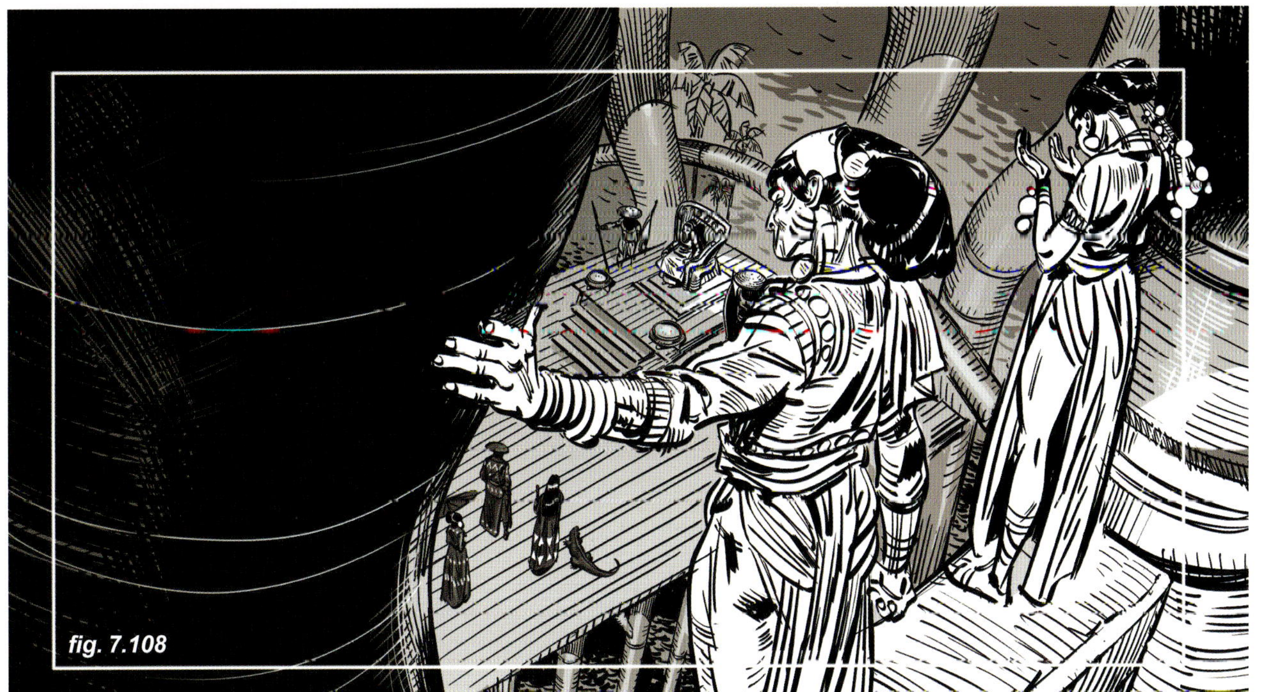

fig. 7.108

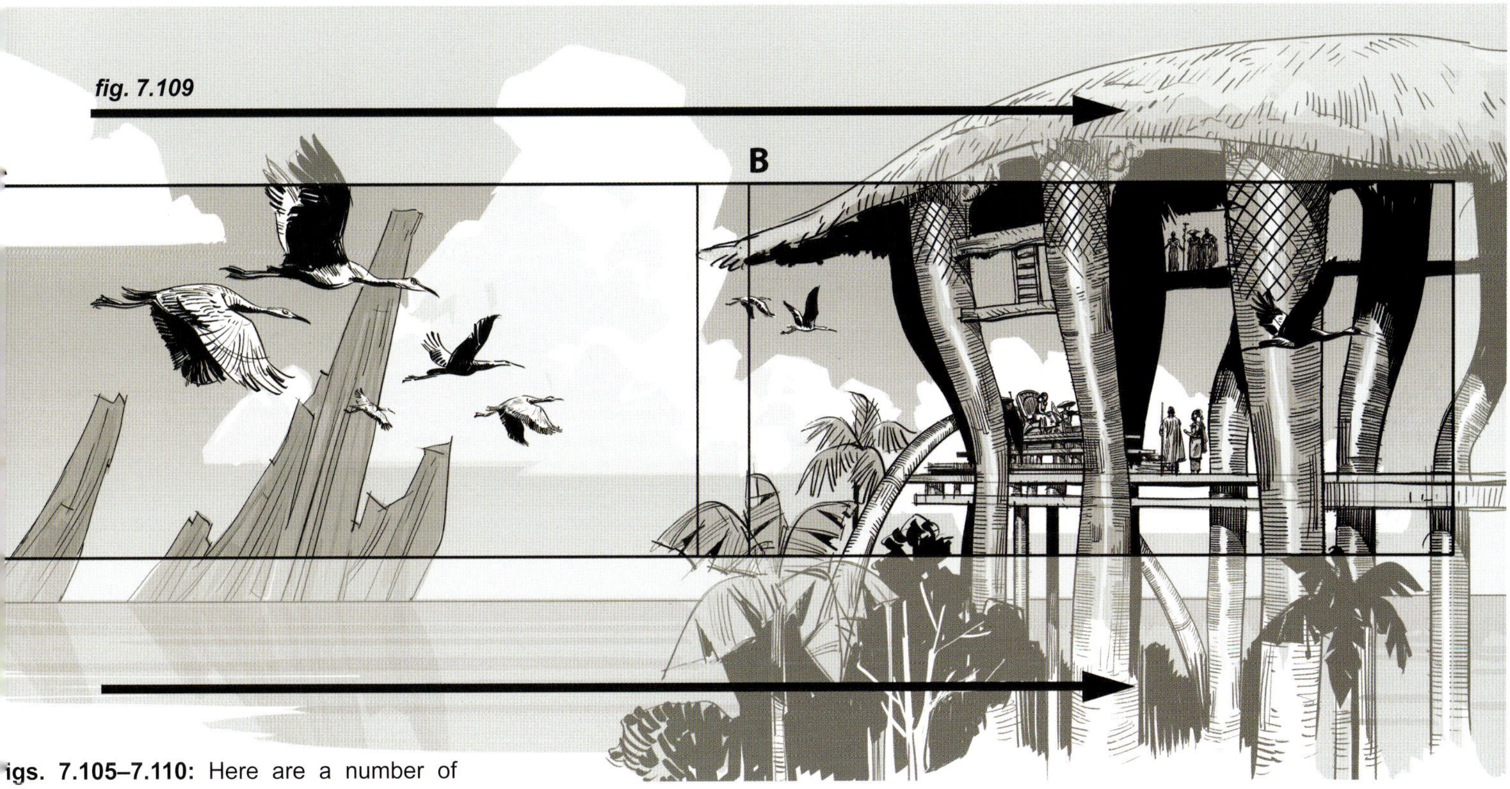

fig. 7.109

 Here are a number of
framing ideas.

Given the airy, open space of this location, we
can use devices such as birds to help create
interesting moments of depth and motion
in the shot. These cranes really add to the
cinematic feel and can motivate a camera
move, if needed (see *Framed Ink,* page 060).

The long tracking shot in fig. 7.109 above
shows how these flying cranes lead us from a
view of the open sky **(A)** directly to an exterior
wide shot of the village's throne room **(B).**

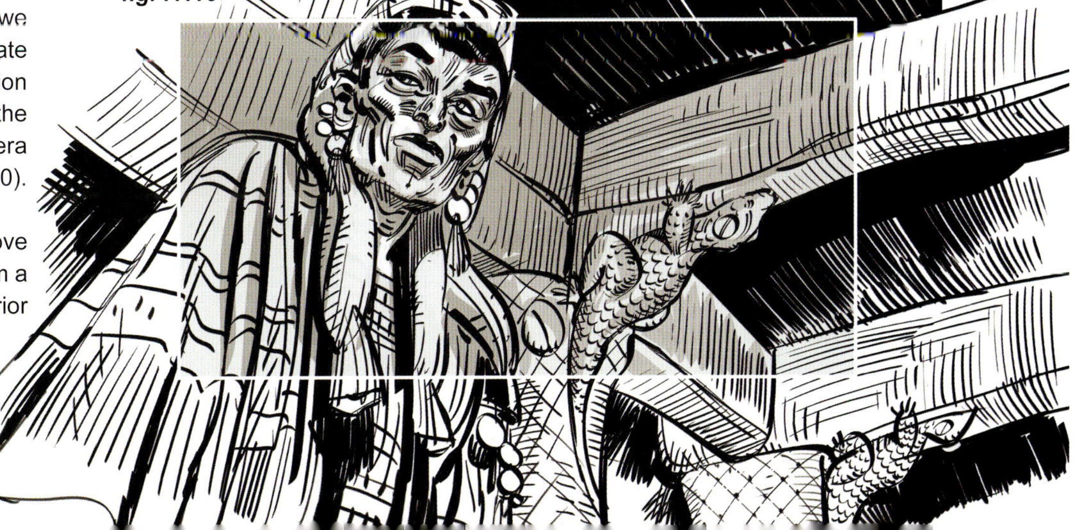

fig. 7.110

A BIG, FINAL CELEBRATION

To complete the design of our village, let's finish with a general view of a big, outdoor celebration next to the enticing ocean.

The idea is to create a view with a large central structure surrounded by a ceremonious crowd, right next to the ocean, in epic scale. This allows for great bridges and other structures consisting mainly of the bamboo materials of the area, as was already established by the previous designs.

This time, let's push it to the extreme (within a sense of believability), with structures that feel solid yet show a certain aura of weightlessness, expressed through their flowing shapes and designs that bring to this space a sense of mystic and magic.

The central altar could have a number of platforms that lead to it, as a reflection of the spiritual stages one would need to go through in order to achieve the ultimate, ethereal power. Also, the whole area would be surrounded by spectacular, natural environments.

Figs. 7.111–7.117: These are different options and ideas that were considered. The handwritten notes explain both positive and not-so-positive aspects of each concept. Turn the page to see the final design (fig. 7.118).

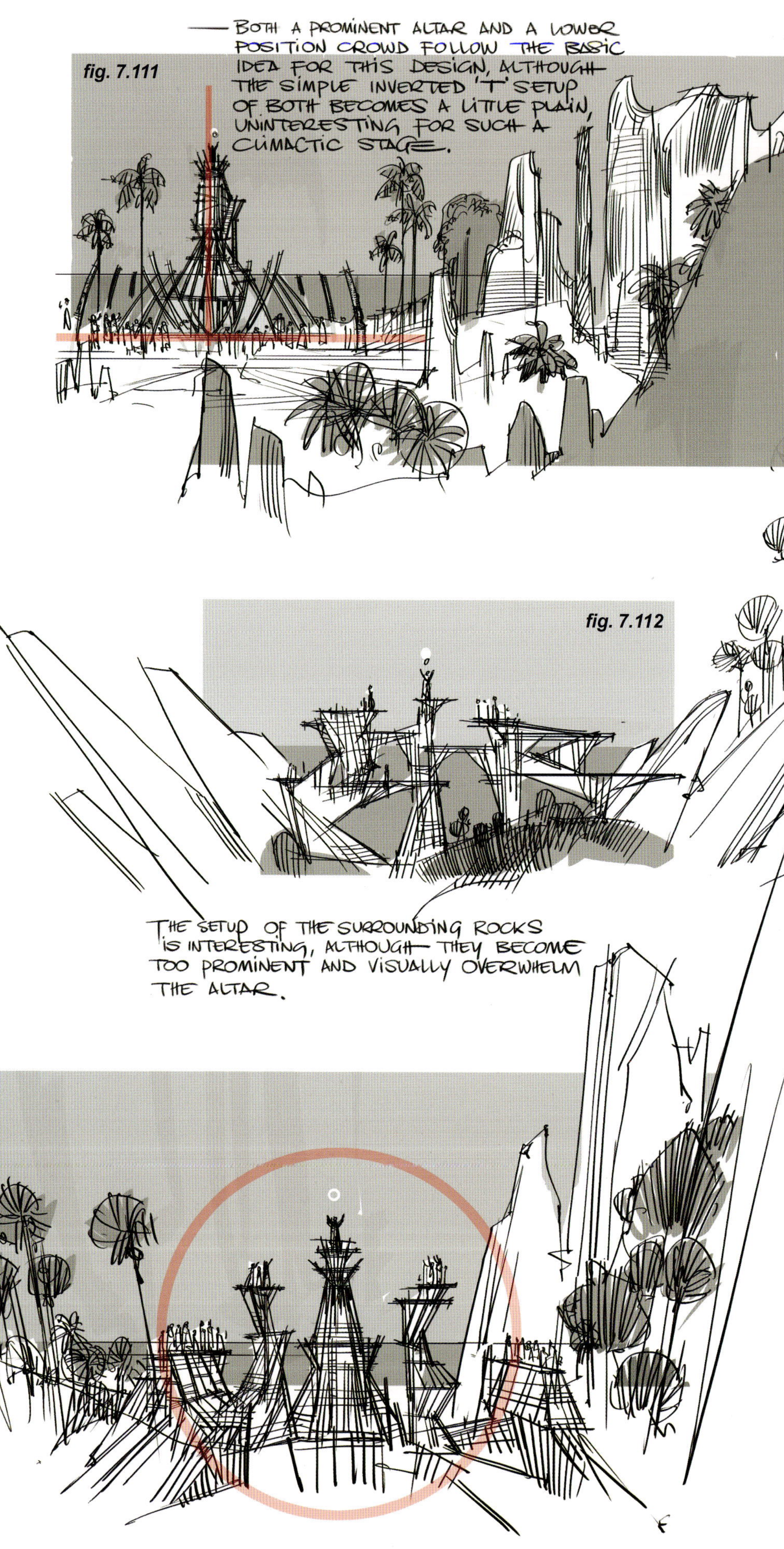

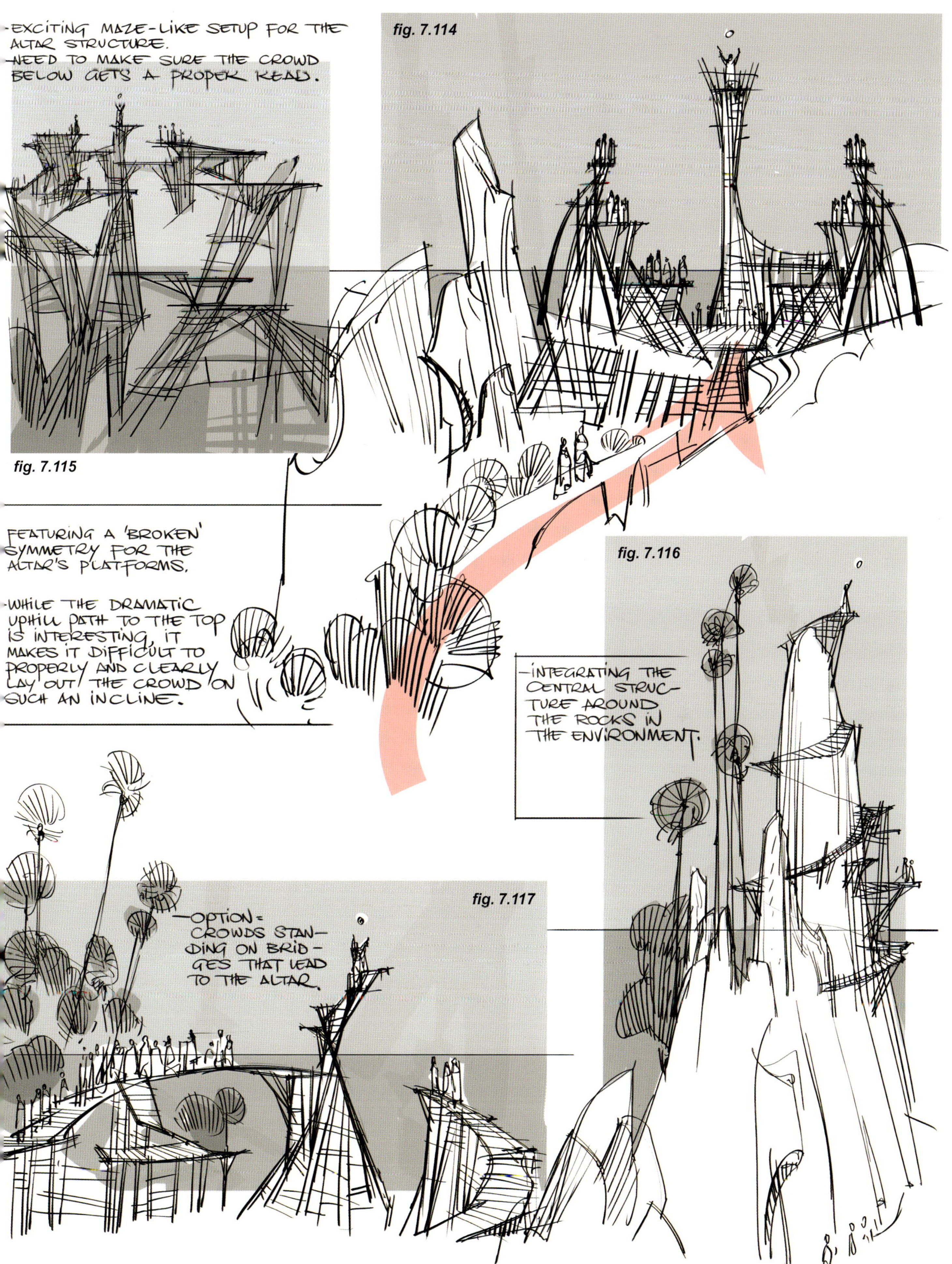

-EXCITING MAZE-LIKE SETUP FOR THE ALTAR STRUCTURE.
-NEED TO MAKE SURE THE CROWD BELOW GETS A PROPER READ.
fig. 7.114
fig. 7.115
FEATURING A 'BROKEN' SYMMETRY FOR THE ALTAR'S PLATFORMS.
-WHILE THE DRAMATIC UPHILL PATH TO THE TOP IS INTERESTING, IT MAKES IT DIFFICULT TO PROPERLY AND CLEARLY LAY OUT THE CROWD ON SUCH AN INCLINE.
fig. 7.116
-INTEGRATING THE CENTRAL STRUCTURE AROUND THE ROCKS IN THE ENVIRONMENT.
fig. 7.117
-OPTION= CROWDS STANDING ON BRIDGES THAT LEAD TO THE ALTAR.

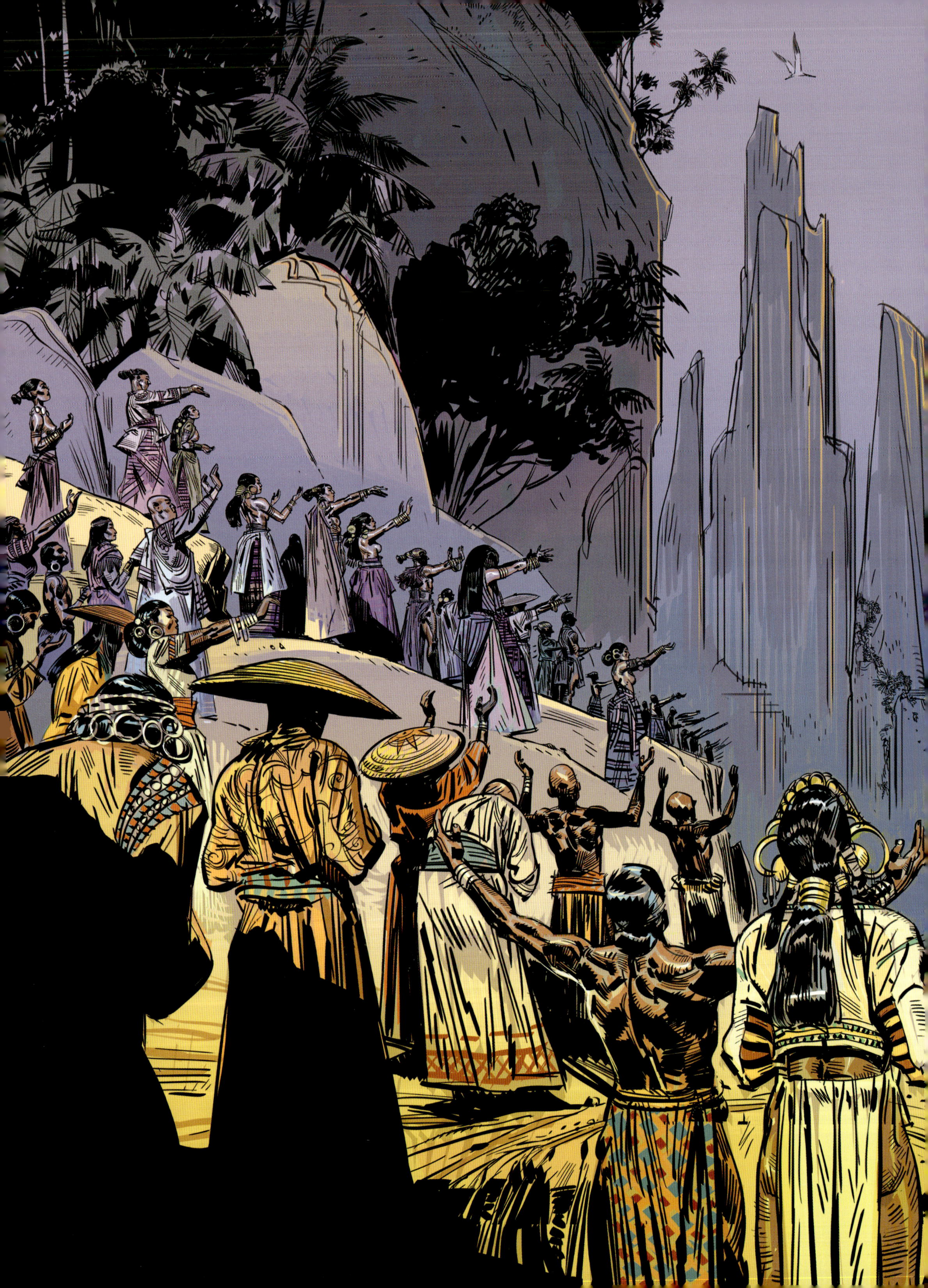

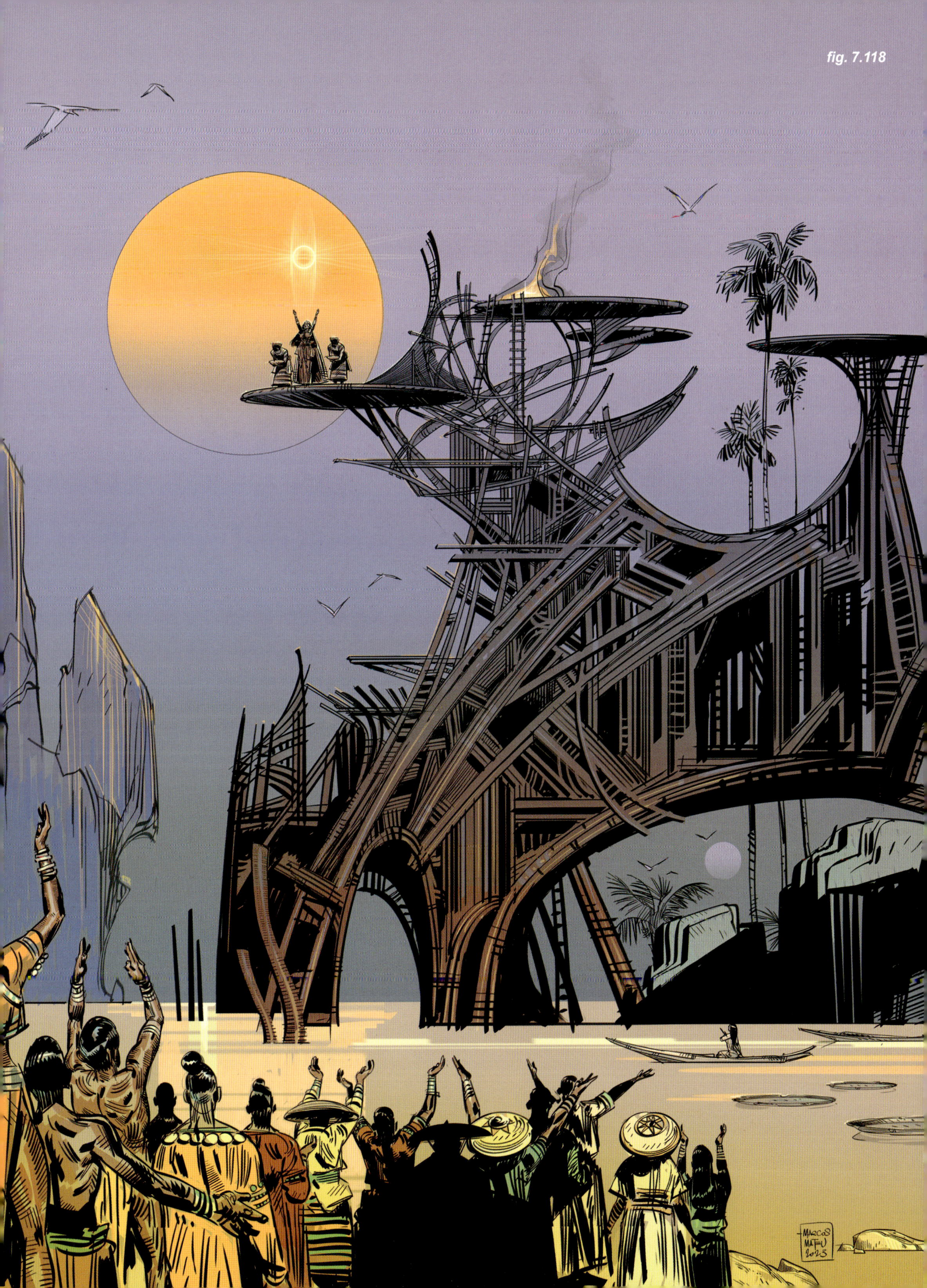

fig. 7.118

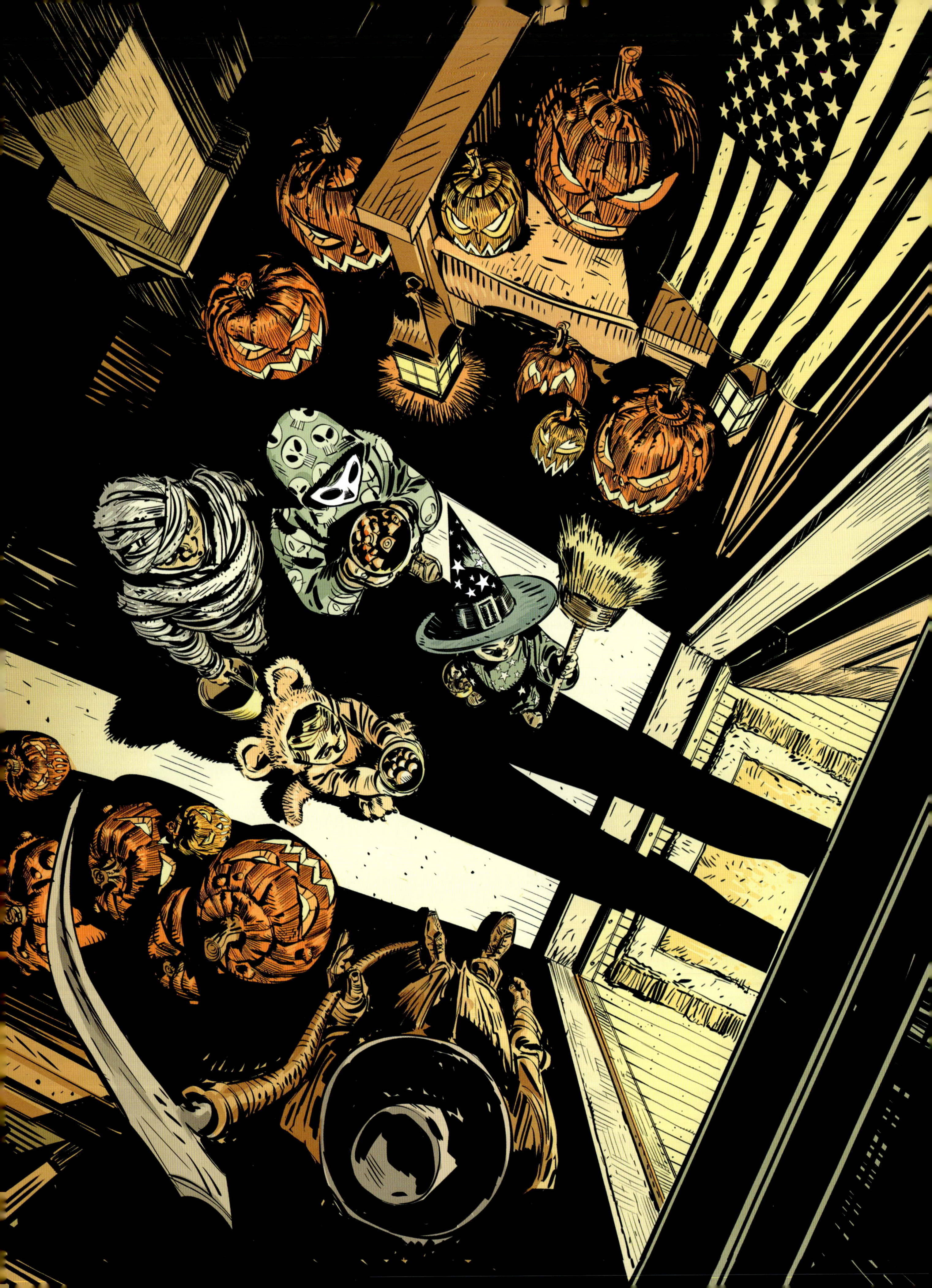

—EPILOGUE

We live in a wonderful world filled with characters and their stories, and none of these stories take place in a void but in environments that can be realistic, fantastic, natural, human-made, or a combination. But no matter what, they all need the mind and hands of a designer to become these purposeful spaces where things happen and emotions are felt.

Remember, the art of storytelling is about engaging with an audience through environments, camera, lighting, acting, music, sound, etc., or the lack of any of these. Make them feel and understand each moment, and make them identify with the characters from beginning to end. In the process, integrate all of this with your artistic vision and sense of style.

Whether complex or plain, quiet or exciting, the possibilities are endless. So, imagine, explore, dare. Especially at the beginning of the process, the sky is the limit, and then some. There will always be time to specify, rationalize, and put things into a proper structure when needed.

Thank you for sharing this time and interest on creating environments. From here my wish is for you to enjoy each and every challenge as the magnificent exercises in communication that they are. Remember, this investment of your passion, time, and occasional disappointment—but fun, excitement, and inevitably progress and evolution—is what links you to your audience and lets this process become a shared experience that you and your designs bring into existence, and that is a wonderful thing.

INDEX

A

angularity, 102
arches, 56–57, 178, 180, 186
architectonic elements, 89
architectural design, 21
    details, 26, 34–35, 61, 68, 80, 97, 167, 171
    elements, 21, 26–27, 28–29, 35, 38, 66, 80–81, 96, 184
    nuance, 99, 167
architectural styles, 25–28, 35, 68, 129;
    American, 28, 34–35, 124, 129;
    Baroque, 26–27;
    European, 23, 25, 28;
    Federal, 28;
    futuristic, 96;
    Georgian, 28, 124;
    Gothic, 25, 28;
    Neoclassical, 28;
    Renaissance, 25–26;
    Rococo, 26–27
asymmetric components, 26
atmospheric elements, 37, 131, 151

B

background, 23, 57, 71, 85, 101, 106–07, 110, 127–28,
                131, 149, 171, 175;
    artist, 17;
    atmospheric, 49;
    elements, 84
backlighting, 99
body language, 40

C

camera angle, 73, 85, 93, 115, 118, 128, 144, 152, 190
camera position, 10–11, 40, 86, 92, 115
character close-ups, 88, 125, 127
character expression, 85, 125, 138
cinematic devices, 81, 153
cinematic shots, 84, 206–07
circular elements, 21
close-up shots, 73, 96
color, 27–28, 40, 86, 104, 118, 121, 134, 175, 184, 187,
                197, 202;
    bright, 26, 39;
    muted, 81;
    pastel tones, 27
composition, 22–23, 49, 70, 73, 82, 92–93, 99, 106, 138,
                151, 153, 159, 190
compositional elements, 35
compositional options, 44
compositional solutions, 94
concentric layers, 101

concept sketches, 51, 113
construction techniques, 66
costumes, 13–14, 17, 25, 27, 75, 78, 164, 194, 197

D

domes, 21, 176, 178, 190, 200

F

fishbone layout, 68
flat plane, 58
flatter elements, 27
flow of lines, 20
foreground, 23, 71, 84, 86, 101, 106–07, 110, 127, 131, 149
Framed Drawing Techniques, 49, 76, 113
Framed Ink, 49, 88, 107, 207
Framed Ink, Vol. 2, 151, 190
Framed Perspective, Vol. 1, 18, 51, 58
Framed series, 22
framing, 81, 88, 92–93, 152, 186, 207

G

geographical area, 34
geographical landmarks, 12
geographical location, 10, 25, 29, 34
geographical orientation, 11
grayscale, 49, 51, 60, 76

H

historical context, 15
historical period, 14–15, 138
historical styles, 28

I

industrial style, 11, 21, 34, 36–37, 39–40, 56

L

layout, 28, 35, 64, 66, 68, 171, 175, 182
lighting:
    backlighting, 11, 23, 99, 106, 124, 153–54;
    contrast, 10, 23, 26, 29;
    dark environment, 10, 136;
    fixtures, 48;
    front lit, 11;
    soft, 61, 125;
    spotlight, 49, 61, 101, 127, 131;
    sunlight, 11, 60, 68, 79, 84, 147, 166;
    tonal contrast, 127;
    tonal range, 130;
    well-lit environment, 10
lighting conditions, 130
lighting range, 127
lighting scenario, 82, 127, 186
lighting setup, 127
lighting solutions, 84
lighting tonals, 49, 60, 76

line languages:
   curved, 21, 44, 113;
   straight/angular, 21, 44, 93, 151;
   straight, 79, 93–94, 129, 150;
   vertical, 114, 116, 119;
line sketches, 49

M

maps, 11–12, 36, 49, 68, 114, 152–54
mid-ground, 84, 110, 128, 131
mid-tones, 127

P

perspective, 37, 40, 42–43, 51, 56, 58, 86, 94, 99, 106;
   sketches, 47, 51, 60
photo references, 35, 38, 41–42, 61, 69, 155, 166.
    See also reference types
Photoshop, 43
point of view, 34, 85, 92, 94, 103, 150
preliminary sketch, 21, 37, 54, 64, 116, 128
props, 28, 49, 52, 61, 75, 80, 87, 142, 194

R

reference gathering, 44, 56, 68, 70, 105, 129, 162
reference types:
   books, 16–17, 34;
   cultural, 68–70, 80, 87, 170, 175, 186, 194;
   natural and organic, 172
   on-site, 18;
   photographic, 34–35, 38, 41–42, 61, 69, 155, 160, 166,
      168
reference library, 14, 17
research:
   archaeological, 14, 66, 68;
   characters, 14, 75;
   costume design, 14, 75, 164;
   environments, 14;
   online, 16;
   photo, 54;
   process, 14, 16–17, 34, 68;
   textiles, 164;
   tools, 75, 164, 192;
   trip, 14;
   visual, 10, 13, 15, 29, 32

S

script, 10–13, 32, 34, 36, 48–49, 51, 102
shape language:
   angular, 47–48, 92, 96, 102, 106, 129, 144, 149–50, 157,
      159, 171;
   angular vs. curved, 10;
   angular vs. round, 19–20;
   broken, 92;
   choppy, 92;
   circles, 90, 97, 113;
   cubic, 21, 96, 103;

   curved, 26, 54, 96, 101, 112, 114–16, 118–19, 136, 144,
      149, 159, 176, 202;
   flat, 10, 27, 92;
   jagged, 10, 92–93;
   quadrangular, 70;
   random, 92;
   rectangular, 66, 70, 79, 106;
   rectilinear, 60, 101;
   regular patterns, 92;
   round, 10, 19–20, 54, 60, 77, 112–14, 116, 142, 150, 157,
      171, 176;
   soft, 10, 19, 21, 92, 154, 157–58, 205;
   settled, 92;
   solid, 14, 92, 96, 100, 104, 113, 149, 159, 205, 208;
   straight, 21, 136, 147, 155, 171, 201;
   straight vs. curved, 19;
   triangular, 97, 149;
   unbalanced, 92;
   uniform, 92
vertical, 21, 60, 92, 144, 147, 155, 160, 168, 171, 176, 182
shot composition, 23
staging, 35, 134, 142
storytelling, 29, 92–93, 213

T

time period, 10, 14, 16, 25, 27, 124, 127

V

visual language, 19, 28, 44, 73, 86, 153
visual order, 23, 144
visual philosophy, 71
visual reference library, 14
visual references, 16–17, 28–29, 48, 162
visual rhythms, 10, 32

W

weather conditions, 10, 15, 18, 34–36, 124, 128–32, 138,
      140, 142, 171
wide-angle lens, 99, 107, 190

MORE FROM MARCOS MATEU-MESTRE

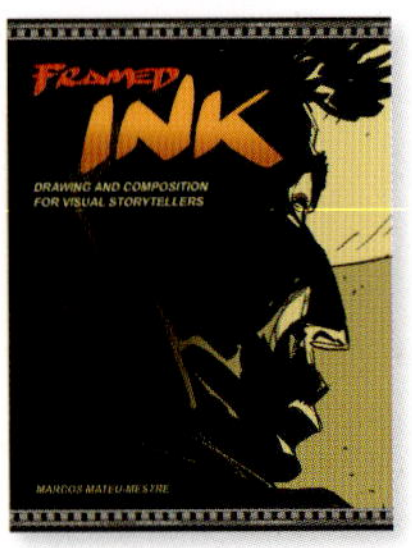 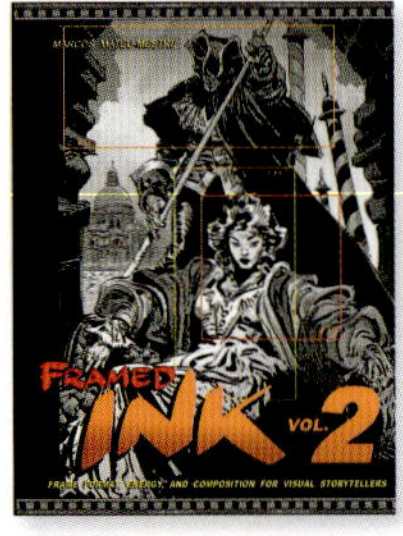 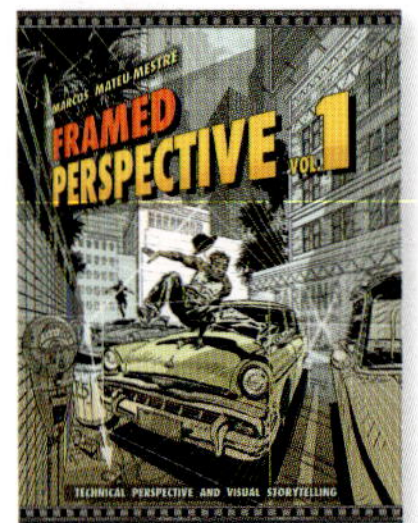 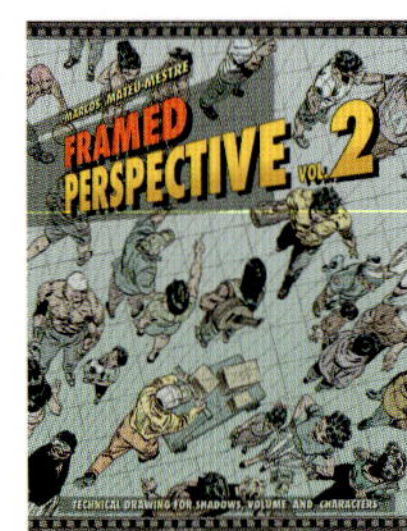 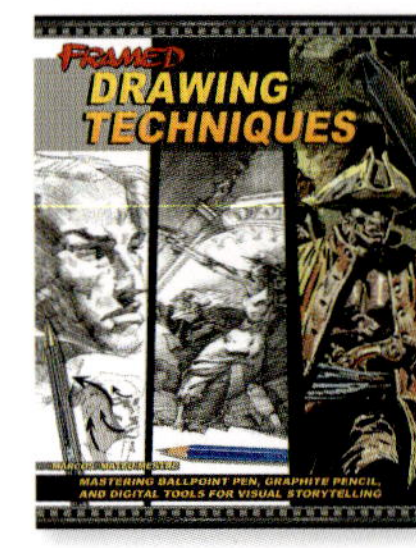

Paperback: 978-1-933492-95-7   Paperback: 978-1-624650-53-6   Paperback: 978-1-624650-30-7   Paperback: 978-1-624650-32-1   Paperback: 978-1-624650-40-6

INTERNATIONAL EDITIONS

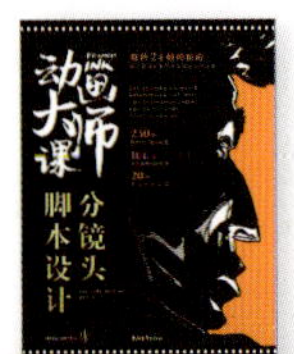
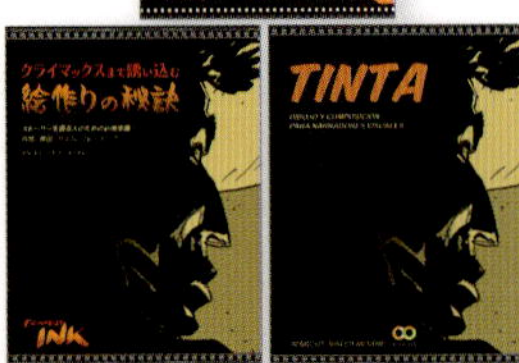
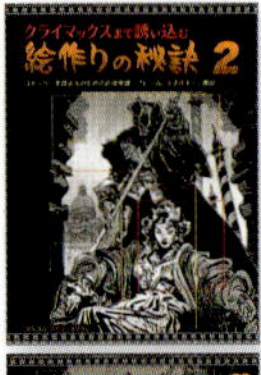
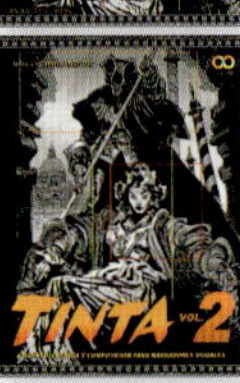
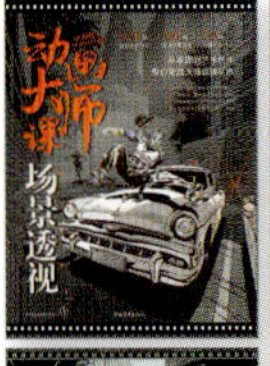
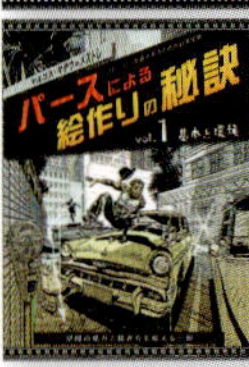
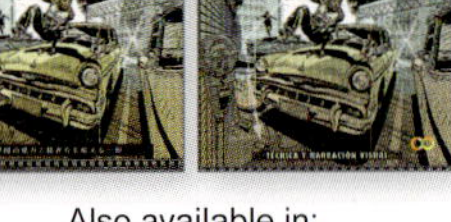
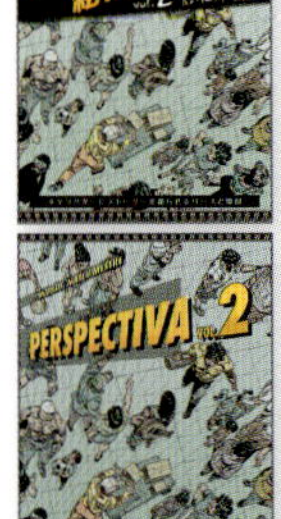
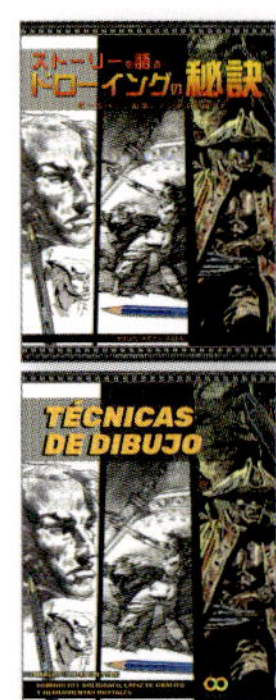

Also available in:
Chinese • Japanese • Spanish

Also available in:
Japanese • Spanish

Also available in:
Chinese • French • Japanese • Spanish

Also available in:
Japanese • Spanish

Also available in:
Japanese • Spanish

OTHER TITLES BY DESIGN STUDIO PRESS

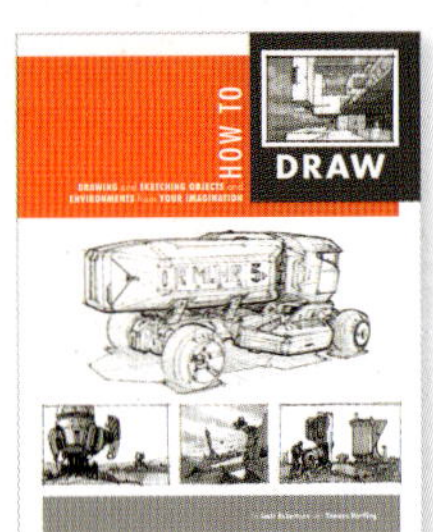 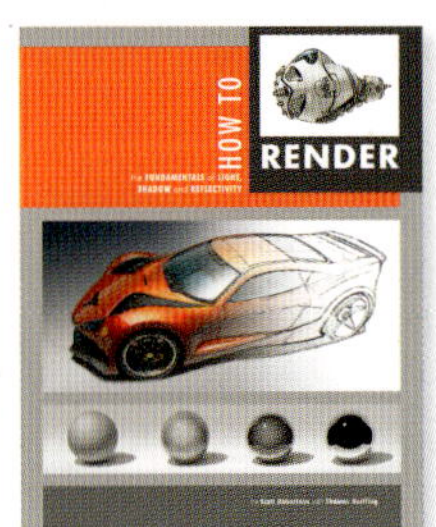 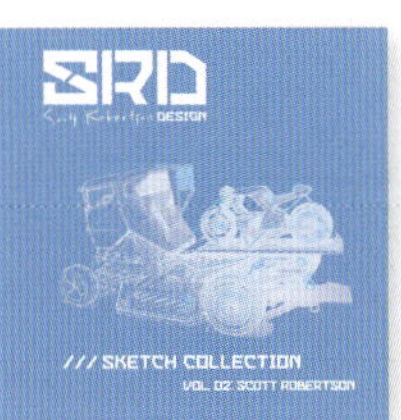 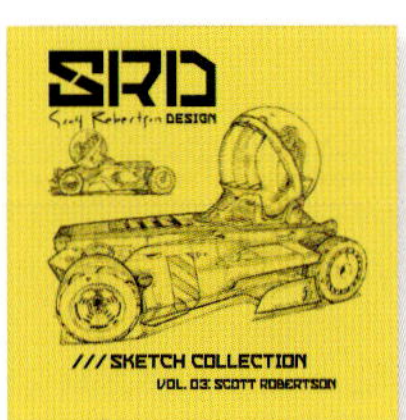

Paperback: 978-1-933492-73-5
Hardcover: 978-1-933492-75-9

Paperback: 978-1-933492-96-4
Hardcover: 978-1-933492-83-4

Hardcover: 978-1-624650-37-6

Hardcover: 978-1-624650-97-0

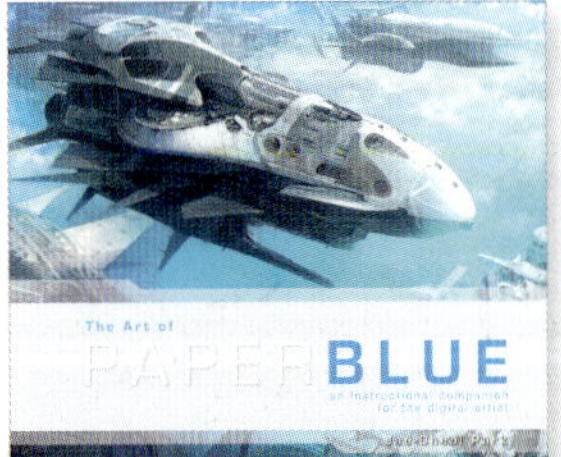 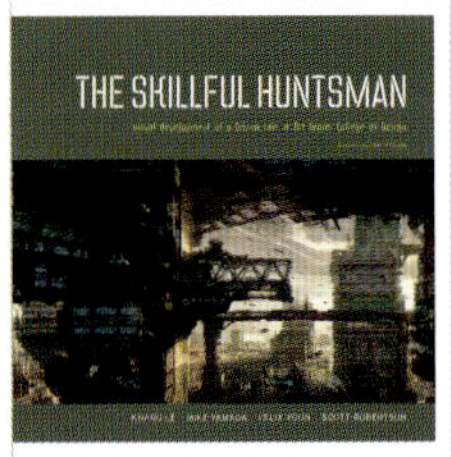 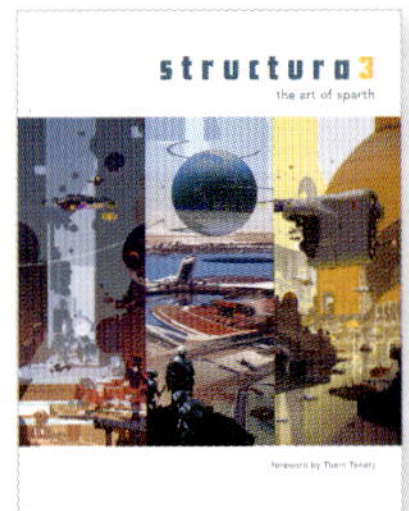 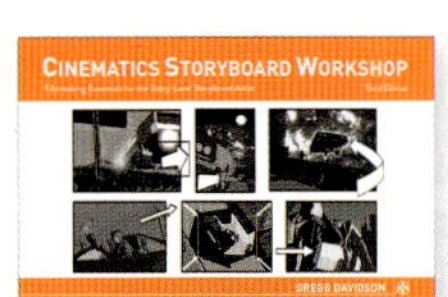

Paperback: 978-1-624650-14-7

Paperback: 978-0-972667-64-7

Paperback: 978-1-624650-12-3
Hardcover: 978-1-624650-11-6

Paperback: 978-1-624650-41-3

To order additional copies of this book, and to view other books we offer, please visit **www.designstudiopress.com**.

For volume purchases and resale inquiries, please email: **info@designstudiopress.com**.

tel: 310.836.3116

To be notified of new releases, special discounts, and events, please sign up for our mailing list on our website. Follow us on social media:

 www.instagram.com/designstudiopress

 www.facebook.com/designstudiopress

 www.threads.net/designstudiopress

 www.x.com/DStudioPress

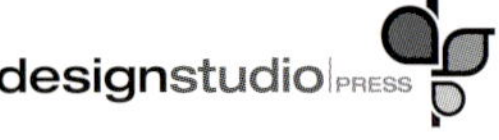 designstudio PRESS